ÁINE NÍ CHÁRTHAIG
AND AIDAN O'SULLIVAN

NEW APPRECIATING

ART

VISUAL STUDIES

FOR LEAVING CERTIFICATE

g **GILL** EDUCATION

Gill Education
Hume Avenue
Park West
Dublin 12
www.gilleducation.ie

Gill Education is an imprint of M.H. Gill & Co.

ISBN: 978-0-7171-88697

Design: Anú Design (www.anu-design.ie)

Illustrations: Oxford Illustrators and Designers, Sarah Wimperis, Keith Barrett, Derry Dillon and Katie Allen

At the time of going to press, all web addresses were active and contained information relevant to the topics in this book. Gill Education does not, however, accept responsibility for the content or views contained on these websites. Content, views and addresses may change beyond the publisher or author's control. Students should always be supervised when reviewing websites.

The authors and publisher have made every effort to trace all copyright holders. If, however, any have been inadvertently overlooked, we would be pleased to make the necessary arrangement at the first opportunity.

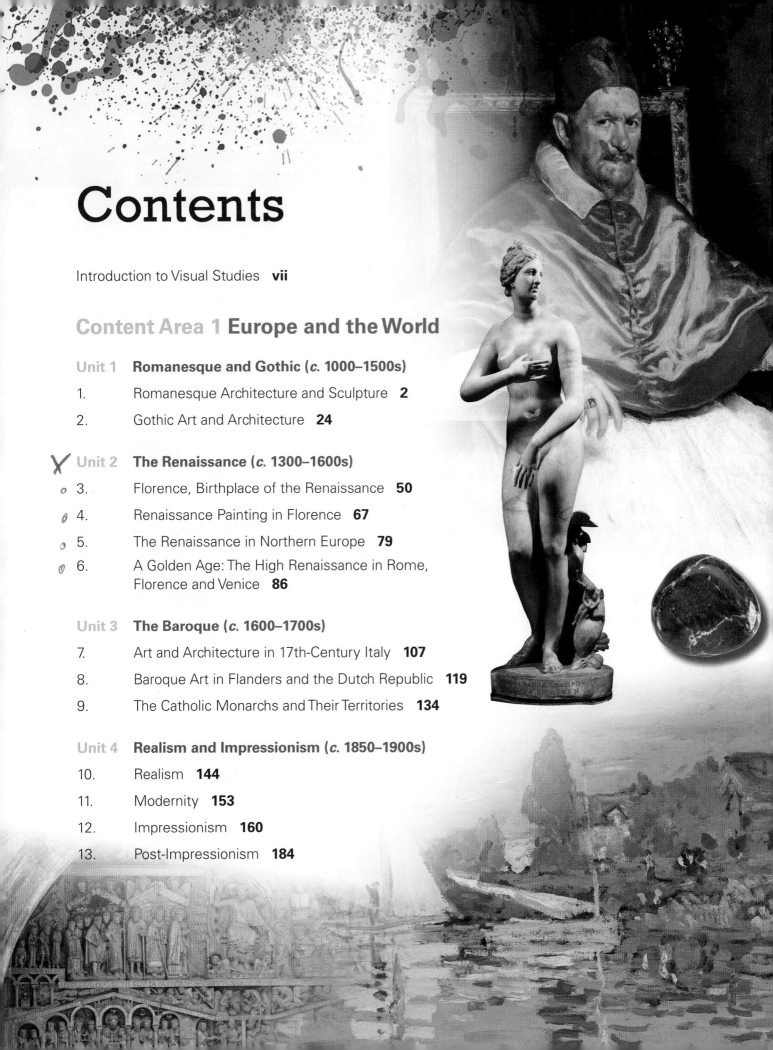

Contents

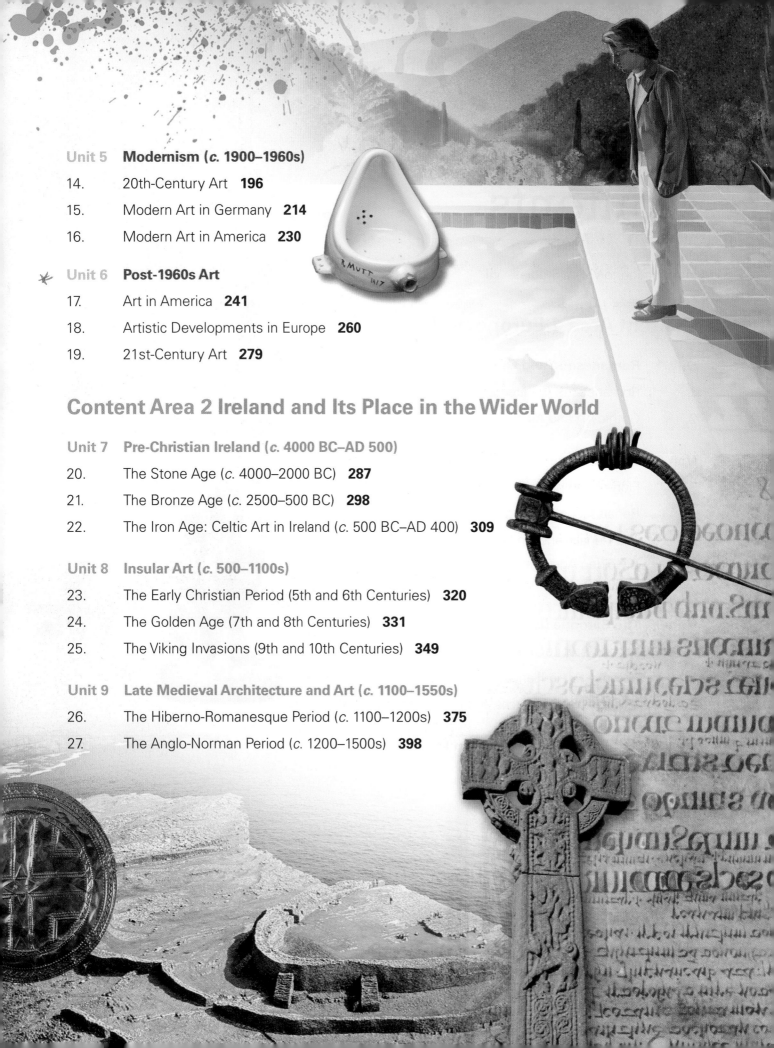

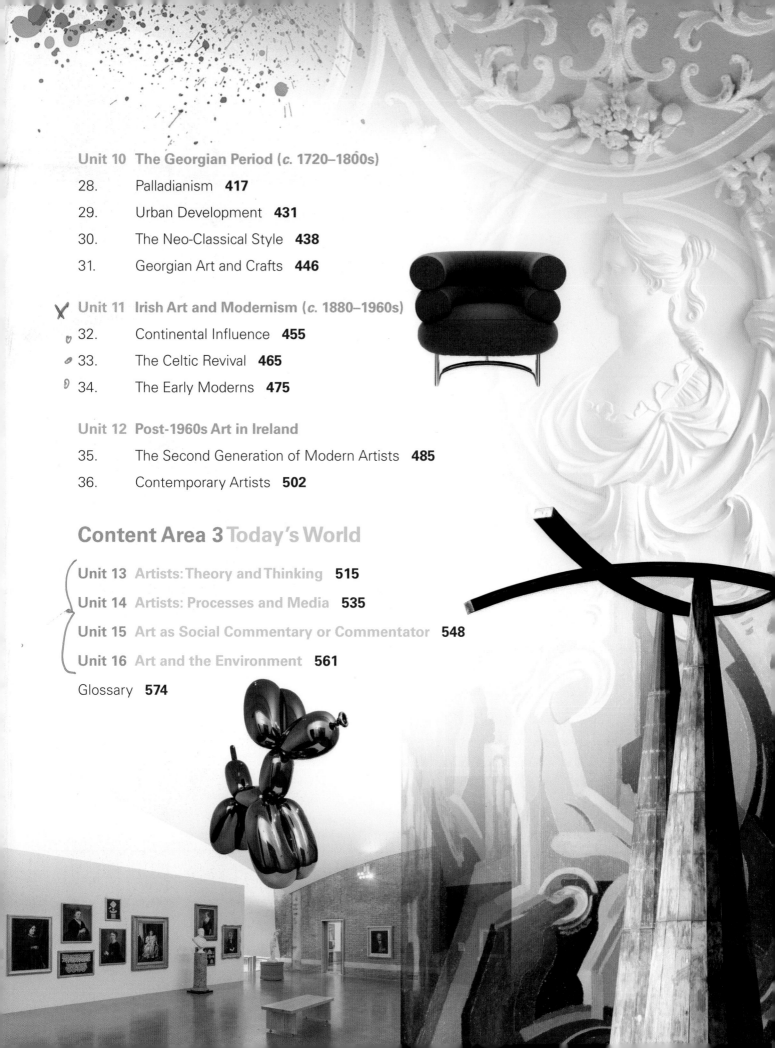

Introduction to Visual Studies

By the end of this chapter I will ...

* have detailed knowledge and understanding of how Art at Senior Cycle is structured

* understand that the course is structured in three strands of Research, Create and Respond

* recognise that these strands are interdependent as well as interconnected

* understand how working with a process will help with my creative journey

* understand how visual studies and practical studies are a fully integrated part of the creative process

* know that my own research on artists and artworks will form an important part of my studies

* recognise why knowledge of other artists and their work should inform and help to develop my own individual and innovative work

* understand that the creative process will involve responding to a stimulus, interpreting primary sources, developing and finally realising my own individual and imaginative works of art.

* know that responding to my own art and the art of others will involve both visual and written formats.

Art

For thousands of years, people have been creating, looking at, criticising and enjoying art. The word can refer to the visual arts, including painting, sculpture, architecture, photography, decorative arts, crafts, or other visual works that combine a range of traditional, contemporary, new and digital media.

Art involves the arranging of elements in a way that appeals to the senses or emotions. It is a visual language used to give form to ideas and to communicate those ideas with an intended audience.

Studying art and experiencing a wide variety of ideas, practices and media encourages self-expression and creativity. It can also build confidence as well as nurture a sense of individual identity because it promotes critical thinking and supports the development of problem-solving skills.

Art strengthens the ability to communicate ideas. As you learn to express ideas in your own work, you should also be better able to make connections across other subjects at Senior Cycle.

Art in Senior Cycle is structured to include Practical Studies and Visual Studies in a process of three interlinked and interdependent strands: **Research**, **Create** and **Respond**.

Leaving Certificate Study Areas

Practical Studies

There are a broad number of disciplines available for you to study within your Art course. These may not all be available within your specific school setting, but you can study any disciplines available in a range of traditional, contemporary, new and digital media, or a combination of these. You should also use media to interact, create, connect and communicate with others as part of your chosen discipline.

Visual studies of artists and artworks past and present should form an integrated part of and an inspiration for your own practical work during Senior Cycle. This could include:

- visiting publicly funded arts venues like art galleries, museums or heritage sites, nationally or within your own county

- engaging with the built environment in your own area or beyond

- working with an artist or designer in a school-based programme or by visiting them at work in their studio.

These are the primary and therefore the best and most direct ways to engage with art, but there is, of course, a huge range of visual culture from numerous sources past and present to be found worldwide. Today's globalised society allows easy access to vast amounts of visual imagery in books and magazines, on television and in cinema and video. However, the internet provides us with imagery and information in a way that would have been unthinkable in previous generations with the simple touch of a screen on our smartphones.

Assessment of Practical Work

Initial research work for your final pieces of artwork should be kept in your Art sketchpad. For the final assessment, you will be required to produce **one realised work**, developed from a stimulus, over an **extended time period** in Sixth Year.

The use of primary sources, including **observational drawings** of objects from life and from the imagination, will form the basis of this work.

Your final submission will include your **artist's statement**. This will fully explain what you have created, how it was created and why it was created.

During the extended time period, you will also be required to develop work towards a **second piece of artwork**. This will be realised during a **five-hour invigilated examination**. This will also include your artist's statement, which explains what you have created, how it was created and why it was created.

Visual Studies

The term 'Visual Studies' refers to culture expressed visually in the past and by contemporary societies. Visual Studies will consider media and disciplines, and the ways in which artworks are shaped by society.

As you study the art of the past, a vast world of culture and developments will open up as you access the work of other artists. This will help you to consider how other cultures represented thoughts and ideas though visual means.

Visual Studies and Practical Studies

Visual Studies should be a fully integrated part of your practical studies, because learning about art and artworks can inspire your own work.

Understanding and being able to analyse the work of other artists should help in the development of imaginative and innovative ideas in your own creative journey.

> Note: Examples of student work showing inspiration and interlinking of visual studies with practical studies are included here (see Figures 18–21), but further examples can be seen on **www.gillexplore.ie**.

Visual Studies: Written Examination

For the written component of the examination, you will study:

- **one** of the following sections of focus within **Content Area 1: Europe and the World**. These include:

  - Romanesque and Gothic (*c.* 1000–1500s)
  - the Renaissance (*c.* 1300–1600s)
  - the Baroque (*c.* 1600–1700s)
  - Realism and Impressionism (*c.* 1850–1900s)
  - Modernism (*c.* 1900–1960s)
  - Post-1960s Art.

- **one** of the following sections of focus within **Content Area 2: Ireland and Its Place in the Wider World**. These include:

  - Pre-Christian Ireland (*c.* 4000 BC–AD 500)
  - Insular Art (*c.* 500–1100s)
  - Late Medieval Architecture and Art (*c.* 1100–1550s)
  - the Georgian Period (*c.* 1720–1800s)
  - Irish Art and Modernism (*c.* 1880–1960s)
  - Post-1960s Art in Ireland.

Note: BCE/CE can be used as alternatives to BC/AD. BCE stands for Before Common Era and corresponds to the same time frame as BC (Before Christ). CE stands for Common Era and corresponds to the same time frame as AD (*Anno Domini*).

- **all** sections of focus in **Content Area 3: Today's World**. These sections are quite interconnected and one can be referred to, where relevant, when studying the others. They will help to draw and build on the range of skills that you have gained through engagement in the three strands of *Research*, *Create* and *Respond* and give you the opportunity to experience and study art that exists in your everyday life. This will support your creative thinking, making and reflective processes. The four areas of focus are:

  - Artists: Theory and Thinking
  - Artists: Processes and Media
  - Art as Social Commentary or Commentator
  - Art and the Environment.

Creative Engagement Project

Figure 1 These students are working with an artist on large batik wall hangings for the school. The images were developed from studies of trees in the school grounds. From left: a. Students hanging their preparatory studies in the school; b. Students learning to wax using brushes and batik tools (tjantings); c. batiks in progress.

Creative Engagement is an arts-in-education programme involving a local artist or arts group who comes into the school. The creative engagement takes place as the artists impart their skills, knowledge and enthusiasm to the students.

Since its inception, nearly 20 years ago, there have been over 1,000 Creative Engagement projects funded by the National Association of Principals and Deputy Principals (NAPD). This is supported by the Department of Education and Skills, the Heritage Council, and the Department of Tourism, Culture, Arts, Gaeltacht, Sport and Media.

Content Area 3: Today's World should help you to develop skills of inquiry as you experience a range of art-led experiences. This can be done by visiting galleries, museums or heritage sites, whether locally, nationally, internationally or virtually.

It can also mean engaging with artists in the community or working with them in school-based projects.

Using this Book for Practical and Visual Studies

- Study your two chosen content areas and the four areas of **Content Area 3: Today's World** for your written exam.

- Use all Content Areas as inspirational sources for your practical studies.

- Use material provided online at **www.gillexplore.ie** in any areas of special interest to your studies.

- Use the internet as a valuable research tool to find out more about artists and artworks. Suggestions for video links and internet sites can be found in the Further Research panel at the end of each chapter.

Further Research

www.youtube.com – Search for 'Linear Perspective: Brunelleschi's Experiment' (4:16) to watch a short video on Brunelleschi's exploration of linear perspective.

www.youtube.com – Search for 'Florence's Gates of Paradise' (4:55) to watch a video on Ghiberti's third set of baptistery doors.

- Activities are included throughout the book. Select any that fit with your Practical Studies or that help with learning and understanding of Visual Studies. These are presented in the form of Research, Create and Respond panels.

CREATE Classroom activity: Sit in groups at a table. Take photographs as you act out the gestures of Jesus and the apostles. Say aloud what you think each one is saying. Make sketches of the gestures.

- Respond to artists and artworks in both Visual and Practical Studies by answering questions in the Chapter Review section at the end of each chapter.

Chapter Review

1. How was Italy ruled in the 15th century?
2. Why did patrons commission works of art?

The Three Art Strands

The three strands of **Research**, **Create** and **Respond** are fundamental to the process of studying art.

Working with a process will encourage and promote innovation as you make new art work, develop new methods and generate new ideas. It is, of course, possible to begin a piece of artwork from any one of the three strands, as they are interlinked and interdependent, but it is important to experience all three.

Visual Studies should play a very important role, alongside and as part of your practical work. The **learning outcomes** within each of the three strands reflect the relationship between the practical making of a work and the knowledge, skills, values and understanding of relevant examples of Visual Studies.

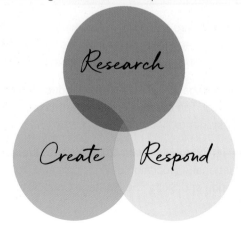

Research Strand

As an artist, you will become a visual researcher, a conceptual explorer and a cultural archaeologist. You will explore and investigate, delve into the past and present and discover possibilities for the future.

The **Research** strand should focus on:

- **looking**, using primary sources or examples of significant works of Visual Studies
- **recording and documenting** your thoughts, ideas, findings and observations in your sketchpad
- **experimenting with and interpreting** what you have observed, further developing your observations and experimenting with the work and ideas
- **contextual enquiries**, researching and discovering more about the context (circumstances or situation) with regard to own work and the artwork of others in Visual Studies
- **following a process** in your research.

Researching works of art is a meaningful and lasting experience. Look, read, sketch, take photos and make written notes using appropriate visual and critical vocabulary. Close observation, careful thinking, researching and discovering more about works of art, the artists who made them and the context in which they were created is both rewarding and satisfying.

One of best ways to appreciate a work of art is to investigate it through its subject or theme, its art elements, context and background. It is best to engage with the work directly in a site-specific location or in a museum or gallery, but it can also be done with reproductions in a classroom discussion.

Analysing a Work of Art or Design

Look – Take time to look at the work of art, paying close attention to details.

- What do you notice?
- Continue to look for 30 seconds and then turn away.
- What details do you remember?
- Look back again.
- What did you overlook?

Describe – Use visual and cultural language to describe what you see.

Art style – Is it Abstract, Realist, Expressionist …?

Theme or subject matter – What is this painting about? What do you see? What do think it means?

Composition – How have the art elements and design principles in the artwork been put together? In what direction is your eye drawn? Is the composition:

- landscape (horizontal) or portrait (vertical)?
- following the rule of thirds (Fig. 2)?
- in a triangular shape (Fig. 3)?
- based on the Golden Mean (Fig. 4)?

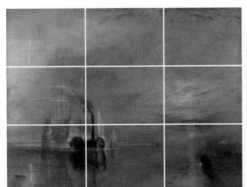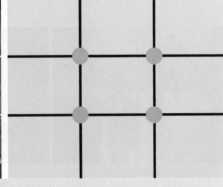

Figure 2 The rule of thirds. The rule of thirds is more of a guideline than a rule. It helps the artist with the placement of art elements and the focal point within the composition.

Figure 3 The triangle or pyramidal composition is used to draw the viewer's attention to a figure or to give an impression of stability. To construct a pyramidal composition, an artist places objects and figures within the outline of an imaginary triangle or pyramid on the picture plane. It was very popular with Renaissance artists.

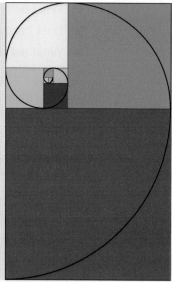

1:1.618

Figure 4 The Golden Mean, also known as the Golden Section or Golden Ratio. Based on a mathematical ratio, the Golden Mean is used to achieve beauty, balance and harmony in art. It creates flow and movement by directing the eye around the space in a balanced manner. It comes back on itself in an almost circular motion. The Golden Mean was used extensively by Leonardo da Vinci and other Renaissance artists.

Perspective – Is there perspective in the painting?

- Linear perspective: Does it suggest depth or distance and give the impression of three dimensions on a flat, two-dimensional surface (Fig. 5)? Are objects reducing in size over distance?

- Atmospheric or aerial perspective: Has the artist created the impression of distance by reducing clarity, colour and tone as objects fade into the distance (Fig. 6)?

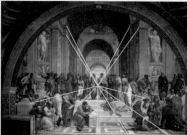
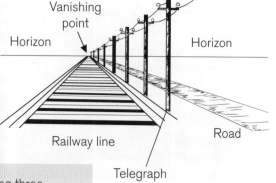

Vanishing point

Horizon   Horizon

Railway line

Telegraph poles

Road

Figure 5 Linear or single-point perspective. A method of representing three-dimensional objects on a two-dimensional picture plane. In linear perspective, all parallel edges and lines converge toward a single vanishing point.

Figure 6 *The Madonna of Chancellor Rolin*, 1435, by Jan van Eyck, 66 × 62 cm, Musée du Louvre, Paris. Atmospheric perspective (or aerial perspective) is highly characteristic of Flemish painting of the 15th century. The device of a landscape seen through a series of arches – a kind of picture within a picture, was used again and again, but Jan van Eyck's painting is the first example. It creates a contrast between the soft light of the interior and the stronger sunlight outside. It also gives the picture a very real sense of depth, heightened by the brilliant light on the horizon, along the line of blue-coloured mountains.

Media and Area of Practice

- Is the work, for example, a painting, drawing, sculpture, photograph, video, sound work or installation, digital image or graphic design?
- What medium is used?
- Is it painted with oils or acrylic, printed, filmed, constructed with plaster, carved in marble or cast in bronze?

Process

- How do think the artist prepared – did she/he sketch or construct?
- Was this a collaborative work or a work of participatory art? (Were others involved or did others take part in its making?)
- How is it displayed? If it is in a frame, what is the frame like?

The Art Elements

The elements of art are the visual components or 'building blocks' for creating a work of art. Not every work contains every element, but at least two will always be present. Examine the work:

- How many art elements can you find?

Figure 7 *Parachute*, 2005, by Dorothy Cross, parachute and gannet, dimensions variable, Irish Museum of Modern Art, Dublin. *Parachute* is a good example of bricolage – an artwork composed of different and unusual materials that happen to be immediately available.

- How has the artist manipulated these?
- Have they been mixed with design principles?

Figure 8 Studies and sketches for *Guernica*, 1937, by Pablo Picasso, Museo Reina Sofía, Madrid. Photographed in the process of creation over five short weeks in May 1937, Picasso's sketches and studies for *Guernica* (see Unit 5, Fig. 14.19) are perhaps the best-recorded examples of a work in progress in the history of art.

The Art Elements

Dot	A small, round mark. This the simplest element of art and drawing.
Line	A point moving in space. Line may be two-or three-dimensional, descriptive, implied, or abstract.
Shape	Can be two-dimensional, flat, or limited to height and width.
Colour	Colour is made up of three properties: hue, tone and intensity. • Hue is the name of the colour • Tone is the hue's lightness and darkness • Intensity is the quality of brightness, strength and purity.
Tone	A colour's value of lightness or darkness.
Texture	The tactile sensation or feel of a surface (rough, smooth, spiky, etc.) or how something appears to feel.
Form	Suggests the physical nature of the work or the element of shape
Pattern	A repeating unit of shape or form organised in a consistent, regular manner.

The Design Principles

The design principles are the other visual components of a work of art or design.

Symmetry	When elements are arranged in the same way on both sides of an axis. Designs are asymmetrical if the arrangement of elements are different on both sides of an axis.
Harmony	Elements that work together and complement each other.
Tension	Creates contrasts and rhythm and flow through a design.

Balance	The arrangement of both positive elements and negative space in such a way that no single area of the design overpowers other areas.
Light	Affects how the viewer perceives the other elements and principles of design.
Space	The distance or area around or between elements of an artwork.
Scale	The relationship of sizes between different parts of a work.
Contrast	The difference in quality between two art elements. The greater the contrast and the more something will stand out.

Figure 9 (left) *Girl before a Mirror*, 1932, by Pablo Picasso, 162 × 130 cm, Museum of Modern Art, New York. Almost all the art elements and several design principles have been included in this painting.

Figure 10 (right) *The Arrest of Jesus Christ*, the Book of Kells, 9th century. Many art elements are included in this work, but there is particular emphasis on the design principles of symmetry, harmony and balance.

Interpretation – finding a meaning or message in the work.

- Is there a narrative and what might that be?
- What emotion is conveyed by the work?

Research – finding out about the context and circumstances associated with the work.

- When and where did this work take place?
- What were the social or historical circumstances of the time?

- Who was the artist? When and where did they work?

Evaluation – bringing together what you have discovered or decided about the work and its context. Note your own feelings and reactions.

- How does it make you feel?
- Would you like to have the work in your house or in your school?
- Would you like to see more examples in similar styles?

Examine these examples of painting, sculpture, graphic design and architecture and notice how each require slightly different methods of analysis. Use the following questions as a guide.

Analyse a Painting

Figure 11 *Time Flies*, 1887, by William Gerard Barry, Crawford Gallery, Cork.

Subject or Theme

● What do you think is going on in this work?
● What do you think the title of this painting refers to?
● Do you think the artist feels optimistic or pessimistic about the passing of time?
● How does he convey this mood?
● Compare the painting to another work you know with a similar style or location. Do you think the works might be connected? Why do you think that?

Light

● Can you tell from the light direction what time of day it might be?
● Why might the time of day be significant?

Composition

● How has the artist used the art elements like colour, line or shape in the painting?
● Has he achieved harmony and balance?

Colour

● Does the colour contribute to the meaning?
● Are the tones strong or soft?

Materials

● What size is the painting?
● What medium do you think the artist has used?
● What is the evidence to support your opinions?

Technique

● Has the artists used gentle or vigorous brush marks?
● Are the figures rendered expressively or naturalistically?
● Is the surface textured or smooth?

Context

● Who was the artist and where did he live and work?
● What artists or art movement was he involved with or influenced by?
● Would knowing more about the artist help you understand the work better?

Analyse a Sculpture

Subject

● What is happening in the work?
● Does it have a purpose or a function?

Form

● Has the sculpture a strong presence? Why do you think this?
● How does the lighting pick up aspects of the surface?
● Would brighter, softer or coloured light change its visual impact?

Context or Location

● Do you think this work was made for this location (site-specific)? Would it be different or have more/less impact in another setting?
● Positive and negative space.
● How does the sculpture react with the space inside and around it?

Figure 12 *Garry Hynes*, 2017, by Vera Klute, 164 × 54 × 45 cm, National Gallery of Ireland, Dublin. This portrait of the director and co-founder of Druid Theatre is made of porcelain and concrete, and is set on a timber plinth.

Scale

- Would the piece still work at a much larger or a more intimate scale?

Material

- Do you think the material affects the content?
- What words would you use to describe the same figure if it was made from wire and paper?

Sculptural Method

In additive sculpture, the artist builds up materials to create the sculpture's form.

In subtractive sculpture, the artist starts with a larger piece of material and removes some of it until only the desired form remains.

- Which method was used by the artist?

Compare

- Which subject appeals to you most? Why is that?
- Does the location, scale and materials used to create the work influence your preference?

Context

- Would you like to know more about these artists and their circumstances?
- Would this help your understanding of their work?

Figure 13
The Gaelic Chieftain, 1999, by Maurice Harron, Curlew Mountains, Co. Roscommon. Made of stainless steel and bronze pieces welded together, the sculpture stands dramatically on a hill overlooking Lough Key. He guards the way to the South, at the Curlew Mountains.

Analyse a Work of Graphic Design

Posters were the traditional medium used to convey information to an audience, but in modern times, they are part of a marketing strategy to attract attention, not just to events, but to businesses. Creative poster design conveys a message to its audience in a unique way. If the imagery and layout has an emotional appeal, this message will be more meaningful.

The effective use of art elements, and design principles like colour, typefaces and images must stand out, but to be fully functional the poster must also be quickly and easily read.

Examine the two posters below using the following questions.

Function

- Does the poster communicate its message or advertisement clearly?
- Is it readable from a distance?
- Does the imagery stand out?

Aesthetic Appeal

- Is the design appealing to senses?
- Does it carry a message or a narrative?

- Is this message positive?
- Is it humorous or playful?
- Is the colour choice striking?

Aesthetic: Concerned with beauty or the appreciation of beauty.

Design

- Which art elements been used most effectively?
- Which design principles contribute most to visual impact?
- How has space been incorporated into the design?

Scale and Proportion

- How big are all the elements in the poster in relation to each other?

Typography

- Is the font choice effective?
- Has the lettering made good use of contrast, scale and balance?

Figure 14 *Tournée du Chat Noir de Rodolphe Salis*, 1896, by Théophile Steinlen. The poster is one of the most famous and evocative images from 19th-century Paris. Rodolphe Salis was an eccentric showman and his Black Cat Cabaret in Montmartre was hugely popular. The poster advertises a tour of its Shadow Theatre.

Figure 15 *Maytime Melodies* by Una Healy. Una Healy Design is a creative graphic design and branding studio based in Dublin.

Figure 16 (top) Lewis Glucksman Gallery, University College Cork. The timber building, designed by award-winning architects Sheila O'Donnell and John Tuomey, incorporates landscape and building, plinth and pathway. Raised to nestle among the treetops, the interlocking suite of rooms have views up and down the river.

Figure 17 (bottom) Guggenheim Museum, Bilbao, Spain. The Guggenheim Museum is an example of 'articulation'. A combination of architectural qualities – shape, size, scale, articulation, texture and colour – also come together in this work.

Analyse Architecture

The built environment in which we live, including buildings, roads and pavements and other artificial surfaces, has been constantly evolving since humankind first lived in dwellings. In today's crowded, urbanised world, the scale, complexity and demand for manmade structures is increasing rapidly.

Good planning is essential for sustainable development of human activity in cities and towns and to reduce any impact on the environment.

Architecture is the art, the science and the business of building. The Lewis Glucksman Gallery in the grounds of UCC is a must-see building for art, design and architecture fans.

When examining a work of modern architecture such as the Lewis Glucksman Gallery in Cork, or the Guggenheim Museum in Bilbao, Spain, consider the following aspects:

Shape

● How have the surfaces and edges been placed together?

Size

● What is the size or the actual bulk of the building?

Scale

● How do you perceive the scale of the building? Are the components such as doors and windows, for example, designed so they are at a human scale? Are its proportions in harmony with other nearby buildings or the surrounding landscape?

Proportion

● What is the relationship of some parts, to the whole building?

Rhythm

● Can you see rhythm in the repetition of some architectural elements such as windows?

Articulation

● How have the surfaces come together to create form?

Articulation in architecture is basically a method of styling the joints by which surfaces are joined together. It can, however, mean a number of things in architectural terms. For example, details that provide shadow could be used to articulate a flat façade, or an entrance could be articulated (emphasised) by using steps.

Texture and Colour

● How have materials and colour been used to create the look of the building?

Light

● How has the effect of light and shade on surfaces been included in the design of the building?

Create Strand

As part of your creative journey in art, you will begin with a stimulus and have the opportunity to fully engage in the process of making art from its earliest conception to its final realisation. You can make full use of your own range of skills, choose your area of practice and use whichever materials are suitable for your choice.

Always work from primary sources and as your work develops, you should take some time to reflect, respond and make decisions. This reflection will help you realise if further research may be necessary.

An important part of creating is also recognising when a work is complete and knowing when to stop.

The **Create** strand should focus on:

- **making**, using primary sources to generate concepts. Interpret these in imaginative and creative ways. Sources of inspiration could include the natural and built environment or the human figure.
  - Apply appropriate skills, knowledge and techniques.
  - Create realised work based on your research.
- **contextual enquiries**, applying the art elements and design principles in the creation and evaluation of your work and that of others.
  - Apply experiences gained from Visual Studies to your own art work.
  - Examine art styles, artists and artworks and apply aspects of style or content that you find interesting to your own work.
  - Learn from other artists, past and present and allow their work to inform and inspire your own art.
  - Find out what inspired and motivated these artists. Incorporate some of their ideas into your own creative process as you develop.

- **process**, thinking about your motivation, area of enquiry and sources of information.
  - Create a selection of drawings, studies and realised work.
  - Experiment and edit your work.
  - Justify your selection and explain the reasons for your choices.
  - Relate the research, processes and decisions that led to your realised work.
- **realisation**, presenting your work. There should be an interwoven link between your practical work and Visual Studies. Present the finished artwork in a considered way, along with a rationale that explains the choices and decisions made.

Note: A good sketchpad is an excellent way to develop good art practice. Draw, sketch and write down your thoughts.

The Creative Process

Following a process is an excellent guideline for creating artwork, but as an artist you can of course start at any point in the following process. Remember, however, that each exploration or finished artwork will lead, influence or inform your next creation.

In the beginning, the most important part is probably your idea and everything generated from that one moment, but once you get the ideas down on paper by making rough sketches, move on quickly to drawing more refined sketches using primary sources. Following this process is both satisfying and rewarding and with each step along the journey, your artwork will evolve and become more interesting.

Curate: To select, organise and look after art objects, often used in relation to a museum setting.

The Creative Process

Think
Take some time to think about making art. Sometimes a word, a picture, a film or an event might set ideas in motion. Jot down your thoughts and scribbles – allow one word to suggest another – and next time you look, you may have a mind map.

Explore
Draw from primary sources to develop your observation and insight.
The simple plan of looking hard and then drawing is like the mind asking a question and the hand answering. Imagining, thinking and looking – through sketching – is an excellent way to explore ideas.

Media Exploration and Experimentation
A sketchbook is the ideal space for risk taking and experimenting with new ideas and materials.
It is a safe place to explore, reflect and refine.
Try a range of materials and combinations of media. Make mistakes – make a mess – it's all part of the fun!

Develop
Explore a theme. Try it out – work on it.
Examine the work of other artists, past or present. Study the art elements and design principles they have used and see how they have resolved artistic issues.
Experiment with ways of expressing ideas inspired by their work and motivation.
Try another way of expressing your thoughts and then another again. After all, it is only the start of your journey – there is a long way to go and there may be several new turns along the way.

Refine
Make new decisions. Which areas work best and why? Look again at your chosen artworks.
Could there be a better solution? Learn from other artists and make new drawings towards the realised imagery.
Should some parts be scaled up or down? Make more drawings.
Could some areas be brighter or clearer? Make new drawings.
Could the idea be better expressed in simpler form? Make a drawing.
Now make sketches of your proposed final artwork.

Realise
Prepare, sketch, plan or begin construction of your final artwork.
Choose your media and materials carefully. Make some small trial pieces if necessary.
Work from your own sketches, but change and refine as you continue. The final piece will evolve through a series of small decisions and consultations with your teacher. New issues will require new solutions.

Present
Curate and present your work in a considered way.
Choose which work to submit and communicate its meaning and context by including your artist's statement.

Reflect
Consider your work. Look and think.
Are you happy with it?
What satisfied you most?
What changes or adjustments might you make, next time?
How will the learning process inform your response to the written component of the examination to come?
How will this inform art choices you may make in the future?

Figure 18 (top left) Sketches and drawings of the dog in action;
(bottom left) Landscape studies inspired by Martin Gale;
(above) *Walking the Dog*, acrylic on canvas, 42 × 50 cm.

Examples of Student Artwork

The examples above and on the following pages of students' work demonstrate the creative process and show how the three strands of Research, Create and Respond and are interlinked. Each learner responded to an initial idea by researching, exploring and drawing from primary sources. They also responded to their studies of visual art by researching artists, art movements and artworks that informed, inspired and influenced their journey towards the creation of their own individual artworks.

Anna – Figure 18

Anna's ideas developed in response to her dog's behaviour and their walks together in the local area. Anna was captivated by the beauty of the coastal landscape in the early morning, as well as the nearby woodlands.

She photographed the sunrise over the headland, made studies of the dog's movements, and quick outdoor drawings in her sketchbook but as her work developed she became very interested in the Irish artist, Martin Gale. His contemporary realist style greatly inspired her own painting, and she loved his depiction of the Irish countryside and weather especially the winter skies and wet roads.

Daniel – Figure 19

Daniel was immediately inspired by the work of Egon Schiele. He found the 20th-century Austrian artist's portrayal of the body very interesting, and, in response, Daniel began to explore more contorted poses. He used a friend as a model and researched life studies by other artists. Michelangelo's love of complicated poses and Leonardo da Vinci's fascination with unusual faces all influenced the creative process as his ideas developed towards a finished piece.

Figure 19

(left) *Trapped*, pencil and coloured pencils on grey sugar paper, 42 × 59 cm.

(far left) Preparatory studies. Initial exploration inspired by Egon Schiele and development of the pose.

Figure 20

(above) *A Terrible Beauty*, acrylic and oil pastel on acrylic paper, 30 × 42 cm.
Preparatory studies (left, top to bottom)
Initial exploration inspired by Francis Bacon and Surrealism; Studies in distortion and Oskar Kokoschka's expressionist colour and style; Exploring the Op Art style of Victor Vasarely and Bridget Riley.

Figure 21 Study of a rope, pencil on paper.

Darragh – Figure 20

In his efforts to represent the internal battle within the individual self, Darragh initially drew inspiration from the poetry of W.B. Yeats and the Surrealist art movement. He responded to Francis Bacon's existential imagery and the surrealist artists René Magritte and Salvador Dalí's work by experimenting with distortion. He made drawings in his sketchbook from his own reflection in concave reflective surfaces, including spoons.

He then researched other art styles like Expressionism and Op Art. The Expressionist work of the early 20th-century Austrian artist and poet Oskar Kokoschka particularly intrigued him. He admired the artist's use of gestural brushstrokes and bright colours, because this had exactly the kind of energy he wanted to create in his own work.

To create a psychological space of orderly disorder and controlled chaos in his final piece, Darragh used a combination of media and styles. In his work *A Terrible Beauty* (named after W.B. Yeats's poem 'Easter 1916'), he painted with acrylic and oil pastels and fused bright expressionist colours and gestural brush marks with the carefully executed black and white squares of Op Art.

Lucy – Figure 21

A drawing of an old piece of rope found on the beach led Lucy to create a figure with an unusual hairstyle. She is now open to new ideas as she responds to the fantasy art of Canadian artist Susan Seddon Boulet and the Art Nouveau style of artist Alphonse Mucha (see Unit 5) but her research of the fashionable Renaissance ladies' hairstyles in studies by Leonardo da Vinci and Botticelli (see Unit 2) will offer further possibilities as her development continues.

Respond Strand

This strand is an opportunity to respond to your work and to that of others. Now that you understand the process better, you should have more confidence to respond emotionally, critically, aesthetically or contextually, or even respond through a combination of these.

As you develop an understanding of the process of being an artist, you will better trust your own decisions. You can better edit and select from your ideas and explain the choices and decisions that you have made.

The **Respond** strand should focus on:

- **analysis**, learning to discuss examples from Visual Studies should help you to:
  - recognise artistic thinking and elements in your own work and that of others
  - question established and new ideas.

- **contextual enquiries**, finding out more on the context, on the social and historical content should help you to:
  - further your understanding and knowledge
  - locate your own work in relation to other artworks within a particular context, such as style, social, political, ethical, etc.

- **impact and value**, looking at ways to judge the value of your own work and the work of others should help you to:
  - argue the merit of artworks using the appropriate information
  - experience art through your own sensory and/or emotional responses.

- **critical and personal reflection** should help you to:
  - discuss the development of ideas and work from conception to realisation
  - present evidence of a sustained and varied investigation of a stimulus
  - value sustained and varied investigation of a stimulus.

- **process**, learning to think about and rationalise this process should help you to:
  - describe your motivation and your area of inquiry
  - interpret sources of information
  - respond to a selection of drawings, studies and realised work
  - justify your research, processes and decision-making within your realised work.

Reflecting on Your Own Art and That of Others

Artist's Statement

The artist's statement is the written text that will accompany your final work. It is most effective when it is true and original; length is not particularly important.

Your statement is a very important introduction to your art practice, as it describes your motivation.

It explains your ideas and concepts, outlines which artistic processes and techniques you have used and gives you the opportunity to reveal some aspects that are sometimes difficult to convey in visual format.

Your artist's statement should include:

- the thinking process, background and ideas involved in your work

- why you made the work and what interests you

- the media, materials, techniques and processes you use

- the way you like to work and how the work was produced

- the processes required and specific methods and ideas that challenge and interest you

- interesting links to other artists and the research you have undertaken.

Writing about Art

In writing about art movements, artists and artworks, it is important to use correct art terms and visually expressive language. Learn from the descriptions and use the vocabulary found throughout this book but also make particular use of the glossary at the end.

Read as much as possible also from other sources to help you to develop confidence in the use of critical and visual language.

Responding to a Question in the Written Examination

Read the question carefully and identify the subject or theme of the question.

Plan and develop the key elements of your discussion by identifying the task words.

As you write you should:

- **evaluate** by examining and bringing together what you have learned about the art works, the artists who made them and the context in which they lived and worked.

- **respond** with emotion to the artwork because your task as a writer is to convey an enthusiastic and individual response that makes sure your reader will appreciate the work.

Reflect and Respond

This could involve a question that requires you to consider a particular aspect of a subject, in which case it is important to discuss this fully and qualify your points with examples

This could involve finding out why something happened or what the meaning of something is.

Discuss: to give information, ideas, and opinions about a topic

Explore: to find out

This could involve the use of words like: however, nevertheless, nonetheless, still, although, even though, though, but, yet, despite, in spite of, in contrast, in comparison, while, whereas, on the other hand, on the contrary.

Contrast: to note the obvious differences between persons or things

Compare: to examine the similarity or dissimilarity between persons or things

Study: to absorb the facts

Analyse: to understand and appreciate

This could involve finding out who, what, where, when and how.

This could involve the use of words like: similarly, likewise, also, like, just as, just like, similar to, the same as, compared to.

This could involve what you conclude from something and why you think that?

- **summarise** with a brief ending that outlines the main points of your argument.

Read and Respond

The use of visual and descriptive language in describing a work of art is really important because words and language should convey a vivid mental picture of the work for the reader.

Read the following descriptions of *A Connemara Village* in the National Gallery of Ireland and *Top of the Hill* in Limerick City Gallery, which have been adapted from information about the paintings on the gallery websites. Then respond in writing using visual and descriptive language to the questions that follow.

A Connemara Village, 1930–3, by Paul Henry, National Gallery of Ireland, Dublin

> *A cluster of tiny, white-washed cottages is picked out by the sunlight against a dark backdrop of mountains and a large cloudy sky.*

> *These cottages emphasise the grandeur of the local scenery, but they also convey a sense of isolation and the dependence of rural communities on the land.*

> *There is no sign of human activity in the work. Instead, the landscape is focused more on the play of light and the bold patterns and shapes of the clouds.*

> *The painting is typical of Henry's mature work and although it was painted in his Dublin studio, it clearly shows his experience and careful observation in the west of Ireland. Like similar works by the artist, it is celebrated as being quintessentially Irish.*

Top of the Hill, 1920, by Grace Henry, Limerick City Gallery of Art

> *It is interesting to contrast Paul Henry's iconic views of Ireland with the images presented by his wife, Grace. She shows more awareness of life in Ireland at that time not just by depicting everyday social scenes, but also by using modern design techniques. She plays with perspective, designing the composition of this painting by placing the three figures in the upper part of the composition so that the viewer is naturally encouraged to look upward and follow the incline of the slope towards them at the top of the hill.*

1. What images came to mind as you read the above descriptions?

2. What did you learn about both artists?

3. Look at these images in Unit 11 (page 470, Fig. 33.8 and 33.9). Compare these with the mental pictures you formed while reading.

4. How do you think your response might differ if you had the opportunity to engage with the real paintings in the galleries?

5. Make a sketch outlining the compositional lines of both works and use this a stimulus for a drawing, painting or print based on your own ideas.

6. Select another image from Chapter 33 or another area of your choice from this book and write your own description of the work.

Analysis

As you engage with the fundamental concepts of Art in both Practical and Visual Studies and learn to work within the three strands of study, you will develop key skills. These will develop as you research the work and ideas of other artists and you will learn to think critically and creatively, through your own recorded observations and drawings of the world around you.

These observations and knowledge will inform and inspire your innovative and creative journey in the making of and communicating your art with others.

Further Research

www.nationalgallery.ie – Ireland's National Gallery in Dublin

crawfordartgallery.ie – Crawford Art Gallery, Cork

gallery.limerick.ie – Limerick City Gallery of Art

www.ouririshheritage.org – Search for 'Grace Mitchell Henry' to find out more about the Irish artist

www.veraklute.net – Sculptor Vera Klute's official website

www.mauriceharron.com – Sculptor Maurice Harron's official website

www.unahealydesign.com – Click on 'Our Work' then select 'Leaflet, Poster and Menu Design' for more examples of contemporary Irish graphic design from the featured artist

www.youtube.com – Search for 'Beginning Graphic Design: Fundamentals' (6:26) to see how the basic art elements are used in graphic design

www.youtube.com – Search for 'Lettering Artistry with Jessica Hische' (4:57) to learn more about the process of creating typography

www.guggenheim-bilbao.eus/en/the-building – Explore the Guggenheim Museum building in Bilbao

odonnell-tuomey.ie – Select 'Projects' from the sidebar to see more of the award-winning architects' designs

www.youtube.com – Search for 'In conversation with Sheila O'Donnell' (4:06) to find the architect presenting the ideas underpinning award-winning O Donnell and Twomey projects

Unit 1

Romanesque and Gothic

(*c.* 1000–1500s)

1. Romanesque Architecture and Sculpture
2. Gothic Art and Architecture

Before

The Early Middle Ages (Dark Ages)

Romanesque (*c.* 1050–1250)

Basilica of St Magdalene Vézelay (12th century)

Tympanum Autun Cathedral Gislebertus (12th century)

Romanesque and Gothic (*c.* 1000–1500s)

Gothic (*c.* 1250–1450)

Chartres Cathedral (13th century)

Sculpture of Ekkehard and Uta, Naumburg Cathedral (13th century)

The Well of Moses, Dijon (15th century)

International Gothic (*c.* 1375–1450)

The Wilton Diptych (1395–9)

Les Très Riches Heures du Duc de Berry (1412–16)

After

The Renaissance in Florence and Rome (*c.* 1420–1500)

Romanesque Architecture and Sculpture

* be able to discuss social conditions in 11th- and 12th-century Europe
* understand why the Christian Church was so powerful
* understand the important role of monasteries in society
* know why people made long pilgrimages throughout Europe
* understand why new churches were needed along pilgrimage routes
* be able to discuss the need for stone vaulting and the problems this caused
* be able to discuss experiments and solutions to these structural problems
* understand the relationship between Romanesque architecture and sculpture
* be able to identify, describe and discuss examples of Romanesque pilgrimage churches
* be able to analyse examples of Romanesque sculpture.

Before Romanesque

The medieval era, or Middle Ages, was a period in Europe after the fall of the Roman Empire in the 5th century. The Early Middle Ages was for a time referred to as the Dark Ages because the rich Roman lifestyle had disappeared and invading tribes had ravaged towns. A good deal of knowledge on science, technology, medicine and literature was also lost.

Life was hard and very few people could read or write. It was not, however, a time of ignorance. Information was transmitted orally and retained through memory.

The Christian Church was the most powerful institution in medieval Europe. The land was divided into small tracts and rulers were constantly at war with one another, but kings and queens drew much of their authority from the pope, so none had absolute power.

The Roman Empire never reached Ireland, but its influence arrived with Christianity. Irish monasteries became internationally famous, as centres of learning (see Chapter 23), but Irish monks also travelled abroad. They established new centres of learning in monasteries throughout Europe, and even today dioceses in France, Germany, Austria, Switzerland, Holland and Italy have an Irish saint as their patron (Fig. 1.1).

 Find out more about the places where Irish monks established settlements in Scotland and the European continent.

The rise of monasticism greatly strengthened the medieval Church.

Figure 1.1
Bobbio, Northern Italy. The Abbey of St Columbano was founded by the Irish missionary St Columban (Columbanus) before AD 615. He had previously established a number of other monasteries around Europe.

St Benedict, or Saint Benedict of Nursia, founded the great Benedictine monastery of Montecassino in Italy during the 6th century (Fig. 1.2). In doing so, he established a new kind of monastery with the motto *ora et labora* – 'pray and work'. The idea of working was very new for monks, who had until then been holy men living like hermits in caves or travelling about performing charitable acts.

St Benedict's monastery became the model for many religious orders, but the Benedictines also greatly valued art and culture as a means of giving glory to God. This gave rise to a remarkable flowering of religious art, music, architecture and learning.

> **Illuminated manuscript:** A handwritten book that has been decorated with gold or silver, brilliant colours, or elaborate designs or miniature pictures.
>
> **Historiated initial:** An enlarged letter at the beginning of a paragraph or other section of text that contains a picture.

Research some important Irish or European illuminated manuscripts. Write your name in calligraphy or fine handwriting and decorate the initial letter in colour and gold based on an example of your choice.

Figure 1.2 An early 14th-century illuminated manuscript, featuring St Benedict on the left, as well as a number of historiated initial letters. Monks wrote or copied books in a scriptorium or writing room. They illustrated these and their handwriting was very skilled.

UNIT 1 ROMANESQUE AND GOTHIC (c. 1000–1500s)

Context

By the 11th century, Europe had developed into larger more stable territories and cities had begun to form. Increased trade and improved farming methods led to a growth in population and a better economy. Education became more established, and this encouraged developments in art and architecture.

The Feudal System

Medieval Europe was organised in a pyramidal structure known as a feudal system.

The king awarded land grants to important nobles, barons and bishops in return for the service of their knights in battle.

The Lord of the Manor owned the land and small communities formed around the castle, church, village and surrounding farm-land. The lord kept peasants safe and gave them land to grow crops, but the rigid system prevented real progress.

> **Note:** In the later centuries of the first millennium AD, there was a widespread fear that the year 1000 would be the year of the last judgement and therefore the end of the world. However, the new millennium actually brought a new spirit of enthusiasm, optimism and cultural unity to people throughout Europe.

The Christian Church

The Christian Church was the strongest, most organised, and powerful force in medieval society. It guided the lives of everyone from the richest king to the lowest serf, and had huge influence:

- It was outside of the feudal system so clever men could to rise to positions of power.
- It received a significant amount of taxes and donations
- Bishops and Church leaders had influential roles in government.
- Abbots of monasteries often came from noble and influential families and this made them powerful political figures.

Find out more about the feudal system and the communities that formed around the lord of the manor. What role did women and girls play within the hierarchy or order of this society?

> **Abbot:** The head of a monastery. His role was to lead and inspire all the monks, and they had to obey him. The word 'abbot' comes from the Greek *abbas*, which means 'father'.

Monasteries

Religious orders played a crucial role in the medieval Church. Monasteries were set on large estates and were almost entirely self-sufficient. They were places of peace, prayer and work that housed travellers, nursed the sick and assisted the poor. They were also centres of learning where the monks safeguarded ancient manuscripts and wrote and illustrated beautiful hand-made books. They built fine churches and created beautiful art objects for religious services – for the glory of God.

Monks, and especially abbots, were well connected to the aristocracy, so despite their closed nature, monasteries had considerable wealth and were a strong influence in society.

Church Influence

This was a time of a deep faith in God and religion, and there was widespread devotion to popular saints. Life was short and hard, with ever-present dangers from hunger, disease, war and fire. Church leaders offered hope with the promise of comfort and happiness in the next life.

One can only imagine the effect of the richly decorated and intricately designed churches on those who lived in poor conditions. It is little wonder that art was such a powerful medium for the Church.

> **Note:** Death was seen as the passage to the next life. This could be sudden and unexpected, so prayer, penance and pilgrimage were always essential.

The Crusades

A series of religious wars was initiated to stop the spread of Islam towards Europe. The Church supported Christian knights in recovering the Eastern Mediterranean – or Holy Land of Jesus – from the Muslims.

The Crusades are now seen as bloody campaigns of violence and self-interest, but Europe did benefit from new trade opportunities and the Church became even more prosperous.

Pilgrimages

The Church greatly encouraged the Christian practice of pilgrimage during the Middle Ages as a penance for sins. Pilgrimages were long, hard journeys made by believers to holy places. They often lasted several years, and were undertaken by millions of people all over Europe, usually on foot.

After the Crusades, a steady flow of important relics had come to pilgrimage sites. People believed in the curative power of these holy relics and numerous miracles were associated with them.

> **Relic:** Something from a saint, for example a part of their body, like hair or bone, or an object they touched, such as clothing. They were extremely valuable to churches or monasteries.

Figure 1.3 The relic hand of St James of Compostela, St Peter's Church, Marlow, UK.

Santiago de Compostela

By the 11th century, the popular pilgrimage routes to Rome and Jerusalem had become too dangerous due to the presence of bandits and pirates. The tomb of St James the apostle was then discovered at Santiago de Compostela, on the most western tip of Spain. This very quickly became the most famous pilgrimage destination in Europe.

Figure 1.4 Modern pilgrims at Santiago de Compostela Cathedral, Spain.

 Find out more about the 800-year-old legend that connects James the Great, son of Zebedee, brother of St John, and Apostle of Jesus with Spain and Santiago de Compostela. Why did the scallop shell become the symbol of this pilgrimage?

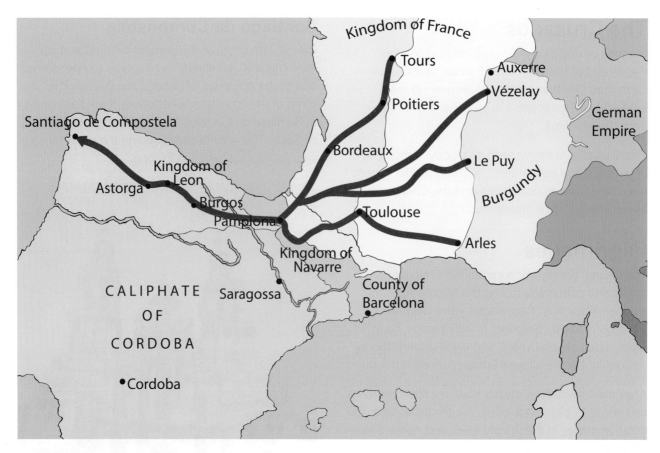

Figure 1.5 The four traditional routes through France to Santiago de Compostela.

Pilgrimage Churches

As more and more people made their way to Santiago de Compostela, the 11th and 12th centuries saw a frenzy of building activity with the construction of hostels, hospitals, bridges and – most dramatically of all – large churches along the pilgrimage routes in France.

Many churches acquired an important relic, and this made them pilgrimage destinations in their own right (Fig. 1.5).

Innovation and Invention

Romanesque means 'Roman-like'. The term was first used in the mid-19th century, when it was judged one of the great phases of Western culture. The art and architecture of the Middle Ages had been regarded as heavy and crude compared to the Renaissance.

Architecture

Ruins of Roman buildings, bridges and aqueducts were scattered around parts of Europe. Romanesque architects used these and especially the round Roman arch as inspiration.

Church designs were based on the Roman basilica, but were adapted to suit the needs of pilgrims (Fig. 1.6–1.9).

Crosswise transepts made them cruciform in shape and broke up the long nave. This allowed pilgrims to walk about without interrupting religious services and an ambulatory or walkway around the back of the altar facilitated the viewing of the relics.

Radiating chapels, each with a minor relic, were built out from the ambulatory and a central tower or cupola (dome) was added to bring light to the centre at the crossing.

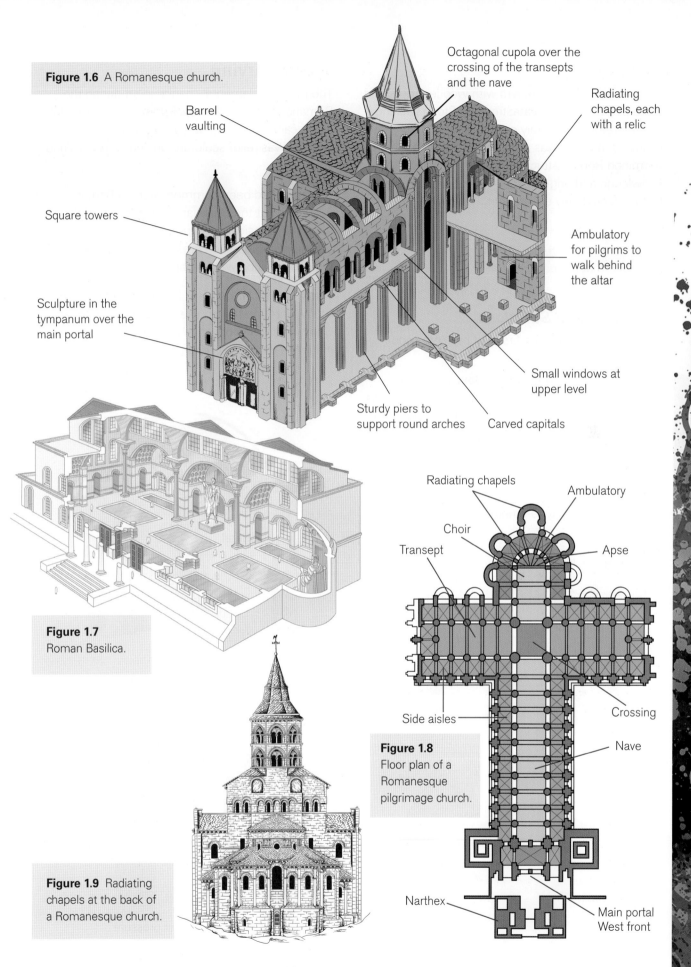

Figure 1.6 A Romanesque church.

Octagonal cupola over the crossing of the transepts and the nave

Radiating chapels, each with a relic

Barrel vaulting

Square towers

Ambulatory for pilgrims to walk behind the altar

Sculpture in the tympanum over the main portal

Small windows at upper level

Sturdy piers to support round arches

Carved capitals

Figure 1.7 Roman Basilica.

Figure 1.9 Radiating chapels at the back of a Romanesque church.

Radiating chapels

Ambulatory

Choir

Transept

Apse

Side aisles

Figure 1.8 Floor plan of a Romanesque pilgrimage church.

Crossing

Nave

Narthex

Main portal West front

Vaulting

Fire was a constant problem with wooden roofs and there had been many catastrophes. Stone vaulting was therefore absolutely essential in the new churches, but this was not an easy task. Masons examined Roman structures, but the technical knowledge and original plans were lost. Medieval builders could only experiment.

> **Vault:** An architectural term for the arched space that supports a roof.

Problems and Solutions

- Barrel vaulting came first, but problems soon developed
- Heavy stone roofs pressed **down**, but also pressed **out**. This caused arches to flatten, walls to push outward and, without intervention, the roof would collapse (Fig. 1.10).
- Pointed barrel vaulting was an improvement, but problems continued.
- Groin vaulting seemed to solve the issue, but problems slowly re-emerged.

Figure 1.10 Vaulting in Romanesque churches.

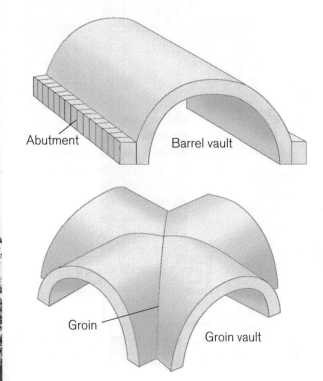

Abutment · Barrel vault

Groin · Groin vault

Stone Carving

The most fundamental change in art during the Romanesque period was a return to monumental stone carving. The most important art form to emerge was relief sculpture on church portals and capitals.

Sculpture had been commonplace on Roman buildings, but the Christian Church had traditionally regarded Classical sculpture, especially free-standing statues, with great suspicion because of their association with pagan gods.

The sculptors at the great Benedictine Abbey of Cluny were the first to use the human figure in Christian art, and because of Cluny's enormous influence the idea spread to other pilgrim churches.

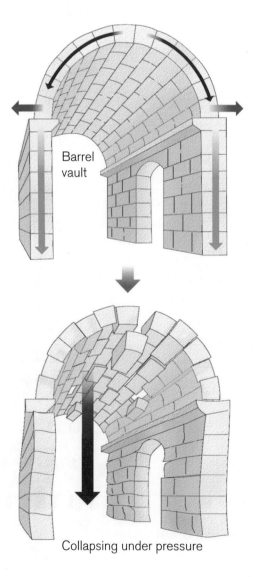

Barrel vault

Collapsing under pressure

> **Relief sculpture:** A wall-mounted sculpture in which the three-dimensional elements are raised from a flat base.
>
> **Classical:** Something related to the civilisation of ancient Greeks and Romans, especially in literature, art and architecture.

Architectural Sculpture

Architectural sculpture represented a new and powerful medium for the Church because, although very few people could actually read, everyone could understand the picture stories in stone.

Monumental scenes of Christ in Majesty and the Last Judgement in the tympana over church doors was one of the most significant innovations of the period.

> **Tympana, plural of tympanum:** The word comes from Latin and Greek meaning 'drum'. This is a semi-circular or triangular decorative wall surface over an entrance, door or window, which is bounded by a lintel and an arch.

Historiated Capitals

Stylised figures and decorative foliage on capitals were another very innovative element. Decorative or narrative imagery was often compressed to fit these awkward spaces (Fig. 1.11).

> **Historiated capital:** In architecture, the capital is the top part of a column. This is sometimes decorated with figures of animals, birds, or humans, used either alone or combined with foliage.

Design a relief sculpture for a rectangular space, of a Romanesque-style demon, that combines animal and human features to symbolise the sin of gluttony (over-eating) or pride. Include natural forms as part of the design.

Figure 1.11 Historiated capital symbolising Lust and Despair in the Basilica Church of St Magdalene, Vézelay, France. Despair, depicted as an open-mouthed demon with dog-like features and burning hair, plunges a sword into his own stomach. Lust is portrayed as a nude woman bitten by serpents.

Artists and Artworks

Church building and sculptural decoration was the main focus of Romanesque art and architecture. Much of this work may have been executed by the monks themselves and the influence of illuminated manuscripts can be seen in the decorative sculpture.

Architect or Sculptor?

Romanesque builders were not architects as we know them today but were skilled masons. They had little formal mathematical knowledge, but were inspired creators who visualised the finished buildings and experimented as they worked. That sometimes meant completely revising the plan and even demolishing the building to improve the overall composition.

The remarkable unity between decorative sculpture and churches built of stone suggests that sculptors may have begun their career as stone masons.

Gislebertus

Gislebertus is the only Romanesque sculptor known by name. He produced some of the most original work of the period and his expressive and imaginative style suggests he may have worked at Cluny, and possibly at Vézelay. However, his signature is all that is known of him. The inscription *Gislebertus hoc fecit* (the Latin for 'Gislebertus made this') appears on the lintel, directly below the feet of Christ, on the tympanum at Autun Cathedral.

Influences

Gislebertus' influence is seen on other church sculptures in France, and his techniques helped to pave the way for the later Gothic style.

> Note: Signatures on works of art were quite common in the Romanesque period, but the position and importance of Gislebertus' name makes it unusual. Earlier examples of signatures in France were placed discreetly either at the base of a column or more frequently on a capital.

Topics

Images of God, the saints or bible stories were carved in relief on architectural spaces. These were used to teach the doctrine of Christ, but judgement scenes were also designed to intimidate pilgrims. Grotesque devils and scenes of hell warned church attendees to recognise their own wrongdoing, and to repent of their sins in good time so they would be saved after they died.

Style

Romanesque sculpture was stylised, distinctive and quite abstract. No attempt was made to portray God or the saints in a natural way and figures were often elongated or distorted.

> **Stylised:** Using artistic forms and conventions to create effects; not natural or spontaneous.

Artistic Expression

Symbolic meaning in religious subject matter was of the utmost importance and no artist could break these fixed laws, but they had a significant amount of artistic freedom in style.

Decorated capitals in particular show great artistic originality. Artists appear to have considerable scope for self-expression, especially in the depiction of legends of local saints. The imagery combines abstract decorative elements with angels, devils and grotesque monsters that are half-animal and half-human.

Romanesque Pilgrimage Churches in France

Cluny Abbey

Cluny in eastern central France is of paramount importance to Romanesque art. By the end of the

Figure 1.12
Engraving of Cluny Abbey before its demolition in the early 19th century.

11th century, this Benedictine Abbey was extremely wealthy and powerful. It was famous for its great splendour (Fig. 1.12).

Cluny III

Cluny's great power was reflected in its vast abbey church, known as Cluny III. This was the third church built on the same site and remained the largest and most beautiful in Christendom for several centuries.

Built from a combination of brick and ashlar masonry, the huge basilica had five aisles, two transepts, an ambulatory and numerous radiating chapels at the east end. The central crossing was surmounted by an octagonal tower, and additional towers over the transept arms allowed light to penetrate the interior.

> **Ashlar masonry:** A type of stone masonry which is built in layers. The stones have been finely dressed (cut) to have the same shape, size and surface texture.

Influences

Cluny's influence extended all over Europe. Many smaller abbeys followed its rules and were inspired by its art. The artists are unknown, but accounts describe the Abbey's beautifully ornamented arches, windows and carved capitals.

Demolition

The abbots of Cluny were very powerful, and some even became popes. However, by the time of the French Revolution, they were identified as part of the old establishment, and therefore undesirable in the new republic. The abbey was taken over by the state and closed. It was then sold and used as a stone quarry until 1823, during which time it was almost completely demolished.

Only one transept arm stands today (Fig. 1.13), but scholars have reconstructed how the interior would have looked. The three-storey elevation with its high pointed barrel vaulting would surely have been a magnificent sight.

Carved Capitals

Most of Cluny's wonderful artwork was lost or

Figure 1.13 The majestic Clocher de l'Eau-Bénite (Holy Water Belfry) that towers over the south transept is the only part of the Abbey Church of Cluny that remains today.

demolished, but some carved capitals were found more or less intact in the rubble of the choir during excavations. These delightful sculptures represent the Gregorian chant as sung by monks. Some are playing instruments and others seem to sway in dance-like movements (Fig. 1.14 and 1.15).

> **Gregorian chant** was sung in unison to accompany mass or other religious services. It is named after Pope St Gregory I AD 509–604.
>
> **Mandorla:** a panel in the shape of an almond.

Search for Cluny Abbey on the Khan Academy website, *www.khanacademy.org.* Why was Cluny so important and how did it influence art and architecture in the surrounding area?

Figure 1.14 (left) Original capitals on reconstructed columns from the ambulatory around the choir of the abbey church of Cluny (*c.* 1088–1130). They represent the eight tones of music, personified as small figures standing in almond-shaped mandorlas.

Figure 1.15 (right) In the third tone, a figure holds a lyre, which rests on his left knee.

St Foy de Conques

Originally an abbey, the Church at Conques became a popular stop for pilgrims after it acquired the bones of St Foy (St Faith).

The 12th-century church has a solid geometric exterior appearance with no real ornamentation except for buttresses, which were added later to counteract the outward thrust of the walls. The towers on either side were added in the 19th century (Fig. 1.16).

The Tympanum

Towering over the Western portal, a series of dramatic sculpted images in the tympanum greeted pilgrims as they passed beneath (Fig 1.17).

> **Portal:** The architectural composition surrounding and including the doorways and porches of a church.

This famous Last Judgement scene is full of activity. Christ in Majesty presides over the souls and a large doorway beneath his feet leads to Paradise on

Figure 1.16 St Foy de Conques, France.

Figure 1.17
The tympanum at
St Foy de Conques.

Figure 1.18
Detail from the
tympanum St Foy
de Conques. In the
kingdom of hell, the
devil is wearing a
crown and seated on
a throne. He hands
out punishment
according to the
severity of the sins.

the one side but on the other to the terrifying and monstrous mouth of hell.

Various sins are depicted, with some figures representing well-known characters from the area's local history. A knight is tossed from his horse into the fires. The hanged man is a reference to Judas. One man is roasted on the spit, while above him another is dangled by the legs in punishment for the sin of gluttony (over-eating). Clothing being stripped from the wealthy is also depicted (Fig 1.18).

Several inscriptions in Latin are clearly readable on the tympanum. Some are in rhyme, but a long band at the very bottom of the scene along the whole length reads: 'O Sinners, if you do not change your ways, know that you will suffer a dreadful fate.'

St Magdalene, Vézelay

The Basilica Church of Vézelay is the largest Romanesque church in France (Fig. 1.19). This Benedictine abbey acquired relics of Mary Magdalene in 1037 and it became a major stop on the Compostela route. It was rebuilt around 1150, after 1,200 pilgrims lost their lives in a fire there.

Figure 1.19 The Basilica Church of St Magdalene overlooks the town of Vézelay.

UNIT 1 ROMANESQUE AND GOTHIC (c. 1000–1500s)

Vaulting

Groin vaulting was quite innovative for the time. It made it possible to have thinner walls, which in turn allowed for larger windows than in most Romanesque churches.

It did not, however, solve the structural problems, and the arches can clearly be seen to have flattened out as a result of pressure from the weight of the stone vaulting. The outward-leaning piers also show the classic signs of outward thrust, which was only solved in later years when flying buttresses were added to support the walls from the outside.

The monks at Vézelay also added a new choir (the area around the altar) at the end of the 12th century. This was built in the new and lighter Gothic style and allowed even more light to pour into the nave.

The Central Tympanum

The portal inside of the narthex (or porch), has three relief sculptured scenes. Over the central doorway, the Pentecost, represents Christ's command to his apostles to preach the good news (Fig. 1.21). The great Christ in majesty, enclosed in a mandorla, faces forward, motionless and serene. His arms are thrown open, to symbolise of the glory of his resurrection. With knees bent to one side, his beautifully pleated robe is arranged in whirling spiral patterns.

Other figures in the scene include:

● St Peter – identified by the key to the Kingdom of Heaven
● the apostles of Jesus – flames of the Holy Spirit fall on their heads, giving them the strength to teach the word of God
● people of the world – arranged in the semi-circular surround (some are pagans and have animal heads or donkeys' ears).

> **Pentecost:** An event after the death of Jesus when the Holy Spirit in the form of tongues of fire descended on his disciples.

Figure 1.20 The interior of the Basilica Church of St Magdalene, Vézelay.

Interior

The exterior of the Basilica Church of St Magdalene suffered great damage during the French Revolution in the late 18th century, but the interior survived. The semi-circular arches that divide the nave into groin-vaulted bays create a soaring upward structure.

One of Vézelay's most notable characteristics is the ochre and white stone that gives a chequered effect and shows the influence of Islamic architecture (Figure 1.20).

Figure 1.21 Basilica Church of St Magdalene, Vézelay. The main scene in the tympanum over the central doorway of the narthex represents the Pentecost.

Carved Capitals in the Nave

Some of the capitals in the nave are typical of the Romanesque fascination with the grotesque, with depictions of devils, beasts and monsters.

The Mystic Mill

Meaning

The most famous scene in Vézelay shows Moses pouring the grain, which represents the law given by God while St Paul the Apostle gathers the flour that has been milled by Christ (Fig. 1.22).

Light

The composition was cleverly designed to take full advantage of natural light. The figure of Moses representing the Old Testament faces west and St Paul representing the New Testament faces east, meaning they were either in shadow or light depending on the time of day. The wheel of the mill, symbolising Christ and creating the central motion of the scene, picks up constant light from the south.

Figure 1.22 The Mystic Mill capital.

Autun Cathedral

The Cathedral of St Lazare was built in the mid-12th century after relics of St Lazarus were discovered in Autun. It was hoped the relics would make Autun a major pilgrimage destination like nearby Vézelay.

The main core of the church and its magnificent sculptures are Romanesque, although several Gothic-style additions, including the choir and great spire, were added later after a fire (Fig. 1.23 and 1.24).

Figure 1.23
The Cathedral of St Lazare, Autun.

Figure 1.24
The interior of St Lazare, showing the original Romanesque pointed barrel vaulting and sculpture on the capitals. The fluting on the columns was inspired by Roman structures which were widespread around the area of Autun. The innovative inclusion of high clerestory windows and the later addition of a new choir brought extra light to the nave. A clerestory is a high section of wall containing windows above eye level. The purpose is to admit light, fresh air or both.

The Tympanum: The Last Judgement

This is probably the most recognisable of all Romanesque church sculptures (Fig. 1.25).

The large figure of Christ is portrayed as an impassive judge, placed in a mandorla.

The narrative starts on the lintel below the tympanum. Figures rise from their coffins at the sound of the trumpets and are guided by an angel towards St Peter, with a large key.

Pilgrims, one with a cross for Jerusalem on his satchel, the other a shell for St James, ascend upwards to heaven, but an angel with a flaming sword turns others away. They are bent over and ashamed, with mouths open in anguish. Farther along they become even more curled in on themselves and their expressions more exaggerated. One is grabbed by two claw-like hands.

The Weighing of Souls

The most famous section in the tympanum is the Weighing of Souls (Fig. 1.26). Archangel Michael weighs the souls, while terrified figures hide beneath his robes. A grotesque devil tries to pull down the scale and another sits in it to make it heavier before a laughing demon pours those condemned forever down a chute towards the gaping jaws of hell and the fires below.

Meaning

The gruesome images represents a struggle between good and evil as souls line up to be weighed in favour of heaven or hell.

Pilgrims always entered by the western door and the dramatic scene above them was calculated to inspire fear as well as hope as they ascended the steps (Fig 1.27).

Form and Style

Carved in quite high relief, some figures are almost free standing. They are stylised, thin and elongated, some distorted to fit the space. These characters show real emotion, but the devils – with grinning animal faces and feet – are particularly repulsive.

> **High relief:** Forms and figures that stand out from the background to half or more than half of their natural depth.

Figure 1.25
The Last Judgement, the tympanum at St Lazare, Autun.

Materials and Techniques

Large white limestone blocks were cut into shape and sculpted before mounting. These were designed to fit neatly together within the architectural space.

Colour

The sculpture would have been even more dramatic originally when it was painted in full colour.

> *Note:* The Last Judgement scene survived the French Revolution because the Church had grown ashamed of the crude Romanesque imagery and had covered it over with plaster in the 18th century. It was rediscovered in the 19th century.

Narrative Scenes on the Capitals

Some of the most charming and touching works of Romanesque sculpture are found on the capitals at Autun. The figures are cleverly combined with ornamental foliage to fit within the awkward shapes.

The Flight into Egypt

Having been warned in a dream that Herod seeks

Figure 1.26 The Weighing of Souls.

to kill Jesus, the holy family leave for Egypt on a donkey (Fig. 1.28). Mary sits upright in the traditional pose. Her lap forms a throne for the solemn figure

Figure 1.27 The western portal, St Lazare, Autun.

Figure 1.28 The Flight into Egypt capital.

of the Christ child. The donkey is quite naturally portrayed.

The Suicide of Judas

This capital portrays the moment that Judas, full of guilt and despair at his betrayal of Jesus, hangs himself. His tongue hangs out and the head falls grotesquely to one side as two demons pull the rope, forming a balanced triangular composition (Fig. 1.29).

Figure 1.29 The Suicide of Judas capital.

The Dream of the Magi

The story is told in three simple gestures. The angel points to the star, gently touches a hand and a king opens one eye. This is a warning not to return to King Herod after they have seen the baby Jesus in Bethlehem. The semi-circular lines of the bed cover unite the composition (Fig. 1.30).

Figure 1.30 The Dream of the Magi capital.

Imagine you are a pilgrim in the 12th century and you have been walking towards Santiago de Compostela for two years or more. How do think you would react to the imagery in the sculpture of these Romanesque churches?

RESPOND

Art Elements and Design Principles

Architecture

Shape

Romanesque architecture had a massive, solid appearance.

Pilgrimage churches were all quite similar. The shapes were geometric and they were symmetrical in plan.

Typical characteristics included:

- rounded Roman-style arches on doors, windows and towers
- thick walls to hold the weight of heavy stone vaulting

- sturdy piers (columns) to support arches
- dark interiors due to the lack of large windows, which would have weakened the walls
- large towers over the crossing to allow light into the interior
- blind arcades – a series of arches on the surface of walls. These were decorative elements, not windows or openings
- cut-stone blocks of ashlar masonry.

Architectural Features

The tympanum: A space enclosed by the arch of the doorway, frequently filled with carved relief sculpture.

Archivolts: Ornamental moulding or bands surrounding the arches that frame the tympanum.

A lintel: A horizontal beam over a window or door, or between two posts

A trumeau: The central doorpost supporting the lintel.

Jambs: The sides of a doorway. These were sometimes in the form of columns decorated with abstract carvings.

Voussoir: A wedge-shaped stone, used in the building of an arch or vault.

Rhythm and Light

The interior of St Magdalene in Vézelay is one of the most beautiful examples of stately Romanesque dignity. The chequered pink and white stone arches create harmony in a perfect balance of rhythm and light.

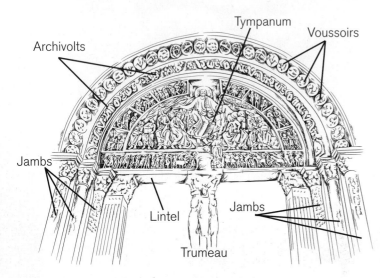

Figure 1.31 Romanesque portal.

Figure 1.32 Window arch piers and blind arcade.

Figure 1.33 The interior of St Magdalene in Vézelay.

Sculpture

Sculpture of the Romanesque period was firmly tied to architecture.

Form

It was carved in high and low relief.

Decorative Elements and Motifs

- Patterns based on foliage and animal forms.
- Texture based on the spiral. This was one of the most significant motifs of Romanesque design. It was used in both figurative and non-figurative sculpture.
- Narrative scenes from the bible or lives of the saints.

Style

The human figure was often distorted to fit the semi-circular shape of the tympanum or the rectangular shape of the column capital.

Characteristics of human in figure in sculpture were:

- largest for Christ or God
- smallest in the lintel – souls rising from the dead
- sometimes bestial or grotesque
- portrayed like dogs with snarling mouths; devils in hell had animal hooves.

Historiated Capitals

Images on the capitals had a strong narrative element but often combined abstract decoration. They included:

- figures from bible stories
- grotesque imaginary creatures
- stylised foliage
- abstract patterns.

Colour

Sculpture and the surrounding decorative features on the architecture would originally have been fully coloured. Traces of the original colour still survive on the tympanum at St Foy de Conques.

Media and Areas of Practice

Architecture

The main focus of the Romanesque period was on church building. Designs were based on Roman structures.

The building materials differed greatly across Europe, as they depended on locally available stone and building traditions. Brick was used in northern countries and rubble or uncut stone was used in early Romanesque buildings.

Smooth ashlar masonry was more widely used in the 12th century for the churches on the pilgrimage routes in France, where easily worked limestone was available.

A vast volume of stone was quarried and many masons were required. They worked as free craftsmen, organising themselves into societies or guilds and oversaw everything from apprenticeships to the quarrying of stone. They also did all the cutting and placing at the building site.

The basic tools had barely changed from ancient times, but they had large saws driven by waterwheels to cut stone, as well as considerable machinery for raising and moving materials.

Note: Ashlar masonry uses layers of stones to make walls. Sometimes referred to as 'dressed stone', the stones are all cut to have the same shape, size and surface texture.

The stones fit tightly, making structures strong and sturdy, but ashlar is expensive because of the time needed to prepare and chisel them down to a finished appearance.

Sculpture

Monks first used sculpture in stone as decoration on capitals in their own private areas of worship.

The human figure first featured in Christian imagery towards the end of the 11th century, but this never took the form of free-standing statues.

Over the course of the 12th century, the façades of the new Romanesque churches were decorated with relief sculpture around the portal, using the Roman arch of triumph as a model.

Analysis

When examining the architecture of pilgrimage churches, look for the use of the Roman rounded arch and other typical characteristics of structure and decoration. Note also how the elements of architecture have been used.

When examining sculpture, remember that most people outside of the monasteries could not read so sculpture was used to guide and teach ordinary people the doctrine of Christ and religious truths. Consider the essential link between architecture and sculpture.

Compare the style and form of the works and consider any influences. Note the use of material, space, and elements of art in prominent works of sculpture and how the composition contributes to the narrative or message.

As Europe returned to political stability and economic growth, art and architecture developed. The Christian Church had grown to a position of strength and power, and the Romanesque period of the 11th and 12th centuries saw a dramatic surge of large-scale church-building, decoration and visual storytelling.

Narrative sculpture over the doors and on the capitals at the top of the interior columns of the new pilgrimage churches were powerful works of art, but their main purpose was to teach and guide the faithful.

The rounded Roman arch was widely used in the architecture of pilgrimage churches, and the threat of fire meant that stone vaulting was absolutely necessary. Early churches had barrel vaulting, but structural problems led architects to experiment with a pointed arch and groin vaulting. This, however, did not fully resolve the problem of outwards thrust, which continued to plague the Romanesque builders until Gothic architecture began to develop ribbed vaulting and buttressing towards the end of the 12th century.

Chapter Review

1. Discuss why the Christian Church developed such a strong and influential position in society.

2. Why were so many stone churches built in France during the 11th and 12th centuries?

3. Describe the characteristics of a typical Romanesque pilgrimage church in France and the problems caused by heavy stone vaulting.

4. Describe and discuss the interior of St Magdalene of Vézelay.

5. Examine 'The Mystic Mill' (Fig. 1.22). Discuss the composition, decorative techniques, treatment of the human figure and use of space. What is the meaning of this work?

6. Gislebertus is the only named Romanesque artist that we know. Which aspect of his work do find most interesting or appealing? Give your reasons for this.

7. Look at the detail from the tympanum at Autun (Fig. 1.34). Describe and discuss:
   - the subject matter and its meaning or message
   - the artist's use of space and treatment of the human figure
   - the style and decorative techniques that convey emotion
   - the meaning of the inscription in Latin.
   - how the imagery might have affected viewers at that time.

Figure 1.34
Detail of the sculpture on the tympanum on the west portico at the Cathedral of St Lazare, Autun.

Further Research

www.youtube.com – Search for 'The Abbey of Montecassino | Italia Slow Tour' (7:45) to discover the path of St Benedict that leads to the great Abbey of Montecassino

www.youtube.com – Search for 'Pentecost and Mission to the Apostles Tympanum, Vézelay' (6:08) to see how the spreading of the Gospel in the 12th century is reflected in the sculpture

www.wga.hu – Search for 'Gislebertus' on Web Gallery of Art to see detailed information on his work at Autun

www.khanacademy.org – Search for 'Last Judgment Tympanum, Cathedral of St. Lazare, Autun' on Khan Academy to see the full details of the Last Judgement

www.theatre-antique.com/en – Select 'The Triumphal Arch and the Remains of the Temple' from the DISCOVER menu to see one of the Roman structures that influenced Romanesque building

Chapter 2

Gothic Art and Architecture

By the end of this chapter I will ...

* understand Abbot Suger's role in the new style of architecture
* be able to discuss the concept of an 'architecture of light'
* be able to identify, describe and draw the distinctive features of Gothic architecture and compare them with those of the Romanesque
* understand how the imagery in Gothic sculpture was used for teaching purposes
* be able to describe and discuss how Gothic sculpture progressively became more naturalistic
* be able to describe and discuss a work by Claus Sluter
* be able to describe the technique of stained glass
* understand the atmosphere created by stained glass in cathedrals
* be able to identify the unique characteristics of paintings in the International style
* be able to describe and discuss a work of art in the International style.

Context

Medieval Europe was at a peak in the 13th century. The population had risen, food supply was better and merchant classes had developed in towns. Travel and communication had also become faster, safer, and easier.

Rich monasteries, controlled by powerful abbots, still held an important role and the Church remained the dominant force in every aspect of society. In particular it controlled intellectual thinking, teaching and learning.

Universities

Scholasticism had developed in schools attached to cathedrals and these evolved into universities in places like Oxford and Paris. However very few young women attended university because all tuition was in Latin and generally only young boys received an early education in this.

Scholasticism: A way of thinking and teaching knowledge in the Middle Ages. It was influenced by the Italian Dominican friar, St Thomas Aquinas (1225–1274). This influential theologian combined the thinking of Aristotle, the ancient Greek philosopher, with Christian religious doctrine.

13th-century France

Culturally and intellectually, France was the most important 13th-century country in Europe. Paris was, of course, the hub, but other large towns like Chartres, Tours, Orléans and Reims were also renowned centres of learning, each with their own universities and cathedrals.

Burgundy

There were also several independent states within France. The most powerful of these was the duchy of Burgundy, which was located between France and the German Empire. It included Flanders (northern Belgium today), the Netherlands and a good part of part of northern France. The dukes of Burgundy were almost like kings and their extravagant court was famous for its magnificence and visual splendour.

Cathedrals

The 13th century was the age of the great cathedral. These soaring new structures were important status symbols in a town, and were associated with universities.

> **Cathedral:** From the Latin word *cathedra*, meaning 'seat'. A cathedral houses the seat of the bishop and is the central church for a wider area or diocese.

Cathedrals today are solemn, quiet and sacred places, but in medieval times, this was not so. Religious services would have taken place in the choir, which was separated from the public by a screen. The nave served the community and this would have been a hub of all kinds of noise and activity.

The vast space, the music, the incense and coloured light from the stained-glass windows would have made the cathedral a unique experience for pilgrims, especially when both inside and outside structures were painted in bright colours.

Art

The Church spread the message of Christ through the medium of art. Some of the most advanced intellectual ideas were reflected in the glass and the sculpture, but ordinary pilgrims also found simple messages and stories of much-loved saints.

The 14th Century

By the 14th century, people were living more independently of the Church. Wealthy patrons paid high prices for small but delicate religious works, usually for private chapels in their own luxurious homes.

Innovation and Invention

Today, Gothic art and architecture is greatly admired, but the term was first used in a negative way during the Italian Renaissance. This linked it to the art of the barbarian Goths, who were notorious invaders and thought of as uncivilised.

The 'Creator of Gothic'

The Benedictine Abbey of St Denis just north of Paris was in a dilapidated state when the new abbot, a man named Suger, took over. He decided to restore the Abbey Church (Fig. 2.1) to its former glory. The result was a major event in the history of architecture.

This deeply intellectual and spiritual man believed that beauty honoured God. His fascination with 'divine' light led to a completely new concept – 'an architecture of light'.

Suger and his architect combined elements of Romanesque architecture with the highly innovative ribbed vaulting (Fig. 2.2).

Thinner walls allowed for more window openings and light to penetrate the building. Stained glass was used extensively and included the first ever Gothic rose window on the west façade.

> A **rib vault** or **ribbed vault** is an architectural feature used to cover the width of a church nave. It is composed of a framework of crossed or diagonal arched ribs.

Figure 2.2 Ribbed vaulting in the nave, Basilica of St Denis.

Figure 2.1 St Denis in Paris. A cleaning technique known as micro abrasion was used on the building in 2015. This helped to reveal the many colours in the stone.

Gothic Architecture

The soaring vertical lines and skeletal structures of Gothic cathedrals soon replaced the massive walls of Romanesque buildings. They first appeared in Paris and the Île-de-France, but spread rapidly to the rest of northern France, in places like Amiens, Chartres, Rouen, Reims, Orléans and Beauvais.

The new 'French style' spread to other parts of Europe, like Cologne in Germany and Milan in Italy, as well as to England.

Find out more about Gothic Cathedrals in Ireland in Chapter 27. Compare these to the Cathedrals of Salisbury, Canterbury, Exeter and others in England. Why was the Gothic style called 'Anglo-Norman' in England and Ireland?

New building techniques included:

- the pointed arch (Fig 2.3)
- the ribbed vault (Fig 2.4)
- the clustered column (multiple columns standing together as one to support the vaulting)
- buttresses on exterior walls (Fig 2.5)
- tall thin walls with large openings for pointed lancet windows
- flying buttresses – arches to support the walls on the higher areas. This allowed for greater height and more openings for large upper-level windows (Fig. 2.5 and 2.6)
- stained glass in the windows
- tracery – ornamental stonework of delicate, lacelike patterns supporting the glass in the windows (Fig. 2.7).

Figure 2.3 Pointed arches.

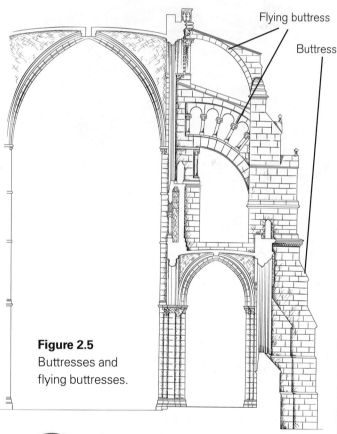

Flying buttress

Buttress

Figure 2.5
Buttresses and
flying buttresses.

Figure 2.4 Ribbed vaulting.

Go to YouTube and watch the video 'Explaining the Flying Buttresses' (1:25). Have some fun trying it out in the classroom or with a group of friends

UNIT 1 ROMANESQUE AND GOTHIC (c. 1000–1500s)

Figure 2.6 Chartres cathedral was one of the first buildings to utilise the full potential of flying buttresses. There are three levels along the exterior of the nave.

A third flyer of arches stretch from the top of the buttresses to just below the gutter of the upper nave

The second level is connected by small columns arranged like spokes of a wheel

The first level takes the form of a simple arch.

Figure 2.7 Tracery on a rose window from Chartres Cathedral.

The Gothic Spire

Romanesque church spires had been simple, four-sided structures, but Gothic spires evolved into taller, slimmer, eight-sided structures that also symbolised aspiring towards heaven. Small pinnacles blended the square base with these octagonal forms.

Spires are quite fragile in bad weather. One of the spires in Chartres was destroyed by lightning in 1506 and was rebuilt in the later Flamboyant style.

Pinnacle: A miniature spire which was used both as a decorative and functional element.

Figure 2.8 A drawing of the Cathedral of St Denis with the north tower before its demolition in the 19th century.

Sculpture on the Doorways

One the most original and unique features of Gothic sculpture were column statues. They first appeared on the doorway of St Denis and reflected the new architecture.

Figure 2.9 (above) Figures on the main doorway of Reims Cathedral include the famous 'Smiling Angel', which has become the emblem of the city.

Figure 2.10 (right) The main doorway of Reims Cathedral is dedicated to Mary.

New Imagery in Art

Gothic art was still didactic (for teaching), but a huge shift in religious thinking by scholars and intellectuals brought great changes in the imagery.

As art became more refined, the message of death and damnation was replaced by a vision of hope, and the distorted shapes and grotesque Romanesque demons disappeared.

Religious figures also became more naturalistic (Fig. 2.9 and 2.10).

Devotion to Mary increased in this age of chivalry, which had a high regard for the 'honour' of women.

Many Gothic cathedrals were called Notre Dame (Our Lady) and dedicated to the Virgin. Mary became one of the most important figures in art (Fig. 2.10).

Chivalry, or the **chivalric code**, was a code of conduct associated with the medieval Christian institution of knighthood. This moral system established the notion of honour and courtly manners.

Stained Glass

Abbot Suger of St Denis was the first to fully explore the possibilities of stained-glass windows. Coloured glass has been made since ancient times, and had come to Europe with Christianity, but Suger's journal tells us that he wanted the Abbey Church to 'shine with the wonderful light of luminous windows'. He considered light to be the manifestation of God himself, and employed very skilled craftsmen to install large stained-glass windows because he believed their beauty would lift people's souls closer to God.

As the sun poured through these huge windows, the walls appeared to dissolve in a magnificent, translucent haze, almost like heaven on Earth.

Media and Areas of Practice

Architecture

Gothic architecture evolved over 250 years. Rivalry and competition led builders to construct higher, grander and ever-more decorative structures, but the style ended abruptly in the 15th century.

The three distinct phases of Gothic architecture were:

- Early Gothic
- High Gothic
- Rayonnant Gothic.

Note: Flamboyant Gothic was a later adaptation of the Rayonnant style. This developed from the mid-14th century onwards and was very decorative in appearance. It featured elaborate patterns in curving shapes that resembled tongues of flame (*flambe* in French) which gives the style its name.

Construction

The great cathedrals were built with heavy stones, but the skeletal lines and open construction created an appearance of lightness and fragility.

The stones were carved on the ground before they were set in place. Larger blocks were carved at quarries, which made them lighter and easier to transport.

Heavy stones were brought to the site in carts pulled by oxen, and scaffolding was used to reach higher parts of the building. Arches were supported using wooden frames called centrings, which held the stones steady before the keystone at the top locked the whole structure into place.

RESEARCH Find out more about the Neo Gothic style or the Gothic Revival of the 19th century. Research examples in Ireland like St Colman's Cathedral in Cobh, St Finbarr's Cathedral in Cork and St Mary's Cathedral in Killarney. Does a church in your local area have Gothic features? Find out when and how it was built.

Sculpture

As in the Romanesque period, sculpture was closely tied to architecture. Doorways were filled with sculptural decoration, but supporting columns on the interior were decorated only with abstract or foliage designs.

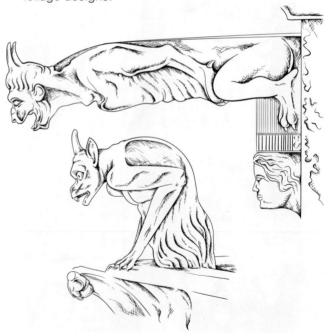

Fig. 2.11 One of the most notable decorative and functional features of Gothic cathedrals is the gargoyle. The grotesque creatures project from the gutters of roofs and spires. Rainwater gushes through their open mouths and falls to the ground, well clear of the building.

Monumental sculpture assumed an increasingly prominent role during the High and Late Gothic periods, as more and more statues were placed on the facades of cathedrals, often in their own niches.

Stained Glass

The term stained glass comes from the silver stain applied to the outer surface of the glass. This turned yellow when the glass was fired.

Over time, images in stained glass get darker. A patina or thick black crust forms on the outside, due to exposure to wind and rain. The windows have to be removed and painstakingly cleaned pane by pane.

Making a Stained-glass Window

The exact details and colour scheme of the narrative in a stained-glass window required careful pre-planning. The basic method has changed very little from medieval times.

1. **Design:** The artist made a drawing called a cartoon directly on the surface of a whitewashed table. This was used as a pattern for cutting, painting and assembling the window.

2. **Cutting:** Each piece of glass was selected for the desired colour and cut into rough shapes. An exact fit was ensured by 'grozing' the edges with an iron and nibbling off small pieces.

3. **Painting:** Details of faces, hair and hands were painted onto the inner surface of the glass using a special glass paint. The pieces are then fired in a kiln to fuse the paint to the glass.

4. **Leading:** The pieces of glass are joined with narrow strips of lead to form a panel. These strips are referred to as 'lead came'. Lead is soft and flexible, which makes it easy to cut and bend. It's also inexpensive and durable.

5. **Glazing:** This is the term used for assembling the glass and setting it into a window. After firing, the pieces of glass are placed in position on the cartoon and joined together with lead came to form a panel. In the Middle Ages, a combination of a knife and hammer was used for this. Once in position, the joints of the came are soldered together.

6. **Cementing:** The panels are cemented all over to keep the lead from bending and the excess is cleaned off with dry brush. The panels may also need to be reinforced, with metal bars attached to the back before placement in the window opening.

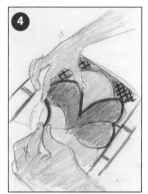

Fig. 2.12 Steps for making a stained-glass window.

Art Elements and Design Principles

Architecture

Two aspects of Gothic architecture particularly set it apart – the luminous quality of light and its unique structure.

- **Light:** Gothic walls have a particularly delicate and porous appearance. Light seems to filter through them and windows appear to float, as the solid patterns of the stone tracery dramatically disappear when articulated by light.

- **Structure:** The carefully developed structure and the precision in which every single block was cut and set showed a new delight in – and regard for – the tectonic system.

> **Tectonics:** In architecture, this is the science or art of construction, both in use and artistic design. It refers not just to the activity of construction, but the raising of this to an art form.

Decorative Features

Many decorative features on Gothic cathedrals also had a structural purpose. Flying buttresses kept walls from falling outwards, and the ornate pointed pinnacles added weight to corners to keep them strong.

As the style progressed, these features became more ornate and decorative. They included:

- complex rib vaulting
- arched and ornate flying buttresses
- intricate window tracery and moulding
- highly ornamented spires and pinnacles
- elaborate sculpture on the portals.

Sculpture

Jamb figures like the tall linear and elegant statues on either side of the Royal Portal at Chartres were carved from the same block as the column. They

Figure 2.13 Exeter Cathedral in England is famous for its 14th-century vaulted ceiling.

are slender, elongated and column-like with long straight lines of finely pleated drapery. This contrasts with the rich and varied abstract patterns of the other jambs and the lower part of the columns, which act as a plinth (Fig. 2.14).

Naturalism developed over the 13th century and figures became more individual, with natural expressions and gestures. During this time, these figures became almost freestanding.

> **Jamb:** From French word *jambe*, meaning 'leg', this is the side-post of a doorway or window opening.
>
> **Plinth:** Heavy base supporting a statue.

Figure 2.14 Column statues on the central doorway of the Royal Portal at Chartres reflect the soaring vertical lines of the architecture.

Stained Glass

Stained-glass windows featured detailed and complicated stories of the life of Christ or the saints. They also often included symbols or motifs of the individual or guild who paid for them.

The height, intricate patterns of the tracery and the latticed web of intense colour make Gothic windows very difficult to 'read', but the coloured light creates a beautiful atmosphere and mood.

The windows of Sainte Chapelle in Paris are famous for their magnificence but by the time of their making in the 14th century, less care was taken in separating the colours. This means the red and blue blend together in a purplish haze and no detail in the individual scenes or figures can be identified in the imagery (Fig. 2.16).

Figure 2.15 The South Portal, Chartres Cathedral.

UNIT 1 ROMANESQUE AND GOTHIC (c. 1000–1500s)

Figure 2.16
Stained glass at Sainte Chapelle. The narrow lancet windows create an atmosphere of fragile beauty and envelop everything and everybody in a purplish light.

Artists and Artworks

Medieval workers ranged from unskilled labourers to master craftsmen and sculptors. Many moved about to work on cathedrals in England, Germany and other parts of Europe.

Masons were highly skilled and experts in architecture, building, crafts, design and engineering. Master masons grew increasingly wealthy, powerful and proud. They signed their work with a mark or even a name, like the inscription on the south transept of Notre Dame Cathedral in Paris: *'Master Jean de Chelles commenced this work for the Glory of the Mother of Christ on the second of the Ides of the month of February, 1258.'*

Sculptors

The skilled Gothic sculptors had probably worked on the major Romanesque churches. Some of the whirls and patterns on the figures at Chartres are similar to those at Autun and Vézelay, but more attention has been given to detail.

The names of individual artists are not known but unique characteristics can be identified.

Gothic Cathedrals
Chartres Cathedral

Notre Dame de Chartres, about 60 km from Paris, is the best preserved of all French Gothic cathedrals (Fig. 2.17). Built in the 13th-century High Gothic style, most of its sculpture and original stained glass are still intact.

Figure 2.17 Chartres Cathedral.

The 'Sancta Camisia'

Chartres was dedicated to Our Lady, and its most sacred relic, the 'Sancta Camisia' (Fig. 2.18), made it a major pilgrimage site. This was the gown said to have been worn by the Virgin during childbirth.

Figure 2.18 The 'Sancta Camisia', the most sacred relic of Chartres.

Disaster and Divine Intervention

The cathedral was rebuilt after the older Romanesque church was destroyed by fire in 1194. The west front and the two towers that survived the blaze were incorporated into the new design.

The sacred relic was first thought lost, but when it was found some days later beneath the charred embers in the crypt, it was seen as a miracle from the Virgin herself. Donations quickly poured in from all over France as rich and poor helped to cart stones up the hill. The new cathedral of Chartres took only 80 years to build, which was a remarkably short period for that time.

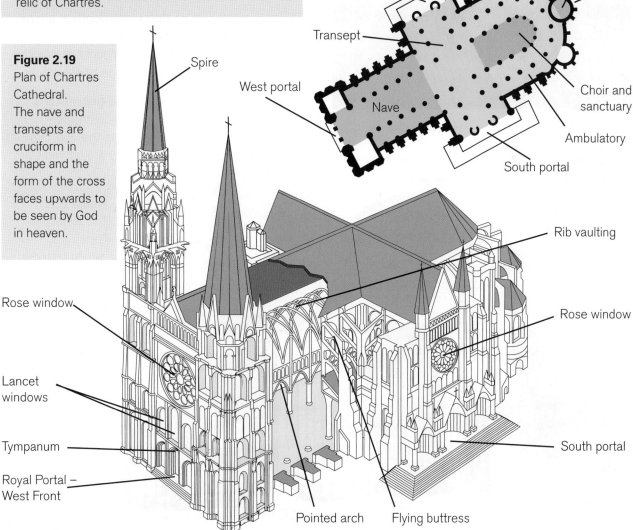

Floor plan

Apse
East
North portal
Transept
West portal
Nave
Choir and sanctuary
Ambulatory
South portal

Figure 2.19
Plan of Chartres Cathedral. The nave and transepts are cruciform in shape and the form of the cross faces upwards to be seen by God in heaven.

Spire

Rib vaulting

Rose window

Rose window

Lancet windows

Tympanum

Royal Portal – West Front

Pointed arch   Flying buttress

South portal

Figure 2.20 Ribbed vaulting over the choir, Chartres Cathedral.

Interior

Clustered slender columns soar dramatically upwards to support rib vaulting. This, along with the massive upper level clerestory windows and three large rose windows, creates an intense feeling of light in the interior (Fig. 2.19).

Sculpture

The sculpture on the exterior doorways developed from Early Gothic on the west, to High Gothic on the north and south transept.

The West Front

The towers and tall lancet windows on the west front date back to the 12th century, but the imagery on the Royal Portal shows a clear transition in style from Romanesque to Gothic (Fig. 2.22).

Jamb Figures on the Royal Portal

The column statues on the central doorway are more accomplished than most of the others, suggesting they were the work of the master sculptor. Work on the side doors may have been done by assistants.

Nobody knows exactly who these graceful and elegant figures represent, and the extremely elongated bodies have very little in the way of natural human form. Instead, they are carved from

Figure 2.21 The 'Royal Portal' is so named because the statues are thought to represent the kings and queens from the Old Testament, who were Christ's royal ancestors.

Figure 2.22 Column statues from the Royal Portal at Chartres.

the same blocks of stone as the columns on which they stand, and the long vertical lines in the folds of the drapery emphasise their tall and narrow appearance. Only the faces, with their serene yet lifelike expressions, are naturalistic (Fig. 2.22).

The North Portal

The north portal is dedicated to the Virgin Mary. Her mother, St Anne, holds the baby Mary on the central trumeau, while above she is crowned Queen of Heaven (Fig. 2.23).

Figure 2.23 The ornate North Portal, Chartres Cathedral.

The sculptures on the cathedrals were originally painted in full colour. Make a drawing of a doorway at Chartres and colour the stonework and sculpture as you think it might have looked.

Jamb Figures on the North Portal

Column statues of apostles and prophets face each other on either of the central doorway. These are significantly more natural than earlier figures and are almost free-standing (Fig. 2.24).

Figure 2.24 Abraham and Isaac, jamb figures from the north porch (centre), Chartres Cathedral. Abraham is just about to sacrifice his son for God, but an angel above his right shoulder comes to save the boy.

Women

Blanche of Castille paid for the decoration of the north portal. She was a strong and powerful figure in medieval France, so this doorway features many women.

RESEARCH Find out the story of Abraham and Issac and see how cleverly the artist has included the details in the figures and their surroundings. Knowing more about the biblical characters makes 'reading' the sculpture on the cathedrals easier and far more interesting.

Figure 2.25
The graceful figure of St Modeste lifts her mantle and raises her hand. In a gesture typical of the refined High Gothic style, she gently inclines her head to one side.

The South Portal

The south portal is dedicated to Jesus Christ, his apostles and his Church. It is 13th-century High Gothic style (Fig. 2.26).

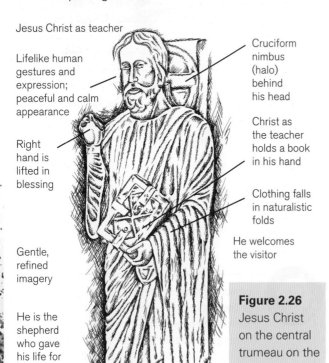

Jesus Christ as teacher

Lifelike human gestures and expression; peaceful and calm appearance

Right hand is lifted in blessing

Gentle, refined imagery

He is the shepherd who gave his life for mankind

Cruciform nimbus (halo) behind his head

Christ as the teacher holds a book in his hand

Clothing falls in naturalistic folds

He welcomes the visitor

Figure 2.26
Jesus Christ on the central trumeau on the south portal of Chartres.

Stained-glass Windows at Chartres

Chartres Cathedral has one of the most complete and precious collections of medieval stained glass in the world. Its windows are:

- large round or 'rose' windows on the west front and both transepts
- tall pointed lancet windows at ground level in the nave
- huge clerestory windows at the top level of the nave.

The Northern Rose (Fig. 2.27) is dedicated to the glorification of the Virgin. She is placed in the central light and is surrounded by doves and angels on the outer sections.

Figure 2.27 The rose window from the north transept, Chartres Cathedral.

Design a stained-glass window. Draw on the tracery and make out a pattern based on a lancet window from a Gothic cathedral. Make out a story and colour the figures in small sections broken by black lines. Make the window by cutting out the main shapes from black card. Glue coloured tissue or cellophane over the cut areas. Create the leading by drawing lines with a large black marker. Place this against a sunny window for effect.

CREATE

Figure 2.28 The Blue Virgin or 'Notre Dame de la Belle Verrière', Chartres Cathedral. Four panels with the Virgin and Child in this famous window survived the fire at Chartres in 1194. They were incorporated into the tall lancet window in the new cathedral.

Figure 2.29 The Blue Virgin or 'Notre Dame de la Belle Verrière', Chartres Cathedral. As Queen of Heaven and Earth, Mary wears an ornate gold crown over a white veil and a beautiful blue cloak. Her lap forms a throne for her son, and she rests her hands on his shoulders. His right hand is raised in blessing and his left holds an open book containing the prophecy of his birth.

Notre Dame, Paris

Notre Dame Cathedral was rebuilt in the 13th century, when Paris was developing as the main centre of political power and commerce. Its construction was supported by King Louis VII himself and it was intended be more impressive than those in all nearby towns (Fig. 2.30).

Different Styles

The west front, with its distinctive towers, was started in around 1200, but many different styles were added as construction continued through the years.

There were also many later alterations, and considerable destruction took place during the French Revolution in 1793.

The sculpture on the west front, the lead-covered wooden spire (which collapsed in the fire of 2019) and the famous gargoyles date to a restoration by Eugène Viollet-le-Duc in the mid-19th century.

Fire in 2019

A fire in 2019 destroyed the spire and part of the roof of Notre Dame. Debate continues on which style to use for the present-day restoration. President Emmanuel Macron called for an international competition and some have suggested that a modern, streamlined style, with a glass roof to let sunshine in, would be appropriate.

Figure 2.30 Notre Dame Cathedral in Paris before the fire in 2019. The famous flying buttresses were not part of the initial architecture, but were included when the weight of the vault began to cause structural problems.

RESPOND

In 1506, after the spire at Chartres Cathedral was destroyed by lightning, it was replaced with a contemporary 16th-century design. Do you think that a new spire for Notre Dame in Paris should be a 21st-century design, or should the reconstruction of such a famous Paris landmark match the original 13th-century architecture?

Reims Cathedral

Reims Cathedral was the place of the coronation for of the kings of France (Fig. 2.31). This piece of Rayonnant Gothic architecture is particularly famous for the complicated tracery on its windows. Building began in 1211 and continued until 1516, but following the Revolution and damage during World War I, a good deal of restoration has taken place. Fortunately, most of its sculpture has survived and the statues on the doorways are the originals.

The central portal of the main entrance is dedicated to the Virgin Mary, but instead of the traditional tympanum, it is surmounted by a rose window framed by a triangular sculptured arch.

Rouen Cathedral

Rouen has been called the 'City of a Hundred Spires' because of its many church spires. Towering above them all is the 150 m cast-iron masterpiece on the city's cathedral. This was erected in 1876.

Figure 2.31 Reims Cathedral. Seven towers were planned for the cathedral, but only two on the western façade were completed. The spires were never added.

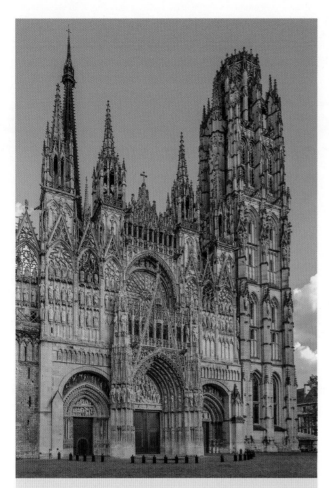

Figure 2.32 Rouen Cathedral. The cathedral began in the 13th century, but several later additions included a mixture of styles from Early Gothic, High Gothic and Rayonnant on its façade and ornamental spires. Its elaborate tracery is almost lacelike.

In 1507, the south tower, which is in the Flamboyant Gothic style, was the last major part to have been completed. It has an octagonal crown but never had a steeple. It is known as the Tour de Beurre (Butter Tower).

Look at Claude Monet's series of paintings on Rouen Cathedral page 169 (Fig. 12.14 and 15). Why do you think he chose this subject? Do you think he was successful in representing it in paint?

Make some sketches in colour of a church or other stone building in your area at different times of the day. Try to capture the 'mood' of the building in your chosen medium.

Sainte Chapelle

This small but perfect example of Rayonnant Gothic architecture was a royal chapel within the palace, the residence of the kings of France in medieval Paris. It has deep buttresses and ornate pinnacles.

The Sainte Chapelle (meaning 'holy chapel') was built by King Louis IX to house relics, including the crown of thorns.

A ground-floor chapel served as a parish church for the palace. The upper chapel is especially magical because of its magnificent stained-glass windows.

Figure 2.33 The Sainte Chapelle, Paris.

Destruction during the Revolution

The Sainte Chapelle was badly damaged during the Revolution but, amazingly, the glass windows remained intact. The interior wooden statues survived because they were placed in storage, but sculpture on the exterior was hacked off and the original spire was pulled down. Louis's precious relics were scattered and today only fragments survive in the treasury of Notre Dame Cathedral.

The Naumburg Master

Medieval artists often travelled for work, and one French sculptor's finest work is in Naumburg, Germany, where he carved twelve statues of the patrons and founders of St Peter and Paul's Cathedral. He is known only as 'the Naumburg master'.

Figure 2.34 Ekkehard and Uta, Naumburg Cathedral, Germany. The poses and gestures have a real human quality, especially in the amazing detail of clothing, faces and hands. Uta, who appears to feel the cold and pulls her heavy ermine cloak to her face, is said to have influenced some of Walt Disney's cartoon queens.

Count Ekkehard and his wife Uta (Fig. 2.34) are the most famous of the Naumburg master's sculptures. These were created long after their deaths, but they are so realistic that they could have been portraits. Some of their original bright colours can still be seen.

Claus Sluter (1340–1405/6)

When Philip the Bold became Duke of Burgundy, his first major project was the restoration of the Charterhouse of Champmol, a Carthusian monastery outside Dijon. He employed Claus Sluter, a sculptor from the Netherlands, to create the sculptures. *The Well of Moses* is Sluter's most celebrated work.

Figure 2.35
A drawing showing the great cross at The Well of Moses with the single kneeling figure of Mary Magdalene.

NEW APPRECIATING ART EUROPE AND THE WORLD

The Well of Moses (1396–1404)

The six figures – Moses, David, Jeremiah, Zachariah, Daniel and Isaiah – are extremely realistic. A weeping angel hovers over each one, but the great cross that stood over the group was destroyed when the monastery was ransacked during the French Revolution (Fig. 2.35).

Composition

The life-sized prophets (Fig. 2.36) are set in a hexagonal structure in the centre of the fountain at eye level. The viewer meets them face to face as it were, before looking high up to the cross, with its single weeping figure, to contemplate Christ's agony.

Figure 2.36 Daniel the Prophet (L) and Isaiah the Prophet (R) on the Well of Moses, 1402–5, by Claus Sluter, painted and gilded limestone, Chartreuse de Champmol, Dijon, France.

Meaning of the Work

The original name of the Well of Moses, *Fons Vitae*, means 'fountain of everlasting life'. The water surrounding the figures symbolised the blood of Christ that brought redemption to all those who drank it.

Style

Claus Sluter was one of the first artists to show a transition in style from Gothic to the earthly naturalism of the Early Renaissance. Each of the figures is an individual character with a distinct personality and expression, making them almost like actors on a stage. The exquisite detail on the faces, flowing drapery, rich skin and hair textures are some of the work's most admired qualities.

Materials

Sluter and his assistants carved the figures, pillar and crucifixion scene in limestone. It was then handed over to artists who painted and gilded them. Traces of the bright colours can still be seen.

International Gothic (*c.*1375–1450)

A late Gothic style that extended across Europe during the late 14th and the early 15th centuries became known as the 'International style'. Artists moved from country to country, working in royal households and producing small and sophisticated works of art. Typical characteristics of this refined style included:

- decorative patterns and rich colours
- raised areas of gold-leaf patterned surfaces (gilding)
- highly realistic floral and landscape details
- elongated elegant figures in curved poses wearing fine clothing
- delicate facial features, blond hair and sweet gentle expressions and gestures.

Diptych: Two panels together.
Triptych: Three panels together.
Polytych: Many panels together.

Figure 2.37 *Richard II presented to the Virgin and Child by his patron saint, John the Baptist, and Sts Edward and Edmund (The Wilton Diptych)*, 1395–9, artist unknown, egg tempera on oak, 53 × 59 cm, National Gallery of London.

The Wilton Diptych

The Wilton Diptych (Fig. 2.37) is one of the most beautiful yet mysterious paintings. Painted on wooden panels, it closes over like a hinged book to measure 53 × 37 cm. It is a royal portrait of Richard II, King of England (1377–99) and also a religious work of art, as the young king is being presented to the Virgin and Child by his patron saints.

The artist is unknown, but was likely to have been French or English.

Style and Composition

The figures' gentle expressions and long thin fingers are typical of the International Style, as are their elegant curved poses and robes falling into soft folds.

The figures on both panels are subtly connected to each other by looks and gestures. Mary holds her tiny son's foot to show where the nails will be driven, but the Christ child leans forward to bless the king. He receives it with open hands.

Materials and Techniques

Thin glazes of egg tempera paint were applied on oak panels. The background and other details are decorated with gold tooling.

Colour

The clothing is very detailed. The Virgin wears ultramarine blue, a colour made from the highly expensive lapis lazuli, and the Christ child wears a cloth of gold. The delicate pattern in the young king's velvet cloak is depicted in gold and vermilion red, which were also very expensive pigments.

Materials

The manuscript is painted onto parchment, made with sheep or goat skin. The paint pigment (powder) was mixed with water and thickened with gum arabic to make sure it would stick to the vellum.

The Limbourg Brothers (1385–1416)

The three brothers, Jean, Herman and Pol de Limbourg came from the Netherlands. Their very realistic style was common in northern Europe, but new to France when they came to work for Jean, Duc (Duke) de Berry. The duke was the son of King John II and brother of the Duke of Burgundy, and he was extremely wealthy. He had many splendid and luxurious castles and was a keen patron of the arts.

Les Très Riches Heures du Duc de Berry (The Very Rich Hours of the Duke of Berry)

It was the custom in the Middle Ages to illustrate, or illuminate, calendars with the labours of the month. These prayer books were called 'Books of Hours'.

Bound with red leather,the Duke's Book of Hours, *Les Très Riches Heures*, is one of the most lavish Late Gothic books. It is also one of the biggest at 29 x 21 cm (the size of an A4 page).

Figure 2.38 *January, Les Très Riches Heures du Duc de Berry*, 1412–16, illumination on parchment, Musée Condé, Chantilly. The scene shows a feast with elegant courtiers in colourful clothing. The Duke is on the right, wearing his brilliant blue velvet robe decorated with gold and a fur hat. His prized gold tableware is on the table, as well as his small dogs, who are eating the scraps.

The Subjects

The illustrations feature the duke and his beautiful castles, possessions and courtiers in precise detail. The most famous pages are the calendar months.

The duke and the Limbourg brothers all died in 1416, possibly of the plague. before the book was finished. It was later completed by another artist.

A high-quality copy can be seen today in the Musée Condé in Chantilly, France. The delicate manuscript itself is kept in an ornamented box.

Figure 2.40 *April, Les Très Riches Heures du Duc de Berry*, 1412–16, illumination on parchment, Musée Condé, Chantilly. It is early spring and green is the dominant colour. Blossoms show on the fruit trees inside the walled garden and ladies pick flowers. The scene shows the engagement of the Duke's granddaughter and indicates a political alliance between two families previously at war.

Figure 2.39 *February, Les Très Riches Heures du Duc de Berry*, 1412–16, illumination on parchment, Musée Condé, Chantilly. Peasants go about their chores in the snow-covered land. This picture of medieval life show a farm with sheep pen, beehives, barrels, bales of straw and even the hooded crows pecking at the straw on the ground.

Analysis

> As Gothic sculpture became more naturalistic, the meaning in the imagery also profoundly changed. Study some examples of Gothic sculpture and consider the treatment of the human figure. Compare this to figures of the Romanesque period. Examine the materials and techniques used by the artists and note the elements of art like colour, line and pattern, while also looking for meaning in the work.

The Gothic style was born with the rebuilding of the Basilica of St Denis on the outskirts of Paris and was inspired by its patron, Abbot Suger. This new style of architecture developed as a result of Suger's desire for natural light. Ribbed vaults allowed for taller buildings, and took the eye upward, away from the solid mass, making the space look larger and lighter.

Church leaders used art to convey ideas of new religious thinking. Scholars and intellectuals absorbed and understood this. They searched for the deeper meaning and symbolism in the imagery, but ordinary people also found simple messages of hope and salvation in the stained-glass windows and statues in the porch.

After the Gothic Period

The International style of the late 14th century was a bridge between Gothic art and that of 15th-century Renaissance art. Art and culture during the Renaissance was also inspired by a new and major intellectual movement called Humanism. This movement, which greatly valued the philosophy and classical culture of ancient Greece and Rome, was centred mainly in Florence.

Figures became more three-dimensional and the human form was more naturally depicted with lifelike features, expressions and gestures. The new theories of perspective featured in detailed landscapes and architectural settings, though the shift in style was sometimes quite slow. Even in Florence, some of the sculpture and painting during the first half of the 15th century remain rooted in the older tradition.

1. Where did the Gothic style of art and architecture begin?

2. What were the most important innovative features of Gothic architecture?

3. Why was it called the 'architecture of light'?

4. What effect do you think the great cathedrals might have for pilgrims visiting them for the first time?

5. What form did the statues on the doorways of Gothic cathedrals take and how did they reflect the architecture?

6. Do you think the stained-glass artists expected people to be able to 'read' the windows? What purpose could they have had in the cathedral otherwise?

7. Examine the *Coronation of the Virgin by Christ* from Notre Dame de Reims Cathedral (Fig. 2.41) and describe the scene. What does the imagery symbolise and what meaning can be taken from this? Compare the treatment of the human body and the use of architectural space, as well as the style and sculptural techniques to those of earlier figures on the Royal Portal at Chartres (Fig. 2.14 and 2.22).

Figure 2.41 *Coronation of the Virgin by Christ*, Reims Cathedral.

Further Research

www.parisdigest.com – Search for an article on the reconstruction of the St Denis spire

www.chartrescathedral.net – Explore the stained-glass windows in Chartres Cathedral

www.frenchmoments.eu/reims-cathedral – Discover Reims Cathedral

www.youtube.com – Search for 'Gothic Cathedrals' (5:14) by Engineering Models to learn how Gothic cathedrals were designed and built

www.youtube.com – Search for 'The Cathedral of Notre Dame, Paris (before the fire)' (4:49) to learn more about what is arguably the most famous church in the world

www.youtube.com – Search for 'Sluter, Well of Moses' (4:51) by Smart History to see more of the famous sculpture

www.nationalgallery.org.uk – Search for 'Wilton Diptych English French' to see the Wilton Diptych in detail and discover its heritage

www.khanacademy.org – Search for 'Limbourg brothers, Très Riches Heures du Duc de Berry' to learn more about the enigmatic manuscript

Unit 2

The Renaissance

(*c.* 1300–1600s)

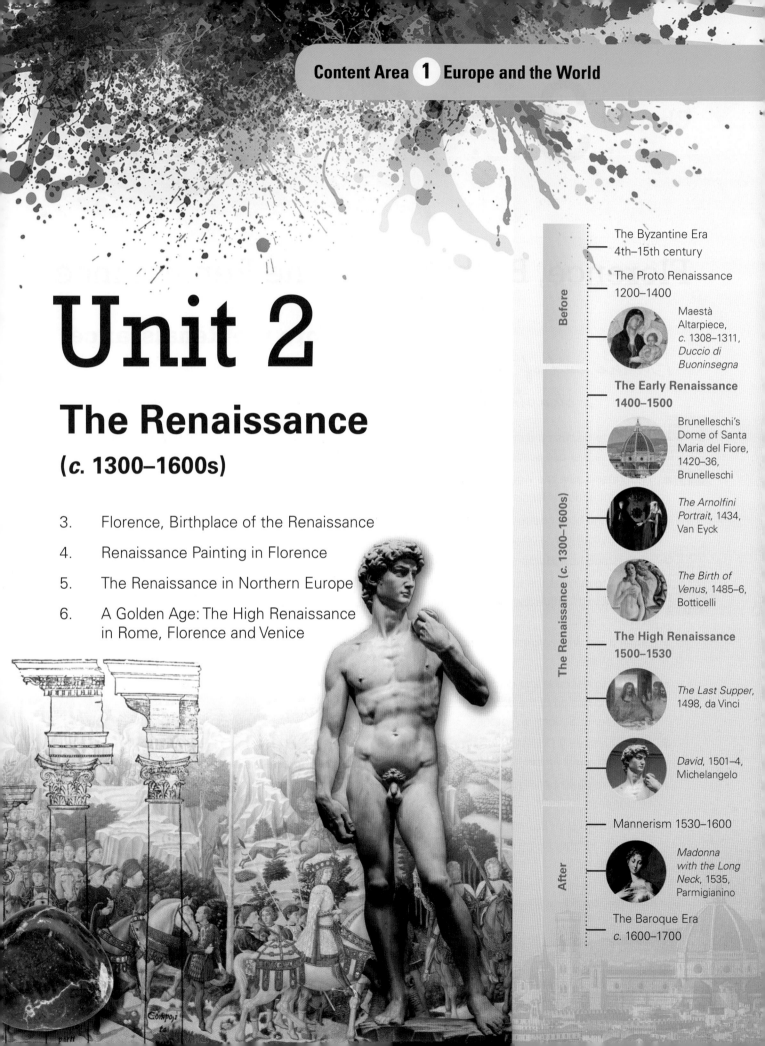

Before

The Byzantine Era
4th–15th century

The Proto Renaissance
1200–1400

Maestà
Altarpiece,
c. 1308–1311,
*Duccio di
Buoninsegna*

**The Early Renaissance
1400–1500**

Brunelleschi's
Dome of Santa
Maria del Fiore,
1420–36,
Brunelleschi

*The Arnolfini
Portrait*, 1434,
Van Eyck

*The Birth of
Venus*, 1485–6,
Botticelli

**The High Renaissance
1500–1530**

The Last Supper,
1498, da Vinci

David, 1501–4,
Michelangelo

Mannerism 1530–1600

*Madonna
with the Long
Neck*, 1535,
Parmigianino

After

The Baroque Era
c. 1600–1700

The Renaissance (c. 1300–1600s)

Chapter 3

Florence, Birthplace of the Renaissance

By the end of this chapter I will …

* be able to discuss the influence of Byzantine Art on the Sienese school of painters
* understand how the work of Cimabue and Giotto influenced Renaissance artists
* understand how wealth in Italian cities benefitted artistic production
* understand how Humanism influenced art
* be able to discuss the Classical ideal of beauty and its influence on Renaissance Art and architecture
* understand why patrons commissioned works of art
* be able to describe and discuss the themes, layout and design of the doors of the Baptistery of St John in Florence
* understand why Donatello was one of the most influential artists in 15th-century Italy
* be able to describe and discuss at least one of Donatello's works
* be able to explain Brunelleschi's new methods for the design and construction of the dome for Santa Maria del Fiore.

Before the Renaissance

In the 1st century AD, the Roman Empire stretched from Hadrian's Wall in Scotland all the way to Turkey. After the Roman Emperor Constantine became a Christian, he moved the capital of the Roman Empire to Byzantium (present-day Istanbul). He renamed the city Constantinople, after himself. This Eastern hub was known as the Byzantine Empire. After the fall of the Roman Empire in the West, Italy maintained strong links with the Byzantine Empire through trade, and this was expressed in religious art.

The Proto Renaissance

The late medieval period in Italy is sometimes called the Proto Renaissance. The term – which essentially means 'pre-Renaissance' – refers to a time in which art began to foreshadow Renaissance characteristics such as naturalism, realism and Humanism.

Siena and Florence

The Byzantine tradition, with its solemn, repetitive imagery, never quite caught on in Florence. It was, however, fully absorbed in nearby Siena, and the elegant Madonnas of the period can still be seen in the city's museums and church altars. The Hodegetria icon was believed to have been painted from life by St Luke the apostle. Replicas of this in Italy greatly influenced paintings of the Madonna in the 13th century (Fig. 3.1).

An event in 1260 particularly links the Byzantine style with the art of Siena. On the eve of a crucial battle with the rival city of Florence, the governor of Siena called upon the intersession of the Virgin. Following Siena's victory, the Virgin and Child became the permanent image of Siena and artistic workshops produced images of the Madonna for churches all over Tuscany.

Artists of Siena
Duccio di Buoninsegna (unknown–c. 1319)

Duccio was the founder of Sienese painting. He blended a degree of realism into the Byzantine style, but maintained the solemn devotional atmosphere.

The Virgin Mary was Siena's patron and queen, and Duccio's huge *Maestà* was carried by the people in a triumphal procession from the artist's workshop accompanied by the sound of bells and music to the Cathedral of Siena on 9 June 1311.

Figure 3.1 *Madonna and Child with Two Angels (Crevole Madonna), c.* 1283–4, by Duccio, tempera and gold on panel, Museo dell'Opera del Duomo, Siena.

Figure 3.2 *Maestà* Altarpiece, *c.* 1308–11, by Duccio di Buoninsegna, gold and tempera on panel, 370 cm × 450 cm, Museo dell'Opera del Duomo, Siena. Maestà or 'Majesty' was the name given to devotional pictures of Mary. Duccio has balanced sacred symbolism and realism with a gold background and solemn rows of angels and saints. In contrast to the traditional Byzantine Madonna, the Virgin wears a blue mantle. This suggests that the Queen of Heaven has descended to take her place on an earthly throne.

The Sienese School of Painting

Situated on the main pilgrimage route to Rome, Siena was a wealthy, cultural and artistic centre in the 13th and 14th centuries. It developed its own painting tradition or school, and its artists became very famous and greatly admired.

Simone Martini (c. 1284–1344)

A pupil of Duccio, Simone Martini learned to portray three-dimensional space from his master but was very influenced by the courtly art of France where he had spent some time. His serene and elegant paintings became famous internationally.

In Martini's altarpiece *The Annunciation and two Saints*, the Angel Gabriel holds an olive branch – the symbol of peace – instead of a lily, the symbol of Mary's purity. The lily was the civic emblem of Florence and this is a reference to the ongoing feud between the two city-states.

The great painting is perhaps the most splendid example of 14th-century Sienese craftsmanship, with its beautifully tooled gold background and relief inscription from the Angel Gabriel's mouth, containing the words of the Annunciation.

Pietro (active 1306–c. 1348) and Ambrogio Lorenzetti (1319–c.1348)

The Lorenzetti brothers worked in Siena in the early 14th century, but Ambrogio's work is probably better known than his sibling's. This can be seen in a great fresco and city portrait for the Palazzo Pubblico in Siena. The figures in *Allegory of Good Government* show the influence of Giotto in a lifelike depiction of peace and harmony in a well-governed land. This refined masterpiece was, of course, political propaganda for the government of Siena.

Figure 3.3 *The Annunciation and Two Saints*, 1333, by Simone Martini, Uffizi Gallery, Florence. The painting is quite flat and pattern-like, but the delicate figures are in very natural poses. The Virgin pulls her cloak around her but her eyes are drawn to the central pot with lilies and to the symbol of the Holy Spirit above.

It is thought that the brothers died in the plague that swept through Europe in 1348, devastating the population of Tuscany and greatly undermining the creative talent of the next generation.

Allegory: A work in which the character represents particular ideas or qualities that relate to morals, religion or politics.

Figure 3.4 *Allegory of Good Government*, 1338–9, by Ambrogio Lorenzetti, Palazzo Pubblico, Siena. An allegorical figure of Justice and the Common Good watches over as young girls dance. Business flourishes in the city as farm workers from the surrounding countryside bring their produce to market.

Saint Francis and Realism in Art

Saint Francis of Assisi lived in the 13th century, and had urged people to meditate on Christ's passion and to picture his life. This brought a new awareness of naturalism in religious art.

After his death, Francis's followers – the Franciscan order of monks – employed the Florentine artist Cimabue (c. 1251–1302) to paint the walls of the Church of St Francis in Assisi. His assistant was Giotto di Bondone, who was later known as the 'father' of the Renaissance.

Giotto di Bondone (c. 1267–1337)

Giotto learned from Cimabue, but his painting developed to a further level of realism.

For the first time, biblical characters showed genuine human emotion. Giotto's innovations included:

- an illusion of depth on a flat surface
- natural and lifelike scenes with real people and real backgrounds
- correct proportions and foreshortening
- light and shade to emphasise modelling in the human form
- real facial expressions and gestures.

Proportion: The relative size of parts of a whole, or objects, in comparison to each other.

Foreshortening: Portraying an object or view as closer than it is, or as having less depth or distance.

Giotto also developed a new technique in fresco painting ('fresco' means 'fresh'). While his teacher, Cimabue, painted *a secco*, meaning painting directly onto a dry surface, Giotto discovered that it was better to paint onto wet plaster, a technique now known as *buon fresco* (pure fresco). The paint flaked off over time when painting a *secco*, but painting *buon fresco* meant that the pigment fused with the lime in the plaster, making the colour secure and long-lasting (Fig. 3.5).

Scrovegni Chapel (Arena Chapel)

Giotto's greatest surviving work is in Padua. It was painted in the family chapel of Enrico Scrovegni, a wealthy merchant and patron of the Franciscans. Giotto covered the walls of the chapel with scenes from the life of Jesus.

He planned his compositions very carefully.

The Lamentation of Christ

In scenes like *The Lamentation of Christ* (Fig. 3.6), Giotto used the diagonal lines of the mountains to draw the eye to Mary cradling the head of her lifeless son.

Figure 3.5 The *buon fresco* technique:

1. The bare masonry is covered in a layer of plaster.
2. A composition is sketched in *sinopia* (red chalk).
3. Enough smooth plaster is applied for one day's work (*a giornata*) and painted while still wet.
4. Azurite blue was sometimes added *a secco*, or on dry plaster, at the end.

Figure 3.6 *The Lamentation of Christ* (also known as *The Deposition*), 1305, by Giotto di Bondone, fresco, 231 × 236 cm, Scrovegni (Arena) Chapel, Padua.

This scene is like a drama on stage: Jesus has just been taken down from the cross and presented to his mother. She is surrounded by mourners, each of whom shows individual gestures of grief and real human emotion.

Saint John the apostle throws his arms back in despair, and foreshortening creates an upward motion. In the sky, distraught angels weep and wring their hands in sorrow.

The artist also chose authentic colours like bold greens, yellows, oranges and reds.

The Flight into Egypt

This panel shows a problem with the fresco – Mary's mantle and the sky has flaked off because Giotto used azurite to make blue (Fig. 3.7).

> *Note:* *Lapis* means stone in Latin, and *azul* means 'blue' in Arabic. This deep blue gemstone is ground down to make ultramarine ('from beyond the seas'), which is one of the most important colours in art. The stone is found only in the mountains of Afghanistan, making it so expensive that artists usually quoted prices for blue separately.

Figure 3.7 (above) *The Flight into Egypt* by Giotto di Bondone, 1304–6, fresco, 200 × 185 cm, Scrovegni (Arena) Chapel, Padua.

Figure 3.8 (right) Lapis lazuli.

This mineral was not compatible with the lime in the plaster, and had to be applied *a secco*. Ultramarine would have been much better, but the lapis lazuli needed to make it was probably too expensive to use in such a large amount (Fig. 3.8).

Giotto's Legacy

Giotto never studied anatomy or perspective, but he had grasped something far more important. He portrayed human emotion in a powerful and meaningful way.

After his death, realism in art fell out of favour again. It was 100 years before the Renaissance artist Masaccio revived Giotto's discoveries.

The Renaissance
Context

The Renaissance was an extraordinary period of art and culture that spread throughout Europe in the 15th and 16th centuries. It was inspired by ancient Greek and Roman literature and art. The period is

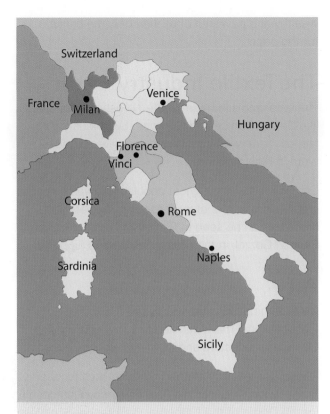

Figure 3.9 Renaissance Italy. The Italian peninsula was a series of independent states ruled over by dukes and princes.

also called the Quattrocento, which means 400 and refers to Italy in the 1400s (Fig. 3.9).

The plague had wiped out nearly one-third of the population of Italy in the 14th century, but by the early 15th century, cities in northern and central Italy had recovered and become important centres of trading and commerce.

Italian textiles were sold throughout the Christian and Muslim worlds, funding artistic patronage.

Powerful princes ruled cites like Milan, Ferrara, Urbino and Mantua, but a series of disastrous wars eventually forced the merchants and traders of Siena and Florence to form guilds and executive councils. These two small city-states became independent republics.

Note: The word 'Renaissance' is French and means 'rebirth'. A French historian first used the term in the mid-19th century.

Humanism

Humanism was a new cultural and intellectual movement that was based on the rediscovery and re-evaluation of Classical (ancient Greek and Roman) literature, art and civilisation.

Humanist scholars promoted the study of original Classical literature and believed that:

● humanity and life on earth were important
● the individual has beauty, worth and dignity
● the human ability to learn and create were God-given gifts
● there was harmony between Classical philosophy and Christian belief.

Patronage

The city of Florence was small, and its sculptors and painters lived and worked in one area. Painters and sculptors were considered merely craftsmen, and they had to work hard to get good commissions. Sometimes they entered competitions to make money, but it was much more important to have a patron.

Commissioning art and architecture was part of the wealth and power structure. It showcased the patron's taste, sophistication, financial status and ambition. Patrons commissioned religious art for monasteries, churches or private chapels within a church. They chose the artist, the subject matter, the media and the style of the piece, and determined the cost. Patrons could be:

● wealthy private citizens and families
● religious orders
● the guilds of Florence
● rulers of the Italian states.

The guilds of Florence: The guilds were associations of master craftsmen. They were extremely powerful and virtually controlled the city's government.

The Medici: Rulers of Florence and Patrons of Art

The Medici family made their fortune in banking for the pope. Cosimo de' Medici, known as 'il Vecchio'

(Cosimo the Old) became ruler of Florence in 1434. He was followed by his son, Piero, and his grandson, Lorenzo the Magnificent.

The Medicis were tough rulers, but Florence prospered and the arts flourished. They were patrons to artists like Donatello, Botticelli and Michelangelo. Florence became the cultural inspiration for other Italian states.

Visit **www.museumsinflorence.com** to research Benozzi Gozzoli's *Procession of the Magi* in the Magi Chapel, Medici Palace (Fig. 3.10).

Innovation and Invention
Banking
Modern accounting and banking were invented in Florence. The Medici family became extremely wealthy and powerful after they became bankers for the pope.

The Textile Industry
The wool and silk trade created prosperity for cities like Genoa, Venice and Florence. Luxurious Italian fabrics made with quality dyes in brilliant shades were in high demand.

Crimson red was the most popular, followed by bright green and sapphire blue. These silks, velvets and brocades can be seen in *Procession of the Magi* by Benozzi Gozzoli in the Medici Palace (see Fig. 3.10).

Art
New learning was inspired by the rediscovery of Classical texts. This in turn led to a new appreciation of Classical architecture and art in 15th-century Florence.

Filippo Brunelleschi studied Classical architecture in Rome, which inspired his new and innovative design for the Dome of the Cathedral in Florence. Sculptors

Figure 3.10 *Procession of the Magi*, by Benozzo Gozzoli, Magi Chapel, Medici Palace, Florence. The fresco depicts the arrival of the three Kings to Bethlehem, but it is also a Medici family portrait.

The magnificent horses and costumes demonstrate the family's wealth and power as they are accompanied by visiting envoys from nearby states. The background shows hunting and exotic animals such as cheetahs. An African servant holding a Syrian bow is dressed in white and red hose (tights), as befits a servant, but his prominent position suggests he is held in high regard by the family.

of the period, such as Donatello and Nanni di Banco, were inspired by Classical statues and drew from life models. They developed a new and very lifelike style of sculpture.

One-point Linear Perspective

Brunelleschi also discovered linear perspective (Fig. 3.11). He observed that parallel lines appear to converge at a single 'vanishing point' on the horizon. He then calculated the scale of objects within a painting in order to make them appear realistic.

This shift from empirical perspective to linear perspective was monumental, and artists began to use the method with astonishing effects in their paintings.

Empirical perspective: What an artist observes without using a method or rules.

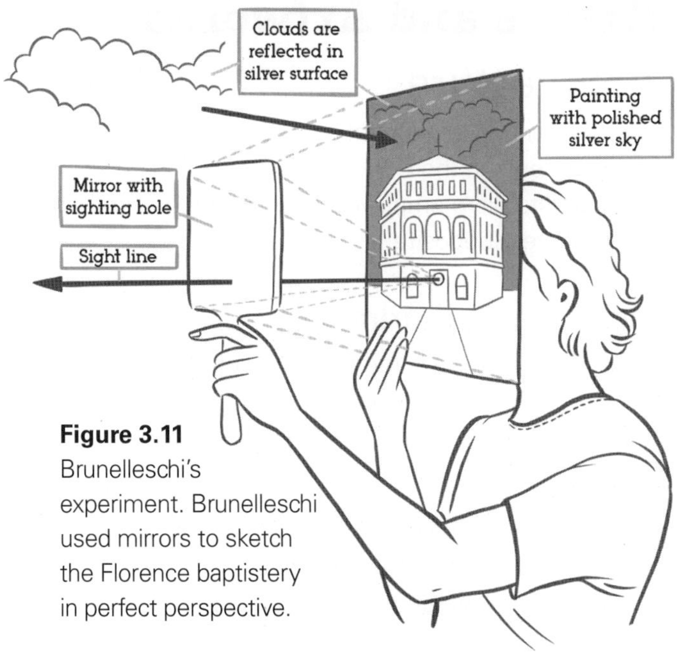

Clouds are reflected in silver surface

Painting with polished silver sky

Mirror with sighting hole

Sight line

Figure 3.11 Brunelleschi's experiment. Brunelleschi used mirrors to sketch the Florence baptistery in perfect perspective.

Art Elements and Design Principles

Sculpture

The Classic ideal of beauty was based on lines, harmony and proportion. The rule of proportions, based on the ratio of lengths of body parts to each other, governed the depictions of both male and female figures.

The distribution of weight on one supporting leg, the counterbalance of weight throughout the torso, and the head slightly inclined towards one shoulder suggested energy and movement (Fig. 3.12).

Renaissance artists adopted these ideals.

Contrapposto: A pose used in sculpture. It was first developed by Classical Greek sculptors to create movement in the pose. The weight of the figure is on one leg, causing the shoulder line and the hips to slant in opposite directions – *contrapposto* means 'opposite' in Italian.

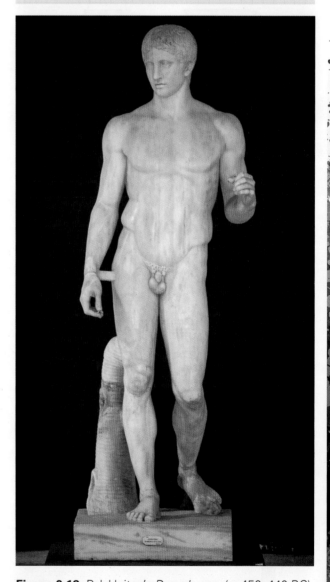

Figure 3.12 Polykleitos's *Doryphoros*, (c. 450–440 BC) marble, 212 cm, an early example of Classical *contrapposto*.

Architecture

Renaissance architects visited Rome to study Classical buildings and ruins, like the Colosseum and the Pantheon. They incorporated Classical elements into their own designs, but also tried to create buildings that would appeal to both emotion and reason (Fig. 3.13).

The architects looked to the ancient Roman architect Vitruvius. His mathematical proportions and measurement were based on the human scale.

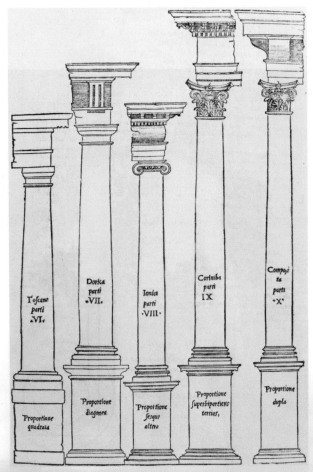

Figure 3.13 (above) Classical orders of architecture. Greek temples were built with very strict rules (orders). There were three basic types of column: Doric, Ionic and Corinthian.

Media and Areas of Practice

The new appreciation of Classical sculpture led to a preference for marble, which was the medium of choice in ancient Rome.

Bronze also came increasingly into use. It was strong and durable, could be polished in various ways and was very suited to gilding.

The main examples of bronze work in Florence are the bronze doors by Andrea Pisano and Lorenzo Ghiberti on the baptistery and several key works of Donatello.

> **Gilding:** A decorative technique for applying a very thin coating of gold leaf to a solid surface like metal.

Artists and Artworks
Architecture

Civic authorities implemented practical building improvements in the city of Florence (Fig. 3.14). Many artists were employed on the cathedral and the baptistery opposite.

Florence Cathedral

Santa Maria del Fiore, the Cathedral of Florence, was traditionally the responsibility of the Calimala (the wool and cloth merchants' guild). Its construction had been ongoing for most of the 14th century.

The cathedral's baptistery had been restored in 1200 with green and white marble cladding, and new bronze doors by Andrea Pisano had been installed in 1329 (Fig. 3.15).

Figure 3.14 (below) City of Florence, Italy.

Figure 3.15 Florence Cathedral and Baptistery.

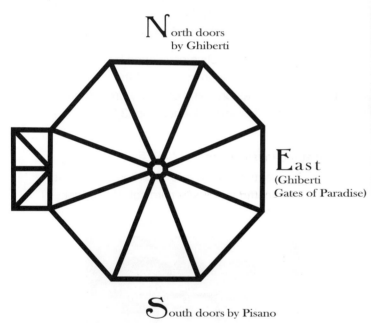

N orth doors
by Ghiberti

E ast
(Ghiberti
Gates of Paradise)

S outh doors by Pisano

Figure 3.16 Plan of the baptistery showing the position of the doors.

Quatrefoil: A shape commonly used in medieval architecture of four arcs linked together.

The Competition for the Second Baptistery Doors

The year 1400 in Florence began with one of the most famous competitions in the history of art. To celebrate the new century, the Calimala instigated a

Figure 3.17 Baptistery of St John, south door, by Andrea Pisano, Florence. Fourteen scenes each on the left and right doors illustrate the life and death of John the Baptist in quatrefoil shapes.

competition to design new doors on the east of the baptistery to match those already in place on the south by Pisano.

Contestants were required to submit a relief panel. The strict rules dictated that it must:

● include the subject of the sacrifice of Isaac, from the biblical story

● be the same format of quatrefoil panels as Pisano

● be made of gilded bronze.

Seven artists took part, but this was reduced to two intense young rivals: Filippo Brunelleschi and Lorenzo Ghiberti (Fig. 3.18). Ghiberti's was selected due to his superior technical skills, and Brunelleschi was bitterly disappointed. He immediately left for Rome.

Figure 3.18
Models of the sacrifice of Isaac, 1401
– (left) Brunelleschi's competition
piece; (right) Ghiberti's competition
piece – hanging side by side in the
National Museum of the Bargello,
Florence.

Lorenzo Ghiberti (1378–1455)
The Second Baptistery Doors

Ghiberti trained as a goldsmith and worked on
the baptistery doors for his entire career. The new
doors took 27 years to make. The subject was
the life of Christ, and while the panels maintained
the quatrefoil shape, they were fuller and more
adventurous than Pisano's (Fig. 3.19).

The new art of perspective developed by his rival
Brunelleschi can be seen in some of the scenes
and the lifelike gestures and correctly proportioned
figures show Classical influence (Fig. 3.20).

The Third Baptistery Doors

Once in place, the doors were such a success that
the Calimala commissioned a third set. These took

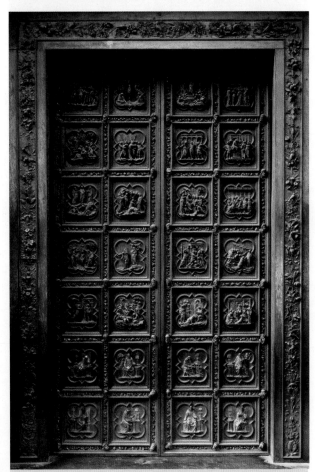

Figure 3.19 Baptistery of St John, north door, by
Lorenzo Ghiberti. These doors originally faced the
cathedral but were later replaced by the 'Gates of
Paradise'.

Figure 3.20 The Flagellation of Christ panel
by Lorenzo Ghiberti on the north door of the
Baptistery of St John, Florence. Note the Classical
influence: Jesus has a gently curved *contrapposto*
pose and is set against an architectural background
of Classical Corinthian columns.

a further 27 years for Ghiberti to complete, but by this point Ghiberti was a master craftsman and was allowed to make his own design decisions. He changed the framing system and created an entirely new design scheme of fully gilded panels on each side (Fig. 3.21).

The panels show real space and correctly proportioned figures with lifelike gestures and movement. The panel depicting the story of Jacob and Esau in particular shows how much Ghiberti's work had changed and how much he had learned from other artists over the years (Fig. 3.22). The continuous narrative is clearly told in six sections reading from left to right, but a Classical influence and Ghiberti's knowledge of the new art perspective is now obvious. Lines of perspective lead the eye to the Classical arch in the centre of the panel; in the foreground, the almost freestanding women in Classical gowns stand in *contrapposto* poses.

Continuous narrative: A visual story that illustrates multiple scenes of a narrative within a single frame.

Figure 3.22 The Jacob and Esau panel by Lorenzo Ghiberti from the east doors of the Baptistery of St John, Florence. Esau was so hungry after work in the fields that he gave up his inheritance to his brother Jacob in exchange for food. In his blindness, their father Isaac mistakenly blesses his younger son, watched by his wife, Rebecca, who set up the deceit.

Figure 3.21 A copy of the east doors, or 'Gates of Paradise', by Lorenzo Ghiberti on the Baptistery of St John, Florence. The original gold panels from 1425–52 have been fully restored and are on display in the Museum of the Cathedral.

Note: The third set of doors on the baptistery is also known as the 'Gates of Paradise'. Legend has it that Michelangelo called them that because of their beauty.

Impressed by their splendour, the Calimala moved the second doors to the north façade. Contrary to religious protocol, Old Testament subject matter was now facing the main cathedral door. This major decision was probably the first that placed the value of the art itself over its religious subject matter.

Filippo Brunelleschi (1377–1446)

Brunelleschi was not formally trained as an architect; he had trained as a goldsmith, studied mechanics and had a keen interest in mathematics. During his time in Rome, he learned about Classical design from ancient buildings like the Pantheon.

The Dome of Santa Maria del Fiore

The Cathedral in Florence had been under construction for more than a century. A massive drum was already in place to support the roof, but no one had any idea how to design a dome large enough to fit on top. In 1418, the governors of the city announced a competition to design the dome.

Brunelleschi was determined to win, and enlisted the help of two of the most innovative sculptors of the day: Donatello and Nanni di Banco. They produced a model that was so technically brilliant that the judges immediately awarded Brunelleschi the commission.

Brunelleschi's Design

Brunelleschi's design was unique. Other designs included wooden scaffolding, but there was no wooden beam long enough to span the diameter. Brunelleschi's innovative double-shell, self-supporting cupola solved the problem (Fig. 3.23). His system also included:

- scaffolding that started at the top of the drum instead of the ground
- an access walkway between the walls
- massive stone ribs to bind the inner and outer shells together
- a series of stone chains embedded within the masonry (Fig. 3.24) to prevent the dome buckling under its own weight
- a herringbone brickwork technique copied from the Pantheon in Rome (Fig. 3.25)
- a circular interior within octagonal walls (Fig. 3.26).

The construction of the cupola was a huge undertaking that required the invention and use of new machinery, in addition to Brunelleschi's extensive knowledge of geometry, mathematics and Classical architecture.

Cupola: A rounded dome forming a roof or ceiling.

The Lantern

Brunelleschi also later designed the lantern for the top of the dome, but died the year before construction began.

Figure 3.23 (below) Santa Maria del Fiore, Florence. Like 'a great umbrella over the city', the vast curved silhouette of Brunelleschi's Dome, 1436, stands out as the landmark of Florence. The white ribs make a striking contrast with the russet tiles. This two-colour effect was a characteristic of Renaissance architecture.

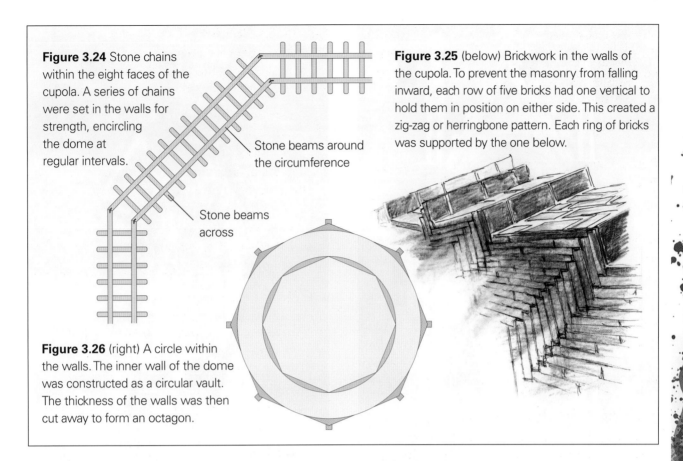

Figure 3.24 Stone chains within the eight faces of the cupola. A series of chains were set in the walls for strength, encircling the dome at regular intervals.

Stone beams around the circumference

Stone beams across

Figure 3.26 (right) A circle within the walls. The inner wall of the dome was constructed as a circular vault. The thickness of the walls was then cut away to form an octagon.

Figure 3.25 (below) Brickwork in the walls of the cupola. To prevent the masonry from falling inward, each row of five bricks had one vertical to hold them in position on either side. This created a zig-zag or herringbone pattern. Each ring of bricks was supported by the one below.

Public Sculpture
Donatello (1386–1466)

Donato di Bardi, better known as Donatello, was a master of marble and bronze sculpture, and one of the most influential artists in 15th-century Italy. His highly emotional works completely changed the popular approach to sculpture.

His career began in Ghiberti's workshop, where he worked alongside Nanni di Banco on the doors for the Baptistery of St John. However, it was his studies in Rome and learning the rules of proportion and perspective with his friend Filippo Brunelleschi that had the greatest influence on Donatello.

The Statues of Orsanmichele

In the early 15th century, the Signoria (city governors) of Florence asked each of the guilds to produce statues of their patron saints for the new Church of Orsanmichele.

The huge new statues were placed in niches around the exterior walls of the church, just above street level. The people of Florence were delighted with the lifelike figures.

Donatello was commissioned by the armourers' guild to create a statue of St George. His life-sized depiction of the saint (Fig. 3.27) marked an important moment in the development of sculpture, showcasing a new realism with a Classical influence.

Donatello's warrior-knight stands firm, feet resolutely apart, tense and determined, intended to reflect the strong Florentine spirit. Yet the figure also shows emotion, vulnerability and softness in facial expression, representing the humanity of St George.

Note: The statue of St George on Orsanmichele today is a bronze copy. The original marble statue and its recess are preserved in the Bargello Museum. The statue once had a real sword and metal helmet.

Figure 3.27 *St George*, 1416, by Donatello, marble, 214 cm, Orsanmichele, Florence. The marble panel at the base shows St George slaying the dragon. It is carved in very low relief, called *rilievo schiacciato*, or flattened relief. This was the first time that linear perspective was used in public sculpture.

Donatello's friend, the sculptor Nanni di Banco, was commissioned by the Stonemasons' Guild to create a sculpture called *Four Crowned Saints* for the Orsanmichele. Find out more about Nanni di Banco's life and work.

David

The story of David, the heroic young shepherd boy who killed the giant Goliath, comes from the Bible and was a favourite in Florence during the Renaissance.

Donatello's bronze depiction of David (Fig. 3.28) was the

Figure 3.28 *David*, c. 1440, by Donatello, bronze, 158 cm, Bargello Museum, Florence.

first life-sized freestanding nude figure since Classical times. It stood for many years in the courtyard of the Palazzo Medici and probably symbolised that family's struggles against its own powerful enemies.

The sculpture shows Classical influences, but the slim youth is unlike the powerful nudes of ancient Greece; his graceful *contrapposto* stance is sensual and somewhat effeminate. The skin is highly polished, but the hair and hat have a rougher finish.

The Feast of Herod

The Feast of Herod was Donatello's first relief in bronze, and is one of six panels on the baptismal font in the baptistery in Siena (Fig. 3.29). The rules

Figure 3.29 *The Feast of Herod*, 1427, by Donatello, Siena. This relief recounts an episode at King Herod's birthday feast, after he asked the beautiful Salome to dance for him. She agreed, but only if he gave her the head of John the Baptist on a platter. The highly emotional scene shows the king recoiling in horror from the ghastly sight.

of perspective have been applied rigorously to the composition: the continuous narrative moves inwards from the immediate foreground through the banqueting hall and into the rooms behind it. The execution itself can be seen at the very back.

Penitent Magdalene

This haunting image of Mary Magdalene is one of Donatello's most emotional works (Fig. 3.30). The tall (nearly two metres high), slender figure is carved from poplar wood and was once painted and gilded. Now only traces of the sad blue eyes stare out from hollow sockets, and partially opened lips show broken white teeth. Her long hair is matted and twisted around her body.

Analysis

Study Brunelleschi's advances in architecture and why his new theory of perspective

affected both painting and sculpture. Note Ghiberti's skilled use of materials and the influence that Donatello's emotionally expressive and very human figures had on other artists.

Humanist philosophy and a new appreciation of the culture, learning and values of ancient Greece and Rome led to a host of new developments in art, especially in Florence. Works of art were commissioned by the civil governments and wealthy individuals. These major works of painting, sculpture and architecture were to influence not only other artists of that generation, but many more in the future.

Figure 3.30 *Penitent Magdalene,* c. 1450, by Donatello, polychrome wood, 188 cm, Florence. This harrowing figure is a timeless image of human suffering.

Look up the sculpture *Famine* by Rowan Gillespie in Chapter 36, page 507, then go to YouTube and watch the video 'Famine Way Walkers 2017 at The Rowan Gillespie Memorial, Spencer Dock, Dublin' (0:38).

Do you think the Irish artist was influenced by Donatello's *Mary Magdalene*?

Look up Donatello's famous statue of *Gattamelata* in Padua. Find out why this first equestrian statue of the Renaissance caused such a sensation. Check out the similarities with the famous statue of the Emperor Marcus Aurelius in Rome. Do you think that this influenced the artist's work?

Chapter Review

1. How was Italy ruled in the 15th century?

2. Why did patrons commission works of art?

3. What is meant by 'Humanism'?

4. Describe and discuss the Classical influence on Renaissance art and architecture.

5. How did Ghiberti's art develop during the production of the Florence Baptistery doors?

6. In your opinion, which is the most special of Donatello's works? Include your reasons for this.

7. How do you think Brunelleschi came up with such a clever design for the dome of Florence Cathedral?

Further Research

www.youtube.com – Search for 'Linear Perspective: Brunelleschi's Experiment' (4:16) to watch a short video on Brunelleschi's exploration of linear perspective

www.youtube.com – Search for 'Florence's Gates of Paradise' (4:55) to watch a video on Ghiberti's third set of baptistery doors

www.youtube.com – Search for 'Donatello and the Renaissance' (6:27) for an introduction to Donatello's most important works

www.youtube.com – Search for 'How an Amateur Built the World's Biggest Dome' (3:50) for an explanation of Brunelleschi's design for the Santa Maria del Fiore cupola

www.italianrenaissance.org – Search for 'Donatello's *Gattamelata*' to see one of the artist's most beloved works

Chapter 4

Renaissance Painting in Florence

By the end of this chapter I will ...

* understand why patrons were so important for Renaissance painters
* be able to discuss Masaccio's innovations
* be able to describe and discuss a work by Masaccio
* understand how artists used perspective
* understand how Botticelli's themes took an entirely new direction
* be able to discuss Botticelli's use of art elements and media
* be able to describe and discuss a painting by Piero della Francesca.

Context

The Republic of Florence was one of the most powerful and prosperous city-states in Europe. It provided the perfect intellectual conditions for Humanist patrons who believed in the dignity and importance of man.

Patrons of Art

The Brancaccis

The rich and powerful Brancacci family commissioned established painter Masolino da Panicale to paint the walls of the family's private chapel in the church of Santa Maria del Carmine.

The Medicis

Cosimo de' Medici was deeply religious and paid for the construction, restoration and decoration of many churches.

The Dominican Monastery of San Marco was his favourite place of worship. He organised its renovation and chose one of the monks, Fra Giovanni – better known as Fra Angelico (angelic) – as his artist.

Twenty-one-year-old Lorenzo de' Medici became ruler of Florence after his father Piero's death in 1469. He was a skilled politician, but also a Humanist poet, with a passionate interest in Classical antiquity. A generous patron of the arts, he is best known for his sponsorship of Botticelli and Michelangelo.

The people of Florence awarded him the title 'Lorenzo the Magnificent'.

Federico da Montefeltro

During the 15th century, the remote hilltop town of Urbino became a centre of culture and learning, and its influence carried far into Europe.

Federico da Montefeltro, the Duke of Urbino, was a renowned Humanist with a deep interest in philosophy, Latin, Greek and mathematics. His favoured painter was Piero della Francesca, who shared these intellectual interests.

Media and Areas of Practice

Artists learned in the *bottegas*, or workshops, from a master artist. Talents were nurtured, new techniques were developed, and new artistic forms came to light. Artists worked together, but also competed among themselves.

As well as large paintings, artists did jobs such as painting sculpture, presenting drawings for architects, making small devotional images and producing banners for festivals.

Painting

Egg tempera on wooden panel was the most popular painting medium in the early Renaissance, as it was almost unaffected by humidity and temperature changes. Tempera was composed of egg yolk and powdered pigment. It was very versatile, and dried quickly so the colours did not mix with the underlying layer. Unfortunately, this made the colours difficult to blend, and the tones were always quite muted.

Artists gradually switched to oil-based paints, but some, like Botticelli, continued to use egg tempera. Botticelli was the first to use tempera on canvas: he added oil or water to the tempera in a process known as *tempera grassa*, making the paints stronger and fuller. He kept colours fresh by applying varnish to the piece, and used little brushstrokes of gold as a decorative element in many of his paintings.

RESEARCH Find out more about Botticelli's painting techniques and then look closely at his paintings. See if you can identify the technique he used to create a delicate gold ornamentation on veils and drapery.

Innovation and Invention

Masaccio was the first to really study Giotto's frescoes on the walls of Santa Croce. He learned from the older master's realism, expressive gestures and lifelike facial expressions.

In his short life, Masaccio radically transformed Florentine painting and created some of the most innovative and monumental works of the early Renaissance.

> ***Chiaroscuro:*** The treatment of light and shade in drawing and painting (Italian for 'light-dark').

Artists and Artworks
Masaccio (1401–1428)

Figure 4.1 The Brancacci Chapel. The artist followed the direction of the natural light from the chapel window on the figures. Shadows form dark sculptural pockets on the garments and the dramatic *chiaroscuro* greatly enhances the painting.

Masaccio was the most remarkable painter of the early 1400s. He worked under the master Masolino, who had been commissioned by the Brancacci family to paint the Brancacci Chapel. Masaccio worked alone in the Brancacci Chapel when Masolino left to work elsewhere.

He continued with the frescoed panels in his unique and classically restrained style. They are some of the finest works of the early Renaissance.

Unfortunately, his untimely death left it unfinished for many years.

Adam and Eve

Masolino and Masaccio both painted Adam and Eve. Facing each other on opposite walls, the fresh realism of Masaccio's early Renaissance style contrasts sharply with Masolino's elegant Late Gothic style.

Figure 4.2 (far left) *The Temptation of Adam*, 1426–7, by Masolino, fresco, Brancacci Chapel, Florence.

Figure 4.3 (centre) *Expulsion from the Garden of Eden*, c. 1426–7, by Massaccio, fresco, Brancacci Chapel, Florence. The outline around Adam's head shows *a giornata* or 'one day's work' in fresco. The blue azurite painted *a secco* has completely faded and only the grey blue primer applied to wet plaster remains.

Figure 4.4 (right) *Venus Pudica*, marble, 153 cm, Uffizi Gallery, Florence.

Masolino's long slender figures in *The Temptation of Adam* (Fig. 4.2) have gentle facial expressions and stand quietly in the garden, whereas Masaccio's (Fig. 4.3) simple but dramatically expressive figures in *Expulsion from the Garden of Eden* show raw emotion. Eve lifts her head to cry out in anguish and Adam covers his face in shame and regret as they stumble forward in sorrow and awkward nakedness. In spite of their despair, the figures show dignity and beauty.

Eve's gestures echo those of the Classical statue, *Venus Pudica* (Fig. 4.4).

The Tribute Money

The cycle of frescoes in the Brancacci Chapel is based on the life of St Peter, but overall it represents the salvation of mankind. The panel known as *The Tribute Money* (Fig. 4.5) relates to the yearly tax for the temple in Jerusalem.

Figure 4.5 *The Tribute Money*, 1426–7 by Masaccio, fresco, 247 × 597 cm, Brancacci Chapel, Florence.

The scene features Jesus and his disciples, who, according to the Gospel of Matthew, arrived at the gates of the city of Capernaum. The tax collector asked Peter: 'Does your master not pay the half shekel?' Peter was reluctant to pay, but Jesus said: 'Go to the lake and cast a hook; take the first fish that bites, open its mouth and there you will find a shekel. Take it and give to them for me and for you.'

Masaccio told the story in a three-part continuous narrative (Fig. 4.6):

- Part 1: Christ is the focal point. He points towards Peter, who is hesitating.
- Part 2: Peter is crouched at the lakeside, taking money from the fish's mouth.
- Part 3: Peter gives the coin to the tax collector.

Links in the Composition

In Part 1, Peter's pose is almost identical to Christ's, and on the two occasions when Peter is confronted by the tax collector, the poses mirror each other. This locks the main characters together within the composition.

The figures are strong and sculptural, with carefully modelled features. They show the clear influence of Classicism and are wearing Greek tunics.

Figure 4.6 Perspective in *The Tribute Money*.

Perspective

Crisp lines of perspective lead directly to the vanishing point over Christ. The architecture acts as a frame for the figures and the receding landscape creates depth.

Make a continuous narrative drawing in several episodes to fit in a square or a long rectangular composition.

Note: A fire in the Brancacci Chapel many years ago blackened the frescoes, but after restoration in the 1980s, details on the faces and distant farmhouses became clearer.

The Trinity

This painting creates an image of the Holy Trinity situated within a small chapel (Fig. 4.7). It is seen from a low viewpoint, so we are looking up at Christ and the barrel-vaulted ceiling above.

The Trinity is a masterpiece of perspective. All the lines of perspective converge to a single vanishing point at eye level. To construct them, a nail was placed in the wall and strings were pulled outwards to mark the central point (Fig. 4.8). The marks made in the wet plaster can still be seen.

Part 2

Part 1

Part 3

Figure 4.7 *The Trinity*, 1428, by Masaccio, fresco, 667 × 317 cm, Santa Maria Novella Church, Florence.

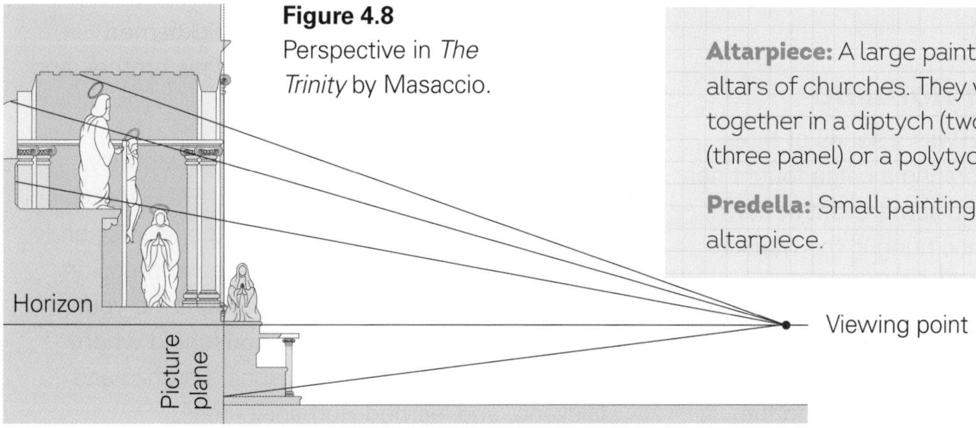

Figure 4.8
Perspective in *The Trinity* by Masaccio.

Horizon

Picture plane

Viewing point

Fra Angelico (1395–1455)

After Masaccio's death, Fra Angelico emerged as the city's most sought-after artist. Cosimo de' Medici commissioned him to paint a series of frescoes in the dormitory cells and corridors of the Dominican Monastery of San Marco. The sacred scenes have a simple, restrained style (Fig. 4.9).

Cosimo de' Medici commissioned a grand altarpiece for the church of San Marco of the Virgin and Child with saints. The story of the saints was told in nine small pictures in the predella, one of which is now in the National Gallery of Ireland (Fig. 4.10).

Figure 4.9 *The Annunciation*, *c.* 1450, by Fra Angelico, 230 × 321 cm, a fresco in a cell at San Marco, Florence. The perspective in the arches suggests the influence of Masaccio.

Altarpiece: A large painting placed on the altars of churches. They were sometimes hinged together in a diptych (two panels), triptych (three panel) or a polytych (many panels).

Predella: Small paintings at the bottom of an altarpiece.

Figure 4.10

The Attempted Martyrdom of Saints Cosmas and Damien, 1439–42, by Fra Angelico, tempera on panel, 91 × 117 cm, National Gallery of Ireland, Dublin.

Paolo Uccello (1397–1475)

Paolo Uccello also trained with Ghiberti, and was highly regarded in his time. He worked in the International Gothic style, and developed a profound interest in linear perspective. He also had a love of decorative effects, such as gold and silver leaf.

> **International Gothic:** A style of painting that developed across many countries in Europe during the late 14th and early 15th centuries. It was characterised by mainly elegant and delicately elongated figures and an emphasis on the decorative drapery, foliage or setting. See Chapter 2, page 43.

The Battle of San Romano

The Battle of San Romano was a series of three large paintings commemorating a battle fought near Florence. They depicted the same event at dawn, midday and dusk. They once hung in the Medici Palace, but have now been split up and are on display in Paris, Florence and London.

The colourful scene in London's National Gallery (Fig. 4.11) shows the Florentines attacking the Sienese at dawn. The artist was probably aiming for a high degree of realism, but the end result is more ornament than history and the stiff figures and horses look a little like wooden toys.

Technique

Original gold and silver leaf decorations were lost in early restorations. The gold on the bridles has remained bright, but the silver leaf on the soldiers' armour has oxidised to a dull grey or black. This would have been quite dazzling in its time.

Sandro Botticelli (1445–1510)

Alessandro Filipepi was brought up in the backstreets of Florence. He was nicknamed Botticelli, meaning 'little barrel', by his brother, and the name stuck.

He developed his signature style – a wistfully delicate beauty – under his master Fra Filippo Lippi (Fig. 4.12). Fra Filippo worked for the Medici, and his young apprentice made quite an impression on Piero de' Medici. He even brought the young Botticelli to stay in the family household where he grew up with the Medici sons, Lorenzo and Giuliano, and learned Humanist ideas.

Figure 4.12 *Madonna and Child*, 1460–5, by Fra Filippo Lippi, tempera on panel, 92 × 63.5 cm, Uffizi Gallery, Florence.

Marriage Paintings

Marriage was the most important family ceremony in Renaissance Florence, so Botticelli's most famous works are linked to Florentine wedding customs. Paintings of love were traditionally displayed in the newly married couple's bedroom in the groom's family home.

Mythology

Mythological themes were popular in the Medici household. Botticelli's paintings took these themes in a completely new direction, inspired partly by Classical poetry and partly by the Renaissance ideal of beauty.

The paintings *Primavera* and *The Birth of Venus* clearly show Botticelli's interest in the themes of love and mythology. *Primavera* symbolises the fruition of love in marriage and *The Birth of Venus* symbolises the birth of love in the world. Both paintings were loosely based on the mythological poetry of the Florentine poet Boccaccio and feature some of the most beautiful nude figures of the Renaissance.

Primavera

Venus, the ancient Roman goddess of beauty and fertility, is surrounded by allegorical figures of virtues and gods (Fig. 4.13). All the women are pregnant as they celebrate the arrival of spring.

Over the head of Venus, Cupid, her blindfolded son, shoots his arrow. It is aimed at the Three Graces dancing in an endless circle of life.

Flowers representing fertility fall from her mouth.

The leaves are laurel (*Lorenzo* means 'laurel' in Italian, a reminder of the Medici patronage).

Mercury, the messenger of the gods, holds up his staff and removes a cloud that hides the truth. Mercury is a likeness of Giuliano, Lorenzo de' Medici's murdered younger brother.

She transforms into Flora, scattering blossoms before her.

Zephyr, the wind, pursues Chloris, the wood nymph.

Figure 4.13 *Primavera* (Allegory of Spring), 1477–82, by Sandro Botticelli, tempera on panel, 202 × 314 cm, Uffizi Gallery, Florence.

Allegorical figures: Characters that stand for an abstract idea or a symbol.

Composition

The painting reads from right to left. Venus is framed in an arc of blue sky among the trees like a Madonna. The elegant Three Graces (daughters of Jupiter), dressed in delicate translucent gowns, dance in a never-ending circle, while Mercury's uplifted arm directs the composition to the little Cupid above.

The Birth of Venus

Botticelli's radical style reached a new level with *The Birth of Venus* (Fig. 4.14). Designed to hang above a marriage bed, it refers to the creative power of love. Unlike anything in its time, this nude figure remained highly controversial and was kept behind closed doors for years afterwards.

Subject

The birth of Venus at sea was a well-known legend. She is blown ashore on her shell by the gods Zephyr and Aurora. Hora the nymph reaches out to cover her with a cloak.

Figure 4.14 *The Birth of Venus*, 1480s, by Sandro Botticelli, tempera on canvas, 172 × 278 cm, Uffizi Gallery, Florence. Venus is the perfect image of grace and elegance. Her face is considered one of the most beautiful in art.

Despite the unnatural pose and neck-line, Botticelli's Venus represents the Renaissance ideal of feminine beauty. The elongation of the figure's limbs and neck add to an air of elegance and mystery. Venus remains still and serene while all around her is motion: the billowing cloth, her hair blowing in the breeze, falling roses and gently breaking waves have no effect on her.

Technique

The Birth of Venus was painted on canvas, but its fresco-like appearance was achieved with *tempera grassa*, which made the paint more transparent. Colour was applied with tiny brushstrokes and a crosshatching technique to achieve perfect smoothness. It was built up slowly in layers before hardening to a compacted, enamel-like surface.

Restoration

The artist's refined technique is best seen in the central figure's translucent skin and rich golden hair. The delicate textures and colours were restored in

Note: Botticelli had all but disappeared into obscurity until he was rediscovered in the 19th century.

recent cleaning and the faintest of pink blushes can now be seen in the cheeks, the nose and mouth.

A Change of Direction

In later life, Botticelli became a follower of the Dominican monk Savonarola, who preached fiery public sermons in the city. Influenced by the religious frenzy in Florence, Botticelli destroyed many of his earlier paintings and turned his attention to religious subjects. The artist quickly fell out of favour with his patrons and he died in 1510, neglected and forgotten.

Piero della Francesca (1416–92)

Piero della Francesca came from the small Tuscan town of Borgo Sansepolcro. He was apprenticed to

Figure 4.15 *Portraits of the Duke and Duchess of Urbino, c.* 1473–75, by Piero della Francesca, tempera on wood, each 47 × 33 cm, Uffizi Gallery, Florence.

a local painter at a very early age and soon moved to Florence. He later became part of the court of Urbino, where he thrived in the Humanistic and creative atmosphere. He formed a close relationship with Federico da Montefeltro, the Duke of Urbino.

Portraits of the Duke and Duchess of Urbino

Piero painted a double portrait of Federico da Montefeltro with his wife, Battista Sforza (Fig. 4.15).

The art of portraiture was quite new. In keeping with Classical influence, the faces are depicted in profile, like the medals of ancient Rome.

Piero showed his patron's intelligent dignity, but has literally depicted him warts and all. The left side of the duke's face was disfigured in a jousting tournament. He lost his right eye and part of his

nose, and these characteristics have been copied faithfully in the painting.

Battista was highly regarded for her intelligence, and her fine clothing reflects her high status as a member of the important Sforza family of Milan. The portrait may have been painted after her death at age 25, shortly after the birth of her ninth child and only surviving son. The duke greatly mourned her loss, but in this portrait, they remain together in a poignant, never-ending partnership.

The Flagellation of Christ

This is a very small but highly impressive masterpiece (Fig. 4.16). It shows Christ being whipped at the pillar before Pontius Pilate. The identity of the three figures on the right remains a mystery. The crystal-clear morning light produces a quiet atmosphere and the pale colours make the torture of Christ all the more brutal. This contrasts sharply with the red and

Figure 4.16
The Flagellation of Christ, 1455–60, by Piero della Francesca, oil and tempera on panel, 58 × 82 cm, Galleria Nazionale delle Marche, Urbino.

Figure 4.17 Expanded drawing of the pattern in the paving tiles and the space.

especially the fashionable blue and gold damask of the splendid costumes on the figures on the right.

Composition

The composition is separated in two with perfect one-point perspective. The floor tiles are dramatically foreshortened, but the pattern is very accurate (as shown by the expanded drawing above). The

detail can clearly be worked out by projecting the perspective (Fig. 4.17).

Art Elements and Design Principles

Perspective and Line

Masaccio's ground-breaking use of mathematical perspective had a powerful effect on Florentine Renaissance art. Perspective is the primary element of *The Trinity* (see Fig. 4.8). It is thought Brunelleschi may have helped him with this.

One-point linear perspective is key to Paulo Uccello's *The Battle of San Romano* (see Fig 4.11). It can be seen in the lines of the composition and individual objects like the lances and the foreshortening of figures like the fallen soldier.

Piero della Francesca's interest in mathematics and the use of line is evident in his very carefully and geometrically planned compositions, as seen in *The Flagellation of Christ* (see Fig 4.16).

Light and Shadow

Masaccio was renowned for his sculptural use of light and shade on the human figure, which is evident in *The Expulsion from the Garden of Eden* (Fig. 4.3).

Fra Angelico adapted some of Masaccio's methods and pioneered many stylistic trends, including the treatment of pictorial space and modelling of forms with light and shadow. This can be seen in *The Annunciation* (see Fig. 4.9).

Decoration

Botticelli painted almost entirely with line. He used very little light and shade and rarely used perspective. He did, however, often add decorative effects to the painting's surface, like the little 'Vs' on the waves in *The Birth of Venus* (see Fig 4.14).

Paulo Uccello also applied decorative gold and silver to his painting of *The Battle of San Romano* (see Fig. 4.11).

Analysis

Look for perspective, foreshortening, proportion and the depiction of the human form in 15th-century Renaissance paintings. Consider the subject matter but note particularly the use of symbolism in both religious and mythological themes, which gives meaning to the work.

The Humanist ideas of wealthy patrons and innovative techniques in Florence brought a new and distinctive character to the Renaissance. Belief in the individual and the value placed on the dignity and importance of man was reflected in a new approach to painting, although traditional religious subject matter remained strong. Giotto's influence, sculptural developments and the new rules of perspective encouraged an interest in the depiction of real space and naturalism in the human figure.

For the first time, Classical mythology and the female nude appeared in subject matter, mostly due to the strong influence of the Medici family. Landscapes also increasingly began to reflect nature as experienced in the real world.

Chapter Review

1. Who were the main patrons for painters in 15th-century Florence?

2. How did painters and sculptors learn their skills during the Renaissance?

3. How did Masaccio apply what he learned from Giotto to his own work?

4. Describe and discuss *The Tribute Money* by Masaccio.

5. Compare two paintings where perspective is key to the composition.

6. What was so new about Botticelli's mythology themes?

7. Describe Botticelli's use of art elements and media in *The Birth of Venus*.

8. Describe and discuss the *Portrait of the Duke of Urbino and his Wife* by Piero della Francesca.

Further Research

www.youtube.com – Search for 'Florence, Italy: Medici Sights' (5:27) – a short introductory video on Renaissance Florence

www.khanacademy.org – Search for 'Masaccio, The Tribute Money in the Brancacci Chapel', an article on the painting's structure

www.travelingintuscany.com – Click on 'Art in Tuscany' on the right of the webpage, then select 'Fra Angelico' for an overview of the artist's life and works

www.youtube.com – Search for 'A celebration of beauty and love: Botticelli's Birth of Venus' (4:56) – a video on its symbolism and structure

www.youtube.com – Search for 'Piero della Francesca, Portrait of Federico da Montefeltro and Portrait of Battista Sforza, 1466' – a video on this early example of portraiture

Chapter 5

The Renaissance in Northern Europe

By the end of this chapter I will ...

* understand how the Northern Renaissance differed in character to the Renaissance in Italy
* be aware that illusionism and symbolism were important elements in painting
* be able to describe the technique of oil painting
* be able to describe and discuss the artist's use of fine detail and illusionistic techniques
* be able to discuss the symbolism in *The Arnolfini Portrait*
* understand how Erasmus's ideas of Humanism were different from the Italian concept
* understand how the development of printing affected the distribution of ideas but presented opportunities for artists
* be able to describe and discuss Albrecht Dürer's work in painting and printmaking.

Context

The term 'Northern Renaissance' refers to two areas of development in fine art. The first was in the Netherlandish Low Countries of Flanders and Holland, and the second took place later in Germany.

Flanders

During the 15th century, the region of Flanders was spread over a significant part of present-day Belgium and northern France. It was controlled by the Dukes of Burgundy.

As in Florence, the wealth created in industrial Flemish cities like Ghent and Bruges allowed a large middle-class population to flourish. The Duke and his court were the most important patrons of art, but wealthy private citizens also commissioned religious pieces.

Humanism

The Northern Renaissance in Flanders and the Italian Renaissance in Florence took place at the same time, but they had quite different characteristics.

The Italian Renaissance was based on Humanism and the rediscovery of Classical Greek and Roman culture, whereas the Flemish movement drew more influence from its Gothic past.

Desiderius Erasmus was a Dutch scholar and theologian in 16th-century Germany (Fig. 5.1), He was a Humanist, but his philosophies were very different

Figure 5.1 *Portrait of Erasmus of Rotterdam*, 1523, by Hans Holbein the Younger, oil and tempera on panel, 74 × 51 cm, National Gallery, London. Erasmus (1466–1536) was critical of the Catholic Church and called for reform, but continued to recognise the authority of the pope.

to those of his Italian counterparts. He felt the world was in great danger and needed God's help.

He inspired a generation of thinkers and clerics to speak openly of their discontent. These ideas spread rapidly due to new printing processes.

Art

Art in Renaissance Italy was based on mathematically calculated linear perspective. Artists sought a scientific and rational understanding of the world.

Flemish artists, on the other hand, relied on empirical perspective and learned from direct and precise observation. They painted what they saw

and captured every single detail of objects like flowers, jewels, fabric and glass.

Netherlandish art placed less emphasis on perfection of the human form. Elements of the Gothic style can still be seen in the solemn facial expressions and quite awkward poses of the painted figures.

Symbolism was a very important feature in most paintings.

> **Symbolism:** Using an object to represent an idea.

> *Note:* The International Gothic style of late medieval art extended across Western Europe during the last quarter of the 14th and the first quarter of the 15th centuries. It acted like a bridge between the Gothic and the Renaissance. See Chapter 2, page 43.

Northern Europe was never comfortable with the pomp and majesty of the Roman Church. Religious devotion was much more austere, as seen in the characteristics of both the early Flemish and later German art of the Renaissance.

The Reformation resulted in a backlash against religious imagery. This meant that patronage for religious works of art disappeared.

> **Reformation:** Also called the Protestant Reformation, this was a religious revolution that took place in the Western Church in the 16th century.

Innovation and Invention

One of the most significant developments in Northern Renaissance art was the perfection of oil-based paint. Oil in painting had been in use since the 8th century, but the Flemish artist Jan Van Eyck and his brother Hubert took it to the next level with a startling realism and luminous finish.

Graphic arts and printmaking developed significantly in Germany due to the invention of the printing press in the 1450s.

Media and Areas of Practice

Painting

Oil painting produced deep, rich colour and a smooth surface that dried to an enamel-like finish.

Oil paint was made with finely ground dry pigment mixed with oil. Works were built up with repeated layers of paint, and coloured glazes were added over time. This all dried slowly and evenly, giving the artist time to correct or change the work as they saw fit. The method was a lengthy one, and each picture generally took six to twelve months to complete.

Printing

As paper became more widely available, woodcuts became popular for religious printing.

In a similar process to lino printing, areas to remain white are cut into the wood before inking the piece and pressing it onto paper to produce an inverted image.

In etching and engraving, the artist engraves or etches the lines on a metal plate. The ink, retained only by the incised lines, is absorbed under pressure by a sheet of paper.

Art Elements and Design Principles

Painting

Flemish paintings were often 'illusionist' and artists used techniques like perspective, foreshortening or shading to create an illusion of reality.

Realistic depictions of space included interior settings and detailed landscapes seen through open windows or doors.

Artists also developed the technique of atmospheric perspective, in which the landscape became hazy or blurry as it faded into the distance.

Printing

Engraving and etching produced fine, intersecting lines, but it was some time before woodcuts arrived at the stage of perfection that allowed half-tones.

Figure 5.2
Dance by Torchlight, Augsburg, 1516, by Albrecht Dürer.

Make two observational drawings of a room with furniture:

1. The first should use empirical perspective.
2. The second should use single-point linear perspective. Include a window showing atmospheric perspective in the distance in one of your drawings.

Artists and Artworks

Jan van Eyck (1390–1441)

Jan van Eyck worked alongside his brother Hubert in their native city of Ghent. The Duke of Burgundy regarded him highly, not only for his artistic talents, but also for his intellectual and scientific achievements.

Van Eyck was chiefly a portrait painter, and his use of the three-quarter pose was quite unique at the time. His work was popular and he was in high demand with wealthy merchants and nobles.

His portrait of Giovanni Arnolfini and his wife is considered to be one of the greatest paintings of all time.

> **Three-quarter pose:** A representation of a head or figure posed about halfway between front and profile views.

The Arnolfini Portrait

This small portrait was the first to show real people in full length in a real-life event (Fig. 5.3). It is famous for its realism, illusionism, symbolism and attention to detail.

This formal picture shows a solemn couple holding hands in the bedroom of their home as they celebrate their marriage contract. They are Giovanni Arnolfini, a successful merchant from Lucca in Italy, and his fiancée, Giovanna Cenami, who lived in Bruges. Symbolic references are found throughout the painting (Fig. 5.4).

How do we know this couple was wealthy? Find as many clues in the painting as you can!

Figure 5.3 *The Arnolfini Portrait*, 1434, by Jan van Eyck, oil on oak panel, 82 × 60 cm, National Gallery, London.

Colour

Colour is significant in the painting:

- **Black and purple:** Giovanni wears a black beaver hat, tunic and stockings, as suits a dignified man. Over this he wears a fur-trimmed coat of purple, a colour associated with Christ.
- **Blue and green:** Giovanna wears a blue dress and a fashionable green over-gown. The colours symbolise the sky, spring, youth and fertility.
- **Red:** The vivid red draperies represent passion.

Illusionism

Ten tiny scenes around the mirror (Fig. 5.5) show Christ's passion, but the mirror itself is a remarkable piece of illusionism. It is a miniature picture of the complete room with figures, floor, ceiling, sky and the garden outside all fitting in the convex glass. Even the painter at his easel can be seen in the

One candle burning represents the presence of Christ and the taking of an oath.

The crystal beads and spotless mirror indicate Mary's purity.

The fruit on the windowsill could refer to man's innocence in the Garden of Eden or that the couple could afford to buy it.

The shoes on the floor show it is a holy place for a sacred ceremony.

Children of the marriage are suggested by a carving of St Margaret (patron saint of childbirth) on the back of a wooden chair, overlooking the marriage bed.

The bride stands in a way that suggests pregnancy.

The dog could represent faithfulness in marriage or that the couple could afford to keep a pet.

Figure 5.4 Symbolic references in *The Arnolfini Portrait*.

Figure 5.5 Mirror detail of *The Arnolfini Portrait*.

reflection of the mirror. This suggests the artist was a witness, and to emphasise this he has signed his name on the wall. The formal decorative handwriting says '*Johannes van Eyck fuit hic 1434*' (which means 'Jan van Eyck was here 1434').

Albrecht Dürer (1471–1528)

Albrecht Dürer was the leading artist of the German Renaissance in the early 16th century. He was noted for his mastery of drawing, printmaking and woodcuts, as well as his portraits and nature studies.

He was a learned man and was inspired by the philosophies of Erasmus. He travelled to Italy and was very envious of the high status that artists enjoyed there. He was influenced by Italian art, but his own style remained very individual.

Self-portraits

Dürer painted a series of self-portraits between the ages of 22 and 28. The most striking of these shows the artist full-face, with flowing hair, staring coldly out of the picture (Fig. 5.6).

Figure 5.6 *Self-Portrait in a Fur-Collared Robe,* 1500, by Albrecht Dürer, oil on panel, 67 × 49 cm, Alte Pinakothek, Munich.

The head-and-shoulders image is clearly an imitation of the head of Christ, reminding the viewer that artistic talent is a God-given gift.

The pyramidal composition shows the influence of Italian High Renaissance artists such as Leonardo da Vinci, but the precise detail shows Dürer's northern origins. The developments in oil paint facilitated the use of fine detail, notably in the eyes and textures of the subject's hair, beard and fur collar.

Woodcuts

Woodcuts formed a large part of Dürer's work. Responding to a wave of apocalyptic (end of the world) feeling that was circulating in the 16th century, he produced a series of woodcuts from the apocalypse revelations of St John. They were terrifying visions of the future, and they were wildly popular.

The Four Horsemen of the Apocalypse

The most famous of these woodcuts is *The Four Horsemen of the Apocalypse* (Fig. 5.7). The riders represent Conquest, War, Famine and Death, and bring plague, war, hunger and death to mankind.

An avenging angel in the sky urges them to descend upon the earth, trampling all beneath their hooves. Hades, a hideous Leviathan (representing Hell) in the bottom left of the composition, swallows everything that Death has passed in his enormous jaws.

Composition

The dramatic scene builds up stunning detail in subtly graded tone. The powerful horses and riders are set against closely worked horizontal lines, and the background emphasises the strong diagonal in the composition.

Figure 5.7 *The Four Horsemen of the Apocalypse,* 1497–8, by Albrecht Dürer, woodcut, 40 × 29 cm, Kupferstichkabinett, Staatliche Kunsthalle, Karlsruhe.

Analysis

Consider the influence of oil painting on painting in Northern Europe. Examine the rich colour, minute detail and use of atmospheric perspective. Note the importance of symbolism in religious subject matter.

Compare the features that clearly distinguish these paintings from those in Italy of the same period.

The Humanism of Florence and Classical Greek and Roman culture had little or no influence on the Northern Renaissance, so painting developed in quite a different manner. Jan van Eyck perfected the technique of oil painting, but he and other artists also borrowed the techniques of perspective, naturalistic observation and a realistic approach to painting from Italy. However, patrons and artists had a very different idea of beauty to that of the Italians: northern Humanism was more austere, with a strong spirit of reform.

Printmaking and the mass production of images was an exciting opportunity for artists. Books, prints, engravings and pamphlets also facilitated the distribution of the ideas of the Reformation.

Further Research

www.artstor.org – Search for 'The many questions surrounding Jan van Eyck's Arnolfini Portrait' for a closer look at the details of the Northern Renaissance masterpiece

Chapter Review

1. What important symbols are seen in *The Arnolfini Portrait*?

2. Why do you think this picture was painted?

3. Describe the technique of oil painting.

4. Why do you think illusionism and symbolism had such an important role in Northern Renaissance paintings?

5. Describe and discuss the use of fine detail and illusionistic techniques in a Northern Renaissance work of art. Compare this to another artist's work of the same period or later.

6. Why do you think Italian Humanism and Erasmus's ideas of Humanism affected art in such different ways?

7. What opportunities did the development of printing present for artists?

8. Why do you think Albrecht Dürer's printmaking is so much more widely known than his painting?

UNIT 2 THE RENAISSANCE (c. 1300–1600s)

Chapter 6

A Golden Age: The High Renaissance in Rome, Florence and Venice

By the end of this chapter I will ...

* understand the Classical ideals of beauty and its influence on artists
* be able to discuss the developments in painterly techniques
* understand the psychological aspects of Leonardo da Vinci's paintings
* understand how Pope Julius II wanted to return Rome to its former grandeur
* understand how the interaction between Pope Julius and Michelangelo resulted in some of the finest art of the Renaissance
* be able to discuss the expressive qualities of Michelangelo's sculpture
* be able to describe and discuss a painting by Raphael
* understand why colour was so important in Venetian painting
* be able to discuss a painting by Titian.

Context

The High Renaissance was a brief but extremely brilliant period in Italy. It spanned the first two decades of the 16th century.

Rome was in a state of disrepair. The economy was weak, and over the years the city's structures and infrastructures had been badly neglected.

There were many ancient ruins, but no modern monuments like those in Florence.

Two popes set out to rectify this:

* In 1503, Pope Julius II (Fig. 6.1) set out to rebuild the great city and restore it to its former glory. He employed craftsmen, architects and artists to build churches, refurbish streets, build bridges and create some of the world's most treasured works of art.
* Pope Leo X (Fig. 6.2), son of Lorenzo de' Medici, was a Humanist, and he continued his predecessor's work.

The Status of the Artist

During the High Renaissance, the status of the artist changed completely. No longer considered mere craftsmen, they were now seen as special, creative individuals who could share and discuss intellectual ideas with patrons as equals. This change in status was largely due to the new Renaissance practice of writing about arts and artists.

Figure 6.1 (left)
Portrait of Pope Julius II, 1511, by Raphael, oil paint, 108 × 80.7 cm, National Gallery, London.

Figure 6.2 (right)
Portrait of Leo X, 1518–19, by Raphael, oil on wood, 154 cm × 119 cm, Uffizi Gallery, Florence. The pope's delicately brocaded white cassock and lush red velvet cape are a reminder of the love of fine fabrics in Florence.

Note Renaissance Writers

- Giorgio Vasari, a 16th-century painter, was the first to write about art.
- Leon Battista Alberti was a leading Humanist writer. He wrote that artists should be well educated, respected and valued in society. His views were highly regarded.
- Leonardo da Vinci also wrote about art. He placed a higher value on painting than other disciplines and argued that it was a natural science.

Ideals of the High Renaissance

Humanism gave the art of the Renaissance a unique quality.

Artists worked with religious themes that glorified God through the achievements of mankind.

High Renaissance painting and sculpture were based on the study of nature and the human figure: artists were not just interested in clever realism, but in striving towards the ideal of human beauty in Classical Greek and Roman culture.

Rome

In 1506, Pope Julius II embarked on the most breathtaking project of the age.

The basilica erected on the burial site of St Peter by Constantine in the 4th century was in a very poor state of repair. This was one of the Catholic Church's most holy sites, but the pope had it completely demolished. In its place, he would build a new and truly spectacular church that would impress generations to come (Fig. 6.3).

Excavations of ancient Roman ruins in the city were ongoing. In 1506, the ancient sculpture *Laocoön and His Sons* (Fig. 6.4) was rediscovered. Michelangelo was present when it was removed from the ground, and this experience had a strong influence on his later sculptures. Pope Julius II purchased the statue and moved his growing collection of ancient Roman sculpture – which also included the *Apollo Belvedere* – to the Vatican (Fig. 6.5).

Venice

Venice was the most splendid city in 16th-century Italy. Built on a network of canals and lagoons, the 'Queen of the Adriatic' shimmered and glistened in a soft radiant light. It was the centre of seaborne trade for the north-east of the country and one of the wealthiest cities in the world.

Clockwise from top: **Figure 6.3** St Peter's Basilica, Rome. Started in 1506, numerous architects worked on the building over 150 years until its completion in 1626. **Figure 6.4** *Laocoön and His Sons*, 208 cm. Discovered in several pieces in a Roman vineyard in 1506, this marble statue is dated to 323 BC–AD 31. After it was re-assembled, it was placed in the Vatican, where it remains today. **Figure 6.5** *Apollo Belvedere*, 224 cm. This marble statue from the 2nd century AD is considered to be a copy of an original bronze statue of 330–320 BC. It was part of Cardinal Giuliano della Rovere's collection and when he was elected pope as Julius II (1503–1513) it was transferred to the Vatican.

These trade networks were fundamental to painting practices. Luxurious, exotic pigments were imported from the east, while trade with Northern Europe brought the new technique of oil painting into the mainstream.

Innovation and Invention

Innovations in painting and sculpture of the High Renaissance included:

- correct proportion in the human figure
- more natural facial features and expressions
- a greater range of human movement
- more natural interaction between figures
- idealised beauty.

Artists and Artworks

Leonardo da Vinci (1452–1519)

The most famous of the great Renaissance masters, Leonardo da Vinci, was an artist of exceptional ability. He was the ultimate Renaissance man – as well as being a painter, he was also a sculptor, architect, musician, scientist, inventor and writer.

Da Vinci came from a little town in the Tuscan hills and became an apprentice to the sculptor Andrea del Verrocchio in Florence. He soon outshone his master. His earliest known painting is of a beautiful young angel in Verrocchio's *Baptism of Christ* (Fig. 6.6).

Milan

Da Vinci moved to Milan to become court artist for Ludovico Sforza, one of the wealthiest and most powerful princes of Renaissance Italy. In this position, da Vinci not only painted but organised elaborate festivals, as well as designing buildings, drainage systems, weapons of war and flying machines.

Scientific Interests

Da Vinci's reflections on mathematics, geology, the human body and other scientific subjects were recorded in thousands of manuscript pages and sketches. He discovered many features of the human body that contributed to his accuracy of proportion and his ability to show motion (Fig. 6.7). However, these

Figure 6.6 *Baptism of Christ*, 1472–5, by Andrea del Verrocchio, oil on wood, 177 × 151 cm, Uffizi Gallery, Florence. Leonardo painted the beautiful young angel in his master's work. Legend has it that when Verrocchio saw Leonardo's angel, he stopped painting and concentrated only on sculpture.

studies absorbed him so much that he completed only 15 paintings and one fresco in his lifetime.

Portraits

Portraiture was one of da Vinci's main subjects, and he painted many women. Traditionally, female portraits were painted in profile and a woman would never look directly at the viewer. Da Vinci, however, chose a three-quarter pose that gave his subjects a stronger presence, and placed them in a pyramidal composition.

Mona Lisa

Da Vinci's most famous portrait is the *Mona Lisa* (Fig. 6.8). She is thought to be Lisa Gherardini, wife of a Florentine cloth merchant named Francesco del Giocondo.

Controversially for the period, she looks directly at the viewer, and her arms, torso and head are each

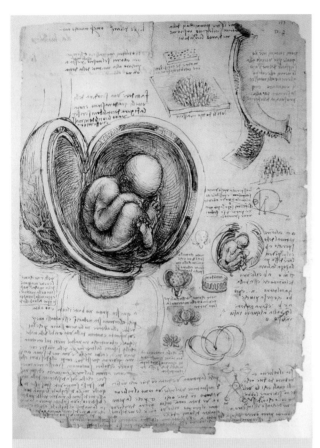

Figure 6.7 Page from Leonardo da Vinci's notes, Royal Library, Windsor Castle, England.

Figure 6.8 *Mona Lisa*, *c.* 1503–5, by Leonardo da Vinci, oil on poplar, 77 × 53 cm, Musée du Louvre, Paris. Mona Lisa's mysterious, unfathomable smile has made her more famous than any of Leonardo's other works. It is possibly a visual representation of happiness, a pun on the subject's husband's name (*gioconda* means 'happiness' in Italian).

subtly twisted in different directions. Her hands are joined in the centre of the foreground.

Da Vinci used the technique of *chiaroscuro* (seen earlier in Masaccio's work) to create a softness around the face and neck. He also developed a new technique called *sfumato*, which adds a sense of mystery. The figure seems to dissolve into the background, with its winding rivers and strange rock formations.

> **Sfumato:** Also known as 'Leonardo's smoke', this is a painting technique that softens outlines and blends areas of light and shade together.

The Virgin of the Rocks

The Virgin of the Rocks shows how da Vinci idealised religious figures and abandoned halos (Fig. 6.9). Mary tenderly watches over the infant

Christ and John the Baptist. Next to them is a smiling, pointing angel with soft, dreamy eyes.

The figures are grouped in a structured pyramidal shape. Detailed rocks, water and plants all studied from nature surround the figures.

The subject comes from a popular legend about St John the Baptist, but da Vinci uses the story to express a deeper and more meaningful concept (idea) of Christianity. In a dark landscape, four figures are illuminated by inner divine light.

Like most of da Vinci's paintings, *The Virgin of the Rocks* shows only a small range of natural colours,

but he has used these effectively to show the effect of rain and dust on colour and distance. Da Vinci was one of the first artists in Italy to use atmospheric perspective.

The Last Supper

Leonardo's most famous work is undoubtedly *The Last Supper*, a fresco in Sante Maria delle Grazie in Milan. Ludovico Sforza paid for the construction of this church and asked da Vinci to paint a fresco on one of the walls in the nearby monastery.

Da Vinci was not happy with traditional fresco techniques. For him, it dried too quickly, and prevented the use of fine detail. To counteract this, he mixed his paints with oil and worked *a secco*. The experiment proved disastrous, and in less than 20 years the great painting began to disintegrate.

Figure 6.9 *The Virgin of the Rocks*, 1495–1508, by Leonardo da Vinci, oil on panel, 199 × 122 cm, Musée du Louvre, Paris. The figures are treated with great tenderness, but Leonardo's love of mystery shows in the gestures, expressions and strange lighting.

Figure 6.10 *The Last Supper*, 1480, by Domenico Ghirlandaio, fresco, 400 × 810 cm, Church of Ognissanti, Florence.

Figure 6.11 *The Last Supper*, 1498, by Leonardo da Vinci, tempera and oil on plaster, 700 × 880 cm, Convent of Santa Maria delle Grazie, Milan.

Apostles react with horror, anger and disbelief

Gestures of upset and shock

Figure 6.12 and **6.13** (above left and right) Leonardo's picture tells the story in a silent but dramatic language of gestures and expressions.

Figure 6.14 (left) The figure of Jesus is placed at the vanishing point for all perspective lines.

Studies have shown that the colours were originally bright and vibrant, but today only traces remain.

The subject of *The Last Supper* was a traditional one, but its execution was highly original. In traditional depictions of the Bible story, Judas sits alone and isolated on the opposite side of the table to Jesus and the other disciples (Fig. 6.10). Da Vinci took an entirely different approach: he imagined the chaos when Jesus announced, 'One of you will betray me' (Fig. 6.11). His depiction of denial, disbelief, confusion and self-doubt is a powerful study of human emotion (Fig. 6.12 and 6.13).

Composition

To solve the problem of so many figures making a very long composition, da Vinci broke the figures into groups and connected them through their individual reactions. To the right of Jesus, one disciple seems to say, 'Lord, is it I?' and clasps his hands to his chest.

In the group to the left of Jesus, Peter, clutching a knife, leans forward to John and whispers in his ear. This action isolates Judas and pushes him out in a pose that directly opposes that of Jesus.

Framed by the window, Jesus is serene and dignified, his pyramidal shape placed in the exact centre of the composition (Fig. 6.14). He is alone in the midst of turbulence, but remains calm despite the knowledge of his suffering to come.

Perspective

The picture was painted for the refectory (dining room) and the artist used strong diagonals and sharp linear perspective to create an impression of a receding wall. This makes it look as if the group are sitting at the top table in the room and the vanishing point is centred on the face of Jesus.

Classroom activity: Sit in groups at a table. Take photographs as you act out the gestures of Jesus and the apostles. Say aloud what you think each one is saying. Make sketches of the gestures.

Michelangelo (1475–1564)

Michelangelo Buonarotti came to prominence in Florence at only 17 years old. He spent a short time in the studio of the artist Ghirlandaio and studied Masaccio's frescoes in the Brancacci Chapel, but always maintained he was self-taught.

He was accomplished in painting, sculpture and architecture, but he considered himself primarily a sculptor. Lorenzo the Magnificent had a school of sculpture, and Michelangelo benefitted greatly from his patronage. Lorenzo brought the young man to live in the Palazzo Medici, where Michelangelo studied the collection of Classical statues in the Medici gardens. Patronage provided the money for Michelangelo's grand schemes, but he always expressed his own personal vision through his art.

The Human Figure

Michelangelo believed that all beauty could be seen in the human body and strove to become an expert in its portrayal. He drew from life, making hundreds of detailed sketches, but also studied anatomy from human corpses.

However, difficult poses proved a challenge for the artist and his figures were often twisted and curved. He also bent the rules of realistic anatomy and proportion, if necessary, to increase the power of expression.

Sculpture
The Pietà

After Lorenzo the Magnificent's death, Michelangelo had to look elsewhere for work. His first major commission was for an elderly cardinal who wanted a statue for his tomb. The Virgin grieving over her dead Christ son was a very common subject in Northern Renaissance sculpture, but the 23-year-old Michelangelo was the first to bring it to Italy. The Classical elegance of his *Pietà* was unlike anything seen before (Fig. 6.15).

Pietà: The word means 'pity' in Italian, and refers to the Virgin Mary mourning the death of Jesus.

The figures are idealised and the drama is restrained. Mary appears serene; her youthful beauty suggests spiritual purity.

Composition

Carving two figures together was a difficult task, but the artist drew the composition together by forming a pyramid (Fig. 6.16), as seen in da Vinci's work. The harmonious symmetry immediately draws the eye to the Virgin's downcast expression.

Technical Problems

The sculpture was crafted from a single block of marble, and stretching a grown man over the seated woman was a complicated problem. Michelangelo solved this by building a support of folded drapery on the Virgin's lap. It made her a little larger and gave him the opportunity to cut deeply into the marble with a drill. The deep folds and curves look more like cloth than stone.

A Signature in Marble

When the *Pietà* was unveiled in 1500, some doubted that an artist so young could produce such an accomplished work. Michelangelo responded by carving his name on the sash running down the Virgin's chest – it was the only work he ever signed.

Later Pietàs

Michelangelo returned again and again to the subject of the *pietà*. This may have been because his own mother died when he was very young, but it also reflected his deep religious faith.

Look up Michelangelo's Pietàs. Compare his early work in Rome with the later Florence *Pietà*.

David

Michelangelo returned to Florence in 1500 to make a large statue for the cathedral. He was given a huge block of marble and from this he produced *David* (Fig. 6.17), the young hero from the Bible story of David and Goliath. This flawlessly beautiful male nude is idealised like a Greek god, posed similarly to Botticelli's Venus and the *Apollo Belvedere*.

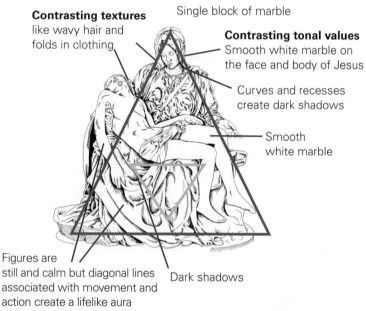

Contrasting textures like wavy hair and folds in clothing

Single block of marble

Contrasting tonal values Smooth white marble on the face and body of Jesus

Curves and recesses create dark shadows

Smooth white marble

Figures are still and calm but diagonal lines associated with movement and action create a lifelike aura

Dark shadows

Figure 6.15 (left) *Pietà*, 1500, by Michelangelo, marble, 174 cm, St Peter's Basilica, the Vatican.

Figure 6.16 (right) Pyramidal composition of the *Pietà*. Mary's head is at the top of the triangle and her foot is on the block; Jesus's head and feet form the other points. The position of Jesus' body makes another, less obvious triangle, inverted inside the main one.

Figure 6.17
David, 1501–4, by Michelangelo, marble, 517 cm, Galleria dell'Accademia, Florence. At over three times life size, *David* was the first monumental freestanding statue seen since Roman times.

David is depicted before the battle, holding a stone in his hand and a sling over his shoulder. His gaze is fixed on the distance and his brow is furrowed in concentration.

The elongated shape of the marble block may have determined the composition. A more active pose could have caused problems with balance. The head and hands are too large for the body, but this may be due to the original intention of displaying the statue high up: people looking upwards would have seen the proportions as perfect.

The Signoria (city governors) were so impressed that *David* was placed in the Piazza del Signoria in the centre of the city. It was later removed to a museum for safety and replaced with a copy outside the Palazzo Vecchio (town hall).

Painting

The Sistine Chapel Ceiling

Michelangelo had a difficult relationship with Pope Julius II, but the holy man managed to persuade the artist to paint the ceiling of the largest chapel in the Vatican, the Sistine Chapel. Though Michelangelo argued that painting was inferior to sculpture as an art form, the project proved to be one of his greatest achievements (Fig. 6.18).

Based on the book of Genesis from the Bible, the painting's scenes begin with the creation of the world and continue to the fall of man. The Creation of Adam and the Creation of Eve are at the centre. At the sides are the prophets and sibyls who foretold the coming of Christ, and in the corners are idealised nude figures, whose meaning is unclear.

> **Sibyl:** A woman in ancient times who was thought to utter the prophecies of a god.

The ceiling is divided into nine narrative scenes, arranged in three groups of large and small panels.

Figure 6.18 The ceiling of the Sistine Chapel, 1512, by Michelangelo, the Vatican. The panels are separated by painted architecture. They begin with the creation over the altar to the story of Noah at the end door.

Legend:

- The Creation
- The Downfall of Adam and Eve
- Three Stories of Noah
- Pendentive/architectural space
- Prophets
- Sibyls
- Ancestors of Christ
- The Last Judgement

Figure 6.19 Design scheme of the ceiling.

Around them are medallions and triangular spandrels formed by illusionistic painted architecture (Fig. 6.19).

Michelangelo began painting at the end of Genesis – the story of Noah – but took a break after the Creation of Eve. Having studied the work from the ground, he simplified the next composition, the Creation of Adam, which has become the most celebrated of the ceiling's scenes. It shows the artist's deep understanding of the human form and the influence of Classical sculptures such as the *Apollo Belvedere*.

Technique and Colour

The artist worked entirely alone on a high scaffold using *buon fresco*. Contrary to popular myth, he did not lie on his back, but stood, and, in a great burst of energy, completed the huge task in just four years.

The strong colour contrasts of soft grey painted architecture with golden yellows, pinks, deep blues and peach made the complicated scenes easier to follow from nearly 20 metres below, especially in the natural lighting of the time.

The colour was restored in cleaning during the 1980s.

Depiction of God

Michelangelo's depiction of God the Father was a complete departure from traditional imagery. In the Creation of Light, the stern, bearded figure surges across the empty sky with his great billowing

Figure 6.20
The Creation of Adam, 1512, by Michelangelo, fresco, Sistine Chapel, the Vatican.

cloak filled with angels and the spark of life passes from his commanding pointed finger to Adam's accepting hand (Fig. 6.20) with barely a touch.

> **RESEARCH**
> Pope Julius II's plans for the Sistine Chapel ceiling revolved around a depiction of the 12 apostles, but Michelangelo had bigger plans. Find out more detail about the scenes he painted from scripture that feature over 300 figures.

The Last Judgement

Twenty years later, Pope Paul III invited Michelangelo back to the Sistine Chapel, this time to paint a large fresco over the altar.

The pope was now dealing with issues raised by the Protestant Reformation, and he wanted *The Last Judgement* (Fig. 6.21) to be part of a message confirming the Church's authority. The scheme itself is quite traditional, but the figures are not.

Michelangelo was now working in the Mannerist style, which favoured more artificial and less naturalistic elegance. This can be seen in the variety of exaggerated, foreshortened, and dynamic poses of the 300 or so muscular figures that fill the wall.

> **Mannerism:** An overly stylised 'manner' of painting that became popular in the late Italian Renaissance. The human body was portrayed in an exaggerated way and there was often a use of elaborate decoration and artificial colour.

The focal point of this complex composition is Christ in Judgement (Fig. 6.21). The figure is like a Greek god who lifts his hand in a sweeping gesture to banish the damned from his presence, while simultaneously calling the saved towards him. Beside him, the Virgin Mary sits in a strange twisted position.

Figure 6.21
The Last Judgement, 1436–41, by Michelangelo, fresco, Sistine Chapel, the Vatican. The martyred saints hold the instruments of their gruesome deaths.

The imagery is Christian, but it incorporated an element of Classical mythology. The golden light behind Christ could be the sun, around which the whole event moves. This may suggest Christ's resemblance to Apollo, the Greek god of the sun, around whom all the planets revolve.

Architecture

St Peter's Basilica

In 1546, Michelangelo took over as chief architect for St Peter's Basilica. He was 81 years old.

Michelangelo redesigned the basilica to a square format, and centralised the entire space with a huge semi-circular dome. Only the drum with its double Corinthian columns was in place when he died, and the design of the dome was changed to an egg shape for structural reasons. The double Corinthian columns on the drum give the structure its strong upward movement (Fig. 6.22).

Figure 6.22 The dome of St Peter's Basilica, the Vatican.

Raphael (1483–1520)

Raphael Sanzio was a highly accomplished artist, and his easygoing personality greatly helped him to progress his career.

Raphael grew up in the court of Urbino, where his father introduced him to painting, artistic ideas and Humanist philosophy.

For a time he worked as an assistant to the artist Perugino, from whom he gained extensive professional knowledge. He arrived in Rome in 1504 and almost immediately attracted the attention of Pope Julius II and his successor, Pope Leo X.

Raphael's career was, however, unfortunately short. The artist died on his 37th birthday.

Madonnas

Raphael is probably best known for his images of the Virgin Mary, and probably the most loved of all is the *Madonna della Seggiola* (Fig. 6.23).

The *tondo*, or circular shape, was very popular during the Renaissance, but made for a difficult composition. Raphael cleverly adapted the

Figure 6.23 *The Madonna della Seggiola* (The Madonna of the Chair), 1513–14, by Raphael, oil on panel, 71 × 71 cm, Pitti Palace, Florence.

interlocking limbs of his figures and made the baby's elbow the pivotal point of the image.

Make a drawing in a circle. Work out a harmonious composition that has balance and symmetry.

The School of Athens

The frescoes in the *Stanze Raphael* (Raphael Rooms) in Vatican are the artist's most celebrated work. These rooms were once part of Pope Julius II's private residence. The most famous fresco, *The School of Athens* (Fig. 6.24), is in the *Stanza della Segnatura* (the pope's personal library), so it reflects his interest in philosophy, law and poetry.

The theme of *The School of Athens* is the Renaissance Humanist idea of harmony between Christian and ancient Greek philosophy. The ancient Greek philosophers Plato and Aristotle stand at the

Figure 6.24
The School of Athens, 1510–12, by Raphael, fresco, 500 × 770 cm, Stanze Raphael, the Vatican. The great philosophers and mathematicians of ancient Greece are shown as colleagues in a great academy.

Figure 6.25
The School of Athens – composition. The perspective lines converge at the centre with the philosopher Plato. The groupings and poses of the figures interacting in philosophical debate were unlike anything seen in earlier painting and resulted in a harmonious, balanced composition.

UNIT 2 THE RENAISSANCE (c. 1300–1600s)

centre, and on either side great mathematicians, philosophers and scientists are engaged in lively debate. The figures appear against an imaginary setting that may include part of the new St Peter's, as well as the Baths of Caracalla and the Pantheon in Rome.

Composition

The characters in the 'drama' are divided across the two sides. The eye of the viewer is led up the steps to the two central figures, Plato and Aristotle, who are set against daylight. The vanishing point of the perspective lines converges at the philosopher Plato with his finger pointing to the heavens (Fig. 6.25).

Venice

Giorgione (1477–1510)

Little is known about the life of Giorgione (which means 'big Giorgio'), but his mysterious, dreamlike paintings brought the concept of *poesie*, or visual poetry, to Renaissance art. His mysterious pictures are halfway between dream and reality (Fig. 6.26).

Titian (1485–1576)

Tiziano Vecellio, or Titian, was one of the most famous artists of 16th-century Venice. Early in his career, Titian worked with Giorgione and was so affected by his style that, for a while, it was difficult

Figure 6.26 *Fête Champêtre* or *Concert Champêtre*, 1508–9, Giorgione (possibly finished by Titian), oil on canvas, 105 × 137 cm, Musée du Louvre, Paris.

Figure 6.27 *The Assumption of the Virgin*, 1516–18, by Titian, 690 × 360 cm, oil on panel, Santa Maria Gloriosa dei Frari Basilica, Venice.

to tell the two artists' works apart. Fortunately, Titian's own style changed and developed over the years. He painted altarpieces, portraits, mythological subjects and landscapes with figures.

Assumption of the Virgin

Titian's huge painting *The Assumption of the Virgin* (Fig. 6.27) is set over the high altar in the basilica of Santa Maria Gloriosa dei Frari, Venice. It established Titian's reputation as an artist in the city.

Composition

The innovative composition shows Mary as she is assumed 'body and soul' into heavenly glory. Its three sections are linked by colour:

- In the lowest section the disciples react with amazement.
- In the middle section the Virgin Mary soars upward, surrounded by angels.
- The top section represents heaven, where God awaits.

Figure 6.28
Venus of Urbino, 1538, by Titian, oil on canvas, 119 × 165 cm, Uffizi Gallery, Florence.

Venus of Urbino

Venus of Urbino (Fig. 6.28) was probably painted as a marriage gift. It is a similar to Giorgione's *Sleeping Venus* and contains many symbolic references.

The picture suggests that the perfect Renaissance woman would be like Venus: a goddess of love who is sensual, beautiful and aware of her charms. The little dog sleeping at her feet is a symbol of faithfulness.

Media and Areas of Practice

Oil paint was now in more common usage than tempera, meaning colours were richer and more naturalistic. Painting was mostly on wood panels, and occasionally on stretched canvas.

This gave Leonardo da Vinci the freedom to paint in extremely fine detail. He worked slowly and methodically, beginning with brown tones and building up the image in layers of very thin paint. He often used his fingers to smooth and soften the edges while the paint was still wet.

Michelangelo worked in white marble, emulating the Classical statues he had studied in Florence and Rome. His precise choice of marble blocks was key to his practice, and he spent months in the quarry at Carrara finding the perfect stones for his sculptures.

In Venice, the most significant development was oil painting on canvas. In Florence, drawing was the most important thing; paint was added only when this was perfect. In Venice, however, colour was an end in and of itself. Oil paint particularly suited artists in Venice because the damp atmosphere made fresco painting on plastered walls impossible. They were among the first to stretch canvas over wooden frames. The canvases were primed with white gesso, so the light shimmered and glowed through the oily paint and glazes.

> **Gesso:** White chalk powder mixed with thin glue. Gesso on canvas or wood gave the surface more texture and prevented paint sinking into the fibres.

Art Elements and Design Principles

Artists of the High Renaissance achieved a high degree of realism, and they emphasised the Humanist values of ideal beauty, harmony and balance.

Leonardo da Vinci's stunningly realistic figures show his studies of human proportions and anatomy. His pyramidal compositions influenced many of his contemporaries and later artists, while his use of *sfumato* was an innovative development in the use of light and shade.

Michelangelo absorbed the ideals of ancient Greek philosophy. These values included correct proportions, muscular bodies, an oval face and a straight nose. He also had a keen eye for light and shade and understood its role in creating volume and shape in sculpture.

Raphael was renowned for his perfectly balanced and harmonious compositions. He learned from da Vinci's pyramidal compositions and painterly techniques. From Michelangelo, he learned to study antiquities and the human figure. He incorporated these techniques into his own Classical and serene style.

Titian fully explored the possibilities of oil painting. He painted directly onto the canvas with rich, vibrant colours, often making changes to the work as he went along. He used soft, fluffy brushwork and had a distinctive smooth, velvety textured style. His figures burst with energy and life. The twisting and complex poses add to the emotion, power and drama of his work.

Analysis

Examine the great works of art in both Rome and Florence and study Leonardo's unique style, Michelangelo's mastery in the depiction of the human figure in both painting and sculpture and how Raphael learned from the two older masters.

The Early Renaissance in Italy belonged to the city of Florence, but the High Renaissance was centred on Rome and Venice. By the 16th century, the status of the artist had had been elevated to a new level.

Pope Julius II was the greatest patron of the High Renaissance in Rome. He supported many important artists, including Michelangelo and Raphael.

Venice had long been the link with the 'exotic' East, and this gave its Renaissance art a distinctly different character to the rest of Italy. Colour was of great importance and oil painting on canvas allowed artists to fully explore its possibilities.

After the Renaissance

The influence of the Renaissance was profound and lasting, but art and architecture were expensive, and by the mid-16th century the Italian states had come under financial pressure. Tastes had changed too, and a more ornate style became popular.

In Northern Europe, the Protestant Reformation resulted in a strong reaction against religious imagery and ideals associated with the Roman Catholic Church. The belief that devotion to images verged on idolatry resulted in the destruction of religious art, including statues, altarpieces and stained glass. Patronage for religious art disappeared and artists had to turn to secular work, such as portraiture, landscape, and mythology, to survive.

Eventually, the Renaissance style evolved into the style known as Mannerism. While Renaissance art emphasised balance and proportion, Mannerism was more artificial and exaggerated. By the 17th century, European artists and architects had adopted a highly elaborate style of art known as Baroque. It was characterised by an ornate, over-the-top aesthetic that developed largely as part of the Catholic Church's response to the Reformation.

Idolatry: The worship of false gods, or devotion to an image of God.

Mannerism

In 16th-century Florence and Rome, a new artistic style evolved. Derived from the Italian word *maniera*, meaning 'style', Mannerism is also sometimes called the 'stylish style' because of its emphasis on an artificial rather than realistic depiction.

Renaissance art had emphasised balance and proportion, but Mannerism was more exaggerated, with unusual colours, elongated proportions and convoluted, serpentine poses in fluid and graceful S-shaped forms.

Artists and Artworks

Jacopo da Pontormo (1494–1557)

The Deposition from the Cross by Pontormo, with its unusual colour palette, elongated figures in distorted poses, and creation of an unrealistic pictorial space, marked the arrival of the Mannerist style.

Although the subject is the deposition of Christ, the artist has very imaginatively left out the cross, but included many figures not traditionally part of this scene.

Parmigianino (1503–1540)

One of the first artists to develop an elegant and sophisticated Mannerist style, Girolamo Francesco Maria Mazzola, known throughout his artistic career as Parmigianino (a nickname meaning 'the little one from Parma'), was an adventurous artist.

Drawn more towards the supernatural than the natural, he pushed out the traditional boundaries with an exaggerated style and paved the way for other bold artists to create works that are still seen as very modern for their time.

Parmigianino's style is characterised by elongated human figures, often with long necks and limbs. His paintings were notable for vivid colours and considerable freedom in brushstrokes.

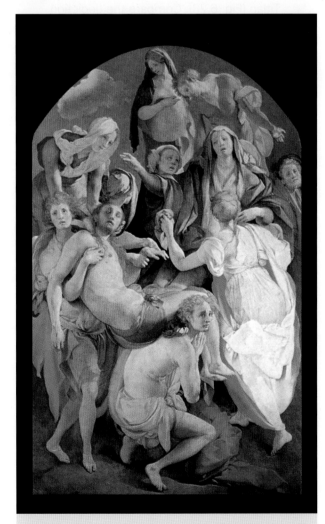

Figure 6.29 *The Deposition from the Cross,* 1528, by Jacopo da Pontormo, Church of Santa Felicita, Florence.

Figure 6.30 *Madonna with the Long Neck,* c. 1534–40, by Parmigianino, Uffizi Gallery, Florence.

Possibly the work most associated with the Mannerist style is the *Madonna and Child with Angels and St Jerome*, now better known as *Madonna with the Long Neck*, due to the Madonna's most prominent feature.

This work focuses on the Madonna, whose elongated limbs and monumental scale fill the centre of the composition. Seated on a high pedestal in graceful robes, holding her elegant long fingers to her heart, she smiles down at the nude infant Jesus on her lap. To the left, four angels crowd around, gazing admiringly on Christ. A row of marble columns on the right emphasise that the Virgin's neck resembles a great ivory tower or column.

The End of the Renaissance

In Northern Europe, the Protestant Reformation resulted in a strong reaction against religious imagery and ideals associated with the Roman Catholic Church.

Mannerism is seen as a link between the High Renaissance and the emotionally charged and dynamic art that followed as part of the response to the Reformation by the Roman Catholic Church.

In the 17th century, European artists and architects adopted a highly elaborate style of art that later became known as Baroque.

Chapter Review

1. What were the Classical ideals of beauty?

2. How did artists depict religious figures during the High Renaissance?

3. Which of Leonardo da Vinci's paintings do you think expresses his understanding of human emotion best? Give your reasons.

4. Describe and discuss a sculpture by Michelangelo.

5. Michelangelo considered himself a sculptor first and foremost. Do you think he was more pleased with the Sistine Chapel ceiling than his sculptural works?

6. Describe and discuss the *Creation of Adam* by Michelangelo from the Sistine Chapel ceiling.

7. Below (Fig. 6.31) is Raphael's *Madonna of the Goldfinch*. Describe and discuss this painting under the following headings:
   - Religious imagery
   - Symbolism
   - Composition
   - Art elements and design principles.

8. Search online for *Sleeping Venus* by Giorgione and look at *Venus of Urbino* by Titian (Fig. 6.28). Compare the depiction of the nude figure by both artists. How do both of these works compare to Botticelli's earlier depiction of Venus (Fig. 4.14)?

Figure 6.31 *Madonna of the Goldfinch*, c. 1506, by Raphael, oil on wood, 107 x 77 cm, Uffizi Gallery, Florence.

Further Research

www.metmuseum.org – Search for 'Design for the Tomb of Pope Julius II della Rovere'

www.youtube.com – Search for 'The Warrior Pope: Raphael's Portrait of Pope Julius II' (23:09) to learn more about Julius II and his relationship with the artist

www.leonardodavinci.net – Search for 'Leonardo da Vinci, his Life and Artworks' for an overview

www.youtube.com – Search for 'What did Leonardo da Vinci's "Last Supper" really look like?' (42:26) for an in-depth examination of da Vinci's methods and how the fresco originally appeared

www.youtube.com – Search for 'Leonardo da Vinci: The Renaissance Man' (19:41) to learn more about the famous artist

www.youtube.com – Search for 'A 10-minute tour of the Sistine Chapel' (9:56) for a virtual tour of the chapel and its artworks

www.youtube.com – Search for 'The School of Athens Raphael Art Analysis (Video Essay)' (5:29) for an up-close examination of the painting

Unit 3

The Baroque

(*c.* 1600–1700s)

Before

The Renaissance
c. 1300–1600s

The Baroque
Baroque Art in Rome

The Taking of Christ, 1602, Carravaggio

St Peter's Square, 1656–67, Bernini

The Dutch Golden Age
1650–1680

Still Life with Cheeses, Almonds and Pretzels, 1615, Peeters

The Night Watch, 1642, Rembrandt

Baroque Art in France
and Spain

Portrait of Innocent X, 1650, Velázquez

The Palace of Versailles, 1682

After

Rococo
1750–1785

Baroque Art (*c.* 1600–1700s)

Chapter 7

Art and Architecture in 17th-Century Italy

By the end of this chapter I will ...

* understand why the Baroque style developed
* be able to discuss innovations of the style
* understand why particular themes were favoured
* be able to describe and discuss a painting by Caravaggio
* be able to describe and discuss a sculpture by Bernini
* understand how town planning in the 17th century changed the city of Rome.

Before the Baroque

The Renaissance was influenced by the rediscovery of Classical Greek and Roman philosophy, culture and art. This great period of art and culture ended towards the mid-16th century as Florence, Rome and other Italian states came under financial pressure and tastes changed.

The more ornate style of Mannerism became popular in Italy. This was a more stylised and exaggerated form of Classicism, and is regarded as a bridge between the High Renaissance and the Baroque period.

Mannerists abandoned the more naturalistic colours and often used quite garish tones. This is famously associated with El Greco, a Spanish painter who adopted the Mannerist style when he moved to Rome (Fig. 7.1).

Figure 7.1 *Saint Francis Receiving the Stigmata*, 1590–95, by El Greco, oil on canvas, 114 × 104 cm, National Gallery of Ireland, Dublin.

The Reformation

In 1517, German monk Martin Luther called for reform in the Church, questioning some of Catholicism's fundamental beliefs. Those who supported him became known as Protestants.

The Church split, and wars erupted when some governments adopted Protestantism and others remained faithful to the Catholic Church.

The Reformation set new religious and political boundaries, but these came at a great cost, with decades of rebellions, wars and bloody persecutions.

Protestants rejected the ideals of beauty associated with the Roman Catholic Church. They believed devotion to religious imagery was a form of idolatry, and this caused a loss of patronage for artists in religious subjects.

In August 1566, a wave of iconoclasm spread across cities in the Netherlands. Rioting Calvinist mobs took over local churches and smashed Catholic statues, stained-glass windows and paintings.

Iconoclasm: The social belief in the importance of the destruction of icons and other images or monuments, most frequently for religious or political reasons.

Calvinists: Followers of John Calvin, a leader during the Protestant Reformation.

Context

The Baroque style overlapped with the Renaissance, but was far more extravagant, dramatic and exuberant in both its art and architecture.

The Baroque style began in Italy and spread through a large part of Europe during the 17th century. The word 'baroque' comes from the Portuguese and Spanish words for a large, irregularly-shaped pearl – *barroco* or *barrueco*. In informal use, the word describes something elaborate and highly detailed, but as the style went out of fashion, the word was used in a more offensive way. Compared to the more ornamental and decorative style popular during the 18th century, the works of the 17th century appeared bizarre, absurd and misshapen.

The Council of Trent (1545–1563)

The Catholic Church had been slow to respond systematically to Luther and the other reformers but eventually a great gathering of Church leaders was held in Trent in Northern Italy.

The Council of Trent made sweeping orders for reform and staunchly defended virtually every doctrine contested by the Protestants. This was the start of the Catholic Counter-Reformation.

By 1600, the Roman Catholic Church had emerged triumphant and optimistic.

Doctrine: A principle or system of belief.

The Jesuits

The Society of Jesus was founded by Ignatius of Loyola, a Spanish soldier turned priest, in 1534. Jesuits were soldiers of God and their role was to combat the spread of Protestantism. They played a leading role in the Counter-Reformation and had a direct effect on art.

Baroque Art

One of the ways the Catholic Church re-established its authority was through art. The Council of Trent's Decree on Sacred Images upheld the importance of religious art. The value of art as education, particularly for those who could not read or write, was officially recognised, and it was implied that the more grandiose and extravagant the art, the greater its appeal. Church leaders therefore encouraged artists to produce religious works of art that directly engaged with emotions and had as much involvement as possible with the viewer.

The imposing style of Baroque architecture was incorporated into grand palaces in several countries.

Ceilings were painted in the illusionistic manner and the grandiose style was popular because it emphasised the image of power for absolute rulers of those countries.

Rebuilding Rome

Anxious to rebuild Rome's reputation as a holy city, several successive popes embarked on extensive building, decoration and urban planning projects. The idea was to link the city's ancient glory with the church's divine authority. Hundreds of artists and architects were attracted to Rome by the new building work.

Media and Areas of Discipline

Some of the qualities frequently associated with the Baroque are grandeur, drama, vitality, movement, tension and emotional exuberance. This tendency towards intensity and passion was found in painting, sculpture, interior decoration and architecture.

Innovation and Invention

Baroque artists used the Renaissance technique of *chiaroscuro* and developed it into tenebrism, creating new and dramatic effects with intense light and dark shadows.

Artists chose moments of high drama to depict the subject matter in both painting and sculpture.

Chiaroscuro: Contrasts of light (*chiar*) and dark (*oscuro*).

Sculpture in the Round

Dynamic movement (especially upwards) in sculpture created a new energy in the depiction of human forms (Fig. 7.2).

Sculpture was created for large spaces, so that people could walk around and encounter them through various perspectives. This was highly innovative for the time.

Tenebrism: (from the Italian word *tenebroso*, meaning dark) A very intense form of *chiaroscuro*. It was used to create extreme contrasts of light and dark in figurative compositions to heighten their dramatic effect.

Figure 7.2 *The Rape of Proserpina*, 1621–22, by Gian Lorenzo Bernini, marble, 225 cm, Galleria Borghese, Rome. This example of energy and upward motion is pure Baroque. The figures are fraught with emotion and tension and it shows Bernini's expert handling of marble.

New Churches

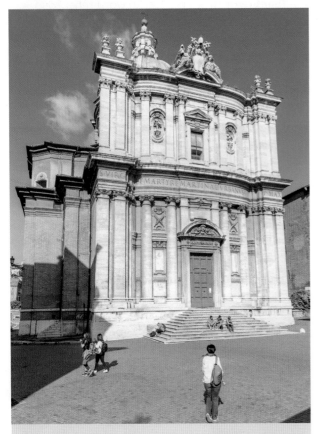

The Catholic Church had a pressing need for new churches, and these had to be impressive. This gave architects the freedom to experiment and express personal ideas.

Classical-inspired Renaissance elements in architecture were replaced with flowing curves. New buildings, like the Santi Luca e Martina, were more sculptural in design (Fig. 7.3).

The Church of the Gesù in Rome became the model for other churches of the newly founded Jesuit order. The interior echoed theatrical techniques: the rooms were large and open to allow full access to ceremonies and preaching. Hidden windows illuminated domes, altars, sumptuous gold leaf and marble décor. Elaborately painted illusionist ceilings appeared to be open to the sky (Fig. 7.4).

Figure 7.4 Interior of the Church of the Gesù, Rome.

Figure 7.3 Santi Luca e Martina, 1635, by Pietro da Cortona. This was the first curved Baroque church façade in Rome. Dramatic effects of light and shade were incorporated into the design.

Art Elements and Design Principles

Baroque painting was noted for:	Baroque sculpture was noted for:	Baroque architecture was noted for:
• dense and detailed compositions, intended to have an emotional impact on viewer • a strong sense of movement, with swirling spirals and upward diagonal lines • strong and sumptuous colour schemes in order to dazzle and surprise	• larger-than-life-size figures • broken form and textured draperies • an active use of space • extra elements like concealed lighting or water fountains added to sculpture • groups of figures and sculpture 'in the round'	• the creation of spectacle and illusion • enlarged domes and roofs • interiors constructed for spectacular effects of light and shade

Artists and Artworks

European Baroque painting developed between two very opposite poles. The idealised perfection of Annibale Carracci and the intense new realism of Caravaggio.

Annibale Carracci (1560–1609)

Annibale Carracci, his cousin Ludovico and his older brother Agostino founded an Academy for painting in Bologna. The academy transformed Italian painting in the late 16th century. The brothers

Figure 7.5 *The Assumption of the Virgin,* 1600, by Annibale Carracci, oil on wood, 245 × 155 cm, Cerasi Chapel, Rome. Carracci's painting over the altar was designed as part of the decoration of the chapel, but it was overshadowed by Caravaggio's paintings of the *Life of St Paul* on either side.

rejected the artificiality of Mannerist painting and promoted a return to nature and the study of the great painters of Renaissance Venice (Fig. 7.5). Annibale Carracci was a driving force in the creation of the Baroque style, and many of the great painters of the 17th century attended his academy.

Note: Carracci's insistence on painting directly from life and nature was quite exceptional in its day. Even the saints and other divine persons are absolutely human in gesture and pose, and show real-life emotion.

Caravaggio (1571–1610)

Michelangelo Merisi, who came from the small town of Caravaggio, was orphaned at age 11. He was apprenticed with a painter in Milan and, following his arrival in Rome in 1592, he was completely destitute.

Life changed when Cardinal del Monte welcomed him to his court. Influential connections meant commissions from some of Rome's wealthiest patrons and collectors. His paintings were stunning and impressive, but both his work and his scandalous lifestyle made Merisi – now known as Caravaggio – a very controversial figure.

Criticism of His Style

Caravaggio's dramatic art was exactly what the Church wanted but, for some, his realism went too far.

Unlike more traditional painters, he did not 'idealise' religious characters. He depicted them as ordinary people in contemporary clothing, and conservative members of the clergy considered this vulgar and disrespectful.

He was also becoming famous as a painter of feet. This was particularly controversial because feet were the lowliest part of the body, and not often portrayed in art at the time.

Caravaggio's painting style was unique, in that he rarely made preliminary drawings and instead painted directly from life onto the canvas, using just the handle of his brush to outline his compositions.

He chose extremely close viewpoints – almost like close-ups in modern-day film – but his use of *tenebrism* (extreme dramatic contrasts of light and dark tones) was probably his most impressive innovation. To achieve the desired effect, he used a single source of light, possibly a hole in the roof, as a spotlight for added drama.

He also used co-extensive space that brought his compositions out of the picture plane and into the viewer's space.

> **Co-extensive space:** An illusionary extension of space in the composition beyond the picture plane and into the viewer's space.

The Calling of St Matthew

Cardinal del Monte used his influence to secure Caravaggio his first commission, the decoration of the Contarelli Chapel in the Church of St Luigi dei Francesi. This consisted of three scenes from the life and death of St Matthew.

The Calling of St Matthew (Fig. 7.6) is set against a deeply shadowed background, divided by a sharp, diagonal beam of light.

Figure 7.6 *The Calling of St Matthew*, 1599–1600, by Caravaggio, oil on canvas, 322 × 340 cm, Church of San Luigi dei Francesi, Rome.

The painting was highly regarded for its realism and dramatic light and shade, but it was also severely criticised for showing Jesus and St Peter as real and ordinary people with bare feet.

The setting would also have been controversial. It looks like a tavern, and the figures in 17th-century Italian clothing would likely have been recognised as gamblers.

The Supper at Emmaus

Caravaggio soon found another patron in Cardinal Girolamo Mattei, who was from one of the foremost noble families in Rome. The artist moved into the Mattei family palace and completed several important paintings, including *The Supper at Emmaus* (Fig. 7.7).

The action centres on a moment of surprise when two apostles recognise the stranger they have invited to supper is none other than Jesus himself.

There is no distance or perspective in the painting, but the two apostles' dramatic gestures and the innkeeper's blank expression draw the eye towards the central point of the composition, Jesus breaking and blessing the bread.

Co-extensive Space

Caravaggio's use of co-extensive space not only projects the figures outwards but also draws the viewer inwards.

The dramatic foreshortening makes the apostle's hand come sharply towards us and the elbow on the left appears to rip through the canvas. This is further accentuated by the tear in the jacket.

The table is laid out like a still life, but the basket of fruit on the edge of the table looks as if it will fall at any moment, not on a floor but at our feet.

Caravaggio became well known in Rome as an unpredictable, aggressive individual. He was frequently in trouble and eventually had to flee for his life after being accused of murder. Go to YouTube, watch the video 'Caravaggio: His life and style in three paintings | National Gallery' (30:50) to learn more about Caravaggio's tempestuous life and career.

Figure 7.7
The Supper at Emmaus, 1601, by Caravaggio, oil on canvas, 141 × 196.2 cm, National Gallery of Art, London. By breaking down the traditional barrier between what is real and what is painted, Caravaggio transforms something that happened in the past into something happening now. We become involved and experience the shock and astonishment for ourselves.

The Taking of Christ

Another painting commissioned by the Mattei family, *The Taking of Christ* tells the story of Christ's betrayal by Judas (Fig. 7.8). The powerful story of disloyalty is told in all four gospels and was a traditional subject for art.

The juxtaposition of the two faces is the focal point of this composition. The contrast draws the eye to Christ's pale, sensitive face and the rough and sunburned face of Judas.

> **Juxtaposition:** Placement of very different objects close together for a contrasting effect.

Figure 7.8
The Taking of Christ, 1602, by Caravaggio, oil on canvas, 134 × 170 cm, National Gallery of Ireland, Dublin. The painting was presumed lost until it was discovered in August 1990 in a Jesuit house on Leeson Street, Dublin.

Composition

An affectionate gesture has become an act of aggression: Judas pulls the enormous force of the composition to the left. Christ instinctively draws back from the embrace and the cold, shining metal armour of the soldier's arm. He seems calm, but his vulnerability and distress are evident from his furrowed brow and downturned eyes. At the very bottom of the picture, highlighted by a bright pool of light, we see Jesus's hands clasped, fingers entwined and palms pushed towards the viewer in resignation.

Lighting

The scene is lit by moonlight from the upper left; a man holds a lantern but it has no effect. This is Caravaggio painting his own self-portrait as a passive spectator to the event.

Experiment with Caravaggism by taking a photograph on your phone of a group of friends in a dark space using bright lighting. Use the grid on your camera to create a balanced composition using the rule of thirds. Crop the photo to compress your composition and figures.

The rule of thirds: A compositional rule that suggests dividing the image into thirds and placing the subject on one of those sides, instead of in the centre.

Go to YouTube and watch the RTÉ video 'Ken Doherty: The Taking of Christ' (3:01). Why do you think Ken Doherty thinks Caravaggio might have been a good snooker player?

Artemisia Gentileschi (*c.* 1593–after 1651)

Caravaggio's amazing ability to engage the viewer and depict real human feeling inspired generations of artists to imitate and experiment with Caravaggism.

Orazio Gentileschi was the most lasting of these Caravaggists. He had known and worked with Caravaggio and he shared his vision with his gifted daughter, Artemisia.

Artemisia Gentileschi was one of the only female artists to achieve success in 17th-century Italy. She would have known Caravaggio when she was young, but she learned his style and techniques from her father.

Gentileschi was the first woman artist to be elected a member of the Academy of Art in Florence and was greatly admired by art collectors and her fellow academicians. She used her position as an artist to comment on the male-dominated nature of society and present female heroines in an entirely new way.

Artemisia Gentileschi was sexually assaulted by a painting tutor at the age of 17, and for a time her work was viewed only as an expression of this experience. Today, however, she is recognised as an extremely successful artist, who gained support and patronage at the highest level.

Gentileschi's paintings are often marked by violent themes. However, her well-known subjects are presented from a female point of view, and her female characters are powerful and defiant (Fig. 7.9).

Note: Artemisia Gentileschi used her own self-portrait for Judith (Fig. 7.9) and was clearly proud of it because she signed it in the lower right corner.

How do you think a girl studying art in 1600s Italy would have been treated by her peers and by society as a whole?

Judith Beheading Holofernes

The story from the deuterocanonical Book of Judith was especially popular in the Baroque period. It was seen as an example of the victory of virtue over vice.

The Assyrian general Holofernes was about to destroy Judith's home city of Bethulia, but she went to his tent in her finest clothing pretending she wanted to negotiate a truce.

Struck by her beauty, Holofernes invited Judith to a lavish banquet, but she got him drunk and he passed out. Judith then killed him, with the assistance of her servant, Abra.

Gentileschi has depicted a scene of graphic violence at the moment that Holfernes awakens from his stupor. She shows the brutality of the beheading in detail, with plunging arms, gripping hands, and sawing of the blade through spine and sinew. She places particular emphasis on the blood spurting from the victim's neck.

> **Deuterocanonical:** Refers to those books and passages of the Old and New Testaments about which there was controversy at one time in early Christian history. These include the Book of Judith and the Books of the Maccabees.

Composition

The sword runs along the painting's central axis, which extends from Abra's arm to the blood running down the edge of the bed. Judith's hand is clenched on the hilt of the sword. This is the very centre of the composition, emphasising that her hand has become the hand of God, possessed of divine strength.

> **Axis:** A real or imaginary line through part of the composition that divides it into two equal halves.

Note: *Judith Beheading Holofernes* is an expression of women's power. In previous versions of the same subject by other artists, Judith's servant Abra waits to collect the severed head from Judith, but in Gentileschi's interpretation Abra actively participates in the killing. This adds to the savage realism by reminding us that it would probably take two women to kill a grown man of this size and strength.

Figure 7.9 *Judith Beheading Holofernes*, 1610, by Artemisia Gentileschi, oil on canvas, 146 x 108 cm, Uffizi Gallery, Florence. Due to its graphic nature, the painting was initially hidden away and remained in a dark corner of the Uffizi Gallery until the late 20th century. Gentileschi wasn't even paid for it until years after its completion.

Colour and Texture

Judith's dress and elaborately curled hair is in keeping with the biblical description of her fine clothing, but the rich colours and textures – like the red velvet draped over Holofernes and the golden damask gown – show Gentileschi's awareness of the taste in Florence for sumptuous fabrics.

Gian Lorenzo Bernini (1598–1680)

Gian Lorenzo Bernini dominated the artistic scene in Rome for 60 years. He was a sculptor, architect, urban designer, painter and theatrical designer. His 'total works of art' incorporated several disciplines like sculpture, painting and architecture. His incredible passion, along with his extreme religious piety, made his art the very epitome of the Baroque style.

Bernini's sculpture was especially celebrated for its emotional expressionism and drama. He created tension, texture, and naturalism in 'living marble', like soft skin, curling hair and crinkling fabric. He also used light and shade effects that would have been traditionally more associated with painting.

The Human Form

Bernini studied the human form from life, and focused on portraying real human expression. He brought a new expertise and sensuality to depicting flesh in stone, and believed the truest way to convey personality was to capture someone in mid-conversation. He called this a 'speaking likeness'.

Saint Peter's Square

The ambitions of Pope Alexander VII, elected in 1655, led to some extraordinary architectural changes in Rome. These designs connected new and existing buildings, and opened up streets and squares in the city.

The pope chose Bernini, his favourite architect, to design St Peter's Square, and this forever changed the face of the city. Also known as Piazza San Pietro, the area was redesigned as part of the pilgrimage approach to St Peter's Basilica (Fig. 7.11).

According to Bernini, the oval shape of the Piazza symbolised the embracing welcome of 'the mother Church of Christianity'.

The square includes two fountains. One was already there when Bernini took on the project, so he designed another to balance it out. There is also a huge Egyptian obelisk, brought to Rome in 37 BC by the Emperor Caligula.

The square is framed by Doric colonnades. Above them, 96 huge statues by Bernini welcome pilgrims and guide them to the basilica.

Doric: A style of ancient Greek architecture identified by the simple circular capitals (the topmost feature) of the columns. See Chapter 3, page 58.

Theatricality

Bernini was deeply religious, but he also had a theatrical side. Theatre was a major part of his life and he wrote, directed, and acted in plays. This flair for drama influenced his architecture and sculpture, and especially inspired his 'total works of art', which combined drama, colour and design.

The Ecstasy of Saint Teresa

The Ecstasy of Saint Teresa is one of Bernini's 'total works of art'. It is pure emotion and a perfect example of Bernini's 'living marble' (Fig. 7.10).

Saint Teresa of Avila was a Spanish nun, mystic and writer during the Counter-Reformation. Bernini interpreted her account of a vision she had of an angel, in which she wrote:

> 'In his hands I saw a great golden spear, and at the iron tip there appeared to be a point of fire. This he plunged into my heart several times ... and left me utterly consumed by the great love of God. The pain was so severe that it made me utter several moans'.

Bernini wanted to interpret the divine event in human terms. The saint's closed eyes, open mouth and arms and feet hanging limp represent the reality of her mystical union with God. The angel prepares to pierce her heart with his spear of divine love. Another angel floats above her on a cloud, and a hidden window creates theatrical lighting that reflects the golden rays of the sun behind the figures.

Dramatic Effect on the Viewer

As the viewer approaches the chapel in which the sculpture is displayed, they see galleries that look like theatre boxes on either side. Inside these, members of the Conaro family, who commissioned the work, appear to be discussing the scene.

Figure 7.10 *The Ecstasy of Saint Teresa*, 1647–52, by Gian Lorenzo Bernini, marble, 350 cm, Santa Maria della Vittoria, Rome. Set in an elevated position above the altar, the sculptural group is a perfect combination of movement and absolute stillness. Fluttering drapery conveys the agitation of the swooning nun and contrasts with the purity of her face.

This drama 'on a stage' very clearly demonstrates one of the most important elements of Baroque art. The barrier between art and reality is broken down to include us in the intensity and passion of Teresa's vision.

Analysis

Examine how architecture, painting and sculpture worked together in a unique and unified way. Study the drama, vitality, movement, tension and emotional exuberance in the works of art and note the use of art elements like sumptuous colour and spectacular light and shade.

Figure 7.11 Saint Peter's Square (Piazza San Pietro) Rome, 1667, by Bernini. This is one of the largest and most beautiful squares in the world.

Baroque was a powerful style of art that developed as a response to Protestantism. This impressive art had a strong emotional appeal that directly involved the viewer.

Grandiose and exuberant works of art were encouraged because Church leaders at the Council of Trent had decided that the arts should communicate religious themes in response to the Protestant Reformation.

Go to YouTube and watch the video 'Bernini, Ecstasy of Saint Teresa' (7:32) by Smarthistory. Consider the theatrical devices used by Bernini to engage the viewer and describe how you might react if you were a visitor to the chapel.

Chapter Review

1. Describe the historical events that led to the development of the Baroque style.

2. What were the main characteristics of the Baroque style?

3. Name the most important Italian painters of the 17th century.

4. Explain the terms 'chiaroscuro' and 'tenebrism'.

5. Describe the compositional techniques in both *The Supper at Emmaus* and *The Taking of Christ* that the artist used to connect with the viewer and draw them into the action.

6. Artemisia Gentileschi's painting *Judith Beheading Holofernes* shows two women killing a man. What art elements of the painting best convey violence and horror in the scene?

7. According to Bernini, St Peter's Square symbolised the embracing welcome of 'the mother Church of Christianity'. Make a drawing of how you think he visualised this design.

Further Research

www.youtube.com – In 'Caravaggio's The Supper at Emmaus' (7:54) by OpenArtsArchive, Dr Emma Barker explores Caravaggio's unusual and innovative approach to depicting a story from the Bible

www.khanacademy.org – Search for 'Caravaggio, Calling of Saint Matthew and Inspiration of St. Matthew' for a detailed look at the painting

www.youtube.com – In 'Beyond Caravaggio at National Gallery' (4:07), broadcaster Kate Bryan explores the phenomenon of Caravaggism

www.nationalgallery.ie – Search for 'How did a masterpiece by Caravaggio end up in a Dublin dining room?' for an article on the rediscovery of *The Taking of Christ*

stpetersbasilica.info – The official site of St Peter's Basilica and Square in the Vatican

Baroque Art in Flanders and the Dutch Republic

* know how the Dutch Republic and Flanders developed as separate states
* be able to discuss Rubens' hugely successful artistic career
* know the meaning of genre painting
* know why smaller-scale paintings suited the artistic tastes of the middle class
* discuss Rembrandt's expression of human feeling in his self-portraits
* be able to discuss Rembrandt's exceptional use of light
* know why women painters in the Dutch Republic had careers and were respected
* be able to describe and discuss works by Vermeer
* understand the connection between Vermeer's art and the camera obscura.

Context

At the beginning of the 17th century, the Netherlands was marked by conflict. The country was, at that time, ruled by the Spanish, who were Catholics. The predominantly Protestant Dutch merchant class revolted against the Spanish, leading to 12 years of war, which weakened the once-powerful commercial centres of Bruges, Ghent and Antwerp.

In 1609, the two opposing sides signed a treaty – the Treaty of Antwerp – that established an independent republic in the north (Fig. 8.1).

The terms of the Treaty of Antwerp were as follows:

* The United Provinces of the Dutch Republic was recognised as an independent state, free from the political influence of the Spanish Catholics.
* The Southern Netherlands, which included Flanders and the city of Antwerp, would remain under the control of Catholic Spain.
* All Protestants had to leave Antwerp within two years. Many artists, craftsmen and wealthy merchants went north to Amsterdam, creating a hub for artists and intellectuals.

The Dutch Republic

The north had historically been less developed than Flanders, but during the course of the 17th century, it became one of the wealthiest nations in Europe. The Dutch Republic consisted of seven provinces, including Holland. The new country became an important naval power, and merchant fleets sailed the world's seas. They set up

Figure 8.1 The Netherlands, 1609–72.

prosperous colonies in Asia, the Dutch East Indies, Africa and America.

Note: New York used to be called New Amsterdam.

Artistic Style

The Baroque style developed in different ways across Europe, as it was governed by individual political systems and religions.

In the Southern Netherlands, or Flanders, the style of art was known as Flemish Baroque. Civic and religious leaders were anxious to re-establish Catholic identity by restoring churches and religious art to their full glory.

In the Dutch Republic, people were proud of their achievements and their land. Art flourished in the self-confident environment and the period 1600–80 is widely referred to as the Dutch Golden Age.

The state religion of Protestant Calvinism prohibited the use of images in places of worship. This created an independent art market, as there was no state demand for religious art.

Artists were paid well and were highly respected, but success and failure depended on who was in power. In order to develop a good reputation and have a profitable business, artists tended to specialise in one particular subject, such as landscape or still life, or even the representation of a particular type of animal or fabric.

The School of Delft

Delft is a canal-ringed city in the Dutch Republic. The School of Delft is known for its genre scenes of domestic life, church interiors, courtyards and the city streets. The paintings are distinguished by a strong sense of calm, a careful observation of light, clear perspective and measured compositions. Pieter de Hooch and Johannes Vermeer are two of the school's best-known artists.

School: A term used for a group of artists who follow the same style, share the same teachers, or have the same aims.

The Guild of St Luke

Most painters in both parts of the Netherlands were members of the Guild of Saint Luke. A master painter needed Guild membership to take on apprentices or to sell paintings to the public.

Women Painters

Several women in the Dutch Republic became well known and successful during the Dutch Golden Age. Some, like Judith Leyster, painted portraits, while others specialised in still life or floral compositions. Clara Peeters, Rachel Ruysch and Maria van Oosterwijck all achieved fame by painting objects rather than people.

Media and Areas of Practice

The Dutch Republic

In the Dutch Republic, the dominant form of visual art featured ordinary subjects, like portraits, landscapes, still life and genre works (Fig. 8.2). Large numbers of small oil paintings depicting everyday scenes were produced to decorate homes. Even relatively modest Dutch households would purchase them because they were a way of making a statement. The paintings were generally displayed in the large front rooms where business was conducted and visitors were entertained.

Southern Netherlands

In the Southern Netherlands, refurbishing the altars of Antwerp's churches was the main priority. Sacred art in the Netherlands had suffered badly from the Protestant iconoclasm, and producing large colourful oil paintings on canvas of religious subjects kept the artist Peter Paul Rubens's workshop busy for many years (Fig. 8.3).

Artists' Materials

There was healthy trade and a high level of expertise in art materials – especially paint – both

Figure 8.2 *Woman with a Child in a Pantry*, 1656–60, by Pieter de Hooch, oil on canvas, 65 × 61 cm, Rijksmuseum, Amsterdam. Space is represented by two 'through views': one leads into the cellar, and the other to the entrance hall. The two windows behind the figures are sources of light, but there is another coming from the viewer's space.

Figure 8.3
The interior nave of Antwerp Cathedral, which houses four altarpieces by Rubens.

in raw and refined form. Linseed oil was made in Flemish windmills by crushing locally grown linseed. Painters had a choice. They could:

- buy raw materials, grind them, and mix in the oil and drying agents before storing them in pig bladders. They could stretch and mount their own canvases before priming them with multiple layers of gesso.
- buy expensive ready-made artists' materials. Ground-up pigments, ready-made paints, tied-up pig bladders, liquids and various sizes of canvases were available off the shelf from specialised art dealers. A supply grocer was nicknamed 'the colourman'.

Innovation and Invention

The Dutch Golden Age resulted in a number of innovations in painting the natural world. The Dutch words *stilleven* and *landschap* were adopted into English as 'still life' and 'landscape'. Flemish and Dutch painters tended to name individual subjects as 'breakfast piece' or 'winter snow scene'.

The Dutch Republic

Artists reached great heights of mastery in specialist areas:

Figure 8.4 *Windmill at Wijk bij Duurstede*, 1668, by Jacob van Ruisdael, oil on canvas, Rijksmuseum, 83 × 101 cm, Amsterdam. Ruisdael is generally considered the pre-eminent landscape painter of the Dutch Golden Age.

- **Genre painting:** subjects featuring contemporary lifestyle, trends and the interests of the Dutch people of the time were popular.
- **Portrait painting:** wealthy tradespeople were far more willing to commission portraits than in other countries.
- **Landscape painting:** landscape painting took on a Classical style in the mid-1600s. It emphasised the unique characteristics of Dutch landscape, like villages and rural life, as well as trees, windmills, cloud-filled skies and strong contrasts of dark and light (Fig. 8.4).

Figure 8.5 *Vanitas with Violin and Glass Ball*, 1628, Pieter Claesz, oil on oak, 36 × 59 cm, Germanisches Nationalmuseum, Nuremberg. The glass, drained to the very last drop, symbolises the briefness of worldly pleasures. The violin represents the rivalry between the two arts of painting and music.

- **Still life painting:** a dominant feature of the Dutch Golden Age, it developed a number of sub-types:
  - *Pronkstilleven* were grandiose displays of food and expensive tableware. The genre began in Antwerp and was quickly taken up by the Dutch Republic.
  - Religious art had disappeared due to the Reformation, but a demand grew for small-scale works containing a Christian message or moral lesson. Artists responded by producing a type of still life painting known as 'vanitas' (Fig. 8.5).
  - *Ontbijtjes*, or 'breakfast pieces', showed the ingredients of a simple everyday meal.
  - Floral still life was painted with scientific accuracy. One of the most highly paid forms of still life, floral painting attracted both male and female artists.

Southern Netherlands

Flemish Baroque artists – artists from the Southern Netherlands – specialised in religious, mythological and allegorical scenes, as well as still life and family portraits.

Artists and Artworks
Southern Netherlands
Peter Paul Rubens (1577–1640)

Peter Paul Rubens was the pre-eminent Flemish Baroque painter in Antwerp in the early 1600s. He spent time in Rome and brought elements from the Italian Renaissance style together with Flemish realism. His powerful and exuberant paintings emphasised movement, colour, drama and sensuality.

He was not only a superb artist but also a brilliant manager. A constant stream of work poured out from his thriving workshop. Handsome, cultivated and well educated, he lived in a magnificent townhouse with his wife Isabella. He had a shrewd business sense and also acted as a diplomat throughout his life.

Patronage

Rubens was highly sought after as a court painter and portraitist. He was commissioned by several important figures and groups in the Catholic Church and in the royal courts of Europe.

Figure 8.6
Galerie Médicis, Richelieu wing, Palais du Louvre, Paris. The series of paintings were intended for private display, in Marie de' Medici's newly constructed home of the Luxembourg palace, but there is a sense that the queen wanted to impress those around her. For this, Rubens was a wise choice.

One of his largest commissions came from Marie de' Medici, who was married to the King of France. He painted a series of large canvases for the Italian-born French queen, depicting her as a heroine emerging through trials and tribulations to fulfil her destiny (Fig. 8.6).

Style, Technique and Subjects

Rubens instilled passion into his painting and depicted the human emotional and psychological state in an imaginative and energetic manner.

He is probably best known for his portrayal of the female form – the term 'Rubenesque' is still used today to describe a voluptuous nude (Fig. 8.7).

His works are mostly oil on canvas, wood or panels, but he also made many sketches and drawings in chalk and ink.

His diverse range of subject matter included religious paintings, figures from ancient Greek and Roman mythology and royal portraits.

Rubens favoured diagonal compositions, which can be seen clearly in *The Elevation of the Cross*, his first commission after his return from Italy.

The Elevation of the Cross

The central panel of the huge triptych painting commissioned for the Church of St Walburga in Antwerp depicts the dramatic moment when Christ, having been nailed to the cross, is raised to an upright position (Fig. 8.8).

Rubens created a strong diagonal emphasis by placing the base of the cross at the lower right of the composition and the top of the cross in the upper left. This makes Christ's body the focal point.

This strong diagonal also reinforces the notion that the event is happening right in front of the viewer, as the men struggling to lift the weight of the cross look as if they are about to burst out of the picture.

The dramatic *chiaroscuro* and the muscular figures pushing past the boundaries of the picture plane are a reminder that Rubens would have seen Caravaggio's work in Rome.

Figure 8.7
The Judgement of Paris, 1632–36, by Peter Paul Rubens, oil on oak, 145 × 194 cm National Gallery, London. In the tale from Roman mythology, Paris was forced to judge the most beautiful of three goddesses: Venus, Minerva and Juno. Rubens is said to have modelled the figure of Venus on his second wife, Hélène Fourment.

Figure 8.8 *The Elevation of the Cross*, 1610, by Peter Paul Rubens, oil on wood, 462 × 341 cm, Cathedral of Our Lady, Antwerp.

Symbolism

The subject had a specific function. During Mass, the people would look up as the priest elevated the host, and also see the elevation of Christ's cross above the altar. This was a visual reminder of Christ's sacrifice.

> **Triptych:** From the Greek word for 'threefold', this work of art is usually a panel painting that is divided into three sections. These sections are sometimes hinged together and can be folded shut or displayed open.

Artists of the Dutch Republic
Clara Peeters (1594–after 1657)

Clara Peeters' still life paintings featured valuable objects alongside exotic flowers, fruit and confectionery. Not a great deal is known about Peeters, but she is credited with introducing the 'breakfast piece' (Fig. 8.9). These compositions showed everyday foods arranged on narrow ledges and viewed from low vantage points, typically against dark backgrounds.

Judith Leyster (1609–1660) was a highly regarded portrait painter of the Dutch Golden Age. Find out about the life and successful career of this extraordinary artist and why her name remained largely unknown until the late 19th century.

Set up a group of objects including a shiny spoon or another convex or concave shape. Include your own distorted image in your drawing.
Variation: Set up several shiny objects for multiple tiny bits of your self-portrait.

Figure 8.9
Still Life with Cheeses, Almonds and Pretzels, 1615, by Clara Peeters, oil on wood, 35 × 50 cm, Mauritshuis, The Hague. A hole in the cheese would have been made to check its quality. The silver bridal knife is decorated with figures representing the virtues of Faith and Moderation and two intertwined hands. The artist signed the painting on the knife. A woman with a white cap can be seen on the pewter lid of the earthenware jug. This is a self-portrait and Clara's second signature.

Rembrandt van Rjin (1606–69)

Rembrandt van Rjin was undoubtedly the most important of all the Dutch realists and one of Europe's greatest old masters. He is especially famous for his outstanding ability to portray deep human feeling alongside human imperfection.

Rembrandt Harmenszoon van Rijn was born into a family of ten in Leiden in 1606. He showed little interest in school; painting and drawing were his only interests and his parents had no choice but to apprentice him to Rubens in Antwerp.

Rembrandt set out to emulate Rubens, but unfortunately he never reached the same level of success. He was greatly admired as an artist and he made a good income from portrait painting and teaching.

His marriage to Saskia van Uylenburgh also brought him a considerable fortune, but by the age of 35 he had lost his grip on his finances and by 50 he was disastrously bankrupt.

His personal life was also marked by tragedy. Saskia died young and three of his five children died in infancy. His lover Hendrickje also died, and he lost his only son Titus just a year before he died himself.

A Unique Style

Rembrandt never went abroad, but became aware of new developments in Italian art by studying prints and the work of artists who had lived in Italy.

He was an extremely versatile artist. Each painting was individual and he never lapsed into a routine. His unique and innovative style included broad, loose brushstrokes and heavy, opaque passages of lighter tones. No one is exactly sure how he created texture in the *impasto* areas, but he may have used a palette knife or rag. One of the key characteristics seen in his paintings today is the use of a sharpened brush handle to scratch through wet paint and create individual lines.

Impasto: Thick paint strokes.

His limited palette of colours was dominated by dark earth tones and golden highlights. Large areas were covered in shadow with pockets of deep darkness, and the works were finished with layers of transparent glaze.

Rembrandt's Subjects
The Old Testament
Portraits and Self-portraits

In his early career, Rembrandt was very much in demand for painting individual and group portraits, but his progress in painting people is better demonstrated by the large volume of self-portraits the artist created throughout his career.

Figure 8.10 *Self-Portrait at Age 34*, 1640, by Rembrandt van Rijn, oil on canvas, 91 × 75 cm, National Gallery, London. The artist's expensive-looking clothes date from around 1550, and are therefore fancy dress. The clothes and pose reference paintings by Dürer, Titian and Raphael. He is both praising the great Renaissance painters and directly comparing himself to them.

Figure 8.11 *Self-Portrait of the Artist at his Easel*, 1660, by Rembrandt van Rijn, oil on canvas, 80 × 67 cm, Musée du Louvre, Paris.

From his early 20s until his death at the age of 63, Rembrandt made paintings, drawings, and etchings of himself. Seen together, they offer a unique insight into the life, character and psychological development of Rembrandt, both as a man and as an artist.

The early self-portraits are very lifelike, and those from his middle years show a confident and successful man (Fig. 8.10). Later works show the ravages of his sad life and the reality of his ageing face (Fig. 8.11).

These works helped advance his career and shape his public image. Self-portraits of well-known artists were popular with art buyers from all walks of life. This presented Rembrandt with the opportunity

to promote himself as an artist while practising facial expressions and refining his techniques of light and shadow, skin texture and fine clothing.

Rembrandt's paintings were made by looking at himself in a mirror, but the image was reversed in his etchings by the printing process. Find some of these prints and compare them to his paintings to see how the artist really appeared to his contemporaries.

Go to *blog.britishmuseum.org* and search for the post 'Rembrandt's depictions of women'. Look at Rembrandt's studies and watch the video at the end of the post. Which do think is more impressive: Rembrandt's pen drawings or his brush drawings?

The Night Watch

At the height of his career, Rembrandt received a commission for a group portrait for the Amsterdam civic guard company (Fig. 8.12). The *arquebusiers*, or musketeers, were the guardsmen of the city gates,

Figure 8.12
The Night Watch,
1642, by Rembrandt van Rjin,
oil on canvas, 363 × 437 cm,
Rijksmuseum, Amsterdam.

policed the streets, put out fires, and generally maintained order.

Subject

Originally known as the *Musketeers' Militia Company of the Second Precinct*, the painting now called *The Night Watch* features the company's captain, Frans Banning Cocq, wearing the formal black attire and white lace collar of the upper class. He is accompanied by his lieutenant, Willem van Ruytenburgh, dressed in bright yellow satin. He wears a military style gorget around his neck and carries a weapon called a partisan.

Composition

Each member of the company had to pay for his face to be included in the painting, so only those who could afford it were included. Higher ranks meant better placing, but all would have expected to be equally visible. There were some, of course, who paid extra to be in the best positions.

Rembrandt kept to the structure that was, by this point, expected of him, but instead of placing his sitters in rows, he brought them to life, like characters in a drama. He also included some 'extras' to create the appearance of a full company.

Symbolism and Pride

A chicken hanging by its claws from the waist of one of the girls dressed in gold and blue is a direct reference to the emblem of the guards. She is not a real person, but a personification of the company.

The Night Watch was cut down to make it fit between two doors when it was transferred to the town hall in around 1715. This did not significantly devalue the painting, which has become an icon of national pride representing the very essence of 'Dutchness'.

 RESPOND Which members of *The Night Watch* do you think paid more for their portraits?

Note: The title *The Night Watch* came about as a result of layers of dirt and varnish that had darkened the painting, but it is actually set in daytime.

Gabriel Metsu (1629–67)

Despite his early death at the age of 37, Gabriel Metsu was one of the leading Dutch genre painters of the 1600s. He was a gifted visual storyteller and his work provides an insight into 17th-century Dutch life, especially into affairs of the heart among the upper class (Fig. 8.13 and 8.14).

Man Writing a Letter and *Woman Reading a Letter*

Painted as companion pieces, these works tell a story, where every little detail has a meaning. Both figures sit at a window: he is writing a letter and she is reading it. We immediately assume it is a love letter.

The pieces show the influence of Johannes Vermeer and an interesting sign of rivalry among artists. Metsu would have known that yellow jackets were one of Vermeer's trademarks.

Read the descriptions of both paintings at **onlinecollection.nationalgallery.ie.**

Write and draw your own graphic novel-style account of the story.

Pieter de Hooch (1629–84)

De Hooch is best known for his domestic scenes of middle-class women and children painted in Delft.

Figure 8.13 *Man Writing a Letter*, 1664–6, by Gabriel Metsu, oil on wood panel, 53 × 40 cm, National Gallery of Ireland, Dublin.

The Courtyard of a House in Delft

A young maid in a white cap, holding the hand of a little girl, steps into the sunny courtyard (Fig. 8.15). A shadowy figure, presumably the child's mother, is seen in the passageway.

Composition

The picture reads in two parts. On the left, the house and the passageway are defined with strong verticals and painted in precise architectural detail. The mother stands here, while on the right, the maid and the child are in the older part of the house. The crumbling brickwork and falling greenery are less formal looking.

Symbols and Meaning

A discarded broom in the foreground is symbolic of a well-ordered household.

A change in household circumstances occurred during the 17th century which meant that men worked less in home, businesses and industries.

Figure 8.14 *Woman Reading a Letter*, 1664–6, by Gabriel Metsu, oil on wood panel, 53 × 40 cm, National Gallery of Ireland, Dublin.

Figure 8.15 *The Courtyard of a House in Delft*, 1658, by Pieter de Hooch, oil on canvas, 74 × 60 cm, National Gallery, London.

They went instead to warehouses or offices and the house became more the domain of women.

Johannes Vermeer (1632–75)

Today, Johannes Vermeer is one of the most highly regarded artists of the Dutch Golden Age, but in his own time his paintings received far less attention. He worked very slowly and produced only 35 paintings in his lifetime. He lived his entire life in Delft and several of his paintings depict the city.

Style and Technique

Vermeer's paintings mostly involve one or two figures, usually women, engaged in everyday simple tasks. Models were often family members or relatives of patrons, and many of his paintings include the same furnishings or motifs. Other characteristics include a delicate pearly light, and a translucent effect achieved by the application of thin glaze over opaque paint layers.

Vermeer used the expensive pigment *lapis lazuli* – ultramarine – in the most lavish way. Paint was often applied broadly, and definite brushmarks can be seen in the work.

His best-known characteristic is little dots of bright light created with unmixed colour. It is thought that these relate to the artist's use of a camera obscura, an early form of camera that projected an image onto a drawing or painting surface (Fig. 8.16).

The evidence suggesting his use of the camera obscura are:

- exaggerated perspective, in which figures and objects look very large in the foreground compared to those farther back
- sparkling highlights and tiny specks of light that resemble light seen through an out-of-focus lens.

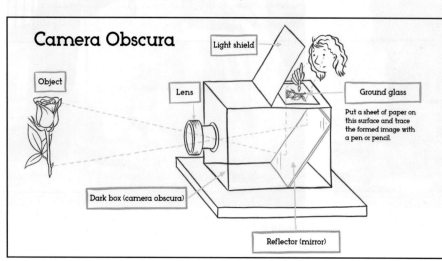

Figure 8.16
The camera obscura, 'dark chamber' in Latin. This optical device preceded the modern camera. A lens was attached to the side of a darkened box and light was admitted through a single tiny hole. An image of the outside scene could then be cast on a wall or surface opposite.

Lady Writing a Letter, with her Maid

A woman sits at a table writing a letter and a maid looks out the window (Fig. 8.17). The maid crosses her arms and waits, but the artist has avoided any narrative or story.

The maid is the central figure, standing calmly, still and straight like a column. Her mistress, in marked contrast, is deeply engrossed in writing. The bright light falls on her writing arm and the angular folds on the pure white sleeve are sharply defined against background shadows.

The mood of painting is one of stillness and calm, but there are small clues to its meaning. The red wax seal indicates that the crumpled letter on the floor was received; as letters were prized in the 17th century, it must have been thrown aside in anger. The empty chair at the table suggests someone has recently been sitting there, since chairs of this type were placed against the wall when not in use.

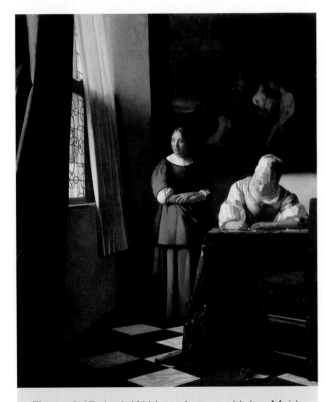

Figure 8.17 *Lady Writing a Letter, with her Maid*, 1670, by Johannes Vermeer, oil on canvas, 72 × 60 cm, National Gallery of Ireland, Dublin.

Composition

The artist has chosen a low viewpoint, which makes the space seem higher. Lines of perspective join the two figures from the upper and lower window to the vanishing point of the mistress's left eye. The viewer's eye is drawn first to the maid, but it quickly passes to the woman at the table.

Colour

The black and white marble floor contrasts with the sumptuous red Persian rug on the table.

Ultramarine has been used throughout. It is even part of the mix in the green fabric on the chair and the rich blue-grey shadows in the white linen sleeves.

Art Elements and Design Principles

Floral and still life painters in the Dutch Republic were primarily concerned with depicting their subject in fine detail. Compositions were carefully planned, and textures such as fabric and fruit were exquisitely rendered, as was light on reflective surfaces like metal and glass. However, these luxury goods often included a skull or an hourglass to remind the viewer that such luxuries would be of little use in the afterlife.

Genre scenes often promoted piety and a devout lifestyle, and landscapes might stress aspects like the hopeful light of a new dawn or the dark threat of an approaching storm. However, these perfectly depicted illusions of space, solidity, texture, and light were also *memento mori* (reminders of mortality).

Johannes Vermeer's paintings usually feature one or two figures in a clearly defined and delicately lit architectural space. The light source is often a window. Compositions are meticulously constructed and the eye is drawn around the interior by his careful placing of objects. These individual objects were chosen so that their position, proportions, colours and textures worked in harmony with the figures, and little dots of bright unmixed colour form highlights.

Religious art in Flanders was much in demand under the influence of the Counter-Reformation. It was injected with a new energy, especially with influences from Italy through the work of Rubens.

Rubens was known for the vigour and passion of his work, and his use of bold, swift strokes added to the drama.

He often worked from a dark background, painting over this in bright reds and golds. He also created rich undertones to add depth, define light and create fine textures.

Chapter Review

1. Who paid for art in the 17th century in (a) Flanders and (b) the Dutch Republic?

2. Compare and contrast the style, composition and colour of a religious painting and a portrait of royalty by Peter Paul Reubens.

3. Why do think women artists painted flowers and still life and not genre paintings?

4. Why did Rembrandt paint so many self-portraits?

5. Amsterdam and Antwerp were both in the Netherlands. Do you think that Rubens and Rembrandt knew each other personally? Why do you think that?

6. Why do you think Vermeer's paintings are considered timeless?

7. Examine *The Lacemaker* by Johannes Vermeer on the right (Fig. 8.18). How do you think the composition and the artist's use of light and shade, detail and colour suggests the young woman's concentration on her work?

Analysis

Study the work of artists in the Dutch Republic, who produced numerous small but exceptionally fine paintings of ordinary subjects, like portraits, flowers, landscapes, still life and genre paintings of everyday scenes.

Compare these to the much larger works produced by a small group of artists working in the Southern Netherlands.

The Dutch Golden Age came to an abrupt end in 1672, when the French invaded the Netherlands. To deter them, the Dutch broke the dykes protecting their homes and flooded much of the land. The economy crashed, many artists went bankrupt and the art market never recovered.

Figure 8.18 *The Lacemaker*, 1669–70, by Johannes Vermeer, oil on canvas, 25 × 21 cm, Musée du Louvre, Paris.

Further Research

www.bbc.com – Search for 'Why Rembrandt's *The Night Watch* is still a mystery' for an interesting look at the seminal painting

www.youtube.com – Search for Rachel Ruysch. Find out how much she learned from her father and why she chose to become a flower painter. Two recommended videos are 'Rachel Ruysch: Painter of the court and mother of 10 | National Gallery' (6:46) and 'Rachel Ruysch, Fruit and Insects' (4:04)

www.youtube.com – Search for 'Peter Paul Rubens, Elevation of the Cross' (8:33) for a closer look at the triptych

www.european-traveler.com – Click on 'Belgium' on the navigation bar, then scroll down to the article 'Visit the Antwerp Cathedral with Rubens Paintings'

www.youtube.com – Watch 'Andrew Graham-Dixon on the genius of Rubens' (7:37) for an examination of Rubens' technique and artistic style

www.rembrandthuis.nl – Meet the Baroque period's most enigmatic figure at the Rembrandt House Museum, Amsterdam

www.youtube.com – 'Self-Portrait, *c.* 1630, Judith Leyster' (1:55) gives a quick overview of the master's most famous work

www.youtube.com – Search for 'Behind the Painting: Vermeer's "Lady writing a Letter, with her Maid"' (6:55) for an informative video on the painting from the National Gallery of Ireland

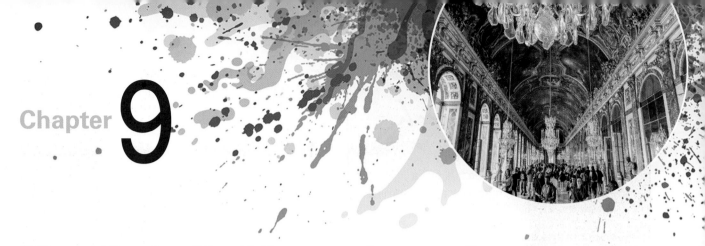

Chapter 9

The Catholic Monarchs and Their Territories

By the end of this chapter I will ...

* know about the Classical influence on the French
* understand how Versailles was designed to reflect the glory of King Louis XVI
* know about the influence of French artists in Rome
* know Velázquez's position as a great artist in Spain.

Context

Catholic Europe adopted the Italian Baroque style with great enthusiasm. Powerful religious orders with their extensive network of monasteries and convents played a significant role in the spread of the style to northern Italy, Spain and Portugal, then to Austria and southern Germany.

France

By the middle of the 17th century, France was Europe's largest and most powerful country.

In France, it was accepted that the king ruled by divine right, that his authority came directly from God. King Louis XIV famously declared '*L'état, c'est moi*' ('I am the state'). He linked his ancestry to the ancient Greek god Apollo and declared himself to be the centre of the universe. He became known as *Le Roi Soleil*, the Sun King (Fig. 9.1).

Note: Five-year-old Louis XIV became King of France when his father died in 1648. His mother, Anne of Austria, served as regent. Anne's advisor, Cardinal Richelieu, helped to centralise power and paved the road for the absolutism of the monarchy.

Absolute monarchy: A form of monarchy where the monarch has absolute power and is not restricted by law or custom.

Spain

Catholic Spain had difficulties coming to terms with the changing face of 17th-century Europe. In spite of the immense wealth pouring in from the Americas, its military force in Europe was badly affected by its wars with Portugal, Catalonia, France, and, of course, the Netherlands. These wars had a catastrophic effect on the economy, but the Spanish

Figure 9.1 *King Louis XIV*, 1701, by Hyacinthe Rigaud, oil on canvas, 277 × 194 cm, Musée du Louvre, Paris. The famous portrait of Louis XIV was made by personal request of the king. A copy hangs over the fireplace in the Apollo room of Versailles.

Inquisition made sure that vast resources were still spent on religious art and architecture.

King Philip IV ruled Spain for 44 years, and he too spent large amounts of his wealth on art and entertainment (Fig. 9.2). For artists, this was a golden age.

Note: The Spanish Inquisition was a powerful office set up within the Catholic Church in the 12th century to root out and punish heresy (belief or opinion against the faith). It continued for hundreds of years throughout Europe and the Americas and resulted in some 32,000 executions.

Figure 9.2 *Philip IV of Spain in Brown and Silver*, *c.* 1631–2, by Diego Velázquez, oil on canvas, 195 × 110 cm, National Gallery, London.

Media and Areas of Practice

Spain

Religious architecture thrived in Spain. Elaborate church façades, stunning, gold-ornamented chapels and strikingly realistic-coloured sculpture emerged both at home and in its new colonies.

King Philip IV collected art and sponsored several painters.

France

The relationship with Baroque art in France was more secular in architecture. Rome had less influence because the monarchy preferred a more Classical style.

With the help of his chief advisor, Jean-Baptiste Colbert, King Louis XIV established an elaborate system of government and court policy which gave him complete control. Architecture and the visual arts played a vital role in this plan.

Louis XIV prohibited the purchase of luxury goods from abroad, and instead used his own large retinue of architects, painters and sculptors to fashion a court of great splendour. Artistic freedom simply did not exist – the king was the main patron of the arts and all artists were under strict government supervision and control.

Elements of the Italian Baroque fused with Classical elements created a distinctive style of art and architecture in France. This reached its full potential in art produced specifically for King Louis XIV, which visually linked him to the might of Imperial Rome.

Innovation and Invention

To ensure the arts in France remained of high quality and continued to reflect the superiority of France in Europe, King Louis XIV set up specialised academies of the arts in Paris. These included schools for dance, painting and sculpture, sciences, architecture, music and crafts.

Charles Le Brun was appointed as the director of the Royal Academy of Painting and Sculpture in 1648. He imposed a strict curriculum of practical and theoretical studies that were firmly based on the Classical style. Disciplines were ranked in order of respectability: historical or narrative painting rated highest. The Renaissance artist Raphael and the art of antiquity were held in the highest regard, and Nicolas Poussin was considered the greatest contemporary artist. At the other end of the spectrum was still life painting, which was considered an inferior art. Venetian Renaissance painters, like Titian, who preferred colour to drawing, were also disregarded. This included the Baroque artist Rubens, who was inspired by them.

The colour versus line debate between *Poussinistes*, who believed in the importance of drawing, and *Rubénistes*, who maintained the importance of colour, extended well into the next century and beyond.

Le Brun also founded the French Academy in Rome in 1666 as part of the Royal Academy in Paris, and the Prix de Rome scholarship was established in 1674. This was awarded to the most promising painters, sculptors and architects in France. The scholars were also given a period of three to five years of study in Rome.

Artists and Artworks
Georges de La Tour

Georges de La Tour was named painter to the king in 1639. He was well known in his own time, but after his death in 1652 much of his work was forgotten. He painted mostly religious *chiaroscuro* scenes, which show a strong influence from Caravaggio. De la Tour's meditative candlelit scenes have a deep sense of wonder and stillness (Fig. 9.3).

- Place an object or figure in a darkened space and illuminate it with a single source of bright light, such as an anglepoise lamp.
- Sketch in charcoal or pastel to create an atmospheric drawing with deep contrasts of light and dark.
- Include a mirror for added effect.

Versailles

In 1682, Louis XIV of France, his court and government moved into the magnificent Palace of Versailles, just outside of Paris (Fig. 9.4). The transformation and expansion of the old hunting lodge had been the major royal project of the 17th century.

Figure 9.3 *The Penitent Magdalen*, 1640, by Georges de la Tour, oil on canvas, 133 × 102 cm, Metropolitan Museum, New York. Mary Magdalen is shown with a mirror, symbol of vanity; a skull, emblem of mortality; and a candle that probably represents her spiritual enlightenment.

Versailles was intended to demonstrate the wealth and power of France. Louis XIV was the embodiment of the nation and so it also served as a visual expression of his divine right to rule.

Charles Le Brun (1619–90)

Charles Le Brun entered the service of King Louis XIV in 1647. He was promoted to first painter to the king in 1664 and received an increasing number of commissions. His influence eventually went far beyond his role as an artist.

He was responsible for the decoration of Versailles and he understood the importance of propaganda.

Propaganda: Biased or misleading information used to influence an audience, usually to promote a political cause or a particular point of view.

He knew that the main purpose of the art at Versailles was the glorification of the Sun King.

The enormous, gilded and mirrored palace, with its equally splendid gardens, was built along an east-west axis so that the sun would rise and set in alignment with the estate.

The sculpture, the paintings and even the fountains in the gardens all focused on the glory of the Sun King. The formality and grandeur of the gardens symbolised Louis XIV's absolute power, even over nature, and he attached a supreme importance to the fountains' water effects.

The Hall of Mirrors

The Hall of Mirrors was the centrepiece of the palace (Fig. 9.4). The ceiling, painted by Le Brun, consists of 30 individual compositions and depicts the glorious history of Louis XIV illustrated through allegories from antiquity.

Nicolas Poussin (1594–1665)

Like many European artists of his generation, Nicolas Poussin was drawn to Rome, but the popular Baroque style held no interest for him. He was more inspired by Raphael's paintings and the works of Classical Greece and Rome.

A man of extraordinary learning, Poussin soon built up an audience for his distinct but very poetic paintings. He was summoned to Paris in 1640 to act as Louis XIV's principal painter, but, dissatisfied with life in the French court, he returned to Italy after just a couple of years.

Poussin soon became a central figure in European art, and his preference for Classicism continued to dominate tastes in French art right up until the 19th century.

Figure 9.4
Hall of Mirrors, Versailles.

The Abduction of the Sabine Women

Poussin's painting *The Abduction of the Sabine Women* illustrates a scene from the history of ancient Rome (Fig. 9.5). There were not enough women in the city, so to ensure the future of Rome, the early Roman men invited the neighbouring Sabine people to a feast. They then drove off the men and seized their women and children.

Stories like *The Abduction of the Sabine Women* were popular in the 17th century. It allowed male and female bodies to be depicted in complicated poses together, as Bernini had done in sculpture, but it also allowed for a variety of expressions and, especially in painting, this created an impression of crowds and panic.

Figure 9.5
The Abduction of the Sabine Women, 1633–4, by Nicolas Poussin, oil on canvas, 155 × 210 cm, Musée du Louvre, Paris. Romulus, founder of Rome, can be seen on the left, directing the action. He stands in a pose inspired by ancient Roman statues. The central section of the composition emphasises panic and confrontation. It is set against an architectural background that provides an opportunity for linear perspective, and that gives the work its depth.

Diego Velázquez (1599–1660)

Diego Velázquez is one the most admired European painters of all time. He had a marvellous gift for conveying a sense of truth and gave the best of his talents to portraits. These capture the appearance of reality in a seemingly effortless way.

Velázquez came from Seville in Spain and in 1623, at age 24, he was summoned to Madrid to paint a portrait of King Philip IV (see Fig. 9.2). He remained attached to the court for the rest of his life and painted several major portraits of the royal family. He was eventually made Marshal of the royal household, with responsibility for the planning of royal events and ceremonies.

From 1629 to 1631, the artist travelled around Italy, where he studied artists like Caravaggio. However, his job of painting royal portraits meant that he had to portray rigid characters with little or no individual personality.

Velázquez made a second trip to Italy in 1649 and of all the painters then in Rome, he alone was granted permission to paint the pope (Fig. 9.6).

In his final decade, his handling of paint became increasingly free and luminous. This style can be seen in the beautiful portrayal of the royal family, *Las Meninas* (Fig. 9.7).

As most of Velázquez's work was carried out for the king, very few people saw it until much later. In the 19th century, however, his paintings made an enormous impact on artists.

Portrait of Innocent X

The *Portrait of Innocent X* has a severe and bitter expression. This suggests that the artist might have expressed himself more freely if he had the freedom to do so. By all accounts, Innocent X was far from an attractive man, and Velázquez depicted exactly what he saw – a suspicious, paranoid old man.

Unsurprisingly, the pope initially thought the portrait was too realistic. He eventually came around, however, and became a supporter of Velázquez. He even had the painting hung in his official visitors' waiting room.

Figure 9.6 *Portrait of Pope Innocent X*, 1650, by Diego Velázquez, oil on canvas, 141 × 119 cm, Galleria Doria Pamphilj, Rome.

Style and Technique

Velázquez's use of light and masterful portrayal of silk, linen, velvet and gold were inspired by Titian and Raphael. The red of the pope's traditional robe dominates the scene, and adds to the atmosphere of oppressive power.

The atmosphere of power emphasises the realism and shows Velázquez's insight into the real man within the powerful robes of office. His loose, almost imperceptible brushstrokes infuse the work with vitality and energy.

Influences

The British expressionist artist Francis Bacon considered *Portrait of Pope Innocent X* to be one of the most successful portraits ever painted. He produced many variations on the image (see Chapter 18, Fig. 18.12).

Las Meninas

In the 1650s, King Philip IV gave Velázquez the Grand Room of the Royal Alcazar Palace to use as his personal studio. The complex and mysterious *Las Meninas*, which was painted here, has intrigued all who have looked at it since (Fig. 9.7).

The Spanish court was renowned for its rigidity and formality, but King Philip IV was an amateur artist and a good friend of Velázquez. This resulted in a rare, intimate depiction of the Spanish royal family and their attendants.

The artist stands to the left in front of an enormous canvas, on which it is thought he may be painting the king and queen, because their reflection can be seen in the mirror in the background. However, the real subject of the picture is the princess, the little Infanta, who has come to watch Velázquez at work. She stands between two young ladies-in-waiting, who seem to be coaxing her to behave.

Further to the right stand the diminutive Mari Barbola and court jester Nicolás Pertusato (or Nicolasito), who were a part of the royal household. Velázquez had painted some of these characters previously and individual portraits of them also hung in the palace. Nicolasito rests his foot on a large, gentle dog, which was possibly a mastiff.

Art Elements and Design Principles

The Palace of Versailles was designed to glorify the king. The rooms incorporate both ornate Baroque decoration and Classical elements. They are filled with marble, gold and painted decoration. The basic structure of the exterior is Classical: symmetrical

Figure 9.7 *Las Meninas*, 1656, by Diego Velázquez, oil on canvas, 320 × 281 cm, Museo del Prado, Madrid. In her memoirs, Madame de Motteville, who was present at the scene, writes of the young princess, 'She is waited on with great respect, few have access to her and it was a special favour that we were allowed to linger at the door of her chamber.'

and repetitive, it is based on simple elements directly borrowed from ancient Greek temples. This was one of Louis XIV's ways of making a direct link between himself the great thinkers and builders of antiquity.

Nicolas Poussin's paintings were notable for his emphasis on line and form, and he meticulously planned every detail of his composition for maximum impact. He believed colour was essential for setting the mood of a painting, and was interested in its relationship to light. He was influenced by antique art and architecture, but his mature paintings became increasingly theatrical. For him, every pose, gesture and facial expression was essential to the work's overall meaning.

Diego Velázquez was a realist and painted exactly what he saw, rendering textures and fabrics exquisitely without the need for ornamentation. He learned the advantages of using a very limited colour palette from Caravaggio; subtle harmonies of grey and black can be seen in many of his portraits. His clever blending of colour, light, space, line and mass gave equal value to each element of his paintings. He created form with colour and light rather than drawing precise lines, and his unusually fluid and free brushstrokes created realistic imagery when seen from afar, though on closer inspection it seems almost abstract.

Note: Because of Velázquez's great skill in merging colour, light, space, rhythm of line, and form in such a way that all have equal value, he was known as 'the painter's painter'.

Analysis

Examine the architecture and decoration of the magnificent Palace of Versailles and the works of art by architects, painters and sculptors who honoured King Louis XIV, and fashioned a court of incredible and lasting splendour.

France emerged as a major world power in the 17th century and became a cultural centre to rival Rome as the Baroque style spread throughout Europe.

After Baroque

By the end of the 17th century, the grand Baroque style was in decline, its fall mirroring that of its principal sponsor, Italy.

France became the dominant European power of the 18th century, and a new and contrasting style of decorative art emerged. This more whimsical style soon encompassed all new architecture, interior decoration, furniture, painting, sculpture and ceramic design. It became known as Rococo.

Chapter Review

1. How did the Baroque style change in France?

2. Why was Louis XIV known as the Sun King?

3. How did his Palace of Versailles reflect the image of the Sun King?

4. How was the work of Nicolas Poussin different to that of other artists working in 17th-century Rome?

5. Why was Diego Velázquez known as the painter's painter?

6. Why do you think Pope Innocent X liked his unflattering image?

7. What do think Velázquez was trying to say in *Las Meninas*?

UNIT 3 THE BAROQUE (c. 1600–1700s)

Further Research

www.nationalgallery.org.uk/artists/ nicolas-poussin – Learn more about Nicolas Poussin from his paintings in London's National Gallery

en.chateauversailles.fr – Visit the Palace of Versailles official website to fully explore the palace and the gardens

www.metillumination.wordpress.com – Search for 'The Penitent Magdalen' to learn about Georges de La Tour's striking painting

www.youtube.com – Watch 'Why Diego Velázquez's *Las Meninas* Continues to Inspire New Interpretations' (3:53) for a closer inspection of the elements of *Las Meninas*

www.youtube.com – Learn more about Velázquez by watching 'Diego Velázquez – National Gallery Documentary' (50:30)

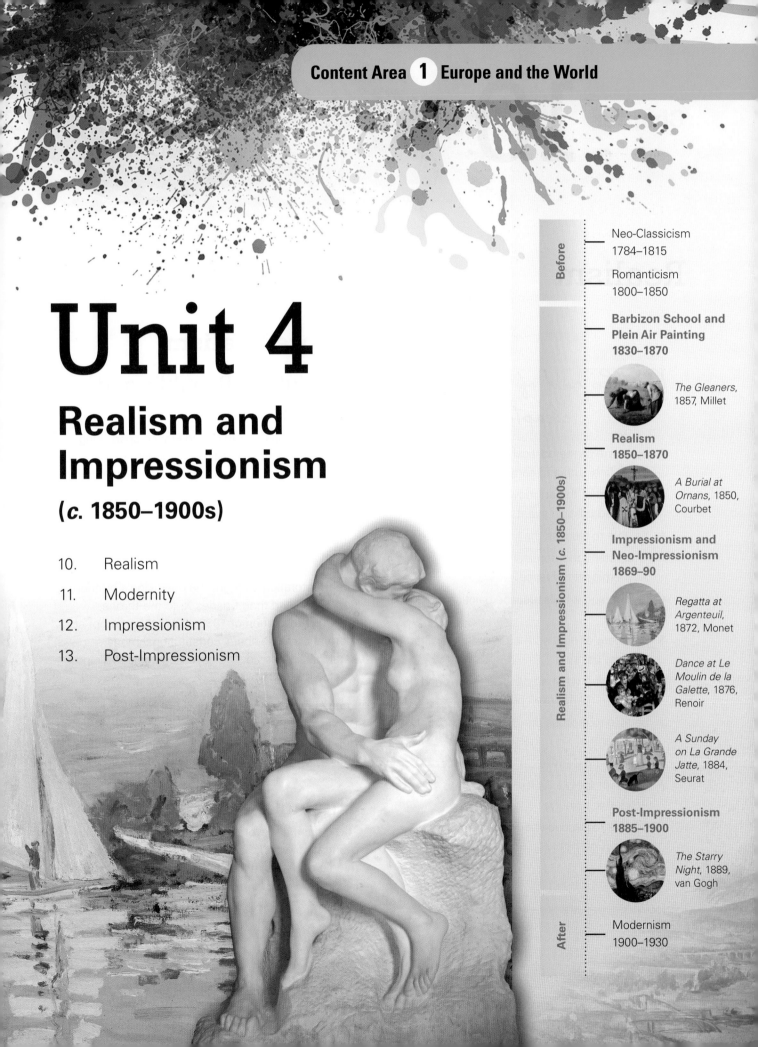

Unit 4

Realism and Impressionism

(*c.* 1850–1900s)

Before

Neo-Classicism
1784–1815

Romanticism
1800–1850

**Barbizon School and
Plein Air Painting
1830–1870**

The Gleaners,
1857, Millet

**Realism
1850–1870**

*A Burial at
Ornans*, 1850,
Courbet

**Impressionism and
Neo-Impressionism
1869–90**

*Regatta at
Argenteuil*,
1872, Monet

*Dance at Le
Moulin de la
Galette*, 1876,
Renoir

*A Sunday
on La Grande
Jatte*, 1884,
Seurat

**Post-Impressionism
1885–1900**

*The Starry
Night*, 1889,
van Gogh

After

Modernism
1900–1930

Realism and Impressionism (*c.* 1850–1900s)

Chapter 10

Realism

Before Realism

Revolution, Republic and Empire

The Revolution of 1789 ripped France apart. King Louis XVI and his wife Marie Antoinette were executed, and tens of thousands were killed during the bloody and chaotic years of 'The Terror'.

Napoleon Bonaparte brought stability and solidarity when he took power, but his reign ended with defeat at the Battle of Waterloo in 1815.

The 'Restoration' brought the dead king's brothers, Louis XVIII and then Charles X, to the throne. The July Revolution of 1830 ended the attempt at restoration and a liberal constitutional monarchy was established instead. The new King Louis Phillippe was overthrown in 1848.

Prince Louis Napoleon, nephew of Napoleon Bonaparte, was elected president of the Second Republic, but in 1852 he declared himself emperor. The Second Empire lasted until 1870.

The Industrial Revolution

The Industrial Revolution in the early 19th century brought railways, machinery and a rich new middle class, but it also created a social class that lived and worked in appalling conditions.

Figure 10.1 *The Oath of Horatii*, 1784, by Jacques-Louis David, oil on canvas, 330 × 425 cm, Musée du Louvre, Paris.

Neo-Classicism

Art reacted to politics first with Neo-Classicism. This restrained, disciplined and austere style reflected the mood of the revolution. Jacques-Louis David became the official artist for the government (Fig. 10.1) and he looked back with nostalgia to the heroic deeds of ancient Greek and Roman warriors.

Romanticism

The Romantic movement emphasised emotion and imagination. Artists embraced themes of struggles for freedom and justice. *Liberty Leading the People* by Eugène Delacroix (Fig. 10.2) is one of the most famous and influential Romantic paintings. It commemorated the July Revolution of 1830, but is allegorical rather than representative of an actual event.

> **Allegory:** A picture that can be interpreted to reveal a hidden meaning, typically a moral or political one.

The Academy of Fine Art

The Royal Academy of Painting and Sculpture was established by King Louis XIV in the 17th century (see Chapter 9, p. 136). After the Revolution it was renamed the Academy of Fine Arts and included an art school, the École des Beaux-Arts. Teaching was firmly based on the Classical style.

Line vs Colour

A debate on the importance of drawing over colour began in the Royal Academy in 1671. The *Poussinistes*,

Figure 10.2
Liberty Leading the People, 1830, by Eugène Delacroix, oil on canvas, 260 × 325 cm, Musée du Louvre, Paris.

followers of the painter Nicolas Poussin, believed that drawing was the most important part of the artistic process, whereas the *Rubénistes*, named after Peter Paul Rubens, championed use of colour.

This line versus colour issue continued over the years, but it was rekindled in the 1830s by a very public argument between Eugène Delacroix, who favoured strong colours, and Jean-Auguste-Dominique Ingres, who promoted classical drawing.

Landscape – *Plein Air* Painting

Landscape painting emerged quite early in the 19th century. Painters in Holland and England had begun to work out of doors and directly with nature. When some of these painters visited France, French artists were inspired by the new style of painting.

Joseph Mallord William Turner (1775–1851)

The English painter Turner was highly influential in the development of landscape painting. He was called 'the painter of light' because of his brilliant use of colour and his interest in skies (Fig. 10.3).

John Constable (1776–1837)

John Constable grew up on a farm in Suffolk. He sketched and observed atmospheric effects in the area surrounding his home, but his large paintings were always done in the studio.

His pictures were not particularly well received in England, but when *The Hay Wain* (Fig. 10.4) was exhibited at the Paris Salon of 1824 it created a huge impression.

The painting shone a new light on everyday subjects of the countryside.

Context

In 19th-century France, the government-controlled Academy set the standard for artistic taste.

Academic artists believed that art, like science, could be governed by rules. Drawing was considered the basis of all artistic practice and art was taught through a series of repetitive exercises.

Figure 10.3
Shipwreck Off Hastings, 1828, by William Turner, watercolour on paper, 19 × 29 cm, National Gallery of Ireland, Dublin.

Figure 10.4
The Hay Wain, 1821,
by John Constable,
oil on canvas,
130 × 185 cm National
Gallery, London.

Academic Teaching and Training

High ideals of truth and beauty were structured in a technical manner. Appropriate subject matter was ranked in three levels of importance and artists were expected to remain firmly within these areas.

- **Level 1:** history painting, considered the noblest of subjects. Derived from the Italian word *istoria*, meaning narrative, it related to high-minded or heroic depictions of battles, coronations, religious themes, mythology and ancient history.
- **Level 2:** literature and portraiture.
- **Level 3:** this included landscape and outdoor settings as suitable backgrounds for historical scenes. Genre scenes were part of level 3. These depicted ordinary people and peasants contently engaged in ordinary activities, and their lives were highly idealised.

Composition and Uplifting Ideals

Strict rules of composition, perspective and proportion were rigorously applied. Realistic figures and objects were to be be placed in a harmonious manner in carefully organised three-dimensional space.

Artists were encouraged to pay particular attention to historical details of costume and setting, and the Academy also stressed aesthetic qualities like expression. Noble and uplifting values were to be presented in a clear, readable manner.

Surface

A highly finished surface like polished enamel was essential in Academic painting. This required that brushstrokes should always be fully blended and smoothed in the creation of a high degree of realism.

The Salon

The Salon exhibition was essential for any aspiring artist. It was originally held for select members in the Royal Palace of the Louvre's *salon carré* (square room), but was later opened to all artists. It remained known as the Salon.

In the 19th century, the Salon was held in large commercial halls and the opening night was always a grand social occasion. A carefully selected jury of artists, Academicians and important officials chose the works to be displayed, and they were famously picky about what they would allow into the Salon.

Innovation and Invention

The invention of the collapsible tin painting-tube and small, folding easels made outdoor sketching a great deal easier for artists.

Before this, painting outside had seemed too impractical, as artists would have to carry all their equipment and materials, which were heavy and cumbersome. It was more common to make watercolour sketches in the field and make finished paintings in the studio.

Watercolour paint: William Reeves developed small water-soluble blocks of colour in 1780. Winsor and Newton of London had been selling oil paint in collapsible tin tubes since 1841. In 1846, they introduced moist watercolours in metal tubes.

Make a watercolour sketch of a landscape, object or animal out of doors. Use this as inspiration for a more finished work indoors.

How did the change from outdoor to indoor change the character of your work? What tools and materials would you need to produce a finished work painted entirely out of doors?

The newly developed railway system of the 1830s made it easier to access the countryside or the coast. The Barbizon School of Painters was one of the first groups to work outdoors and the train from Paris made regular journeys there much easier.

Artists and Artworks
Camille Corot (1796–1875)

Corot devoted almost the whole of his long life to painting nature. He painted out of doors in Normandy, Brittany and Burgundy (Fig. 10.5). He never lived in Barbizon with the other painters, but regularly joined them to paint woodland scenes in the forest of Fontainebleau.

He trained in the studio of a Neo-Classical artist but preferred painting outside. He travelled around Paris and spent time in Rome. He painted some of the historical monuments directly from nature, and, on his return to France, continued to paint *en plein air*.

By the 1860s, his work was accepted by the Academy and shown regularly at the Salon.

Gentle Landscapes

Corot's paintings were always finished in the studio and in line with the Salon tradition, he often 'improved' them by adding trees, animals or

Figure 10.5
Recollections of Mortefontaine, 1864, by Jean-Baptiste-Camille Corot, oil on canvas, 65 × 89 cm, Musée de Louvre, Paris. This carefully assembled recollection was painted in the studio. The artist looks back to the ponds of Mortefontaine where he had studied surface reflections and the play of light. He added in three girls on the left for compositional balance.

nymphs into landscapes. However, his landscapes have a fresh, country-air feeling with a gentle, still, silvery-toned mood of slightly overcast days. There is a good collection of Corots in the Hugh Lane Gallery in Dublin.

 RESEARCH Camille Corot was an Academic painter trained in the Neo-Classical style. Find out more about why he chose to paint out of doors and why he was considered one of the forerunners of Impressionism.

Jean-François Millet (1814–1875)

Millet grew up on farm near Cherbourg in Normandy. He once said: 'I have never seen anything but fields since I was born.'

He was raised in the expectation of taking over his family's farm, but his talent for art was such that he began taking art lessons locally.

Millet arrived in Paris in 1837, but the Academic system of teaching and painting was entirely unsuited to him. Eventually, he took his family away from the city and spent the rest of his life painting the great harvest fields near Barbizon.

He depicted French rural life with insight and compassion. He was one of the first artists to portray peasant labourers with the grandeur reserved for heroes in Academic art (Fig. 10.6 and Fig. 10.7).

The Gleaners

Having grown up on a farm, Millet understood farm workers. His distinctive and personal scenes showed people working in the fields in a low-key but deeply emotional manner.

However, the conservative art establishment was suspicious that his paintings reflected 'socialist issues' and, when *The Gleaners* (Fig. 10.6) was shown at the Salon in the summer of 1857, it was greeted with hostility.

Gleaning was one of the lowest jobs in society, but the three women picking up the leftovers from the harvest are the central focus of the picture and have an air of quiet nobility.

Millet's paintings were eventually accepted because he showed peasant life in a kind of idealised manner. Religious overtones helped.

The composition contrasts the three phases of the backbreaking repetitive task: bending over, picking up and straightening up again.

Figure 10.6
The Gleaners, 1857, by Jean-François Millet, oil on canvas, 84 × 110 cm, Musée d'Orsay, Paris.

Light

The slanted setting sun picks out the workers' hands, necks, shoulders and backs. It also brightens the colours of their clothing, making their labour seem worthwhile and beautiful.

The Angelus

Set against the pink light of evening and a low horizon, the hard-working couple take a break to bow their heads in prayer. It is almost possible to hear the peal of bells across the field from the spire of the distant church.

The Angelus (Fig. 10.7) is often thought to be a religious work and it does have a timeless, monumental quality, but Millet said: 'The idea came to me because I remembered working in the fields and my grandmother, hearing the church bell ringing, always made us stop to say the Angelus prayer for the poor departed.'

Look up *Peasants Bringing Home a Calf Born in the Fields*, 1864, in the Art Institute of Chicago.

Have a class discussion on what aspects of the scene you think best show Millet's own farming background.

Gustave Courbet (1819–1877)

A farmer's son from Ornans in south-eastern France and a larger-than-life character, Gustave Courbet was often at the centre of controversy. He was, however, one of the most influential mid-19th century French painters.

Figure 10.7 *The Angelus*, 1858, by Jean-François Millet, oil on canvas, 56 × 66 cm, Musée d'Orsay, Paris.

Note: Courbet was one of a group of artists and intellectuals who often met in a Paris café called the Brasserie Andler. The term 'Realism' was first used in 1846 and they renamed the café the 'Temple of Realism'.

'Truth, Not Prettiness'

He wanted 'truth, not prettiness' and shocked society with straightforward images of farmers, gravediggers, woodsmen and poachers in a way that glorified their work.

He had difficulty getting work shown at the Salon, but in the freer atmosphere of 1848 there was no selection committee and Courbet won a gold medal. Courbet's award meant an exemption from the selection process for life. He was now free to show his Realist paintings.

A Burial at Ornans

A Burial at Ornans (Fig. 10.8), depicting the funeral of Courbet's great uncle, was shown at the 1850 Salon. The effect of the huge painting, with nearly sixty life-sized people, was stunning but the Academic establishment was utterly shocked and considered it 'a glorification of vulgarity'.

The frieze-like composition follows the line of the background hills and the family, friends and local dignitaries at the graveside remain below that line. Only the crucifix is above their heads.

The atmosphere is muted and austere. The greens and browns, as well as the cloudy evening sky, suggest the passage of day into night and the coffin passing from light into dark.

A 'Pavilion of Realism'

In 1855, Courbet submitted thirteen pictures to the World Fair in Paris. Not all were accepted, so he reacted by building a 'Pavilion of Realism' outside the official event. He organised his own exhibition, which included *A Burial at Ornans*, so that his work could be available to the whole of society.

Figure 10.8
A Burial at Ornans, 1849,
by Gustave Courbet,
oil on canvas,
315 × 668 cm, Musée
d'Orsay, Paris.

Realism

Gustav Courbet was the first to challenge Academic rules and he established the Realist movement. Large-scale paintings were traditionally reserved for grand and noble subjects, but Courbet chose ordinary subjects and everyday country people. He presented them on large-scale canvases, which was considered shocking and vulgar.

Art Elements and Design Principles

As part of his reaction against Academy painting, Courbet often chose compositions that seemed crude to the preferences of the time. He also abandoned the careful modelling and finished appearance in favour of more emphasis on surface texture with broken and thick application of flecks and slabs of paint.

Millet's mature works in Realism were devoted to genre paintings of poor peasants and toiling farmers, but his later works also had looser, more gestural brushwork.

Analysis

Consider the reasons why Camille Corot and Jean-François Millet were so influential on younger artists and examine how they were inspired by painting directly from nature.

Study the large-scale compositions by Gustav Courbet and examine why his paintings of ordinary farmers and rural working people were so shocking to society.

Figure 10.9 *The Meeting* or *Bonjour Monsieur*, 1854, by Gustave Courbet, 129 × 149 cm, Musée Fabre, Montpellier, oil on canvas. Courbet portrays himself with one of his rich patrons in Montpellier. Dressed casually, he holds his head high in a direct, anti-bourgeois gesture against the image of the 'respectable' artist. It was based on a popular 19th-century print called *The Wandering Jew*. This would have been associated with an outsider, which is how Courbet would have identified himself.

Media and Areas of Practice

Landscape

The Barbizon School of *plein air* painters moved from Paris in the 1830s to live and work on the edge of the Forest of Fontainebleau. The peasants, houses, the forest and the plain near the village were an endless source of inspiration.

Gustav Courbet established himself as one of the leading Realist artists in France. The modern movements that followed were influenced by his philosophy and greatly admired his challenge to the Academic system, but Realism had no direct followers.

The rigid Academic system remained the only way an artist could achieve success and respectability. It proved extremely difficult for any artist who took a different path.

Chapter Review

1. How did English landscape painting influence the development of *plein air* painting in France?

2. What new inventions made painting out of doors easier?

3. Why do you think artists wanted to work *en plein air*?

4. Why was Camille Corot so influential on younger artists?

5. Examine the work by Camille Corot (Fig. 10.10) opposite. Discuss the artist's use of imagery, colour and light. Would you describe it as a Realist work?

6. Why was the conservative establishment suspicious of Jean-François Millet's paintings of peasants in the fields?

7. Why do you think Gustave Courbet set out to shock his audiences?

8. What were the main characteristics of Realism?

Further Research

www.apollo-magazine.com – Search for the article 'Peasant company – Jean-François Millet among the moderns' to learn about Millet's inspiration on later artists like van Gogh

www.musee-orsay.fr/fr – Read more information about Courbet and his further works in the Musée d'Orsay, Paris

www.youtube.com – Search for 'David, Oath of the Horatii' (6:24) to discover more about the context of this painting

www.youtube.com – The video 'Liberty Leads the Way in Delacroix's Revolutionary Portrait' (3:10) looks at the how this painting depicts the ideas of the French Revolution

www.youtube.com – 'Ingres, Princesse de Broglie' (3:23) takes a close look at the details of the painting by Jean-Auguste-Dominique Ingres

www.youtube.com – Search for 'Ingres's Madame Moitessier | Talks for All | National Gallery' (24.23) for a talk about the work of Ingres from the National Gallery in London

www.youtube.com – Look up 'Barbizon: The Cradle of Impressionism' (13:45) for an overview of Barbizon, how artists spent their time there, and how it influenced their art

www.youtube.com – In 'Gustave Courbet – Understanding Modern Art Part 3' (18:21) you can learn more about Courbet and how he began a movement towards political art

www.youtube.com – 'Courbet, Burial at Ornans' (6:24) analyses the details of this painting

Figure 10.10 *A Morning. The Dance of Nymphs*, 1850, by Jean-Baptiste-Camille Corot, oil on canvas, 98 × 131 cm, Musée d'Orsay, Paris.

Chapter 11

Modernity

By the end of this chapter I will ...

* understand why Manet wanted success at the Salon
* understand why Manet chose contemporary subjects
* know the rules of Academic painting and how Manet went against these
* be able to discuss Manet's influence on the Impressionist artists.

Context

At the beginning of the 19th century, Paris was a chaotic, overcrowded city. Crime and disease were rife.

One of Napoleon III's first acts in 1852 was to re-enact the vision of his uncle's plans to 'modernise' the city. He hired civic planner Baron Georges-Eugène Haussmann, who completely transformed the structure of Paris. In this grand new urban landscape, quays and bridges were built, neighbourhoods were demolished, streets were widened and thousands of trees were planted on new boulevards. A massive network of sewers was constructed under the city streets.

Figure 11.1
The Grand boulevards at the corner of Place de l'Opéra, Paris.

Figure 11.2
Music in the Tuileries, 1862, by Édouard Manet, oil on canvas, 76 × 118 cm, Hugh Lane Gallery, Dublin and the National Gallery, London. This 'snapshot' of modern life and the figures cut off on the edge of the canvas show the influence of the new art of photography.

The booming economy allowed for a more convenient leisurely lifestyle and newly developed open spaces encouraged the bourgeois to flaunt their new wealth (Fig. 11.1).

Musical concerts took place regularly in the gardens of the Tuileries Palace, where fashionable people liked to meet and be seen. *Music in the Tuileries* by Édouard Manet shows this (Fig. 11.2). He included his brother, Eugène, in the centre and his own portrait on the extreme left.

 Find out how Manet has suggested the theme of music rather than showing the actual activity in *Music in the Tuileries*.

 Why do you think the artist chose to depict himself as well as his brother in this painting?

Art

The art market was dominated by collectors from the new middle class. Insecure and fearful, they looked on anything radical with suspicion and that included new art. They depended on 'experts' in the Academy.

The Academy favoured 'safe' Classical subjects. Jean-August-Dominique Ingres (Fig. 11.3) was a professor at the École des Beaux-Arts and he

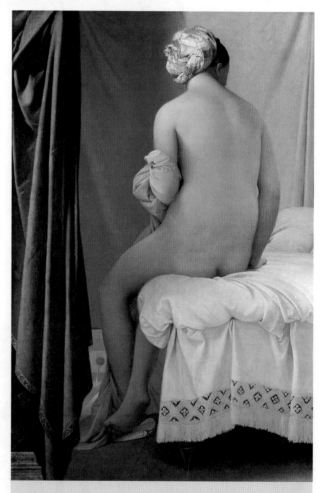

Figure 11.3 *The Valpinçon Bather*, 1808, by Jean-Auguste-Dominique Ingres, oil on canvas, 146 × 98 cm, Musée du Louvre, Paris.

represented the establishment. Those who were against him were seen as rebellious and dangerous.

The 'noble and ideal' Classical style was rigidly applied to all artistic training.

The Salon

The Salon was now held in the huge new Palais d'Industrie. It was visited by art dealers, collectors and critics from all over the world.

Artwork that the jury liked best was hung at eye level; lesser art was hung high above.

Refused work had a large 'R' stamped on it. Artists tried to hide this stamp, because nobody wanted a painting refused by the Salon.

Salon des Refusés

The jury of 1863 rejected more than two-thirds of the submitted paintings, which caused uproar among the artists and the wider public. The protests were so emphatic that the emperor intervened. As a compromise, the committee set up the now famous 'Salon des Refusés' as a separate exhibition.

Manet's *Le Déjeuner sur l'Herbe* caused the biggest furore at the Salon des Refusés. Manet became a celebrity, but critics accused him of only trying to shock (Fig 11.4).

Artists and Artworks
Édouard Manet (1832–1883)

Manet was born into a prosperous upper middle-class family. His father was a wealthy lawyer with aristocratic connections.

Manet spent six years in the studio of respected painter Thomas Couture. He admired his teacher, but Academic instruction frustrated him. He said, 'I paint what I see, and not what others choose to see,' and after he left Couture's studio, Manet developed his own ideas and style.

His ambition was to be a well-established Academic artist. He certainly never intended to lead a revolt against the traditions of French art.

Manet had the highest regard for the Paris Salon and his goal was to gain recognition there. This never changed throughout his life, in spite of official rejection and even ridicule.

Manet's experience with *Le Déjeuner sur l'Herbe* deeply upset him, and he was slow to submit again. His friends persuaded him to submit *Olympia* (Fig. 11.5) in 1865 and the jury amazingly accepted it (they were probably more lenient following the Salon des Refusés). Sadly, Manet's fears were more than confirmed: the critics savaged the painting and the jury ordered it moved to the top corner.

What the Critics Said

Manet was described as 'a brute that paints green women with dish brushes'. Some critics thought he mocked Renaissance art, but all agreed the painting had a 'childish ignorance of drawing'.

He never repeated this kind of powerful imagery or bold colours again, but his work continued to cause controversy.

People naturally assumed that Manet was a rough, almost revolutionary type, but he was a man of elegance and charm. Even the critics wrote about his 'agreeable character and correct appearance'.

Association with the Impressionist Group

Manet was financially independent and had a wide circle of friends and supporters from the artistic and literary communities. The artist Berthe Morisot was a close friend of Manet's, and she shared his passion for painting. She married his brother and features in several of his works.

Morisot encouraged him to try painting *en plein air*. As a result, his paintings became brighter and he began to use colour in shadow instead of grey or black, and to observe the effect of light on water.

He was happy to play the part of modern master to younger artists. They admired his modern ideas and were thrilled by his use of loose, unblended brushstrokes, but he always refused to take part in their independent exhibitions and remained committed to success in the Salon.

Many scenes by Edouard Manet were set in cafés or café concerts. Use the suggested web links in the Further Research section on page 159 to find out more about these painted snapshots of bohemianism, urban working people, as well as some of the bourgeoisie.

Success came in 1881, when Manet won a medal. He died the following year, aged 51.

Within a year, an exhibition of his paintings, pastels, drawings and prints was shown to great admiration at the École des Beaux-Arts in Paris.

Le Déjeuner sur l'Herbe

The painting references *Fête Champêtre*, by Venetian artist Giorgione in the Louvre (see Chapter 6, Fig. 6.26). The model is Victorine Meurant, who was well-known in artistic circles. She is far from demure, and looks directly at the viewer.

Composition and Meaning

The picture includes some visual contradictions. A nude woman at a picnic with men in indoor dress is very strange. The model is painted from life but the bather in the background appears to come from another painting.

Olympia

The comparisons to Titian's famous *Venus of Urbino* (see Chapter 6, Fig. 6.28) were clear and intended and Victorine Meurant was again the model.

Olympia was a name for prostitutes in Paris and this shocked spectators. Respectable gentlemen certainly did not want to be reminded of this hidden reality in an art gallery.

Colour and Tone

The picture has once again gone against Academic rules. Instead of smooth shading it is simplified into two planes of light and dark and vigorous brushstrokes are clearly visible on the surface instead of careful blending.

Note: It was scandalous for any woman, not to mention this type of woman, to stare at the viewer so directly.

Figure 11.4
Le Déjeuner sur l'Herbe, 1863, by Édouard Manet, oil on canvas, 208 × 265 cm, Musée d'Orsay, Paris. The painting was originally called *Le Bain* (The Bath), and its meaning continues to intrigue spectators to this day.

Figure 11.5 *Olympia*, 1863, by Édouard Manet, oil on canvas, 131 × 190 cm, Musée d'Orsay, Paris. Manet considered *Olympia* to be his masterpiece and kept it until his death. Afterwards, Claude Monet organised a fund to purchase it and offered it to the French state. It is considered one of the finest works of 19th-century French painting.

Style and Symbolism

This very real and modern young woman raises her head with confidence. The neck ribbon, the bracelet, ribbon in her hair and satin slipper are symbols of wealth and sensuality, but they emphasise her nakedness. The dog (a symbol of fidelity in marriage) has been replaced with a black cat, which suggests immorality.

A Bar at the Folies-Bergère

Like so much of his work, the meaning of *A Bar at the Folies Bergère* (Fig. 11.6) is somewhere between reality and illusion. A young woman in a neat blue dress stands alone at the bar with her hands placed firmly on the marble countertop. She has a detached, melancholy look and a locket around her neck.

Figure 11.6 *A Bar at the Folies-Bergère*, 1881–2, by Édouard Manet, oil on canvas, 96 × 130 cm, Courtauld Gallery, London. Manet persuaded a barmaid he knew from the nightclub to pose in his studio for the picture. It captures all the coolness, glamour and cruelty of modern life.

Lighting

The lighting and the chandelier in the mirror indicate the new and modern electric lights in the Folies-Bergère at Montmartre. It was the most famous and modern of Paris's café-concert halls.

The girl's reflection does not match with her figure and this creates a sense of dislocation. It suggests that Paris is a hall of mirrors where she floats helplessly, and the only solid realities are the bottles, a bowl of oranges and the flowers.

Media and Areas of Practice

Classical themes were popular Academic subjects and often depicted nude female figures. These mostly took the form of nymphs or goddesses rather than real characters.

Shapes had to be attractive, but even the most graceful of poses could be seductive and sensual.

Nymph: A mythological spirit of nature imagined as a beautiful maiden living in places like rivers or woods.

The Birth of Venus by Alexandre Cabanel (Fig. 11.7) was the hit of the 1863 Salon exhibition. It was everything visitors to the Salon expected.

Academic artists built up paintings in layers of paint. These took time to dry, so artists frequently added layers without the model present. The surface was glazed over at the end for a smooth finish.

Manet was a Realist and preferred to paint from life with the model in front of him at all times. He preferred natural light to the 'false' Academic lighting and completed his paintings quickly, without layering or glazing at the end. This meant he had to choose the perfect colour and he placed them side by side, instead of mixing on a palette. If he made a

Figure 11.7 *The Birth of Venus*, 1863, by Alexandre Cabanel, 130 × 225 cm, Musée d'Orsay, Paris. Venus is completely lacking in character, but the idealised, sexually passive figure is perfection itself. The smooth brushwork and polished surface make this the perfect Academic work.

mistake, he scraped off the paint, down to the bare canvas, and then repainted that area.

He painted with loose brushstrokes, leaving parts of the canvas sparsely covered.

Art Elements and Design Principles

Manet used sharp contrasts of light and shade instead of the carefully constructed perspective and smooth Academic shading. This meant his figures tended to 'flatten out'. In *Olympia*, for example, the picture divides into two simplified planes (Fig. 11.5).

Manet was influenced by the new art of photography. The frontal or 'flat lighting' popular in studio photography bleached out flesh tones, creating a sharper contrast between light and dark, which reduced the grades of tone.

Innovation and Invention

Seventeenth-century Dutch and Spanish painting greatly inspired Manet. He particularly admired Venetian art and had a very clear vision of how to modernise these great traditions to create very modern French art for the very modern city of Paris.

Analysis

Examine whether Édouard Manet achieved his ambition to work in a 'truly modern style'. Study *Le Déjeuner sur l'Herbe* and *Olympia* and see why the subject matter, as much as the colour, tone and painting techniques used in these works, caused such controversy.

Manet's struggle against the Academic system cost him dearly and he suffered rejection and ridicule throughout his life. The meaning or message in his work may not have been entirely understood by viewers of the time, but his unique style and developments in painting bridged the gap between Realism and Impressionism.

Chapter Review

1. Why was Manet so anxious to succeed with the official Salon?

2. Describe how Manet's style went against the tradition of Academic art

3. Why do you think contemporary subjects were so important for him?

4. The meaning of both *Le Déjeuner sur l'Herbe* and *The Bar at the Folies-Bergère* has been debated for a long time. What do you think?

Further Research

www.manetedouard.org – Click on the 'Biography' tab to learn more about Manet's life and works

www.youtube.com – Look up 'Manet, Le déjeuner sur l'herbe' (6:14) to discover the details of this painting

www.youtube.com – Search for 'Manet, A Bar at the Folies-Bergère' (5:38) for a closer look at this painting

Chapter 12

Impressionism

By the end of this chapter I will ...

* understand the innovations developed by Impressionist artists

* know why these artists chose to exhibit independently

* understand the reasons for public rejection of the style

* be aware of Durand-Ruel's role in the success of Impressionism

* be able to discuss the individual characteristics of each artist's work

* understand why Claude Monet was the leader of the group

* be able to describe and discuss a typical Impressionist painting

* be able to discuss the different methods used by Edgar Degas

* understand the innovative nature of Auguste Rodin's sculpture

* understand how scientific Impressionism developed

* be able to describe and discuss a work of Neo-Impressionism.

Context

During the 1860s, Paris was a leading centre for finance, commerce, fashion and the arts. Its redevelopment continued under the direction of Baron Haussmann.

The new age of railways and the enormous increase in travel required new train stations, large hotels, exhibition halls and department stores in Paris. These were built in the decade leading up to 1875 when many new squares, parks and gardens were also created.

Napoleon III greatly admired London, where he had spent some years in exile. He was especially impressed with Hyde Park with its lake and winding paths. The development of a leisure park in Paris became his special project and he personally oversaw the transformation of part of the king's old hunting grounds in the Bois de Boulogne. Several lakes were encircled by a carriage path and islands were constructed in the centre. The '*tour des lacs*' soon became a highly fashionable afternoon activity for Parisians in their carriages.

The Bois de Boulogne is the setting for Berthe Morisot's painting, *A Summer's Day* (Fig. 12.1). The park presented her with an opportunity to work *en plein air*, because respectable women artists could not otherwise work outdoors alone.

The sketchy 'impression' is an effort to capture a fleeting moment in time. To convey this idea, she has used loosely textured brushwork, but she has also included a carriage moving swiftly along the far shore.

Figure 12.1 *A Summer's Day*, 1879, by Berthe Morisot, oil on canvas, 46 × 75 cm, Hugh Lane Gallery, Dublin and the National Gallery, London.

The two stylish women in the boat wear the very latest Parisian fashions.

A New Racecourse

Part of the royal land was allocated for a racecourse and, in April 1857, the emperor and his wife attended the first-ever race at the now famous Longchamp.

Several artists, including Édouard Manet (Fig. 12.2), depicted horseracing scenes at this extremely modern and highly fashionable venue. The horses also became a favourite subject for Edgar Degas (see Fig. 12.25).

The Franco-Prussian War (1870–71)

Napoleon III's Second Empire ended abruptly when he led the country into disastrous war with Prussia. In 1871, the emperor signed a humiliating armistice. Paris had been under siege, but even as the Prussian army left, the city was hit by a new terror.

Left-wing communist revolutionaries took over the streets. Barricades were erected and huge damage was done before government troops brutally crushed the uprising. Thousands were executed.

Under the Third Republic, Paris tentatively began to rebuild.

Art

The Académie des Beaux-Arts continued to dominate standards in painting in both content and style. The Academy preferred realistic images with precise and well-blended brushwork. Colours were muted and often toned down further with varnish.

Independent Artists

On 15 April 1874, the Anonymous Society of Painters, Sculptors and Engravers held an independent exhibition. Despite being very individual artists, they all had a shared distaste for the Academic system, and were all completely frustrated by rejection after rejection from the Salon.

Figure 12.2 *The Races at Longchamp*, 1866, by Édouard Manet, oil on canvas, 85 × 44 cm, Chicago Institute of Art.

The exhibition was held in the studio of the photographer Nadar in the centre of Paris. Critics wrote that they couldn't draw, that their colours were vulgar and that their compositions were strange.

The Impressionists

One art critic, Louis Leroy, described *Impression,*

Sunrise by Claude Monet (Fig. 12.3) as 'an impression of nature, nothing more. Wallpaper in its preliminary state is more finished!' He wondered, 'Who were these "Impressionists"?'

Following the exhibition, all the artists except one – Edgar Degas – agreed to use this new name.

Figure 12.3
Impression, Sunrise, 1872, by Claude Monet, oil on canvas, 48 × 63 cm, Musée Marmottan Monet, Paris.

A Break with Tradition

An impression, in Academy terms, was a quick outdoor sketch made in preparation for a finished studio painting. The Impressionists, however, showed these as finished works. The public, who attended the Impressionists' exhibitions in great numbers, laughed at the work, perhaps to hide the fact that they found it dangerously anti-establishment.

The Impressionists' first exhibitions made huge losses and, of the original 30 artists, only Claude Monet, Edgar Degas, Pierre-Auguste Renoir, Camille Pissarro, Berthe Morisot, Alfred Sisley and Paul Cézanne remained associated with the Impressionist movement.

The Influence of Édouard Manet

Édouard Manet was a leader, inspiration and huge influence. The artists met with him regularly in the Café Guerbois in Paris for lively discussions on art. He advised, worked and learned with them, but he never partook in their exhibitions, despite them constant begging him to do so.

RESPOND

Compare *Madame Monet and Her Son* (National Gallery of Art, Washington) by Auguste Renoir with *The Monet Family in the Garden* by Manet (Fig. 12.4).

Consider the composition, use of colour and brushstrokes in both works. Which appeals to you most? Why is that?

The Impressionists had six more exhibitions in Paris and one in New York. Over time, the new style became more accepted.

Sculpture

Auguste Rodin is considered an Impressionist sculptor because of his interest in the effect of light on sculpted surfaces. His experimental methods also show how much he was influenced by modern movements in painting.

Neo-Impressionism

George Seurat challenged Impressionism with a new direction for modern art. When Pissarro insisted that Seurat's *A Sunday on La Grande Jatte* (see Fig. 12.32) should be included in the Paris Impressionist exhibition of 1886, Monet and Renoir refused to exhibit.

This marked the end of Impressionism. Each artist's career took a very different path, but each had a modern approach to art.

Seurat disliked the term 'Neo-Impressionism' and preferred to use 'Divisionism' or 'Pointillism' to describe his method of painting in small strokes or points of colour.

When Pissarro adopted this method, he called it 'scientific Impressionism', but he abandoned the method completely after he found the compositional rules too strict.

Figure 12.4
The Monet Family in the Garden at Argenteuil, 1874, by Édouard Manet, oil on canvas, 61 × 100 cm, Metropolitan Museum of Art, New York. Just as Manet was beginning this picture of Claude Monet with his wife Camille and their son Jean, Auguste Renoir arrived and borrowed paint, brushes, and canvas. Standing next to Manet, he also painted the mother and child.

Figure 12.5
The Railway Bridge at Argenteuil, 1874, by Claude Monet, oil on canvas, 54 × 71 cm, Musée d'Orsay, Paris. The old bridges at Argenteuil were destroyed during the Franco-Prussian War and replaced by modern structures of cast iron and concrete. Monet painted them a number of times.

Innovation and Invention

Impressionism took painting in a new direction at a time when society was changing fast.

The artists painted street scenes, cafés and theatres in the new city, as well as bridges, railway stations, trains and factories (Fig. 12.5).

The New Role of Art Dealer

Paul Durand-Ruel was fundamental to the success and recognition of the movement. He was also the forerunner of the modern art market (Fig. 12.6).

Durand-Ruel inherited an art gallery in Paris from his father in 1865. He soon established a new professional philosophy based on innovative principles, such as the organisation of individual exhibitions, the promotion of art, and the creation of an international network of galleries.

During the Franco-Prussian War of 1870, Durand-Ruel opened a gallery in London. In his search for new artists, he met Claude Monet and Camille Pissarro, both of whom had taken refuge in London. He immediately saw potential in the

Impressionist style. He bought several paintings and, in doing so, provided financial relief for artists like Pissarro, Monet and Renoir. He encouraged the Impressionists to mount their first independent exhibition in 1874 and eventually took complete charge of business arrangements for the group.

American artist Mary Cassatt set up the connections and, in 1886, Durand-Ruel organised a huge and successful exhibition in New York. American buyers paid high prices for these modern paintings.

Figure 12.6 Paul Durand-Ruel in his gallery, 1910.

The Hugh Lane Collection

Irish art collector Sir Hugh Lane bought several paintings from Paul Durand-Ruel in Paris in 1904. These included *Music in the Tuileries* by Édouard Manet (see Chapter 11, Fig. 11.2) and *The Umbrellas* by Auguste Renoir (see Fig. 12.21).

Learn the full story of the Dublin Art Gallery dispute that resulted in shared paintings between the National Gallery London and the Hugh Lane in Dublin.

The Industrial Revolution

Technological advancements during the 1860s played a large part in the artists' lives and painting methods.

The Railway

New railway lines radiating out from the city made it convenient for Parisians to travel to the countryside. Every weekend, they poured into villages like Bougival and other leisure areas along the River Seine. In the summer of 1869, Monet and Renoir took the train to paint at the popular bathing spot of La Grenouillère (Fig. 12.7).

Photography

Photography was now a fashionable art form, and it inspired artists to pursue other means of creative expression. They developed aspects like colour, which photography then lacked.

Edgar Degas' paintings were aided by photographic images. The cropping of the compositions at the edges shows its influence (see Fig. 12.26 and 12.27). Later in his career, Degas even took up photography.

Japonism

Japanese wood block prints helped artists like Monet and Degas to develop an interest and understanding of Japan.

These *ukiyo-e*, or 'pictures of the floating world', were first seen by French audiences at the World Exposition in 1867. Artists were fascinated by the simple, everyday subjects presented in such an appealing and decorative manner.

New Colour Theory

In the early 19th century, scientist Michel Eugène Chevreul had developed a theory on colour perception and was the first to develop a colour

Figure 12.7
Bathers at La Grenouillère, 1869, by Claude Monet, oil on canvas, 73 x 92 cm, National Gallery, London. The scene is constructed entirely with detached brushstrokes. These emphasise the patterns of light on water and colour on the jetties, tree trunks, bathing sheds and the boats moored in the shadows.

wheel. These theories had an impact on French painters' use of contrast and harmony in colours.

They preferred to paint *en plein air* because they could better observe colours.

New Materials

New materials contributed to a new way of painting.

The French easel, although not a new invention, became lighter and more compact.

The circular metal clamp, or ferule, which secures brush heads to the handle was pressed flat, creating a flatter, wider shape. This allowed artists to use a much more expressive brushstroke.

Oil paint came in tubes, and synthetic pigments had been invented by industrial chemists in new and vibrant shades like cobalt blue, cerulean blue, French ultramarine, zinc white, viridian green and chrome yellow.

Neo-Impressionism

Georges Seurat studied Michel Eugène Chevreul's colour theories, but also those by American physicist Ogden Rood. He applied these formal scientific principles to painting light and colour.

Sculpture

Rodin's innovations in sculpture included capturing movement. He famously had his models move around him while working with preliminary clay studies.

He abandoned the narrative approach and Classical themes of Academic sculpture and placed more stress on the dignity of simple human moments.

Artists and Artworks
Claude Monet (1840–1926)

Claude Monet was a key Impressionist artist. He was fascinated by natural light and its effects, and devoted his life to painting outside. He painted in and around Paris, the Normandy coastline and his own gardens.

Early Influences

Oscar Claude Monet grew up in Le Havre in Normandy. He was encouraged to paint *en plein air* at home by artist Eugène Boudin, but later continued his studies in Paris. Camille Pissarro introduced him to Camille Corot and they soon began taking painting expeditions to Barbizon.

Monet also encouraged fellow students Frédéric Bazille, Alfred Sisley and Auguste Renoir to paint outside. Friendships with these and other young artists, including Paul Cézanne and Edgar Degas, proved to be extremely significant.

Meeting with Édouard Manet

Claude Monet met Édouard Manet when his two seascapes were shown in the Salon of 1865. They were hanging next to the infamous *Olympia*. When Monet saw the huge nude, it inspired him to try painting large figures. He spent the summer months working exclusively on *Women in the Garden* (Fig. 12.8) and poured all his creative energy and expensive art materials into this one huge painting. He was deeply shocked and depressed when it was rejected by the Salon of 1866. The jury criticised its lack of subject and narrative. They said it was unfinished and careless.

Monet returned to painting landscapes and worked with his friends Pissarro and Renoir. By 1869, they had developed the unique Impressionist style.

Argenteuil

Life became very difficult for Monet after the birth of his son. He and his wife, Camille Doncieux, lived in miserable poverty, but his meeting with Durand-Ruel in London helped. On his return to Paris, he lived in Argenteuil (Fig 12.9), which was only fifteen minutes from the city by train. Monet was enthralled with the loveliness of the River Seine and produced over seventy pictures of the river, boats and bridges.

An Independent Exhibition

Durand-Ruel's business ran into temporary difficulty and he had to stop buying paintings, but he encouraged Monet and the other Impressionists to mount an independent exhibition.

Giverny

Monet eventually had success and bought a house in the little village of Giverny in Normandy. His wife Camille had died, but he lived here with his new wife Alice, his two sons and her six children. He became increasingly attentive to light and colour until eventually his painting came close to abstraction.

Inspired by Japonism, he created a beautiful water garden and a large water lily pond spanned by a Japanese-style bridge (Fig. 12.10).

In the last 30 years of his life, Monet spent a great deal of time painting the pond in varying light conditions and from different vantage points.

Despite becoming partially blind, Monet continued painting almost until his death in 1926, at the age of 86.

Figure 12.8 *Women in the Garden*, 1866, by Claude Monet, oil on canvas, 255 × 205 cm, Musée d'Orsay, Paris.

Women in the Garden

This huge canvas was painted entirely *en plein air*. To reach the top, Monet dug a trench in the garden so that it could be lowered down.

Monet's first wife, Camille Doncieux, was the model for all the women (Fig. 12.8).

Colour and Shadow

Manet's influence can be seen in the simplified treatment of the faces but Monet's unique purple-blue shadows are one of the painting's most dominant features.

Dappled light on the figures and foliage carries the eye around the composition.

Regatta at Argenteuil

In this simplified composition, long brushstrokes and small slabs of colour suggest the shimmering water. The rust reds, oranges and green reflections make the creamy white triangles all the more striking against the blue sky (Fig. 12.9).

Water Lily Pond: Green Harmony

The composition is entirely focused on the bridge and the trees. The bright light suggests morning, but there is only the slightest suggestion of sky and the artist has closed off the background and sides.

Everything is compressed into a square and the edges of the Japanese bridge have been absorbed into the planting, but its graceful curves form a natural division across the centre (Fig. 12.10).

Monet's Series

In later life Monet had no further interest in working with other artists. He firmly believed that only he held true to modern ideals and he was very anxious to maintain his status as the leader.

He developed a way of working in 'series' that depicted the same object at different times of the day (Fig. 12.12–12.15).

Figure 12.9 *Regatta at Argenteuil*, 1872, by Claude Monet, oil on canvas, 48 × 75 cm, Musée d'Orsay, Paris.

Figure 12.10 (left) *Water Lily Pond: Green Harmony*, 1899, by Claude Monet, oil on canvas, 90 × 93 cm, Musée d'Orsay, Paris. **Figure 12.11** (right) *The Bridge with Wisteria*, 1856, by Utagawa Hiroshige, woodblock print, 34 × 22 cm, Galerie Janette Ostier, Paris.

Grainstack Series

These huge stacks of wheat silhouetted against the sky were in the fields behind Monet's house in Giverny. They are not so much realistic depictions of these objects but more studies based on nature.

Composition

The simple compositions have strong geometry. The distant hills are reduced to parallel bands extending across the entire canvas.

Rouen Cathedral Series

Monet's Rouen Cathedral series reflects the artist's love of French culture. He rented a room opposite the cathedral for the best view of the sun moving over the façade and painted over 30 close-up views in a variety of colours and moods. As the light changed, he put one canvas away and worked on another.

Colour and Texture

Textured brushstrokes of yellow, orange, pink,

Figure 12.12 (left) *Stacks of Wheat (Sunset, Snow Effect)*, 1891, by Claude Monet, oil on canvas, 65 × 100 cm, Art Institute of Chicago. **Figure 12.13** (right) *Stacks of Wheat (End of Day, Autumn)*, 1890–1, by Claude Monet, oil on canvas, 66 × 101 cm, Art Institute of Chicago.

Figure 12.14 (left) *Rouen Cathedral in Full Sunlight*, 1893, by Claude Monet, oil on canvas, 107 × 74 cm, Musée d'Orsay, Paris.

Figure 12.15 (right) *Morning Sun, Harmony in Blue and Gold*, 1893, by Claude Monet, oil on canvas, 91 × 63 cm, Musée d'Orsay, Paris.

Figure 12.16 Monet's *Water Lilies* in the Orangerie Museum.

green, blue and white convey the atmosphere of sculpted grey stone dissolving in bright colours as the sun moved across the sky or was suddenly lost behind clouds.

Water Lilies

Monet's last works were giant wall canvases painted during World War I. They were left to the state in remembrance of the war and are displayed in accordance with his wishes, in specially-built oval rooms in the Orangerie Museum in Paris (Fig. 12.16).

Camille Pissarro (1830–1903)

Camille Pissarro spent his childhood in the Virgin Islands but was educated in France.

He met Claude Monet and the other Impressionists during their studies in Paris. He was about 10 years older and he encouraged and advised them.

Pissarro's Career

Pissarro admired Camille Corot in particular. He worked with the Barbizon painters and his early work was accepted in the Salon.

Pissarro absorbed the ideas of light and colour in nature in the new style, but he never forgot the importance of solid structure. He painted in summer and winter, and was the first Impressionist artist to paint snow (Fig. 12.17).

Figure 12.17
The Versailles Road at Louveciennes (The Snow Effect), 1869, by Camille Pissarro, oil on canvas, 38 × 46 cm, Walters Art Museum, Baltimore. Loose brushwork creates the effect of snow and thick blotches of pink, lilac and violet blend with the white.

The Franco-Prussian War of 1870 forced the Pissarro family to move to London. Here, the artist met the Parisian art dealer Paul Durand-Ruel and introduced him to his friends.

Pissarro organised the first Impressionist exhibition in 1874 and was the only artist to exhibit in all eight of the group's exhibitions.

Neo-Impressionism

Pissarro moved in the direction of Neo-Impressionism for a short time, but found the method too laborious and returned to Impressionism.

Success in later life meant he could at last offer his wife and seven children security. He bought a house in the little town of Eragny (Fig. 12.18) and painted some of his finest works in the countryside nearby.

Auguste Renoir (1841–1919)

Pierre-Auguste Renoir trained as a painter on porcelain, in his native town of Limoges. He studied in Paris where he met Camille Pissarro and Claude Monet. Monet encouraged him to paint *en plein*

air and during the summer of 1869, he and Monet painted on the banks of the River Seine. They remained very close friends.

Renoir's Subjects

Renoir painted people in cafés, dance halls, boats or riverside scenes. He also painted portraits of women and children. These images of happy, smiling people had instant appeal and Renoir achieved artistic success quite early.

He said, 'Why shouldn't art be pretty? There are enough unpleasant things in the world.'

Beyond Impressionism

After Renoir visited Italy and saw the work of Raphael, he changed to what he called his 'harsh' style.

Later, Renoir lived in the south of France and developed his 'pearly' method. He painted female nude figures in half-tones of pink and white. He worked in natural sunlight and returned to his earlier free brushwork style.

Figure 12.18
The Church and Farm of Eragny, 1895, by Camille Pissarro, oil on canvas, 74 × 60 cm, Musée d'Orsay, Paris. The light is diffused and the colours are warmer than in his earlier works, but the artist has remained faithful to the origins of Impressionism.

Figure 12.19
Dance at Le Moulin de la Galette, 1876, by Auguste Renoir, oil on canvas, 131 × 175 cm, Musée d'Orsay, Paris.

Dance at Le Moulin de la Galette

One of the artist's largest works was painted on location over one summer (Fig. 12.19). It was the first time that such a large painting with so many figures had been painted completely *en plein air*. It was displayed on a wall of its own at the third Impressionist exhibition in 1877.

It captured a moment of movement, noise and light. The modern, working-class Parisians, dressed in the latest fashions, are enjoying a Sunday afternoon at Le Moulin de la Galette in Montmartre. The bar had an outdoor dancefloor and served *galettes* (a kind of pancake).

Composition

Renoir's characteristically blurred outlines capture the carefree mood of the party. Dappled sunlight unites the picture and moves with the dancing figures.

Luncheon of the Boating Party

The woman on the left with the dog is Renoir's wife, Aline Charigot. She and a group of friends are enjoying lunch on a sunny afternoon on the balcony of the restaurant Maison Fournaise (Fig. 12.20). The composition is linked by interactions between these figures.

The painting depicts a scene from modern life. This is also emphasised by the inclusion of supports for a new railway bridge that can be glimpsed in the distance through the greenery under the canopy.

Figure 12.20 *Luncheon of the Boating Party*, 1881, by Auguste Renoir, oil on canvas, 130 × 173 cm, Phillips Collection, Washington.

The Umbrellas

This busy street scene (Fig. 12.21) was created in two distinct stages, with an interval of about four years between them.

Figure 12.21 *The Umbrellas*, 1881–6, by Auguste Renoir, oil on canvas, 180 × 115 cm, Hugh Lane Gallery, Dublin.

Change in Fashion and Painting Style

Changes can be seen both in the women's fashion and painting style. The women on the right wear fashions of the 1880s, while the woman on the left is wearing the simpler style of 1885, when hats had gone out of fashion.

The figures on the right are painted in Impressionist style, with bright colours and soft, feathery brush-strokes. The colours on the left are more subdued and show Renoir's new, more 'finished' style.

Composition

A carefully planned and abstract geometric rhythm of blues and greys spreads across the painting. The cut-off figures – or 'snapshot' frame – shows the influence of photography.

Berthe Morisot (1841–1895)

Berthe Morisot was one of the founders of the Impressionist movement. She was a very progressive artist and the only woman to participate in the first three Impressionist shows. She was, however, never taken seriously as a professional artist, and this hurt her more deeply than any criticism.

Early Influences

Morisot came from an upper-class family. She grew up in Bourges. When the family moved to Paris, she and her sister Edma studied painting.

Édouard Manet was a considerable influence on both women, but Edma gave up painting after marriage. Berthe married Manet's brother, Eugène, and continued to work.

Morisot and Impressionism

As an artist, there were significant restraints on a woman of Morisot's social background. The focus

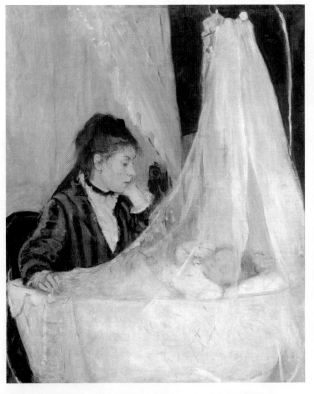

Figure 12.22 *The Cradle*, 1872, by Berthe Morisot, oil on canvas, 56 × 46 cm, Musée d'Orsay, Paris.

on drawing from the male nude made it difficult to gain admittance to the Academy, and she had to be chaperoned when painting outdoors (Fig. 12.1). She could not visit cafés like her male colleagues, so she concentrated largely on family scenes, domestic interiors and gardens.

The Cradle

This very tender portrayal of motherhood (Fig. 12.22) features Edma as she watches over her sleeping baby daughter, Blanche.

The curtain sweeps across in a wave and the mother's gesture is mirrored by the baby's arm. Her left hand resting on the little bed completes the triangular composition.

The small painting was shown at the Impressionist exhibition in 1874.

Edgar Degas (1834–1917)

Edgar de Gas was the son of a well-to-do banker in Paris. Using the altered surname of 'Degas', he was one of the founders of the Impressionist movement, but he always hated the term; he preferred to be called a Realist or Independent painter.

His rigorous Academic artistic training was the solid foundation for everything he did, and he always valued quality drawing and line over colour. He

spent long periods in Italy and was very impressed by Renaissance paintings and frescoes.

Impressionist Period

Degas' paintings were accepted in the Salon, but he was unhappy with their hanging.

Degas and Édouard Manet had a similar background. By the early 1870s, Degas was following Manet's example of painting modern Paris in motion.

He enjoyed the discussions in Café Guerbois, but the other artists found him difficult. They accepted his complaining and cantankerous personality because of his spectacular talent, but he constantly tried to move them on to more 'Realist' subjects.

Working Methods

Degas was interested in modern subjects and capturing a moment in time, but he had absolutely no interest in painting *en plein air*.

Figures

The figure was his primary subject and his outstanding drawings included working-class women's occupations like ironing or making hats. Controversially, he depicted private bathroom scenes of women washing. Female dancers (Fig. 12.23)

Figure 12.23
Two Ballet Dancers in a Dressing Room, 1880, by Edgar Degas, pastel drawing, 49 × 64 cm, National Gallery of Ireland, Dublin.

became one of his favourite themes, but there was often a deep psychological element to his works.

In his last years, his eyesight, which had troubled him all his life, began to fail. He kept creating until his death, turning increasingly to sculpture to express himself. Ironically, he painted his most impressionistic and colourful works in his final years.

He sometimes combined pastels and oil paint to create paste. He also dampened the surface of the paper and stuck on pieces at the ends or sides.

Family Portrait

This painting shows Degas' relatives, the Bellelli family, who lived in Italy. This disturbingly frank family portrait of tension and disharmony was shown in the Paris Salon of 1867 (Fig. 12.24).

The artist's aunt Laure, the woman in the painting, had confided in him how unhappy she was with her husband and life. She stands severely upright, her face set and her head held high. Behind her on the wall is a Degas drawing of her father, Hilaire de Gas,

a subtle indicator of the artist's relationship to the subjects.

Composition

The huge size, simple composition and sober, cool colours create a sense of melancholy. The dark triangular shape of Laure Bellelli and her daughters holds the composition together. Her shape suggests pregnancy, but there is an empty baby cradle in the background. A son born to the family did not survive. The white candle on the mantelpiece may well be symbolic of this.

Baron Gennaro Bellelli is turned away from the viewer and does not engage with the family. Barricaded behind his armchair, he forms a separate frame.

Colour

The most striking feature is the black and white of the little girls' dresses against the muted blue background. Laure Bellelli's father had just died, which explains the black clothing.

Figure 12.24
Family Portrait, 1858–67, by Edgar Degas, oil on canvas, 200 × 250 cm, Musée d'Orsay, Paris.

Figure 12.25
Race Horses in Front of the Tribunes (also known as *The Parade*), 1866–8, by Edgar Degas, oil on canvas, 46 × 61 cm Musée d'Orsay, Paris.

Race Horses in Front of the Tribunes

Encouraged by Manet, Degas went to the race track and made hundreds of sketches in preparation for paintings (Fig. 12.25).

Composition and Colour

The nervous action of a horse in the background is the only indication that a race is about to begin.

The painting relies on strong diagonal lines. The flat colours show the influence of Japanese prints and the cropped edges imitate the effect of a photograph. The contrasts of light, especially the long shadows of the horses, reinforce the perspective lines.

Degas used a significant amount of turpentine in this painting and, although the colours are bright and clear, the overall effect is muted.

The Dance Class

Degas was a frequent visitor to the ballet at the Paris Opera. He observed the young dancers' movements, gestures and poses in the rehearsal room, and they came to pose for him in his studio. *The Dance Class* (Fig. 12.26) was shown at the first Impressionist exhibition of 1874.

Ballet master Jules Perrot is the main focus of the painting. He had been a famous dancer in his youth,

Figure 12.26 *The Dance Class*, 1873–6, by Edgar Degas, oil on canvas, 84 × 77 cm, Musée d'Orsay, Paris.

but now he leans on his cane and gives advice to the ballerinas.

Composition

The painting conveys a charming image of dancers relaxing – one scratches her back and another twists her earring as she reads – but it is in fact a highly complex composition. The edges are cropped, but the large floorspace is the key element.

A raised viewpoint, the small figures on the opposite side and a heightened perspective exaggerate the linear perspective and strong diagonal lines accentuate it even further.

Music, the life-blood of dance, is suggested by the cello reflected in the mirror.

> **Heightened perspective:** The higher the base of an object, the further away it seems.

The Absinthe Drinker

L'Absinthe, or *The Absinthe Drinker*, is one of Degas' most compelling works (Fig. 12.27). The toxic,

highly addictive liquor was known as 'the queen of poisons' or *la fée verte* ('the green fairy') and was later prohibited.

A man and a woman sit side by side. The mood is sombre and the woman's slumped shoulders, splayed out legs and downcast eyes convey a feeling of hopelessness. Absinthe, in the glass in front of her, is easily identified by its greenish colour. The woman's companion is looking away.

Composition

The strange composition is a fundamental element of the psychological impact. Like a photo taken from a nearby table, the figures are off-centre and the frame is cropped.

A matchstick holder looks like a small pot of paint on the table in the foreground and this, along

Figure 12.27 (above) *The Absinthe Drinker*, 1876, by Edgar Degas, oil on canvas, 92 × 68 cm, Musée d'Orsay, Paris.

Figure 12.28 (right) *The Absinthe Drinker* sketch.

Morning light reflection — Hopeless expression — Absinthe — Frame is cut off

Folded newspaper — Folded newspaper — Match container — Zigzag composition

with Degas' signature on the baton, creates the impression that the artist has just left.

The white café tables come forward in a zigzag pattern. We realise we have taken his place and are now staring at the couple opposite.

> *Note:* This scene was carefully set up in the studio. Degas used the well-known actress Ellen Andrée and an artist friend, Marcellin Desboutin, as models.

Mary Cassatt (1844–1926)

Mary Cassatt was the only American artist to exhibit with the Impressionists. She studied in Paris in the strict Academic system before making a successful career in France. Her superb talent in both painting and printmaking was recognised and supported by her colleagues, particularly Edgar Degas. Her subjects were women, mostly mothers and children, but like her friend Berthe Morisot, she experienced difficulty as a woman artist.

Cassatt's friendships and professional relationships on both sides of the Atlantic established her taste for modern art, which was key to developing the market in America. Her connections enabled Durand-Ruel to organise the hugely successful Impressionist exhibition in New York in 1886.

In the Loge

The stylish woman in the theatre box (*loge*) at the Comédie-Française in Paris uses a pair of opera glasses to look at the stage (Fig. 12.29). Cassatt subtly suggests that members of the well-dressed audience also put on performances for one another. The black of her dress is echoed in the clothing of other figures, and a man several boxes down can be seen watching her through his own glasses.

Auguste Rodin (1840–1917)

Auguste Rodin is generally considered the forerunner of modern sculpture. He did not set out to rebel against the past, but his sculpture broke barriers with strongly realistic figures, charged with emotion and sexuality.

Rodin grew up in a working-class district of Paris and was refused entrance to the École des Beaux-Arts. This meant that he had to serve a long and difficult apprenticeship, though he escaped the rigid Academic training.

For many years, he was employed as an assistant for some of the monumental stone sculptures in the new public squares and buildings in Paris. In 1876, he travelled to Italy, and was deeply impressed by the work of Michelangelo. This would influence his sculpture for years to come.

By the 1890s, Rodin's commissions enabled him to employ studio assistants, one of whom was Camille Claudel. Claudel also became his model and mistress. She hoped they would marry, but the relationship ended unhappily in 1893, partly because

Figure 12.29 *In the Loge*, 1878, by Mary Cassatt, oil on canvas, 81 × 66 cm, Museum of Fine Arts, Boston. When the painting was exhibited in Boston in 1878, one critic wrote that Cassatt's work 'surpassed the strength of most men'.

of Rodin's reluctance to abandon his lifelong companion Rose Beuret.

The Kiss

Camille's face and body haunted Rodin; she was the inspiration behind many of his expressions of love, passion, ecstasy and suffering.

The Kiss (Fig. 12.30) depicts a deeply sensual embrace. The woman's feet barely touch the ground as her whole being is uplifted in this most graceful of gestures. Tension flows through both bodies and the kiss itself is barely suggested in a gentle meeting of the lips.

Figure 12.30 *The Kiss*, 1882, by Auguste Rodin, marble, 182 cm, Tate Gallery, London. This is one of three full-scale versions that Rodin made. Its blend of eroticism and idealism makes it one of the great images of sexual love.

Camille Claudel (1864–1943)

Camille Claudel was a daring and innovative artist, and her work is sometimes considered superior to that of Rodin. Women artists were not taken seriously at the time and this was especially true for Claudel due to the sexual nature of her work. Her work was constantly compared to Rodin's, and she had to collaborate with him to get commissions. Only Rodin's signature would appear on those pieces and only Rodin got the credit.

In 1913, Claudel was committed to a mental institution where she spent the last thirty years of her life.

She destroyed a lot of her work and as result, her talent as an artist has only been realised recently.

The Waltz

Claudel made various versions of this sculpture from 1889 to 1903, each with slightly different poses, hoping for a public commission to create a half-life-size marble sculpture.

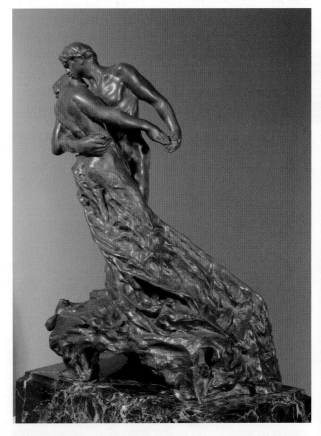

Figure 12.31 A bronze cast of *La Valse*, 1889–1903, by Camille Claude.

A green-glazed stoneware version (Fig. 12.31) emphasises the vegetation around the base. This extends up and threatens to unbalance the swaying couple.

Look up Rodin and Camille Claudel and find out why she never reached the same level of success as he did.

Georges Seurat (1859–91)

After his studies, Georges Seurat began experimenting with colour theory and started a new movement in painting.

He was not interested in painting quickly *en plein air*. Instead of fleeting moments of time, he wanted solidity, clarity and timeless grandeur. He preferred to work slowly from sketches in his studio, and planned his paintings in meticulous detail.

Scientific Impressionism

A Sunday on La Grande Jatte (Fig. 12.32) was exhibited in Paris in 1886. The huge painting attracted ridicule and sarcasm from the press, but one art critic, Félix Fénéon, was impressed by this 'scientific Impressionism'. He described it as 'Neo-Impressionism' and wrote a pamphlet that set the stage for a battle between the Neo-Impressionists and the Impressionists.

A Sunday on La Grande Jatte

A Sunday on La Grande Jatte is built up entirely with contrasting dabs or points of colour placed side by side.

The scene by the riverside is crowded with respectable, well-to-do Parisians in fashionable dress, enjoying their weekend.

The painting is like a modern version of a frieze from ancient Greece. Arranged in groups and facing only sideways or straight ahead, the statuesque and monumental figures look dreamlike and frozen in time.

Composition

The picture is carefully proportioned. The large, grassy area with figures is balanced by the busy river on the left, while receding diagonal lines draw the composition back to create an illusion of space.

Make a painting using only dots of colour. Place the primary colours side by side to allow optical mixing in the eye of the viewer to make secondary colours.

Figure 12.32
A Sunday on La Grande Jatte, 1884–6, by Georges Seurat, oil on canvas, 208 × 308 cm, Art Institute of Chicago.

Media and Areas of Practice

In an effort to capture a fleeting moment in time, the Impressionists painted light and movement. They observed light reflecting on surfaces like water or dappled sunlight filtering through trees, clouds and steam.

The *Tache*

One of the most striking Impressionist techniques was a thickly applied, bold, even stroke of one single colour (see *Bathers at La Grenouillère*, Fig. 12.7). The *tache* – French for 'blot' or 'stain' – was made with flat brushes and was a move away from the traditional method of blending colours.

Wet-on-Wet

Artists used pure unmixed colour and added new layers of paint before the previous layer had dried. This resulted in a blurred effect.

Unvarnished Surface

Instead of the thick golden varnish used by their predecessors, Impressionist artists left the canvas surface unvarnished to keep their colours bright. Their colours were shocking to those accustomed to the more sober colours of Academic painting.

Some artists, especially Edgar Degas, diluted the paint with turpentine to eliminate shine. This created a smooth, velvety, matt surface (see *Race Horses in Front of the Tribunes*, Fig. 12.25).

Pastel

Impressionist artists increasingly began to exhibit their prints and drawings as finished works of art. Berthe Morisot, Edgar Degas and Mary Cassatt worked in pastel, a medium that presented them with an opportunity for a bold new radiance.

Degas built up texture in layers and experimented with a wide range of media, including oil, watercolour, chalk, pencil, etching and photography. However, he found that pastel gave him the opportunity to use the drawing line he so enjoyed.

Sculpture

Rodin worked primarily with his hands, moulding clay or plaster into casts rather than carving wood or stone.

Art Elements and Design Principles

Japanese Influence

Impressionist compositions were often inspired by photography and Japanese prints.

Monet's collection of Japanese woodblock prints was a significant influence on his work. The flat planes of bright colour and irregular shapes offered an alternative approach to traditional landscape painting.

The inspiration for his *Water Lily Pond: Green Harmony* (Fig. 12.10) came from Japanese prints.

Colour and Light

Artists noticed how colours changed in different lights. This encouraged a shift towards a colour-priority system. Instead of deep darks and lights, they used mid-range tones that were more reflective of natural light.

They also avoided black and grey, and instead mixed complementary colours for shadows. They noticed shadows in snow were blue and purple and used slabs of colour and small strokes to simulate reflected light on water (see *Bathers at La Grenouillère*, Fig. 12.7).

'Optical mixing' involved placing vivid colours together and allowing them to mix in the eye of the viewer.

Loose Brushstrokes

Short, thick brushstrokes and broken colour techniques like the *tache* captured movement or quivering light and the essence of the subject.

Degas

Edgar Degas' painting methods were the exact opposite of the Impressionists'. He did not use quick brushstrokes, and everything was studied, planned and executed in the studio in controlled conditions.

His paintings are defined by meticulous compositions, precise drawing and clever use of light. The texture was built up in layers to achieve rich surface effects.

Seurat

Seurat's new painting techniques were:

- **Divisionism**: separation of colour.

- **Pointillism**: The application of small strokes or points of colour to the canvas.

- **Optical mixing**: From a distance, colours blend together in the spectator's eye. For example, small dots of blue and red side by side become purple in an optical illusion. The main advantage was vibrancy of colour, but it was a very laborious technique.

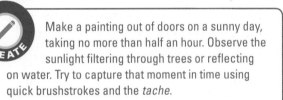

Make a painting out of doors on a sunny day, taking no more than half an hour. Observe the sunlight filtering through trees or reflecting on water. Try to capture that moment in time using quick brushstrokes and the *tache*.

Sculpture

Instead of polished surfaces Rodin produced quite rough and unfinished surfaces. He sculpted lifelike figures in distinctly modern expressions of love, thought, and proud physical strength.

The mark of the artist, that is fingertips visible on the surface of the clay, was also quite a new departure.

Analysis

Examine why painting directly from nature out of doors rather than working in a studio from sketches was so important to the Impressionist artists. Consider the impact of new materials and study the techniques that artists developed to help them work quickly and capture the changing effects of sunlight on the scene.

Painting out-of-doors or *en plein air* gave Impressionist artists a greater awareness of the effect of light on colour. Newly developed scientific theories on colour and the availability of new artistic equipment and materials also influenced Impressionist art.

The Impressionists' work was ridiculed and scorned when it was first seen in the Independent Exhibition, but this was the first distinctly modern movement and the beginning of a pronounced shift in artistic practice.

Chapter Review

1. Describe the innovations in painting by Impressionist artists.

2. Why do you think the public reaction to Impressionism was so strong?

3. Why was Durand-Ruel so important for the success of Impressionism?

4. Describe and discuss a typical Impressionist painting.

5. Discuss the psychological element in a work by Edgar Degas.

6. Describe and discuss one of Claude Monet's series of paintings.

7. What was new and different about Neo-Impressionism?

8. Compare a sculptural work by Auguste Rodin to one with a similar theme by Camille Claudel.

9. Describe and discuss *A Sunday on La Grand Jatte* by Georges Seurat.

10. The painting below by Mary Cassatt (Fig. 12.33) is set in the Bois de Boulogne. Describe the scene and discuss the composition, as well as the artist's use of light, colour and painterly techniques.

Figure 12.33 *A Woman and a Girl Driving*, 1881, by Mary Cassatt, oil on canvas, 90 × 131 cm, Philadelphia Museum of Art. The models were Cassatt's sister, Lydia, and Degas' young niece.

Further Research

www.youtube.com – Search for 'The Story of Hugh Lane: The Dublin Art Gallery Dispute' (4:25) to learn more about the tumultuous history of the gallery

www.youtube.com – Look up 'Claude Monet Biography – Goodbye-Art Academy' (4.56) for a deeper look at Monet, his life and work

www.youtube.com – 'Renoir, Bal du moulin de la Galette' (4:56) gives a close look at the details of this painting

www.youtube.com – Watch 'Berthe Morisot: Inventing Impressionism' (2:47) to discover more reasons why Morisot never gained the same recognition as her male contemporaries

www.youtube.com – Learn more about the career and life of Degas by watching 'Degas Biography from Goodbye-Art Academy' (4:45)

www.youtube.com – Look up 'Degas/ Cassatt at the National Gallery of Art' (4:53) to learn more about the relationship between these two artists

www.musee-rodin.fr/en – Select 'The musée Rodin – Paris' from the 'The Museum' dropdown list in the navigation bar. Click on 'The Visitor Experience' to learn more about this museum, Rodin's work and the room in the museum dedicated to Camille Claudel's work

www.museecamilleclaudel.fr/en – The official site of the Camille Claudel Museum

UNIT 4 REALISM AND IMPRESSIONISM (c.1850–1900s)

13

Post-Impressionism

By the end of this chapter I will ...

* understand how and why artists moved beyond Impressionism
* be able to discuss Cézanne's techniques in working with nature
* be able to describe how van Gogh expressed emotion through colour
* understand why Gauguin was attracted to exotic places
* understand why Post-Impressionists were so influential on younger artists.

Context

After the Franco-Prussian War ended in 1871, France became a republic again. This Third Republic was politically unstable because of rivalry between monarchists and republicans, but it was also a period of imperial expansion and considerable scientific and artistic achievement.

The French Colonial Empire developed during the Third Republic. The largest and most important colonies were in North Africa and Indochina in the East (Vietnam today), but it also covered islands in the Pacific or French Polynesia, including Tahiti.

At the core of the project was the 'civilising mission', the idea that it was Europe's duty to bring civilisation to local populations. Missionaries travelled with administrators and soldiers, and dedicated themselves to converting the people to Christianity.

Art

In the 1870s and 1880s, Impressionism dominated avant-garde art in France. Some artists, however, had difficulty with the movement's focus on style rather than subject matter and struck out on an individual career path.

The most influential of these were Paul Cézanne, Paul Gauguin and Vincent van Gogh.

Avant-garde: A group of people who develop new and often very surprising ideas in art.

Post-Impressionism

These stylistically different artists all worked outside of Paris but, like the Impressionists, they shared their work with the public through independent exhibitions in the French capital.

'Primitivism'

So-called 'primitive' art played a significant role in changing the direction of European painting at the turn of the 20th century. It reflected the fascination

Figure 13.1
Tahitian Women on the Beach, 1891, by Paul Gauguin, oil on canvas, 61 × 91 cm, Musée d'Orsay, Paris.

for less industrially developed cultures and a romantic notion that non-Western people might be more genuinely spiritual, or closer in touch with nature, than the more 'artificial' Europeans.

Paul Gauguin dreamed about establishing a colony in the tropics, far from any taint of European civilisation. He spent many years in Tahiti and *Tahitian Women on the Beach* (Fig. 13.1) tells its own story. One of the native women wears the traditional white and red floral printed wrap-around skirt and a flower in her hair. She is turned away and is completely unoccupied, but the other woman wears a western style dress and is busy making a basket.

Innovation and Invention

Cézanne

Paul Cézanne rejected Impressionism because, in his opinion:

- it was limited because of the artists' obsession with colour and light

- the paintings lacked structure and were little more than a brightly coloured haze.

He wanted to 'make of Impressionism something solid and durable, like the art of the museums'.

Van Gogh

Vincent van Gogh's personal and highly expressive style developed after he arrived in Paris. Connection with the French avant-garde led to significant changes in colour. Instead of dark colours, he adopted bright, pure tones and experimented more in matching them with emotion.

Gauguin

Paul Gauguin developed a new theory, known as 'synthetism', in which he:

- simplified forms and eliminated details
- used thick lines and large flat areas of colour
- got rid of shadows and linear perspective
- suggested depth with planes of colour.

Artists and Artworks

Paul Cézanne (1839–1906)

Paul Cézanne wanted to exhibit and have success at the Salon, but harsh criticism and ridicule of his work caused him to become suspicious and bitter.

He was born in Aix-en-Provence. His father was a banker and expected his son to follow in his footsteps.

Paul chose to study art, but found Paris very difficult. He was a sensitive, shy and timid man and had a rude and blustering manner.

His artistic progress was slow and tortuous but after he began working with Pissarro out of doors his painting went through a transformation. He now focused entirely on nature. *The Hanged Man's House* (Fig. 13.2), a key work from this time in his career, shown at the first Impressionist exhibition of 1874.

Post-Impressionist Development

Shortly after the exhibition, he returned to his home in Aix-en-Provence. After 1878, he had become such a recluse that many in the Paris art world thought he was dead, until the art dealer Amboise Vollard took an interest.

Figure 13.2 *The Hanged Man's House*, Auvers-sur Oise, 1873, by Paul Cézanne, oil on canvas, 55 × 66 cm, Musée d'Orsay, Paris.

Cézanne exhibited his painting in Paris during the 1890s and, as a result, his work became widely appreciated and his place as a leader in modern art was firmly established.

> *Note:* Cézanne hoped to create a 'harmony parallel to nature.' He believed it was the painter's job to translate nature on to the painted surface.

Madame Cézanne in a Red Armchair

Cézanne only painted people he knew well. He painted nearly thirty portraits of his wife, Hortense (Fig. 13.3), but as he treated figures as 'human still life', she was expected to sit completely still for hours.

Figure 13.3 *Madame Cézanne in a Red Armchair*, 1877, by Paul Cézanne, oil on canvas, 72 × 56 cm, Museum of Fine Arts, Boston.

Figure 13.4 *Still Life with Apples and Oranges*, 1899, by Paul Cézanne, oil on canvas, 74 × 93 cm, Musée d'Orsay, Paris.

Still Life with Apples and Oranges

The main objects are arranged in a pyramid shape. In a formal composition, the tabletop line would form the base of the pyramid, but this table is at another angle entirely (Fig. 13.4). The leg is vertical, but the plates are tilted, and the objects are leaning.

Montagne Sainte-Victoire

Cézanne painted numerous versions of 'his' mountain in both oil and watercolours, but different viewpoints and weather conditions mean no two paintings are alike.

In *Montagne Sainte-Victoire with Large Pine*, the mountain is framed with a tree (Fig. 13.5) and includes details like roads, viaducts and houses.

The tree acts as a framing device, but the high viewpoint makes the distant mountain appear closer and larger.

The branches echo the outline of the mountain and draws the composition into the landscape around the mountain. It follows the lines of the viaduct in a circular motion before returning to the foreground.

Later views of the mountain were painted from the hill just above Cézanne's new studio. *Mont Sainte-Victoire* (Fig. 13.6) shows a greater freedom of expression and the mountain is larger than in his 1887 painting. The strong pattern of dense brushstrokes are arranged in slabs of vibrant colour that fit together like a mosaic and bring the painting close to abstraction, but the mountain never loses its form or sense of grandeur.

Vincent van Gogh (1853–1890)

Van Gogh's painting career was one of the shortest but most intense in the history of art. He died at 37, only eight years after he began painting.

Figure 13.5 (left) *Montagne Sainte-Victoire with Large Pine*, 1887, by Paul Cézanne, oil on canvas, 67 × 92 cm, Courtauld Gallery, London.

Figure 13.6 (right) *Mont Sainte-Victoire*, 1902–4, by Paul Cézanne, oil on canvas, 57 × 97 cm, Metropolitan Museum of Art, New York.

Early Life

Born into an upper-middle-class family in Holland, van Gogh became quite religious and wanted to be a preacher. However, his personality was not suited to the life of a holy man and his despair at this drove him to painting. The poverty and the hardship of peasant life affected him deeply and was the subject of his early paintings.

Paris

Van Gogh arrived in Paris for formal art training in 1885. His brother Theo supported him both financially and psychologically, and continued this throughout his life.

South of France

Van Gogh wanted brightness and sunlight, so he moved to Provence in the south and settled in Arles. He worked with a new intensity and drive. His strokes broadened, his drawing grew more confident and his colours became stronger and brighter.

Some of his most powerful and emotional works came from this period, when he was living alone in the 'Yellow House'. Paul Gauguin joined him and they lived and painted together for a short period. The two men quarrelled badly, however, and when Gauguin left, van Gogh fell into depression and famously cut off part of his own ear.

Search for 'Van Gogh and Gauguin in the Yellow House in Arles'. Find out the full detail of this very productive period for van Gogh, as well as the depression that led him to cut off his own ear.

After this episode, he spent time in a psychiatric facility in Saint-Rémy, but in July 1890, he shot himself.

This may have happened in the wheat field in which he had been painting, but he managed to walk back to the inn where he was staying. He was attended by a doctor, but died three days later.

Van Gogh's Room

In preparation for Gauguin's arrival, van Gogh painted his room. The simple interior and bright colours (Fig. 13.7) were to convey notions of rest and sleep. To celebrate the end of his solitude, he included two of everything, such as pictures on the wall, pillows on the bed and chairs.

Figure 13.7
Bedroom in Arles, 1888, by Vincent van Gogh, oil on canvas, 72 × 90 cm, Vincent van Gogh Museum, Amsterdam.

Composition

The scene is very simply painted with pure yellows, browns and pale blues. Shapes are strongly outlined, but the strange perspective is one of the most striking aspects of the painting. The corner of the house was in fact slightly skewed, but the artist exaggerated the downward tilt.

Sunflowers

For van Gogh, the sunflower symbolised the sun's energy and this had religious associations. It expressed the brightness of the Provençal summer sun and his own feelings of optimism. He painted four pictures in six days (Fig. 13.8).

A vase of flowers was a traditional subject, but van Gogh breathed new life into this with a simple direct composition and his use of colour, line and texture.

The entire lifespan of the flowers has been expressed, from full yellow bloom to wilting and dying blossoms in faded ochre.

The Starry Night

Vincent wrote to Theo of his terrible need for religion. When he felt like this he wanted to paint the stars. Paul Gauguin had encouraged him to paint more from memory and imagination so the picture (Fig. 13.9) is partly invented.

Figure 13.8 *Vase with Fourteen Sunflowers*, 1888, by Vincent van Gogh, oil on canvas, 95 × 73 cm, National Gallery, London.

Composition

Huge stars gleam like great yellow fireballs in contrast to the cool, undulating lines of the ultramarine

Figure 13.9
The Starry Night, 1889, by Vincent van Gogh, oil on canvas, 74 × 92 cm, Museum of Modern Art, New York.

sky. The crescent moon shines an intensely bright yellow and orange.

The strong vertical silhouette of the cypress tree in the foreground balances the composition and contrasts the rhythm, energy and emotion of the richly textured and sweeping impasto brushstrokes.

Self-portraits

Van Gogh painted more than 30 self-portraits. This was a conscious link to the 17th-century Dutch artist Rembrandt (see Chapter 8, p. 126) and was part of his desire to be taken seriously.

The candid images record not only the changes in his painting technique, but also a psychological decline.

One of the last of these shows van Gogh in a very agitated state. (Fig. 13.10). He is wearing a suit instead of his usual working jacket, but the piercing eyes are the most tightly drawn feature. They illustrate the mental anguish that lies behind the stern and passive expression.

Figure 13.10 *Self-Portrait*, 1889, by Vincent van Gogh, oil on canvas, 65 × 54 cm, Musée d'Orsay, Paris.

The painting pounds with energy. Swirling patterns ripple throughout in a churning, turbulent motion; the furrow in van Gogh's forehead completes this terrifying image.

Colours

Cool blues and greens are normally calm colours, but these appear differently when seen against the fiery orange of the artist's hair and beard.

Look up van Gogh's self-portraits and trace his depictions of himself as a confident artist though to his images with a bandaged head, following his act of self-mutilation on his ear.

Examine van Gogh's *Self-Portrait* (Fig.13.10) and write a paragraph on why you think he chose to represent himself this way. Compare the work to other self-portraits made by the artist.

Paul Gauguin (1848–1903)

Paul Gauguin grew up in Peru, but returned to France with his mother after his father died.

A 'Sunday Painter'

Gauguin spent many years as an amateur 'Sunday painter', but he gave up his comfortable job and his wife and children for a life of poverty, bitterness and suffering as an artist. He worked with Pissarro and became involved with the Impressionists for a short time.

Pont Aven

Gauguin established an artist's colony in Pont Aven in Brittany. He considered establishing another in Provence, but after the disastrous period with van Gogh he began to think further afield.

Tahiti

Eventually he decided on the South Sea island of Tahiti. This turned out to be not quite the paradise he had expected, but he was fascinated by the local women's gentle beauty (Fig. 13.11).

Figure 13.11
Two Tahitian Women,
1899, by Paul Gauguin,
oil on canvas, 94 × 72 cm,
Metropolitan Museum of
Art, New York.

Financial Difficulties

In spite of his efforts to live in a completely natural way, Gauguin needed money and he found it difficult to get his paintings sold.

In his search for the perfect place, he left Tahiti and travelled to Hivaoa in French Polynesia. He refused to pay taxes to the French colonial authorities and was imprisoned. He died soon after.

Two Tahitian Women

This gentle depiction of beautiful, mysterious women shows Gauguin's image of a mythical paradise (Fig. 13.11).

The women carry a basket of mango blossoms, like an offering of their innocence and purity. It follows the artistic tradition of comparing a woman's breasts to flowers or fruit.

Art Elements and Design Principles

Cézanne called his pictures 'constructions after nature'. He translated nature into patterns, shapes and colours. He said: 'Treat nature by means of the cylinder, the sphere and the cone.'

Working slowly and methodically, he carefully placed each brushstroke using small dabs of colour. He used horizontal strokes for breadth and vertical ones to suggest depth.

He often worked with the same motif. He distorted objects and compositions to prevent them becoming rigid, but always maintained order.

A key characteristic was his use of multiple viewpoints, such as:

- objects seen from different positions at one time
- tabletops tilted upwards or at a slant.

The relationship of one object to another is more important to the artist than traditional single-point perspective. This can be seen in *Still Life with Apples and Oranges* (Fig. 13.4).

Van Gogh learned the methods and aims of both Impressionism and divisionism from Camille Pissarro. The strongest characteristic of his painting was his energetic brushstrokes, but he is most famous for his *impasto*. This produced more visible brushstrokes, added texture and reflected light.

Impasto: Thick paint strokes.

Yellow was van Gogh's favourite colour and he used variations of chrome yellow, chrome orange, cadmium yellow, geranium, Prussian blue and emerald.

Gauguin dreamed about nature and painted from imagination. He placed an emphasis on pattern and colour harmonies and instilled his paintings with a profound sense of mystery.

Media and Areas of Practice

After Cézanne returned to Provence, he painted the landscape of his childhood, especially the Montagne Sainte-Victoire in the mountains near Aix.

He also painted in his studio and produced over 200 still life paintings of apples, oranges, onions, bottles and ornaments on a white tablecloth (Fig.13.4).

Van Gogh was entranced by the landscape of Provence. He worked frenetically all day in the open air, in all weathers. He weighted his easel into the ground when the strong 'mistral' wind blew. He even painted the stars at night and stuck candles in the brim of his hat to see.

Gauguin's inspiration came from non-naturalistic imagery like Japanese woodblock prints. Harsh reds, blacks and whites characterise some of his work. He also revived the art of woodcutting and produced some fine lithographs.

Analysis

Examine the work of Post-Impressionist artists and see why their ideas and vision of art took them on a distinctly individual career path that went far beyond Impressionism.

Study their unique techniques and note the use of brushstrokes, colour and composition. Consider how and why these particular styles developed and why this was so influential on 20th-century art movements.

It was many years before Paul Cézanne's genius was appreciated, but he had a widespread influence on generations to come.

After Van Gogh's death, his brother Theo's wife and son promoted his work. It quickly became widely known and appreciated.

Gauguin wrote a good deal about his art and his time in Tahiti. His writing and paintings were very influential on 20th-century painting.

In 1910, the noted art critic, historian and curator Roger Fry coined the term 'Post-Impressionism' for his show in London. None of the artists lived long enough to see it.

After Impressionism

Gauguin and Les Fauves

'Les Fauves' ('the wild beasts') was a group of French painters with shared interests. Henri Matisse became its leader. This 20th-century modern art movement was inspired by the rejection of naturalism.

In response to Gauguin's ideas, the artists used more intense colour and simplified forms. Above all, they emphasised personal expression.

Cézanne and Cubism

Cézanne's art directly influenced Spanish artist Pablo Picasso, one of the founders of Cubism. He referred to Cézanne as 'the father of us all'.

Cubism

Cubism was one of the most influential of all artistic movements in the early 20th century.

Cézanne's ideas that nature can be depicted with the cylinder, sphere and the cone and his use of multiple viewpoints directly inspired it.

Van Gogh and Expressionism

Vincent van Gogh's energetic brushwork, distortion of form and use of strong colours to convey emotion was a major influence on the development of Expressionism. Gauguin and Fauvism were also influences.

Expressionism

Expressionism emphasised an emotional response to subjects and events.

The artists expressed themselves with bold brushwork, distortion, exaggeration and imagination. Their colours and shapes were strong and vivid.

Among the Expressionist artists were the German Max Beckmann, Franz Marc and Ernst Ludwig Kirchner.

The Norwegian Edvard Munch was also related to this movement and, during his stay in Germany, the Russian Wassily Kandinsky became involved with Expressionism.

As Modernism developed, artists continued to push the limits of traditional representation.

Chapter Review

1. Why did Post-Impressionist artists want to go beyond Impressionism?

2. What part did memory and emotion play in the work of Vincent van Gogh?

3. Describe and discuss a work of art by van Gogh.

Figure 13.12 *Where Do We Come From? What Are We? Where Are We Going?* 1897, by Paul Gauguin, oil on canvas, 139 × 375 cm, Museum of Fine Arts, Boston.

4. Why do you think that Paul Cézanne left Paris and returned to work in Aix en Provence?

5. Cézanne described his paintings as 'constructions'. Why do you think he used such a term?

6. What do you think Paul Gauguin hoped to achieve in Tahiti?

7. How did Post-Impressionist artists influence 20th-century art movements?

8. Gauguin never fully explained the imagery in his huge painting on page 193 (Fig. 13.12). What do you think it might mean?

Further Research

www.youtube.com – Look up 'Post-Impressionism' (8:29) for an overview of this artistic movement

www.youtube.com – Watch 'Cézanne: "The Father of Modern Art"' (14:15) for a closer look at the life and work of this artist

www.youtube.com – Search for 'A Closer Look: Van Gogh and Gauguin' (3:34) to learn more about the relationship between these artists

www.artsy.net – Search for the article 'Inside Vincent van Gogh and Paul Gauguin's Nine Turbulent Weeks as Roommates'

www.youtube.com – 'Vincent van Gogh: The colour and vitality of his works | National Gallery' (29:33) gives an in-depth look at his life and the details of his paintings

www.artsy.net – Read a fascinating article 'How Vincent van Gogh's market was tirelessly built up by his sister-in-law Jo'

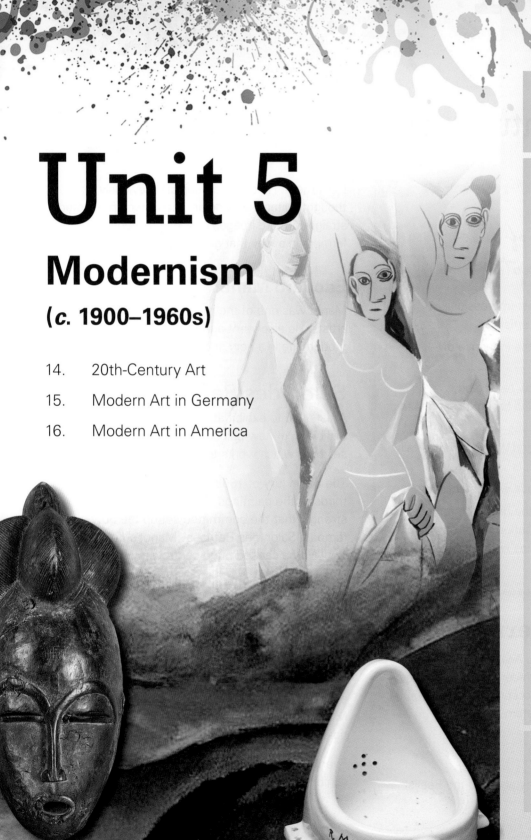

Unit 5

Modernism

(*c.* 1900–1960s)

14. 20th-Century Art

15. Modern Art in Germany

16. Modern Art in America

Édouard Manet and
Modernism 1863–83

Impressionism 1874–90

Post-Impressionism
1886–1905

**Advertising Posters
1889–1910**

Divan Japonais,
1893, Toulouse-
Lautrec

**Modern Art Movements
1890–1930**

The Scream,
1893, Munch

*Les Demoiselles
d'Avignon,* 1907,
Picasso

Bauhaus 1920–1934

The Bauhaus
Building, Dessau,
Germany

Surrealism 1920–1936

*The Persistence
of Memory,*
1931, Dali

**New York School of
Painting 1946–1960**

*One: Number
31,* 1950,
Pollock

Contemporary art
1960–Present

Before

Modernism (c. 1900–1960s)

After

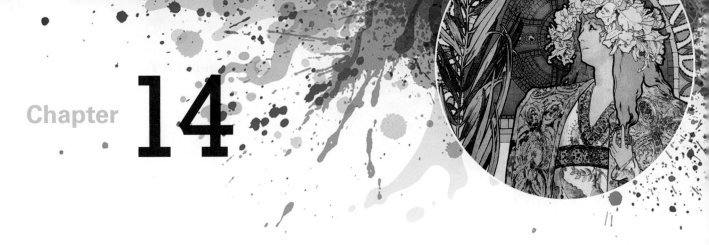

14

20th-Century Art

By the end of this chapter I will ...

* understand how Post-Impressionism influenced modern artists
* be able to discuss the influence of Primitivism on art
* understand how new technology encouraged ideas and brought changes to art practices
* understand that World War I fundamentally affected art and artists
* understand why Dada was established
* be able to discuss the development of Surrealism and the influence of new psychological theories and techniques.

Before Modernism

The government-controlled Académie des Beaux Arts set standards for art in 19th-century France. Artists found it very difficult to succeed professionally if they did not conform to this system.

Realism

In 1846, Gustav Courbet established the Realist movement. He avoided subjects previously thought suitable for fine art and instead presented straightforward images of everyday people like farmers in a way that glorified their work.

Édouard Manet

Manet was one of the most influential 19th-century artists. He also went against tradition by painting modern life in a new style.

Salon des Refusés

Artists had to exhibit at the Salon, a huge public exhibition of new painting and sculpture. A jury selected which works to hang.

The Salon jury of 1863 rejected more than two-thirds of the paintings. Artists protested so strongly that the committee set up the now famous 'Salon des Refusés'. Manet's *Le Déjeuner sur l'Herbe* caused huge controversy at this (see Unit 4).

Impressionism

Impressionists challenged the Academic tradition again when artists began painting outdoors in a very new style. At their first Impressionist exhibition in 1874, critics singled out Claude Monet's painting *Impression, Sunrise* for particular ridicule and gave the group its name.

Eventually the style was accepted and the last exhibition was held in New York in 1886. This firmly established the place of French art and Paris as the international centre of Modern Art.

Post-Impressionism

Post-Impressionist artists, Paul Cézanne, Vincent van Gogh and Paul Gauguin, inspired the modern art movements of the early 20th century.

Context

The period 1871 to 1914 in France was known as the Belle Époque. The Franco-Prussian war had ended the Second Empire and brought down Napoleon III. The defeat humiliated France, especially with the loss of the south-eastern states of Alsace-Lorraine to a new united German Empire.

There followed a succession of short-lived governments, but standards of living greatly increased for the upper and middle classes. There was also huge growth and innovation in the arts, sciences and engineering.

Paris developed especially rapidly at the start of the 20th century and grand railway stations like the Gare d'Orsay were works of art in their own right. Modern engineering marvels also saw the opening of a new subway system on 14 July 1900 (Fig. 14.1).

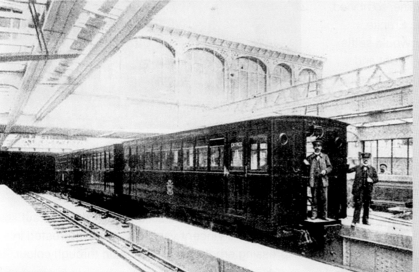

Figure 14.1 (left)
The Paris Métro opened in 1900.

Figure 14.2 (below)
Parisian fashion c. 1900.

Classe 52   EXPOSITION UNIVERSELLE   1900   Classe 85

Félix Jungmann

106-108, rue Montmartre.

A huge growth took place in design for urban architecture, fashion and the applied arts as demand rose for quality products.

Paris was the fashion capital of the world and by the 1900s, young ladies from as far away as New York and St Petersburg would come twice a year for their new outfits (Fig. 14.2).

> **Applied art:** The term used for the application of artistic design for practical objects.

World War I (1914–1918)

The Belle Époque came to a crashing halt in 1914. Ongoing anger at the loss of Alsace-Lorraine, combined with a growing fear of the new German Empire, had led to a belief that only a new war would settle the score. Few were prepared for the horror and devastation of the first fully mechanised war in Europe.

Primitivism

In late 19th-century Europe, an artistic movement known as 'Primitivism' reflected the fascination for less industrially-developed cultures. This romantic notion saw people of far-off lands as more spiritual, or closer in touch with nature, than the more 'artificial' European society.

Tribal arts from Africa and the Pacific Islands presented artists with a new visual vocabulary and played a major role in early modern art.

Twentieth-century artist Pablo Picasso saw an exhibition of archaic African art at the Ethnographic Museum in Trocadero, in Paris. He simplified and adapted the figures he saw and used them in his own work (Fig. 14.3 and 14.4).

Figure 14.3 A Baule African mask. Ivory coast, early 20th century. Wood, 36 x 15 x 14 cm. Leopold Museum, Vienna.

Figure 14.4 *Female bust*, 1907, by Pablo Picasso, oil on canvas.

Modern Art Movements

Paul Cézanne depicted solid form in nature. Paul Gauguin and Vincent van Gogh were interested in expressing emotion or imagination through colour.

The three artists worked entirely alone, but their ground-breaking work encouraged modern artists to explore new possibilities.

Influence of the Subconscious

Psychologist Sigmund Freud's book *The Interpretation of Dreams*, published in 1899, also inspired artists.

After the war, art movements became all the more diverse. Artists began questioning exactly what art should do for society and found more unconventional ways to express themselves.

Exhibiting Art

The Society of Independent Artists was formed in Paris in 1884. It allowed any artist to exhibit upon payment of a fee.

The Salon d'Automne was established in 1903. It rapidly became the most progressive, showcase for modern artists. A sensational exhibition at the Salon d'Automne in 1905 introduced Fauvism to the public. This was followed with a retrospective for Paul Gauguin in 1906, and a landmark retrospective for Paul Cézanne in 1907. These exhibitions established international reputations and inspired many younger artists.

Art Collectors

Wealthy middle-class people in 19th-century Europe were often art collectors, but American collectors were especially interested in Modern European art.

Paul Durand-Ruel (1831–1922)

Durand-Ruel was an art dealer of French Impressionism in Paris (Fig. 14.5). He established a market in America and opened a gallery in New York in 1887.

America's First Museum of Modern Art

The Phillips Collection Museum was founded by

Figure 14.5 *Paul Durand-Ruel*, 1887, by Auguste Renoir, oil on canvas, 65 × 54 cm.

Figure 14.6 Marjorie and Duncan Phillips in 1954, seated in front of *Luncheon of the Boating Party*.

Duncan Phillips and Marjorie Acker Phillips in 1921 in Washington DC. The collection includes works by Paul Cézanne, Edgar Degas, Henri Matisse, Pablo Picasso and Vincent van Gogh.

As a painter herself, Marjorie was interested in Impressionism, especially the works of Paul Cézanne and Pierre-Auguste Renoir. In 1923, she bought the gem of their collection, Renoir's *Luncheon of the Boating Party* (see Chapter 12, Fig. 12.20) from the Durand-Ruel gallery (Fig. 14.6).

The Walter-Guillaume Collection, Musée de L'Orangerie, Paris

Paul Guillaume collected works of Impressionism and modernism from 1914 until his premature death in 1934. His wife Domenica took this over and later remarried the architect Jean Walter. When the French State acquired the collection in the late 1950s, she insisted on retaining the name.

Peggy Guggenheim (1898–1979)

Peggy Guggenheim built up an important collection of Modern European art (Fig. 14.7). She came from a wealthy New York family but lived in Paris during the 1920s. She became friendly with avant-garde writers and artists.

After 1940, when World War II disrupted the flow of art from Europe, she continued to support avant-garde artists in the US.

> **Avant-garde:** French for 'vanguard'. It usually refers to people like writers and artists and their ideas that are ahead of their time.

Figure 14.7 Peggy Guggenheim in Paris, 1930. The silhouette of Notre Dame is clearly visible and *Dutch Interior II* by Joan Miró hangs on the wall behind her.

An American documentary film about art collector Peggy Guggenheim is available on YouTube. Search for 'Peggy Guggenheim: Art Addict (2015)'.

Innovation and Invention
The Eiffel Tower

The Eiffel Tower was the centrepiece of the World's Fair in Paris in 1889, the centenary year of the French Revolution.

Gustave Eiffel's engineering firm won the contest for its design and the wrought-iron structure demonstrated France's industrial prowess to the world.

Iron had been used as support structures for factories and bridges, but this was a completely new use of the material. Elevators were deliberately included so that Parisians and their visitors could enjoy the views.

Street Art

The poster emerged as a new form of art during the 1890s, and large colourful advertisements transformed the streets.

Figure 14.8 *Le Pays des Fées*, 1889, by Jules Cheret. A poster advertising an attraction at the World's Fair of 1889 in Paris.

Their development was due to new techniques in lithographic printing.

Artists and advertisers had been using this method in black and white for many years, but Jules Cheret produced colour lithographs from his own press in Paris (Fig. 14.8).

> **Lithography:** A printing process that begins with drawing on a flat limestone with a greasy substance. The ink adheres to this, and the non-image areas are ink-repellent. Copies can be made as long as the stone is kept wet.

Henri de Toulouse-Lautrec (1864–1901)

In late 19th-century Paris, cabaret was a new and popular form of entertainment all over the city.

Figure 14.9 *Divan Japonais*, 1893, by Henri de Toulouse-Lautrec, lithograph, 81 × 62 cm. When the Divan Japonais, a cabaret club in Montmartre, was newly redecorated in 1893, its owner, Édouard Fournier, commissioned this poster depicting singers, dancers and patrons, to attract customers.

Henri de Toulouse-Lautrec saw real artistic possibilities for the poster as a work of Modern art (Fig. 14.9). His lifestyle and work made him the classic stereotype of the anti-establishment bohemian modern artist.

> - Look up *At The Moulin Rouge* by Henri de Toulouse-Lautrec.
> - Look for paintings and posters by Toulouse-Lautrec that tell you more about singers and dancers like La Goulue, Jean Avril and Aristide Bruant.
> - Consider whether the artist has depicted them sympathetically.

Art Nouveau

Between 1890 and 1910, a new style of art and design evolved in several countries in Europe. Artists drew inspiration from natural forms like blossoms and leaves and abstracted them into elegant, organic motifs. The style was used in architecture, interior design, jewellery and glass design, posters and illustration.

Alphonse Mucha (1860–1939)

The most famous Art Nouveau posters were made by Czech artist Alphonse Mucha, who came to Paris in 1887. His instantly recognisable works featured beautiful women with long tendrils of hair, decorative botanical motifs and delicate colours.

He originally found fame with his stunningly original poster *Gismonda* for the legendary actress, Sarah Bernhardt (Fig. 14.10). The long narrow shape revolutionised poster design. It emphasised the slimness of the actress and created a resemblance to a goddess. The stillness and subtle colours of the near life-size figure introduced dignity and calm to what had been up to then garish street art.

Bernhardt was enthralled and commissioned several more posters for her next productions.

Sculpture

The Romanian sculptor Constantin Brancusi helped shape non-representational Modernism and changed the way future generations would make and view sculpture.

Figure 14.10
Gismonda, 1894, by Alphonse Mucha, lithograph, 216 × 74 cm.

Figure 14.11 *The Kiss*, 1916, by Constantin Brancusi, stone, 58 x 34 x 25 cm, Philadelphia Museum of Art. This is one of the few works that Brancusi made for a specific commission. It was requested by John Quinn, Brancusi's patron in New York.

According to Brancusi, 'What is real is not the external form, but the essence of things.'

His most famous work is *The Kiss*, and he created several versions around this theme (Fig. 14.11). The juxtaposition of smooth and rough surfaces combined with dramatically simplified human figures suggests the influence of African sculpture.

Modern Architecture

Charles-Édouard Jeanneret, better known as Le Corbusier, was one of the most imaginative and influential architects and urban planners of modern times (Fig. 14.12).

Together with contemporaries like Ludwig Mies van der Rohe and Walter Gropius, he developed the International Style of Architecture.

Le Corbusier outlined five key features necessary for modern architecture. According to him buildings should:

1. be raised off the ground on *piloti* (reinforced concrete pillars)
2. have one façade that was not part of the structure
3. be free of internal structural walls
4. have large windows
5. have a roof garden to replace the area of landscape taken from the ground.

Modern Art Movements

Les Fauves

A group of artists held an exhibition at the Salon d'Automne in 1905. Their work was so brightly coloured that when art critic Louis Vauxcelles saw them in the same room as a small, bronze Renaissance sculpture, he exclaimed, '*Ah, Donatello chez les fauves!*' – 'Ah, Donatello among the wild beasts!' The artists kept the name 'Les Fauves', and their style of painting is known as Fauvism as a result.

Fauvist artists were influenced by Paul Gauguin and Vincent van Gogh's use of colour, and its potential to draw out emotions and sensations.

The movement centred on the vision of Henri Matisse. In the summer of 1905, he and his wife Amélie travelled to the little village of Collioure on the Mediterranean coast of France. The artist was captivated by the colour, light and vitality of the little Catalan fishing port, and persuaded his friend André Derain to join him there.

They spent the summer painting side by side around the coastline. Matisse sometimes painted through open windows, which acted as a frame for the colourful scenes (Fig. 14.13).

Derain's paintings were a little more conventional in but his use of colour was every bit as powerful.

Figure 14.13 *The Open Window, Collioure*, 1905, by Henri Matisse, oil on canvas, 55 × 46 cm, National Gallery of Art, Washington D.C.

Maurice de Vlaminck was a friend of Derain and, although he never came to Collioure, his vividly coloured scenes were shown at the famous exhibition of 1905.

Fauvism ended suddenly in 1908 and the artists went their separate ways.

Fauvist Artists and Artworks

Henri Matisse (1869–1954)

Matisse was fascinated by colour, but was also interested in Islamic art and the sculpture of Africa. He developed a personal style that relied on pure colour, flat shape and pattern.

His *Portrait of Madame Matisse* (Fig. 14.14) was one of the most controversial exhibits at the 1905 Salon d'Automne. It was heavily criticised for its loud colours and roughly textured surface.

In 1917, Matisse moved permanently to Nice in the south of France. Views seen through windows continued to be a favourite theme.

Success came in the 1930s, but in 1941, after an operation for cancer, he was confined to a wheelchair. He continued to expand his work, experimenting with line drawing and cut-out shapes.

Before he died in 1954, Matisse's work featured in a large retrospective exhibition in the Museum of Modern Art, New York.

Portrait of Madame Matisse (The Green Line)

The model is the artist's wife (Fig. 14.14). The traditional head-and-shoulders portrait format is broken up with colour. The artist has used extremely bright colours, and the textured handling of paint is a feature of the new Fauvist style.

- Look up some Matisse paintings on the theme of the open window.
- Draw or paint a view of an interior that includes a view from a window.

Figure 14.14 *Portrait of Madame Matisse (The Green Line)*, 1905, by Henri Matisse, oil on canvas, 40 × 32 cm, Statens Museum, Copenhagen.

Cubism

Pablo Picasso and Georges Braque established the Cubist movement. They worked together in Paris from 1907 to 1914 and their styles were so alike that their work can be hard to separate.

The initial influence came from African masks, but the work of Paul Cézanne was pivotal. Cézanne had rejected traditional perspective and explored the notion that objects can be seen from many points of view at any one time.

His comment that 'nature can be reduced to cubes and spheres' was a starting point for Braque and Picasso, but *Les Demoiselles d'Avignon* (Fig. 14.16) was considered to have been the first step towards Cubism.

By 1911, Picasso's and Braque's paintings were almost completely abstract, but now the artists moved to a second phase. They began to mix materials such as sand, sawdust, plaster, metal filings and even ash with paint to create surface texture.

Next they used 'real' material like *papier collé* (collage). The purpose, according to Picasso, was: 'That different textures can enter into a composition and become reality.'

The artists tried to get rid of *trompe l'oeil* and instead find a *trompe l'espirit*.

> **Trompe l'œil:** An artistic technique that uses realistic imagery to create the optical illusion of a three-dimensional object.
>
> **Trompe l'espirit:** Something that can deceive the mind in the same way that a trompe l'oeil deceives the eye.

Look up *Bottle of Vieux Marc, Glass, Guitar and Newspaper* by Pablo Picasso at the Tate Gallery, London.
Make a collage by choosing scraps of paper or other material that represent the 'real world' and give them an 'unreal' role in a flat, pictorial space.

Cubist Artists and Artworks

Pablo Picasso (1881–1973)

The son of an art teacher, Picasso was born in Málaga, Spain, and moved with his family to Barcelona. He became part of the avant-garde artistic movement before moving to Paris in 1900.

A cold blue began to dominate his palette at this time and he painted young, sad, bloodless women, sickly children and old and emaciated beggars (Fig. 14.15). This was followed by a 'Rose Period', which showed harlequins, acrobats and circus performers.

Picasso and Cubism

Picasso saw Paul Gauguin's and Paul Cézanne's work in their Paris exhibitions.

He was particularly interested in Gauguin's work from Tahiti and this encouraged him to explore Primitive art, especially African art.

Figure 14.15 *The Old Guitarist*, 1903–4, by Pablo Picasso, oil on panel, 123 × 83 cm, Art Institute of Chicago. During his so-called 'Blue Period', Picasso painted melancholy scenes showing the difficulties of life for ordinary people. The blue colouring in the elongated figure adds to the sense of despair.

He began to work with Georges Braque, and together they developed Cubism.

Les Demoiselles d'Avignon

The source for the strange faces in *Les Demoiselles d'Avignon* (Fig. 14.16) was Picasso's own collection of African masks.

The combination of several viewpoints in one painting was an entirely new departure, but Cézanne's influence can be seen in the angles of figures and background.

The painting also broke new ground in its brutal sexual frankness. The five figures represent sex workers from a brothel called Avignon in Barcelona,

Figure 14.16 *Les Demoiselles d'Avignon*, 1907, by Pablo Picasso, oil on canvas, 244 × 234 cm, Museum of Modern Art, New York. The painting was seen by friends and artists from 1907, but it wasn't until 1916 that it was displayed in public.

and the viewer is placed in the position of the client. The women's expressions are far from attractive or inviting and the sharp angles of the composition, as well as the pointed, almost weapon-like shape of the melon in the foreground, all contribute to a deeply threatening atmosphere.

Still Life with Chair Caning

As Picasso's ideas developed, his paintings became 'real objects' and not representations. He created reality without illusionism by assembling a piece of commercially made oil cloth printed with a cane chair pattern, with a pipe, a glass, a lemon, an oyster and a newspaper.

JOU means 'game' in French, but is also the first three letters of the French word for newspaper. This, the chair caning and the oval shape suggest a café setting. A thickly textured piece of real rope acts as a frame around the work (Fig. 14.17).

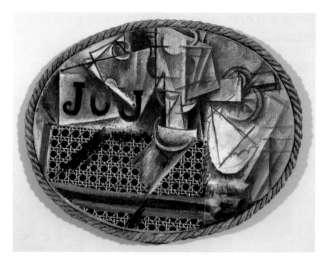

Figure 14.17 *Still Life with Chair Caning*, 1912, by Pablo Picasso, oil on oil-cloth over canvas edged with rope, 29 × 37 cm, Musée Picasso, Paris.

Experience of World War I

As a citizen of neutral Spain, Picasso took no part in World War I. He saw many friends, however, including Georges Braque, go to war, and the experience radically changed him.

He abandoned Cubism and returned to Classicism. His wife, Olga, was his model at this time (Fig. 14.18).

Figure 14.18 *Portrait of Olga in an Armchair*, 1917–18, by Pablo Picasso, 130 × 89 cm. Olga Khokhlova was a Russian ballet dancer.

Picasso came under the influence of Surrealism in the late 1920s, and, while it never transformed his work, it encouraged him to move in a new direction.

Guernica

By 1932, Picasso had become very successful and a huge retrospective exhibition in Paris confirmed his position as a major artist of the 20th century.

His life became more complicated however, and by 1937 he was separated from Olga. She and their son Paolo were living in the south of France. His new lover, Dora Maar, was living nearby and his young mistress, Marie-Thérèse Walter, was living in the country with their baby, Maya.

 Find out more about the women in Picasso's life and how he represented each of these new relationships with a different artistic response.

Separation had involved giving up his studio flat and this interfered with his ability to work. He had received a large commission for the Spanish Pavilion in the World's Fair in Paris to be held in May, but by mid-April he had still not even begun.

Inspiration came suddenly with a shattering event in his native Spain, where a civil war was raging with increasing ferocity.

When Picasso heard of the bombing of the little Basque town of Guernica, he began to sketch. In a rush of creative energy, the giant canvas Guernica was finished within five weeks (Fig. 14.19).

Nothing in the painting specifically alludes to Guernica. The profoundly disturbing imagery could reflect any atrocity of war, but it conveys the strong message that something terrible has happened.

At the base, the corpse of a dead warrior lies decapitated, splintered and crushed, and above him a horse screams in agony. Most poignant of all is the distraught mother holding the limp body of her dead child: standing impassively behind her is the dark and massive figure of a bull. Only the wind blowing across the canvas lifts his tail.

Reflecting the newspaper headlines and pictures, the black, white and grey created a sombre mood. Picasso had a special matt house paint made so that the surface could be flat in every way. Brushmarks and textures are kept to a minimum, but there are some scratch marks.

 Picasso's giant painting of Guernica was on loan to the Museum of Modern Art in New York for 42 years. It was returned to Spain in 1981. Find out why this happened and why it became an anti-war painting.

South of France

Picasso remained in Paris during the German occupation of 1940 to 1945 and although the Nazis

Figure 14.19 Guernica, 1937, by Pablo Picasso, oil on canvas, 349 × 777 cm, Reina Sofia Museum, Madrid.

regarded his work as degenerate, they gave him little or no trouble. After the war, he moved to the south of France where he remained for the rest of his life.

With his amazing range and diversity of style, Picasso remained one of the most dominant and influential artists of the 20th century.

Georges Braque (1882–1963)

Georges Braque hugely admired Cézanne, but gradually, through working with Picasso, he began to see how Cézanne's solid style could be pushed a little further.

Together the artists developed Cubism. They fragmented everyday objects almost to the point where they no longer existed – in other words, abstract art – but they did not quite cross that threshold.

Braque was injured in World War I and returned to Normandy to live quietly. He continued to paint but his work became gentler, more colourful and patterned.

Woman with a Guitar

The use of text and muted colour scheme makes this a typical Cubist work (Fig. 14.20).

Multiple viewpoints are seen as the woman looks down to the guitar, out of the composition and also to the right.

There is no formal perspective and there is no sense of where the background ends and the subject begins.

Figure 14.20 *Woman with a Guitar*, 1913, by Georges Braque, oil and charcoal on canvas, 130 × 73 cm, Centre Georges Pompidou, Paris. The mood is sober and although the guitar with strings is suggested, there is nothing frivolous about the image.

Dada

This complex international anti-war movement started in Zurich, Switzerland, among a group of artists and writers. It was a reaction to World War I and the nationalism that many thought had led to the war.

The movement ranged from performance art to poetry, photography, sculpture, painting and collage. It became a powerful influence on artists in many cities, including Berlin, Paris and New York, all of which had their own groups.

French poets André Breton and Louis Aragon established the Paris-based Dada. They had been medical students at a military hospital in Paris during the war.

The name came from the French word *dada* ('hobby horse'), chosen at random from a dictionary, partly for its nonsensical sound but also for its association with childhood freedom.

Writers and artists questioned a society that could start such a terrible war and, more alarmingly, how they could justify its continuation.

Artists believed that art was admired only for its material value rather than beauty or truth. They saw 'reason' and 'logic' as part of the problem, so they favoured imagination and randomness.

Dada Artists and Artworks

Marcel Duchamp (1887–1968)

As an alternative to representing objects in art, Marcel Duchamp presented the objects themselves as art. He selected mass-produced, commercially available objects, or 'readymades', which he designated as art by giving them titles like *Trébuchet (Trap)*, for a wood and metal coatrack (Fig. 14.22). He argued they were works of art because the artist chose to make them such.

The first of his 'readymades' was created in 1913, but he is best-known for the urinal, entitled *Fountain*, which he signed 'R. Mutt' (Fig. 14.21). He submitted this to an exhibition of the Society of Independent Artists in New York in 1917, where it created huge controversy.

His ideas disrupted centuries of thinking about the artist's role as a skilled creator of original handmade objects.

Figure 14.21 *Fountain*, copy 1966, original 1917, by Marcel Duchamp, ceramic, Philadelphia Museum of Art. Presenting everyday objects as art was meant to challenge the art establishment.

Note: By the early 1900s, Americans were using the term 'readymade' to distinguish manufactured items from those that were handmade.

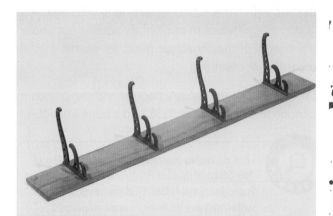

Figure 14.22 *Trébuchet* (Trap), 1917, by Marcel Duchamp. This was shown at the Bourgeois Art Gallery and Duchamp asked that it be placed near the entrance. Nobody noticed this piece of 'art' during the show.

Make your own 'readymade' by selecting three objects from your surrounding environment. Spend time choosing suitable titles and then take photos of your readymades along with their titles.

Did humour play a role in the titles you selected?

How did the titles affect the way you or others perceived these everyday objects as art?

Surrealism

Dada went a step further into the art of the subconscious, imagination and dreams with Surrealism. Louis Aragon's *Perpetual Motion: Poems (1920–1924)* became the manifesto for the new movement. Artists were also inspired by Sigmund Freud's book, *The Interpretation of Dreams* (1899), which suggested a complex and repressed inner worlds of sexuality, desire and violence.

Surrealist artists believed that creativity came from deep within the subconscious and that this was more authentic than conscious thought. They used psychoanalyst's techniques like dream analysis and automatic painting to access feelings and desires within the subconscious. In psychology, 'automatism' refers to involuntary actions not under the control of the conscious mind, for example dreaming or breathing.

Surrealism became widely popular and exhibitions in London and New York in 1936 had a huge impact.

 Look up *Hell* by Hieronymous Bosch (1504) and *The Sleep of Reason Produces Monsters* by Francisco Goya (1799). Find elements of these works that you think might have influenced Surrealist artists.

Surrealist Artists and Artworks

Salvador Dalí (1904–89)

Salvador Dalí was one of the 20th century's most infamous artists. A flamboyant figure, he was born in Figures, Spain, and experimented with Impressionism, Fauvism and Cubism before moving to Paris in 1926. He was introduced to the Surrealists by Joan Miró.

Dalí was intrigued by the mental images that occur between sleeping and waking. He experimented with ideas for generating and capturing these vivid or bizarre mind pictures.

His favourite technique was to put a tin plate on the floor and sit beside it holding a spoon. He would totally relax and when he began to doze the spoon would slip. The clang on the plate would wake him and set off images.

The Persistence of Memory

A set of melting clocks are scattered across the composition. Only a pocket watch, which remains closed, has retained its structure, but an army of ants cover this (Fig. 14.23).

The clocks evolving from solid to liquid exemplify one of the key concepts in the Surrealist movement: the transformative power of dreams and the Freudian emphasis on the dream landscape. For Dalí, these 'soft watches' suggest that the concept of time loses all meaning in the unconscious world.

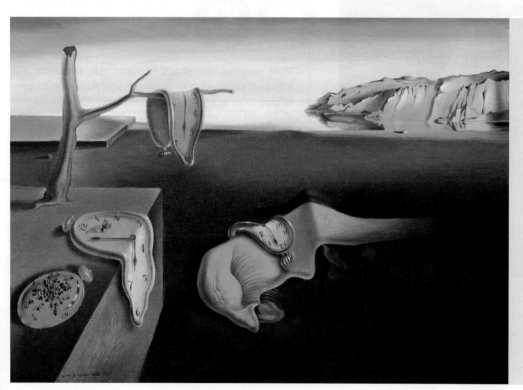

Figure 14.23
The Persistence of Memory, 1931, by Salvador Dali, oil on canvas, 24 × 33 cm, Museum of Modern Art, New York.

The scene may also allude to scientific advances like Einstein's Theory of Relativity, which referenced the distortion of space and time.

The clocks may symbolise the past, present and future, but they are not the only references to time in the painting. The sand refers to the sands of time and sand in the hourglass. The ants have hourglass-shaped bodies. The shadow that looms over the scene suggests the passing of the sun overhead, and the distant ocean may suggest timelessness or eternity.

The painting is one of Dalí's best-known works, but it is only slightly larger than a sheet of notepaper, approximately 24 cm × 33 cm.

Joan Miró (1893–1983)

Miró moved from Spain to Paris in 1919. He experimented with Fauvism, Cubism and Dadaism before signing the Surrealist manifesto in 1924. He developed automatic painting and created private symbols of fertility and nature.

Carnaval d'Arlequin

The long-necked white figure with a blue and red head is the harlequin, but otherwise the composition is full of unexplained, strange symbols. The viewer is left to find their own structures and meanings in this loosely arranged collection of shapes and forms (Fig. 14.24).

The images are painted in flat oil paint on a thin background. Miró made marks by using the automatic drawing technique and responded by changing or expanding them.

René Magritte (1898–1967)

Born in Belgium, Magritte was a leading figure in the Surrealist movement. His paintings are puzzles – nothing is ever as it seems.

On the Threshold of Liberty

The room is divided into panels, with seemingly unrelated images in each panel. A large field gun is placed in the foreground but, as always, we have no idea what anything means.

All the spaces are balanced from left to right. Only the gun, pointing diagonally at the female torso, breaks the harmony.

Figure 14.24
Carnaval d'Arlequin (Harlequin's Carnival), 1924–5, by Joan Miró, oil on canvas, 66 × 93 cm, Albright-Knox Art Gallery, New York.

Figure 14.25 *On the Threshold of Liberty*, 1937, by René Magritte, oil on canvas, 239 × 185 cm, Art Institute of Chicago.

Media and Areas of Practice

Collage

Collage was invented by Pablo Picasso and Georges Braque in 1912. The materials were fragments of the 'real world', which were given new and unreal roles in a flat, pictorial world.

Braque first added wood-grain effects and then Picasso introduced graphic art in the form of letters and numbers. Eventually they stuck objects, such as tickets, pieces of newspaper and printed images, to the surface.

Dada artists chose non-artistic methods like collage made of rubbish and photomontage using words and images cut from newspapers and magazines. These were placed in unlikely combinations.

Painting

Dalí and Magritte painted realistically in great detail. Dalí's oil-painting technique was smooth and accomplished and Magritte's images were almost photographic. This realism sometimes made the images all the more disturbing.

Art Elements and Design Principles

The Fauves rejected traditional methods of light and shade in favour of line and colour. To them, painting was first and foremost a flat surface to be covered with colours assembled in a certain order.

Cubism explored the notion that objects can be seen from many points of view at any one time. These multiple repeating shapes were used to create symmetry across the composition.

Dadaist works took the form of:

- assemblage with objects nailed, screwed or connected together
- readymades: manufactured objects with signatures or titles.

Surrealist Artists

Joan Miró's compositions are full of unexplained, strange symbols. The viewer is left to find their own structures and meanings in a loosely arranged collection of shapes and forms.

Automation

Joan Miró allowed his hand to move about unconsciously with a minimum of control while dribbling paint or making rubbings or scrapings. He then responded to the marks he made.

Dream Pictures

Salvador Dali and René Magritte painted carefully executed realistic scenes that made no rational sense. Objects were distorted and placed in odd combinations.

Analysis

Consider the broad range of styles and forms that developed in the new art movements of the early 20th century. Examine how these news ideas eventually led to abstract art and, in particular, why the use of new materials changed the perception of painting.

New art movements developed during a period of great change, when new technology was developing rapidly. World War I deeply affected art, and artists experimented in its aftermath as they looked at ever-more unconventional ways to express themselves.

New directions in modern art led to Surrealism, and the anti-art movement of Dada before eventually becoming completely abstract.

Chapter Review

1. How did new art movements respond to the work of Paul Cézanne, Vincent van Gogh and Paul Gauguin?

2. What was 'Primitivism' and how did this influence artists?

3. Why do you think new technology in the early 20th century encouraged so many new ideas in art?

4. How did modern works of art end up in art museums in both France and America?

5. Why do you think artists reacted to World War I by challenging so completely what a work of art can be?

6. Discuss the influence of Sigmund Freud's psychological theories and techniques like dreams and automation on art. Which element played a stronger role in Surrealist imagery?

7. Several objects represent the passing of time in *The Persistence of Memory* by Salvador Dalí (Fig. 14.23). What symbolic meaning do think the artist wanted to convey with this?

8. *Odalisque with Red Trousers* (Fig. 14.26) is one of a series painted following Matisse's visits to North Africa. What art elements in this work make it typical of the artist's style? How does it show the influence of Islamic art?

Figure 14.26 *Odalisque with Red Trousers*, 1924, by Henri Matisse, oil on canvas, 50 × 61 cm, Musée de l'Orangerie, Paris.

Further Research

www.bbc.com – Search for 'How a small African figurine changed art' for an overview of the development of Fauvism and Cubism

www.arthive.com/alphonsemucha – Browse Mucha's archive of work, including the poster for *Gismonda*

www.musee-orangerie.fr/fr – Learn about the history of the Walter-Guillaume Collection

www.youtube.com – Search for 'Picasso, *Les Demoiselles d'Avignon*' by Smarthistory (5:57) for an informative video about one of Picasso's most famous works

www.theartstory.org – Go to 'Artists' and find Henri de Toulouse-Lautrec to learn more about this unique artist

www.youtube.com – Search for 'Salvador Dalí at the MoMA: The Persistence of Memory' (7:06) for a closer look at the 'soft watches'

15

Modern Art in Germany

By the end of this chapter I will …

* understand the impact of political events in Germany in the early 20th century on art and society
* understand how separate Expressionist movements developed in Berlin and Munich
* be able to discuss the Bauhaus ideas for design in mass production
* understand how Expressionist artists tried to convey emotion
* be able to describe and discuss a typical Expressionist painting or print
* understand how World War I and its aftermath affected artists' work
* understand how 20th-century printmakers picked up on a long tradition in German art
* understand how the development of abstract art changed modern art.

Context

After the Franco-Prussian War of 1870–71, individual German states united and Wilhelm I of Prussia became Emperor. This happened in spite of significant geographical distance and religious, linguistic, social and cultural differences among the people.

The Prussian politician Otto von Bismarck had long wanted a single state, with Prussia at its core, and victory in the Franco-Prussian war presented the opportunity.

This new state, the *Kaiserreich*, dominated European politics at the close of the 19th century and start of the 20th, but defeat in the Great War forced the Kaiser into exile. Germany became a republic.

Berlin and Munich

As the capital city of Prussia, Berlin had come through a remarkable transformation during the 19th century. It developed even more rapidly after 1871 when it was assigned as official capital of the newly united Germany.

It was also a very confident period for Munich, the capital city of Bavaria.

In 1889, a group of young painters from Berlin took part in the Paris International Exhibition. In 1892, Norwegian artist Edvard Munch's work was exhibited in Berlin. An association of progressive artists called the Berlin Secession was established as a result.

> **Secession:** The breaking-away of younger and more radical artists from an existing academy or art group to form a new grouping.

Expressionism

Expressionism developed across various cities in Germany from about 1905. It responded to widespread social concerns that mankind had lost its way and that truth and spirituality no longer mattered.

Vincent van Gogh (see Chapter 13, p. 187) and Edvard Munch were particularly influential on the artists.

Expressionism was also inspired by the Symbolist ideas of late 19th-century art.

> **Symbolism:** This was both an artistic and a literary movement that suggested ideas through symbols and emphasised the meaning behind forms, lines, shapes, and colours.

Expressionist Groups

Die Brücke (The Bridge)

In 1905, four architecture students – Ernst Ludwig Kirchner, Erich Heckel, Karl Schmidt-Rottluff and Fritz Bleyl – founded a group in Dresden called *Die Brücke*. They saw themselves as transitional figures, connecting outdated German art traditions with Modernist ideals for the future.

The work became a form of social criticism and artists sometimes included people like sex workers as examples of those who suffered emotional isolation in the modern city (Fig. 15.1).

> **RESEARCH** Look up *Die Brücke*. Find out why the artists found the work of Matthias Grünewald (1470–1528), Albrecht Dürer (1471–1528) and James Ensor (1860–1949) influential. Find similarities and differences in the work of Ernst Ludwig Kirchner, Erich Heckel, Karl Schmidt-Rottluff and Fritz Bleyl.

Der Blaue Reiter (The Blue Rider)

The *Neue Künstlervereinigung München* (Munich New Artists' Association), or NKVM, was also a secession movement dedicated to forwarding ideas of Expressionism. In 1909, after a bitter disagreement, Wassily Kandinsky left the association to form *Der Blaue Reiter* with Franz Marc and Paul Klee as a more abstract counterpart to the style of *Die Brücke*.

Figure 15.1 *Berlin Street Scene*, 1913, by Ernst Ludwig Kirchner, oil on canvas, 121 × 95 cm, Neue Galerie, New York. The street life in Berlin captured Kirchner's eye and inspired a series of paintings.

Wassily Kandinsky is usually credited with having produced the first abstract picture around 1910. Unfortunately, this cannot be proved, as the painting is lost.

> **Abstract art:** A term used to describe 20th-century work in which the traditional European concept of art as imitation of nature has been abandoned. Abstract paintings do not represent any recognisable objects.

> **RESEARCH** Find out more about artist Hilma Af Klint and why she is now recognised as having produced the first abstract painting. A great starting point is the article 'The first abstract artist? (And it's not Kandinsky) Focus Hilma Af Klint', in the Tate Galleries' magazine, *Tate Etc*. Search for the article on **www.tate.org.uk/tate-etc**, click 'Browse all issues' and select 'Issue 27: Spring 1013' and the article above from the contents list.

Worpswede – An Artists' Colony

In 1884, the artist Fritz Mackensen became fascinated by the landscape of the Teufelsmoor area in northern Germany. It marked the beginning of an artists' colony in the little village of Worpswede outside of Bremen.

Art After World War I

Many artists, writers and intellectuals initially welcomed the war in 1914, either from a sense of patriotic duty or the opportunity for 'adventure'. Others believed the war was necessary to ensure future peace.

The dreadful reality of the war left an indelible mark on German art (Fig. 15.3). It became inward-looking, angry or even violent, especially during the chaotic years of the Weimar Republic in Germany (1919–33).

De Stijl (The Style)

This abstract, pared-down aesthetic movement developed in the Netherlands in response to World War I. It was an effort to bring harmony back to the shattered world. Artists chose simple forms with only the primary colours of red, yellow and blue, along with black and white (Fig. 15.16).

This visual language, considered appropriate for the modern era, was applied to sculpture, industrial design, typography and even literature and music. It also inspired the International Style of architecture (Fig. 15.2) in the 1920s and 1930s.

Aesthetics: A philosophy based on the appreciation of beauty, and what is pleasing to the senses.

Figure 15.2 Villa Tugendhat, Brno, Czech Republic, 1928–30, by Mies van der Rohe. Many aspects of the International Style had already been worked out by the architects of the De Stijl and Bauhaus movements.

Figure 15.3
Der Krieg (The War), 1932, by Otto Dix, oil on wood, 264 × 306 cm, Galerie Neue Meister, Dresden. Inspired by his horrific experiences in the trenches over ten years earlier, Otto Dix made a series of anti-war drawings, paintings and prints.

Innovation and Invention

The Bauhaus

The Bauhaus was the most influential art and design school of the 20th century (Fig. 15.4). Literally meaning 'building house', its approach to industry and society had a major influence on design education in Europe and the USA.

The school was founded in Weimar in Germany in 1919 to compete with British and American industry. Walter Gropius was its first director.

The intention was to unify art, craft and design in the production of useful objects and mass production. They adopted a slogan: 'Art into Industry'. It emphasised a strong understanding of basic design, especially the principles of composition, colour theory and craftsmanship.

In 1925, for political and financial reasons, the Bauhaus moved to Dessau. Walter Gropius designed the new buildings and a number of famous artists taught courses.

The Bauhaus style had five important characteristics:

1. **Form follows function**: This means that in design, a form should always be applied because of its function instead of its aesthetic appeal (Fig. 15.5).

2. **True materials:** Designers did not try to modify or hide materials for the sake of aesthetics.

3. **Minimalist style:** Bauhaus artists favoured linear and geometrical forms. Only line, shape and colours mattered.

4. **Gesamtkunstwerk:** The German word *Gesamtkunstwerk* means 'a work of art that makes use of all or many art forms'. The term is now accepted in English.

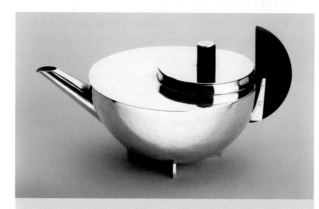

Figure 15.5 Teapot in silver and ebony, Bauhaus design, *c*. 1924, by Marianne Brandt. The clean lines and simple geometric shapes of this teapot are typical of Bauhaus designs for industry. The function of the teapot from its non-drip spout to the heat-resistant ebony handle was just as important as its appearance.

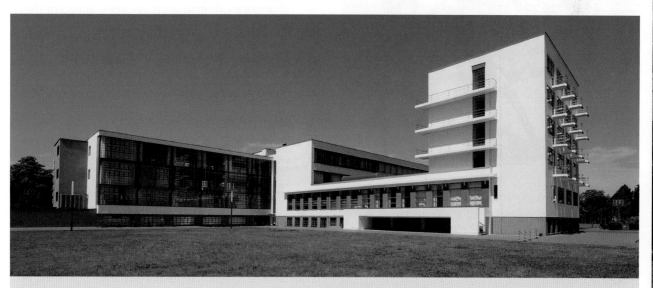

Figure 15.4 The Bauhaus Building, Dessau, Germany. The Bauhaus Building is a flat-roofed construction of steel and concrete. Three wings, arranged asymmetrically, connected the workshops and dormitories.

5. **Uniting art and technology:** In 1923, Bauhaus organised an exhibition called 'Art and Technology: A New Unity'. From then on, there was a new emphasis on technology and prototypes of products suitable for mass production.

Media and Areas of Practice

Printmaking

Expressionist artists are perhaps most famous for their printmaking. Germany had a long tradition in this medium, but the Expressionist artists, and later Max Beckmann (Fig. 15.6), revolutionised wood cutting, etching and lithography.

The Bauhaus used their own furniture and fittings. Tubular steel construction in lightweight, modern, stackable chairs became a standard worldwide before suitable plastics were invented (Fig. 15.7).

Bauhaus buildings, constructed in concrete, steel and glass, became a standard form of modern architecture.

Figure 15.6 *Group Portrait, Eden Bar*, 1923, by Max Beckmann, woodcut, 50 × 49 cm, Museum of Modern Art, New York. The bar in the Hotel Eden was a popular meeting place for Berlin's artistic and literary crowd in the 1920s. Tightly compressed into this angular composition, the patrons stare away from each other blankly, reflecting the alienation Beckmann perceived in Berlin's café society.

Figure 15.7
Cesca Chair/Knoll by Marcel Breuer. Tubular steel construction for furniture was invented in the Bauhaus by Breuer.

CREATE Find some examples of famous Bauhaus posters. Choose one of these as a inspiration for a poster design of your own choice. Include the Bauhaus Universal typeface as part of your design. Does your computer have a 'Universal' font?

Graphic Design

Some of the key elements of the Bauhaus style are still used in graphic design today. This includes:

- **Primary colours:** Or just black and white combined with a single colour, like red or blue.

- **Collage graphics:** Isolated figures and human features, like hands and eyes, giving them a Surrealist style.

- **Experimental layouts:** Bauhaus students were abandoning formal grids decades ahead of their time.

- **Geometric and minimalist typography:** Herbert Bayer's experimental Universal typeface is probably the best known of the Bauhaus types.

RESPOND How much do you think today's design industry today owes to the Bauhaus movement? Find examples that show this.

Art Elements and Principles of Design

Die Brücke is characterised by strangely shaped figures, bold colours and swirling, swaying, brushstrokes. This conveyed the artists' emotional reaction to the anxieties of modern living.

Figure 15.8 Cover design for *The Blue Rider Almanac*, 1911–12, by Wassily Kandinsky, watercolor, ink and pencil on paper, 27.9 × 21.9 cm, Städtische Galerie im Lenbachhaus, Munich.

Der Blaue Reiter compositions were dramatic, vibrant and chaotic with an underlying sense of violence and angst, but this also hinted towards spiritual harmonies (Fig. 15.8).

Abstract art developed in two basic ways. Artists reduced nature to very simplified forms, or used non-representational forms, like geometric shapes.

De Stijl was a completely abstract style, based on rectangles, verticals and horizontals.

Bauhaus instructors had high skill levels and understanding in their art or craft. Each had a unique interpretation of the underlining values.

- **Josef Albers** focused on formal qualities of harmony or balance, free or measured rhythms, geometric or arithmetic proportion, symmetry or asymmetry.

- **Wassily Kandinsky** encouraged his students to understand abstraction. His written theory 'Point and Line to Plane' was based on the analysis of individual art elements.

- **Paul Klee** concentrated on the theory of colour movement. His findings did much to change ideas on colour in the 20th century.

Artists and Artworks
Edvard Munch (1863–1944)

Edvard Munch grew up in rural Norway and studied in the Royal School of Art and Design of Kristiania (now Oslo).

His childhood was overshadowed by illness, death and depression in his family. Following his mother's death from tuberculosis when he was five years old, he became very close to his older sister Sophie. Unfortunately, she also died from the same disease some years later.

His father, a Christian fundamentalist who suffered from depression and anger, saw this as a punishment from God. All of this deeply affected the young artist, and his worries about human mortality, religion and sexual liberation were expressed in his mysterious, semi-abstract paintings.

Influence on German Expressionism

A painting of Sophie, during her last illness in 1885 (Fig. 15.9), was an important breakthrough in Munch's artistic career. He described this deeply emotional work as his farewell to Realism.

He visited Paris in 1889 and was captivated by the works of Paul Gauguin and Vincent van Gogh, but an invitation by the Union of Artists to exhibit in Berlin in 1892 presented him with a huge opportunity.

All however did not go so smoothly. The director of the Imperial Academy of Fine Arts in Berlin objected to the modern style and unfinished quality to his work, and the exhibition was closed. This also made Munch a celebrity with younger artists.

The exhibition went on to tour in Düsseldorf and Cologne, before returning to Berlin. Very few paintings were sold, but Munch earned quite a bit from ticket sales. He became part of the Berlin circle of intellectuals and artists before returning to Norway.

He continued to work until his death in 1944.

During the Nazi years, Munch's works were labelled 'degenerate art' and removed from German and Norwegian museums. Munch was deeply upset by this as he considered Germany his second home.

The Sick Child

The figure is centrally placed, and all detail has been stripped from the simple composition. The young girl's face is turned away and her gaze rests on the head of the older woman (Fig. 15.9). Their hands are tightly clasped.

The paint is applied with thick brushstrokes as well as fluid thin trickling lines. The surface of the canvas is scratched and scored, and the dull tones of green and brown emphasise the bright red hair against the white pillow.

Figure 15.9 *The Sick Child*, 1885–86, by Edvard Munch, oil on canvas, 120 × 119 cm, National Museum, Oslo.

The Scream

Munch was walking along a bridge overlooking Oslo at sunset when, in his own words, 'the faces

Figure 15.10 *The Scream*, 1893, by Edvard Munch, oil, tempera, pastel and crayon on cardboard, 91 × 74 cm, National Gallery, Oslo. Munch's most famous work depicts a conflict between the individual and society, and expresses the artist's most intimate emotions.

of my comrades became a garish yellow-white,' and 'the sky turned as red as blood. I stopped and leaned against the fence … shivering with fear. Then I heard the enormous, infinite scream of nature' (Fig. 15.10).

Composition

The picture is in two parts. The sharply plunging left-right diagonal lines of the bridge and its fence separates the figures walking and the anguished, central figure from the whirling chaos behind. The scream echoes beyond the bay and upwards towards the heavens.

Colour Contrasts

The dramatically falling lines contrast with the curves, lines and swirling brushstrokes. The skull-like figure, set against the colour contrasts of blood-red and orange sky and blues, transforms this otherwise beautiful sunset scene into an expression of fear and loneliness.

NEW APPRECIATING ART EUROPE AND THE WORLD

Make an Expressionist painting.

Examine the art elements of line, colour, texture and pattern in *The Scream* by Edvard Munch and *The Starry Night* by Vincent van Gogh (see Chapter 13, Fig. 13.9).

Taking these paintings as inspiration and in a subject of your own choice, use:
- contrasts of colour and line
- gestural and textured brushstrokes

to express emotion and convey an atmosphere such as joy, excitement, anxiety or sadness.

Ernst Ludwig Kirchner (1880–1938)

When Kirchner arrived in Berlin in 1911, life in the city inspired him to paint a dramatic series of works. They captured the energy with jagged strokes, dense forms and sharp colours.

Following his involvement in World War I, Kirchner had a nervous breakdown. He then moved to Switzerland and painted mainly landscapes.

In 1937, the Nazis condemned his work as degenerate and had much of it destroyed.

Self-Portrait as a Soldier

When war broke out in 1914, Kirchner volunteered to serve as a driver in the military, but was soon declared unfit for service due to issues with his general health. *Self-Portrait as a Soldier* shows his psychological distress and is a reference to van Gogh's *Self-Portrait with a Bandaged Ear*.

The eye, unseeing and empty, reflects the blue of his uniform and the nude figure in the background has a resemblance to his lover of the time, Erna Schilling (Fig. 15.12).

Figure 15.11 (left) *Self-Portrait with a Model*, 1910, by Ernst Ludwig Kirchner, oil on canvas, 150 × 100 cm, Kunsthalle, Hamburg. **Figure 15.12** (right) *Self-Portrait as a Soldier*, 1915, by Ernst Ludwig Kirchner, oil on canvas, 69 × 61 cm, Allen Memorial Art Museum, Ohio.

UNIT 5 MODERNISM (c. 1900–1960s)

The amputated, bloody arm is not a real injury, but a metaphor for an injury inflicted on his identity as an artist.

The painting can be compared to *Self-Portrait with a Model* (Fig. 15.11), painted before the war, which shows the young artist at the height of his confidence wearing a brightly coloured striped robe.

The shallow space and two-figure compositions are similar, but the artist in the later painting shows little connection with the model who looks more like a carved statue. The sharp, jagged lines, the dark, cold colours, and even the cigarette hanging limply from his lips contrast with the fuller, more rounded earlier figure confidently smoking his pipe.

Kirchner the soldier is surrounded by everything he needs to make art, but cannot do so.

> **Metaphor:** An object or action expressed in a way that isn't literally true, but helps explain an idea or make a comparison.

Franz Marc (1880–1916)

Franz Marc and Wasily Kandinsky met in 1911 in Munich and the two artists formed *Der Blaue Reiter* together. After their first exhibition, Marc invited members of the Berlin *Die Brücke* group to participate in a second show.

When World War I broke out in August 1914, Marc immediately enlisted. He was killed France in 1916.

In spite of his short career, he had a tremendous impact on the various Expressionist movements that came after World War I.

Marc turned away from modern life, from which he felt increasingly estranged, and focused instead on the natural world and animals. This offered meaning in his life.

He believed in a mystical relationship between colour and form. The glowing colour and rhythmic geometry of his paintings present an ideal and mystical world where everything is in harmony. He understood how colour could affect mood, and developed a specific theory of colour symbolism. He associated blue with the masculine, yellow with the feminine, and red with the physical – often violent – world.

Large Blue Horses

Marc's use of colour to symbolise man's relationship with nature is perfectly captured in *Large Blue Horses*. This is one of a suite of paintings made by the artist in 1911, which followed other primary-colour compositions like *Red Horses* and *Yellow Cow*.

In this semi-circular arrangement, the horses take up most of the canvas. They are formed with curving

Figure 15.13
Large Blue Horses, 1911, by Franz Marc, oil on canvas, 106 × 181 cm, Walker Art Center, Minneapolis.

lines; all are pointing to the left and are integrated with the foreground foliage and the contrasting red of the hilly landscape and yellow sky.

The horses are encircled, almost like a halo, by a pair of white lines. These long, abstract, free-floating lines are often present in Marc's work.

Wassily Kandinsky (1866–1944)

Born in Russia, Kandinsky gave up a legal career to become a painter, printmaker and art theorist. He trained in Munich and encouraged an interest in French avant-garde painting in his fellow students. In 1911, he established *Der Blaue Reiter* with Franz Marc.

Music and the idea of music appears everywhere in Kandinsky's work. He believed shades resonated with each other to produce visual 'chords' that had an influence on the soul.

The titles of his 'Compositions', 'Improvisations' and 'Impressions' made between 1907 and 1939 demonstrate this. The first three of the series were destroyed during World War II, but sketches and photographs show them to have been a cycle of 'symphonies'.

His specific theories on colour played a big part in enabling his imaginative leap into abstraction. He attributed particular emotional or 'spiritual' qualities to each shade.

Complete Abstraction

By 1914, Kandinsky had evolved a completely abstract style in which line, colour and shape were used independently of each other, and traces of subject matter had almost disappeared (Fig. 15.14).

At the outbreak of World War I, Kandinsky moved back to Russia, but he returned to Germany in 1921, where he took up a teaching post in the Bauhaus.

When the Nazis closed the Bauhaus in 1933, Kandinsky went to live in France.

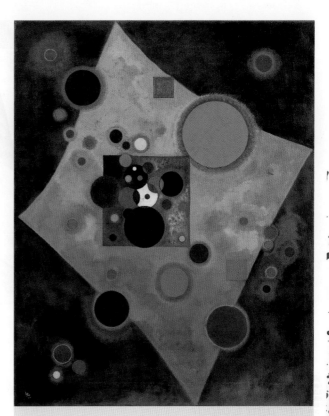

Figure 15.14 *Accent on Pink*, 1926, by Wassily Kandinsky, oil on canvas, 101 × 81 cm, Centre Georges Pompidou, Paris. This is a painting without traditional subject matter. Based on geometry, the free-floating shapes are nothing but themselves: harmonies in shape and colour.

Composition IV

This abstract painting has no subject other than its own shapes and colours, but there is a suggestion of a castle as well as human figures and landscape (Fig. 15.15).

Composition

The eye follows colour and line around the composition, picking up more details and points of interest in the centre of the canvas, then right to the two 'figures', and down through the two larger diagonal shapes to the bottom.

Style, Technique and Materials

The artist believed that colour affects the viewer in the same way as music and his painterly abstract style uses brushmarks and blended colour to create

Figure 15.15
Composition IV, 1911, by Wassily Kandinsky, oil on canvas, 160 × 251 cm, Kunstsammlung Nordrhein, Westfalen. There are still traces of figures and landscape in these early compositions.

a harmonious composition. Broad areas of blended colour are overlaid with strong, dark lines applied with a brush.

Line and Colour

Composition IV is a symphony of line and colour. The lines vary in thickness: some are heavy, like the two verticals that divide the composition; others are lighter, like the interlacing lines that suggest galloping horses on the top left.

Bright yellows and reds, which contrast with the softer tones of the sky, are outlined by black lines. Two elongated figures emerge from the bottom right against a blue hill with a castle on top. A rainbow in the middle left of the picture signifies a bridge.

Piet Mondrian (1872–1944)

The artist Piet Mondrian founded the magazine *De Stijl* in 1917 and became the leading exponent of the new style. He called it Neo-Plasticism ('new-forming').

Composition with Large Red Plane, Yellow, Black, Grey and Blue

In this abstract composition, blocks of colour and white in varying sizes are separated by black lines of different widths (Fig. 15.16). Everything is reduced to its most basic form in search of a universal harmony. Only primary colours with grey, black and

Figure 15.16 *Composition with Large Red Plane, Yellow, Black, Grey and Blue*, 1921, by Piet Mondrian, oil on canvas, 95 × 95 cm, Gemeentemuseum, The Hague.

white are used, but the flat colour and straight lines are painted very precisely in oil paints.

Paula Modersohn-Becker (1876–1907)

Paula Modersohn-Becker was one of the most important Worpswede artists. Like other women

Figure 15.17 *Seated Peasant Woman with Child on Her Lap*, 1903, by Paula Modersohn-Becker, oil on cardboard, 60 × 49.5 cm, Kunsthalle, Hamburg.

of the time, the young Paula Becker faced significant barriers in becoming an artist, but a lucky inheritance allowed her to study in Berlin. When she joined the artists' colony in Worpswede, she met Otto Modersohn, whom she later married.

Modersohn-Becker made several trips to Paris, where she was inspired by the work of Cézanne, Gauguin and van Gogh. Her own style was a blend of French Modernism and Germanic Humanistic ideals.

Modersohn-Becker had a very short career, but she completed more than 700 paintings and 1,000 drawings and prints. Her distinct style and daring subject matter made her a leading artist of her generation.

Mothers, babies and wistful children (Fig. 15.17) were Modersohn-Becker's favourite subjects. She felt both pity and admiration for Worpswede peasants with their great 'Biblical simplicity'. Her most radical step was in taking herself as a subject, and she became the first modern woman artist to

have depicted herself nude, and to have painted herself pregnant.

At the age of 31, Modersohn-Becker gave birth to a daughter. The new mother died two weeks later.

Self-Portrait with Amber Necklace

Modersohn-Becker portrays herself as strong and muscular like the peasant mothers in her paintings. She is crowned with pink flowers and wears an amber necklace.

The warm orange and pink flesh tones are set against the rich blues and greens of the background frieze.

Figure 15.18 *Self-Portrait with an Amber Necklace*, 1906, by Paula Modersohn-Becker, oil on canvas, 61 × 50 cm, Kunstmuseum, Basel.

Käthe Kollwitz (1867–1945)

Käthe Kollwitz's drawings, sculptures and prints are celebrated worldwide.

As a student, Käthe Schmidt studied at the Women's Academy in both Munich and Berlin. A series of

Figure 15.19 *The Widow I*, cover of the War portfolio, 1921, by Käthe Kollwitz, 37 × 24 cm, woodcut, Käthe Kollwitz Museum, Berlin.

etchings called *The Weavers* first brought her critical attention in 1898, and she joined the Berlin Secession in 1901. Schmidt remained part of the

movement until 1913, alongside Emil Nolde, Ernst Ludwig Kirchner and Max Beckmann.

Following marriage, she moved to a working-class area of Berlin, where her husband, Karl Kollwitz, worked as a physician. Käthe shared her studio space with his clinic, so his patients became the subject of her works, along with her own two sons.

The loss of her younger son, Peter, on a Belgian battlefield in October 1914 dominated Käthe Kollwitz's life and work from that point. She was a committed pacifist for the rest of her life.

In response to those 'unspeakably difficult years', she produced a series of seven woodcuts simply titled *Krieg* – War (Fig 15.19).

Under Nazi rule, Kollwitz's husband Karl was forbidden to work, and she was not allowed to exhibit. He died in 1940, and in 1942 their grandson, also named Peter, was killed while fighting with the German army in Russia.

Kollwitz was evacuated from her home in Berlin shortly before bombs destroyed the house and many of her works. She died in 1945.

The Volunteers

The only print of the War portfolio to show soldiers, *The Volunteers*, clearly demonstrates the sacrifices demanded in the name of honour and glory (Fig. 15.20).

Figure 15.20
The Volunteers, from the War portfolio, 1921, by Käthe Kollwitz, woodcut, 49 × 35 cm, Käthe Kollwitz Museum, Berlin.

Kollwitz's younger son, Peter, is next to the grotesque figure of Death.

Linked by a dramatic rainbow-like arc, the pared-down images of the young men are drifting in a trance-like state to the beat of a drum. The central figure with outstretched arms pushes the boy into the arms of death.

Otto Dix (1891–1969)

Unlike many of his contemporaries, Otto Dix lived through World War I, World War II and post-war Germany. This fed a deep-rooted interest in dark social contexts and the human types that emerge from them.

During his four years as a gunner in World War I, Dix witnessed casualties, destruction and senseless violence. Ten years after the conflict, he created a cycle of paintings and prints that shows the full horrors of trench warfare and the aftermath of battle, with the dead, dying, and shell-shocked

soldiers, bombed-out landscapes, and graves (Fig. 15.21).

After 1918, Dix turned towards social satire and developed a grotesque, exaggerated style associated with the *Neue Sachlichkeit* (New Objectivity) movement, whose artists sought to unsentimentally portray the social and political realities of the Weimar Republic.

Dix depicted World War I veterans with grossly distorted features, emphasising their war-damaged bodies, and said, 'I had the feeling that there was a dimension of reality that had not been dealt with in art: the dimension of ugliness.'

Max Beckmann (1884–1950)

Max Beckmann resisted any move towards abstraction and remained a figurative painter for his entire career. He had strong links with German Expressionism as well as Cubism, but refused to join either group.

His intense subject matter sought to convey the mysteries of human existence and numerous self-portraits are a moving record of the artist's inner

Figure 15.21 *Abandoned Position near Neuville*, 1924, by Otto Dix, etching and drypoint, 19 × 14 cm, Museum of Modern Art, New York.

Figure 15.22 *Night*, 1918, by Max Beckmann, oil on canvas 133 × 153 cm, Kunstsammlung Nordrhein-Westfalen, Düsseldorf, Germany. In a devastated Berlin, the city's inhabitants torture one another, clamp their eyelids shut, and dance frantically.

spirituality, but he never lost a firm belief in the strength of the human spirit.

He served as a medical corpsman in World War I. Like many he had believed war could cleanse the individual and society, but shocking images of the dead and maimed changed him. Completely disillusioned, his work depicted sordid, often horrifying imagery (Fig. 15.22).

Prosperity and public recognition helped him to recover, but under the Nazi regime Beckmann was classified as a 'degenerate'.

During his later years, he was recognised in America as a major force in modern art.

Analysis

Examine the reasons why Expressionism became one of the most influential 20th-century art movements. See how distortion of form and strong colours were used to express emotion.

Study paintings and prints of the *Die Brücke* and *Der Blaue Reiter* artists and note how they experimented with a new formalism and profound spirituality.

World War I profoundly affected German artists, and many turned to angry or even violent themes in reaction.

The Bauhaus was the most influential German art and design school in the 20th century. When it closed in 1933, some of the staff emigrated, which brought Bauhaus design to America. There, many of the leading architects and designers were accepted into American universities.

Chapter Review

1. Which Expressionist movements developed in Berlin and Munich?

2. Name and describe the five characteristics of Bauhaus design.

3. Compare and contrast the subject, composition and colours in Ernst Ludwig Kirchner's paintings of *Self-Portrait with a Model* (Fig. 15.11) to *Self-Portrait as a Soldier* (Fig. 15.12).

4. Describe and discuss an Expressionist painting that conveys an image of emotional isolation in the modern city.

5. Why do you think World War I and its aftermath affected German artists' work so much? Select an artist and artwork and compare this to a French artist's work from the same period.

6. Discuss how formal art elements are emphasised to create a harmonious composition in an abstract painting by Kandinsky.

7. Compare the theme, composition, medium and use of tone and line in *The Widow I* (Fig. 15.19) by Käthe Kollwitz and *Abandoned Position near Neuville* by Otto Dix (Fig. 15.21). Which of these images do you find most moving? Why is that?

8. Compare the composition, use of perspective and colour in *Evening on Karl Johan Street* by Edvard Munch (Fig. 15.23) with *The Scream* (Fig. 15.10). What significance do you think can be taken from the single figure who moves against the flow of traffic and walks in the middle of the street?

Figure 15.23
Evening on Karl Johan Street, 1892, by Edvard Munch, oil on canvas, 85 × 121 cm, KODE Art Museum of Bergen, Norway.

Further Research

German Expressionist Woodcuts, ed. Shane Weller, Collections of Fine Art in Dover Books, 1998

www.youtube.com – Watch 'Ernst Ludwig Kirchner: Germany's Picasso' (5:40) to find out more about this enigmatic figure

www.youtube.com – Watch 'Visual Analysis of Edvard Munch's The Scream' (6:52) for a look at the details in Munch's most famous work

www.edvardmunch.org – A website documenting Edvard Munch's paintings, biography and quotes

shop.bauhaus-movement.com – Search for 'Discover the Bauhaus' to learn how the movement influenced design history with its emphasis on theory and practice as taught by the masters

www.youtube.com – Search for 'PAULA: Film Clip (English)' (6:15) to see an extended trailer for a German film about Paula Modersohn-Becker

www.youtube.com – For more on Max Beckmann, watch 'Max Beckmann - A Close Look at His Work | Arts 21' (5:08)

www.moma.org/artists/429 – Search for Max Beckmann at the Museum of Modern Art (MoMA) in New York. Follow the links on the site to learn more about this important Modernist painter, printmaker, draftsman and writer

www.ottodix.org – The Online Otto Dix project

16

Modern Art in America

By the end of this chapter I will ...

* understand why the centre of artistic activity shifted to New York
* be aware of the importance of art collectors and museums in the promotion of artists and their work
* understand how politics was influenced by the new movement of Abstract Expressionism
* be able to discuss the formal elements of an Abstract Expressionist work.

Context

The Nazis' repressive artistic programmes caused significant changes in European artistic development. Many leading avant-garde artists left for America, taking their ideas with them.

The United States was largely unscathed by the war and while Europe was recovering, the American economy rose rapidly. New York and then California emerged as important centres of artistic activity and for the first time America developed its own major art movement that became known as Abstract Expressionism.

Peggy Guggenheim – Art Collector

Bohemian and socialite Peggy Guggenheim (Fig. 14.7 and 16.1) was a collector of Surrealist and Dada art. By 1938, she had left Paris and was living in London where she opened the Guggenheim Jeune Gallery. She had further plans for London, but the outbreak of World War II intervened. However, she continued

Figure 16.1 Peggy Guggenheim and the Art of This Century Gallery.

to travel to Paris, collecting works of modern art and left only days before the German invasion in 1940. She arrived in New York along with hundreds of artworks and opened her Art of This Century Gallery in 1942, showcasing the work of European artists like Kandinsky, Miró and Braque.

Austrian architect Frederick Kiesler designed the interior with concave walls and protruding, razor-thin wooden frames. This gave the paintings the appearance of free-floating within the gallery.

The gallery was short-lived, but it played a crucial part in launching the careers of many American artists, including Jackson Pollack. Guggenheim moved back to Europe in 1947 and settled in Venice.

The Museum of Modern Art (MoMA), New York

New York's Museum of Modern Art – or MoMA – was key to the promotion of new American art.

The idea of a museum for modern art came from a group of wealthy women in 1929. Known as the 'daring ladies', their primary purpose was to educate the public in Modern European art.

The first director, Alfred H. Barr Jr, was a huge fan of the Bauhaus and of Picasso. He greatly expanded the

institution and, in 1934, he hired a young, formally trained curator named Dorothy Canning Miller.

MoMA moved to its permanent home on West 53rd Street, New York in 1939. The building was designed by Philip Goodwin and Edward Durell Stone, who were known for their innovative 'International Style'.

Politics and Art

During the Cold War of the late 1940s to the 1960s, America was seen as an economic and military power that defended the 'free world' against the threat of Communism. Abstract Expressionism was officially recognised as a sign of a modern, liberal America to show abroad.

Women and the Male Art World

In the USA in the 1940 and 1950s, artistic independence was considered incompatible with female identity. Although women regularly exhibited in New York galleries, they were still marginalised.

This attitude can be noted in particular by a very famous photograph from 1950 (Fig. 16.3). A group of American abstract artists had signed an open

Figure 16.2
MoMA, New York, designed by Philip Goodwin and Edward Durell Stone.

Figure 16.3 The Irascibles. The iconic group photograph appeared in *Life* magazine and established the artists as the first generation of the Abstract Expressionist movement.

letter to the president of the Metropolitan Museum of Art, rejecting the museum's exhibition American Painting Today and complaining about the selection of the jury of works in the show. They noted that several jurors were openly biased against abstraction and that one had even called abstract art 'unhuman'.

The letter was published on the front page of *The New York Times*. The next day, *The Herald Tribune*, a competing paper, published an article defending the Met. This labelled the signatories 'The Irascible 18', a label that greatly helped the artists become better known.

Hedda Sterne, the only woman in the famous photograph, said of the artists in 1981: 'They all were very furious that I was in it because they all were sufficiently macho to think that the presence of a woman took away from the seriousness of it all.'

Innovation and Invention

Abstract Expressionism was an intensely creative and innovative development that took place in New York in the 1940s and 1950s. The huge scale and romantic mood of Abstract Expressionist paintings were seen to embody the American spirit of rugged individual freedom. Also known as the New York School, it was the first American art movement to achieve global recognition as New York overtook Paris as the world centre for innovation in modern art.

For decades, the art market had been dominated by European art, but the flow was badly disrupted by the war and Paris had not recovered from occupation by the Nazis. Demand for contemporary American art had never been that strong, but galleries and magazines now began to promote new works from the USA.

New American Painting Exhibition

Dorothy Miller curated six different shows devoted to Modern and Abstract American artists between the early 1940s and mid-1960s. She also curated the ground-breaking New American Painting exhibition that visited eight European countries in 1958–9. This forever changed the way Europeans viewed American art.

Find out more about Alfred H. Barr Jr, Dorothy Miller, and the artists that became successful due to promotion by MoMA. Refer to Chapter 18, page 244 to see how the exhibition New American Painting influenced artists in London.

Media and Areas of Practice

Within American Abstract Expressionism, there were two broad groups: Action Painting and Color Field Painting.

Action Painting

The term 'Action Painting' related to an artist's inner impulses that directed their actions in an energetic and impulsive manner. Highly influenced by Surrealism and automation, they improvised as they went along, using large brushes and gestural, expressive brushstrokes. Sometimes they even splashed and dripped paint onto canvas.

The American art critic Harold Rosenberg first used the term 'The American Action Painters' in *ARTnews* in December 1952. According to Rosenberg, the act of creation was more important than the work itself.

Action painter Jackson Pollock sometimes used sand, broken glass, pebbles, string, nails and other 'foreign matter' on the surface. He also famously danced around the canvas while pouring paint from the can or trailing it from the brush or a stick.

Color Field Painting

Within the Abstract Expressionism movement, there was a small but distinct group of painters who became known as the Color Field painters. Their working method was very different from the gestural mark-making of the Action painters and was characterised by large areas of a more or less flat single colour.

The American scholar Irvine Sandler used the title 'Color Field Painters' for a chapter in his book, *Abstract Expressionism*, published in 1970. It dealt with the work of three abstract painters who worked in the 1950s and 1960s: Mark Rothko, Barnett Newman and Clyfford Still. These artists were deeply interested in religion and myth.

Art Elements and Principles of Design

Clement Greenberg was arguably the most influential American art critic of the second half of the 20th century. He championed Jackson Pollock and fully supported Abstract Expressionism. In his 1960 essay, 'Modernist Painting', he explained his concept of formalism.

He argued that the 'rationale' of Modernist painting, like all the Modernist arts, was to employ its own methods to criticise itself and establish its area of competence more firmly.

According to Greenberg, painting could not:

- be three-dimensional, because this was the domain of sculpture
- be representational, because this was the domain of literature
- generate dramatic effects outside its material, because this was the domain of theatre.

The second aspect of painting's critique of itself was a stress on the limitations that constitute the medium of painting. These limitations consisted of three things:

- the rectangular shape of the supports
- the properties of pigment (paint)
- the flat surface of the support.

The flatness of the support was the most important limitation because, according to Greenberg, flatness was unique to the medium of painting.

He believed the artist was engaged in a natural and unstructured 'struggle' with painting. Gestural marks with roughly worked, thick *impasto* paint was evidence of this.

Artists and Artworks
Jackson Pollock (1912–1956)

Arriving in New York in 1930 as a young art student from Los Angeles, Jackson Pollock quickly became absorbed by Surrealism and the subconscious. He was, however, an unstable, solitary character, who struggled with alcoholism for most of his life.

As his work developed, he abandoned all shape and form and painted in a completely spontaneous manner. His technique of flinging, dripping and flicking thinned enamel paint onto an unstretched canvas laid on the floor brought him international fame in 1947.

He argued: 'The painting has a life of its own. I try to let it come through with actions.' He preferred to 'express feelings rather than illustrate them'.

Figure 16.4
One: Number 31, 1950,
by Jackson Pollock, oil and
enamel paint on canvas,
270 × 531 cm, Museum of
Modern Art, New York.

He said: 'On the floor I am more at ease. I feel nearer, more a part of the painting since this way I can walk around it, work from the four sides and literally be in the painting.'

One: Number 31

A landmark in the history of Abstract Expressionism, *One: Number 31* is one of Pollock's largest and most famous works (Fig. 16.4). It was one of three wall-sized paintings produced in quick succession in 1950.

Pollock's skill and technical prowess can be seen in the looping cords of colour that animate and energise every part of the composition. Despite its enormous size, it appears to expand even more in the eyes of the viewer.

Lee Krasner

Lee Krasner met Jackson Pollock in 1936 and became an important influence on his career. They supported each other during a period when neither's work was well appreciated. They married in 1945.

Krasner painted abstractly but rejected the idea that her work had no content. She 'wouldn't dream' she said of creating a painting from a fully abstract idea.

She was a central figure of Abstract Expressionism but had problems both as a woman artist and as the wife of Pollock. As late as 1958, she was referred to as 'Mrs Jackson Pollock'. It was even noted in one publication that was she was 'primarily a housewife'.

Figure 16.5
Gaea, 1966, by
Lee Krasner,
oil on canvas,
175 × 319 cm,
Museum of
Modern Art,
New York.

She signed her works simply 'L.K.'

She took over Pollock's legacy after he died in 1956, at the age of 44. She promoted his work and donated some to New York's Museum of Modern Art (MoMA).

Today, Krasner's work (Fig. 16.5) is accepted on its own terms. Unfortunately, she did not live to see a long-planned retrospective of her own work at MoMA in 1984.

Willem de Kooning

Willem de Kooning was one of the most prominent and celebrated Abstract Expressionist painters. He was famous for his bold, spontaneous brushwork, clashing colours and *impasto* textures. He typified the energetic, gestural painting style of the New York school, and fused elements of Cubism, Surrealism and Expressionism in his work.

Holland

Born in Holland in 1904, de Kooning was quite poor growing up, but he took evening classes at the Rotterdam Academy of Fine Arts and Applied Sciences. His rigorous training in both fine and commercial art continued to underpin even his most abstract creations.

When he moved to America in 1926, he worked as a house decorator. Large brushes and fluid paints remained part of his art even after he no longer needed to paint houses for money.

He remained committed to a blend of figuration and abstraction, but was criticised by Abstract Expressionist purists for what they saw as a conservative return to figure painting. He responded by stating, 'Even abstract shapes must have a likeness.'

Glimpses

Unlike other Abstract Expressionists, de Kooning was inspired by observation. Glimpses of the world around him, such as bits of colour or random objects seen while passing through Manhattan or Long Island, could inspire a painting or an entire series.

He would rework paintings over and over, letting mistakes guide the next step.

Women

In his *Women* series, de Kooning developed a wide, toothy smile from a mouth seen briefly in a magazine. He was inspired by van Gogh and Picasso's women and Renaissance Madonnas. During the 1940s, he also spent a good deal of time in New York's Metropolitan Museum where he studied portraits by Jean-Auguste-Dominique Ingres.

Woman 1

In this parody of male sexual preference, the face and massive pillow-like breasts are an obvious exaggeration of clichéd, stereotypical images of women. The wide-open eyes, virtually lipless mouth and long teeth creates an image of a strangely fixed grin rather than a smile (Fig. 16.6).

Figure 16.6 *Woman 1*, 1950–52, by Willem de Kooning, oil and metallic paint on canvas, 193 × 147 cm, Museum of Modern Art, New York. To prepare for this work De Kooning produced drawing and collages. It took two years to complete, during which time he prepared huge quantities of paint and continuously altered the colours and textures.

Colour

Painted in a blend of sweeping brushstrokes, colour is the essential element. Thick, lustrous strokes ranging from yellow, orange, green and blues, to pink with white and grey, go off in multiple directions, create a dazzling impression of activity.

Technique

The surface is built up with angular strokes, streaks and slashes, all executed vigorously. A mainly black outline distinguishes the form from the background. The textured surface shows that the artist painted it over several times with *impasto* layers of oil paint thinned with kerosene and even water.

Working fast and energetically, he applied, smeared and removed paint with spatulas and knives.

Elaine de Kooning

Elaine Fried was introduced to Willem de Kooning in 1938. She was just 20, and already greatly admired the 34-year-old's artwork. The couple married in 1943.

De Kooning successfully infiltrated the male-dominated New York art scene to become closely associated with Abstract Expressionism in the 1940s and 1950s. She was a prolific and versatile painter, writer and teacher who, over the course of her 40-year career, painted a wide range of subjects in both abstract and figurative styles. Portraiture was her passion, and men were her longest-running fascination.

The ultimate male subject was President John F. Kennedy. A commission to paint his portrait turned the tide in her career and made her name as recognisable as her husband's.

Portrait of President John F. Kennedy

De Kooning flew to Kennedy's 'Winter White House' in Palm Beach, Florida and made numerous sketches from late 1962 through early 1963. She described him as 'incandescent, golden – bigger than life' (Fig. 16.7).

Composition

The massive 120 cm × 240 cm canvas is a lean, vertical portrait of traditional dimensions.

Figure 16.7 *John F. Kennedy*, 1963, by Elaine de Kooning, oil on canvas, 120 × 240 cm (cropped view), National Portrait Gallery, Washington D.C. De Kooning was still working on her portrait in November 1963 when the president was assassinated. She was so emotionally affected by his death that it took her months to return and complete the painting.

The seated Kennedy looks up while turning a page of a book in his lap, as though the artist has caught him off-guard. He leans forward towards her in a gesture of familiarity.

De Kooning took her sketches back to her New York studio where she laboured for months over the portrait. In the end, however, she managed to convey his restlessness in gestural rhythms of loose brushstrokes, in a semi-abstract style.

Mark Rothko

Mark Rothko spent many years searching for a style that would adequately express his ideas. Eventually his style matured into rectangular fields of shimmering colour and light.

Marcus Rothkovich was born in Dvinsk, Russia (now Latvia), but like other Jewish families, they had to leave. They came to the United States in 1910 when Mark was a young boy, but his father died within a few months. This made life hard growing up and he had to leave school early for work. Later, he was awarded a scholarship to Yale which he did not complete.

Throughout his life he remained preoccupied with politics and retained the social revolutionary ideas of his youth. He was also heavily influenced by the philosophies of Nietzsche, Greek mythology and his Russian-Jewish heritage.

Note: Friedrich Nietzsche was a 19th-century German classical scholar, philosopher and critic. He became one of the most influential of all modern thinkers.

His signature style was very strong in formal elements such as colour, shape, balance, depth, composition and scale, but Rothko always maintained that his art was full of content and brimming with ideas. It was intended to convey a sense of spirituality.

Rothko felt words were inadequate to explain his ideas. He preferred to let the works speak in silence, but his strong views clashed with the established art world. This sometimes caused him to refuse commissions, sales and exhibitions.

In 1958, he agreed to provide murals for the Four Seasons, a new luxury restaurant in New York's Seagram building, but he developed doubts about whether a restaurant was an appropriate setting. The commission was then withdrawn.

The works, which are still known as the 'Seagram Murals', were donated by the artist to the Tate Gallery in London.

Red on Maroon

Rothko said of his *Red on Maroon* mural: 'I was much influenced subconsciously by Michelangelo's walls in the staircase room of the Medicean Library in Florence. He achieved just the kind of feeling I'm after.'

Composition

The muted maroon forms a base colour and over this a large red rectangle encloses a narrower maroon rectangle, suggesting a window-like structure. This simplified composition of unbroken colour produces a flat plane (Fig. 16.8).

Colour

The red paint forms a solid block of colour, but the edges seep slightly, blurring into the areas of maroon. Different pigments have been used within the maroon, blending shades of crimson and mauve

Figure 16.8 *Red on Maroon*, 1959, by Mark Rothko, oil paint, acrylic paint and glue tempera on canvas, 239 × 267 cm, Tate Modern Gallery, London. The 'Seagram Murals' have since been displayed almost continuously at the Tate, albeit in different arrangements, in what is commonly termed the 'Rothko Room'.

colour. This changing tone creates a sense of depth in an otherwise abstract composition.

Analysis

Study the paintings of the Abstract Expressionists and examine how gestural brushstrokes created an impression of spontaneity.

Compare the style and techniques of the Action painters to those of the Colour Field painters and consider why this American movement is particularly associated with a 'macho' image of a paint-splattered man.

The flow of European artwork to America had stopped during World War II when Paris was occupied by the Nazis. American art became stronger in response and, after the war, the centre of artistic activity shifted to New York.

Abstract Expressionism was the first truly American international art movement, and it was strongly supported by the Museum of Modern Art in New York. However, it presented a problem for younger artists who wanted to move beyond its stifling hold on intellectual ideas.

After Modernism

From around 1960, a more purely abstract form of Color Field painting emerged, in which a special role was played by the artist Helen Frankenthaler. She is perhaps the only female artist who was admitted to have had a decisive influence on the subsequent development of non-figurative art.

Mountains and Sea (Fig. 16.9) caused a sensation and established her career in 1952. Inspired by a trip to Nova Scotia, this large painting had the appearance of watercolour but was, in fact, oil paint that had been heavily diluted with turpentine. The colours were poured directly onto unprepared canvas so that they soaked into the material.

Frankenthaler's characteristic 'soak-stain' painting technique emphasised the flatness of the medium and pointed the way for a new direction in modern painting. It differed from Abstract Expressionism in that it eliminated both the emotional, mythic or religious content of the earlier movement, and the highly personal and painterly or gestural application associated with it. This influenced younger artists in a second generation of Abstract Expressionists.

Figure 16.9
Mountains and Sea, 1952, by Helen Frankenthaler. Oil and charcoal on unsized, unprimed canvas, 219.4 × 297.8 cm. Collection Helen Frankenthaler Foundation, New York, on extended loan to the National Gallery of Art, Washington, D.C.

Clement Greenberg entitled this 'Post-Painterly Abstraction', a term often also used to describe the work of the 1960s generation and their successors.

Chapter Review

1. How was art in America affected by World War II?

2. Who supported American art and how was it promoted?

3. What is meant by the term 'Action painting'?

4. Describe and discuss the concepts that led to Abstract Expressionism.

5. Does Willem de Kooning's *Woman 1* make fun of male sexual preferences, or is it just a grotesque depiction of a woman? What do you think?

6. Mark Rothko always said his paintings were full of meaning. Do you agree? Why?

7. Do you think Elaine de Kooning captured the personality of John F. Kennedy? Why do you think that?

8. Look at *No. 8* by Mark Rothko (Fig. 16.10). Is this an Action painting or a Color Field painting? Discuss the painting with reference to the formal elements of line, colour, tone, shape and pattern. Compare this to Rothko's later 'Seagram Murals'. What might the artist have wished to convey with these brighter colours?

Figure 16.10 *No. 8*, 1949, by Mark Rothko, oil and mixed media on canvas, 228.3 x 167.3 cm, National Gallery of Art, Washington D.C.

Further Research

www.youtube.com – In the summer of 1950, Hans Namuth, a German-born photographer, captured the essence of Pollock's work in a ten-minute film, simply called *Jackson Pollock 51*. Search for 'Jackson Pollock by Hans Namuth' (10:14) to see it

www.artsy.net – Search for '11 Female Abstract Expressionists You Should Know, from Joan Mitchell to Alma Thomas'

www.tate.org.uk – Search for 'Art Term Abstract Expressionism' to explore the movement's art and artists

www.youtube.com – Watch 'Portrait in a Minute: Elaine de Kooning – National Portrait Gallery' (4:33) to learn more about Elaine de Kooning

www.youtube.com – Watch 'Helen Frankenthaler, Mountains and Sea, 1952 by Smarthistory' (4.29) to learn more about the artist's celebrated soak-stain technique

Unit 6
Post-1960s Art

Before

Modernism in Europe
(1918–1939)

Accent on Pin
1926, Wassily
Kandinsky

American Regionalism
(1930–40)

American Got
1930, Grant
Wood

Social Realism in
America (1930–40)

Nighthawks,
1942, Edward
Hopper

Abstract Expressionisr
(1946–60)

One: Number
1950, Jackson
Pollock

Pop Art (1955–70)

Marilyn Dipty
1962, Andy
Warhol

Contemporary Art
(1960–2000)

Harran II,
1967,
Frank Stella

Maman,
2000, Louise
Bourgeois

The Pont Neu
Wrapped, Par
1975–85, Chr
and Jeanne-
Claude

Technological
Developments and Art
(2000–10)

Love is Calling
2013, Yayoi
Kusama

Post-Internet Art

The Katastwo
Karavan, 2017
Kara Walker

Post-1960

Art in America

* understand how changes in 1960s society influenced art
* understand why artists reacted against Abstract Expressionism
* have examined the reasons for the development of Pop Art
* be able to analyse a Pop Art work
* understand the concept of Minimalism
* understand how ideas can be works of art
* be able to relate Land Art with other Conceptual Art ideas.

Figure 17.1 *American Gothic*, 1930, by Grant Wood, oil on beaverboard, 78 × 65 cm, Art Institute of Chicago. The painting was inspired by 15th-century Flemish Renaissance art, which the artist had seen in Europe in the 1920s.

Before 1960

American Regionalists

Modernist art in America in the early 20th century had been dominated by European developments, which were centred in Paris.

Some painters like Grant Wood, however, deliberately turned their attention back home towards the hard-working rural population of America during the Great Depression. *American Gothic* (Fig. 17.1) brought him instant fame in 1930.

Note: The Great Depression was the worst economic downturn in US history. It began with the stock market crash of October 1929. By 1933, unemployment was at 25 per cent and more than 5,000 banks had gone out of business.

Social Realism

Urban life was reflected in art at a time of heightened racial conflict and the rise of fascism internationally.

The teachings of German philosopher Karl Marx, and the Russian political leader Vladimir Lenin inspired artists with left-wing sympathies.

When President Franklin Delano Roosevelt instigated a Works Progress Administration (WPA), artists began painting murals in the city. This gave them a purpose and a sense of community.

Note: **Karl Marx** (1818–83) was a German economist, sociologist and philosopher. He was also an influential Communist thinker.

Vladimir Lenin (1870–1924) was founder of the Russian Communist Party, leader of the 1917 Revolution and was the first head of the Soviet state.

Frida Kahlo (1907–54) was with her husband, Diego Rivera. While he was painting murals she painted *Self-Portrait on the Borderline between Mexico and The United States* (Fig. 17.2).

The couple returned to Mexico and Frida became known for her brutally honest self-portraits.

 RESEARCH Self-portraits by Frida Kahlo. Find out how these depictions reflected the frustration and life-long pain that followed her injuries received in a bus accident as a young woman.

Edward Hopper (1882–1967) was a Realist who offered a deep insight into the isolation of life and real human experience in the modern city. His figures are often disconnected from their environments, often by glass windows, and there is usually an emotional undercurrent that suggests a psychological inner life (Fig. 17.3).

Andrew Wyeth (1917–2009) was one of America's most popular Realist painters of the 20th century. His scenes of everyday life in rural Pennsylvania and

Figure 17.2
Self-Portrait on the Borderline between Mexico and the United States, 1932, by Frida Kahlo, oil on metal, 31 × 35 cm, Detroit Institute of Arts. This was the artist's response to the conflict she observed between nature and industry.

Figure 17.3
Nighthawks, 1942,
by Edward Hopper,
oil on canvas,
84 × 152 cm, Art Institute
of Chicago. The people in
a downtown diner late at
night are seen through a
large glass window. The
exteriors of the buildings
across the street are also
depicted.

Maine were also quite mysterious (Fig. 17.4). He worked mainly in watercolour and tempera instead of the more typical oil or acrylic.

Wyeth's reputation declined in the 1960s, but the artist had no wish to change his style to suit new trends in art.

Georgia O'Keeffe (1887–1986) was an important modern American artist with links to European avant-garde movements of the early 20th century.

Figure 17.4 *Christina's World*, 1948, by Andrew Wyeth, tempera on panel, 82 × 121 cm, Museum of Modern Art, New York. Wyeth was inspired by his neighbour, Anna Christina Olson, who as a young girl developed a degenerative muscle condition that left her unable to walk. She refused a wheelchair, preferring to crawl. Wyeth wanted to 'do justice to her extraordinary conquest of a life which most people would consider hopeless'.

Figure 17.5 *From the Faraway, Nearby*, 1937, by Georgia O'Keeffe, oil on canvas, 91 × 102 cm, Metropolitan Museum, New York. The poetic title suggests longing and loneliness in an emotional state of mind as well as a physical location.

Her primary subjects were landscapes, flowers and bones. They related mostly to the places in which she lived, especially the landscape of New Mexico, where she spent her summers painting before returning to New York in winter to exhibit her work (Fig. 17.5). She moved to New Mexico permanently in 1949.

O'Keeffe's art was based on intense observation of nature, experimentation with scale, and subtle use of line and colour. From the 1940s through the 1960s in particular, her work was outside the mainstream but she remained true to her own vision.

Abstract Expressionism

American Abstract Expressionism became an internationally recognised movement in 1952 (see Chapter 16).

The artists were supported and promoted by:

- the Museum of Modern Art, New York
- Peggy Guggenheim's Art of This Century gallery in New York
- Betty Parsons, an influential art dealer with her own gallery
- Clement Greenberg, an influential art critic who was fundamental to the success of the movement.

An exhibition called New American Painting toured Europe in 1958 and 1959. This firmly established the importance of contemporary American painting.

Pop Art

The dominance of Abstract Expressionism caused problems for younger American artists with new ideas. They felt excluded from what they saw as a small, elitist group, who were out of step with the new consumer society.

This gave rise to Pop Art in the late 1950s and early 1960s.

Context

After World War II, the United States and the Soviet Union were the world's superpowers. Although they never declared war on each other, they fought a war of ideas called the Cold War throughout the 1950s and 1960s. They also fought indirectly through involvement in the Korean War and the Vietnam War, the development of nuclear weapons (the arms race), and through space technology (the space race) in which man eventually landed on the moon.

The 1960s was one of the most turbulent and divisive decades in world history. A 'generation gap' developed between young and old, and unrest came with civil rights demands for African Americans, anti-war protests and the political assassinations of John F. Kennedy, Robert Kennedy and Martin Luther King, Jr.

Contemporary Art

Put simply, the term 'contemporary art' refers to art produced today. However, this definition can be a bit fuzzy. Most art historians accept the late 1960s or early 1970s as the decade when artistic values changed, from Modernist to Postmodernist.

Postmodernist art is sometimes used as an alternative word for contemporary art.

Pop Art in Britain

The term 'Pop Art' originated in Britain in the 1950s. Popular culture from America, like movies, comic books and advertising, began to influence society and art.

Just what is it that makes today's homes so different, so appealing? (Fig. 17.6) is considered to be the first genuine work of Pop Art. The collage was created by Richard Hamilton for the catalogue of an exhibition at London's Whitechapel Gallery, entitled 'This is Tomorrow'.

Find out why Richard Hamilton is considered to be the first Pop Artist, and what influenced his art.

Figure 17.6
Just what is it that makes today's homes so different, so appealing?, 1956, by Richard Hamilton, collage, 26 × 25 cm, Kunsthalle Tübingen, Germany. Images were cut from American magazines for a modern Adam and Eve. They are surrounded by all the consumer items considered necessary for the good life – or temptation.

Innovation and Invention

Pop Art in America reflected the new popular culture of music, advertising and consumerism.

Neo-Dada was a term applied to artists during the 1950s. This was a reference to the early 20th-century Dada movement (see Chapter 14, p. 208). During World War II, the French Dada artist Marcel Duchamp had moved to New York. By 1950, his ideas were becoming increasingly influential on younger artists in their use of new materials such as found objects.

Conceptual Art developed as boundaries were pushed out and new experimental forms of visual art began to develop.

Minimalism developed in the 1960s, but it is still prevalent today. The basic idea was to keep personal expression and artistic input to an absolute minimum.

The Feminist Art movement emerged in the late 1960s amidst the fervour of anti-war demonstrations, civil and gay rights movements.

Contemporary Art Movements
Land Art

Also known as Earth Art, Land Art was part of the wider Conceptual Art movement in the 1960s and 1970s. Creating site-specific art was a very new idea.

> **Land Art:** Site-specific art designed specifically for a particular location.

Pop Art

Pop Art developed in New York City along with the spread of pop music and youth culture, it was brash, young, and fun. In direct contrast to the heavy intellectualism of Abstract Expressionism, the bold, simple, everyday imagery and vibrant block colours gave works a modern 'hip' feel.

Jasper Johns and **Robert Rauschenberg** laid the foundations in the 1950s by questioning how we look at, perceive and make art.

Pop Artists and Artworks
Jasper Johns (b. 1930)

Johns was influenced by Dada ideas and in particular by Marcel Duchamp's found objects or 'readymades' (see Chapter 14). Johns used 'found images' like flags, targets, letters and numbers.

Jaspar Johns' art was *about* art, and this broke down traditional boundaries separating fine art from everyday signs and symbols. His exploration of **semiotics** and perception of how we see set the stage for both **Conceptual Art** and the Postmodern movement of the following decades.

Flag

Johns' first major work was *Flag* (Fig. 17.7). A real object, the very familiar American flag, was a direct

> **Semiotics:** The study of signs and symbols as a significant part of visual communications.
>
> **Conceptual:** Related to ideas and concepts formed in the mind.

move away from the Abstract Expressionist model of non-representational painting. He chose this as the ideal symbol for his first visual exploration of the 'things the mind already knows'.

Symbolic Meaning

It presented viewers with a contradiction because the American flag had a very different symbolic meaning for different people.

He referred to his paintings as 'facts' and did not provide explanations. When he was asked if it was a painted flag, or a flag painting, he said it was both because the meaning of the artwork is determined by the viewer, not the artist.

Style and Technique

Flag is painted in encaustic, an ancient method of painting with wax, and the artist mixed this with shredded newspaper. The very distinct texture echoed the gestural brushwork of the Abstract Expressionists. When the wax cooled, pieces of text

Figure 17.7
Flag, 1954–5, by Jasper Johns, encaustic, oil, and collage on fabric mounted on plywood, 107 × 154 cm, Museum of Modern Art, New York.

were forever preserved. This idea was at the very heart of Jasper Johns' career-long investigation into 'how we see and why we see the way we do'.

Robert Rauschenberg (1925–2008)

Robert Rauschenberg was a crucial figure in the transition from Abstract Expressionism to modern movements.

His very innovative techniques included collage and assembling all kinds of found objects together. These included printed images, but also things like stuffed birds, umbrellas and even car tyres that he found while wandering around New York City.

He called his assemblages 'combines', but meaning and interpretation were left entirely up to the viewer.

Monogram

One of Rauschenberg's most famous combines was an assemblage placed on top of an abstract oil painting on canvas.

Monogram (Fig. 17.8) is a stuffed angora goat encircled with a tyre Rauschenberg picked up in street rubbish.

He painted the goat's nose with gestural brush-strokes and surrounded it with objects, like a tennis ball, a wooden plank and reproduced images.

Meaning

Despite various interpretations, Rauschenberg consistently refused to offer any explanation. Some, however, have suggested that it references the artist's homosexuality, and his own artistic monogram.

> **Monogram:** A motif of two or more interwoven letters, typically a person's initials, used to identify a personal possession or as a logo.

Andy Warhol (1928–1987)

Andy Warhol is undoubtedly Pop Art's most famous artist. He had worked as a commercial artist, and, as a result, popular imagery of the advertising industry fascinated him. Over-exposure made it banal and void of emotion, but this made it even more interesting for him.

Figure 17.8
Monogram, 1955–9, by Robert Rauschenberg, 107 × 161 × 164 cm, Moderna Museet Stockholm. oil paint, printed paper, printed reproductions, metal, wood, rubber heel and tennis ball on canvas, with oil paint on Angora goat and tyre on wooden base mounted on four casters.

Figure 17.9
Campbell's Soup Cans, 1962, by Andy Warhol, synthetic polymer paint on thirty-two canvases, each 51 × 41 cm. When the work was first shown in 1962 the paintings were displayed on shelves, like grocery products. The images look exactly like mass-produced, printed advertisements, but they are, in fact, hand-painted.

Banal: Boring, ordinary and not original. Too often used and therefore not interesting.

He celebrated the banal in a series of works ranging from soup cans to celebrities. His detached approach was the same in a painting of *Campbell's Soup Cans* (Fig. 17.9), a *Car Crash*, actress *Elizabeth Taylor* or an *Electric Chair*. He said: 'I think every painting should be the same size and the same colour so they're all interchangeable and nobody thinks they have a better or worse painting.'

Style and Technique

Inspired by Duchamp's 'readymades', Warhol was completely against the idea of skill and craftsmanship. He wanted to be like a machine and said: 'If you want to know all about Andy Warhol, just look at the surface of my paintings and films and me, there I am. There's nothing behind it.'

Note: Marcel Duchamp used real objects which he called 'readymades' in his art. This came from the American term 'readymade' that distinguished manufactured items from those that were handmade (see Chapter 14).

From autumn 1962, Warhol began to produce photo-silkscreen works, which involved transferring a photographic image on the porous silkscreens.

Silkscreen printing: A stencilling method that involves pressing printing ink through stencils on a porous fabric mesh stretched across a frame called a screen.

In 1964, Warhol moved to a studio, which he called 'The Factory'. This marked a turning point in his career. He could now create films and even more repetitive, mass-produced and meaningless images.

 Find out more about Andy Warhol's Factory. What films did he make there, and which artists/collaborators worked there with him?

Marilyn Diptych

Warhol had a lifelong fascination with Hollywood and especially Marilyn Monroe.

Marilyn Diptych (Fig. 17.10) was shown in his first New York exhibition in 1962. This was just weeks after the famous actress died from acute barbiturate poisoning. The silkscreened images are based on a 1953 publicity photograph for the film *Niagara*.

Composition

The two silver canvases form a diptych, a format traditionally used in religious painting. This probably reflected the artist's devotion to the Hollywood star.

Warhol grew up in Pittsburgh, but his parents were emigrants from what is today Eastern Slovakia. They remained devout Eastern Catholics and Andy always attended mass.

> **Diptych:** A painting, especially an altarpiece, on two hinged wooden panels that may be closed like a book.

Style and Techniques

The huge scale gives the subject importance, but repetition debases the real person. It also ensures the eye will wander about the composition without a focal point.

On the left, a crudely coloured photograph is repeated, but on the right, some of the black and white images are fading as if the printing ink has run out. This suggests the temporary nature of fame and the power of celebrity to both create and destroy.

Roy Lichtenstein (1923–1997)

Early in his career, Roy Lichtenstein developed a style based on the comic strip. His paintings had the hard-edged look of mechanically produced commercial graphic images. These had been designed to fit efficiently on a book-sized page, but Lichtenstein enlarged his painting to the grand scale of Abstract Expressionism.

Style and Techniques

Lichtenstein copied source photographs or pictures by hand. He adjusted the composition to suit his idea, and then used a projector to trace his drawing onto the canvas. His use of Ben Day dots, the method used

Figure 17.10 *Marilyn Diptych*, 1962, by Andy Warhol, silkscreen ink and acrylic paint on canvas, 205 × 290 cm, Tate Gallery, London.

Figure 17.11 *Whaam!*, 1963, by Roy Lichtenstein, acrylic and oil on canvas, 170 × 400 cm, Tate Gallery, London.

by newspapers and comic strips to denote gradients and texture, became a signature element of his style.

This commercial imagery also highlighted one of the central lessons of Pop Art: that all forms of visual communication are filtered through code or language.

Whaam!

The left panel painting depicts an American fighter plane unleashing a spurt of fire into an enemy plane on the right (Fig. 17.11). The pilot's words are seen in the yellow speech bubble above: 'I PRESSED THE FIRE CONTROL … AND AHEAD OF ME ROCKETS BLAZED THROUGH THE SKY …'

Composition

Lichtenstein based his piece on an illustration by Irv Novick, which appeared in the 89th issue of *All-American Men of War*, published by DC Comics in February 1962.

Style, Technique and Colour

The explosion is composed of a series of yellow, red and white jagged areas and the title, 'WHAAM!', zig zags diagonally out of the fireball in yellow.

Like machine-printed comic strips, the flat areas of primary colour and lettering are outlined in thin black lines. The purple shading on the main fighter plane and blue of the sky are rendered with Ben Day

dots. These dots were formed with a homemade aluminium mesh, and oil paint was pushed through the holes with a small scrubbing brush.

The outlines and solid colour were painted with acrylic.

Meaning

This is undoubtedly a picture of violence, but it poses a question: Is this a celebration of comics and their glorification of war, or is it an image of the detached, chilling and mechanised nature of modern killing?

Research: Find out more about Roy Lichtenstein's working techniques.
Create: Make a small preparatory drawing based on an image from DC comics in which you adjust the composition to suit a large two-panel format.
Respond: Write a short account on your choice of image and what message your work might have.

Claes Oldenburg (b. 1929)

Claes Oldenburg's sculptures are witty, humorous and full of contradictions. Hard objects like a lipstick (Fig. 17.12) are made of soft vinyl, while soft objects like an ice cream cone are made out of hard

NEW APPRECIATING ART EUROPE AND THE WORLD

material. Small objects like a spoon and cherry (Fig. 17.13) are super-sized.

By changing the form, scale and function of his subjects, Oldenburg forced the viewer to see the object differently.

In the early 1960s, Oldenburg was involved in various 'Happenings'. In fact, his first large-scale public work was part of a student protest against the Vietnam War.

Happenings: Spontaneous, improvised, participatory artistic events.

Lipstick (Ascending) on Caterpillar Tracks

The monumental 7 m high orange-red lipstick emerged from a caterpillar-treaded military vehicle. Oldenburg made the structure in collaboration with architectural students and had it secretly brought to the university campus. The benign 'feminine' beauty product had a bullet-like shape; its sexual associations make it seem masculine or even violent.

Materials

The soft sculpture was never intended to be permanent and Oldenburg, a Yale graduate himself, charged no fee for its creation. Instead, the students and graduates paid for the materials: the base was made of plywood and the lipstick was vinyl, which could be inflated and deflated for comic effect.

Political Statement

It may have seemed a playful, artistic joke, but its position in the square overlooking both the office of Yale's president and a World War I memorial made *Lipstick* a very real anti-war statement. The work was later remade in metal and placed in a less-prominent spot on Yale's campus.

Public Commissions

Oldenburg married Dutch art historian, Coosje van Bruggen and they worked together on many

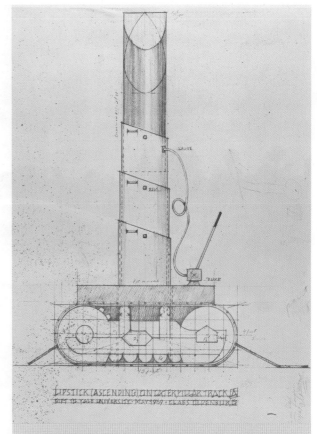

Figure 17.12 *Lipstick (Ascending) on Caterpillar Tracks*, 1969, by Claes Oldenburg, drawing of the sculpture at Yale University, Connecticut. Tate Gallery, London.

colossal, outdoor sculptures (Fig. 17.13) in Europe and the US from late 1976 until van Bruggen's death in 2009.

Make a drawing of a small everyday object. Suggest that this is a large-scale sculpture by including a suitable background.

Minimalism

Sometimes referred to as 'ABC art' or 'Cool art', Minimalism developed in 1960s New York, but it is still prevalent today. This was also a reaction to Abstract Expressionism.

The basic idea of Minimalism was to rid art of its reliance on the artist's emotion and instead to keep personal expression, a guiding hand or thought processes to an absolute minimum.

Figure 17.13 *Spoonbridge and Cherry*, 1985, by Claes Oldenburg and Coosje van Bruggen, steel, aluminium and enamel, 9 × 15.7 × 4.1 m, Minneapolis Sculpture Garden.

Viewers were invited to respond only to what they saw and this was highly revolutionary at the time. This idea of simple, abstract visual appeal made Minimalism quite unique.

Artists also wanted to break down barriers between painting and sculpture. Their works resembled factory-built commodities and they used prefabricated industrial materials and simple, often repeated geometric forms.

Skills and Influences

While it may seem like a simple principle, achieving excellence in the Minimalist style requires great skill. It asks artists, designers and architects to break things down into their essential elements, using simple forms to produce harmonious work.

Minimalism was greatly influenced by Japanese culture and philosophy, and has remained an enduring aesthetic in contemporary art and design.

Its greatest influence was the **Zen philosophy**, which places value on simplicity as a way to achieve inner freedom.

Oldenburg uses the Japanese idea of *seijaku* – peaceful stillness – as inspiration for his designs. Here, aesthetics are used to help encourage tranquillity, harmony and balance. It's easy to see how the clean simplicity of Minimalist design used these same goals.

Note: Japanese aesthetic principles look for the innate beauty in objects. *Wabi-sabi*, finds value in the simple forms of nature. Another principle known as *ma* or emptiness, calls for large open spaces in order to create a spatial emptiness. This forces contemplation of essential forms, which is a key concept for contemporary Minimalist architecture.

Minimalist Artists and Artworks

Frank Stella (b. 1936)

A key figure in Minimalism, Frank Stella is often quoted for saying, 'What you see is what you see.'

In 1966, he produced *Irregular Polygons*. These were very large canvases painted in irregular geometric forms with flat colour.

His *Protractor* series was based on curves, like the instrument used for measuring and constructing angles. The shape and huge scale of these decorative patterns meant they could be seen in terms of painting, sculpture and architecture.

> **Monochrome:** A picture developed or executed in black and white or in varying tones of only one colour.

Harran II

Harran II (Fig. 17.14) is one from the *Protractor* series. The curving and circular decorative patterns and the combination of acrylic and fluorescent paint create an almost psychedelic effect. Harran is the name of an ancient city in Asia Minor and the Roman numeral II indicates that it is from the second of the three design groups – 'interlaces', 'rainbows' and 'fans'.

Feminist Art

A new movement created opportunities for women artists and paved the way for the identity art and activist art of the 1980s.

Feminist Artists and Artworks

Louise Bourgeois (1911–2010)

In 1982, at the age of 70, Louise Bourgeois became the first female artist to be honoured with a major retrospective in New York's Museum of Modern Art.

Born in Paris, she was inspired by the art of the 1930s before moving to New York in 1938. The subconscious, autobiography and identity were important influences on her work.

Figure 17.14 *Harran II*, 1967, by Frank Stella, polymer and fluorescent paint on canvas, 305 × 610 cm, Guggenheim Museum, New York.

Figure 17.15
Maman, 2000, by Louise Bourgeois, steel and marble, 9.3 × 8.9 × 10.2 m, Tate Modern, London. Supported by eight slender, knobbly legs with a sharp-tipped point, the body is suspended high above the ground. The viewer can walk underneath and look up at a meshed sac holding seventeen white and grey marble eggs.

Working Methods

Louise Bourgeois' artwork was often personal and narrative. She employed a wide variety of working methods and materials, working across the disciplines of drawing, printmaking, painting and sculpture, and she was an early champion of installation art.

The artist is most famous for spider sculptures produced in a range of materials and scales. These are usually found in outdoor locations like the Guggenheim Museum in Bilbao, St Petersburg and Tokyo but the largest, *Maman* (Fig. 17.15), was shown in Turbine Hall of the Tate Modern in London to mark the gallery opening in 2000.

Installation art: Mixed-media constructions or assemblages usually designed for a specific place and sometimes for a temporary period.

Maman

This huge steel structure refers to emotional development and motherhood (Fig. 17.15). The artist saw spiders as both fierce and fragile, both protectors and predators. For her, these darkly compelling creatures were a contradictory mix of psychological and biographical references towards her mother and partly to herself. They represented cleverness, industriousness and protectiveness.

Judy Chicago (b. 1939)

One of the major figures of the early Feminist Art movement of the 1970s, Judy Chicago continues to be an influential feminist artist, author and educator. She consistently challenges the male-dominated art world and initially sought to draw attention to traditional women's crafts that were often dismissed, such as needlework and ceramics.

Judith Sylvia Cohen was born in Chicago, and was very influenced by her father's left-wing activism from an early age. She studied at the Art Institute of Chicago and University College, Los Angeles. She began working with feminist content in the late 1960s and changed her last name to Chicago.

The Dinner Party

Chicago's most famous work is *The Dinner Party* (Fig. 17.16). This installation celebrates women's history with a large-scale triangular table. Thirty-nine table places are set for important women including Queen Hatshepsut of Ancient Egypt, artist Artemisia

Figure 17.16 *The Dinner Party*, 1974–9, Ceramic, porcelain, textile, 1,463 x 1,463 cm, Judy Chicago, Brooklyn Museum, New York.

Gentileschi (see Chapter 7, p. 114) and poet Emily Dickinson. The monumental project was made in co-operation with hundreds of volunteers and incorporates embroidery, needlepoint and ceramics.

Conceptual Art

Artists of the 1960s arrived at a new notion that ideas in themselves can be works of art, and can look and be almost anything.

Conceptual Artists and Artworks

Joseph Kosuth (b. 1945)

In his 1969 essay 'Art After Philosophy', artist and theoretician Joseph Kosuth argued that traditional discussion on art history had reached its end. Instead, he proposed a radical new way of looking at how art is accepted as important. 'Being an artist now,' Kosuth wrote, 'means to question the nature of art.'

One and Three Chairs

In 1965, Joseph Kosuth presented an installation of one chair in three ways (Fig. 17.17). These were:

- a manufactured chair
- a photograph of the chair
- a copy of a dictionary entry for the word 'chair'.

The work was therefore composed of an object, an image and words.

The artist did not make the chair, take the photograph, or write the definition. Instead he selected and assembled them.

Kosuth turned a simple wooden chair into an object of debate and a platform for exploring new meanings.

Figure 17.17
One and Three Chairs, 1965, by Joseph Kosuth, Museum of Modern Art, New York.

Classroom debate

With *One and Three Chairs*, Kosuth wanted his viewers to think about how 'art is making meaning'.

Is this art? Which representation of the chair is most 'accurate'?

Yoko Ono (b. 1933)

One of the strongest feminist voices to emerge in the 1960s, Yoko Ono has had a long career. She once said 'I thought art was a verb, rather than a noun.'

She was born into a Japanese aristocratic family in Tokyo, but they had to flee the American bombing in 1945 and later moved to New York.

In the 1960s she gravitated towards 'Happenings' and was always at the cutting edge of art trends in New York. Her very innovative approach was inspired by Zen Buddhism and her involvement of the audience was one of the earliest examples of participatory art.

A crucial element to the meaning of her work was that anyone could make them. For example,

Figure 17.18 *Cut Piece*, photo of performance by Yoko Ono in New Works of Yoko Ono, taken by Minoru Niizuma, 21 March 1965, Carnegie Recital Hall, New York.

in *Cloud Piece* (1963), she instructs her audience to imagine digging a hole in the garden, and putting clouds into it.

Yoko Ono became world famous after she married John Lennon of the Beatles, but she resolutely continued her career, despite huge media attention.

Cut Piece

Cut Piece (Fig. 17.18) was one of the first examples of Performance Art. Ono invited members of the audience to come forward one by one and cut away pieces of her clothing. There were long pauses between each cutting, and all the while the artist knelt still and silently on the stage.

This was intended to harness the Buddhist mentality of giving up material items, but it was also a symbol of female passivity and vulnerability.

Land Art

Land Art, also known as Earth Art, was part of the wider Conceptual Art movement in the 1960s and 1970s.

Works were mostly temporary and artists documented the work with photographs and maps exhibited in galleries. Sometimes Land artists brought in material and used it to create installations in galleries.

The rejection of traditional gallery and museum spaces was one of the defining aspects of a new group of Land artists. Their idea of site-specific art was very new because the work sometimes required wide open spaces. For example *Sun Tunnels* by Nancy Holt is situated in the Great Basin Desert, which lies in the Utah desert between the Rocky Mountains and the Sierra Nevada range. It is four hours from the Gallery of Fine Art in Utah.

This questions the very purpose of art as something to be viewed.

Land Artists and Artworks

Nancy Holt (1938–2014)

In 1976, after three years of planning and many visits to the desert, artist Nancy Holt finished *Sun*

Figure 17.19 *Sun Tunnels*, 1973–6, by Nancy Holt, concrete, each 5.5 m long and 2.7 m in diameter, Great Basin Desert, Utah.

Tunnels (Fig. 17.19). It became her most famous work and defined her reputation at a time when it was still overshadowed by her famous husband, Robert Smithson, who had died in a plane crash three years earlier.

Sun Tunnels

The four massive, cylindrical, concrete forms are large enough to walk inside. Arranged on the cracked desert floor in a cross pattern, they align with the sunrise and sunset on the summer and winter solstices and each of the cylinders is also pierced with smaller holes representing the stars.

Holt's design allows for an ever-changing play of light on the surfaces and the cylinders act as viewfinders which, in her own words, 'bring the vast space of the desert back to human scale'.

Robert Smithson (1938–1973)

Robert Smithson began making landscape art in the 1960s. He used mechanical earth-moving equipment to make his most famous Land Art work, *Spiral Jetty* (Fig. 17.20), built out into the Great Salt Lake in Utah.

Spiral Jetty

This huge coil of black basalt and earth winds in a counter-clockwise spiral into the red-violet lake.

The colour of the water was a direct result of the construction of a causeway for the Southern Pacific Railroad in 1959. The northern section of the lake was cut off from fresh water supplies and a concentration of salt-tolerant bacteria and algae produced its unique colour.

Smithson often picked damaged sites to represent a kind of rebirth, but he particularly liked this one because the colours suggested a ruined science-fiction style landscape.

Figure 17.20
Spiral Jetty, 1970, by Robert Smithson, Great Salt Lake, Utah.

Sun Tunnels by Nancy Holt is situated in the Great Basin Desert, between the Rocky Mountains and the Sierra Nevada range. This is about four hours from the Gallery of Fine Art in Utah. How do you think this affects the purpose of art as something to be viewed?

Media and Areas of Practice

Neo-Dada artists used collage and assemblages of found objects and materials in their work.

Pop Art was influenced by popular culture and mass-produced products. These were transformed into easy-to-understand art.

Encaustic was a very old painting method used by Jasper Johns in which wax and pigment are fused onto a surface with heat. He combined this with newspaper collage to create an interesting and textured surface.

Happenings were staged as live actions that combined painting, poetry, music, dance and theatre. They were influenced by Dada and were taken up by a number of American Pop artists. The experience of the participants was considered more important than an end product.

Minimalist artists sought to break down barriers between painting and sculpture. They sometimes used prefabricated industrial materials and worked with simple, geometric forms.

Conceptual Art is a term for art in which the idea behind the work is more important than the actual product.

Site-specific art was an important element of Land Art.

Art Elements and Design Principles

Roy Lichtenstein's paintings are witty and fun to look at, but the controlled use of formal art elements as compositional elements remains central to the work. These elements included:

- black outlines
- flat primary colours
- strong contrasts
- the clichéd style of comic-book imagery.

Clichéd imagery: An element of an artistic work which has become overused to the point of losing its original meaning or effect, even to the point of being corny or irritating.

- Language and the written word was an important tool for Conceptual artists as part of an emphasis on ideas over visual forms.
- To achieve excellence in Minimalism, artists, designers and architects must break the design down to its essential elements and still produce harmonious work.
- Frank Stella worked in a geometric abstract style and his 'hard-edge painting' focused only on the formal art elements of colour, line and shape.

Analysis

Consider how art could be made from any material and why skilled artistic craftsmanship was no longer needed to produce works of art. Explore the full possibilities of the notion that art could, in fact, be just an idea.

The pop culture of the 1960s swept away the remnants of traditionalism and opened the way for new art forms like installation, performance and video. Pop Art became the symbol of a new lifestyle struggling against the conservative high culture.

Soon, even the need for the physical space of the gallery was challenged, as Land Art became part of the wider Conceptual Art movement.

Chapter Review

1. Why did Andy Warhol choose the Diptych format for his Marilyn Monroe painting?

2. What were the influences on both Minimalist and Conceptual artists?

3. Describe and discuss Judy Chicago's *The Dinner Party*. How does it celebrate women?

4. Conceptual Art can be about anything because the idea is the most important aspect. How does this work for art? Choose one art piece and describe why you think this best expresses a concept.

5. Describe how it might feel to walk under Louise Bourgeois' *Maman*?

6. Would you like to visit *Sun Tunnels* and *Spiral Jetty* in Utah? How do think the remote locations would change your experience of viewing these outdoor works of art?

7. Examine *Dropped Cone* (Fig. 17.21) by Claes Oldenburg and Coosje van Bruggen, made for a busy Cologne shopping mall.
   a. What meaning do you think this work might have?
   b. Why do you think the artists chose this location?

Further Research

www.tate.org.uk – Search for 'Peter Saville on Richard Hamilton' to learn more about the 'godfather of pop art'

www.youtube.com – Watch 'Jasper Johns at The Royal Academy' (19:26) for an up-close look at the artist's key works

www.youtube.com – Watch 'Robert Rauschenberg | TateShots' (5:18) to see how the artist blazed a new trail for art in the second half of the 20th century

www.warhol.org – The official Andy Warhol Museum website has a wealth of information on the artist's life and work

www.youtube.com – Watch 'Frank Stella: A Retrospective' (7:24) to see the artist speak about an exhibition showcasing Stella's work

www.theguardian.com – Search for 'My art is a form of restoration' for a rare interview with Louise Bourgeois

www.youtube.com – Watch 'The Dinner Party: A Tour of the Exhibition' (1:16) to learn more about Judy Chicago and her most famous piece

www.youtube.com – Watch 'Spiral Jetty, Sun Tunnels, and Salt' (11:54) to see Holt and Smithson's famous Land Art constructions

Figure 17.21 *Dropped Cone*, 2001, by Claes Oldenburg and Coosje van Bruggen, steel, plastic and wood painted with polyester gelcoat, 12.1 × 5.8 m, Neumarkt Galerie, Cologne.

Chapter 18

Artistic Developments in Europe

By the end of this chapter I will ...

* be able to discuss American influence on art in 1960s London
* have examined the role of commercial galleries in promoting new art
* understand how the post-war generation of artists had new ideas
* be able to contrast art produced in London with that of Berlin
* be able to discuss why the work of the Young British Artists was greeted with shock
* have reflected on whether the introduction of big money changed how art was produced and promoted.

Context

The 'Swinging Sixties' was a defining decade for Britain. In just 10 short years, London had transformed from a bleak, conservative city, still coping with the aftermath of World War II, into the capital of the world, full of freedom, hope and promise. In spite of the Cold War and the constant fear that one push of a nuclear button could destroy the world in seconds, the mood was hedonistic. London was a city where anything and everything was possible.

A boom in national wealth gave people more spending power. Air travel and sun-seeking holidays became more widely available and most homes had a television showing images of daily life filtered by news photographers, and sometimes invented by the advertising agents.

American influence was everywhere. American servicemen were still around, American films were in the cinemas and American slang was part of everyday speech.

Fashion

Popular culture and fashion trends had shifted towards a new, noisy, bright and happy emphasis on youth.

The 1960s were famous for the emergence of the mini skirt and the self-taught London designer Mary Quant is widely credited with this (Fig. 18.1).

Hedonism: Living and behaving in ways to get as much pleasure out of life as possible, according to the belief that the most important thing in life is to enjoy oneself.

Find out why Mary Quant became the most iconic fashion designer of the 1960s.

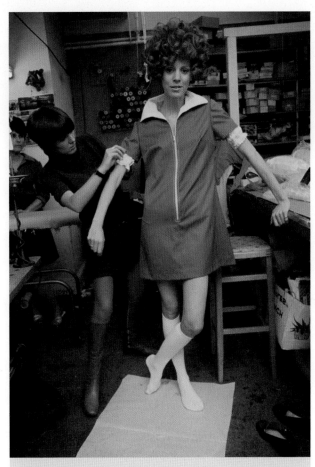

Figure 18.1 Mary Quant fits a zip-up mini dress on a model in her design studio in London, 1967.

Germany

After World War II, Germany was divided. British and American powers occupied the Western part and the Soviet Union occupied the East.

Within the Eastern section, Berlin was also divided, and in 1961 Eastern authorities erected a wall separating the two parts of the city. This prevented the economic problem of the migration of East German workers to the West, but it also meant that families were split, and those employed in the West of the city were cut off from their jobs.

 Thierry Noir became world famous in 1984 for his graffiti on the Berlin Wall. Find out why he thought painting outside was important.

Art

Sculpture

Henry Moore was one of the foremost British sculptors of the 20th century. His work in the 1950s was monumental and figurative.

St Ives School

Barbara Hepworth (1903–1975) was one of the most important artists in the loose-knit group of artists

Figure 18.2
The Berlin Wall. Photo from the West side showing graffiti by several artists, including French artist Thierry Noir.

Figure 18.3 Barbara Hepworth Museum and Sculpture Garden.

that gathered in St Ives, Cornwall. Her abstract sculpture had a major impact on the development of Modern art in Britain (Fig. 18.3).

Picasso Retrospective Exhibition

In the summer of 1960, Britain was overwhelmed by what the newspapers were calling 'Picassomania'. The Picasso retrospective exhibition at the Tate Gallery London (Fig. 18.5) was the most extensive ever staged, and marked the moment when Picasso's work – and Modernism – finally arrived in Britain.

The New Generation

Some of Britain's most influential artists emerged during the 1960s from London art schools, and an explosion of new styles and techniques drew huge attention in the USA and Europe. By 1965, London was hailed as the new world centre of contemporary art and culture.

Figure 18.4 *Family Group*, by Henry Moore. This bronze sculpture was made for Barclay School in Stevenage, Hertfordshire, where it has remained since 1949. In 2010, for security reasons, the school decided it was best to move their prized artwork inside.

Figure 18.5 Picasso Exhibition, 1960, Tate Gallery, London.

Figure 18.6
The Wedding, 1989–93,
by R.B. Kitaj,
oil on canvas
183 × 183 cm,
Tate Gallery, London.
His painting depicts the
wedding of Kitaj to the
American artist Sandra
Fisher which had taken
place in 1983. They first
met in Los Angeles,
where Kitaj was
teaching and met up
again when he returned
to London in 1972.

Figurative Artists – The School of London

The American artist and intellectual R.B. Kitaj (Fig. 18.6) became a leading member of a diverse group of artists that he called the School of London in 1976. They painted in a wide range of styles, but all were interested in figurative painting.

Note: School in this context indicates a group of artists who follow the same style, share the same teachers, or have the same aims.

Figurative painting: A form of art that has strong references to the real world and particularly to the human figure.

Berlin

Even before the Wall went up in 1961, the two sides of Germany were moving apart. In the West, Abstraction indicated freedom of expression, and by the late 1960s this gave way to Pop and Conceptualism.

To encourage West German citizens to move to West Berlin, the government offered incentives such as exemption from mandatory military service. As a result, a free-spirited culture of art and music developed in the city.

Neo-Expressionism

The 1970s and 1980s saw the rise of Neo-Expressionism in Germany. This was a direct challenge to the cool ideas of Pop Art, Minimalism, Conceptual Art and Postmodernism. Artists returned to emotional content with the gestural brushstrokes, bright colours and distorted forms of the early 20th-century Expressionist movements, such as

Fauvism, *Die Brücke* and *Der Blaue Reiter*, and the abstract forms of Abstract Expressionism.

Expressionism had been denounced by the Nazis, but it became symbolic for artists such as Georg Baselitz in asserting their independence from Pop Art.

Young British Artists (YBAs)

Despite having slipped behind New York and Berlin on the art scene in the 1980s, in the early 1990s the 'Young British Artists' (YBAs) burst onto the scene to revive British art.

They deliberately picked up on the mood of the sixties and became part of 'Cool Britannia'. They were actively promoted by dealers and curators who were part of the 'scene'.

Art Dealers

London in the mid-1960s was home to two of the coolest commercial art galleries; The Kasmin Ltd and Robert Fraser galleries were quite short-lived, but were incredibly influential.

The Fraser Gallery showed classic 20th-century art alongside British Pop and artwork from Americans like Andy Warhol. It was the owner, Robert Fraser, who suggested that the British artist Peter Blake should design the (now iconic) cover for the Beatles' album, *Sgt Pepper's Lonely Hearts Club Band* (Fig. 18.7).

John Kasmin, meanwhile, had a passion for the flat, bold colours of American abstract paintings and his new gallery was the first architect-designed space to show these huge-scale works.

Note: Robert Fraser was a close friend of the rock band The Rolling Stones and was present at an infamous 1967 party in guitarist Keith Richards' house that was raided by police for drugs.

Mick Jagger, the lead singer of the group, and Keith Richards were acquitted on appeal, but Fraser pleaded guilty to charges of possession of heroin. He received a jail sentence, but after his release his heroin addiction grew worse. He closed the business in 1969.

Neo-Expressionism and the Art Market

Neo-Expressionism was part of an international return to expressive painting in the 1980s. It had a distinct connection with the art market, in which investment firms were becoming increasingly interested. However, phenomenal success in the 1980s was quickly followed by collapse as the art market lost interest.

Figure 18.7
Pop artist Peter Blake poses beside a copy of the *Sgt Pepper's Lonely Hearts Club Band* album cover, which he co-designed with his wife Jann Haworth in 1967. This dazzling piece of modern art defines its era.

Jean-Michel Basquiat

African-American artist Jean-Michel Basquiat became a huge celebrity in the 1980s (Fig. 18.8). His spray-painted images and scribbled words dominated the art market. They also became tools for highlighting his experiences in the black community and racism issues of his time.

He died tragically in 1988 at the age of 27, but in 2017 one of his untitled paintings set a new record high for any American artist at auction, selling for $110.5 million.

RESEARCH Jean-Michel Basquiat's paintings were responsible for bringing graffiti artists into the realm of the New York gallery scene. Find out more about the artist and how success in the art market affected his life.

Figure 18.8 *Untitled (One Eyed Man or Xerox Face)*, 1982, by Jean Michel Basquiat, oilstick, 183 × 122 cm.

Innovation and Invention

British Pop Art received a powerful impetus from the friendship of the American artist R.B. Kitaj. Ronald Brooks Kitaj came from Ohio in the US but remained in London for much of his life.

The 1960s London 'scene' was a tightly woven interconnection of art, music, poetry, theatre, fashion and film. There was no real distinction as ideas, styles and personnel criss-crossed between the disciplines.

This opened new and exciting opportunities for design, as artists produced album covers, posters, murals and editorial graphics for the alternative press, clubs and events (Fig. 18.9).

Psychedelic Art developed as musicians and artists came into regular contact with LSD, but there was also a strong connection with Op Art, Art Nouveau and even Surrealism (see Chapter 14).

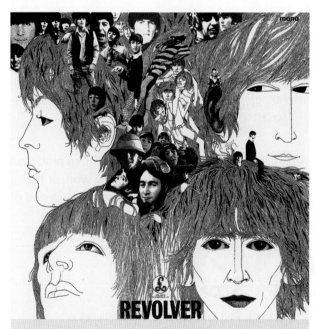

Figure 18.9 Cover art for the Beatles' album *Revolver*, 1966, by Klaus Voormann. The band asked their friend Voormann to design an album cover for their new release. He used pen and black ink to create four large line drawings of the band members, which he then combined with a collage of cut-up black and white photos.

Figure 18.10 *Exploding Hendrix* poster, 1968, by Martin Sharp. The excitement and energy of the American guitarist Jimi Hendrix was combined with psychedelic art. Sharp worked from an original photograph taken by Linda Eastman, wife of Paul McCartney, at a concert in New York in 1967.

Australian-born London artist Martin Sharp produced some of the most overtly psychedelic work of the 1960s. He captured a particular moment with one of the most iconic posters (Fig. 18.10) of the time.

Research: Find out more about the influences on psychedelic art and the colours and imagery used by Martin Sharp in his collaged design for the 1967 record cover *Disraeli Gears* by Cream.
Create: Design your own poster or album cover in psychedelic style by using bright colours, 'flower power' images and bubble writing.
Respond: Identify the influence of Art Nouveau on psychedelic artists.

Painting in 1980s Germany was revitalised with the Neo-Expressionist's strong colours, as well as motifs drawn from Mannerism, Cubism, Fauvism, German Expressionism, Surrealism, and Pop Art.

Young British Artists

In the 1990s, the YBAs became known for their innovative spirit, as well as their notorious shock tactics and a desire to push beyond what many people at the time considered normal and decent.

Members participated in two of the most shocking exhibitions in London of the late 20th century: *Freeze* in 1988 and *Sensation* in 1997. Their Conceptual work was widely criticised in the media.

Media and Areas of Practice

The School of London raised the stature of English painting to one of international significance. It generated enormous interest in **figurative painting** and continued to have a very strong influence well into the 1980s.

The British sculptor Anthony Caro played a pivotal role in the development of 20th century **sculpture**. He worked in steel, bronze, silver, lead, stoneware and wood.

The **New Generation** artists created the visual identity for 'Swinging' London. In spite of the more avant-garde approaches to art, some artists remained dedicated to painting in figurative realism.

Neo-Expressionism turned again to raw emotion in painting, as artists became concerned with the portrayal of genuine ideas and feelings, rather than the final appearance of the work.

Op Art (short for Optical Art) developed as part of a new interest in the technology and psychology of illusion in the 1950s. The fashion, design and advertising industries all borrowed from its graphic, sign-like patterns and its decorative value.

The **Young British Artists** had an open approach to process and materials. Many had studied in Goldsmiths College in London, where a Bachelor's degree in Fine Art was no longer divided into painting, drawing, photography and sculpture. It was instead completely mixed across all disciplines.

Art Elements and Design Principles

British artists in the 1960s reacted in a less emotional way to American Abstract Expressionism. They focused on the abstract properties of painting and sculpture and had a more formal response to space, surface, scale and process.

Neo-Expressionism in 1980s Germany, known as *Neue Wilden* (New Fauves), was particularly intense in its choice of subject matter. These were depicted in highly textured large-scale works, gestural brushwork and very intense colours.

Op Art's distinct style is created with abstract patterns and contrasts. The positive and negative spaces are given equal importance, and the precise mathematically produced geometric shapes confuse and excite the eye. This creates the illusion of a two-dimensional surface that moves, vibrates and sparkles.

Artists and Artworks
Francis Bacon (1909–1992)

Francis Bacon was one of the most unique painters to emerge in post-war Britain. He was born in Dublin, but moved away from Ireland due to a difficult relationship with his father.

He took up painting in his twenties, having made ends meet in the late 1920s and early 1930s as an interior decorator and even a gambler. He settled in London and remained there for the rest of his life.

Charming and sociable, Francis Bacon was an outspoken atheist and he was openly homosexual. He was considered the leader of the London group.

Success came in 1944 with his triptych *Three Studies for Figures at the Base of a Crucifixion*. As a boy in Ireland, he had seen many images of the crucifixion. He was also fascinated by the raw flesh that he saw hanging in a butcher's shop. Bacon obviously saw a connection between the brutality of slaughterhouses and the Crucifixion, and the unsettling result established his reputation as an artist (Fig. 18.11).

He claimed the triptych format enabled him to depict things in 'shifting sequences', like a movie.

Photography and the human form was fundamentally important for Bacon's art but, as an existentialist artist, he captured the contradictions, anxieties and frenetic energy of the 20th century. His figures explored pessimism and death at a time when Europe had been repeatedly savaged by war.

Figure 18.11 *Three Studies for Figures at the Base of a Crucifixion*, 1944, by Francis Bacon, oil on board, each 74 × 94 cm, Tate Gallery, London.

Bacon rejected Abstraction because, in his view, it communicated nothing. His dominant and consistent subject was the human face and body, though he rarely suggested any real space.

Note: In the late-1940s and early 1950s, Existential art drew on the popular philosophy that grew up around the writings of French philosophers Jean-Paul Sartre and Albert Camus. Existentialist themes of alienation, as well as angst in the face of the human condition had a significant impact on the visual arts. Existentialism was also an influence on some American Abstract Expressionists and individual painters and sculptors like the Swiss sculptor Alberto Giacometti and Bacon's friend Lucien Freud.

Figure 18.12 *Study After Velázquez's Portrait of Pope Innocent X*, 1953, by Francis Bacon, oil on canvas, 153 × 118 cm, Des Moines Art Center, Iowa.

Study After Velázquez's Portrait of Pope Innocent X (1953)

Bacon transformed the classic portrait of Pope Innocent X by the Spanish Baroque artist Diego Velázquez (see Chapter 9, Fig. 9.6) into a screaming figure surrounded by a cage-like frame (Fig. 18.12).

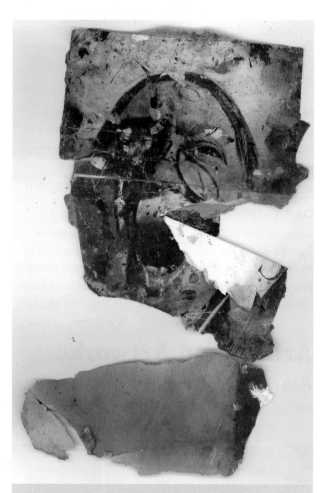

Figure 18.13 Cutting with photographic illustration of the screaming nurse in Sergei Eisenstein's *Battleship Potemkin*, by Francis Bacon, 16 × 17 cm, Hugh Lane Gallery, Dublin.

Note: The friendship between Bacon and Lucian Freud was particularly important for the School of London as well as for both artists' artistic development. They first met in the mid-1940s, and for the next 30 years they saw each other nearly every day. They critiqued each other's work and painted noted portraits of each other.

Figure 18.14
Girl with a White Dog,
1951, by Lucian Freud,
oil on canvas,
76 × 102 cm,
Tate Modern, London.

A scene from the 1920s silent film *Battleship Potemkin* deeply impressed the artist and he used the image of a screaming woman many times (Fig. 18.13).

Lucian Freud (1922–2011)

Lucian Freud was renowned for his portrayal of the human form, and especially for his unflinching, intimate, honest portraits. He worked entirely from life and made several self-portraits.

The grandson of psychoanalyst Sigmund Freud, Lucian was born in Berlin but his family came to London in 1933 to escape the Nazis.

After graduating art school in 1944, he was noted as an artist to watch, despite his very traditional medium and mode of work, painting from life in the studio. While this was not as popular or new as other artistic movements at the time, Freud gained international recognition when his work was included in an exhibition that toured Paris, London, Berlin and Washington DC.

Girl with a White Dog

The portrait of his first wife Kitty, painted in 1951 (Fig. 18.14), is a fine example of Freud's transitional period at a time when he began to paint the nude figure. Her absent stare shows the artist's detachment from his model and, despite the calm atmosphere, her expression shows a kind of weariness. The dog was one of two bull terriers the couple were given as a wedding gift, but the marriage was very short due to Freud's many affairs.

Technique

Girl with a White Dog is painted with linear precision, almost like a drawing. Freud used a fine sable brush to apply the muted colours that give this composition an overall flatness.

The robe has slipped off her shoulder, exposing her right breast. The soft and warm textures are created with pale skin tones and subtle shading.

Bridget Riley (b. 1931)

In 1956, English painter Bridget Riley saw an exhibition of American Abstract Expressionist painters at the Tate Gallery, London. This helped the young artist to shape her creative thinking and gave her a sense of direction. After spending some time teaching and travelling in Italy, she began to work in the Op Art style.

New York

Riley's paintings came to international notice at an exhibition called The Responsive Eye at the

Museum of Modern Art in New York in 1965. The exhibition also featured the French Hungarian-born artist Victor Vasarely and other Op artists, but it was Riley's work that was featured on the exhibition catalogue cover.

The exhibition was a huge hit and Bridget Riley became an art celebrity in Britain.

Technique

Riley paints everything by hand and she never uses rulers, masking tape or mechanical instruments. However, because of the large scale and the need for great precision, she has worked with assistants since the 1960s.

Movement in Squares

Riley started *Movement in Squares* by painting a single square on the canvas, and completed the painting in a single session (Fig. 18.15). When she stepped back at the end, Riley said she was 'surprised and elated' with what she had created.

Composition

The basic unit of the square is used right across the canvas, but it modulates and changes its width. The height remains the same and towards the centre the square becomes little more than a sliver. It then opens up again towards the right edge as if two planes are coming together and bending into each other.

The effect is similar to the pages of a bound book lying open.

Beginning with a square, make a sketch for a work of Op Art in black and white that could be enlarged later.

David Hockney (b. 1937)

David Hockney's long and prolific career has resulted in artwork that ranges from collaged photography to Cubist-inspired abstractions and paintings of the English countryside.

Freedom of Expression

Hockney grew up in Bradford, Yorkshire. He had known he was gay since boyhood, but in London he had the freedom to express it.

He was deeply impressed by the Picasso retrospective in London in the summer of 1960 and noted especially how often the older artist had changed direction and style.

California

Hockney first visited Los Angeles in 1963, a year after graduating from the Royal College of Art, London. In 1976, he moved there permanently.

He was captivated by the relaxed way of life and the modern homes drenched in sunlight. On his first visit, he famously commented that Los Angeles needed to be documented in paint. He said: 'My God! This place needs its Piranesi ... so here I am.'

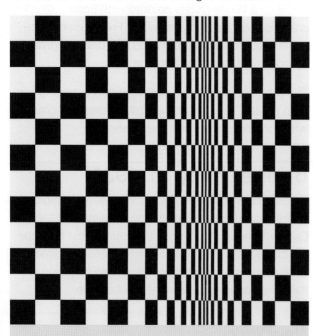

Figure 18.15 *Movement in Squares*, 1961, by Bridget Riley, tempera on hardboard, 122 × 122 cm, Arts Council Collection, London.

Piranesi: Giovanni Battista, aka Piranesi, was one of the greatest Italian printmakers of the 18th century. He was famous for his etchings of Rome.

Figure 18.16
A Bigger Splash, 1967,
by David Hockney,
acrylic on canvas,
243 × 244 cm, Tate
Gallery, London.

He documented life in California by painting people in showers (which were of course very modern in the early 1960s) and with swimming pools, sprinklers, plants and glass houses.

A Bigger Splash

Hockney is most famous for his swimming pool paintings, in which he attempted to represent the constantly changing surface of water.

A Bigger Splash (Fig. 18.16) was part of a series in which Hockney tried to capture the splash of water after a dive into a pool.

Mr and Mrs Clark and Percy

One of the Tate's most viewed paintings, *Mr and Mrs Clark and Percy* (Fig. 18.17) is the intimate and relaxed portrait of Hockney's friends, Celia Birtwell and Ossie Clark. He said: 'My aim was to paint the relationship of these two people.'

Composition

The figures are life-sized and painted from life, but the painting proved troublesome. Hockney had difficulties in capturing the subdued London light and the *contre-jour* effect of the light coming from the centre made it harder.

> **Contre-jour:** The technique of painting against the light – backlighting.

His friends' marriage was already in trouble, and Hockney's reversal of conventional positions, like the man seated and the woman standing, as well as the open window, reinforces the separation.

Perspective

The artist had become fascinated by one-point perspective, a development that coincided with a growing interest in photography. However, by the

UNIT 6 POST-1960s ART

Figure 18.17
Mr and Mrs Clark and Percy, 1971, by David Hockney, acrylic on canvas, 213 × 305 cm, Tate Gallery, London.

mid-1970s Hockney found that naturalism was just a convention that, for him, failed to accurately capture the world.

> **Naturalism:** A true-to-life style that involves the representation or depiction of nature (including people) with the least possible distortion or interpretation.

Christo and Jeanne-Claude

This collaborative artist duo became famous for wrapping architecture in fabric and creating art with natural elements.

Christo Vladimirov Javacheff met Jeanne-Claude Marie Denat while living in Paris. They shared the same birthday – 13 June 1935 – but she was born in Casablanca, Morocco and he in Gabrovo, Bulgaria.

Christo studied art in Sofia, while Jeanne-Claude graduated with a degree in Latin and philosophy from the University of Tunis.

Christo's art had begun with small found objects, but in collaboration with Jeanne-Claude they advanced to larger scale. The couple emigrated to the United States in 1964, where Christo created drawings and collages to help with funding for their artistic endeavours. Over the years, they quickly gained an international reputation for their high-profile projects that were unprecedented in scale. These showcased a contrast between engineered, man-made elements and the site's natural characteristics.

Jeanne-Claude died in 2009, but Christo continued to make work throughout the world under both their names until his death in May 2020.

Pont Neuf, Paris

Pont Neuf is Paris's oldest bridge and one of its most historically significant monuments. The artists had an idea to transform the famous landmark into an art object by wrapping the entire structure in woven polyamide fabric (Fig. 18.18).

The idea of creating this bizarre and distinctly modern illusion in the most ancient part of the city was beautifully simple, but its execution was anything but. It took ten years because the couple had never worked with such a busy city site. In September 1985, the sensational response to the

> **RESEARCH**
> Originally Jeanne-Claude was seen as Christo's publicist and business manager. Find out why the couple chose only to use Christo's name and research some of their collaborations like Valley Curtain, a gigantic, crescent-shaped fabric curtain that stretched across an entire Colorado valley.

bridge's unveiling made Christo and Jeanne-Claude
the most famous artists in the world.

Joseph Beuys (1921–1986)

A major figure of the post-war German avant-garde,
Joseph Beuys practised his art in Europe and the USA
from the 1950s through the early 1980s. He viewed
art as a vehicle for social change, and his performance
'actions' were shamanistic-style experiences
incorporating ritualised movement and sound.

> **Shaman:** A person regarded as having access
> to, and influence in, the world of good and evil
> spirits. Typically, such people enter a trance
> state during a ritual.

His work is especially famous for its inclusion
of animal fat and felt, which had deep personal
significance to the artist.

The Pack

The two common materials, one organic, the other
fabricated, are an essential ingredient in his very
famous work, *The Pack* (Fig. 18.19). The work may
refer directly to his experiences in World War II. He
often described being rescued from a plane crash
over Crimea by a band of Tartars who coated his
body with fat and wrapped him in felt.

Form

A Volkswagen Bus is symbolic for an entire
generation of anti-war demonstration, international
social upheaval and fears of global nuclear Cold War.

Figure 18.19 *The Pack*, 1969, by Joseph Beuys,
Staatliche Museen, Germany. *The Pack* includes a
1961 Volkswagen bus and 24 wooden sleds.

Twenty-four sleds, resembling a pack of dogs, tumble from the back of the van. Each one carries a survival kit of fat, a blanket and a torch. They are leaving the vehicle to find anyone out in the wild in need of rescue.

Anselm Kiefer (b. 1945)

Anselm Kiefer came of age in Germany in the late 1960s, when the shame regarding Nazi crimes made the subject taboo. His artwork forced his contemporaries to deal with this past and redefine what it meant to be German.

In 1970, Kiefer became a student of Joseph Beuys, who encouraged his early use of symbolic photographic images to deal with 20th-century German history. Beuys also encouraged Kiefer to paint and, after his studies in law and languages, Kiefer attended the School of Fine Arts at Freiburg and the Art Academy in Karlsruhe.

Kiefer's art brings complex events of life, death and the universe together in a blend of painting, literature and sculpture.

His work emphasises the importance of the sacred and spiritual and includes paintings, glass, installations, artist books, drawings, watercolours, collages and altered photographs.

His materials vary from lead, concrete, and glass to textiles, tree roots and even burned books.

Your Golden Hair, Margarete; Your Ashen Hair, Shulamite

Kiefer painted a series of two images based on a poem by Holocaust survivor Paul Celan, which was widely read in post-war Germany.

He devoted more than thirty works to 'Margarete', the blonde-haired, blue-eyed Aryan ideal of the Nazis, while in a contrasting series he represents the Jewish women killed in concentration camps.

Your Golden Hair, Margarete (Fig. 18.20) portrays the 'golden hair' as sheaves of wheat in the countryside with real straw collaged onto the canvas. This represents a hope that this base material could be transformed into gold.

Your Ashen Hair, Shulamite (Fig 18.21) shows the German landscape – a source of great pride to the Nazis – as a place of shame and emptiness. The charred black fields and ashen landscape signal despair.

Figure 18.20
Your Golden Hair, Margarete, 1980, by Anselm Kiefer, watercolor, gouache and acrylic on paper, 40 × 30 cm, Metropolitan Museum, New York.

Figure 18.21 *Your Ashen Hair, Shulamite*, 1981, by Anselm Kiefer, oil, acrylic paint, shellac and straw on canvas, Kröller Müller Museum, Amsterdam.

Class discussion
Why do you think that German artists were so deeply affected by the Nazi regime even though they did not live through it?

Damien Hirst (b. 1965)

Damien Hirst changed from a young and unknown artist to an artistic superstar virtually overnight. This was largely due to promotion by the London businessman Charles Saatchi, who saw promise in his work with rotting animal corpses and gave him an open-ended budget to continue.

The Physical Impossibility of Death in the Mind of Someone Living

In 1990, Hirst presented *The Physical Impossibility of Death in the Mind of Someone Living* (Fig. 18.22) at the Saatchi Gallery in London. It consisted of a dead tiger shark preserved in formaldehyde in a glass case.

Hirst devised a fool-proof strategy for grabbing the attention of the public and critics. He well understood how the thrill of seeing a dead shark up-close for the first time would draw visitors to museums.

Sure enough, audiences at the Saatchi Gallery were wowed and repulsed in equal measures. But rather than being something new and shocking, Hirst's artwork was firmly rooted in historical sources. Reminders of death, or *mementi mori,* were, for example, often found in Vanitas paintings of the 17th century with the inclusion of human skulls (see Chapter 8).

Because it was initially preserved poorly, the creature began to deteriorate and, in 1993, the Saatchi Gallery gutted it and stretched its skin over a fiberglass mould. Hirst, however, commented, 'It didn't look as frightening ... You could tell it wasn't real. It had no weight.'

The piece was sold in 2004 for an undisclosed amount, but it is widely reported to have been $8 million.

Hirst's highly controversial work (as well as their enormous price tags) has kept him firmly at the centre of attention in the art world. He is reportedly the UK's richest living artist.

Figure 18.22
The Physical Impossibility of Death in the Mind of Someone Living, 1991, by Damien Hirst.
Glass, painted steel, silicone, monofilament, shark and formaldehyde solution, 217 × 542 × 180 cm.

Figure 18.23
My Bed, 1999, by Tracey Emin, Tate Modern, London. The work was considered very shocking, but it attracted scores of visitors to the museum. It was bought by a private collector but is on permanent loan to the Tate.

Note: Charles Saatchi is a Baghdad-born businessman and obsessive art collector who brought contemporary art to London by showcasing the works of the YBAs. He is considered to have changed the face of the art world in the 1980s and 1990s by changing the way the industry operated.

Tracey Emin (b. 1963)

Tracey Emin's work includes painting, drawing, video and installation, photography, needlework and sculpture. She explores complex personal states and ideas of self-representation in distinctly Expressionist styles and themes.

Her art is based on real-life events, and she visually and verbally dissects everything from 'hideous Brexit', to abortion, relationships and her mother's death with a passion that reveals her hopes, humiliations, failures and successes. These can be both tragic and humorous.

Emin grew up in Margate, where her parents ran a hotel. She suffered many destructive relationships in her teens and twenties because she says she had a very low opinion of herself in those days. As a result, she felt that she deserved to be treated badly.

My Bed

In 1999, all the publicity for the Turner Prize was on Tracey Emin and her notorious installation. Despite this, *My Bed* (Fig. 18.23) did not win the prize, which led Emin to believe that the Tate just used her for publicity and never seriously considered giving her the prize.

Meaning and Interpretation

This artwork explores the common experience of depression in a very personal and intimate way, but it also draws an important distinction between representation and presentation. Unlike a painting or sculpture, this art object doesn't refer to another object. It is itself the object.

At the time, Emin was living in a council flat in Waterloo, London, and this was her real bed, with every kind of intimate and embarrassing object scattered across the crumpled, stained sheets.

The artist was recovering from a traumatic relationship breakdown, but now all these years later, she sees it as a portrait of a younger woman.

Note: The Turner Prize is awarded to a British artist. 'British' can mean an artist working primarily in Britain or an artist born in Britain working globally. It was named after the 19th-century British artist J.M.W. Turner and was first awarded in 1984.

Anish Kapoor (b. 1954)

One of the most influential sculptors of his generation, Kapoor is perhaps most famous for his public sculptures. These are both adventures in form and genuine feats of engineering.

Born in Bombay, India, Kapoor has lived and worked in London since the early 1970s when he moved there to study art.

Kapoor creates elegant sculptures that combine simple materials, geometric shape and organic form (Fig. 18.24). He manoeuvres between vastly different scales and has worked with mirrors, stone, wax and PVC. He has a particular interest in

Figure 18.24 *Sky Mirror*, 2006, by Anish Kapoor, steel, 11 m diameter, New York. The artist described this massive work as a 'non-object' because its reflective surface allows it to disappear. Versions of this piece have been installed in the UK, USA, the Netherlands and Russia.

negative space. 'That's what I am interested in,' he says, 'the void, the moment when it isn't a hole. It is a space full of what isn't there.'

Find out how thousands of people play with Anish Kapoor's *Cloud Gate* every day in Chicago.

Analysis

Examine the works produced by artists born during the inter-war years and how they looked beyond Europe for inspiration.

Compare the technique, style and materials used in these to works of art produced in the 1980s and explore the concepts that inspired them.

The 1960s was a lively and transformative decade for art. The power of commercial galleries in London was a crucial element in its promotion, introducing the new art and artists of America to young artists. Galleries also introduced audiences to new and sometimes controversial ways of making art.

By the 1980s, John Kasmin was still dealing with established artists, but with investment firms increasingly involved in the art market, he described art as 'becoming far more of a counter in financial games'.

The Kasmin Gallery closed in 1992, marking the end of an era.

Chapter Review

1. Why do you think Francis Bacon chose such grotesque imagery?

2. Describe the process in making a work of Op Art.

3. Describe and discuss the use of light, space and objects used by David Hockney in *Mr and Mrs Clark and Percy* to show the deteriorating relationship between the couple.

4. What elements of Anselm Kiefer's paintings do you think viewers in Germany might have found disturbing?

5. How do you think wrapping a bridge in plastic fabric makes it an art object?

6. What do you think of how Tracey Emin exposes her own life experiences in her art?

7. Examine the *Stravinsky Fountain* by Niki de Saint Phalle and her husband Jean Tinguely which was inspired by the music of Igor Stravinsky (Fig.18.25).

   a. Do you think the black and highly coloured sculptures work well together?
   b. Which works do you think best express the musical compositions?

Figure 18.25 *Stravinsky Fountain*, 1983, by Niki de Saint Phalle and Jean Tinguely, fibre-reinforced plastic and steel, Paris.

Further Research

www.vam.ac.uk/articles/introducing-mary-quant – An introduction to Mary Quant and the 'Swinging Sixties'

thierrynoir.com/berlin-wall – Learn more about Thierry Noir's graffiti on the Berlin Wall

www.youtube.com – Search for 'Bridget Riley speaks about her work' (0:58) to hear the artist's take on Op Art

www.youtube.com – Watch '"I assume the best work is yet to come": David Hockney (1980)' (5:07) to see an interview with the iconic artist

martinsharpcovers.blogspot.com – Explore Martin Sharp's Pop Art album cover designs

www.youtube.com – Search for 'Joseph Beuys | Utopia at the Stag Monuments' (5:21) to watch curator Norman Rosenthal and artist Antony Gormley discussing 'Utopia at the Stag Monuments', the most important UK exhibition of Beuys's work

www.khanacademy.org – Search for 'Christo and Jeanne-Claude, The Gates' for an article on one of the artistic couple's most extensive works

Chapter 19

21st-Century Art

By the end of this chapter I will ...

* understand what is meant by Visual Culture
* have considered how artworks selling for vast amounts of money may affect the perception of its value
* have observed how artists responding to a wide range of issues and ideas have changed from traditional disciplines
* be able to discuss how artists use new technology
* be able to describe and discuss the work of artists that addresses historical, political, or environmental issues in today's society.

Context

The 21st century is in its early years, but already art has taken an incredible variety of forms. There are now more artistic tools, techniques, opportunities and ideas than ever before. The spectrum of art is so diverse that it is difficult to find a single movement that defines the current era of artistic production. Issues and ideas are evolving rapidly and new artists are constantly gaining attention and influence. It is possible, however, to look at some of the styles, approaches and philosophies that are beginning to shape this latest era of human creation.

Visual Culture

In more recent times, our understanding of art and communication has shifted dramatically. The interdisciplinary field of study is now known as Visual Culture.

Along with art, students of Visual Culture examine areas like medicine, science, sports, politics, consumer culture, and religion. They also analyse film, television, graphic novels, photography, fashion

Figure 19.1
Rabbit, 1980, by Jeff Koons, steel. Christie's Auction House described it as 'at once cute and imposing', as it is over a metre high.

Figure 19.2 *Portrait of an Artist (Pool with Two Figures)*, 1972, by David Hockney, acrylic on canvas, 210 × 300 cm. Introspective and remote, Peter Schlesinger (who was Hockney's boyfriend and muse) looks down on the swimmer, who we presume is Hockney himself. The painting shows their deteriorating relationship; in contrast to the naturalistic depiction of the landscape, the pool and swimming figure are carefully patterned and abstracted.

design and many other kinds of popular culture in addition to fine-art media such as painting and sculpture.

The Art Market Today

In May 2019, the record was broken for the most expensive artwork by a living artist sold at auction. A stainless steel rabbit sculpture by Jeff Koons (b. 1955) sold at Christie's for a cool $91.1 million (Fig. 19.1).

The price surpassed the previous sale of the celebrated painting *Portrait of an Artist (Pool with Two Figures)* by David Hockney sold at Christie's in New York for just over $90m in November 2018 (Fig. 19.2).

The Italian artist Maurizio Cattelan (b. 1960) came to art relatively late in life, shifting from furniture design to sculpture in his twenties. His work soon captured public attention with its overt wit, but it also provoked more complex interpretations.

Cattelan's famous 1996 sculpture, *The Ballad of Trotsky*, featured a taxidermy horse hanging from the ceiling by a saddle (Fig. 19.3).

The exhibit cleverly 'switched' the function of the saddle from a device for holding up a rider to one for holding up a horse, but it also questioned the traditional function of equestrian art as a means of promoting human power and authority. The piece was auctioned in New York in 2004 for $2.1m (£1.15m).

Identity Art

Identity is the way we perceive and express ourselves. Factors and conditions that an individual is born with will often play a role in defining this. Aspects of a person's identity can of course change throughout his or her life and artists today use their work to express, explore and question this and other ideas about identity.

Innovations and Inventions

Post-Internet Art

The era following the creation of the internet has been a huge development for humanity. The internet goes hand in hand with technological advancements, some of which are feared and others welcomed.

Either way, the internet changed the world and because of that, it has also changed art in its content, its form, its aesthetics, the way we consume it and the way we potentially buy it.

In this new age of technology, artists have taken full advantage of television and video, and the arrival of computers has presented even more opportunities.

The possibilities are endless and just like millions of traditional artists before them, today's practitioners are pushing the boundaries of their resources and finding new solutions.

Participatory Art

Recent decades heralded a new wave of so-called participatory art. The idea is that those experiencing the art are physically engaged in it too.

During recent years, the artist's work has continued to provoke debate. In 2018, Cattelan installed a functioning toilet made of 18-carat gold in Manhattan's Guggenheim Museum, giving it the provocative title *America*. He intended that the golden toilet should be used to criticise the unfair distribution of income and the art market bubble.

RESPOND

Class discussion

When an artwork fetches a record price at auction, the first question everyone silently asks is: 'Could it really be worth that?' But if art is 'worth' whatever someone is willing to pay, how does it change our perception of the work as art?

Neo-Dadaism and Absurdist Art

Dadaism is an art movement of the European avant-garde in the early 20th century. Almost exactly one century since its inception, it has made a huge comeback. Neo-Dadaism is taking on new forms, and this new style of anti-art movement is more popular than ever.

Media and Areas of Practice

Amidst all the diversity of contemporary art, it is easy to forget that the long-standing traditions of painting and sculpture remain central to artistic production. Classic artistic methods are still part of the ultra-modern ones.

Most contemporary artists do not draw rigid distinctions between high art and popular culture. Today, inspiration, imagery, material and concepts come from a wide variety of sources.

Art Elements and Principles of Design

Very little of today's art is based on the traditional forms of visual art, but almost everything that belongs to the domain of the visual uses at least one of the basic art elements. Line, shape, colour, texture and space continue to build our perception of what we see.

Surrounded as we are by colourful imagery, the need to communicate efficiently has never been greater. The contemporary designer must follow the rules to create an effective composition that cleanly delivers a message.

The confident use of the fundamental principles of design, like symmetry, balance and harmony, contrasting colours and white space, are a vital element in guiding the viewer's eye to that important information quickly.

Art and Artists

A key feature of the art scene in the 21st century is the impact of globalisation and the speed of connection of human activity and information across time and space. Awareness of the vitality of contemporary art in localities around the globe has grown so much that anyone with access to the internet can follow developments in communities from Asia to Australia to Africa.

Research ideas and get inspiration for your own art project by finding artists on social media. Many have websites or put their work on other platforms. Check out their followers to find further ideas.

Kara Walker (b. 1969)

Kara Walker has gained national and international recognition for her cut-paper silhouettes depicting historical narratives haunted by sexuality, violence and subjugation. She uses a mixture of drawing, painting, text, shadow puppetry, film and sculpture and sound to expose the power, pain and pleasure of black characters who were caught in the miserable, downtrodden existence of the pre-Civil War American South.

Her work calls into question what black art could and should be, and whether it should even be categorised in such a way.

The Katastwóf Karavan

This performative sculpture, built for Prospect New Orleans, took two years to make (Fig. 19.4). It was

Figure 19.4 *The Katastwóf Karavan*, 2017, by Kara Walker, painted steel, at Prospect New Orleans.

placed at Algiers Point because enslaved peoples were held there before being sold at locations on the East Bank of the Mississippi.

Katastwóf is the Haitian Creole word for 'catastrophe', and it refers to the institution of slavery and its role in bringing Africans to European colonies. The wagon has figures in silhouette on its sides and a 32-note steam calliope that resembles those on Mississippi river steamboats.

> **Calliope:** An American keyboard instrument resembling an organ but with the notes produced by steam whistles, formerly used on showboats and in travelling fairs.

> *Note:* Prospect New Orleans is a city-wide triennial exhibition that was founded in 2008 following New Orleans' devastation from Hurricane Katrina. Running from November 2017 to February 2018, Prospect 4 was entitled *The Lotus in Spite of the Swamp*.

Ai Weiwei (b. 1957)

Ai Weiwei has been an open critic of the lack of democracy and human rights in his native China. In 2011, he was charged with tax evasion and placed under house arrest for four years. He later fled to Berlin, where he established a new studio.

Ai Weiwei's political activism has its roots in a turbulent childhood. Born in Beijing, he grew up in an artistic family. His father, Ai Qing, was one of China's most important poets. Yet shortly after Ai's birth, the Communist government under Mao Zedong accused his father of supporting capitalism, and the entire family was exiled to a labour camp in Manchuria.

Today, Ai lives in Britain and has become a true star of the art world. His fame has earned him increasingly prominent international commissions and his art has taken an incredible variety of forms, blurring the distinction between artist and activist.

Law of the Journey

One of his newest works is an installation consisting of an oversized rubber boat filled with refugees (Fig. 19.5). This is a metaphor for the destiny of the thousands of human beings seeking help and shelter.

This multi-layered, epic statement on the human condition is the artist's expression of empathy and moral concern in the face of continuous, uncontrolled destruction and carnage. He says: 'We need more tolerance, compassion and trust for each other since we all are one … There's no refugee crisis, but only human crisis … In dealing with refugees we've lost our very basic values.'

Figure 19.5
Law of the Journey, 2017, by Ai Weiwei.

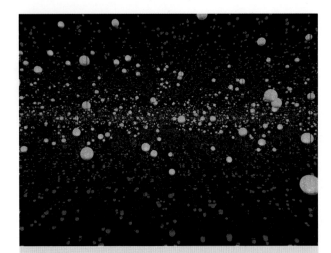

Figure 19.6 *INFINITY MIRRORED ROOM - DANCING LIGHTS THAT FLEW UP TO THE UNIVERSE*, 2019, by Yayoi Kusama, David Zwirner Gallery, New York.

Yayoi Kusama (b. 1929)

At the time of writing, Yayoi Kusama spends every day making art or writing. Globally recognised for her polka dots and pumpkins, Kusama's method of using mirrors to create the illusion of infinite space with a kaleidoscopic effect has made her a pop culture icon.

Born in Matsumoto, Japan, Kusama began creating art as early as age 10. According to her autobiography, she experienced auditory and visual hallucinations from a very early age. These visions prompted her to create art, and included the polka dots that would become her signature motif.

After World War II, Kusama moved to New York City. In the 1960s, she gained massive recognition for her paintings, sculptures and cultural happenings protesting the Vietnam War.

The repetitive nature of her artwork forces the artist to face issues like sexual anxiety, and more recently, dazzling and beautiful installations using light and mirrors to address the concept of eternity and infinity.

Infinity Mirrored Room

Kusama first produced a mirrored installation in 1965, for a solo exhibition at the Castellane Gallery in New York, where she placed thousands of soft, polka-dot-studded male sexual organs against reflective surfaces.

In *INFINITY MIRRORED ROOM - DANCING LIGHTS THAT FLEW UP TO THE UNIVERSE* (Fig. 19.6), her 2019 'infinity' room, a single, suspended globe of light illuminates the mirrored chamber. Then a second, then a third, lights up until the room becomes a constellation of lanterns with the viewer at its centre. The globes then flash to red and after a few seconds of coloured light, the room goes dark again.

Olafur Eliasson (b. 1967)

The Danish-Icelandic artist Olafur Eliasson uses natural elements like light, water, fog and makeshift technical devices to transform galleries and public areas. Known for their elegant simplicity and lack of materiality, his installations are rooted in a belief that art can create a sensitive space for both the individual and communities.

In 2003, he famously installed a giant artificial sun inside the Tate Modern (*The weather project*). Another of his projects, *Green river*, was to pour bright green (environmentally safe) dye into rivers running through the centres of Los Angeles, Stockholm, Tokyo and other cities.

In 2008, Eliasson installed four large waterfalls (*The New York City Waterfalls*) in New York's East River to give the city a sense of dimension. In the summer of 2016, a towering waterfall appeared to fall from mid-air into the Grand Canal at the Palace of Versailles as part of a slideshow. Cascading from high above the surface of the pool, the *Waterfall*

Figure 19.7 *Waterfall*, 2016, by Olafur Eliasson, Versailles.

installation appears as a torrent of water with no actual source when seen from the front steps of the palace (Fig. 19.7).

Analysis

Consider some of the many new trends and experiments that characterise the art of the early 21st century and examine some works that are of particular interest to you. Find out how and why they were created by examining the materials and techniques used by the artist, and by exploring the concept or meaning that she or he intended to convey.

Today, we can enjoy the work of those creating art in many forms and have an open mind towards the millions of artists who create for creation's sake, without worrying about conforming to any rules or movements.

wall was an updated version of an untitled piece from 2007.
a. What do you think of using real animals for making art?
b. Discuss the possible meaning of this work.

Figure 19.8 *KAPUTT*, 2013, by Maurizio Cattelan , taxidermied horses, life-sized.

Chapter Review

1. Is any work of art worth $90 million? Who and why, in your opinion, would someone pay money like that?

2. How has art been directly affected by the internet?

3. What relevance do you think the historical images in Kara Walker's art have to issues in today's society?

4. Ai Weiwei could be considered an activist. Do you think art should have this kind of role?

5. Are Olafur Eliasson's projects just ornamental or do you think they have a role in drawing attention to environmental issues?

6. Maurizio Cattelan's 2013 show was entitled *KAPUTT*. This display of taxidermy horses who had apparently gone headfirst into a

Further Research

www.mymodernmet.com/jeff-koons-ballerina-sculpture – Discover another of Jeff Koons' massive sculptures

www.youtube.com – Watch 'Artist Kara Walker – "I'm an Unreliable Narrator"' (6:00) to learn about how a fountain in London explores the interconnected histories of Africa, America and Europe

www.youtube.com – Find out more about Yayoi Kusama and her signature polka dot style by watching 'Yayoi Kusama – Obsessed with Polka Dots | Tate' (7:24)

www.youtube.com – Search for 'Olafur Eliasson interview: Retrospective opens at Tate Modern' (5:00) to learn more about the artist's seminal works

www.aiweiwei.com – Ai Weiwei's official website

Unit 7

Pre-Christian Ireland

(*c.* 4000 BC–AD 500)

Before

The Palaeolithic Period
c. 10500–4000 BC

The Stone Age
4000–2000 BC

The entrance
stone at
Newgrange
3200 BC

The Bronze Age
c. 2000–500 BC

Sun discs
c. 2000 BC

A gorget
800–700 BC

The Iron Age
(500 BC–AD 400)

The Turoe Sto
c. 50 BC

The Broighter
Collar
1st century B(

After

The Insular Period
c. AD 400–1100

Pre-Christian Ireland (*c.* 4000 BC–AD 500)

The Stone Age (4000–2000 BC)

Before Pre-Christian Ireland

Settled communities were late to develop in Ireland. The first Palaeolithic people who lived here, *c.* 10500 BC, lived by hunting and by gathering wild fruits and vegetables. Farming had developed in the Middle East from *c.* 9000 BC, but did not reach Ireland and the far West and North of Europe until *c.* 4000 BC. The world population was relatively small at the time, so there was no great pressure on people to find new land. Trade and communications were just beginning to develop.

Context

The first permanent dwelling places were made by the first farmers who arrived in Ireland around 4000 BC in what is called the Neolithic period.

> **Neolithic:** The New Stone Age (Neolithic) was from 3700 to 2000 BC in Ireland. The word comes from the Greek words *neo*, meaning 'new' and *lithos* meaning 'stone'. It refers to the time when farming and tool-making evolved and people began to settle in permanent communities.

These farmers seemed to have arrived in the north-east of the country first, where a crossing from Scotland would have been the shortest sea journey from Britain. They probably brought their seeds and animals with them on the crossing, which means they must have had substantial boats or rafts even at this early time. Neolithic people spread out across the country over the course of a few hundred years, because their dwelling and burial sites are found countrywide.

Innovation and Invention

Everything that the Stone Age people built and designed was new in this country. There were no examples for them to work from, so they were a creative and inventive people solving design and construction problems as they encountered them.

Passage mounds, a type of Neolithic burial structure, can be found in countries along the Atlantic coast from Africa to Scandinavia, but the largest and most elaborately decorated examples are in Ireland.

Stone Age art and construction created the foundation for all that followed; these people were the original innovators and inventors. They had no examples to follow; every tool, design and construction technique had to be created from scratch. These innovations were happening all over the world, and found their way to Ireland with the first farmers.

Media and Areas of Practice

Corbelling

Corbelled chambers are the oldest roofed structures still standing in Western Europe (Fig. 20.1).

At Newgrange, grooves were cut in the top surface of the roof stones to help shed any water that might have seeped down into the mound. The roof stones were sloped outward to shed water and to distribute the weight away from the centre, thus reducing the risk of a collapse.

> **Corbelled vaults** were built on the standing stones of the chamber of a passage mound in gradually decreasing circles of large flat stones sloping slightly outwards. These rings of stones became self-supporting as the circles grew smaller, until the dome could finally be closed by a single stone.

Figure 20.1
A section of a corbelled vault.

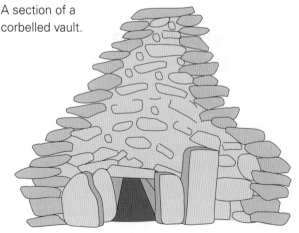

Chip Carving

Lines and patterns on stones were made by cutting into the surface with a sharp flint or obsidian edge, or by picking or pecking with a stone chisel or point driven by a hammer stone (Fig. 20.2). This technique was used to create areas of low relief.

Smoothing

The surface of the stones was sometimes smoothed by hammering or by rubbing with a rough textured stone. The lines on the entrance stone at Newgrange were smoothed and deepened in this way.

Hammer stone

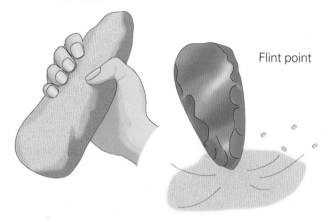

Flint point

Figure 20.2 Chip carving.

> **Stone dressing:** Most of the stones at Knowth and Newgrange have been dressed. This means rough areas and a thin layer of stone have been removed with a stone chisel to improve the colour and surface of the stone.

> **Incision:** Simple cuts or scratches are made using a sharp flint on the less elaborately decorated stones.

> *Note:* Wood and stone were the only materials available for building and making tools and weapons during the Stone Age. Some hard stones like flint could be broken and shaped to produce sharp edges that could be used as knives, scrapers, chisels, axes, spears and arrowheads (Fig. 20.3).

(above left) Blades, scrapers, arrows and lance heads were made from flint, shaped by flaking or knapping the stone to create a sharp edge.	(above right) Polished axe heads were used to chop down trees. They might also have been used as weapons.

Figure 20.3 Stone Age tools and weapons.

Pottery

Clay was dug and hand-built into a variety of simple pot shapes, which would have been heated enough in open fires to turn them into ceramics (Fig. 20.4).

Figure 20.4 Examples of Stone Age pottery.

Create a simple thumb pot, using Stone Age technology to decorate it.

Houses

Domestic buildings were generally round in plan, built with stone wood and mud, with thatched roofs.

Note: Stones for large structures would have been moved by dragging and levering, possibly using logs as rollers to ease the progress of the largest stones. Beasts of burden and the wheel were not yet available.

Art Elements and Design Principles

Stone Age designs are made from the simplest art elements: dot and line with a little low relief. There are 10 different categories of designs:

- five are made of curved lines: concentric circles, spirals, arcs, serpentiforms (snake-like designs) and dots in circle shapes
- five are made of straight lines: chevrons, lozenges (diamond shapes), radials (sticking out from a centre like spokes on a wheel), parallel lines and offsets (lines at angles to each other).

All the shapes are drawn freehand and they are abstract, but they must have held some meaning for the people who made them (Fig. 20.5 and 20.6).

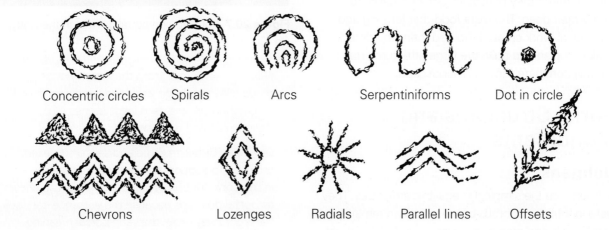

Concentric circles   Spirals   Arcs   Serpentiforms   Dot in circle

Chevrons   Lozenges   Radials   Parallel lines   Offsets

Figure 20.5 Range of Stone Age designs.

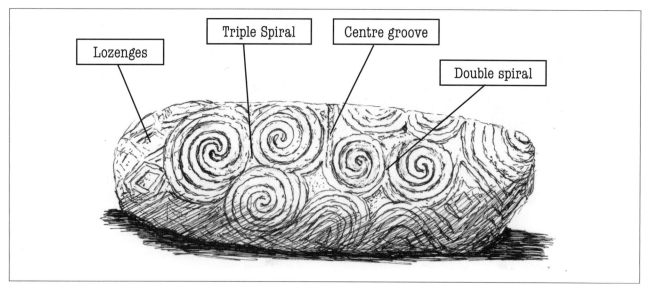

Lozenges

Triple Spiral

Centre groove

Double spiral

Figure 20.6 The entrance stone at Newgrange.

Sketching is a good way to help your memory. Practise things like the entrance stone at Newgrange. Begin your sketch with the groove that marks the entrance, near the top centre of the stone. Draw the three spirals to the left, then the group of spirals to the right. Add in the wave pattern along the lower part of the stone, then fill in the lozenges and curves at each end. Write notes on your sketches pointing out the important features of the design.

Artists and Artworks

The works of art and construction that survive from the Stone Age are generally associated with places of importance to these first people. Little evidence of their language or everyday lives survives, but we can find the remains of the structures they built as places of ritual or to glorify their dead. The extra food that farming and communal work created allowed them the time to think out, plan and build the large structures that can still dominate their local landscape.

Burial Structures and Monuments

Dolmens

Dolmens are the simplest megalithic structures. They were identified as tombs because human remains from burials and cremations were found within them, along with some Stone Age artefacts. Stones at the

back of the tombs are generally lower than those at the front. Some archaeologists believe that this suggests that capstones may have been dragged up an earthen ramp to rest on the upright stones. There are dramatic examples at Poulnabrone in the Burren, Co. Clare (Fig. 20.7), and at Kilcooley, Co. Donegal. There are 170 or so portal dolmens in Ireland.

Capstone

Upright leg

Figure 20.7 Poulnabrone portal dolmen in the Burren, Co. Clare.

Megalithic: Comes from the Greek words *mega* meaning 'large' and *lithos* meaning 'stone'. Megalithic builders used large stones to build their tombs and monuments.

Dolmens: Between three and seven stone legs are used to support one or two large capstones in the construction of a dolmen. These are known as portal dolmens because the entrance can look like a doorway (from the Latin *porta*, meaning 'gate').

Figure 20.8 Court cairn reconstruction.

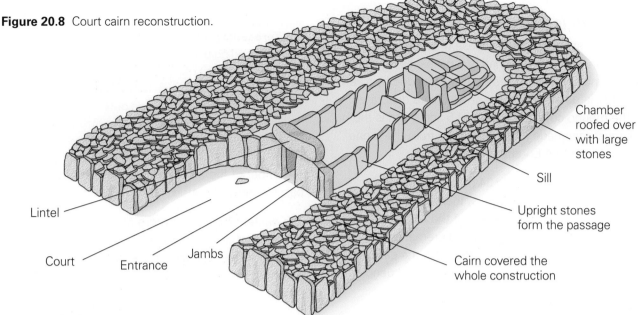

Chamber roofed over with large stones

Sill

Upright stones form the passage

Cairn covered the whole construction

Lintel

Court

Entrance

Jambs

Court Cairns

Court cairns structures are understood to be places of burial, where ceremonies or rituals might have taken place. A covered chamber inside the cairn was sometimes divided by upright stones and sills or lintels, creating 'doorways' between spaces. Outside, a semi-circular area created a formal entrance or ceremonial area (Fig. 20.8). There is an outstanding example at Creevykeel, Co. Sligo.

> **Court cairn:** A combination of a burial chamber inside a mound or cairn of stones with an open court in front of it.

> *Note:* Dolmens and court cairns have no added decoration, but they were built as the result of ideas, which puts them in the realm of art.

Passage Mounds (Graves)

There is a growing preference for the term 'passage mound' rather than 'passage grave' or 'tomb', as our understanding of their function is still growing. There are over 200 known passage mounds in Ireland, in a variety of layouts and sizes. Many have decorated stones as part of their construction.

There is a concentration of these structures in Co. Meath, particularly at Brú na Bóinne, an area 4 km

long and 3 km wide, that is enclosed by a bend in the River Boyne (Fig. 20.9). The site is 8 km east of Drogheda, 40 km north of Dublin. There are close to 40 mounds in this area, including three large mounds at Knowth, Dowth and Newgrange, with smaller satellite mounds surrounding them.

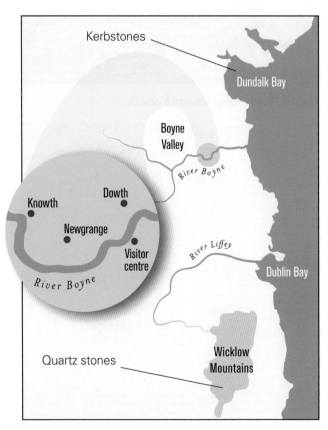

Kerbstones

Dundalk Bay

Boyne Valley

River Boyne

Dowth

Knowth

Newgrange

Visitor centre

River Boyne

River Liffey

Dublin Bay

Quartz stones

Wicklow Mountains

Figure 20.9 Brú na Bóinne, Co. Meath.

Knowth (c. 4000 BC)

The oldest and largest of these mounds is at Knowth (Fig. 20.10). It has two passages, one facing east and one facing west. It is surrounded by a kerb of 127 large stones, most of which are decorated. The mound covers an area of 1.5 acres and is the largest manmade roofed structure from the Stone Age in Western Europe (Fig. 20.11).

The western passage is 34 m long and is of the undifferentiated type; that is, there is no clearly separate chamber at the end of the passage. A basin stone, with the remains of cremation burials and some grave goods, was found in the passage. The grave goods included stone balls and pendants, coloured beads, shell necklaces and stone tools such as arrowheads, knives, chisels and scrapers.

Figure 20.10 Aerial view of Knowth.

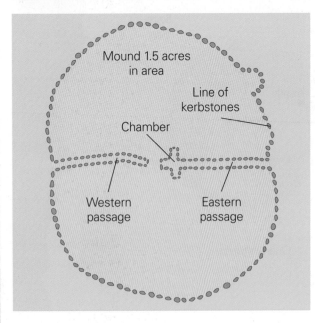

Figure 20.11 Plan of Knowth.

Mound 1.5 acres in area

Line of kerbstones

Chamber

Western passage

Eastern passage

Kerbstones: The large stones laid end to end surrounding the base of many of the passage mounds. Some of these stones are 3 m to 4 m long and over 1 m high. The kerb may have been laid out to define the shape of the mound and to retain the filling material that formed the mound.

A number of the orthostats (upright stones) in the passage are decorated.

The eastern passage is more elaborate. There is a chamber which is cruciform (cross-shaped) in plan and has a corbelled roof at the end of the 40 m passage. The corbelled vault is 7 m tall at its centre. A beautifully decorated basin stone was found in the recess at the northern side of the chamber (Fig. 20.12). The outside of the basin is decorated with horizontal grooves, with concentric circles and curves at the centre. Inside, it is decorated with arcs and radiating lines. A mace head carved from a piece of flint from the Orkney Islands off the west coast of Scotland was also found (Fig. 20.13 and 20.14). It is a remarkably well-made and finely finished piece for such an early date. A mace is a type of hammer, so the heavy end is at the bottom. This mace has often been illustrated upside down because it looks a bit like a face from that angle.

Chip-carved design, about 1 cm deep

Figure 20.12 Knowth basin stone.

Basin stone: A large, almost circular, low profile stone, hollowed out to create a kind of basin. They seem to have been used in passages to hold the cremated remains of the dead and small offerings.

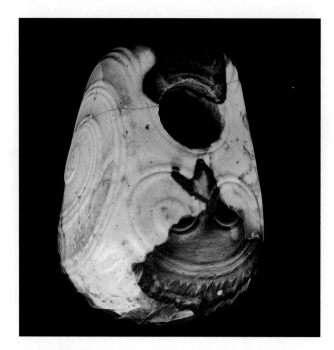

Figure 20.13 Knowth mace head, carved from flint.

Figure 20.14 What the Knowth mace head would have originally looked like with a handle.

Quartz Stones

White quartz stones are laid on the ground in front of the eastern entrance, creating a ceremonial or restricted area. This is a different interpretation of the purpose of the quartz stones to the arrangement made at Newgrange during its reconstruction.

Decorated Stones at Knowth

The greatest number of decorated stones is at Knowth – about half of all the Stone Age art in Ireland. Many of the 127 stones in the kerb are elaborately patterned. Kerbstone 15, which looks like a sundial, can be interpreted as a lunar calendar recording the phases of the moon (Fig. 20.15). Kerbstone 78 is also thought to refer to phases of the moon, although the designs are quite different. Wavy lines and circles dominate the pattern, which flows over the entire surface of the stone (Fig. 20.16).

Figure 20.15 Knowth kerbstone 15, the sundial stone.

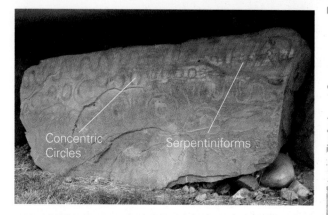

Concentric Circles

Serpentiniforms

Figure 20.16 Knowth kerbstone 78.

Dowth (c. 3200 BC)

Dowth has not yet been thoroughly excavated, but it has two passages facing west. One is a short passage with a circular chamber. The other passage is longer with a cruciform chamber containing a basin stone. There are many decorated stones in this mound as well. We will know more when a complete survey has been done.

Newgrange (c. 3200 BC)

Newgrange was built about 3200 BC. It was excavated from 1967 to 1975, when it was reconstructed into the shape that we see today (Fig. 20.17).

The most well known of the Boyne Valley mounds, Newgrange is famous for the following:

● The 'roof box' over its entrance allows the sun to shine down the long passage into the furthest recesses of the chamber (a total of 24 m) on the days around 21 December (the midwinter solstice, the shortest day) each year.

Between the first and second roof slabs of the passage, over the entrance, is the rectangular opening built in stone, which forms the roof box. The upper lintel stone of this opening is carved to a depth of about 2 mm with a series of triangles, which create a raised pattern of X shapes separated by vertical lines. The large flat slab of stone seen beside the entrance was used to close it, so the light box was the only source of light inside the passage.

- The passage, which is 18.7 m long, is formed by upright stones (orthostats): 22 on the left (west) side and 21 on the right (east) side. These uprights are roofed with flat stones for most of the length of the passage and corbelled at the end nearest the chamber.

- The chamber is roughly 6 m in diameter and 6 m tall. It has three recesses, which create a cruciform plan like the east passage at Knowth. There is a basin stone in each of the recesses which contained ash from human cremations (Fig. 20.18).

Quartz Stones

The wall of white quartz stones and grey water-worn granite stones stands on the row of kerbstones at the front of the structure. The quartz came from Wicklow, 85 km away, and the granite beach stones came from Dundalk Bay, which is 50 km away.

The white stones were arranged as we see them today on the instructions of Professor O'Kelly, the chief archaeologist. Based on his research, he imagined that the mound had been built with a facing of white and grey stones when it was first constructed. There is now some dispute about this theory and the archaeologists at Knowth came to a different conclusion.

- Ninety-seven kerbstones surround the base of the mound at Newgrange. Many have decorations ranging from simple lines and spirals to fully decorated stones like the beautifully patterned entrance stone and kerbstone 52 on the opposite side of the mound. The kerbstones near the entrance are the largest – they are between 3 m and 4 m long and 1.2 m high. They are greywacke stone, which is found at Clogherhead, Co. Louth, about 30 km away. The 97 stones had to be transported by boat or raft along the coast and up the Boyne River to a point near Newgrange and then moved uphill to the site.

Figure 20.17 Newgrange.

The quartz wall

Stones from the Great Circle

The entrance

Kerbstones

- The Great Circle is a ring of standing stones that surrounds the mound, 7 m to 12 m outside it. Only 12 undecorated stones remain standing out of an original 35. This ring of standing stones may be more modern than the mound, possibly from the Bronze Age.

 Research the arrangement of quartz stones at Newgrange and Knowth. Make drawings and write your opinion on which arrangement you prefer and give reasons for your answer.

 Have a class discussion on the merits of one arrangement of quartz stones over the other.

Construction

The mound at Newgrange is 11 m tall and between 79 m and 85 m in diameter.

Building large structures like these was a heroic task for Stone Age people. Their technology was limited to what they could carry, pull or lever into place, yet they moved large stones up to five tons in weight across country that may have been forested.

Layout

Construction probably began with the layout of the passages, as their orientation to the sun or moonlight was an essential part of the purpose of the structure. The line of the kerb would need to be laid out early

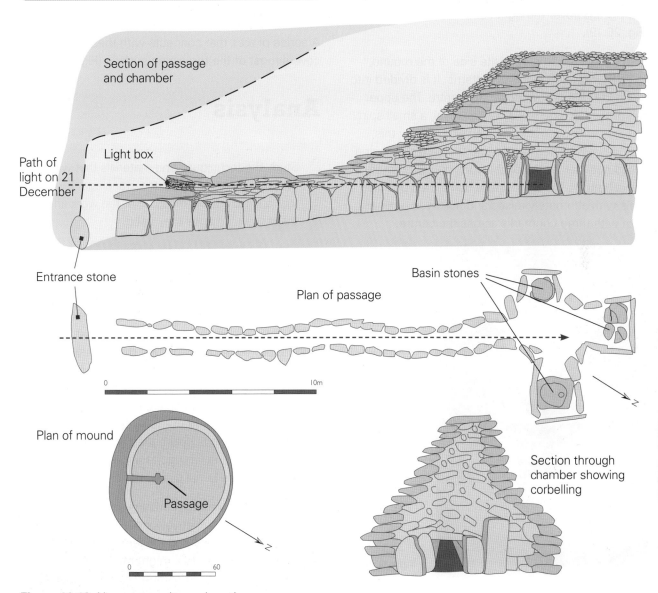

Figure 20.18 Newgrange plan and section.

on, as it was the retaining structure for the stones, sods and earth that made up the body of the mound. The corbelled roof over the chamber might have been constructed as the level of the mound built up allowing access to gradually higher levels.

Decorated Stones at Newgrange

At Newgrange the entrance stone is covered in a curvilinear pattern, which emphasises the size of the stone. A groove at the top centre lines up with the entrance and the roof box. Left of the groove is a triple spiral and beyond this, a series of lozenges covers the end of the stone. Right of the centre, two double spirals sit on top of a wave pattern that connects back to the triple spiral. Lozenges, curves and zigzags cover the right-hand end of the stone (Fig. 20.19).

Kerbstone 52, at the opposite side of the mound, has a more varied range of patterns. It is divided into two parts by a groove down the centre. The upper half of the left side has a double spiral, a small spiral and arcs with cupmarks at each side. Below this, lozenges have been carved into the surface, leaving raised outlines. A row of chevrons makes a border at the bottom. The right side is dominated by three ovals with alternately raised and hollowed outlines, each with three cupmarks across the centre.

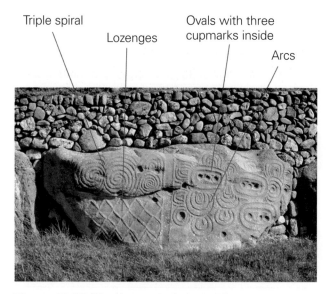

Figure 20.20 Newgrange kerbstone 52.

A series of arcs that connects with these ovals covers most of the remaining surface (Fig. 20.20).

Analysis

Study the techniques and materials that were available to the artists of the stone age. Try to work out the reasons for the work and the range of images they used.

Passage mounds seem to have been so much more than graves for our ancestors. The sheer scale of the commitment from the Stone Age people who spent generations constructing them must have made them the most important thing in the lives of the community. They were the largest structures in the country for thousands of years and were the source of legends. The earliest records describe Brú na Bóinne as the home of the Tuath Dé Danann, the ancient Irish gods descended from the skies to inhabit Ireland. In later generations, they were thought to be the burial places of ancient kings.

The number of cremated remains inside the passage mounds is relatively small in relation to the size of the community and the length of time the mounds were in use. This might mean that only very special members of the community were buried there or that they were ritual or sacrificial burials.

Figure 20.19 Newgrange entrance stone and light box.

Astronomy

There is a growing body of support for the theory that designs on the stones relate to the movements of the sun, moon and planets. This would be a way to keep track of the seasons and important community events. Kerbstones at Knowth in particular can be interpreted as recording lunar events and patterns. A full lunar cycle takes over 18 years, so Stone Age observers must have had ways to remember the phases of the moon.

- The passages at Knowth received the light of the rising and setting sun at the equinoxes, around the 21 March and 23 September. The spring and autumn were important seasons for planting and harvesting in a farming community.

- At Newgrange, the light of sunrise enters the chamber through the light box on the winter solstice, the shortest day of the year, around 21 December. This event may have celebrated the death of the old year and the beginning of the new. Other passage mounds also received the light of the sun or the moon at significant times and are the focus of ongoing research.

Our understanding of the Stone Age in Ireland continues to evolve. Following a period of drought in the summer of 2018, traces of large wooden structures were revealed between Newgrange and the River Boyne. Archaeologists have interpreted these as ritual sites that are later than Newgrange, but connected to it in some way they have not yet worked out.

 Find out more about the recent archaeological discoveries at Newgrange by reading the article 'Archaeological discoveries at the Brú na Bóinne World Heritage Site' on *www.worldheritageireland.ie*.

Chapter Review

1. What range of tools did Stone Age people have and what did they use them for? Draw some tools and describe their use.

2. How do you think the Stone Age structures were built? Make annotated sketches and describe the methods you think they used.

3. Describe the range of designs used by Stone Age people. Do you think they were simply decoration or did they have meaning? Draw, annotate and describe some of the designs.

4. Based on your observations of Stone Age construction, art and design, do you think they were intelligent and resourceful people? Write an illustrated and annotated response to the question.

5. What do you think motivated Stone Age people to build such large structures? Use sketches to explain your points.

Further Research

www.megalithicireland.com – Accounts of a number of megalithic monuments

www.archaeology.ie/nationalmonuments – Lists national monuments by county

www.sacred-destinations.com/ireland/newgrange – A description of Newgrange

www.newgrange.com – A description of Newgrange and a video

www.knowth.com – A short description of Knowth

Chapter 21

The Bronze Age (2500–500 BC)

By the end of this chapter I will ...

* know what bronze is and how it was made
* be able to draw and describe a sun disc, a lunula, a torc, a fibula, a gorget and a lock ring
* know the progression of design from the early to the late Bronze Age
* know the progression of craft techniques from the early to the late Bronze Age
* have opinions on Bronze Age technology and craftsmanship that I can back up with facts.

Context

Bronze technology and more communal living developed in Ireland after 2500 BC. This technology was the foundation of early civilizations, which were beginning to develop by *c.* 1300 BC. The type of sophisticated development that evolved around the Eastern Mediterranean did not reach Ireland until much later.

During the early Bronze Age in Ireland, Stone Age culture continued for some time in the south and west of the country, while the Beaker people (so called because of their cremation burials found under upturned 'beaker'-shaped pots) brought

Bronze Age technology and culture to the north, east and midlands (Fig. 21.1).

The first great civilisations of Egypt, Babylonia and Assyria developed walled cities and figurative art during the Bronze Age. Ireland's pastoral farming and smaller social groups did not lend itself to this type of development.

Figure 21.1 Bronze Age beaker pottery.

A Change in Style

There are clear differences between the freehand, low technology methods of making art in the Stone Age and the mechanically made new technology of the Bronze Age work. This suggests that these were different people who probably came from mainland Europe in search of copper and gold deposits. There is certainly evidence of Irish gold and copper being traded into Britain and Europe, which suggests links with the wider European community.

Innovation and Invention

Metalwork

Mining for gold and copper was carried out at a number of locations in Ireland during the Bronze Age. Evidence of Bronze Age metalworking has been found at Mount Gabriel in Co. Cork, Ross in Co. Kerry, the Vale of Avoca in Co. Wicklow and in the Mourne Mountains.

Gold

Gold was probably found in nuggets or by panning alluvial deposits in rivers. In the panning technique, a mixture of sand, gravel and gold particles is dug up from the riverbed and gradually washed with water, leaving the heavier parts (the gold) in the pan while the lighter material is washed away. The gold particles could then be melted and cast into suitably sized pieces to be worked on later.

Copper

Copper was mined by roasting ore-bearing rock with fire and cracking it by throwing cold water on it. The broken stone was then dug out with wooden shovels and crushed with stone hammers. The pieces with the highest concentration of copper oxides would be selected and smelted over a charcoal fire. The resulting molten copper was poured into stone or sand moulds and cast into the shapes of axes, knives, sickles or whatever shape was required (Fig. 21.2).

Many of the early tools and weapons were made of copper on its own. The alloy bronze, which was harder and held a sharp edge for longer, gradually replaced copper in tools and weapons (Fig. 21.3)

Figure 21.2 Bronze axe in a stone mould.

Figure 21.3 Early Bronze Age objects.

Bronze is an alloy (mixture) of copper and tin. In Ireland, it was made from native copper and tin imported from Cornwall, England.

Media and Areas of Practice

Metalwork

Bronze

Bronze was used to make tools and weapons and a variety of useful and decorative objects. Figure 21.4 shows a cauldron, which may have been used to boil meat for feasts, trumpet which might have been used in battle or ceremonies, some spear and axe heads, a bulla and some rings.

Gold

Early Bronze Age objects were made from a single piece of gold, as the technology for joining

Figure 21.4 Late Bronze Age objects.

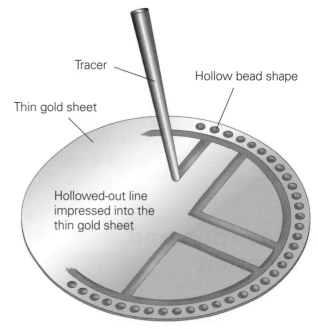

Figure 21.5 The repoussé technique.

pieces together with gold solder had not yet been developed in Ireland. Early decorative techniques were quite simple and direct but carried out with great precision and flair.

Repoussé was a technique used to create a raised design on a flat surface. A thin sheet of gold which had been cut to shape was laid face down on a firm surface so it could be worked on from the back. (In modern times, a leather sandbag or a bowl of mastic would be used by goldsmiths.) A pattern could then be created on the surface using tracers (chisel-like tools with a variety of shapes cut into the tip). These were pressed or hammered into the surface to produce a design. With the work completed, the sheet of gold was turned face up to reveal the design projecting from the surface. The work required careful craftsmanship, as a careless stroke could tear the thin gold sheet and the work would have to be started again (Fig. 21.5).

Incision: Decoration was incised (cut into the surface) with a scriber (a sharp pencil-shaped bronze tool (Fig. 21.6).

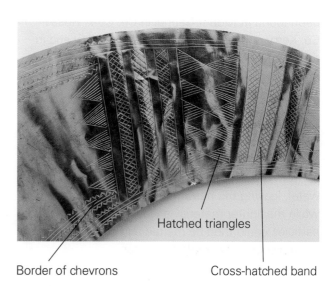

Figure 21.6 A close-up of an area of incised decoration on a lunula.

Pottery

A wider range of pottery shapes and designs were created during the Bronze Age. Pots were better built and more evenly fired, although still completely handmade (see Fig. 21.1).

Bronze Age Structures (Architecture)

Bronze Age human settlements (houses and fences) seem to have been made of wood that has rotted away over the centuries, although evidence of a widespread population has survived through burial sites and finds of Bronze Age objects.

Tomb design changed during the Bronze Age. In most areas of the country the dead were laid to rest in pits or stone-lined cists. In the west of Ireland, wedge tombs, which were related to the court cairns of the Stone Age, were still being built. None of these burial sites had the drama of the Stone Age monuments.

Art Elements and Design Principles

Early Bronze Age gold objects were decorated with simple abstract geometric patterns, such as circles, triangles, dots and straight lines. These elements were repeated and combined in various ways to make up the range of designs used by the first goldsmiths in Ireland (Fig. 21.7).

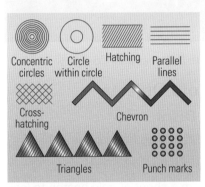

Some combinations of designs

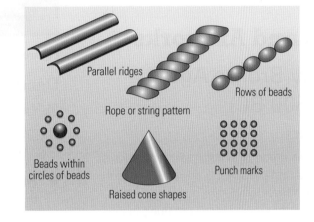

Some combinations of designs

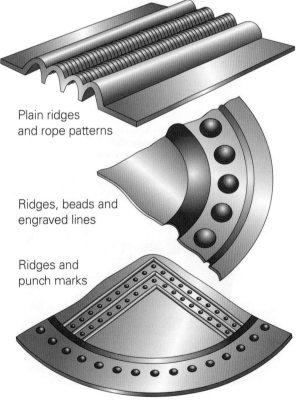

Plain ridges and rope patterns

Ridges, beads and engraved lines

Ridges and punch marks

Figure 21.7
Bronze Age designs.

Respond to the range of patterns in Figure 21.7 by using some of them to **create** a decorative pattern that might be used on fabric or to decorate a piece of pottery. **Research** the techniques you might use to carry out the project.

Create some drawings of natural or manmade forms using line techniques like hatching and cross-hatching to describe form and tone.

Artists and Artworks

The Early Bronze Age (2500–1500 BC)

Architecture

Ceremonial sites made of circular earthen banks or standing stones and hilltop forts once thought to have been from the Iron Age are now believed to be Bronze Age structures, which continued in use into the Iron Age. One such ceremonial site is the Drombeg stone circle in Co. Cork (Fig. 21.8).

Stone carving was not used to decorate burial places but it is found on large stones in the landscape. Examples are found in many parts of the country, for example the rock art found at Derrynablaha, Co. Kerry (Fig. 21.9). Designs were very simple, mainly little cupmarks surrounded by circles, sometimes with radiating lines.

Figure 21.9 Rock art, Derrynablaha, Co. Kerry.

Decorated Gold Objects

Tedavent Sun Discs

The Tedavent Sun Discs date from about 2000 BC (Fig. 21.10).

- **Form:** Made from a sheet of gold beaten to less than a millimetre thick, they have been cut into perfect circles 11 cm in diameter.
- **Function:** Two holes near the centre of the discs suggests that they may have been sewn on to a belt or garment. They may have been status or symbolic objects. Gold is often associated with the sun in primitive cultures.
- **Technique:** The design was applied by the repoussé technique.

Figure 21.8 Drombeg stone circle, Co. Cork.

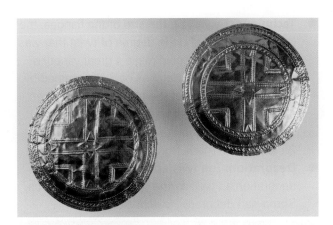

Figure 21.10 Tedavent Sun Discs from Co. Monaghan.

- **Decoration:** A repeating pattern of ridges, dots and chevrons was made around the perimeter with a cruciform (cross shape) at the centre.

Note: The cruciform design on the Tedavent Sun Discs is from 2000 years before Christ. It is simply a geometric pattern and has no Christian or religious symbolism.

Lunula from Ross in Co. Westmeath

- **Form:** The word 'lunula' comes from the Latin *luna*, meaning 'moon', because of its crescent-moon shape.

Figure 21.11 Lunula from Ross, Co. Westmeath.

Draw a lunula. Use two circles to get the shape, then add designs appropriate for the Bronze Age.

- **Function:** A lunula was a neck collar, which was probably worn as a status or magical item.
- **Technique:** A piece of gold was hammered into a thin flat sheet and the shape was cut from this. Lugs at the narrow ends were twisted at right angles to create a kind of catch, which may have been tied shut. Decoration was incised into the surface.
- **Decoration:** The lunula from Ross in Co. Westmeath has a repeating pattern of lines, triangles and chevrons incised into the surface. (Fig. 21.11) The patterns are concentrated in the narrow ends of the crescent. Four patterned areas on each side have parallel lines with chevrons inside, separated by hatched lines. Rows of hatched triangles are on each side of the parallel lines. The main body of the lunula is plain, surrounded by two rows of lines edged with triangles.

The Middle Bronze Age: The Bishopsland Phase (1500–1200 BC)

Torcs

From about 1400 BC, a completely new form of ornament largely replaced sheet gold work. These new objects were made by twisting gold into a variety of decorative forms. Ribbon torcs were made from a flat band of gold, which was twisted into an even spiral. The ends were sometimes worked into a catch with knobs at the end (Fig. 21.12 and 21.13).

Bar and Flanged Torcs

- **Form:** Torcs came in a variety of shapes and sizes. They could be square, triangular, circular or cross-shaped in section and came in a variety of lengths.
- **Function:** Torcs were made to fit the neck, arms, waist and as earrings. They may have been purely decorative or a sign of status.

Torcs were made by twisting flat, round, square or triangular sectioned rods of gold into a spiral shape. A variation of the basic bar torc was made by hammering flanges out from the angles of square or triangular sectioned bars before twisting.

- **Technique:** By varying the size of the flanges, the length of the bar and the degree of twist that was applied, craftsmen could make a great variety of these flanged torcs. Catches could be created by hammering the end of the torc into the required shape. These were sometimes simple hooks or could be more elaborate spirals (see Fig. 21.13). All torcs were made from one piece of gold.
- **Decoration:** The twisted forms were the decoration as well as the structure of the torcs. Some had decorative catches (Fig. 21.14).

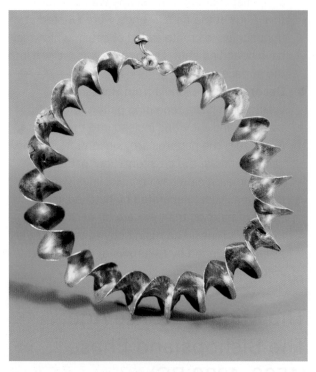

Figure 21.12 Ribbon torc from Belfast.

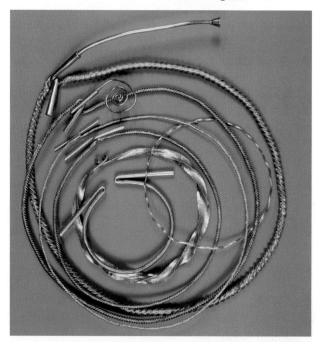

Figure 21.14 Flanged torcs came in a variety of shapes and sizes.

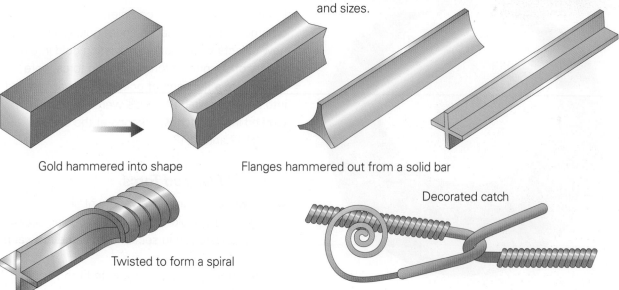

Gold hammered into shape

Flanges hammered out from a solid bar

Twisted to form a spiral

Decorated catch

Figure 21.13 Method of making flanged torcs.

The Derrinaboy Armbands

Some sheet metalwork was still being made during the Bishopsland Phase.

- **Form:** Rectangles of gold sheet were decorated using repoussé and curved to form a cylindrical band.
- **Function:** These bands would have been worn on the upper arm or at the wrist, probably as a sign of rank or status.
- **Technique:** Rectangles cut from a thin gold sheet were decorated with repoussé patterns and heated so they could be curved to form a band.
- **Decoration:** Boldly patterned in alternate rows of smooth and string-patterned ridges of repoussé, there is an area of finer string-patterned ridges arranged vertically beside the opening of the bands (Fig. 21.15).

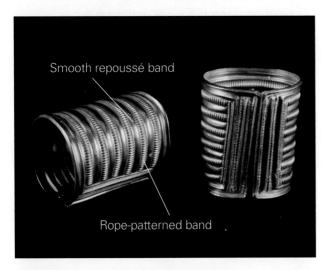

Smooth repoussé band

Rope-patterned band

Figure 21.15 The Derrinaboy Armbands.

The Late Bronze Age: The Golden Age (The Dowris Phase) (1200–500 BC)

Sometime after 800 BC, there was a huge upsurge in metalwork production in Ireland. New types of bronze tools and weapons and gold ornaments have been discovered in buried hoards all over the country, but particularly in the area of the lower Shannon River. This was Ireland's first Golden Age.

The Clones Fibula from Co. Monaghan

A fibula is made up of a gold bow or handle with a flat or cup-shaped disc at each end (Fig. 21.16). The basic form would have been cast and the cups or discs at the end of the bow would be hammered out into the required shape. Fibulae come in a variety of shapes, both decorated and undecorated.

- **Form:** Made from a kilogram of solid gold, the Clones Fibula has large open-cup ends connected by a bow or handle (Fig. 21.17).
- **Function:** Fibulae are often described as dress fasteners, where the button-like ends could have been put through holes on a cloak or tunic. However, some of the shapes you can see in the photograph (see Fig. 21.16) could not have been used in this way. They may have been status or trading items. What do you think?

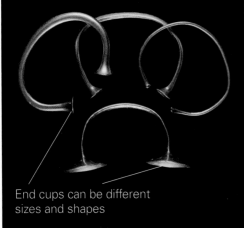

End cups can be different sizes and shapes

Figure 21.16 A selection of fibulae.

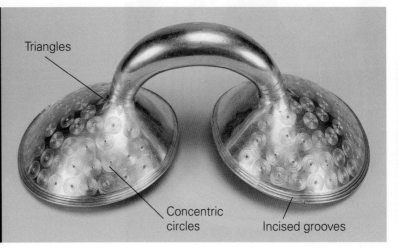

Triangles

Concentric circles

Incised grooves

Figure 21.17 The Clones Fibula.

- **Technique:** The bow was cast and the end plates or cup terminals hammered into the required shape. The decoration was incised into the surface. The work is very skilful and beautifully finished.
- **Decoration:** The terminals are decorated with irregular rows of small concentric circles with a little hollow at each centre. A special tool may have been used to make these patterns. The circles are arranged freehand across the surface, some with their edges touching. The pattern of circles ends in the area below the bow, which might have been difficult to reach with the tool that was used to make the circles. Three ridges surround the outer edge of each terminal. The area where the bow joins the cups is decorated with incised triangles and bands of lines. There are also triangles on top of the bow.

The Gleninsheen Gorget

Gorgets are perhaps the most beautifully made objects from the Bronze Age. There are several examples in the National Museum, the most perfect of which is the Gleninsheen Gorget (Fig. 21.18), which was found in a rock crevice close to the tomb of the same name, near Ballyvaughan in Co. Clare.

- **Form:** A U-shaped gold collar with a gold disc connected to each end.
- **Function:** Gorgets would have been worn at the neck. They were high status items.

- **Technique:** Gorgets were constructed from a number of parts. The outer and inner edge of the collar was finished with a strip of gold wrapped around it to create a smooth finish. The discs were made of two layers, with the edge of the lower, larger disc wrapped over the edge of the smaller upper disc, again to create a more finished edge. The discs were connected to the collar by stitching with gold wire or in some cases by a kind of hinge arrangement. All the parts are made of flat gold sheet decorated by the repoussé technique and incision – all very precise and skilful craftsmanship.
- **Decoration:** The U-shaped body of the Gleninsheen Gorget collar has rows of repoussé decoration, which are alternatively plain and rope patterned. There is a row of beading along the outer and inner edges. The six areas of rope pattern are each made up of three rows of rope design: a small one on each side of a larger one. The discs at each end are patterned in rows of beads and concentric circles, with a smooth cone at the centre of each circle. Similar designs appear on sunflower pins and little round gold boxes

> **Gorget:** A gold U-shaped collar with a gold disc attached to each end.

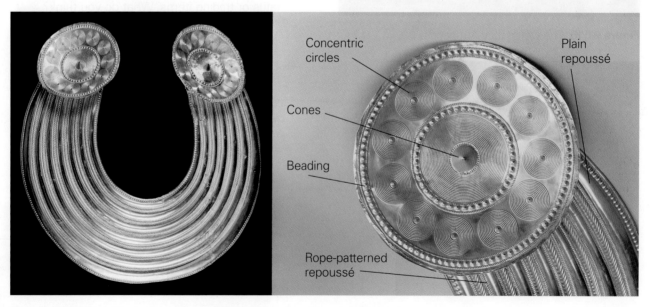

Concentric circles

Plain repoussé

Cones

Beading

Rope-patterned repoussé

Figure 21.18 The Gleninsheen Gorget with a close-up of an end disc.

from the same period. The alternately smooth and textured patterns on the surface catch the light beautifully, creating an impression of movement and dancing light.

The Gorteenareagh Lock Rings

- **Form:** Structurally, lock rings are the most advanced work of Bronze Age goldsmiths in Ireland (Fig. 21.19). They are made of two cones of gold wire joined at their wide ends by a tubular rim. An open-sided tube forms the centre of the cones. Lock rings are sometimes found in pairs.
- **Function:** Lock rings seem to be a uniquely Irish invention. They may have been used as hair ornaments.
- **Technique:** Fine gold wires were soldered together into cone shapes, with an opening at one side. Two cones were then held together at their outer edge by a tube of fine gold sheet. Another bigger tube of gold sheet, with an opening in one side, was then inserted into openings at the centres of the cones. The openings in the cones and the tube would allow a plait of hair to be squeezed into the centre and the tube then turned out of line with the opening in the cones to capture the hair in the centre (Fig. 21.20).

> **Lock rings** take the form of two cones made of fine gold wire connected at their outer edges, with an open-sided tube set in a centre opening.

Create a design for a piece of jewellery based on Bronze Age models. Make a number of sketches showing how your piece might be worn.

Put 'Irish Bronze Age artefacts' into a web search and you will be offered a range of objects that will add to your understanding of Bronze Age design. Make sketches and take notes from some examples you can use in your own work.

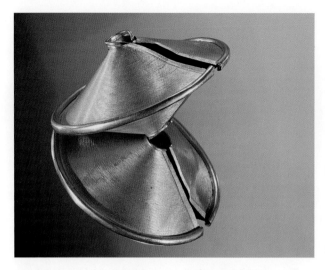

Figure 21.19 The Gorteenareagh Lock Rings.

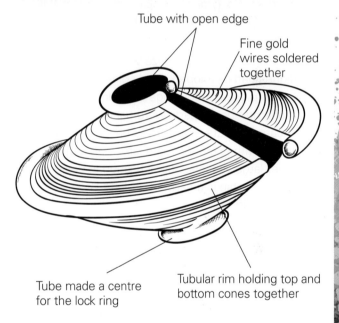

Tube with open edge

Fine gold wires soldered together

Tube made a centre for the lock ring

Tubular rim holding top and bottom cones together

Figure 21.20 The construction of the Gorteenareagh Lock Rings.

Analysis

> Note how the new technology created a new style of art and design. Observe the development of skills and design. Who do you think the work was being made for?

The art of the metalworker reached a very high standard of craftsmanship in the Late Bronze

Figure 21.21 This bronze cauldron was found at Castlederg, Co. Tyrone. It is 56 cm in diameter. It is from the Dowris phase of the Late Bronze Age.

Age, both in gold and in bronze work. Skills and techniques had developed. Gold solder was used to join fine pieces of gold together. Clay moulds made of a number of parts were used to cast more complicated objects. Bronze was beaten into sheets and joined with rivets to create large cauldrons and other large vessels. Sophistication in design and workmanship is a hallmark of Late Bronze Age metalwork (Fig. 21.21).

By the end of the Bronze Age, design and technology had moved forward a long way from the Stone Age. The pace of change was increasing, as traders in gold, copper and other goods from Ireland met up with people from Britain and Europe, creating an exchange of ideas and technology alongside goods. Ireland, situated at the edge of the known world, was at the end of the line in terms of trade and innovation.

Chapter Review

1. Note the changes in design from the Stone to the Bronze Age. Can you explain the radical changes that occurred? Use annotated sketches to help explain your points.

2. Use annotated sketches to describe two methods of metalwork design construction from the Bronze age.

3. Which Bronze Age object appeals to you most? Describe the object in words and sketches and give reasons for your preference.

4. Describe the evolution of design and techniques from the Early Bronze Age through the Bishopsland and Dowris phases. Draw examples of pieces that you think show the changes best.

5. 'Bronze Age designs were influenced by the techniques used to make them.' Discuss this statement and use annotated sketches to illustrate your points.

Further Research

www.museum.ie – The National Museum of Ireland. Go to 'Archaeology' then 'Exhibitions' then 'Ór – Ireland's Gold' to see some of the Bronze Age collection

www.askaboutireland.ie – Search for 'Bronze Age Monuments' for information on stone circles and standing stones

Chapter 22

The Iron Age: Celtic Art in Ireland (500 BC–AD 400)

By the end of this chapter I will ...

* have a definition for La Tène design
* understand the Celtic influence in Ireland
* be able to draw and describe Dun Aengus, the Turoe Stone, the Broighter Collar, the Loughnashade Trumpet and the Petrie Crown
* know how design developed from Insular La Tène to Ultimate La Tène
* have seen new developments in design and craft techniques.

Figure 22.1 *The Dying Gaul of Pergamon.* This Celtic warrior is naked for battle except for a torc around his neck. His weapons and trumpet lie around him on the ground.

Context

Iron technology and Celtic culture arrived after 500 BC, when the Roman Empire expanded into Northern Europe and pushed Celtic people north and west.

The Celts

The Celts were a group of tribes that populated much of Europe from around 700 BC until the 3rd century AD. They were known to the Greeks and the Romans as the *Keltoi*.

They were renowned as warriors, horsemen and craftworkers, skilled in the production of a wide range of goods and weapons (Fig. 22.1). They worked in gold, bronze and iron.

Iron Technology

The Celts had learned iron technology, which improved farming and military equipment and allowed them to expand their area of influence. Some hints of their art and technology reached Ireland by the 6th century BC, but did not seem to take root.

By the 5th century BC, a new style of Celtic art had developed called La Tène art. La Tène art was

Figure 22.2 Scabbard plate design.

Vine scroll ending in a spiral   Decorated trumpet ends

evident in Ireland from the 3rd century BC, first in the form of imports. Gold collars found in Roscommon, scabbard plates found in north-east Ulster (Fig. 22.2) and a sword hilt in the shape of a human figure found in the sea at Ballyshannon, Co. Donegal (Fig. 22.3) were all probably imported from Europe.

The La Tène style combined influences from classical Greek and Roman art, the Etruscans, the Scythians and Oriental art with the Celtic style. This style is called La Tène after a site on the shores of Lake Neuchätel in Switzerland where the diagnostic examples were found. The migrations and invasions of the Celtic peoples throughout Europe in the 5th and 4th centuries BC helped to spread the style.

The Celts in Ireland

Exactly when the Celts arrived in Ireland – and how they got here – is still open to debate. In the early 20th century, it was assumed that the Celts had invaded Ireland, but this is not so certain anymore. Significant sites like hill forts and places of burial seem to have been in continuous use from the Bronze Age into the Iron Age, so Celtic influence may have actually arrived by trading, migration and assimilation, with larger numbers arriving as refugees when the Romans invaded Gaul and Britain. By the 1st century BC, Ireland had a Celtic culture of some depth and substance. A Celtic language was spoken and there was a unified social and political system throughout the country. It was a tribal society based on family ties, with wealth built on cattle ownership. The story of The Táin, written down much later, gives some idea of Celtic society in Ireland.

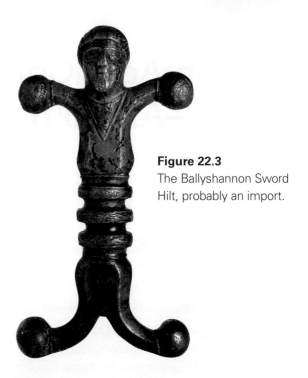

Figure 22.3
The Ballyshannon Sword Hilt, probably an import.

Media and Areas of Practice

Metalwork

Iron

The arrival of iron technology in Ireland improved and simplified the production of tools and weapons (Fig. 22.4). Iron was readily available in the environment in the form of clay ironstone nodules, bog iron and other, less easily worked, sources. In Ireland iron was not melted and cast, but heated until the impurities were burnt off or melted away, then it was hammer forged and shaped.

The smith would have had similar tools and skills as any blacksmith up to the present time.

All metalworkers were highly valued members of society, equal in status with physicians. Metalworkers' skills were associated with magical powers.

Figure 22.4 Iron Age sword.

Bronze

Much of the decorative work from the Iron Age was made of bronze. Horse trappings, tools and utensils, brooches, armbands and rings were all beautifully crafted (Fig. 22.5). The 'lost wax' method of casting in bronze allowed complicated pieces, like horse bits, to be made.

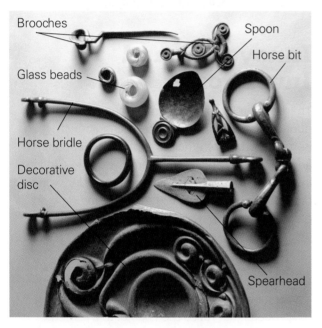

Brooches
Spoon
Horse bit
Glass beads
Horse bridle
Decorative disc
Spearhead

Figure 22.5 Decorative bronze and glass from the Iron Age.

Lost wax casting: Models made of wax were enveloped in a clay mould, which was fired. The wax melted out of the mould, leaving a hollow space, in the shape of the model, which could then be filled with molten bronze, creating an exact copy of the wax model.

Go to YouTube and watch the video 'Lost Wax Casting Process' (9:10) by Silvera Jewelry School for a demonstration of the ancient skill.

Sheet bronze was turned and hammered to produce vessels and decorative items.

Gold

The finest decorative pieces were produced in gold. The ancient techniques of hammering and cutting to shape were still used. Casting techniques were improved and chasing was sometimes used instead of repoussé for relief work.

Chasing is a metalwork technique that brings a design into relief by pressing back the surrounding area by hammering. In some ways it is like a reverse of the repoussé technique.

Architecture

It is difficult to identify specific pieces of architecture as 'typically Iron Age' because some of the larger structures like ring forts were already being built in the late Bronze Age and continued to be built into medieval times. Houses were mainly made of wood, so little remains of them.

Stone Carving

With the introduction of iron tools, it was easier to carve larger-scale stone sculptures. Pieces like the Turoe Stone (see Fig. 22.8) were carved to shape and decorated in relief carving.

Art Elements and Design Principles
Changes in Style

Stone Age art was drawn freehand, without a ruler or compass. Bronze Age art was created mechanically using a straight edge and compass. Both of these styles were abstract, meaning they did not represent objects in the real world.

Iron Age design combined freehand and mechanical elements and has abstract and stylised representational images. There does not appear to be much continuity in design from one age to another, although there are some common elements.

Figure 22.6 Celtic design motifs. These were the basic forms that the La Tène designers elaborated upon.

La Tène Style

The new La Tène style combined leafy palmate forms with vines, tendrils, lotus flowers, spirals, scrolls, lyre and trumpet shapes into a flowing, sinuous, abstract style that the Celts used to decorate ornaments and weapons. (Fig. 22.6).

Insular La Tène: The style of art used by the first native craftsmen in Ireland is called Insular La Tène. It is a modified version of the European style. It consists of scrolls, leaf and vine forms, trumpet ends and spirals. Some of its characteristics are peculiar to the islands off the west coast of Europe, which gives the style the name 'Insular'. The patterns on the Turoe Stone and the Broighter Collar are in this style.

Innovation and Invention

There was a lot of social and economic change during this period; new metal technology in iron created more efficient tools and weapons, and new ideas and design came with the Celtic influence. Trade with Rome and the wider world brought new materials like enamel, and new art elements like the triskele and the pelta.

Enamel is a coloured, glass-like material that can be either opaque or transparent. It can be attached as decoration to metal by a heating process that fuses the enamel to the metal.

Triskele: A motif of three curved limbs that spring from the same point and turn in the same direction.

Artists and Artworks
Iron Age Structures (Architecture)

Much of our knowledge of Stone Age and Bronze Age structures is based on the tombs and burial sites of the time. Little is known about the burial practices of the Iron Age people in Ireland, but habitation sites and ring forts in earth and stone are relatively common throughout the country. Some forts were built for defence, some were ritual sites and smaller ones were just homesteads. The circular enclosure with houses and animal pens inside continued in use in the Celtic areas of Ireland even after the Norman invasion.

Dun Aengus

Dun Aengus (Dún Aonghasa) is an enormous promontory fort that backs onto 100 m cliffs on Inis Mór in the Aran Islands (Fig. 22.7).

- **Form:** The fort has three walls curving around it. The inner wall is 5 m tall and up to 6 m thick in places. It encloses an area approximately 130 m × 100 m. Inside, flights of stairs lead up to defensive ramparts. A second lower wall encloses an area outside the main structure which is surrounded by an area of *chevaux-de-frise* (upright stones set in the ground as a defence against cavalry attacks). A third wall surrounds a large area up to 200 m from the inner wall.
- **Function:** There are some clear defensive features, but archaeological work has shown

evidence of domestic buildings and areas where metalworking has been carried out. It was probably a chieftain's residence, which could have been a centre for ceremonies.

- **Technique:** The whole structure is built in uncut dry stone. No mortar was used to join the stones together. The main wall has a batter (it slopes back from the base to the top), creating a more stable structure. The buttresses that now support the wall were added in the 19th century when the structure was being restored. The building was begun in the Bronze Age, the main wall was enlarged during the Iron Age and it continued in use into medieval times.

Stone Carving

The first objects we can confidently claim to be of Irish manufacture in the La Tène style are a number of large boulders that have been dressed and carved with abstract patterns. The stones at Castlestrange, Co. Roscommon, Killycluggin, Co. Cavan and Derrykeighan, Co. Antrim, have linear patterns carved into their surfaces. The Turoe Stone in Co. Galway has a pattern sculpted in low relief.

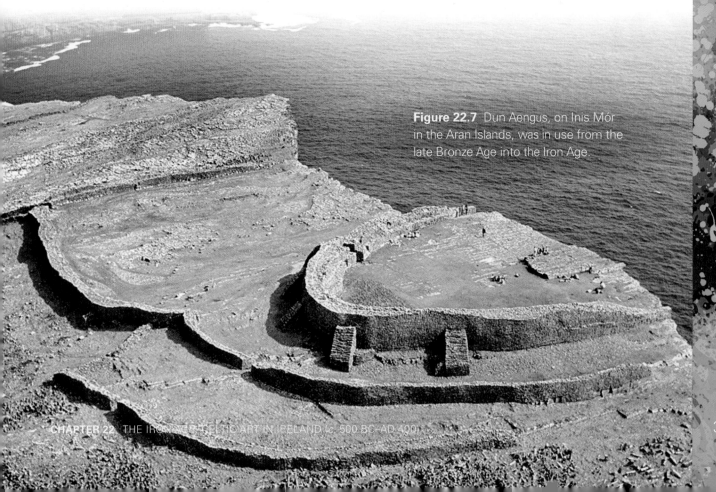

Figure 22.7 Dun Aengus, on Inis Mór in the Aran Islands, was in use from the late Bronze Age into the Iron Age.

The Turoe Stone

The Turoe Stone has been dated to about 50 BC.

- **Form:** This four-ton boulder, which is 1.68 m tall, is pink feldspar Galway granite (Fig. 22.8).
- **Function:** The purpose of these decorated stones is not known. They may have been boundary markers or ceremonial objects.
- **Technique:** The stone was carved with iron chisels to a depth of about 3 mm, leaving a pattern standing out in low relief.
- **Decoration:** The pattern on the Turoe Stone (Fig. 22.9) takes the form of semi-abstract leaf and vine shapes, trumpet ends and spirals, all flowing in a casual symmetry. The design has four segments. Two semi-circular areas of design take up most of the surface. Between these are two smaller, triangular segments of pattern which connect over the top of the stone. A triskele appears in one of the triangular segments. The flowing pattern takes up the domed top of the stone. Some of the spaces between the areas of raised pattern can be read as part of the design, showing the Celtic love of the play between positive and negative shapes. A brick or step pattern forms a band below the decorated dome and separates it from the plain base.

 RESPOND
Compare the decoration on the Turoe Stone with that on the Castlestrange Stone in Figure 22.10.

Figure 22.10 The Castlestrange Stone.

Stone Figures

Some stone figure carvings may also be from the Iron Age, but it is difficult to date them accurately. The triple head from Corleck, Co. Cavan (Fig. 22.11) is generally accepted as Celtic, as is the Tandragee Idol from Co. Armagh (Fig. 22.12). Other figures and heads once assigned to the Iron Age are now thought to be of a later date.

Triskele

Leaf and vine-scroll shape

Figure 22.8 (left) The Turoe Stone. In this photograph, we are looking at the right-hand part of the schematic drawing.

Figure 22.9 (right) A schematic drawing of the Turoe Stone.

Figure 22.11 (left) The Triple Head from Corleck. The three faces rise slightly up the head.
Figure 22.12 (right) The Tandragee Idol.

Visit www.dbsirishstudies.wordpress.com and search for 'Corleck Head' for some interesting background on the artefact. Note the reference to the Celtic three-part designs. Can you find other examples of three-part designs?

Metalwork
The Broighter Hoard

Not many gold finds can be dated to the Iron Age, but the quality of some pieces makes up for the lack of quantity. The Broighter Hoard (Fig. 22.13) was turned up by a ploughman in Co. Derry and includes some of the finest examples of the goldsmiths' art.

The collection consists of a model boat and a bowl made of thin-sheet gold, two chains, two twisted bracelets and a gold collar. The gold chains and twisted bracelets were probably imports of Roman origin. The gold boat is a model of an ocean-going craft, probably a hide-covered boat driven by oars and a square sail. It is an interesting indication of how Celtic people travelled round the coast of Europe.

The Broighter Collar (*c.* 50 BC)

● **Form:** The collar is formed of two tubes of sheet gold with a foliage pattern chased into the

Figure 22.14 The Broighter Collar is the most elaborate piece of craftwork to have survived from the Iron Age.

Figure 22.13 The Broighter Hoard.

surface. Buffer terminals (they look like railway buffers) form a catch at one end. A T-shaped bar is used as the lock that holds the two terminals together. Another terminal, now missing, would have joined the other ends of the tubes together (Fig. 22.14).

- **Function:** The sculpture of the Dying Gaul (see Fig. 22.1) shows a warrior wearing a neck collar like the Broighter Collar. Elaborate collars of this type were high-status items worn by important people on important occasions.

- **Technique:** The collar is the most accomplished piece of Irish manufacture in the Insular La Tène style. The design would have been applied to a flat gold sheet that was raised by chasing. The flat areas between the raised patterns were incised with compass arcs. The patterned gold sheets were then heated and rolled into a tube shape. The tubes were soldered shut and then filled with hot mastic (a wax-like substance) so the tubes could be curved without crushing or tearing them. The cast buffer terminals were riveted onto the ends of the tubes. A row of beading has been raised along the joint to hide the rivet heads.

- **Decoration:** The pattern on the collar is symmetrical. Based on interconnecting S scrolls, it combines a variety of plant-based forms ending in spiral bosses, which are made separately and pinned on (Fig. 22.15). The background area between the patterns has been incised with compass arcs to create a contrast in texture with the smooth surface of the raised design. On the buffer terminals there is a raised pattern of plant-based designs with a little gold bead soldered in the centre, where it meets the tubes. One of the terminals has rows of beading.

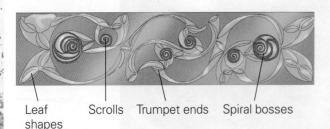

Leaf shapes   Scrolls   Trumpet ends   Spiral bosses

Figure 22.15 Schematic drawing of a section of the Broighter Collar.

Respond to the Insular La Tène designs of the Turoe Stone and the Broighter Collar by **creating** a design in any medium you like to represent Ireland's Celtic past. **Research** the positive and negative shapes and natural elements in the patterns.

A Change of Style (Ultimate La Tène)

Around the turn of the first millennium, there was a new development in the style. Designs became lighter, with more open space around them, and more often arranged around geometric patterns. The following examples are in this new style.

Ultimate La Tène style: In the late Iron Age, patterns became more delicate and more symmetrical. The plant-based designs of the insular style gave way to the more geometric forms of Ultimate La Tène.

The Loughnashade Trumpet

The Loughnashade Trumpet was found in Co. Antrim. It is from the 1st century AD (Fig. 22.16).

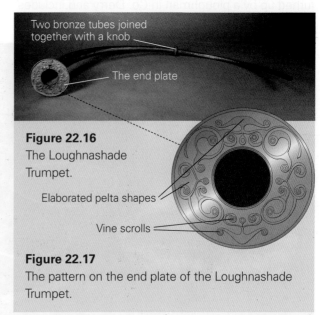

Two bronze tubes joined together with a knob

The end plate

Figure 22.16 The Loughnashade Trumpet.

Elaborated pelta shapes

Vine scrolls

Figure 22.17 The pattern on the end plate of the Loughnashade Trumpet.

- **Form:** The trumpet is made from two tubes of sheet bronze joined by a knob in the middle. It has a decorative plate on the open end.
- **Function:** The trumpet was probably used at ceremonial occasions and for war.
- **Technique:** The tubes are expertly made. The edges were rolled together and riveted onto an internal strip of bronze. The plate at the open end has a four-part pattern raised by the repoussé technique.
- **Decoration:** The Roman pelta design forms the basis for much of the four part pattern, this is combined with vine scrolls and plant forms. The design is almost perfectly symmetrical. Compared to the Broighter Collar, the design is lighter, more linear and more geometric, with broader areas at the ends of the curves (Fig. 22.17).

The Petrie Crown

The Petrie Crown (Fig. 22.18) is an object of unknown origin from the collection of the 19th century antiquarian, George Petrie.

- **Form:** The crown consists of an openwork band with a cone and two discs attached to it.
- **Function:** Petrie called it a crown, but its actual function is not certain. The top and bottom edges of the band are perforated, so it may have been sewn onto fabric or leather, or fixed to wood or metal. The original length of the band is not known or how many cones or discs were fixed to it. What do you think it was used for?
- **Technique:** The raised outlines of the design were made by cutting back the surrounding metal. The cut-out openings in the band create the impression of a series of connected semi-circles. The concave discs that are mounted on the band would have been hammered into shape. Each disc has a boss set slightly off centre, a red enamel bead sits in the hollow centre of one boss. The empty eye sockets of some of the bird heads probably held enamel beads. This is the first surviving example of enamel work in Ireland. The cone-shaped attachment is made of sheet bronze formed into a tapering cylinder.
- **Decoration:** All the parts are decorated with spirals ending in bird heads. The deceptively simple design on the discs combines plant-based and triskele motifs created by the slim trumpet curves. The negative space at the top of the discs forms a pelta (Fig. 22.19). The artist made use of positive and negative shapes to create the design, a tendency that becomes stronger as we move into the Christian period. The bird heads found on the band, discs and cone are among the earliest zoomorphs found in Irish art. There is a little cross in a circle on the right-hand disc. This might be a Christian symbol which would

Figure 22.18 The Petrie Crown.

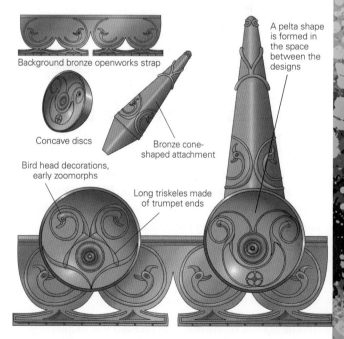

Background bronze openworks strap

Concave discs

Bird head decorations, early zoomorphs

Bronze cone-shaped attachment

A pelta shape is formed in the space between the designs

Long triskeles made of trumpet ends

Figure 22.19 The construction of and patterns on the Petrie Crown.

date the crown to at least the 4th century AD, at the beginning of Christian influence. Otherwise it may be an abstract pattern that just happens to look like a cross. What do you think?

Analysis

Design ideas were beginning to arrive in Ireland from other countries. Identify some of these new shapes and techniques in some of the work you have studied.

Celtic influence brought radical change to Irish art. Elements of design from all over the world were combined in the La Tène style. The natural forms that dominated the early examples like the Turoe Stone and the Broighter Collar gave way to the finer lines, spirals and zoomorphs (animal forms) of the Petrie Crown. The sophisticated techniques and the standard of craftsmanship that developed during the Iron Age created the foundation for the golden age that followed.

The work left to us from this time displays the elements of the designs and patterns that formed the basis for the decorative art that followed in the Christian Celtic period. Plant forms (vegetal decoration), zoomorphs, simplified human figures and geometric patterns were brought together to create a style of art that was flexible, harmonious, imaginative, ambiguous and, above all, beautiful.

After Pre-Christian Ireland

The introduction of Christianity into Ireland in the 5th century brought great social change. Monasteries were built in the same style as ring forts, with little churches and dwelling huts inside. The sculptors turned their hands to making cross slabs with some La Tène decoration. Metalworkers and calligraphers incorporated Christian symbols into the range of designs that had been in use for centuries.

The designers of the Iron Age had laid the foundations for the extraordinary developments in art, craft and design that followed in the next 500 years.

Chapter Review

1. What changes did Iron Age technology bring to Irish art and society?

2. La Tène design is a combination of influences. Can you identify some of these influences? Make sketches of some of the art elements that combined to make the style.

3. What do you think are the best features of La Tène design? Describe in words and sketches the most attractive elements of the style.

4. Iron, bronze and gold were all used to make Iron Age La Tène objects. Can you sketch and describe some objects made from each metal?

5. Describe a piece of craftwork with Ultimate La Tène patterns on it. Use annotated sketches to describe the structure and decoration of the object.

6. What is a zoomorph? Where might you find one from the Iron Age? Describe it in words and sketches.

Further Research

www.bailieborough.com/corleck-head – A piece on the Corleck Head

www.visual-arts-cork.com/irish-sculpture – Click on 'Turore-stone' for an account on the Turore Stone

www.aranislands.ie/dun-aonghasa-inis-mor-island – The official website for Dun Aengus on Inis Mór, Aran Islands

www.youtube.com – Search for 'Loughnashade Trumpet Hidden Heritage NIEA' to watch an informative video on the Loughnashade Trumpet

Unit 8

Insular Art

(*c.* 500–1100s)

23. The Early Christian Period (5th and 6th Centuries)

24. The Golden Age (7th and 8th Centuries)

25. The Viking Invasions (9th and 10th Centuries)

Before

The Iron Age
c. 500 BC–AD 400

The Early Christian
Period (*c.* AD 400–600)

Skellig Michael,
c. AD 588

The Cathach,
c. AD 600

The Golden Age
(*c.* AD 600–800)

Carndonagh
Cross,
7th century

The Book of
Durrow,
late 7th/early
8th century

Ardagh Chalice,
c. AD 750

The Viking Invasions
(*c.* AD 800–1000)

Muiredach's
Cross, 9th/
10th century

The Book
of Kells,
c. AD 800

After

The Irish Romanesque
Period (*c.* AD 1000–1200)

Insular Art (*c.* 500–1100s)

Chapter 23

The Early Christian Period (5th and 6th Centuries)

By the end of this chapter I will ...

✳ know what an early monastery looked like and what construction methods were used

✳ be able to draw and describe the Reask Pillar, some letters from the Cathach and the Ballinderry Brooch

✳ have definitions for vellum, codex, majuscule, *diminuendo* and penannular brooch

✳ have observed the significant changes brought about for craftworkers by the introduction of Christianity.

Before Insular Art

Society had been developing in Ireland throughout the Stone, Bronze and Iron Ages. The first farmers seem to have appeared around 6,000 years ago. They began to create permanent monuments in the landscape to act as places of ceremony or burial sites. They produced the first known art, in the form of abstract, freehand decoration carved into the stones of their monuments. Newgrange Passage Mound is a World Heritage Site with some of the most famous examples of Stone Age Art.

Metal technology was introduced into the country around 2500 BC, and with it came new artforms and craftwork. Bronze Age art was also abstract but based on simple geometry. The quality of craftsmanship reached a very high level; they produced beautiful works in bronze and gold. The Gleninsheen Gorget is an example of their skill.

The Iron Age began in Ireland in around 500 BC. The Insular La Tène style evolved flowing patterns that combined natural elements like leaves and vines with geometric patterns and animal forms. The Insular Art of the Early Christian period, covered in this chapter, was heavily influenced by Iron Age design. Pieces like the Broighter Collar and the Petrie Crown are examples of the level of sophistication achieved in the Iron Age.

Context

Early medieval Ireland had a society based on kinship. The tribe (*tuath*) was the social unit, which expanded into small kingdoms. It was a society without towns or money: trade was by barter, exchanging goods or services of equal value. There is evidence of the import of wine, oils and other luxury goods from the old Roman Empire and from further afield.

Stock-rearing and crop-raising were the main economic activities, which in turn supported craftworkers, musicians, poets, lawyers, priests and nobles. Most people were illiterate – with the exception of Ogham script – and were therefore dependent on an oral tradition (storytelling) to maintain their laws and folklore.

By the 3rd century AD, the Roman Empire was in decline, and the legions finally left Britain in the year AD 406. Irish raiders set up colonies in Wales and took over large areas of Argyll in West Scotland. This new contact with the outside world had a significant effect on lifestyle and art in Ireland.

The Arrival of Christianity in Ireland

Christianity seems to have arrived in Ireland in a number of ways. Traders and raiders in and out of Ireland would have met Christians on mainland Europe and in Britain; this influence may have penetrated back into Ireland. Anchorite monks (religious recluses) and hermits looking for places of isolation along the coast of Europe settled on the islands off the Irish coast (Fig. 23.1). The self-denial and endurance of these hermits would have appealed to an Irish society brought up on tales of the valour and strength of the old Celtic heroes.

Palladius and St Patrick

In the year 431, Pope Julius sent a bishop named Palladius 'to the believers in Christ in Ireland'. The bishop brought with him books and religious objects in the Roman style, as well as a group of craftsmen to make more of them. Following this initiative from Rome, St Patrick and others succeeded in converting the country to Christianity without martyrdom or excessive conflict with the pagan priesthood.

Church Organisation

Initially, the Christians of Ireland were organised under the European model, with the bishop controlling a diocese of parishes in a geographical area. However, this model was better suited to urban areas, and it did not adapt well to the predominantly rural Irish Celtic society.

> *Note:* A system of monastic federations evolved in Ireland based on kinship or allegiance to the founding saint of one of the great monasteries.

The abbot of the leading house of each monastic federation was called the *comharba* and was generally a relative of the founder – in some cases, sons succeeded fathers. Some of these *comharbaí* would have been laymen or in minor orders.

Figure 23.1 The monastery of St Molaise on Inishmurray Island, off the Sligo coast.

Monasticism in Ireland

The founders of monasteries were revered as saints, and their burial places and relics became centres of pilgrimage over the years. Some saints were associated with multiple sites and holy wells, particularly Patrick and Brigid, while others had a more local following.

During the 6th century, Irish monastic sites became great centres of learning and strict spiritual practice. Students came from Britain and Europe, where the Church was in some disarray and scholarship was at a low ebb.

In the following centuries, Irish monks travelled throughout Europe, spreading the word of Christ and founding new monasteries. Columba used Iona as an outpost for the conversion of Scotland, which became a political colony of Ireland at the same time.

Innovation and Invention

Irish art was radically changed by the arrival of Christianity, as most artistic resources were directed towards the production of objects for Church use. Symbolism became an important element in design, emphasising Christian teachings within the images and patterns. Literacy among the clergy and some of the more powerful families fuelled the new craft of book-making.

The Importance of Books in Irish Monasteries

The Bible was, and is, central to the practice of Christianity in Ireland. A monk in an early Christian monastery needed a copy of the Bible and other texts for the daily readings and singing, which were at the centre of his daily life. Before the invention of the printing press in the 15th century, every single book had to be copied out by hand. As well as Bibles, monks needed books of prayers and services, texts on Latin grammar and all kinds of scholarship for the education of the clergy and nobility.

Latin was the language of educated people throughout Europe; clerics and educated nobles could join in Church services and communicate with each other anywhere on the continent. All Church ceremonies were conducted in Latin. Education began with Latin, so that students could read the texts and further their knowledge.

Note: Books were very precious, not simply because of the time and effort that went into their making but as sources of knowledge and the word of God. Carelessly copied texts would be regarded as an insult to God, whose words were being transcribed. Monks offered their work as prayer, so they tried to make it as perfect and beautiful as they could.

Media and Areas of Practice

Architecture

Early monasteries were laid out following the local building style; an enclosing bank or wall surrounded an area with the church or oratory at the centre or southeast corner. A cemetery was located near the church and monastic buildings. The area around the perimeter of the enclosure would have been for domestic dwellings and workshops.

Most of the early monasteries were made of wood or wattle and daub, but they were built over or used as burial grounds in the following years, so little can be discovered about them. In the west of Ireland and on some coastal islands, monasteries were built in stone, and these remains give us a much better idea of how monasteries were laid out.

Stone Carving

As we have seen in relation to the construction of monasteries, stone was not generally the material of choice during the 5th and 6th centuries. The development of carved stone monuments evolved over several hundred years, and because of gaps in the progression of design and technique, it is difficult to work out the reasons for the form and variety of the monuments that remain.

Simple designs were carved using iron chisels.

Making Books

Not only did books have to be written by hand but every part had to be produced from raw materials. There was no source of ready-made pages, inks or pens, so the scribe had to make everything from what was available locally or what could be imported. Pages had to be made and assembled into book form.

Inks and Pigments

Black and dark inks were made in a variety of ways.

Carbon inks made from burnt wood or animal fat remained black, but sometimes flaked off the page.

Iron-gall ink was made by mixing iron sulphate with crushed oak-galls, and gum to bind them together. This was diluted with water, wine or vinegar. It was longer-lasting than carbon ink, but over time the iron etched into the vellum and the gall sometimes faded to brown.

The earliest books that have survived used very little colour.

Pens

Pens were made from the feathers of large birds: geese, swans and birds of prey. The feathers needed to be strong at the tip to hold the nib shape, which was cut with a penknife. Most of the feather would have been trimmed away for ease of use. You can see one on the portrait of St John page in the Book of Kells (see Chapter 25, Fig. 25.22).

Vellum

In Ireland, vellum was the preferred material for making pages, but it was a lengthy production process.

> **Vellum** is calf skin that has been prepared for writing.

The animal skin was placed in a bath of water and lime or excrement for a few days to loosen the hair. Timing was important, because if the skins were left in the bath too long, they could become prone to bacterial attack. The Book of Kells has suffered a little from this problem.

After this preparation, skins were taken to be cleaned and scraped free of hair and impurities with a blade. The skin was then rubbed smooth with a pumice stone, then stretched flat and dried before being cut into pages. The vellum could then be sewn into rolls or made into a book (Fig. 23.2).

Art Elements and Design Principles

Architecture

We have some idea of how early monastic buildings may have looked from written accounts and from images created in other crafts, such as the painting of the temple on the temptation of Christ page in the Book of Kells (see Fig. 25.28), as well as a number of house-shaped shrines. The cap of Muiredach's Cross at Clonmacnoise is also house-shaped. The little 12th-century stone church on St Macdara's Island in Co. Galway copies the detail of the wooden construction of an earlier church, right down to carvings in the shape of shingles on the roof (Fig. 23.3). The simplicity of these early churches reflects the austerity and self-denial of the early Christian monks in Ireland.

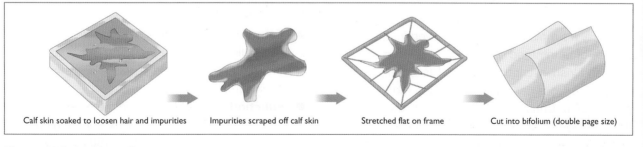

Calf skin soaked to loosen hair and impurities   Impurities scraped off calf skin   Stretched flat on frame   Cut into bifolium (double page size)

Figure 23.2 Making vellum.

Decorative finials

Antae in imitation of timber frames

Shingle shapes carved into the stone roof

Figure 23.3 The church on St Macdara's Island, Co. Galway, copies wooden construction in stone.

Churches had a simple rectangular plan, and varied from being almost square to, more commonly, about twice the length of the width. Small windows in the east gable and the western doorway would have allowed only a little natural light to penetrate. Some later churches had additional small windows towards the eastern end of the sidewalls.

Wooden churches had steep roofs covered in thatch or wooden shingles; this design tradition was replicated when churches were built in stone. While there has been much debate about the age of the simplest stone churches, there is little mention of stone buildings in the texts before the 9th century. Carbon dating has produced a timescale of AD 640 to 790 for some of the corbelled buildings on the Dingle peninsula, which puts them close to the beginning of the development of stone churches in Ireland.

Stone Carving

On early Christian stone carvings, the decoration is usually a simple linear pattern carved into the surface of untrimmed stones. These can include Latin and Irish inscriptions, as well as Greek, Latin or Maltese cross designs. The Chi-Rho monogram (a symbol for Christ), swastikas, simple knots, fretwork, spirals and curves can also appear as part of the design repertoire.

Most of these elements, apart from the Christian symbols, were in the La Tène style already in use during the Iron Age in Ireland.

Symmetry and balance were an important part of these early designs.

Manuscripts

The decoration used by scribes follows on from the La Tène style (trumpet ends, spirals and a few animal and plant forms), and incorporates Christian symbols like the cross and the fish.

The simple shapes and patterns used in book decoration are echoed in contemporary stone and metalwork, the small repertoire of designs forming the basis for the amazingly elaborate work produced by the following generations of craftsmen.

Most of the designs are linear.

Write a piece of script or make some ink drawings, from any source you like, using pens that you have made yourself. You could make them from feathers or bamboo. You will find some tutorials online if you need help.

Metalwork

As Roman designs found their way into Ireland through contact with Britain and Gaul (France), a new range of objects appeared at this time, among them hand pins, penannular brooches, latchets and hanging bowls. They were designed with the same La Tène elements as the other crafts.

Artists and Artworks

Architecture

Skellig Michael

- **Form:** The well-preserved monastic settlement on Skellig Michael off the Kerry Coast consists of a group of corbelled buildings and stone enclosures.
- **Function:** The settlement on the Skelligs would not have been a typical monastery, clinging as it does to the crags of an island 180 m above the

Atlantic, but it does give us an idea of the scale and complexity of early monasteries (Fig. 23.4).

- **Technique:** All the walls, steps and buildings on the island are constructed in the dry-stone walling technique – no mortar is used to join the stones together. Corbelling was an ancient method of construction dating back to the Stone Age (it was used at Newgrange). It allows the builders to create a dome of stone by laying each circular or rectangular course of stone a little inside the one below, creating an inward curve that continues until the walls meet at the top. There are both dome-shaped and rectangular corbelled buildings on Skellig Michael; some are as large as 9 m in diameter and 4.5 m tall.

- **Decoration:** There are some simply decorated crosses in the graveyard, but all the buildings are plain.

Corbelling: A technique for building a roof in stone. Flat stones were laid in decreasing circles or rectangles. Each row was a little smaller than the one below, and the walls gradually got closer together until they met at roof level.

Go to YouTube and watch the video, 'The Wonder of Skellig Michael on the Wild Atlantic Way' (2:25) by Peter Cox Photography.

This short drone video of Skellig Michael gives a good idea of the location of the monastery. Can you imagine what it would have been like living in such an isolated and dangerous place? Why do you think the monks chose it?

Gallarus Oratory

- **Form:** The Gallarus Oratory on the Dingle peninsula is the best preserved and most complete of the group of corbelled rectangular oratories on the mainland (Fig. 23.5).

Figure 23.4 Some of the corbelled buildings and a simple cross in the enclosure of the monastery on Skellig Michael.

Figure 23.5 Gallarus Oratory, Dingle peninsula, Co. Kerry. The thickness of the walls can be noted in the west doorway.

- **Function:** The oratory is the church of a small monastery.
- **Technique:** It is a dry-stone construction using carefully selected stones that are larger at the corners and at the base, and smaller and lighter towards the top and centre, where a cave-in was more likely. The stones were laid down sloping out from the centre of the wall and trimmed to an even surface on the outside to shed the rain and wind. The side walls form one continuous surface from ground to ridge and are supported by inward-leaning gables. The doorway has inclined jambs (the opening is narrower at the top than at the bottom) and a plain lintel. The tiny east window has a round top cut from two stones, so it is not a true arch.
- **Decoration:** It is a plain, undecorated building.

Stone Carving

Ogham Stones

Dating from the 4th and 5th centuries, Ogham stones, which are found mainly along the southern end of the country from Wexford to Kerry, were the earliest form of vertical stone monument from the Christian period (Fig. 23.6). A few examples are found in Britain in areas that once supported Irish colonies, but they are mainly of Irish origin. Ogham was a form of Latin script simplified down to marks across a line or around the corner edge of a stone.

RESEARCH

Go to *www.ogham.ie* and look at the Ogham alphabet.

Why do you think this type of script was used in the early Christian period?

Try writing your name in Ogham.

Cross-inscribed Pillars

Upright pillars and slabs with crosses inscribed into their surfaces are found at some of the earliest monastic sites. These inscribed pillars are often found close to churches, and tradition suggests that some of them mark the grave of the founding saint, which would have become a focus for pilgrimage in the following centuries.

The majority of this type of monument is found in the western part of the country, from Kerry to Donegal.

Reask Pillar

The cross-inscribed pillar in the walled monastic enclosure at Reask on the Dingle peninsula in Co. Kerry dates back to the 7th century (Fig. 23.7).

- **Form:** An untrimmed, upright, stone pillar with carved decoration.
- **Function:** It may mark the grave of the founder of the monastery or it might simply be a focus point for prayer.
- **Technique:** Using iron tools, the cross at the top of the slab is carved in shallow relief. The rest of the design is a thin carved line. The stone is not dressed and the shape is not changed from its natural, uneven surface.
- **Decoration:** A Maltese cross surrounded by a circle takes up the top of the slab. A pattern of spirals extends down from the circle, ending in a pelta shape. The letters D N E are inscribed on the left of the shaft. They probably stand for the Latin word *Domine*, meaning 'Lord', and may refer to 'the Lord our God' or it might mean 'the Lord Abbot'. All the design elements on

Figure 23.6
Ogham stone from Traigh an Fhiona on the Dingle peninsula, Co. Kerry. The inscription is in old Irish and reads: CUNAMAQQI CORBBI MAQQS. It is hard to translate, but it might be 'Cuna (grand) son of Corbbi'.

Maltese cross in circle

Untrimmed stone

Lettering *DNE*

Upturned pelta with spirals

Figure 23.7
Decorated, untrimmed stone pillar at Reask on the Dingle peninsula, Co. Kerry.

this pillar relate to late La Tène design and the delicate line contrasts with the crude surface of the stone on which it was carved.

Manuscripts

The Cathach

The Cathach is probably the oldest surviving Irish manuscript. It was written in the late 6th century and is the second oldest psalter written in Latin in the world. This book is believed to be from the hand of St Columba (Colmcille, 'Dove of the Church') *c.* 521–597. He was the founder of the Columban order of monks who continued the tradition of manuscript writing and missionary work begun by their first abbot.

The name Cathach, an Irish word meaning 'battler', was given to the book by the O'Donnells, clansmen of Columba, who carried it with them into battle, invoking the protection of the saint.

Rubrics

Diminuendo

Pen flourishes

Cross

Animal head

Spring spiral

Figure 23.8 (left)
The opening lines of Psalm 91 in the Cathach.

Figure 23.9 (right)
The capital letter M on folio 21a of the Cathach is decorated with spirals and trumpet ends.

This is reputed to be the book that Columba transcribed in haste without the permission of his master Finnian, bringing about a court case that ruled 'to every cow its calf, to every book its copy'. Columba's clansmen disputed the court case and fought the Battle of Cúl Dreimhne for ownership of the book. The story goes that Columba was so horrified by the death and destruction of the battle that he banished himself on permanent pilgrimage and exile from home. This *peregrinatio* (wandering) involved a life of prayer and self-denial while spreading the word of God to the heathens. His travels took him first to Iona, an island off the coast of Scotland, where he founded a monastery that was to become the chief house of the Columban *paruchia* (family of monasteries) for the next 200 years. The missionary work then continued through Scotland to Northumbria in northern England and to Europe.

- **Form:** A vellum manuscript in the form of a codex measuring 27 cm × 19 cm. Fifty-eight damaged pages remain from an original 110 folios.

> **Folio:** A complete page, front and back.
>
> **Codex:** Groups of pages sewn together into book form. The codex became more popular than the scroll, as it was easier to refer to and to store.

- **Function:** A psalter is a book of psalms. These are sacred poems from the Old Testament of the Bible that were sung or chanted as part of monks' daily practice.
- **Techniques:** The vellum was made in the way described on page 323 (see Fig. 23.2). A dark

ink was used, applied with a quill or reed pen. Red letters (rubrics) are used to write a short introduction (in old Irish) before each psalm. Orange dots are used to outline some of the decorated capitals at the beginning of each psalm.

- **Decoration:** The Cathach is written in a clear majuscule script with enlarged capitals introducing each psalm. The lettering is in a peculiarly Irish style. A small spring spiral, an animal head and a cross are all added to the tail of the Q and a row of flourishes decorates the inside (Fig. 23.8). The letter M that opens the psalm on folio 21a is decorated with spirals and trumpet ends (Fig. 23.9).

> **Majuscule:** A style of rounded capital letter written between two ruled lines with a very few short ascenders or descenders above or below these lines.

Try using a majuscule style of writing in your copy, in a piece of writing, or as part of a design for a poster for an exhibition of ancient manuscripts.

> The *diminuendo* effect is where the initial letter takes up five lines and the following letters gradually reduce in size until they are back to the general text size. This is a characteristic feature of Irish script, not seen in Roman models.

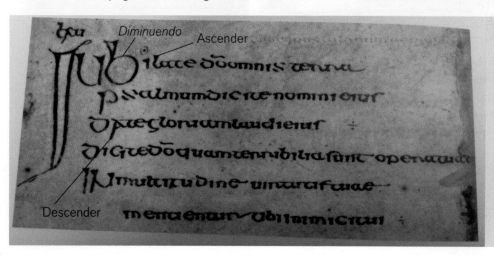

Figure 23.10
Example of script from the Cathach with ascenders and descenders.

Metalwork

Penannular brooches take the form of a broken circle with a pin attached to the ring. The earliest brooches were simple wire dress fasteners. The ends beside the opening in the ring were bent back to retain the pin, which was connected to it by a loop. Later, brooches were cast in bronze or silver (Fig. 23.11). As time went by, the loop on the pin and the decorated areas beside the opening of the ring were enlarged to incorporate more elaborate designs.

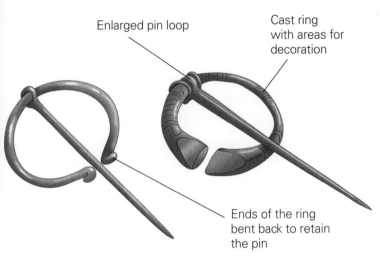

Enlarged pin loop

Cast ring with areas for decoration

Ends of the ring bent back to retain the pin

Figure 23.11 Simple penannular brooches.

The Ballinderry Brooch (*c.* AD 600)

● **Form:** A cast-bronze ring with enlarged areas next to the opening. A pin with an enlarged loop and a bronze spiral are attached to the ring (Fig. 23.12).
● **Function:** The brooch was used to fasten a cloak or tunic.
● **Technique:** The ring and pin were cast in bronze. There is *millefiori* glass decoration on the ends of the ring and on the pin head.
● **Decoration:** A range of textures and patterns on the cast bronze brooch form a zoomorph on each end of the ring. These animal heads are almost abstract; viewed from above, their bulbous noses face the ring. Protruding eyes are met by the shield-shaped areas of enamel that form the tops of their heads, while small rounded ears border the opening.

Millefiori literally means 'a thousand flowers', because an area decorated in this way can look like a field of flowers. Sticks of coloured enamel are melted together and stretched into a long thin rod. Thin sections can be cut from the rod and applied to a metal surface by heating.

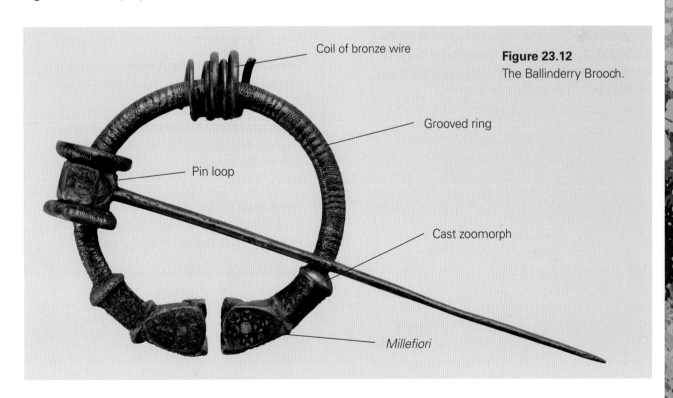

Coil of bronze wire

Figure 23.12
The Ballinderry Brooch.

Grooved ring

Pin loop

Cast zoomorph

Millefiori

The brooch, which was found at Ballinderry Crannóg, is a beautiful example of the developing style. Later brooches became even more elaborate, and new techniques emerged through trade with Europe. Gold wire filigree is found in a few small pieces dating back to the 6th century. A small bird-shaped button was found in Lagore Crannóg, where *millefiori* glass was also discovered in an enameller's workshop. We will see more of filigree and *millefiori* in the next chapters.

Analysis

> Look at how Christian symbolism was combined with Celtic design in the new crafts that came with Christianity.

The Christian mission to Ireland brought with it new ideas and influences from abroad, which were swiftly incorporated into the national craft style. Further opportunities were created by the introduction of decorated books and the demand for beautiful metalwork and stone carving in the new and rapidly expanding monasteries.

During the 5th and 6th centuries, technical skills and the variety of designs gradually increased to the point where all the elements needed for the explosion of creativity that happened in the 7th and 8th centuries were gathered together in the workshops of the larger monasteries.

Chapter Review

1. The Christian mission to Ireland brought new influences and ideas. Can you identify some of these new elements in the crafts of the period using words and drawings?

2. Judging from the buildings of the time, can you imagine the lifestyle of the early monks? Sketch and write about your ideas.

3. What, do you think, was the purpose of cross-inscribed pillars in early monasteries? Draw a decorated example and write your reasons.

4. Can you describe how vellum and inks were made? Illustrate your answer.

5. Can you describe some zoomorphic figures from 5th- and 6th-century craftwork? Draw and describe some examples.

Further Research

www.sacredsites.com – Search for Skellig Michael to learn more about the monastery

www.megalithicireland.com – Look for the section on Reask to see more of the Reask Pillar

www.museum.ie/Archaeology – The National Museum of Ireland (Archaeology) – Visit the Ballinderry Brooch the next time you are in Dublin

www.ria.ie – Learn more about the history of the Cathach by selecting 'The Cathach / The Psalter of St Columba' from the sidebar

Chapter 24

The Golden Age (7th and 8th Centuries)

By the end of this chapter I will ...

* know about new influences on design from Britain and Europe
* be able to draw and describe the Fahan Mura Slab and the Carndonagh Cross
* know how to draw and describe two pages from the Book of Durrow
* understand metalworking techniques
* know how to draw and describe the Tara Brooch and the Ardagh Chalice and some of their decoration
* be able to compare the design of human and animal figures in the different crafts
* have noted continuity and change in each craft from earlier 5th-century work to 7th- and 8th-century examples.

Context

Europe became more stable through the establishment of strong kingdoms in the areas that are now France and Germany. Much of Europe was converted to Christianity, and the papacy had become stronger. Clergy from France converted southern Britain to Christianity.

Political and monastic dynasties in Ireland were also strengthened. The Uí Néill, kings of Tara, controlled the Midlands and a good part of Northern Ireland. They made an alliance with the Dál Riata, who were kings of Antrim and Argyll, which extended their influence into Scotland. The Uí Néill were in conflict with the Eóghanachta of Munster for 400 years.

The Monasteries

Monasteries became more important in Ireland. They had become centres of learning and places of refuge for pilgrims, the sick, widows and orphans. Kells, Armagh, Glendalough, Clonmacnoise and other large monasteries grew in size and population and took on a new economic importance in the community. The simple austerity of the early monasteries was replaced by wealth and power, which even lead to conflicts between monasteries. In AD 790, a war was fought between the monks of Clonmacnoise and the monks of Durrow.

Irish Missionaries in Europe

The missionary work that had begun on Iona in the previous century spread to Britain and Europe in the 600s. Saint Aidan, a follower of St Columba, was invited by King Oswald to build a monastery on the island of Lindisfarne off the east coast of England. Saint Aidan had great success in converting the people of Northumbria to Christianity. Saint Columbanus, another Columban monk, set up monasteries in France, Switzerland and Italy.

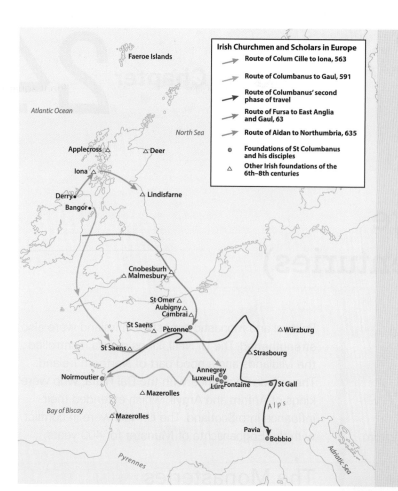

Figure 24.1
Map of Ireland, Britain and Europe, showing Irish monasteries in Europe.

When the Irish monks came into contact with European clergy, differences in their practices created difficulties. The Irish Church, which had been out of direct contact with Rome, had retained some ancient practices. Irish monks had a different tonsure (way of cutting their hair), a different way of calculating the date of Easter, and were not organised in dioceses under a bishop. These irregularities were not acceptable to the Roman authorities. The Synod of Whitby, a gathering of clergy from the Irish and Roman traditions, was called by King Oswiu of Northumbria in 664. It settled these differences, but the Irish clergy were slow to make the required changes.

Insular Manuscripts in Europe

A number of 8th-century gospel books in the Insular style survive. A manuscript from Durham Cathedral Library, the Lindisfarne and Lichfield Gospels, are all in England. Gospel books from Echternach in Luxembourg, Maihingen in Germany and the Abbey

Figure 24.2 The Lindisfarne Gospels, cross-carpet page.

Library of St Gall in Switzerland are all written in the Irish style of script. They all contain portraits of the evangelists, carpet pages, decorated initials, animal interlace and a range of colours. These books give us a wider picture of the style and quality of Irish manuscripts (Fig. 24.2).

Media and Areas of Practice

Architecture

Very little architecture survives that can be dated with any certainty to the 7th and 8th centuries. A few stone churches that would originally have had wooden roofs may date from this time. These churches have antae (projections of the side walls beyond the surface of the gables), which may be an imitation, in stone, of corner posts from wooden buildings.

Stone Carving

Cross-decorated slabs, simple crosses and grave slabs became more common in monasteries in the 7th and 8th centuries. Crosses and slabs were trimmed to shape and carved in low relief using iron tools.

Manuscripts

Book-making Techniques

Books were written on vellum pages (see Fig. 23.2, p. 323). To assemble the pages into a codex, the vellum would have been cut into bifoliae (a bifolium is a strip of vellum, which is folded in half to create two pages), which were then collected into bunches called gatherings. These gatherings were then sewn together to form the codex.

Writing Tools

Pens were generally made from the tail feathers of the goose or swan, but they could also be made from cut reeds. Brushes could be made from a variety of hairs tied into a goose quill ferrule. The hair of the marten could have been used for the finest brushes. Straight edges, compass and dividers would have been needed for ruling out the pages and laying out designs.

Colours

- **Orange-red** was made from red lead. The resulting pigment was quite toxic.

Red from red lead

Eight square panels on the cross

Orpiment yellow

Black ink in the spaces emphasise the colours

Ribbon interlace

Verdigris green has eaten through the vellum

Figure 24.3 The Book of Durrow, folio 1v, the double-armed cross-carpet page.

- **Yellow** could be made from ox gall, but this often discoloured to brown. A purer, brighter yellow was made from orpiment (from the Latin *auripigmentum*, which means 'gold pigment'). It is yellow arsenic sulphate, which had to be imported from parts of Europe or Asia, and is both toxic and foul-smelling. It reacts chemically with lead or copper-based colours (Fig. 24.3).

- **Green** was most commonly made from verdigris, which is copper acetate. Verdigris could be unstable and has eaten through the vellum in some manuscripts, including the Book of Durrow.

Metalwork

The metalwork of the 7th and 8th centuries is of a very high quality. It is easily the most elegant and technically refined work of any country in Europe during the early Middle Ages. It might help to examine some of the techniques before we look at the objects themselves.

- **Enamelling:** A variety of techniques were used in enamelling.
  - *Cloisonné:* Areas of design were surrounded with silver, gold or bronze wire and filled with enamel.
  - *Champlevé:* An old Celtic technique in which areas of a surface were carved away or beaten hollow and the spaces created were filled with enamel.
  - *Millefiori:* Rods of coloured glass were heated and drawn together in a molten state and stretched into long, thin rods from which fine sections could be cut off and applied to enamel surfaces. The sections can look like flowers, hence the name, *millefiori*, meaning 'thousand flowers'.
  - **Studs:** Studs were cast in clay moulds. Some had wire grilles fitted into the mould, which were then filled with coloured glass enamel. Other studs were cast with hollow spaces, which then could be filled with a second colour.
- **Filigree:** Consisted of thin gold wires that were twisted together into a fine rope. Sometimes wires of different sizes were twisted together to create a more glittering effect. The filigree was bent into shape and soldered to a gold foil background that could then be fixed in place (Fig. 24.4).
- **Chip carving:** Chip carving was a technique of carving metal in high relief, creating sharp outlines and deep shadows.
- **Casting:** A variety of methods and techniques were used in casting. Clay and bone moulds were used to create both plain and decorated objects. The lost wax technique was used for more complicated objects. Chip carving was sometimes imitated in cast designs.
- **Engraving:** Engraving involved cutting a design into a metal surface with a sharp point. Sometimes two metals were laid one on top of the other so that the colour below would be revealed when the upper metal was engraved.
- **Die stamping:** Die stamping involved stamping a thin sheet of metal, usually gold or silver, with a design that had been carved into a block of wood or cast into metal.
- **Turning:** A sheet of metal was pressed onto a former (a type of mould), rotated on a lathe, and gradually shaped into a bowl or cone shape as required. The lathe was also used to polish beaten metalwork.
- **Amber:** Amber, which is fossilised resin, was cut to shape and used like enamel studs as a

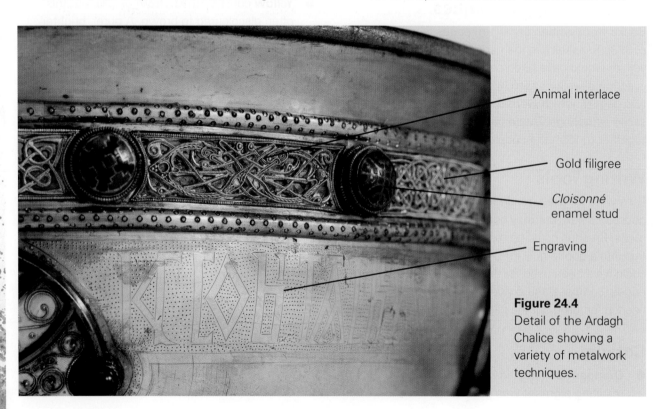

Animal interlace

Gold filigree

Cloisonné enamel stud

Engraving

Figure 24.4
Detail of the Ardagh Chalice showing a variety of metalwork techniques.

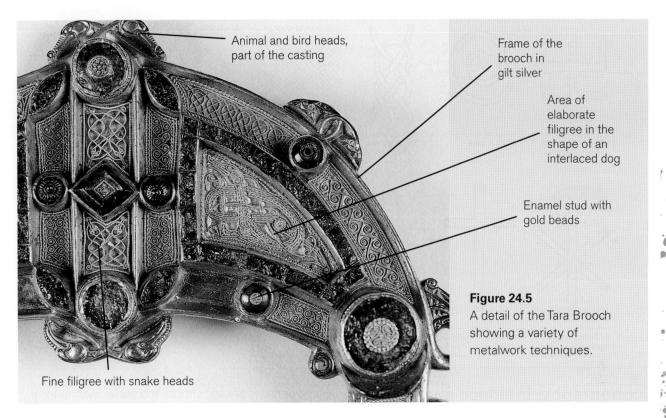

Animal and bird heads, part of the casting

Frame of the brooch in gilt silver

Area of elaborate filigree in the shape of an interlaced dog

Enamel stud with gold beads

Fine filigree with snake heads

Figure 24.5
A detail of the Tara Brooch showing a variety of metalwork techniques.

contrast to areas of filigree or chip carving. The amber could be heated and lightly moulded into shape.

- **Trichinopoly:** Trichinopoly is a type of wire mesh made in copper, silver or gold. It is formed into a chain on the Tara Brooch and is used to cover the rim on the Derrynaflan Paten.
- **Gilding:** There were two methods of gilding bronze or silver:
  - Gold leaf was attached mechanically. This was not often done.
  - In fire-gilding, gold was dissolved in mercury and applied to the surface, which was heated. The mercury evaporated, leaving a thin layer of gold.

Art Elements and Design Principles

The Insular Style

Over a number of centuries, elements from European design were incorporated into the native Irish design sensibility. The Insular style evolved into something unique and original that was used in all the crafts during the 7th and 8th centuries. Notable features of the Insular style included:

- Spirals and pelta shapes, which had their origins in Celtic design and had already been in use for 800 years at this time.
- Interlace, which is of Coptic (the Christian Church of North Africa and the Eastern Mediterranean) origin. This probably came to Ireland via the Mediterranean countries – and Rome in particular – as it had a strong input from the Middle East in early medieval times.
- Animal ornament of Germanic origin. This would have been introduced through Anglo-Saxon influences in Northumbria, which had a close connection to Ireland.

Much of the design was linear, and dots were frequently used. Pattern, shape and colour were key elements.

Interlace: A pattern made of interwoven strands, looped, braided or knotted into a geometric pattern.

A swastika, an old celtic sun symbol

A spiral

A simple two cord knot

A fret pattern

A Chi Rho symbol: A monogram for Christ

A Latin cross: Upright longer than cross piece

A Greek cross: Arms are the same length

A Maltese cross

Figure 24.6
Insular design elements.

Iconography: Interlace and Numbers

It is difficult to be certain about the meanings or significance that the artists of the early Middle Ages intended to put into their work 1,300 years ago, but historians do understand a certain amount.

In some cultures, interlace patterns were considered to provide protection from evil. Intricate patterns, particularly those incorporating animal heads, were thought to confuse and intimidate evil spirits. This may be a reason for including such patterns at the beginning of manuscripts and at the start of the gospels.

Number symbolism is a common theme in early medieval Christian art. It was designed to help the observer find new layers of meaning in the artworks. For example, a four-part design could, depending on the context of the design, imply: the four gospels, the four evangelists, the four cardinal virtues, the four rivers of paradise, the four rings which carried the Arc of the Covenant, the four qualities of Christ, and so on.

Stone Carving

This is the first time we see stone carved to shape, given a clear outline and smooth surface. The figures

and patterns are still simple and linear. Symmetrical patterns cover most of the surface of these carvings. Detail could have been added by painting.

Manuscripts

When new Irish monasteries were set up in Britain and Europe, they would originally have been stocked with books made in Ireland, and Irish monks probably trained the scribes in these monasteries. Influences from British and continental traditions in art also found their way back into Ireland with the monks.

While books in the Insular style survived in many European monasteries, scholars can't be certain where each book was actually written. The script, patterns, colours and balance of the designs all have a strong element of the Irish Celtic tradition.

 Create a design for a T-shirt print using the design elements and style of Insular Art.

Innovation and Invention

Missionary monks travelling through Britain and Europe picked up new designs and techniques that they brought back to Ireland. The patterns we find in the books, crosses and metalwork from the 7th and

8th centuries come from as far as the Middle East, thanks to the trading networks introduced by the Roman Empire.

The animals in the Book of Durrow look similar to Saxon examples from the north-east of Europe.

Greater sophistication in design and technique is evident in stone carving, book painting and metalwork.

Artists and Artworks

Architecture

Unfortunately, no complete buildings from the 7th and 8th centuries have survived to the present day. Some features remain, but most buildings were made of wood and have therefore disintegrated over time.

Monasteries seem to have been laid out in the same way as they were in the 6th century, with a surrounding bank of earth or stone enclosing small stone or wooden buildings. These enclosures could easily be expanded, adding more small buildings and moving the bank farther out to enclose a wider area.

Stone Carving

Cross-decorated slabs, simple crosses and grave slabs became more common in monasteries during the 7th and 8th centuries.

The Fahan Mura Slab

Fahan Mura in Donegal is the site of the monastery founded by St Columba for his disciple Mura. It dates to the end of the 7th century.

- **Form:** A fully trimmed and dressed upright slab of stone, with a low triangular top, the Fahan Mura Slab is 2.10 m tall with low relief decoration related to Pictish slabs found in Scotland (Fig. 24.8). There are little stubs projecting from the sides of the slab, which some commentators regard as the beginnings of the arms that appear on later crosses.
- **Function:** This and other crosses may have been a focus point for prayer, a marker for the boundary of sanctuary, a memorial to a saint or perhaps all three.
- **Technique:** Carved in low relief using iron tools, the details are hard to see except in good light. The shallowness of the decoration has led some commentators to believe that the pattern may originally have been painted.

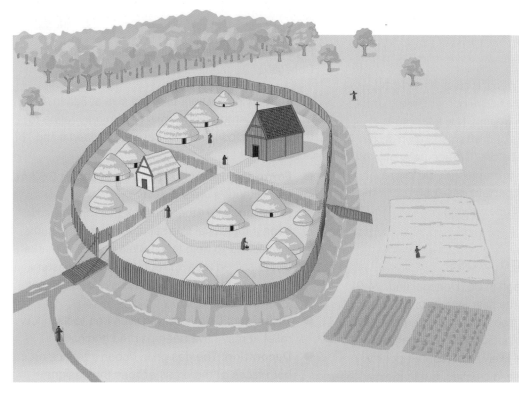

Figure 24.7 A monastic enclosure with a wooden fence and church. Huts were built of wattle and daub, and had thatched roofs.

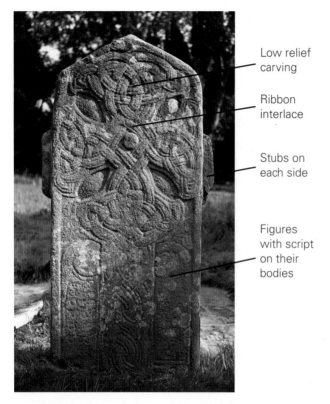

Low relief carving

Ribbon interlace

Stubs on each side

Figures with script on their bodies

Figure 24.8 The west face of the Fahan Mura Slab.

- **Decoration:** A pattern of outlined ribbon interlace is formed into a cross shape on both faces. On the west face, simple human figures stand to the left and right of the cross shaft. Each of these figures has an undeciphered inscription on their tunic.

> *Note:* This decorated slab marks a further development in the art of stone carving in Ireland. It is a far more sophisticated piece of craftsmanship in stone than we have seen before. The accuracy of the design and the refinement of the low relief carving mark an important development in the evolution of Irish stone carving.

The Carndonagh Cross

The cross at Carndonagh in Co. Donegal (Fig. 24.9) has been regarded in the past as the transitional piece between stone slabs and pillars and the fully formed Celtic high cross. Scholars now believe that this cross is more likely to be contemporary with the early wheel-head crosses, but in a

Crucifixion scene

Triskele of birds

Cross shape in ribbon interlace

Pillars with figures

Figure 24.9 East face of the Carndonagh Cross, Co. Donegal.

different style tradition. Like the slab at Fahan Mura, the Carndonagh Cross design may relate to the monastic connections between Donegal and Scotland.

- **Form:** The unevenly shaped cross stands 2.53 m tall, without a wheel head.
- **Function:** Like other crosses this may have been a memorial to a saint, a focus for pilgrims, a visual aid to help teach Bible stories, a marker of the sacred area surrounding the monastery, or a focus for prayer. It could have been any or all of these things.
- **Technique:** Lightly carved with iron tools in low relief, it may have been painted originally.
- **Decoration:** The design in ribbon interlace on both faces of the cross echoes the designs

found on Pictish cross slabs in Scotland. The ribbon interlace on the east face forms a cross on the upper part of the stone, with a little group of birds forming a triskele pattern in the crook of each arm. On the shaft, there is a crucifixion scene and other groups of figures that are not clearly identified. There are small pillars beside the cross, carved with figures representing David playing the harp, Jonah and the whale, and ecclesiastics with bell and crosier, all of which are themes that occur on other crosses.

 You will find more images of the Carndonagh Cross at *www.megalithicireland.com*. Make notes and sketches from these images to help with your written work.

Manuscripts

Not many Irish books survive from the 7th century. There are some from the monastery of St Columbanus at Bobbio in northern Italy, but we are very lucky to have an outstanding example in this country.

The Book of Durrow

- **Form:** The Book of Durrow is the earliest example (late 7th to early 8th century) of a fully decorated manuscript in the Insular style. It is a copy of the Four Gospels with some preliminary texts. The pages are 245 × 145 mm. There are 248 folios (leaves) of vellum, most of which have writing on both sides.
  The text is a copy of the Latin Vulgate version of the New Testament, which St Jerome compiled for Pope Damasus in the late 4th century in an effort to create a correct and standard translation of the books of the Bible.
- **Function:** This is a book of the New Testament, the Four Gospels of the Bible. A manuscript this richly decorated was meant for display rather than everyday use.
- **Technique:** The materials and methods used in making the book are described under the Media and Areas of Practice section of this chapter.
- **Decoration:** There are 12 fully decorated pages and many more with decorated capitals.

The script is in the Irish majuscule style, written in long lines across the page. Books of a similar type written in Lindisfarne and other Northumbrian monasteries with Irish connections were generally written in two columns.

The Decoration Scheme

The Book of Durrow opens with some decorated pages. The first (folio 1v) is a carpet page with a design in the shape of a double-armed cross (see Fig. 24.3). In the Coptic tradition of the eastern Mediterranean, double-armed metal crosses were used to house a fragment of the True Cross. The design may invoke the protection that such a relic would bring. The cross design includes eight squares, which may refer to the eighth day of Christ's passion (the Resurrection). These symbols would announce the core message of the Bible, Christ's death and resurrection, for the sake of his faithful followers and mankind in general.

The Four Gospels

The books of the Four Gospels begin on folio 21v. Each begins with an evangelist symbol page, followed by a carpet page (except in the case of St Matthew's Gospel, where the carpet page was misplaced sometime over the centuries). The first page of each gospel has a decorated capital letter. The opening lines are usually larger than the general text, and surrounded by red dotting.

Note: In a complete Bible manuscript, each gospel would begin with three decorated pages: an evangelist's symbol, a carpet page and an initial capital letter page.

The Man Symbol

The man symbol at the beginning of St Matthew's Gospel is shaped like a contemporary Irish bell. The face is very accurately drawn in fine line, although there is no sign of arms or details of clothing (Fig. 24.10). The check pattern looks like the *millefiori* glass decoration created in 7th- and 8th-century metalwork and the overall shape of the figure is like those on the Carndonagh Cross. An area of plain

Figure 24.10 The Book of Durrow, folio 21v, the man symbol for St Matthew.

a triquetra knot, a symbol of the Trinity. The little cross at the top of the *X* is similar to the one on the tail of the *Q* at the beginning of Psalm 91 in the Cathach. The enlarged letter-size at the beginning of each passage is a development of the *diminuendo* effect we saw in the Cathach. The most elaborately decorated letters are the opening lines at the beginning of each gospel.

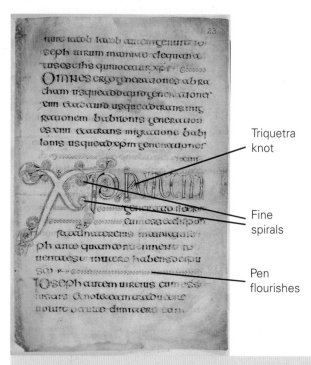

Triquetra knot

Fine spirals

Pen flourishes

Figure 24.11 The Book of Durrow, folio 23r, the Chi-Rho page.

Initial Letter Pages

The Initium page (folio 86r) from the beginning of St Mark's Gospel is the best preserved of the initial pages (Fig. 24.12). The letter *I* takes up three-quarters of the height of the page with a sharp *diminuendo* to the *N*, *I* and *T*. The first three lines are surrounded with red dotting. The spirals and trumpet scrolls that decorate the ends of the *I* and *N* become zoomorphs on closer inspection.

Animal Interlace

The page of interlaced animals on folio 192v at the beginning of St John's Gospel is one of the highlights of the Book of Durrow and is full of number symbolism (Fig. 24.13). The circle in the middle of the page has a cross at its centre, which is surrounded by a three-part interlace pattern in

vellum around the figure creates a well-designed balance with the heavily patterned areas. A border of ribbon interlace in shades of yellow and green surrounds the page. The area between the ribbons has been darkened for dramatic effect and a triangle of plain vellum breaks each dark triangular space into three smaller parts, probably a reference to the Holy Trinity, which is picked up again on the Chi-Rho page.

The Chi-Rho

Folio 23r is the Chi-Rho page (Fig. 24.11). The Chi-Rho is a special decoration where the name of Christ is mentioned for the first time in the gospel.

The letters *X* and *P* are the Greek letters *Chi-Rho*, which is a monogram for Christ. They are beautifully decorated with fine spring spirals and trumpets and surrounded inside and out by a field of red dotting, except for the space between the *X* and *P*, which has little triangles of dots. The centre of the *A* has

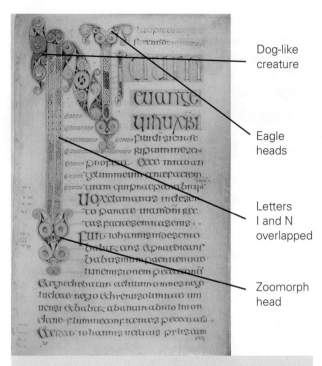

Dog-like creature

Eagle heads

Letters I and N overlapped

Zoomorph head

Figure 24.12 The Book of Durrow, folio 86r, the Initium page from the beginning of St Mark's Gospel.

Figure 24.13 The Book of Durrow, folio 192v, animal interlace carpet page at the beginning of St John's Gospel.

red, yellow and green. The emphasis on three-part patterns within the circle is a reference to the Trinity; the panels of three biting dogs to left and right might also have this underlying meaning. The panels of elongated animals in the top and bottom sections are alike, but they are not mirror images of each other. It can be interesting to unravel an animal interlace and see how the leg, tail or jaw can be extended to loop around other limbs or back on itself to fit the artist's pattern. The inner rows of eight animals refer to the eighth day of the passion of Christ, the Resurrection. The top and bottom patterns have 10 animals in each panel, a reference to St Augustine's perfect number, 10, which symbolised unity. There are a total of 42 animals on the page, which may be a reference to the 42 generations of the ancestors of Christ.

Origins of the Book

The Book of Durrow is associated with the Columban monastery at Durrow in Co. Offaly. It was probably written in the late 7th or early 8th century.

The book we see today is in remarkably good condition considering the ups and downs of its 1,300 years of existence. It was knocked about during its enshrining in a metal *cumdach* (book shrine) in 916 and its value as a miraculous object led its keepers in the 17th century to dip it in water that they used to cure sick cattle, which caused some staining and loss of colour. It has been in the care of Trinity College Library in Dublin since the late 17th century and was completely restored and rebound in 1954.

Search online for more images of the Book of Durrow. Make sketches and take notes to use in your studio or written work.

UNIT 8 INSULAR ART (c. 500–1100s)

Metalwork

At the beginning of this chapter, we noted three sources for the origins of Christian Celtic design. In the following metalwork objects, we will see how these basic elements were elaborated on and distorted to create designs of the most extraordinary quality. There is nothing second-hand or copied in these designs; the elements were used with flair and originality to create a unique and subtly balanced art.

Many penannular and pseudo-penannular brooches ranging in size from 7 cm to 13 cm in diameter are known to date from the 7th and 8th centuries; of these, the Tara Brooch is the finest (Fig. 24.14).

The Tara Brooch

The Tara Brooch was found in 1850 in Bettystown, Co. Meath, near the mouth of the River Boyne. Although some sections are damaged, enough remains to give a clear impression of the quality of craftsmanship and design. The chain attached to one side suggests that it was connected to a matching

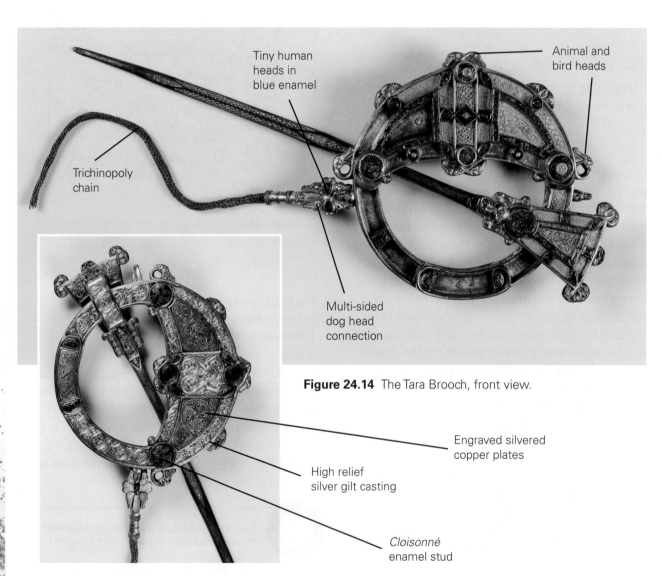

Tiny human heads in blue enamel

Animal and bird heads

Trichinopoly chain

Multi-sided dog head connection

Figure 24.14 The Tara Brooch, front view.

Engraved silvered copper plates

High relief silver gilt casting

Cloisonné enamel stud

Figure 24.15 The Tara Brooch, back view.

brooch, one worn on each side of the chest, with the chain connecting them.

- **Form:** The body of the 8th-century brooch, which is 8.7 cm in diameter, was cast in silver, creating a raised framework. The front face of the brooch is divided into panels of filigree, separated by amber and enamel studs. There is a large area of decoration on the head of the pin.
- **Function:** Brooches were fasteners for cloaks or tunics. There were laws controlling the size and quality of brooches, which could be worn by people from different levels of society. Brooches may have been part of clerical garb. They are shown on some of the figures carved on high crosses.
- **Technique:** The main body and the pin of the brooch are cast, creating frames to hold the decorative parts. Filigree is used in most of the panels on the front, separated by enamel studs. The reverse side of the brooch (Fig. 24.15) has sections cast in high relief, with zoomorphs and spiral patterns separated by enamel studs. Every part of the brooch that has not been decorated separately has been gilded. There are two silvered copper plates with fine spiral patterns engraved into them on the widest part of the ring on the back of the brooch. A cast double head connects the frame to a trichinopoly chain which may have connected to a matching brooch.
- **Decoration:** Fantastic stylised animals seem to be the theme of the Tara Brooch. They appear in the filigree sections, in cast areas, on the back, at several places on the perimeter, on the pin and on the chain connection.
  - The trichinopoly chain is attached to the rim by an intriguing series of animal heads with interlocked jaws. This link also contains two tiny human faces made of moulded blue glass.
  - Most of the filigree is very fine and is wrought into spiral and interlace patterns. In the remaining triangular panel on the front of the brooch, there is a dog design. The creature's body, which is made up of a range of different textured filigree strands, turns back on itself in a pattern that tightly fits the triangular space. There is another dog-like animal design on the head of the pin.
  - One could read the pattern at the centre of the front of the Tara Brooch as a cross, and the animal patterns could have a Christian meaning.

Communion Vessels

The large chalice and paten that survive from the 8th century are in a style not common in Europe. The closest comparable pieces are of an earlier date and are from Syria. This does not necessarily mean that there were direct connections between Ireland and Syria, but it does point to differences in religious practice between Ireland and the rest of Europe.

The Ardagh Chalice

Many of the techniques we have seen used in the Tara Brooch were also used in making the Ardagh Chalice (*c.* AD 750) (Fig. 24.16). It was found in 1868 with a small bronze chalice and three large brooches, in a hoard at Ardagh, Co. Limerick, by a boy digging potatoes.

- **Form:** The chalice is made up of a silver bowl connected to a conical foot by a gilt bronze collar. It is 17.8 cm high and 19.5 cm in diameter.
- **Function:** The large size of the vessel points to ceremonial use. It would have been used to distribute wine to the congregation, and was probably brought to the altar in an offertory procession.
- **Technique:** The silver bowl and foot were made from sheet silver turned on a lathe. Gold filigree is soldered on to fine gold sheet and fixed into framed areas. Glass enamel studs with *cloisonné* decoration separate filigree areas. The stem, which joins the bowl to the base, was cast.
- **Decoration:** The decoration of the chalice is a masterpiece of subtlety and refinement, with an almost perfect balance between areas of sumptuous decoration and the plain silver of the bowl and foot.
  - A band of decoration just below the rim is made up of panels of gold filigree punctuated with 12 enamel studs. The filigree is a mixture of animal and abstract panels. The names of the apostles are lightly

Figure 24.16
The Ardagh
Chalice,
front view.

Filigree

Handle

Turned
silver bowl

High relief
cast-gilt
collar

Filigree and
enamel studs
decorate the
rim of the foot

Medallion
with Greek
cross in circle

Cloisonné
enamel
studs

Engraved
names of the
apostles

Turned
silver foot

engraved in a field of dots just below this band, and are probably symbolised in the 12 studs.

- The handles and the plaques that attached them to the bowl are decorated with gold filigree, red and blue enamel, and glass studs inlaid with silver wire.
- Two medallions in the shape of a Greek cross in a circle are placed centrally on each side of the bowl of the chalice. They are also decorated with filigree and glass studs.
- The collar joining the bowl to the base is cast, in imitation of high relief chip carving, in spiral and interlace patterns.
- A rim around the upper surface of the conical foot is decorated with filigree panels punctuated by squares of blue glass.
- Underneath, at the centre of the foot, is a large crystal that hides the bolt connecting the foot to the bowl. This is surrounded by three bands of decoration. The inner band, an animal interlace, is in gold filigree; the middle band has chip-carved spiral decoration punctuated by small glass studs with gold granulations; and the outer band has an abstract interlace pattern in the chip-carved style (Fig. 24.17).

Figure 24.17 The Ardagh Chalice, underside of the foot.

The Derrynaflan Paten

This paten is the only one of its kind to come to light so far. It was found in 1980 at the monastery of Derrynaflan in Co. Tipperary. It was buried under a bronze cauldron with a chalice and other objects, which we will see more of later. The discovery of this paten shows that work of the quality of the Ardagh Chalice and Tara Brooch was not a rarity in Ireland in the 8th century.

- **Form:** The paten is 35 cm in diameter and made of over 300 components.
- **Function:** The large paten would have been used for distributing communion bread to the congregation and it would have been carried in procession.
- **Technique:** The beaten silver dish has a gilt bronze rim, which is decorated with gold filigree panels and *cloisonné* enamel studs (Fig. 24.18). The rim is riveted on to the silver dish. A ring of trichinopoly wire, in copper and silver, frames the decorated upper rim and conceals the joint between it and the side panels. Die-stamped gold foil panels decorate the sides of the rim and the foot.
- **Decoration:** The design of the filigree panels relate closely to those on the Ardagh Chalice, as do the enamel studs. The quality of the decorative elements is very high.
  - Animal, human and abstract designs are used in the filigree (Fig. 24.19).
  - There are 24 glass enamel studs around the upper rim of the paten; the number is probably a reference to the 24 elders of the Apocalypse who were seated around the throne of God. These studs are in two groups: 12 larger and 12 smaller, perhaps a reference to the apostles. The 12 smaller studs are set in little cups containing fine filigree. These studs hide the rivets that join

the components of the paten together. All the studs are more patterned and colourful than any we have seen before.
  - The die-stamped gold panels on the side of the rim are decorated with interlace and scroll patterns. The panels on the foot are similar, but not as finely made.

Visit *www.100objects.ie/derrynaflan-paten* to see some close-up photographs of the paten. Draw some of the filigree and studs to help you understand how they were made.

Create a painting that makes reference to the people and animals you have seen represented in the works of art we have looked at in this chapter. Think about the colours and patterns that were used in the 7th and 8th centuries.

Silver plate

Cloisonné enamel stud

Filigree

Silver trichinopoly

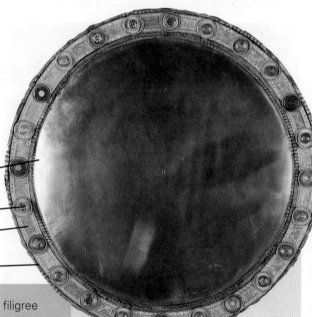

Human interlace filigree

Figure 24.18 (above)
The Derrynaflan Paten, viewed from above.

Figure 24.19 (left)
The Derrynaflan Paten, a section of the rim showing human interlace filigree and enamel studs.

UNIT 8 INSULAR ART (c. 500–1100s)

Shrines and Relics

The fashion for pilgrimage was strong throughout Europe. Relics and shrines dedicated to saints became an essential part of any large monastery. Shrines in a variety of shapes – house-shaped, book shrines and a range of others – were made to display the relics of the saints.

Book shrines were made to contain books associated with an important saint. While this preserved the book from human interference, the pages were often damaged from knocking into the sides of the box when it was moved. This type of damage can be seen on the Cathach and the Book of Durrow.

The Rinnegan or Athlone Crucifixion Plaque

- **Form:** An 8th-century gilt bronze decoration that was probably once attached to a wooden book box. Holes around the perimeter would have allowed it to be pinned to the wood.
- **Function:** Probably a decoration on a book box or shrine box.
- **Technique:** A gilt bronze plaque, cast in low relief, with the areas between the figures cut away (Fig. 24.20).
- **Decoration:** The figures in the crucifixion scene are similar to ones we have seen on the Carndonagh Cross and in the Book of Durrow. An angel sits on each of Christ's shoulders and the sponge and spear bearers are at his sides. The figures are decorated with spirals based on triskeles and bands of interlace.

The Tully Lough Cross

- **Form:** An 8th- or 9th-century wooden cross, almost 2 m tall, with metal decoration (Fig. 24.21).
- **Function:** An Irish altar cross that could be carried in procession.
- **Technique:** The sheet metal parts on the surface of the cross are nailed on to an oak core. The edges are finished in tubular binding strips with animal-head cast terminals. Originally, the decorated areas were gilt and the flat areas were tinned, which would have created a much more glittering effect than the exposed bronze plates and castings that we see today. The central pyramid-shaped boss

Gilt bronze cast

Areas cut away

Figure 24.20 The Athlone (Rinnegan) Crucifixion Plaque.

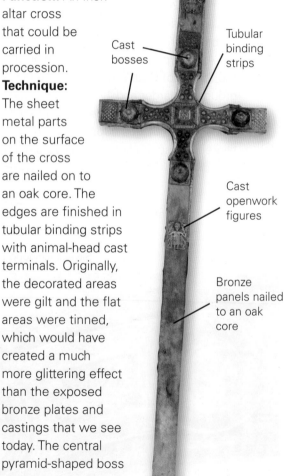

Cast bosses

Tubular binding strips

Cast openwork figures

Bronze panels nailed to an oak core

Figure 24.21 The Tully Lough Cross.

NEW APPRECIATING ART   IRELAND AND ITS PLACE IN THE WIDER WORLD originally had amber studs in the settings at the centre and corners.

- **Decoration:** The front of the cross is more decorative than the back. It is divided into areas of interlace and figure panels interspersed with cast bosses and areas of plain metal. The two openwork figure panels are almost identical. A kilted figure with an open-mouthed animal on each side may represent Christ between two beasts or Daniel in the lions' den. All the bosses have chip-carved designs using a range of La Tène motifs.

Analysis

Compare the use of the human figure and pattern in the different crafts you have studied. Note the development of sophisticated design and technique in all the crafts.

The 7th and 8th centuries were a high point in Irish art and learning, when Ireland was the repository of scholarship for Europe, which was just coming out of the Dark Ages. It is extraordinary that the finest craftsmanship and scholarship of the age should have come from a society without towns and cities. Work of extraordinary technical skill and subtle design characterises the period. The representation of human and animal figures had become an important part of the design repertoire.

All the influences that came together to produce the style that we call Insular Art were fully developed by the 8th century. They created the standards necessary for the production of the amazing work in book painting and stone carving that followed.

The Human Figure

During the 7th and 8th centuries, the human figure was more symbolic than realistic. The figures on the Carndonagh Cross, in the Book of Durrow and on the Tully Lough Cross all have large oval heads with large almond-shaped eyes, small noses and simple, straight mouths. Their bodies and limbs are

Human interlace panel from the Derrynaflan Paten

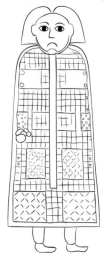

Man symbol for St Matthew in the Book of Durrow

Christ figure from the Carndonagh Cross

Figure 24.22 Human figures in 7th- and 8th-century Irish art.

small and simply treated. The figure of St Mark from the Book of Durrow and some of the minor figures on the Carndonagh Cross are not even given arms. Feet generally face the same direction and are shown in side view. Figures in the filigree sections of the Derrynaflan Paten are more animated but just as stylised (Fig. 24.22).

Animal Figures

Animals are used in a variety of ways as part of designs. Simple birds appear on the Carndonagh Cross. Bird heads appear on the outline of the Tara Brooch and on the Initium page in the Book of Durrow, where we also find a kind of dragon head made of spirals at the bottom end of the letter *I* (Fig. 24.23). This relates back to the terminals on the Ballinderry Brooch. Still on the Initium page, we find a dog-shaped animal clinging to the top left corner of the page. He has relatives on the animal interlace page of the Book of Durrow (folio 192v), which

UNIT 8 INSULAR ART (c. 500–1100s)

are interlaced together in a variety of patterns. The limbs, tongues, tails and crests of these creatures can be extended to any length and intertwined with each other or themselves. Creatures also appear in the areas of filigree, such as the dog in the triangular space on the Tara Brooch and other creatures on the Derrynaflan Paten. All these animals seem to be used for their decorative qualities more than for any meaning or symbolism.

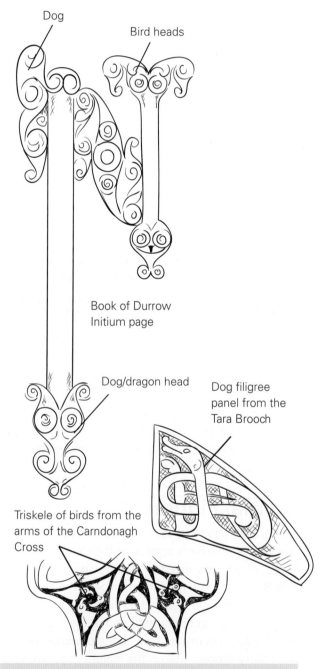

Dog

Bird heads

Book of Durrow
Initium page

Dog/dragon head

Dog filigree panel from the Tara Brooch

Triskele of birds from the arms of the Carndonagh Cross

Figure 24.23 Animal figures in 7th- and 8th-century Irish art.

Chapter Review

1. Describe in words and sketches four different metalworking techniques. Show where they might have been used.

2. Messages and symbols were an important part of design in the 7th and 8th centuries. Describe a page from the Book of Durrow, in words and sketches, where symbolism is a feature.

3. How would you describe human and animal figures from the 7th and 8th centuries in terms of realism? Use examples from sculpture, metalwork and book painting to help your description.

4. Write a description of the Tara Brooch, noting its structure and decoration. Make sketches to illustrate your points.

5. The Ardagh Chalice is considered to be a high point in the history of Irish craft and design. What do you think are its outstanding features? Use drawings to help make your points.

6. What was the function of reliquaries? Write an account of the Athlone crucifixion plaque, which was part of a reliquary, and describe its form and decoration using sketches to help your answer.

Further Research

www.3dicons.ie – Search for the Fahan Mura Cross

www.arthistoryleavingcert.com/early-christian-ireland/manuscripts – An account of the history and decoration of the Cathach and the Book of Durrow

www.museum.ie – Search for the section about The Treasury exhibition, which contains information and images of the collection

www.irishhighcrosses.com – A valuable resource for background and information on high crosses by county

The Viking Invasions (9th and 10th Centuries)

Chapter 25

By the end of this chapter I will ...

* know how the Vikings influenced Irish art
* be able to draw and describe a round tower
* know the origins of the wheel-head high cross
* be able to draw and describe Muiredach's Cross and at least one other cross
* be able to describe two panels from each high cross and understand subjects, style and techniques
* be able to draw and describe at least three pages from the Book of Kells
* know about the changes of style in metalwork
* be able to draw and describe the Derrynaflan Chalice.

Context

Viking raids on Irish monasteries began in the year AD 795, when several islands off the north and west coast were plundered. The island of Iona, where the chief monastery of the Columban order was located, was raided in that year and again in 802 and 804. By 807, the Columbans had moved their headquarters to Kells in Co. Meath, away from the coast and the immediate danger of Viking attack.

In 842, the Vikings overwintered in a defended ship harbour in Dublin and established a settlement there. In the following years, they established settlements at Arklow, Wicklow, Wexford, Waterford, Cork and Limerick. To an extent, they were absorbed into the Irish tribal system, although raids continued until the end of the century.

The Vikings caused a great deal of destruction raiding monasteries, which were the centres of population and wealth in Ireland. Pieces of Irish art have been found in graves in Norway, including parts of book covers and reliquaries that were cut up to make jewellery. The Vikings took slaves, whom they traded for silver in the Middle East. They traded

Note: There was also a positive side to the arrival of the Vikings. They established the first towns and introduced coinage. They paid tribute to the local Irish kings, often in the form of silver, which became more readily available to Irish craftsmen. Precious metals were not easy to obtain up to this time in Ireland, and were used in tiny quantities to gild bronze. Only the most important pieces used pure precious metals.

and raided all over Western Europe, from Russia to the Mediterranean, gathering great wealth, some of which was brought back to Ireland.

In spite of the Viking raids, Irish monasteries continued to grow as centres of learning and pilgrimage, so expansion and reorganisation became necessary.

Media and Areas of Practice

Architecture

Stone buildings, particularly churches, became more common at this point in Ireland's history. As construction materials shifted from wood to stone, workmen needed to have more skill to build the larger churches and the now iconic round towers.

Stone Carving

High Crosses

We can get some idea of how crosses were made from an unfinished cross found at Kells, Co. Meath

(Fig. 25.1). The basic blocks that were needed would have been roughed out at the quarry. All the parts were then transported to the site where the cross was to be erected.

At the site, the stonemason would have marked out the areas for decoration and checked the shape of the stone for accuracy with a square and compass. The measurements of mouldings and panels seem to correspond with inches and feet used in the Imperial system, which was based on the Roman measuring system.

Crucifixion scene

Partly finished panel

Raised panel for deeper figure carving

Figure 25.1 The unfinished high cross at Kells.

Blocks roughed out at the quarry. Mortices and tenons cut to make joints.

Tenon

Mortice

Panels blocked out on site. Different thicknesses allowed for different depths of carving.

Cross erected on site. Carvers begin carving designs.

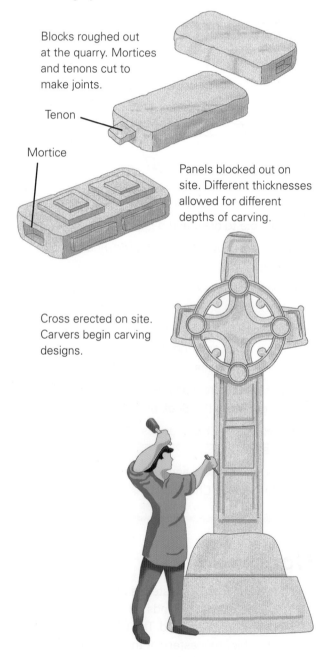

Figure 25.2 The construction of a high cross.

Blocking Out

Different depths of carving were allowed for during the blocking-out process. This can be seen on the unfinished Kells Cross. All the surfaces were first trimmed flat so that drawings could be transferred onto them. When all the preliminary work was complete, the parts would have been assembled in their final position, so that edges and joints could be carefully matched, giving continuity to the design (Fig. 25.2).

Tools

The sculptors would have used iron chisels, similar to the tools used by modern sculptors, but this is only an assumption, since tools from this time have not been found to date. In the 9th and 10th centuries, crosses have a greater depth of carving, which may be accounted for by improved iron technology brought by the Vikings. On Muiredach's Cross at Monasterboice, Co. Louth, drill marks can still be seen in the areas under the arms and ring that have been the least weathered. The drill would have been used to bore down to the deepest areas of the design, followed by a chisel, which would have formed the details of the design (Fig. 25.3).

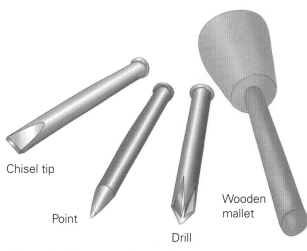

Chisel tip

Point

Drill

Wooden mallet

Figure 25.3 Stone carving tools.

Go to YouTube and watch the video 'Introduction to Stone Carving Tools and Techniques' (5:01) by Minneapolis Institute of Art. You could use this information to add detail to your written work or as guidelines for your own studio work.

Manuscripts

Writing Media

We have seen how pens and paint brushes were made in Chapter 24, page 333; the same techniques were used through the 9th and 10th centuries. Artists would also have needed a ruler, a compass and probably templates to lay out the designs and patterns. Cow horns were used as inkwells.

The portrait of St John in the Book of Kells (folio 291v; see Fig. 25.22) shows the scribe with a pen in his right hand and a book in his left, with the inkwell sitting just above his right foot. Knives were used to scrape away mistakes.

Colours

The range of colours in the Book of Kells includes the yellow, red and green that we have seen in the Book of Durrow, but some more exotic and expensive pigments were also used.

● **Blues** were obtained from indigo (a plant imported from Asia), woad (a Northern European plant) and lapis lazuli, a mineral from northern Afghanistan that is ultramarine blue (ultramarine means 'from across the sea'). Lapis lazuli was a very precious and expensive pigment usually reserved for the most important areas in a design.

● **Kermes red** was obtained by crushing the bodies and eggs of the *Kermes vermillo* insect. **Vermillion** is a red mineral, which probably came from Spain.

● **Folium** comes from marsh plants grown around the Mediterranean. It produces a range of purples and plum colours.

● **White lead** was used both as a colour and a base for over-painting. It was much used in spite of its toxicity.

Note: Colours may have been traded in the form of small rags of dyed cloth from which the colours could be diluted out as required. Colours could be bound in egg white, in yolk, natural gums or animal gelatine so they would stick to the vellum page.

Most of the organic pigments were extracted in ammonium (urine) and fixed in mineral salt (aluminium hydroxide).

Making Books

We can now see that the work of scribes and artists entailed a lot more than simply writing text or painting designs. They had to work with foul-smelling and poisonous materials and spend long hours preparing colours and pages. Even with all this work complete, the book still had to be bound together by sewing groups of pages along the spine and attaching them to wooden boards that formed the covers. A layer of decorated leather was sometimes used to create a final cover.

Art Elements and Design Principles

Stone Carving

The Shape of the High Cross: The Ringed or Jewelled Cross

The reason for the shape of the Irish high cross seems to originate in the large jewelled cross that was erected on the hill called Golgotha (where Christ was believed to have been crucified) in Jerusalem by the Emperor Constantine to celebrate the finding of the True Cross by his mother, St Helena, in the 4th century. Images in early mosaics, manuscripts, sculptures and wall hangings, show the cross on a stepped base, which represents Golgotha.

The cap on the top of crosses is thought to represent the church that Constantine built over the Holy Sepulchre. It can be seen as a symbol of resurrection and eternity (Fig. 25.4).

Note: A wreath or circle surrounds the crossing of the shaft and the arms, this ring represents Christ's victory over death, and at the same time eternity or the universe. Multiple layers of meaning attach to many parts and scenes on Irish high crosses. This was a common element in medieval art and writing.

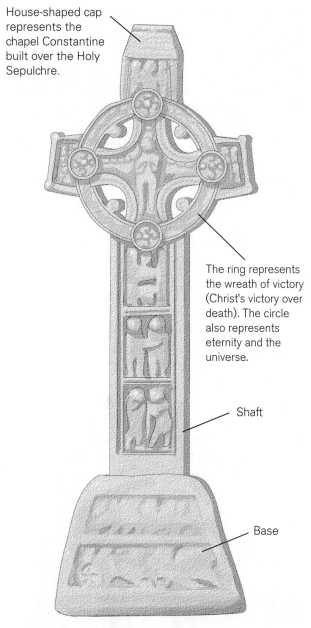

House-shaped cap represents the chapel Constantine built over the Holy Sepulchre.

The ring represents the wreath of victory (Christ's victory over death). The circle also represents eternity and the universe.

Shaft

Base

The whole image represents the cross erected in Jerusalem to celebrate the finding of the True Cross

Figure 25.4 The parts of a high cross.

The Design of the Scripture Crosses

The iconography of the Scripture crosses is not simple to work out. The images and subjects relate to designs found on Roman sarcophagi (box tombs) from about the 4th century AD. These tombs were often re-used for later burials, so an Irish pilgrim, or cleric on Church business in Rome, who went to see the relics of saints or famous

Figure 25.5 (above) The 12 Apostles sarcophagus from the Basilica di Sant'Apollinare in Classe, near Ravenna, Italy. Note that the grouping of the figures in the end panel is similar to panels on high crosses.

Figure 25.6 (right) An ivory book cover. The image is of St Luke writing his gospel.

Churchmen, would have seen many of these sarcophagi (Fig. 25.5).

Some of the subjects and images found in Irish art have origins in the Byzantine Church. Images may also have come second-hand through Britain or the Carolingian Empire, which had contacts with Ireland (Fig. 25.6). There are accounts of written descriptions of the relics and sites of Rome being circulated, so possibly drawings may have been available as well.

Note: However it evolved, a style based on 'classical art' was in use in Ireland in the 9th and 10th centuries. While the subjects and layout were often based on Roman designs, the details were based on local observations; hairstyles and clothing were in the Irish style, not the classical togas seen on the sarcophagi.

Innovation and Invention

Architecture

Stone Churches

In the 9th and 10th centuries, the building of stone churches became more common. There are a number of examples at Clonmacnoise in Co. Offaly. Temple Ciaran, which measures just 3.8 m × 2.8 m internally, may have been an oratory to house the remains of the saint. The cathedral, which originally measured 18.8 m × 10.7 m was the largest stone church in Ireland until Norman times (Fig. 25.8). It was built between AD 908 and AD 909.

A few 10th-century churches have the chancel at the east end separated by a round-headed arch from the nave. These churches have a mixture of ancient and more up-to-date features. The antae are gone, replaced by corbels to carry the roof timbers. The Trinity and Reefert churches at Glendalough, Co Wicklow, which are of this

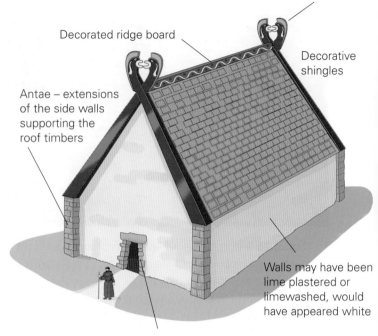
Note: Irish buildings were designed in a conservative style and were very small compared to contemporary European churches. This was probably a result of the rural social structure and the style of monasticism practised here.

type, have small flat-headed doorways and small windows with arches cut from a single stone, in the style of the earliest churches.

Round Towers

From early in the 10th century AD, round towers became part of the range of buildings found in Irish monasteries. An entry in the Annals of the Four Masters for the year 960 is the first written reference to a round tower. It notes that 'the Belfry at Slane' was plundered by Vikings from Dublin.

Figure 25.7 (below) An aerial view of Clonmacnoise. The round tower and the Cathedral can be seen on the left. The monastery covered a much wider area in the 10th century.

Figure 25.8 (above) A conjectural reconstruction of the cathedral at Clonmacnoise.

Round tower

Cross of the Scriptures

Cathedral

Figure 25.9 Round tower at Kilmacduagh, Co. Galway. Note the very high doorway on this tower.

buildings. They would have been important landmarks, pointing out places of pilgrimage and learning, distinguishing monastic sites from secular settlements. Remains of over 60 towers exist today, and there is evidence of far greater numbers having been built during the 250 years before the Norman invasions.

Origins

The origins of round towers are not clear. There is no evidence of wooden predecessors or simpler versions; they seem to have begun as a fully formed idea which may have come from Britain or the Rhineland where there were strong contacts with Ireland through pilgrim monks. Towers in these regions would have been attached to the west front of churches, which were larger than Irish buildings. There was a tradition of freestanding bell towers in Italy, but they were more often square in plan. The Irish towers were generally built at the west end of the main church in the monastery, with the door of the tower facing the west door of the church, which is, in effect, a looser arrangement of the Rhineland style. There are some later Irish churches with towers attached, as at Clonmacnoise and Glendalough, although these do not seem to have been a common type.

Construction

Round towers are a uniquely Irish construction. They were frequently around 100 feet tall (the number 100 was considered to be a perfect number in medieval times). In proportion, towers were often twice the height of the circumference of the base. This not only led to an elegant shape, but also a stable structure. Construction followed the ancient tradition of building on a circular plan. Churches were an exception, as they were built on a rectangular plan. Towers generally had quite shallow foundations, less than a metre deep, constructed of large stones built in layers gradually stepping inwards to the diameter of the base of the tower (Fig. 25.10). The cylinder of the tower was built of an outer and inner skin of carefully selected or cut stone. The space between was filled with rough stone and lime mortar. It was this infill of stone and mortar, which turned to concrete when it set, that gave the towers their structural strength. When construction reached about 1 m in height, a wooden scaffold was built to allow work to continue at a

Obviously the belfry (tower) had to have been built before this date, which gives us an approximate starting point (Fig. 25.9).

The Irish word for a round tower is *cloicteach*, literally 'bell house', which describes its primary function of calling the monks to prayer from their various duties around the monastery and surrounding fields. The towers were also used as the treasury of the monastery, keeping the relics and valuables of the monastery safe, as well as acting as a place of sanctuary in times of trouble.

Round towers would have been outstanding buildings in a society that normally built small-scale low-profile

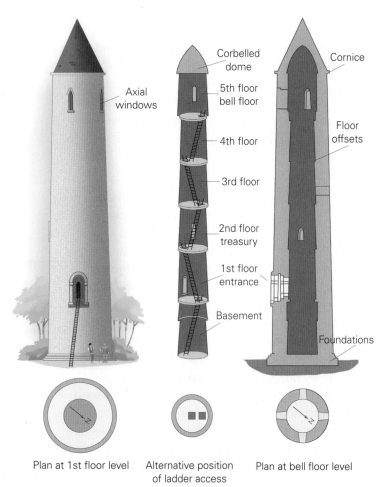

Corbelled dome

Axial windows

5th floor bell floor

4th floor

3rd floor

2nd floor treasury

1st floor entrance

Basement

Cornice

Floor offsets

Foundations

Plan at 1st floor level   Alternative position of ladder access   Plan at bell floor level

Figure 25.10 The structure of a round tower.

higher level. The scaffold was connected to the tower by putlog holes, which would have held wooden beams to build the scaffold upon. Putlog holes can be found on the exterior of many towers, showing where the scaffold was connected to the rising walls.

Discover round towers close to you on the website *roundtowers.org*, which lists the structures by county. You could visit a tower or use the site to collect information for your studio or written work.

The Celtic High Cross

There are many theories about the origins of the Irish high cross and the various local styles of decoration that are used in different parts of the country. The earliest written mention of a high cross is in the Annals of the Four Masters for the year 951, but the crosses are clearly older than this. There are written accounts of crosses made of wood and stone from Northumbria in Britain, an area with

strong Irish connections dating back to AD 750. The Tully Lough Cross, now on display in the National Museum in Dublin, is a rare survivor of these wood and metal crosses, which may have been part of the inspiration for the shape and design of high crosses.

Remains of over 200 high crosses survive in Ireland, but this may represent only a part of the number that once existed. Several crosses are found at some sites, although the same Bible scenes are not often repeated at the same monastery. Not all crosses have figure scenes or decoration – there may be as many as 16 large, plain crosses and over 40 with geometric ornament or an inscription but no figure scenes. The majority of the crosses were erected in the 9th and 10th centuries, when the Columban order, which was based in Iona and Kells, created an impetus for cross construction.

The Function of the High Cross

The high cross standing in a monastic enclosure in Ireland represented the True Cross: the symbol of the Resurrection, which was at the centre of Christian belief. It was also a reminder of the relics and holy places that a pilgrim might see on a visit to Jerusalem, the holiest place in the Christian tradition. Respect for the symbolism of the high cross made them important markers of the boundaries of sanctuary in the monastery.

In a country that had little large-scale art, the high cross's many functions in an Irish monastery, alongside its symbolism and imagery, would have attracted pilgrims and other visitors.

Artists and Artworks
Crosses
The Ahenny Crosses

The Ahenny group of crosses are situated in a river valley north of Carrric-on-Suir, Co. Tipperary, on the border with Kilkenny. They are located at Kilkieran, Killamery, Kilree and Ahenny itself. They seem to be a manifestation of the jewelled cross in Ireland.

The shaft and arms are covered with patterns of curves, knotting, fretwork and spirals, which have close relationships with contemporary metalwork.

A raised border of what looks like woven trichinopoly wire translated into stone surrounds the cross and ring, like the border of the Derrynaflan Paten (Fig. 24.19, p. 345) that hides the edges of the metal plates. Stone bosses appear in high relief at the centre of the cross and, where the ring passes through the arms and shaft, they look like the studs used in metalwork construction to hide the rivets that join metal plates together

Border pattern like woven wire

Bosses

Interlace pattern

Fret or key pattern

Spiral pattern

Adam and the animals

Figure 25.11 The North Cross at Ahenny, Co. Tipperary, east face.

The North Cross at Ahenny

- **Form:** An early 9th-century wheel-head cross, it stands 3.13 m tall on a stepped base (Fig. 25.11).
- **Function:** It seems to commemorate the jewelled cross erected at Jerusalem, and marks the sacred area surrounding the monastery.
- **Technique:** The cross is carved from one piece of stone set in a base. There is fine detail cut with iron chisels.
- **Decoration:** The cross itself is completely encrusted in abstract pattern, including one panel of human interlace on the west face of the shaft. The base is decorated with human and animal figure scenes.
  - On the west face of the base is a group of seven figures with crosiers, representing Christ's mission to the apostles (Fig. 25.12).
  - On the East face a man sits under a palm tree facing a group of animals; Adam being given dominion over the animals.
  - On the north side, David charges into battle on a chariot, while on the south side David carries Goliath's head in a procession, with Goliath's headless body tied to a horse.
  - The style of figure carving is simple and non-Classical, more in the Celtic tradition of symbolism in preference to realism. The low relief panels on the base of this cross

Visit *www.irishhighcrosses.com* and find some close-up photographs of the North Cross. Make some sketches of (a) a figure panel and (b) a patterned panel.

Figure 25.12 The North Cross at Ahenny, west side of base. The figure in the centre facing forward is thought to represent Christ. The three figures facing him on each side may represent the apostles. Note the different styles of crosiers that they carry.

are worn and difficult to see clearly except in good light. The patterns of circles and spirals on the shaft are linked in style to the carpet page (folio 3v) in the Book of Durrow.

The Granite Crosses

Most of the Irish high crosses are carved in sandstone, but in the area around Kildare there are a number of crosses carved in granite. This hard, granular stone presents a problem for the sculptor, as fine lines and small details are not possible and a smooth finish is hard to achieve. Despite these difficulties, interesting, even beautiful, crosses were created in a design style that relates back to the Celtic traditions rather than the more classical style, which we will see on the Scripture crosses from the Midlands.

The Cross of Moone

The monastery at Moone was probably a Colomban house. The cross on the site is unique in style and layout.

● **Form:** Over 7 m tall, it is the second tallest cross in Ireland. Its height is emphasised by the narrow shaft and small wheel head. It is carved from three blocks of granite (Fig. 25.13).

● **Function:** This is an illustrated cross. The theme of the Cross of Moon seems to be the help that God gives his faithful followers, which is illustrated in scenes from the Old and New Testaments. A medieval monk looking at the scenes on this cross would have deciphered layers of meaning in all the scenes. Events recorded in the Old Testament were often understood as a prefiguration of events in the life of Christ and his followers.

● **Technique:** The stone carver was limited in the detail he could achieve by the hard granite he was carving.

● **Decoration:** Most of the upper part of the cross (the shaft, arms and head) is carved with patterns. A figure of Christ in Majesty appears on the crossing on the east side, and animals appear in panels on the west side of the shaft. The tall base, which is almost square in plan, has figure scenes on every side, set in panels. The armless figures of Daniel and the Apostles, and body-less Christ child in the Flight into Egypt

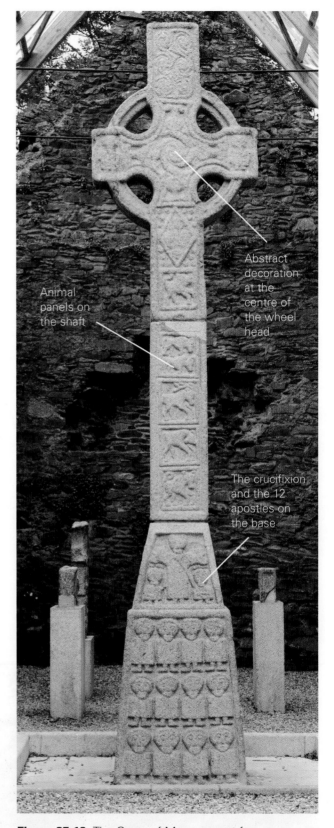

Animal panels on the shaft

Abstract decoration at the centre of the wheel head

The crucifixion and the 12 apostles on the base

Figure 25.13 The Cross of Moone, west face.

scene suggest that some details and decorative elements may have been painted onto the carvings, creating images like those in the Book of Durrow (Fig. 25.14 and 25.15).

The lions in the Daniel scene look like they might be related to the lion symbol of St Mark in the Book of Durrow.

Prefiguration: A term used to note an image or idea that was imagined in earlier times. Scenes on high crosses from the books of the Old Testament in the Bible are understood to 'predict' events that came about hundreds of years later in the life of Christ in the New Testament.

Visit *www.megalithicireland.com* and look for photos of the base of the Cross of Moone. Sketch the scenes from the north and west faces of the base.

The Scripture Crosses of the Midlands

Many high crosses were used to illustrate Bible stories for the illiterate public. They were also a focus for prayer and repentance; most of the crosses with Bible scenes were designed to be read from the bottom up, starting from the eye level of a penitent believer, kneeling in prayer. Scenes on Muiredach's Cross at Monasterboice echo the penitential litanies that the monks would have chanted.

The Crosses at Kells

There is an important group of crosses at Kells, Co. Meath, which was the senior monastery in the Colombian tradition in the years that followed the Viking raids on Iona in the early 9th century. Kells would have been a centre of power and influence in the Irish Church, active in the spread of new ideas and art forms.

The Cross of Saints Patrick and Columba

- **Form:** The Cross of Saints Patrick and Columba is 3.3 m tall. It is a wheel-head cross, carved from one block of sandstone set in a base.
- **Function:** This cross may have been erected to commemorate the founding of the monastery at

The three Hebrews in the fiery furnace are in the top panel

The flight into Egypt is in the middle

The miracle of the loaves and fishes is in the lower panel

Figure 25.15 The Cross of Moone, south face of the base.

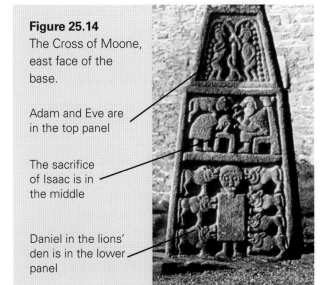

Figure 25.14 The Cross of Moone, east face of the base.

Adam and Eve are in the top panel

The sacrifice of Isaac is in the middle

Daniel in the lions' den is in the lower panel

UNIT 8 INSULAR ART (c. 500–1100s)

David playing
his harp

Abraham
sacrificing
Isaac

St Paul and
St Anthony

Daniel in the
lions' den

The children in
the furnace

Cain killing
Abel

Adam
and Eve

Spiral pattern

Game birds
and animals

Figure 25.16 The Cross of Saints Patrick and
Columba, Kells, east face.

Kells in about AD 804. The inscription '*Patricii et
Columbae crux*', unusually written in Latin, may
indicate an agreement between the paruchia
(group of allied churches and monasteries) of St
Patrick, based at Armagh, and the paruchia of St
Columba, then centred on Iona.

- **Technique:** Carved in relief with iron chisels
  from a single block of sandstone.
- **Decoration:** This cross is unusual among Irish
  crosses because it is not divided into panels;
  figure scenes and areas of decoration meet
  without borders. The figures in the Bible scenes

Visit *www.megalithicireland.com* and find
images of the following Kells crosses:

- West Cross
- East Cross
- Market Cross
- North Cross

Note the different styles of the crosses and
make sketches of one detail from each.

are more vigorous and animated than on other
crosses. Some areas of the cross have different
subjects side by side.

- If this cross can be interpreted as the earliest
  one at Kells, its unusual style could be attributed
  to influences from Iona and the Scottish style of
  carving.

The Cross of the Scriptures at Clonmacnoise

- **Form:** One of the most beautiful and complete
  of the high crosses, dating from the first half
  of the 10th century (Fig. 25.17). It stands 3.9 m
  tall in the interpretive centre specially built to
  protect the crosses at Clonmacnoise. Modern
  copies now stand in the original locations.
- **Function:** The theme of this cross is the
  passion, death and resurrection of Christ. The
  Old Testament scenes on the lower panels of
  the east face of the shaft can be interpreted as
  a prefiguration of the resurrection, illustrated in
  two panels on the base and lower shaft of the
  west side, which would have been the focus of
  a person kneeling in prayer before the cross.
- **Technique:** The sculpted panels are carved in
  high relief, with some of the figures almost

The wheel passes over
the arms of the cross,
with a medallion at
each crossing point

The crucifixion

The betrayal of Christ

The arrest of Christ

Soldiers guarding the
tomb of Christ

Figure 25.17
The Cross of
the Scriptures at
Clonmacnoise, west
face. It is located in
front of the west door
of the cathedral.

projecting free from the surface. The designs are neatly composed and carried out in greater detail than we have seen on previous crosses. The ring at the head of the cross passes over the shaft and arms, which is different from other crosses where the ring is set back from the surface of the shaft and arms.

- **Decoration:** There is a crucifixion at the crossing on the west face and a Last Judgement scene in the same position on the east. Scenes from the Bible fill most of the other panels. Men on horses and chariots and animals seem to follow in procession round the base.

The Crosses at Monasterboice, Co. Louth

Mainistir Bhuite is on the site of the monastery founded by the 5th-century monk, Buite. He prophesied the importance of St Columba; tradition says that Columba was born on the day in AD 521 on which Buite died. This made Monasterboice an important place of pilgrimage, connected to Kells, which may explain similarities in the style between the crosses at Kells and Monasterboice.

Muiredach's Cross

Another local tradition stated that Muiredach's cross was sent from Rome. This may relate to the themes and messages that are on the cross and even to the origins of the designs, which some scholars say are based on images from early Christian tombs in Rome.

- **Form:** The cross stands 5.2 m tall and is one solid piece of stone except for the cap and base. Artistically and technically, it is the finest high cross in Ireland (Fig. 25.18).
- **Function:** Like other crosses with figure scenes, this cross would have been used to instruct pilgrims and to be a focus for the monks' prayers.
- **Meaning:** Because of the layers of meaning associated with each scene, a number of messages can be taken from this cross. Christ the King can be seen in the mocking scene, the crucifixion and the Last Judgement. In fact, the whole west face could be interpreted in this way. The importance of the Eucharist can be

noted in a number of scenes and the passion, death and resurrection of Christ were also emphasised.

- **Technique:** The quality of the carving on Muiredach's cross is unsurpassed by any other Irish cross. There is a crispness of detail and depth of modelling rarely found elsewhere. Features of hairstyles, clothes and weapons can be seen on the larger figures, which are carved almost in the round.
- **Decoration:**
  - The Old Testament scenes on the east face are crowded into panels with multiple subjects or large groups. Across the arms of the cross is a Last Judgement scene with Christ at the centre.
  - On the bottom of the west face of the shaft is an inscription written in old Irish: *'OR DO MUIREDACH LAS NDERNAD – – – – RO'*,

The Last Judgement

Adoration of the Magi

Moses striking the rock

David killing Goliath

Adam and Eve; Cain killing Abel

Figure 25.18
Muiredach's Cross at Monasterboice, east face.

Figure 25.19
(left) Muiredach's Cross at Monasterboice, west face.

Figure 25.20
(right) The lower panels on the west face of Muiredach's Cross at Monasterboice.

Note the brooch on Christ's cloak and the clothes and hairstyles of the soldiers

Cats holding mice lie in front of the inscription

Christ's ascension

Christ's crucifixion

Christ giving keys to St Peter and a book to St Paul

Christ with St Peter and St Paul

The Mocking of Christ

meaning 'a prayer for Muiredach, who had (the cross) made' (Fig. 25.19 and 25.20). This inscription, which gives the cross its name, does not help to clarify a date for the cross, as there were several abbots called Muiredach and the cross can't be associated with one in particular.

- The north and south sides of the cross are decorated with interlace patterns on the shaft and figure scenes on the ends of the arms and at the top of the cross. The base is divided into panels that contain figure and animal scenes on the upper row and interlaced patterns along the bottom.

Note: The style of the figure carving and the design of the scenes on Irish high crosses predates versions in Romanesque sculpture by more than 100 years. Could it be that Irish pilgrim monks brought their sculptural designs to Europe as they had done with their book designs?

Create a modelled plaque in the style of a relief figure panel from a high cross. You may choose the more stylised figures, like those on Moone or Ahenny, or the more realistic figures found on the midland crosses. You can choose your own theme.

Manuscripts

We have already seen how simple the buildings in an Irish monastery were and how few comforts were available for the monks. The beautifully decorated and elaborately laid out books of the 9th and 10th centuries seem to be in contrast with this simple life, but they are also an expression of the attempt by Irish monks to lead a spiritual and intellectual life free from worldliness. Beautiful Bibles had a value beyond the everyday – they were an expression of the commitment of the community to spiritual ideals.

The Book of Kells

Scholars now generally agree that the Book of Kells was written at the chief monastery of the Columban order on the island of Iona and then brought to Kells when Iona became unsafe due to Viking raids. The book could have taken decades to write, so it may have been started on Iona and continued in Kells. These monasteries were regarded as one unit, under the authority of one abbot, in the early part of the 9th century. The book was probably written in the years around AD 800, but it was never fully completed. Two pages are blank and a few have decorative elements that were begun but left unfinished.

- **Form:** The Book of Kells is the most elaborately decorated manuscript codex in the Insular style to have survived the ravages of time. The text is very similar to that of the Book of Durrow. The Four Gospels and related preliminary writings could have been copied from a common exemplar, even though Kells was written 100 years after Durrow. Both books were transcribed in Columban monasteries, which may account for the closeness of the texts.
- **The book today:** The Book of Kells now measures 330 mm × 255 mm. It was cut down for rebinding in 1830, damaging the design of a number of pages. It was badly rebound again in 1895 before it was restored in 1953. The decoration suffered damage from wetting the pages to flatten them at each rebinding. However, the book still preserves some of the most amazing work of the illuminator's skill from any time. Three-hundred and forty folios remain, but it is estimated that about 30 are lost, including some fully decorated pages.
- **Function:** The Book of Kells is a display Bible, made for use on special occasions.
- **Technique:** Calf vellum was used to make the pages for the Book of Kells (see Fig. 23.2, p. 323). Skins of newborn or intrauterine calves were preferred to produce the finest vellum – only one bifolium could be made from each skin of this size. Stronger vellum for the fully decorated pages was obtained from two- or three-month-old calves, producing two bifoliae from each skin, although decorated pages were often on single leaves, which could be worked on separately and sewn into the book later. It has been estimated that the hides of up to 185 calves could have been needed for the complete book; this suggests a monastery of great wealth, capable of affording these resources.

The Scheme of Decoration

The text begins with the canon tables, *Breves Causae* and *Argumenta*, which are supporting texts and commentary on the Bible.

The Four Gospels follow. In the original plan, each gospel began with a Four Evangelists page, a portrait of the evangelist and an initial page.

- St Matthew's Gospel has six fully decorated pages.
- St Mark's Gospel has only three fully decorated pages remaining – his portrait is missing.
- St Luke's Gospel has lost the Four Evangelists and portrait pages, but it does have the beautiful *Quoniam* page, two other fully decorated pages and some decorated capitals.
- St John's Gospel has the three decorated opening pages, but no other fully decorated pages survive. This is the most damaged part of the book.

The Four Evangelists Page from St Matthew's Gospel

Folio 27v (Fig. 25.21), the Four Evangelists page from the beginning of St Matthew's Gospel, is richly coloured and patterned in the style of enamelled jewellery. Translucent layers of colour are built up to create rich blues and purples balanced with bright orpiment yellow.

The central cross form is emphasised by the arcs on the outside of the frame. There is human, animal, bird and snake interlace in the border. Panels of spirals and black and white maze and interlace patterns in very fine lines are used to separate the coloured sections.

The man symbol for St Matthew seems to be skipping lightly forward in his gorgeous robes and wings, holding a processional cross.

St Mark's lion symbol is shown in a leaping pose. He has a curling tongue and mane and fabulously decorated wings.

The ox or calf symbol of St Luke has four wings, the flight feathers entwining with his legs on one side and with the second wing on the other. The three white circles with crosses inside them on his haunch are a reference to the Eucharist.

Matthew

Mark

John

Luke

Human interlace

Figure 25.21 Folio 27v: the Four Evangelists page from St Matthew's Gospel in the Book of Kells by the artist known as 'the Portraitist'.

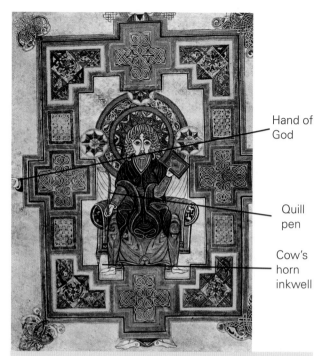

Hand of God

Quill pen

Cow's horn inkwell

Figure 25.22 Folio 291v: portrait of St John from the Book of Kells by the artist known as the Portraitist.

The eagle symbol of St John has a halo with three crosses, a device that recurs a number of times and appears to be a reference to the Trinity. The beautiful tail of this eagle connects to the body in a sweeping S curve.

The Portrait of St John

The painting of St John on folio 291v (Fig. 25.22) portrays the author as a scribe, his quill pen in his right hand, a book held aloft in his left, and an ink horn down by his right foot. The stylised figure of John has an elaborate halo and the folds in his garments are arranged in a very symmetrical way. The patterns in the border seemed to be mirror images of their opposite number until one takes a closer look to discover differences in pattern and colour. The crosses at the top, bottom and sides of the border emphasise the head, hands and feet that protrude beyond the frame, a reference to God the Father, who is behind everything, unseen. Alternatively, the crosses could be a reference to the fact that John was the only evangelist present at the crucifixion of Christ.

The Quoniam Page

The opening word of St Luke's Gospel, 'Quoniam' (Fig. 25.23) is given a full page to itself. The letters

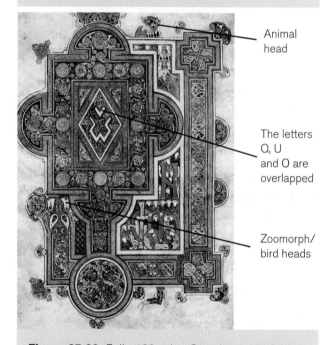

Animal head

The letters Q, U and O are overlapped

Zoomorph/ bird heads

Figure 25.23 Folio 188r: the *Quoniam* page from the opening of St Luke's Gospel in the Book of Kells by the Portraitist.

Q U O are overlapped into one shape framed in purple. The remaining letters *N I A M* are surrounded by little groups of figures. The group to the left and inside the A seemed to be over-indulging in drink, while two at the bottom have their heads in the mouths of lions, which are formed from the ends of the letter *M*. This group of figures is sometimes thought to represent the Last Judgement or the punishments of hell.

Above the lettering is another group of figures forming an interlace pattern. Interlace patterns of a very high quality can be seen inside the circle at the bottom of the letter *Q* and in the panels that make a frame around the right and bottom sides, ending in a large dragon head that shares teeth and outline with lion and eagle heads – the work of an artist with an amazing sense of design. On the Tara Brooch, there is a link connecting the chain to the frame that is designed in a similar way.

Turn in the Path

Some decoration is used to mark the ends of passages, to highlight words in the texts, or to point out a 'turn in the path' or 'head under wing' – where

Decorations separating the turn in the path from the rest of the text

Figure 25.24 Folio 19v: a page from the *Breves Causae* illustrates a 'turn in the path'. The word at the end of the third line from the bottom, 'doce', is finished 'bat' on the line above. The last line is also finished on the line above. A little decoration separates each ending from the rest of the line.

a line is finished in the line above, using up space left at the end of the previous verse (Fig. 25.24). This was a strategy used by scribes to save precious vellum. All the copyists in the Book of Kells seem to have used this device.

Scribes and Artists

A book as large and as elaborately decorated as the Book of Kells would have taken many years to produce, and could have been worked on by many hands over the years. Scribes and artists trained in the same scriptorium would have learnt similar styles and techniques, so the work is not always easy to identify. More than one artist may have worked on individual pages, making it more difficult to separate styles.

The Scribes

Scholars have identified four different scribes, designated Scribes A, B, C and D (Fig. 25.25).

- Scribe A is regarded as the most conservative and wrote in a clear majuscule script. The decoration is controlled and may have been added by another hand. His work appears at the beginning of the book, in the preliminaries, and at the end of St Luke's and St John's Gospels.
- Scribe B has quite a different style. He uses coloured inks and ends his pages in a line of minuscule script. This scribe added the rubrics (instructions and comments on the text, written in red) and other pieces throughout the text. He may have had the task of filling in gaps and finishing off incomplete sections of the book.
- Scribes C and D copied most of the Gospels of St Matthew, St Mark and St Luke. Their work seems to combine both script and decoration, their style is very close and some scholars treat all their work as by the same hand.

The quality of the lettering is very high, but it is sometimes difficult for the modern reader because the conventions of word spaces and punctuation were not yet in use in the 9th century. Some of the more elaborately decorated capitals and the opening pages can be difficult to decipher. Many of the monks reading the book would have known the texts by heart, so they would have known which letters to expect.

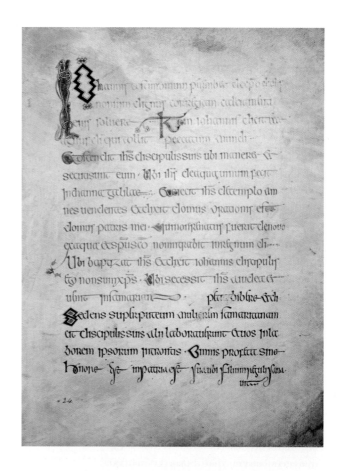

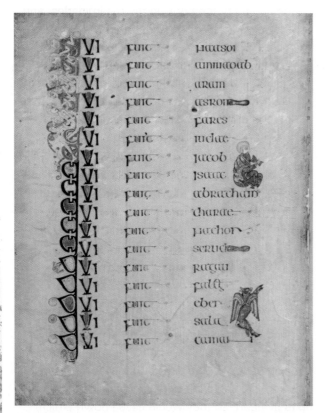

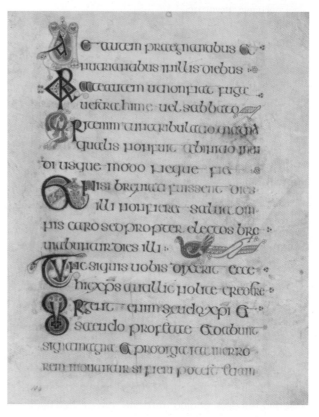

Figure 25.25 Folio 309r is the work of Scribe A. Folio 24r: Scribe B. Folio 118v: Scribe C. Folio 104r: Scribe D.

The Artists

The artists may not have been separate people from the scribes, but so much time would have been needed to complete the decorated pages that it would seem logical that some monks would be dedicated to this work alone. Three main artists have been identified.

The Goldsmith

The first artist is called 'the Goldsmith' because his work looks like metalwork in gold and silver. He is credited with the eight circles carpet page, the Chi-Rho page and the opening words of the Gospels of Saints Matthew, Mark and John, as well as with some smaller pieces of decoration.

It is interesting to compare the Chi-Rho page in the Book of Kells (Fig. 25.26) with the same page

Figure 25.26 Folio 34r: the Chi-Rho page from the Book of Kells. This is one of the pages decorated by the artist known as the Goldsmith. Spend a little time looking for the angels, animals and people hiding in the decoration.

in the Book of Durrow (see Fig. 24.11, p. 340). In both cases, the letters are decorated with spirals and trumpet curves, but in Kells the Goldsmith elaborates on everything. There is an almost endless variety of circles, spirals, triskeles and trumpet ends, twisting and turning together like the wheels of an old-fashioned clock mechanism. Between all these moving parts are panels and spaces filled with interlace, and men, birds, lions and snakes are interwoven in the most intricate patterns.

The colour scheme is subtler than some of the other pages. Delicate blues and violets make a counterpoint to smaller areas of bright red and yellow that outline the letters.

The Portraitist

'The Portraitist' is the name given to the artist who painted the images of Christ, St Matthew, St John and the symbols page for St Matthew's Gospel. We already looked at the Four Evangelists page (see Fig. 25.21) and the portrait of St John (see Fig. 25.22), which demonstrate a use of colour and space that is quite different from the Goldsmith's work. There was less interest in tiny detail, and areas of open vellum were left to contrast with the painted areas.

The Illustrator

'The Illustrator' is thought to be the artist behind the paintings of the temptation, the arrest of Christ and the Virgin and Child, as well as the evangelists' symbols before St John's Gospel. He may also have had a part in some other pages.

The Virgin and Child Page

The first page completely devoted to decoration is folio 7v, a portrait of the Virgin and Child surrounded by angels (Fig. 25.27). Mary wears a purple cloak fastened with a kite brooch. She sits on a throne of gold with a step pattern creating crosses of various shapes on the side. There is a lion's head terminal on the back of the chair. The Christ child is larger than the newborn baby mentioned in the text. He tenderly holds his mother's hand and she enfolds him in her arms.

The four angels at each side of the throne are usually identified as the Archangels Michael, Gabriel, Raphael and Uriel, who will appear a number of times

Figure 25.27 Folio 7v: the Virgin and Child page from the Book of Kells, by the artist known as the Illustrator.

Figure 25.28 Folio 200v: the Temptation of Christ page from the Book of Kells. This is a page decorated by the artist known as the Illustrator.

throughout the book, witnessing important events in the life of Christ. This painting is the earliest surviving image of the Virgin and Child from a Western manuscript, although there are written accounts of panel paintings and icons of this scene, now lost, which may have been models for its composition.

The Temptation of Christ Page

The Temptation of Christ page, folio 200v, (Fig. 25.28) shows Christ at the top of the temple, which can be interpreted as the Church, the body of Christ. To his right is a group of figures, which may represent his faithful followers, whom he protects from the Devil. One of the group holds up a small shield, the shield of truth from Psalm 19:5, which the Devil quotes in the temptation story. The Devil, at Christ's left side, holds up a snare to trap the unwary. Four angels accompany Christ, as they do in the other scenes from his life.

The beautifully decorated temple with the lion's head finials on the roof may give some idea of how

an Irish wooden church looked in the 9th century. The figure in the doorway may represent Christ the judge. The two groups of 13 torsos at the bottom of the page could represent the apostles and the prophets, who were the foundation of the church, or if the rectangle in the middle of the group can be seen as an empty table, they could be clergy fasting to see off the 'Evil One'.

The panels of snake interlace inside the crosses and at the bottom and sides of the border can be understood to represent the presence of evil in this scene.

digitalcollections.tcd.ie has a complete digital record of the Book of Kells. Pages can be enlarged to see details. Take notes and make sketches to help with your studio and written work.

Figure 25.29
A restored page
from the Fadden
More Psalter.

The Fadden More Psalter

Discovered in a bog in Co. Tipperary in 2006, the
Fadden More Psalter appears to be a complete book
of psalms contained in a leather satchel. Damaged
when it was found and suffering from the effects
of spending 1,000 years in a bog, it is still the most
significant discovery in a long time. It is a large-
format codex of 52 or 54 folios (104 or 108 pages)
written in Irish majuscule with some decoration.
Surviving parts of the book are now on display in
the National Museum (Fig. 25.29).

Create a piece of craftwork that responds to
images from the Book of Kells. Research the
designs and patterns that you would like to
use for your project.

Metalwork

Metalwork continued largely in the same style as
the century before, albeit less colourful. Enamel
was not used as frequently and the fine, detailed
filigree work of the 8th century was transformed
into looser, simpler designs. Precious materials
like silver, gold and amber were more widely used.

Craftsmen were still highly skilled and work was
well constructed and carefully finished, but there
was a loss of creative ingenuity. Designs and
patterns were repeated more frequently.

Note: By the 10th century, a Viking
influence was in evidence in
Ireland. An Irish version of the Viking Jellinge
style appeared alongside Irish motifs. Brooches
took on new shapes and forms, probably in
response to a Viking preference for larger pieces
cast in solid silver.

A Brooch from Roscrea

- **Form:** A pseudo-penannular brooch cast in silver
  (Fig. 25.30).
- **Function:** A cloak or tunic fastener and status
  symbol.
- **Technique:** It is cast in silver and decorated with
  gold filigree and amber.
- **Design:** This is a good example of this new
  style. The design is much broader and simpler
  than the Tara Brooch, the pin and ring are boldly

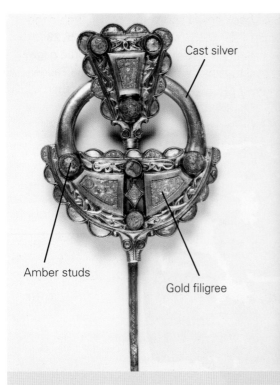

Cast silver

Amber studs

Gold filigree

Figure 25.30 (above) A brooch from Roscrea, Co. Tipperary. It is a pseudo-penannular brooch in cast silver with gold filigree decoration and amber studs.

Figure 25.31 (right top and bottom) Two thistle brooches, two bossed penannular brooches and a kite brooch. Cast-silver brooches became more common during the period of the Viking invasions.

outlined in a crest of semi-circles filled with amber. A band of simple animal interlace, inside this border, surrounds panels of loose spirals in filigree. The overall effect is simpler and bolder than the Tara Brooch but it does not have the subtlety of design and ingenious craftsmanship of the older brooch.

New brooch types were also introduced at this time; large silver kite brooches, bossed penannular brooches, and thistle brooches (Fig. 25.31) became more common in the 10th century. The laws, which dictated the size and value of brooches that could be worn by people from different layers of society, were still very much in evidence at this time.

The Derrynaflan Chalice

The Derrynaflan Chalice (Fig. 25.32), found in the same hoard as the paten that we looked at earlier, is the finest piece of 9th-century metalwork yet discovered.

- **Form:** It is 19.2 cm high and 21 cm in diameter. It is made of silver and decorated with gold filigree and amber studs.
- **Function:** A large decorated chalice for use on special occasions.
- **Technique:** The bowl and foot are turned silver sheet with a cast stem joining them. Filigree sections decorating the rim, foot and stem are separated by amber studs.
- **Decoration:** The decoration is laid out in a similar way to the Ardagh Chalice. There is a band of

Figure 25.32 The Derrynaflan Chalice.

Figure 25.33 (above) A filigree animal from under the rim of the Derrynaflan Chalice.

filigree and amber studs just below the rim; the handles have large decorated escutcheons; and the collar between the bowl and the foot has bands of filigree and amber studs, which are also used on the decorative rim around the foot. Bird and animal shapes are the main elements in the filigree decoration (Fig. 25.33), although the designs are simpler than those on the Ardagh Chalice. The artist uses the contrast between the warm tones of the gold and amber decoration and the cooler silver of the bowl and foot for a rich effect.

Other Metalwork

The manufacture of other kinds of metal artefacts continued in the 9th and 10th centuries, including crosiers, book boxes and shrines. Although none survive in very good condition, they indicate the range of objects that were made at the time. Skills and techniques had not greatly fallen away since the 8th century, but the taste for intricate design seems to have changed in favour of bolder work, maybe more suited to the taste of Vikings, who were important trading partners.

Analysis

Some of the most important works of Irish art, like the Book of Kells and Muiredach's Cross were made at this time. Can you work out why? Note the development of greater realism in some work.

Book painting reached a high point during this time. The Book of Kells is one of the most refined examples of a decorated manuscript from the early medieval period in Europe.

We know from later history that medieval masons in Europe had pattern books of abstract designs and figure scenes from which they could choose when they were carving decorations on churches. Irish masons may have had similar records to help them. In any case, there are close relationships between some of the designs and patterns found on Irish high crosses, which indicates that designers were at least aware of the work on other crosses.

The Human Figure

The way the human figure was represented changed in the 9th and 10th centuries. The figures on the crosses from Tipperary and Kildare were carved very simply, with oval heads, rectangular bodies and simple or no limbs, similar to figures on earlier crosses and books. They were symbols of humans rather than an attempt at realism.

The Midlands Crosses are quite different. The figures are strongly three-dimensional and quite well-proportioned. Details of hair and clothing can be seen and some attempt at individual characters has been made (Fig. 25.34).

Adam and Eve from the west face of the North Cross at Castledermot, Co. Kildare. The figures are simple and symbolic. The circles around the frame are the apples on the Tree of Knowledge.

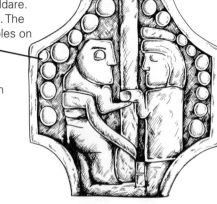

Adam and Eve from Muiredach's Cross at Monasterboice, lowest panel on the east face. The figures are almost three-dimensional and are animated.

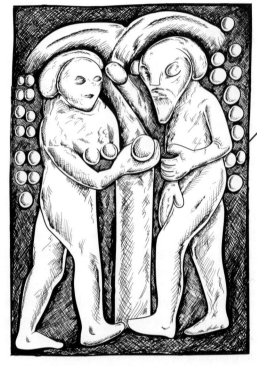

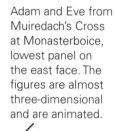

An angel from the top-right corner of the Virgin and Child page in the Book of Kells. Details of hair and clothing are represented, but in a linear and patterned way and are not fully realistic.

In the Book of Kells, the human figures are somewhere between the two. Facial features are simplified and stylised, but they are close to correct proportions. Pattern and shape are more important than realism in the representation of bodies and clothes.

After Insular Art

The period of the Viking invasions brought great change to Ireland. A society that had lived in comparative isolation for nearly 1,000 years was violently opened up to new values and ideas. The notion of an island of saints and scholars was dealt a death blow.

Irish book painting as a recognisable style vanished in a few generations, and although stone carving and metalwork would have a revival in the Romanesque era, the style was heavily overlaid with Viking and European influences. The unique combination of Celtic society and Christianity that proved to be so creative was at an end.

The 11th and 12th centuries were a time of significant religious and social change. The European models of society were becoming the norm in Ireland. The idea that kings could leave their kingdoms to their eldest sons was not the Irish tradition – here, the most able member of a clan could become leader if he passed the tests that were given to him.

Abbots of the leading monasteries in Ireland had been the Church leaders, but now Rome insisted that they take on the hierarchical system that operated in the rest of Europe.

The increased connections with Europe and the invasion of the Normans that followed brought an end to Insular Art. An Irish version of the Romanesque style lasted for about 200 years, but after that there was little that was distinctively Irish.

Chapter Review

1. Were there any positive sides to the Viking invasion? Write a short account naming the positive inputs of the Vikings and how they affected the Irish.

2. There seems to have been a number of uses for round towers. What do you think they were? Describe in words and sketches the structure of a tower and how you think it was used.

3. Can you imagine what work in a 9th-century scriptorium might have been like? Using words and sketches, describe all the jobs that a scribe did and where he worked.

4. Based on your observations of 9th-century designs, do you think the monks had a deep faith in God? Using words and sketches, take examples from sculpture, book painting and metalwork to make your points.

5. What, do you think, was the symbolism of high crosses? Draw a cross and annotate the meanings of the various parts.

6. What are the most interesting aspects of the Book of Kells? Use drawings to illustrate the aspects of the work you find most interesting.

7. Describe in words and sketches a piece of metalwork from the 9th or 10th century, noting the differences from 8th-century work.

Further Research

www.sacred-destinations.com – Search for information on the monastery and crosses at Clonmacnoise

www.irishhighcrosses.com – A useful resource for researching 9th- and 10th-century high crosses

www.visual-arts-cork.com – Contains information about many aspects of Insular Art

digitalcollections.tcd.ie – A digital record of the Book of Kells

www.youtube.com – A video explaining the construction of the Book of Kells

www.youtube.com – Search for 'The Secret of Kells (2009) Trailer' (2:03). This is an animated film by the Cartoon Saloon

Unit 9

Late Medieval Architecture and Art

(c. 1100–1550s)

26. The Hiberno-Romanesque Period (c. 1100–1200s)

27. The Anglo-Norman Period (c. 1200–1500s)

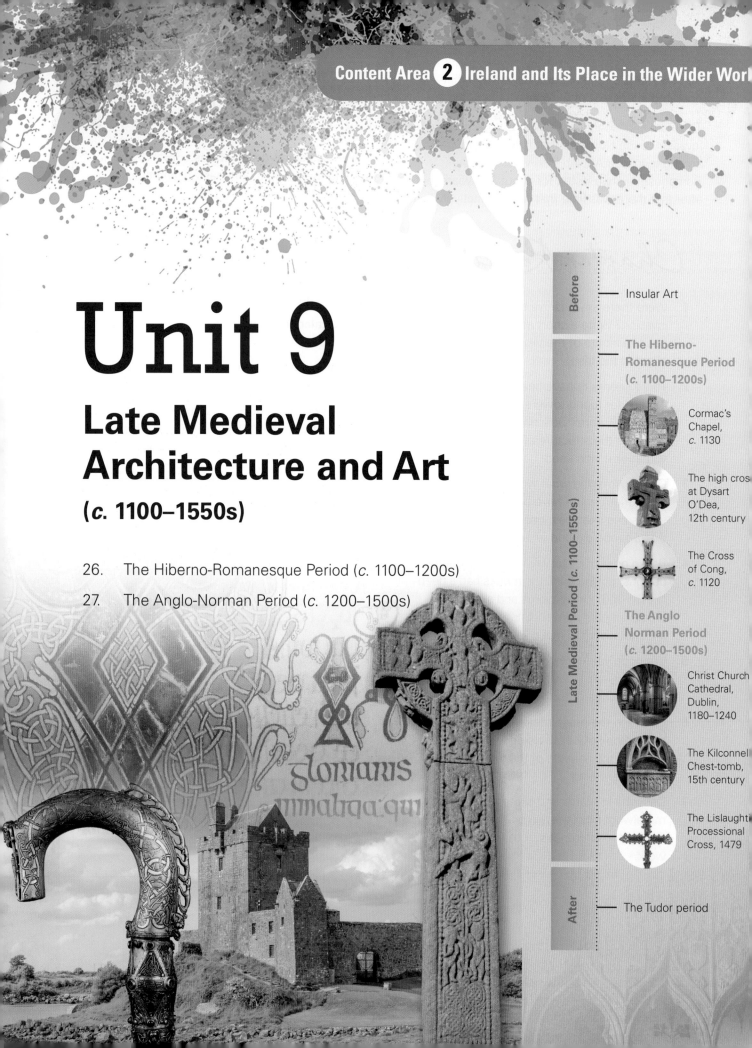

Before

— Insular Art

The Hiberno-Romanesque Period (c. 1100–1200s)

Cormac's Chapel, c. 1130

The high cros at Dysart O'Dea, 12th century

The Cross of Cong, c. 1120

The Anglo Norman Period (c. 1200–1500s)

Christ Church Cathedral, Dublin, 1180–1240

The Kilconnel Chest-tomb, 15th century

The Lislaught Processional Cross, 1479

After

— The Tudor period

Late Medieval Period (c. 1100–1550s)

Chapter 26

The Hiberno-Romanesque Period (*c.* 1100–1200s)

By the end of this chapter I will ...

* understand how outside influence from Britain and Europe brought changes to the arts in Ireland

* have seen the Viking influence on design

* be able to sketch and describe Cormac's Chapel at Cashel and one other piece of architecture

* know about changes in the shapes and decoration of high crosses, and be able to draw and describe at least one cross

* understand the changes in the decoration of metalwork and manuscripts

* be able to draw and describe the Cross of Cong and at least one other piece of metalwork

* know how to draw and describe at least one high cross.

Before the Late Medieval Period

In the early medieval period, Ireland became a Christian country. The social and economic centres were the monasteries that had developed all over the country. The Irish religious and social systems were different from most of Europe, having developed outside of the Roman Empire, which was a more urbanised society. Irish society developed out of small tribal units whose wealth was based on agriculture, notably the ownership of cattle. The monasteries were tied into this tribal system, as the abbot was generally a member of the leading tribal family in the area.

Art, design and craftsmanship reached a very high standard during the Christian Celtic period. The style known as Insular Art was unique to Ireland and parts of Britain and Scotland that had strong connections with Ireland. Some of the most famous pieces of Irish Art, including the Ardagh Chalice and the Book of Kells, were produced in Irish monasteries in the 8th and 9th centuries.

Vikings began their raids on Ireland around the year 800. They came to take valuables, in the form of high-quality craftwork and precious metals, along with slaves that they could trade for goods all over Europe. These Vikings began the process of urbanisation in Ireland, building towns at important trading ports around the country and establishing relationships with the rest of the world.

Context

There was a lot of political and social change in Europe in the 11th and 12th centuries. Population

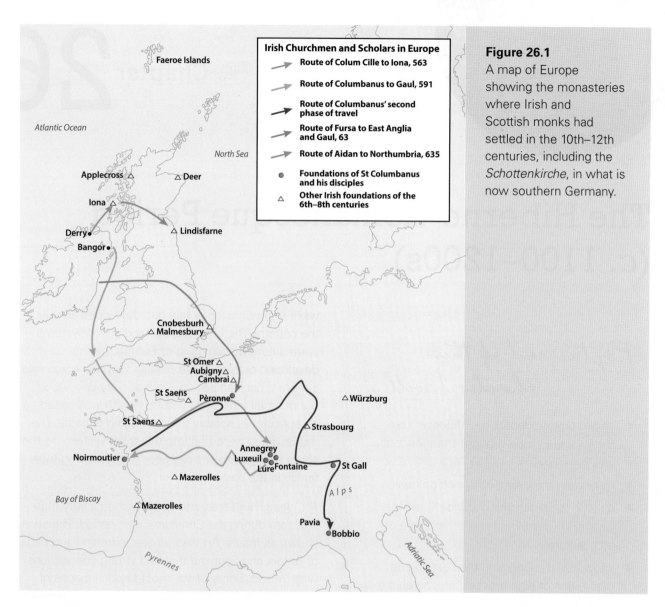

Figure 26.1
A map of Europe showing the monasteries where Irish and Scottish monks had settled in the 10th–12th centuries, including the *Schottenkirche*, in what is now southern Germany.

The map legend reads:

Irish Churchmen and Scholars in Europe
- Route of Colum Cille to Iona, 563
- Route of Columbanus to Gaul, 591
- Route of Columbanus' second phase of travel
- Route of Fursa to East Anglia and Gaul, 63
- Route of Aidan to Northumbria, 635
- ● Foundations of St Columbanus and his disciples
- △ Other Irish foundations of the 6th–8th centuries

and economic growth lead to an increase in the number of towns. There were advances in philosophy, theology and law, leading to the formation of the first universities in Europe. Irish monks were renowned for their scholarship and were welcomed into monastic communities and universities across Europe. By the mid-1100s, there were several Irish monasteries called *Schottenkirche* (literally 'Irish monasteries') of the Benedictine order in southern Germany (Fig. 26.1).

The Normans (who were, incidentally, direct descendants of the Vikings who settled in northern France) were powerful colonists, invading Britain in 1066, taking over southern Italy and leading the First Crusade which captured Jerusalem in 1099. In Rome, the pope was keen to assert papal authority following periods of war and confusion in parts of Europe. Monastic orders were reorganised and new ones formed to improve and standardise religious practice.

Church Reform

The Irish Church had developed its own organisation based on allegiances between monasteries. In the rest of Europe, the Church was organised with the pope at the head, then cardinals, archbishops, bishops and priests. Irish monks in Europe and the new European monastic orders coming into Ireland brought word of these irregularities back to the authorities on the continent, who set about bringing the Irish Church into line.

Pope Gregory VII wrote to King Toirdelbach Ua Briain (Turlough O'Brien) and the archbishops, bishops and abbots of Ireland, offering assistance with reform. A synod (a meeting of clergy) was held in Dublin in 1088 and attended by both the King and the Anglo-Norman Bishop Lanfranc of Canterbury, who represented the pope. The synod was to organise the diocese and archdiocese of Ireland. Another synod, held at Cashel, Co. Tipperary in 1101, was organised by Muirchertach, son of Toirdelbach Ua Briain, where he made a gift of the site to be used as the centre of a southern archdiocese, with Armagh as the centre of the northern archdiocese.

In the following years, further synods were called to set boundaries for diocese and to introduce further reforms. By the mid-1100s, there were archdioceses at Armagh, Cashel, Dublin and Tuam. The boundaries of the dioceses were set more or less as they are today. This period of renewal reinvigorated the Church and created a demand for new building and craftwork.

Patronage

Irish kings were traditionally appointed by their tribe, with the fittest member of the leading families holding office. The land was considered to be held in common by the tribe, not owned by individuals. Under the feudal system in Europe, kingship was passed from father to son as a divine right. The king had full power over his subjects and full ownership of territory. Irish kings soon adopted the feudal system and made themselves patrons of the Church and the arts.

There are inscriptions on doorways, books and pieces of metalwork offering blessings on the kings who paid for their construction and the clergy who commissioned them. The annals often record a king presenting a gift of gold or silver on the occasion of a visit to a church or monastery. The purpose of the gift – to build a church or to enshrine a relic – is often noted. Kings felt that such gifts increased their status and improved their chances of getting into heaven.

Pilgrimage

Pilgrimage was an important part of religious life in the medieval period. Jerusalem, Rome and the shrine of St James in Santiago de Compostella, northern Spain, were the most popular sites for medieval pilgrims, but every local church tried to have its own relics to encourage visits and donations from the public. There were pilgrim paths to all the big monasteries in Ireland, including Glendalough and Clonmacnoise. St Patrick's purgatory at Croagh Patrick, Co. Mayo, and St Brendan's purgatory on Mount Brandon, Co. Kerry, saw huge annual pilgrimages, both of which are still observed today.

Much of the surviving metalwork from the 11th and 12th centuries is in the form of reliquaries, made to house part of the remains or articles associated with a saint. Bones, bells, books, crosiers and other relics were enclosed in cases of decorated and precious metals, often paid for by local royalty.

Media and Areas of Practice

Architecture

There were important changes in the nature of architecture in Ireland during the Romanesque period. Influences from Britain and Europe were added to some existing buildings, while churches were built for the first time completely of stone,

Figure 26.2 St Flannan's Oratory in Killaloe, Co. Clare, was one of the first churches in Ireland built completely in stone. It is a two-storey structure with a barrel vault over the nave and a room under the stone roof.

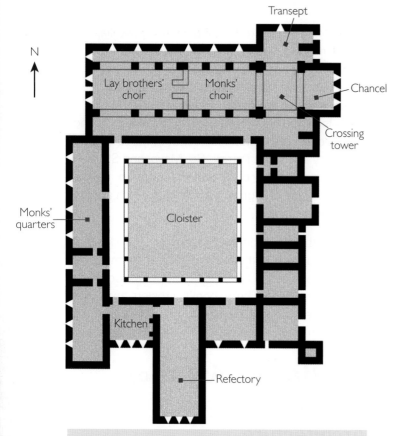

N ↑

Transept

Lay brothers' choir

Monks' choir

Chancel

Crossing tower

Monks' quarters

Cloister

Kitchen

Refectory

Figure 26.3 The layout of a Cistercian monastery. The religious and domestic buildings were organised around the cloister.

with vaulted stone ceilings and roofs. St Flannan's Oratory at Killaloe, Co. Clare (built *c.* 1110), is thought to have been among the earliest of these stone-vaulted churches, and Cormac's Chapel at Cashel in Co. Tipperary is the largest and most elaborate (Fig. 26.2).

Another radical change in architectural design came with the arrival of European monastic orders to Ireland. These new orders built in the European style, with a church and domestic buildings arranged around an open cloister (Fig. 26.3). These buildings were much larger and more elaborate constructions than the traditional Irish monasteries, which were a looser collection of small structures.

Sculpture

Sculptural decoration as part of the structure of a church became a more common feature at this time. Following the building of Cormac's Chapel, around AD 1130, doorways with Romanesque decoration

were added to many of the more important religious buildings, particularly churches at the centre of new dioceses.

High Crosses

After a gap of almost 200 years since the carving of the scripture crosses in the midlands, high crosses in a variety of styles were seen again in Ireland. The cross at Drumcliffe, which is thought to be the earliest of the Hiberno-Romanesque crosses, has a wheel head and figure scenes like its 9th-century counterparts, but others come in a variety of shapes. Most of them have large figures sculpted in high relief.

Manuscripts

There are a number of interesting books from this period. Most are known for their content rather than their decoration, but a few painted books survive. None of these books have full illustrated pages like those found in the Book of Kells, but there are good capitals and interesting decorations. The same techniques and materials that were found in earlier books continued in use. The range of colours is similar to those found in the Book of Kells.

Metalwork

See the range of metalworking techniques in the Insular style on page 334, which were still in use, with a few additions.

Many of the surviving pieces from the Hiberno-Romanesque period are reliquaries, made to house a relic or some treasured item. New designs and techniques were introduced by the Vikings and other European influences.

- **Filigree** – fine gold wires twisted together to form a design – was not generally of a high standard at this time. Sometimes copper or silver wire was used and covered with gold leaf.

- **Gilding** was more frequently executed using gold leaf than by fire gilding, which was used in the 9th and 10th centuries.

- **Studs** were decorated with enamel and *millefiori*.

- **Niello**, a paste of silver and sulphur, was set

into grooves to create a black line. It was often used beside silver ribbons inlaid in bronze. You can see examples of this on the Clonmacnoise Crosier (Fig. 26.4).

● **Casting** in bronze and silver was often of a very fine quality.

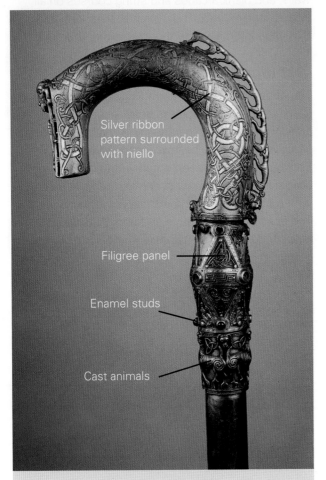

Silver ribbon pattern surrounded with niello

Filigree panel

Enamel studs

Cast animals

Figure 26.4 Some of the new metalworking techniques can be seen on the Clonmacnoise Crosier.

Art Elements and Design Principles

Architecture

Most buildings with Romanesque elements in Ireland are simple structures with carved decoration added. The elements of the decoration are often influenced from outside Ireland. Chevrons, which were often used to decorate arches, are of English

origin. Animal and human heads found on capitals and arches may have come from France, or they may come from older Irish designs. The Viking influence is seen in exotic animals combined with geometric patterns in the Urnes and Ringerike styles, which were an adaptation by the Vikings of Irish zoomorphs and patterns.

Carving style can vary from deeply carved elements to very lightly carved patterns. Some doorways are made up of different coloured stones, which suggests that they might have been painted.

Stone Carving

Techniques had changed little over the years. The same iron chisels and drills would have been used as in former centuries. Styles changed, with larger, deeply carved figures frequently dominating the face of the crosses. Panels of interlace, often with elements of Viking style, appear on the sides and the base.

Urnes elements, elongated animals intertwined with snakes

Animal heads in profile

Ringerike elements, plant forms with flourishes

Figure 26.5 Hiberno-Romanesque design elements.

Snake head viewed from above

Manuscripts

Manuscripts were still written on vellum using black and coloured inks applied with quill pens and brushes. A compass and ruler would have been used for layout and a scraper for corrections. Designs combined animal and human figures with interlace and decorative flourishes. At first glance, the decoration looks like the work from the Book of Kells, but on closer inspection elements of Viking Urnes and Ringerike styles can be noticed.

Metalwork

Many of the metalwork pieces surviving from the Romanesque period take the form of reliquaries, which have probably survived because of their religious significance. The same design elements we have noted in the other crafts – animals, interlace and geometric patterns – form the basis for most decoration here also.

Innovation and Invention

The most obvious innovation was the introduction of large decorated elements on the churches and buildings of the new monasteries laid out in the European style. There were some changes in sculpture, metalwork and manuscript design, including new techniques which we saw above and the new design elements seen in Figure 26.5.

The external influences on design came from the Vikings and new ideas on architecture came from Britain and Europe.

Artists and Artworks

Architecture

Cormac's Chapel, Cashel, Co. Tipperary

Built between 1127 and 1134 under the patronage of Cormac Mac Cártaigh, king of Munster, Cormac's Chapel was constructed on a site donated by Muirchertach Ua Briain in 1101. It was a unique building in Ireland at this time, because it was planned, designed and built as a complete unit. The decoration is integrated inside and out, and has been largely unchanged since it was built.

Form

In plan, the chapel is a simple nave and chancel church. It is a stone structure, with a vaulted ground floor and a stone roof over a chamber above. There are two square towers at the eastern end of the nave, Romanesque doorways in the north and south walls, and blank arcades and string courses on all sides of the exterior. The church is 15 m long and 5 m wide internally, and the towers are 18 m tall.

Technique

The appearance of Cormac's Chapel seems to owe much to the Anglo-Norman style, especially the arcading, chevron decoration and scalloped capitals. Many art historians believe that masons from England may have been employed to build it. The chapel is built of finely cut ashlar; the nave is roofed with a barrel vault and the chancel with a rib vault. The space over the vaults and under the roof can be accessed by a spiral staircase in the south tower.

String courses

Two towers

Blank arcade

Figure 26.6 The view of the eastern end of Cormac's Chapel shows the Germanic influence the towers bring to the building.

> **Vault:** A roof built in the form of an arch or arches.

Decoration: Exterior

The north wall is the most richly decorated. It has a deeply carved doorway with a gable pediment, which is decorated with rosettes and chevrons. This pattern continues east over a tomb recess with a roof over it, which is connected to the pediment hood. Human and animal heads form part of the decoration at this level and at the colonnade (row of columns) supporting the eaves.

The north doorway has five rows of arches: three of them project beyond the wall and two are set in the thickness of the wall. All but one have saw-tooth chevron decoration (Fig. 26.8). The middle arch is the most elaborate, with bar-and-lozenge decoration on the inner face and chevrons on the arris (the outer edge of the arch where the

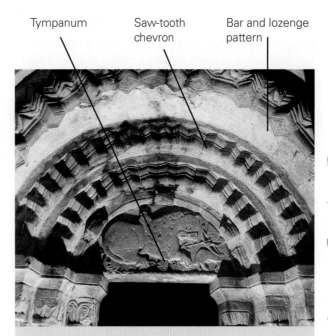

Figure 26.8 A row of saw-tooth chevrons on the inner arch surrounds the tympanum on the north door of Cormac's Chapel. The carving shows a centaur aiming an arrow at a lion.

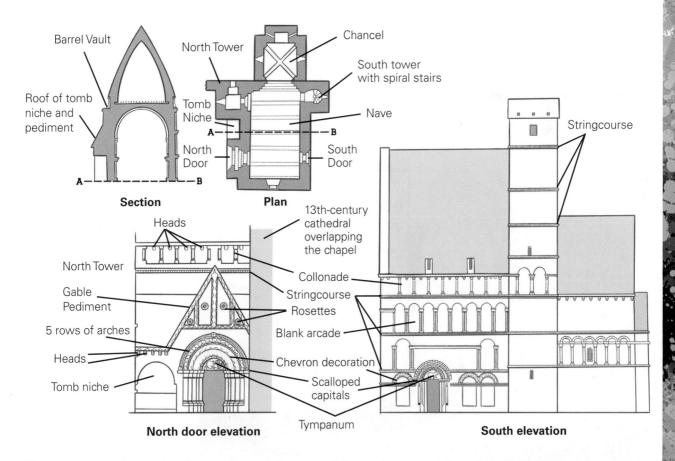

Figure 26.7 Drawings of the plan, section and elevations of Cormac's Chapel at Cashel, Co. Tipperary.

two faces meet). A tympanum over the doorway features a centaur shooting a lion with a bow and arrow. There are two creatures below the lion's feet. The meaning of this scene is no longer understood. The capitals on the pillars supporting the arches have a range of designs, including scallops, tendrils and animal and human heads. This wall originally faced a courtyard in front of the old church (now gone) and the round tower, so this would have been the formal ceremonial entrance to the church. Today, this side of the chapel is partially covered by St Patrick's cathedral, which was built on the site in the 13th century.

The south wall has three stages of arcading with a colonnade above, like the one on the north wall. Saw-tooth chevrons decorate the arch of the doorway and the arches of the arcade at ground level. A simple tympanum is decorated with an animal, probably a lion.

The string courses that run horizontally all around the building, combined with the arcades, create a unity of design not usually seen in Irish churches of this time.

Decoration: Interior

The inside of the nave has two levels of decoration.

At ground level, there are rows of arcading each side of the doorways. Above these, a string course supports engaged shafts, which in turn support the transverse ribs of the barrel vault. These arcades and shafts are decorated in a similar style to the exterior, with chevrons, lozenges and four-leaved plant forms.

A portal is a formal word for an entrance, usually an important one.

The portal to the north tower is large and elaborately decorated with four orders of arches; the outer arch has a roll moulding on the arris, the second arch has saw-tooth chevron, and the inner two are later medieval replacements.

The chancel arch, which separates the nave from the chancel, has five orders of decoration (Fig. 26.10). The most remarkable of these is the second arch, which has a row of human heads radiating out from the centre. The heads continue down to the ground between the pillars that support the arches.

The chancel also has blank arcades at ground level. Above these are three arches in the north and south walls; the centre one on each side is a window opening. The most striking feature of the chancel is the rib-vaulted ceiling, which was painted in the 12th century.

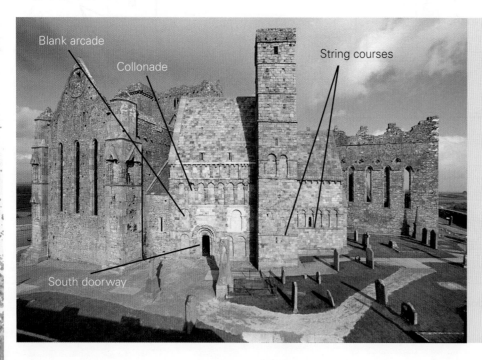

Figure 26.9
This view of the south side of Cormac's Chapel shows how the 13th-century cathedral dominates the space.

Blank arcade

Collonade

String courses

South doorway

Human heads decorate one of the chancel arches

Rib vaulting in the chancel

Figure 26.10 The chancel arch of Cormac's Chapel, featuring a row of carved heads, separates the nave from the rib-vaulted chancel.

Painting

A restoration of the chapel in the 1990s revealed fragments of painted scenes from the early life of Christ, the Magi meeting with Herod, the adoration of the Magi and a scene with shepherds. The paintings may have been prepared for the visit of Henry II in 1171. Other areas of the chapel also show traces of paint, so it's possible that the whole interior was brightly painted.

Function

Cormac's Chapel was designed for ceremonial use. The elaborate north door and the formal doorway to the north tower inside the building suggest important functions. The tomb niche in the north wall and the decorated chest-tomb, still in the church, suggest that important people were entombed there, where they could be visited and commemorated.

Some people think that Cormac Mac Cártaigh wanted to build something very impressive to outshine his rivals for the Munster kingship, the O'Briens. They had built St Flannan's Oratory at Killaloe some years earlier, probably with the assistance of English masons. Cormac must have gathered all his resources to create a royal chapel at the new centre of the archdiocese of Cashel.

Figure 26.11 A scene from the ceiling frescoes in Cormac's Chapel at Cashel, Co. Tipperary. Only fragments remain of the once-colourful bible scenes.

Architectural Decoration

The decorated north doorway of Cormac's Chapel seems to have impressed some influential people, as there were eight other doorways with pediments built in the following years. Most of these doorways are in the midlands; the largest and most elaborate one is at Clonfert Cathedral in Co. Galway.

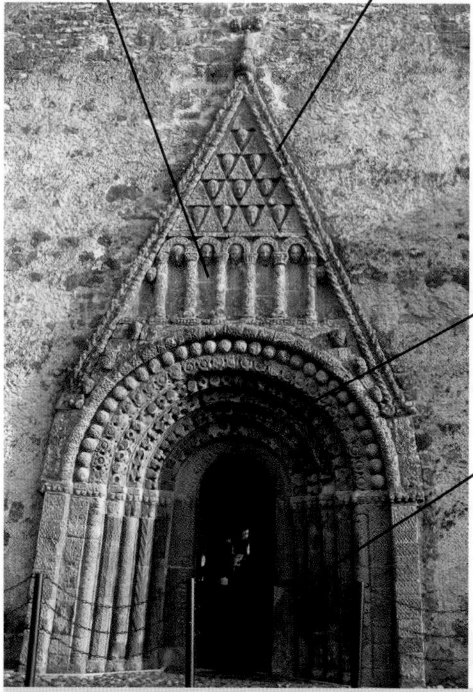

Clonfert Cathedral

Form

Clonfert Cathedral is a typical Irish Romanesque building with a simple nave and chancel plan, altered over the years to include new features like the decorated doorway in the west wall.

Decoration

The decorated area is eight metres tall. It consists of a doorway with six orders of Romanesque arches and a pediment above. The inside arch of grey limestone was added in the late Middle Ages and is not part of the brown sandstone of the original design. The pillars on each side of the doorway are decorated in matching pairs, with lightly carved patterns of geometric and vegetal designs. The capitals have animal heads and human faces, again in matching pairs on either side of the doorway.

The arch rings are deeply carved in a variety of designs. The inner arch is decorated with plant forms, the next one has animal heads holding a roll

Blank arcade with heads

The triangular pediment surrounded with a cable moulding

Six decorated arches

Lightly carved patterns on the pillars

Figure 26.12 The west door of Clonfert Cathedral, Co. Galway.

moulding in their jaws, and the third arch has Greek crosses on both faces with a roll moulding along the outer edge. Flat discs are carved on both faces of the next arch, alternatively pierced or decorated with spirals, serpents and flowers. The fifth arch has circles surrounding bosses on both faces, with a roll moulding running behind them. The sixth arch has hemispherical bosses decorated with interlace and plant forms. The outer ring, which separates the arches from the pediment, is decorated with an interlace pattern of slim, stylised animals in the Viking Urnes style.

The triangular pediment is framed by a double cable moulding. Human heads feature in every area of the design, in the tops of arches in the lower part of the pediment and in the triangular spaces in the upper part. The triangular areas around the heads are decorated with plant forms.

The doorway at Clonfert is one of the most elaborately decorated portals in Ireland. It is deeply carved with a variety of designs, and has features

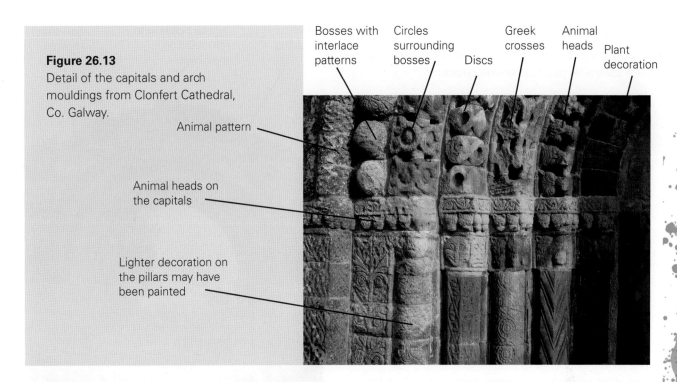

Figure 26.13
Detail of the capitals and arch mouldings from Clonfert Cathedral, Co. Galway.

Bosses with interlace patterns

Circles surrounding bosses

Discs

Greek crosses

Animal heads

Plant decoration

Animal pattern

Animal heads on the capitals

Lighter decoration on the pillars may have been painted

that have parallels in England and France. The portal may have been built at the time of the synod, which was held there in 1179.

The Nuns' Church at Clonmacnoise

There are Romanesque features at over 100 sites in Ireland, in almost every county around the country, ranging from simple chancel arches to elaborately carved doorways. Most of these features are part of small, plain buildings, usually older churches with Romanesque details added to them.

Completed in 1167, the Nuns' Church at Clonmacnoise is an example of how the system of patronage helped to finance the new Romanesque decoration on churches.

Note: The Nuns' Church was sponsored by Derbforgaill, daughter of the king of Meath, who was the patron of Clonmacnoise. This was the same Derbforgaill who was abducted by Diarmaid Mac Murchada, King of Leinster. For this and other reasons, Diarmaid was expelled from Ireland. He went to Wales and got support from some Norman knights to retake his kingdom and unfortunately initiated the Norman invasion of Ireland.

Hood moulding

Saw-tooth chevron

Animal heads with roll moulding in their jaws

Pillars with chevron patterns

Figure 26.14 The western doorway of the Nuns' Church at Clonmacnoise.

Form and Function

This was the main church for a community of nuns at Clonmacnoise. The west doorway and the chancel arch are all that remains of the building.

Technique and Decoration

Deeply carved decoration on the arches contrasts with low relief patterns on the pillars.

The doorway has four decorated arches resting on pillars. Each pillar is decorated on both faces with a chevron pattern. This creates lozenge shapes along the outer edge. Animal heads at the tops of some of the pillars hold the ends of the pattern in their jaws. The inner arch is plain, while the second one has animal heads with patterned faces holding a roll moulding in their jaws. The third arch has saw-tooth chevrons with the points facing out. The outer arch is a hood moulding decorated with small bosses and a herringbone pattern, the outer ends of which terminate in stylised animal heads.

The chancel arch of the Nuns' Church has four orders facing the nave and two facing the chancel. The jambs on the nave side have a simple roll moulding on their outer edge, imitating a pillar. The capitals are almost square; some have patterns and some have small human heads on the outer corner. The inner arch has saw-tooth chevrons on both faces, creating deep, hollow lozenges along the

Animal head terminal   Saw-tooth chevron   Animal heads with roll moulding in their jaws

Animal heads at the tops of pillars   Lozenges formed at the outer edges of the pillars

Figure 26.15 The capitals of the pillars in the western doorway of the Nuns' Church at Clonmacnoise.

Hood moulding   Animal heads with roll moulding in their jaws   Saw-tooth chevron

Pillars with chevron patterns

Figure 26.16 The chancel arch of the Nuns' Church at Clonmacnoise.

outer edge. The second arch has bar-and-lozenge moulding on the outer edge and gapped chevrons on both faces. The third arch has chevrons on both faces, which form an intricate lozenge design along the outer edge. A hood moulding surrounds the arches, decorated with chevrons and ending in animal heads at both ends.

RESEARCH

Explore the patterns and designs on the Nuns' Church at Clonmacnoise. Make drawings and take notes of the features that appeal to you. You could use some of the images as a starting point for your own work.

Other Sites

There are many fine examples of Romanesque decoration on Irish churches around the country.

- Dysart O'Dea in Co. Clare has a doorway with human and animal heads carved in high relief.

- Glendalough, Co. Wicklow, has a collection of Romanesque buildings, some with decoration.
- Killeshin in Co. Laois has a mixture of lightly incised and deeply carved sculpture on different coloured stones, suggesting that the doorway was once painted.
- A large entrance front survives at Roscrea with a contemporary high cross beside it.
- Inside the cathedral at Tuam, Co. Galway, there is a magnificent chancel arch from an earlier church.

These are just a few examples of the buildings in the Romanesque style that can be found all over the country.

Sculpture

During the Romanesque period in Europe, sculpture was a decoration added to architecture. In Ireland, one could almost say that the opposite was true: buildings were small without many architectural qualities, but the sculptural decoration was of a high standard. The decorative carving we looked at under the heading 'Architecture' could just as easily be called sculpture. Many of the design elements (geometric, plant and animal patterns and high relief figure carving) also apply to the design of high crosses.

High Crosses
Drumcliffe High Cross, Co. Sligo
Form and Function

Drumcliffe High Cross is 3.83 m tall and is carved from two blocks of pale sandstone. It has many of the features of the 9th- and 10th-century crosses, like a wheel head and a tall base, but the panels are not as sharply defined.

It appears to be a traditional type of cross, displaying scenes from the Old and New Testaments, which would help pilgrims focus their prayers and thoughts.

Technique

Most of the cross is carved in relief using iron chisels. The outstanding technical feature is the creatures carved in high relief midway up each face of the cross: a lot of stone had to be carved away to leave these figures projecting so far from the rest of the cross.

Decoration

Bead moulding surrounds the decorated areas on both faces, leaving a plain border outlining the form of the cross. Interlace and figure scenes appear on all faces of the cross.

The west face shows scenes from the New Testament. At the bottom, there is a panel of interlace, followed by a scene with three figures (the centre figure holding a baby, may be the

The Last Judgement

Daniel in the lions' den

Possibly Cain and Abel

High relief lion

Adam and Eve

Interlace pattern

Figure 26.17 The east face of the high cross at Drumcliffe, Co. Sligo.

presentation of John the Baptist in the temple). Above this is an animal that may be a camel carved in high relief, then a scene showing the mocking of Christ. In the top panel, there are two figures, one holding a baby. This may represent the holy family returning from Egypt. The crucifixion is shown at the intersection of the cross.

The east face of the high cross shows scenes from the Old Testament. At the bottom, there is an interlace knot-work panel, followed by a representation of Adam, Eve and the serpent. This is topped by another interlace panel, then a high relief figure of a lion. The next panel is Cain killing Abel or David killing Goliath, who may be holding a shield. Just below the intersection of the cross is Daniel in the lions' den. The scene at the intersection is probably the Last Judgement with the heads of the saved and the damned on the arms of the cross. At the end of the arm on the south side is an image of the Virgin and Child – the only one found on an Irish high cross.

> ## Note: Pilgrim Crosses
> The Romanesque high crosses at Tuam, Roscrea and Cashel are badly weathered and damaged, but some details can still be made out. The crucified Christ, for example, is represented by a figure in a long dress or tunic. This figure may be a reference to the Volto Santo, a carved wooden crucifix kept in the cathedral at Lucca in Italy. Lucca was on the pilgrim route to Rome, and small copies of the cross were sometimes carried by pilgrims on the journey to and from Rome. The style of the pilgrim crosses may have influenced Irish stone carvers.

St Patrick's Cross at Cashel
Form and Function

At 4.65 m tall, St Patrick's Cross at Cashel has a unique design, with supports under the arms of the cross. Sockets on the top of the arms and the side of the upper part of the shaft would have held further decoration (angels have been suggested). It stands on a large base.

The location of this cross at Cashel, the centre of a new archdiocese, suggests the large bishop figure was a statement of the importance of the new Church organisation in Ireland.

Technique

The cross is carved from a single piece of stone. The uprights under the arms may be a support for the arms or they may be part of the design, representing the crosses of the thieves crucified with Christ.

Decoration

The large base is decorated with a lamb inside a pattern of concentric circles, a pattern of crosses and a panel of animal interlacing.

Figure 26.18 The west face of the high cross at Cashel, Co. Tipperary. The Christ figure takes up the full height of the cross.

The west face is dominated by a large figure of Christ, almost in the round. On the east face is the figure of a bishop, right hand raised in blessing, left hand holding a crosier. The cross is very weathered and pieces are missing, so we do not have the detail of the original design.

Dysart O'Dea High Cross, Co. Clare
Form and Function

The Dysart O'Dea cross has no wheelhead, but the sockets in the ends of the arms may have contained some further decoration. The large figure of a bishop may have been a reminder to all who saw it that there was a reformed Church order, with bishops in charge of the diocese. A socket at waist level on the bishop's body probably held an arm raised in blessing. The head of the Christ figure is a separate piece of stone. The cross is 3.27 m tall.

Technique

The figures in high relief on the east face contrast with the low relief carving on the rest of the cross. The limestone it was carved from has weathered well, as much of the detail remains crisp.

Decoration

High relief figures of a bishop and Christ take up the east face of the cross. On the remainder of the cross, the work is carried out in low relief, patterns of crosses, animal interlacing and key patterns. The base has figure scenes and patterns of interwoven snakes.

Other High Crosses

Remains of about 20 crosses from the Romanesque period still survive. A group of related crosses at Kilfenora, Co. Clare and on Aran Mór are carved from shallow slabs of local stone, decorated with patterns and figure scenes. Another group is found around Tuam, Co. Galway, made under the patronage of Turlough O'Connor, king of Connacht. The Munster kings seem to have been the patrons of the crosses at Roscrea, Monaincha and Cashel. The cross at Drumcliffe, which we looked at above, along with one at Glendalough and a few others around the country, are more isolated examples of the Romanesque style.

Figure 26.19 The east face of the high cross at Dysart O'Dea, Co. Clare.

Christ figure

Bishop

Low relief patterns

Compare the high cross at Drumcliffe with the one at Dysart O'Dea, noting the similarities and differences in the human figures and patterns. Make drawings of the features that most appeal to you.

Manuscripts

A number of decorated books survive from this time, no full-page illustrations but decorated capitals

UNIT 9 LATE MEDIEVAL ARCHITECTURE AND ART (c. 1100–1550s)

including human and animal forms and interlace. The Viking influence is seen in the designs which include elements of the Urnes and Ringerike styles.

The Liber Hymnorum
Form and Function

The Liber Hymnorum is codex made of vellum pages. It is book of hymns that would have been sung by the monks in a monastery. It measured about 30 × 20 cm before it was trimmed for rebinding. It is now in poor condition due to mishandling over time.

Technique

The same techniques that were used in the 9th and 10th centuries were still in use in the Romanesque period. Quill pens and brushes made of fine animal hair were used to form the letters and apply colour.

Decoration

The Latin text is written in Irish majuscule across the full width of the page. Notes and commentaries in old Irish are written around the formal text in smaller minuscule letters. The first letter of each hymn is a decorated capital. The colour scheme includes white, red, yellow, green and purple. Dotting in a second colour is often added to the capital letters. You can see notes on the making of colours and writing materials in Chapters 24 and 25, pages 333 and 351.

Majuscule letters are large, uncial letters (rounded, unjoined), generally the same height, with few ascenders or descenders. They were most commonly used in European manuscripts of the 4th to 8th centuries. Modern capital letters developed from them.

Minuscule letters are smaller, lower-case letters with ascenders and descenders, like modern handwriting, developed in the 7th century.

The details of the decoration have changed from the 10th-century style. Note the fat paws on some of the creatures, flourishes at the ends of decorations and the simplified interlacing – all influences from the Viking Ringerike style.

Figure 26.20 A capital letter from the Liber Hymnorum in Trinity College Library, Dublin.

The Psalter of Cormac

A codex is a manuscript in book form.

Form

A codex written on vellum, the Psalter of Cormac measures approximately 18 × 14 cm. The book is in particularly good condition, although some decoration was lost when the book was trimmed for rebinding.

Figure 26.21 The capital Q from the 51st psalm, of the Psalter of Cormac which begins, '*Quid gloriaris*' ('What glory').

Function

A psalter is a book of psalms, the religious verses sung or recited in Christian and Jewish worship. This manuscript gets its name from an inscription in Latin at the bottom of a page of musical notation: '*Cormacus scripsit hoc psalterium ora pro eo*', which translates to, 'Cormac wrote this psalter, pray for him'.

Technique

The penmanship and decoration in this small book are of a very high quality, superior to anything else from the Romanesque period.

Decoration

The text is a well-executed Irish majuscule: the smaller capitals that begin each verse have their centres coloured in, and fat paws and animal heads decorate the end flourishes of some of the letters. White, red, yellow, purple, blue and green paints are used.

The book is divided into three sets of 50 psalms by framed pages, which once held illustrations. These illustrations have been scraped out, probably because the style was considered old-fashioned and was intended to be replaced. Large capitals taking up most of the page open each set of fifty psalms.

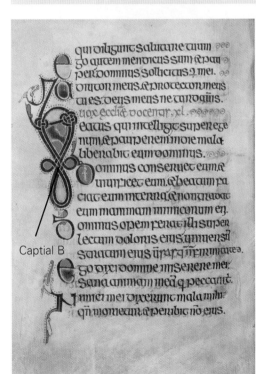

Captial B

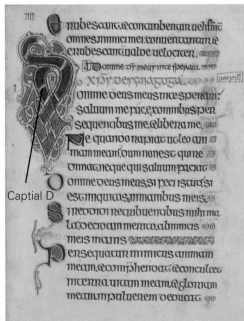

Captial D

Figure 26.22
The Psalter of Cormac. The capital D is a painted ribbon interlace letter. The capital B is in pen and ink with the interior space painted in a variety of colours. Note the white spaces between the pen lines to appreciate the accuracy of the scribe.

Folio 60r begins the second set. The opening words of this psalm, *Quid gloriaris*, begin with a huge purple and blue capital Q, which is surrounded by a tangle of yellow zoomorphic interlace, set against a red background (Fig. 26.21). The interlace ends in animal heads with lolling tongues, all around the outside of the decorated area. Human faces hide among the loops of the pattern. The next three letters – U,I and D – are twice the size of the ordinary letters and made with a broader pen. The interior spaces are painted in red, yellow and purple patches. Animal heads form flourishes at the ends of the letters.

Two different types of capitals begin every second psalm. One type is a ribbon interlace capital with zoomorphs and sometimes human figures, surrounded with yellow interlace on a red background. The other type of capital is in a bold, black pen line, sometimes doubled. The internal areas of the letters are painted in patches of different colours.

These books mark the end of the true Irish manuscript. Most of what followed were written in a common European style. Irish decorated capitals rarely appeared in the following centuries.

Metalwork

Most surviving examples of 11th- and 12th-century metalwork are reliquaries. They have probably survived due to their importance to the Church as objects of veneration. In many cases, they were looked after by generations of the same family who were keepers of the shrine. Some were handed over to state collections in the 19th century, and can now be found in museums. Several of these metalwork pieces have been engraved with a dedication to the bishops and patrons who commissioned them.

Brooches and chalices – which were so important in the 9th and 10th centuries – hardly feature at all in the Romanesque period.

A **shrine** is a place or container considered holy by association with a sacred person or relic.

The Shrine of St Patrick's Bell
Form and Function

The Shrine of St Patrick's Bell is a box made of sheet and cast bronze to hold an ancient iron bell.

It could be carried in procession using a strap through the rings on the sides. It would have been displayed in the church on important occasions.

Technique

According to the inscription on the back panel of the shrine, it was made by Cudulig O'Inmainen and his sons in their workshop in Armagh. The high king and bishop also mentioned in the inscription have helped scholars to date the shrine to between 1094 and 1105.

The box itself is made with bronze plates, which were then decorated with pieces of filigree on the front. Cast openwork silver and gilt silver are used on the sides and on the handle cover. The castings in bronze and silver are particularly well-made.

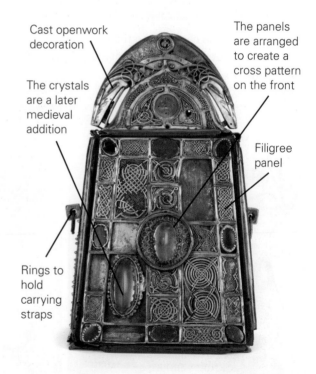

Cast openwork decoration

The crystals are a later medieval addition

The panels are arranged to create a cross pattern on the front

Filigree panel

Rings to hold carrying straps

Figure 26.23 The front face of the Shrine of St Patrick's Bell. A cross is formed by the patterns of interlace. The large crystals are a later addition.

Decoration

The decoration on the front of the shrine is mainly intact, although a number of quartz stones added in the late Middle Ages disrupt the balance of the design. Panels of animal interlace filigree, which were influenced by the Viking Urnes style, create a cross shape with a circle at the centre and mounted stones at the end of each arm. Snakes and ribbon-bodied animals in a thin, linear style are the main elements of the designs.

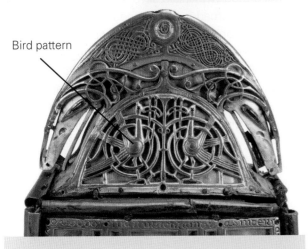

Silver gilt openwork panels on the side of the shrine

Figure 26.24 The Shrine of St Patrick's Bell showing the beautifully cast silver gilt openwork patterns.

Bird pattern

Figure 26.25 The cast silver gilt bird patterns on the handle cover of the Shrine of St Patrick's Bell. The animal heads at each side have been damaged over time.

On the handle cover at the top of the shrine is a fine, silver gilt, openwork casting of a pair of birds intertwined with interlace patterns. Animal heads at either side of the cover have been damaged over time.

The side panels are silver gilt openwork castings in a pattern of snake-like creatures in beautifully balanced curves.

The Lismore Crosier
Form and Function

The Lismore Crosier was found in a walled-up tower of Lismore Castle in 1814. It is a reliquary, made to contain a staff of office associated with an important abbot or bishop. It is a horse-head crosier in the Irish style, made of bronze sheets on a wooden core. An inscription at the joining of the crook with the top knob on the staff asks for a prayer for the bishop who commissioned the object and for the craftsman who made it.

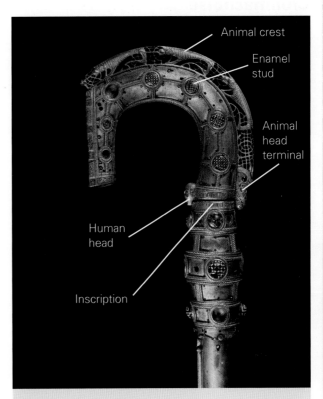

Animal crest

Enamel stud

Animal head terminal

Human head

Inscription

Figure 26.26 The Lismore Crosier. The crest on the crook and the enamel studs are what remains of the decoration, which would have included gold filigree panels in the framed spaces.

Technique

The whole crosier is covered in bronze sheet, held together by three cast-bronze knobs. The gold filigree that once filled the spaces on the crook and knobs is now missing, likely stolen. The casting on the crest is of high quality, as are the enamel and *millefiori* studs.

Decoration

A beautifully cast-bronze crest decorates the top of the crosier. Thin areas of pattern connect three dogs, while the nose of the monster at the end is patterned with interlace, and blue enamel studs create the creature's eyes. The centre knob is divided into small panels decorated with zoomorphs and interlace. The decorated areas would have been covered with gold foil, but this has been lost over the years. A small human face stands out from the inscribed band.

The Crosier of the Abbots of Clonmacnoise

Form and Function

A reliquary kept as a symbol of office for an abbot or bishop. This 12th-century crosier is made of bronze sheet covering a wooden core, held together with cast-bronze knobs.

Technique

Castings and filigree are used in several areas and small enamel studs punctuate the knobs. The inlaid silver and niello on the crook are the technical highlight of the piece.

Decoration

The top and bottom knobs are divided into small triangular panels decorated with vegetal interlace, similar to the type of patterns we saw on Romanesque doorways. Blue enamel studs mark the junctions where the triangles meet. Below the top knob is a band of four creatures in opposing pairs. They have spirals on their haunches and their tails form triquetra (three-part) knots, each ending in an animal head.

The head of the crosier is decorated with what remains of a crest of little animals, each one biting

Figure 26.27 The Clonmacnoise Crosier is a good example of the new techniques of silver inlay and niello.

the rear of the one in front. The sides of the crook are decorated with inlaid silver ribbons outlined in niello. The broader silver bands end in animal heads with long jaws, and form simple figure-of-eight patterns. The thinner lines that intertwine with them make the pattern look more complicated. A human face with an elaborate moustache adorns the reliquary box at the front of the crook; the little figure of a bishop below it is a later addition.

Other Crosiers

Irish crosiers came in other shapes as well as the horse-head ones we have seen, including a tau (T-shaped) crosier and a spiral headed one made of ivory, both of which are in the National Museum in Dublin. The ivory crosier was found near Aghadoe, Co. Kerry, and is carved with an image of Jonah emerging from the whale.

The Shrine of St Lachtin's Arm

Form and Function

At 40 cm in height, the Shrine of St Lachtin's Arm is a fine example of a type of shrine that was once common in Europe. The reliquary was made to hold the limb of a saint, and is made of bronze plaques held together with cast bronze rings.

Technique

Sheet bronze and bronze casting are the structural elements. Grooves were cut into the surface to take silver ribbon and niello which is now lost. Gold foil would have been attached to most of the surface, which is also gone.

Decoration

This shrine is contemporary with the Clonmacnoise Crosier and was decorated in a similar way with silver and niello. The design is a ribbon pattern of thread-like animals with open jaws. The hand is a separate cast with panels of filigree, silver nails and a gilt silver palm, decorated with foliage and tendrils. The band around the middle of the arm is cast openwork in an interlace pattern. The band at the base has interlace panels separated by glass studs.

Figure 26.28 The Shrine of St Lachtin's Arm. The gold leaf, silver and niello that once made this a dazzling object are now gone.

The Cross of Cong

Form and Function

The Cross of Cong is a 76 cm tall processional cross, made of bronze plaques mounted onto an oak core. It is a reliquary made to hold a fragment of the true cross, which was brought to Ireland in AD 1119. The large rock crystal at the centre of the cross is translucent, allowing worshipers to catch

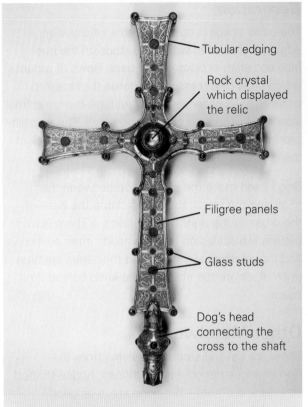

Tubular edging

Rock crystal which displayed the relic

Filigree panels

Glass studs

Dog's head connecting the cross to the shaft

Figure 26.29 The Cross of Cong was made to house a relic of the true cross.

a glimpse of the relic behind it. The cross would have been carried in procession on important occasions and displayed on the church altar during ceremonies. Part of a Latin inscription on the cross states '*by this cross is covered the cross on which the creator of the world suffered*' – a reference to the relic of the true cross inside.

A further inscription in Irish runs all around the sides of the Cross of Cong: it mentions Toirrdelbach Ua Conchobair as the king who commissioned the piece, and Mael Isu mac Bratain Ui Echach as the craftsman who made it. Two other clerics are also mentioned.

Technique

Bronze sheets and castings, filigree, enamel and glass studs, silver and niello inlay are all part of the repertoire of techniques used on this highly decorated piece.

Decoration

The cross shape is outlined with a tubular silver edging, punctuated with glass studs on the front face and enamel discs on the back. Rows of mounts, which once held glass studs, divide the face into panels. These panels are filled with gilt-bronze animal interlace in a version of the Urnes style. The four gilt-bronze openwork plaques that decorate the back of the cross are also in the Urnes style.

Dog heads make the connection between the shaft and the cross; their jaws clamp the base of the cross to the staff that supports it. There is a pattern like scales on the dog heads: their eyebrows and moustaches are niello, and their eyes are blue enamel, as are the studs on the knob behind their heads.

Other Metalwork

There are several shrines surviving from the Romanesque period – book shrines, house-shaped shrines and others – but none are in as good condition as the ones we have examined here.

Metalwork from the Hiberno-Romanesque period is not as highly regarded as 8th-century works like the Ardagh Chalice and Tara Brooch. The 11th- and 12th-century work made its impact with bolder designs and more colour, although pieces like the Cross of Cong are beautifully balanced and subtle in design.

> **CREATE**
>
> Design a piece of art or craftwork based on the designs of animals you have studied from the Hiberno-Romanesque period. Think about the colours, forms and textures that you have seen in the work. Look at the doorways at Clonfert and the Nuns' Church, the capital letters in Cormac's Psalter and the crests of the crosiers.

Analysis

When looking at examples of the arts and crafts in this chapter, it is clear how changes in style affected design and decoration. Note the English, Viking and French influences in architecture, the Viking elements in sculpture, manuscripts and metalwork, combined with native Irish Insular design. Different crafts can be compared, noting how designers used the new style features in their work. The art elements like colour, line and form can be studied in each of the objects.

The changes that began with the arrival of the European monastic orders and the Norman knights created enormous social upheaval in Ireland. The Celtic monasteries that had been at the centre of Irish society for hundreds of years became less important, as large numbers of people joined the new European orders: the Cistercians, Augustinians and Benedictines. Meanwhile, the feudal system was adopted by Irish chiefs and European-style towns were developing, further altering the Irish social structure.

For a time, the patronage of Irish kings and the fashion for pilgrimage in Ireland brought prosperity in building and craftwork. However, pressure from the Norman invaders ended this period of revival of the arts in Ireland.

In the late 19th and early 20th centuries, the Celtic Revival movement took a great interest in the design and decoration of the Insular period, in particular the Hiberno-Romanesque style, which was incorporated into the art and architecture of the period.

Chapter Review

1. Write an account of the structure and decoration of a Hiberno-Romanesque building, using sketches to describe its features.

2. Describe a high cross in the Romanesque style using words and sketches.

3. Using words and sketches, describe the structure and decoration of a piece of metalwork, noting the techniques used in its manufacture.

4. Compare the style and decoration of a piece of metalwork with the decoration on a manuscript. Use sketches to show similarities and differences.

5. What were the outside influences that reached Ireland in the 11th and 12th centuries? What differences did they make to Irish design and craft?

6. Would you describe the decorative elements on Romanesque buildings as sculpture or architecture? Draw examples that illustrate your points.

Further Research

www.what-when-how.com – Scroll to the bottom of the home page and type 'Church reform twelfth century Ireland' into the search bar. Click on the first result for an article outlining the changes to the Church during this period

www.pilgrimagemedievalireland.com – An account of pilgrimage in medieval Ireland

www.google.ie/images – Search for 'Irish Romanesque design' to view images that will help familiarise you with the Hiberno-Romanesque style

irishhighcrosses.com – A description of high crosses by county

www.bl.uk/manuscripts – Type 'Add MS 36929' into the 'Manuscript' search bar to view Cormac's Psalter online

Chapter 27

The Anglo-Norman Period (*c.* 1200–1500s)

By the end of this chapter I will ...

* appreciate the Norman influence on the arts in Ireland
* be able to describe the structure and decoration of a Gothic building
* know about the Gaelic Revival and the affect it had on the arts
* have an understanding of Gothic sculpture in Ireland and be able to draw and describe at least two examples
* have compared the design of the human figure in all the crafts and be able to draw and describe examples
* understand the change to the Gothic style in metalwork and be able to draw and describe two examples.

Context

Europe had experienced a time of prosperity and expansion from about 1150, but the 1300s brought a time of conflict and famine in Europe. A period of bad weather caused crop failures and social unrest. The Hundred Years War between England and France raged from 1337 to 1453. The Black Death swept across Europe from 1346, arriving in Ireland in 1348. A third of Europe's population died from the disease.

Ireland experienced radical change when Diarmaid Mac Murchadha recruited Richard Fitz Gilbert de Clare, a.k.a. 'Strongbow', and other Norman knights from Wales to help him regain his kingdom of Leinster. The first Norman knights arrived in Ireland in 1169, and they captured the Viking cities of Waterford, Wexford and Dublin in quick succession.

Strongbow and King Henry II of England and France had been political opponents, so when the king saw the knights taking areas of territory in Ireland in 1171, he arrived in Waterford with a large army to take control of the situation. The Normans and many of the native kings ultimately acknowledged Henry as Lord of Ireland. This one act changed the political, social and cultural fabric of the country forever.

Initially the Normans built castles, towns and churches in the English style, improving roads and farming practices, and creating a time of prosperity in their territory. Following the Black Death, which affected the English towns more than the Gaelic areas, there was a Gaelic Revival, particularly in the western half of the country. Building, scholarship and the arts flourished for a while in the areas outside the Pale.

The Pale: An area of strong English influence between Drogheda and Dublin.

Innovation and Invention

There was a big change in the arts and crafts following the Norman invasion. Almost everything was made in the English style. Little of the Insular style was seen until the Gaelic Revival, which began in the later 13th century. Buildings and sculpture were in the Gothic style and manuscripts and metalwork were often indistinguishable from European types in the years following the invasion.

Note: Insular art refers to the period from *c.* AD 600 to 900, when Celtic art, with influences of Anglo-Saxon art, was the dominant style in Ireland and parts of Scotland and England. Interlace and other repeating patterns were a significant part of the style. Human (and particularly animal) forms were often stylised and stretched in combination with patterns. The style influenced Romanesque and Gothic art, particularly manuscript decoration. Examples have also been found on the continent where Irish monks had travelled, bringing their manuscripts with them.

Media and Areas of Practice

Architecture

The monastic orders from Europe that had settled in Ireland in the Anglo-Norman period needed larger buildings for their communities. They built in cut stone with well-made arches, door and window openings, finished with stone mouldings. Castles and city walls – also built in stone – appeared all over the country.

Sculpture

English stonemasons built many of the earlier buildings in the English-controlled areas. Stone carving was an integral part of architecture with masons producing the practical work on pillars and arches as well as decorative work.

Manuscripts

Very few manuscripts survive from the 13th century. Some can be dated to the 14th and 15th centuries, but only a few are of notable quality. Books that were produced were mainly in the European style, but the Insular style appeared again in some of the books written under Irish patronage in the west of Ireland.

Metalwork

Almost nothing identifiable as Irish survives from the 13th century. Some fine pieces were made during the Gaelic Revival in the 15th century, but these were in the European style.

Art Elements and Design Principles

Architecture

With the introduction of the Gothic style, architectural forms and decoration were changed. Pointed arches supported on composite pillars were one of the main structural features. Pillar capitals and areas around doorways were often decorated with fine carvings.

Composite pillars: Pillars grouped together to make a support, usually for an arch.

Sculpture

Stone carvers worked on decorated tombs as well as church decoration. The style of the figures and decoration was based on European models. Some wood carvings survive from the 15th century.

Manuscripts

Some capitals in the Insular style survive, but most work was in the European style, even work carried out by Gaelic patrons.

Metalwork

A few quality pieces of 13th-century metalwork survive, but these are again in the European style.

Artists and Artworks

Architecture

In the early years following the Norman invasion, buildings in the towns and cities were made by English tradesmen who had come to work with the knights.

Christ Church Cathedral, Dublin

Christ Church Cathedral was built in the heart of medieval Dublin. Begun in the Romanesque style, the transepts (the arms, in the plan of a cross-shaped church, projecting at right angles from the body of the church) were finished in a transitional style by 1200. The Gothic parts were started in

Triforium · Clerestory windows · The arcade · Rib vault

Figure 27.1 The nave in Christ Church Cathedral, Dublin, is in the 'Early English' Gothic style.

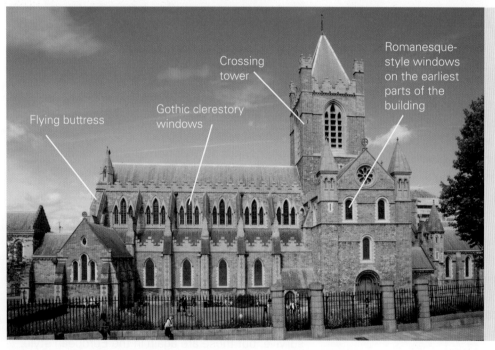

Flying buttress · Gothic clerestory windows · Crossing tower · Romanesque-style windows on the earliest parts of the building

Figure 27.2 Christ Church Cathedral, Dublin. The Romanesque windows surrounded in a pale stone can be seen from here. The flying buttresses supporting the weight of the vault and roof can be identified also.

Rib vaults

Capitals decorated with human heads and leaf patterns

Composite pillars

Figure 27.3
Decorated capitals with human faces and leaves top the columns in the nave of Christ Church Cathedral, Dublin.

the 1230s, during the Anglo-Norman period, and construction finished in about 1240. The cathedral was heavily restored in the 19th century, but many of the important features survive.

Form and Function

This is the cathedral built for the archdiocese of Dublin, beginning in the 1180s. It has a cruciform plan, with a three-stage elevation:

1. An arcade opening onto the aisles at ground level.

2. Triforium arches on the first floor; a gallery which is the upper storey of the aisle is at this level.

3. Clerestory windows allow the light in from above the roof of the aisles.

There is a stone rib-vaulted roof and, outside, flying buttresses support the walls of the Gothic parts of the building.

Technique

This is a full-scale Gothic construction, built in cut stone, requiring teams of stonemasons and labourers. We can get an idea of the time and effort required since the style of architecture changed during the course of construction.

Churches were usually started at the eastern end, where the altar and choir would be built first, so that services could begin while the rest of the church was under construction. Scaffolding was used to build the higher parts and hold up each section of the stone vault while it was being built.

Decoration

The eastern (earlier) end of the building is in the Romanesque style. The south transept still displays some Hiberno-Romanesque features, with chevrons on the arches and capitals with human and animal ornament. The stone and the craftsmen to build the western, Gothic section were imported from Bristol, in the south-west of England. The capitals on the pillars are decorated with human faces peering out from among leaf decoration.

St Patrick's Cathedral, Dublin
Form and Function

Built on a cruciform plan, St Patrick's Cathedral in Dublin also has a three-stage elevation with a rib-vaulted ceiling, like Christ Church. It is the largest cathedral in Ireland.

It was built outside the medieval city walls, to be a cathedral for secular clergy, as a monastic order ran Christ Church. After years of dispute, a 1300

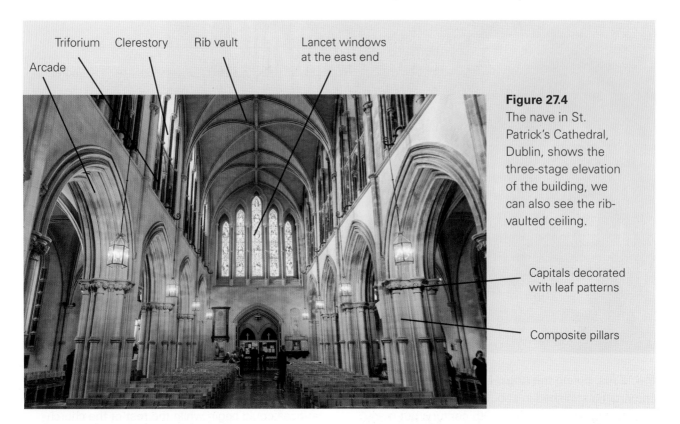

Arcade Triforium Clerestory Rib vault Lancet windows at the east end

Figure 27.4
The nave in St. Patrick's Cathedral, Dublin, shows the three-stage elevation of the building, we can also see the rib-vaulted ceiling.

Capitals decorated with leaf patterns

Composite pillars

agreement made St Patrick's a collegiate church, where the clergy were dedicated to worship and learning. There was a university at the site until the Reformation, and the archbishop of Dublin operated out of both buildings. It is now the national cathedral of the Church of Ireland, while Christ Church is the cathedral of Dublin.

Technique

St Patrick's was built with similar construction techniques to those used for Christ Church.

Decoration

This is a plainer building than Christ Church, and has been much altered over the years. The north wall of the nave gives an impression of the original design.

St Patrick's Cathedral and Christ Church Cathedral are the only 13th-century churches in Ireland with the full Gothic treatment, three-stage elevations and stone-vaulted ceilings. In the rest of the country, full structural Gothic architecture was not often used. Most Irish Gothic churches had wooden roofs, with vaulting used in small areas. The Gothic element was more commonly the decoration on arches, doors and windows.

St Canice's Cathedral, Kilkenny
Form and Function

St Canice's is a cathedral church for the Norman diocese of Kilkenny, built over the period 1210–70. Built on a cruciform plan in the Early English Gothic style, it has a two-storey elevation and a wooden roof over the nave and aisles. There is a low crossing tower supported on tall arches, resting on composite pillars inside the building. The chancel is groin-vaulted.

Technique

The building is made of local limestone. Pointed arches on composite pillars separate the nave from the aisles, while clerestory windows above the arches and a large west window illuminate the interior. The chancel is groin-vaulted and lit by three sets of three lancet windows on the south, east and north walls. All this was the work of skilled masons, who probably came over from England.

Lancet windows: Tall, narrow windows with a pointed arch.

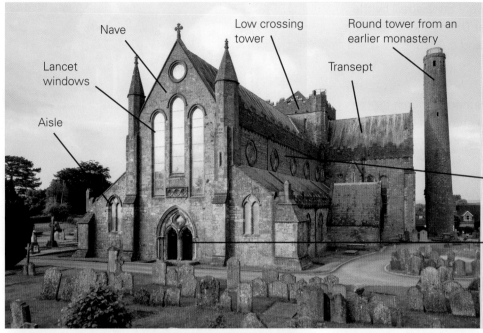

Figure 27.5
St Canice's Cathedral, Kilkenny. Begun in 1210, the cathedral was completed in 1270, in the Early English Gothic style.

Labels on Figure 27.5: Nave; Low crossing tower; Round tower from an earlier monastery; Lancet windows; Transept; Aisle; Clerestory windows in quatrefoil surrounds; West door

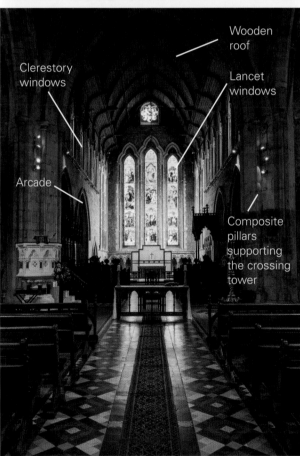

Figure 27.6 The interior of St Canice's Cathedral, Kilkenny, looking east down the nave. The capitals in the nave are plain and there is little decorative carving on the interior fabric.

Labels on Figure 27.6: Wooden roof; Clerestory windows; Lancet windows; Arcade; Composite pillars supporting the crossing tower

Figure 27.7 The west door of St Canice's Cathedral, Kilkenny.

Labels on Figure 27.7: Quatrefoil decoration; Figure and plant carving

Decoration

Quatrefoil (four-leaved) decorations appear in a number of areas. A quatrefoil stone moulding frames the outside of the clerestory windows, the west doorway has a quatrefoil centrepiece and the arches have a four-part decoration.

St Patrick's Cathedral, Cashel

Cashel was in an area of Anglo-Norman influence, even though the archbishops were of Irish decent. It was the centre of an archdiocese, so an impressive building was needed. Cormac's Chapel and the first cathedral (now gone) were quite small by the standards of the churches at Dublin and Kilkenny. It was built between *c.* 1230 and *c.* 1270.

Form and Function

Cashel Cathedral was the cathedral church for the archdiocese of Cashel. It's a cruciform building with a very long choir, a short nave and transepts of equal length. The crossing tower is the only vaulted part of the building. There are no aisles, and the building is lit by lancet windows in the choir and transepts. Because the building is tight up against Cormac's Chapel on its south side, the windows on that side are only at the western end of the nave, beyond the chapel. On the opposite wall, the windows are at the eastern end of the wall so that end of the choir can get light. It's an odd arrangement in terms of the balance of the design.

Technique

The choir is built in sandstone and is the earliest part of the building. Much of the detail in the carving has been weathered away due to this choice of stone. The tower and transepts are built in limestone, which has fared better over the years. The building is constructed with cut stone. Skilful masons carried out the decorative work.

Figure 27.9 The south-eastern pier of the crossing tower at St. Patrick's Cathedral at Cashel, Co. Tipperary.

Decoration

Most of the decoration is very high up, on the ends of the hood mouldings over the windows in the choir. Human faces with downturned mouths and animals from the bestiaries seem to warn of evil. The capitals of the pillars at the crossing are decorated with small human faces among stylised leaf patterns, not quite like the more natural ones in Christ Church Cathedral, Dublin. Again, this decoration is so high up it is difficult to see from the ground.

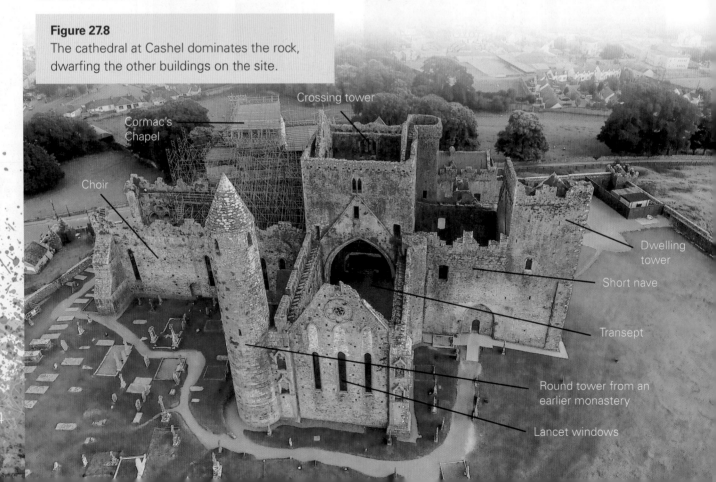

Figure 27.8
The cathedral at Cashel dominates the rock, dwarfing the other buildings on the site.

Crossing tower

Cormac's Chapel

Choir

Dwelling tower

Short nave

Transept

Round tower from an earlier monastery

Lancet windows

Figure 27.10 Faces and foliage from a decorated capital of the crossing tower at Cashel Cathedral.

Research the decorated capitals on some Gothic buildings, Christ Church Cathedral in Dublin or St. Patrick's Cathedral at Cashel have good examples. Make sketches of the faces and natural forms that the sculptors used and make notes to use in your written or studio work.

The Gaelic Revival in Building

A period of famine and the Black Death had a devastating impact on many parts of Europe, but affected English towns more than the rural areas of Ireland. Gaelic chiefs regained territory, and some of the Norman families integrated into Irish society. The settlers who still identified strongly as English were in an area from around Drogheda to below Dublin, called the Pale. Outside this area things were relatively peaceful and prosperous.

The monastic orders that had come in from Europe in the 12th and 13th centuries were now operated by Irish monks. They built a number of religious houses under the patronage of Irish chiefs in the 15th century.

The Franciscans built plain buildings with tall, narrow crossing towers at Quin in Co. Clare, Askeaton and Adare in Co. Limerick, Kilconnell in Co. Galway, and Moyne and Rosserk in Co. Mayo.

Tall crossing tower characteristic of Franciscan friaries

Figure 27.11 Kilconnell Franciscan Friary Co. Galway.

Holycross Abbey, Co. Tipperary

Form and Function

During the Anglo-Norman period, the Cistercians built an elaborate church and abbey at Holycross, Co. Tipperary. They claimed to have a fragment of the true cross, which they kept in a shrine there, drawing pilgrims from all over the country. The contributions made by the pilgrims helped to fund the building of a well-decorated church. The church has been restored and is still used for religious services.

The church is built on a cruciform plan, with a cloister and domestic buildings on the south side. The shrine of the true cross has made the abbey a centre of pilgrimage.

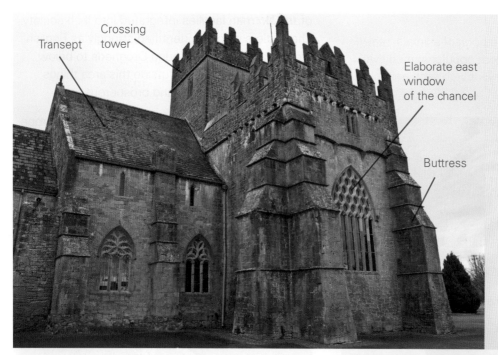

Transept
Crossing tower
Elaborate east window of the chancel
Buttress

Figure 27.12
Holycross Abbey Co. Tipperary, seen from the east. The decorated tracery of the chancel window can be seen.

Technique

Holycross Abbey was constructed in cut stone, with decorative carving of a very high standard. The chancel, north transept, crossing and two chapels in the south transept have good rib-vaulted ceilings.

Decoration

A sedilla (seating place for clergy), known mysteriously as 'the tomb of the good woman's son', has beautifully carved decoration. Three cusped arches edged in decorative leaf patterns surround the openings where the clergy sat. Shields of the Butler family and the kings of England are carved between the tops of the arches. Rows of foliage patterns cover the face of the structure and a stone canopy overhangs it.

> **Cusp:** The pointed end where two curves meet. It can be a projecting point in Gothic decoration.

Other highly decorated parts of Holycross are the walking place (which may have been the location of the shrine of the true cross), some arches and the west doorway.

Canopy
Foliage patterns
Crests of the kings of England
Butler family crest
Cusped arches

Figure 27.13
The sedilla in Holycross Abbey, Co. Tipperary, is decorated with well-executed carvings of leaf patterns.

Tracery

The stone framework that divides large openings into smaller shapes is called tracery. In Ireland, we can see the development of tracery designs, which in turn can help to date the buildings they are found in.

Lancet windows   Switch-line tracery

Cusped tracery   Flamboyant tracery

Figure 27.14 This illustration shows some of the main types of tracery found in Irish Gothic buildings.

The West Doorway at Clontruskert Priory, Co. Galway

A number of decorated doorways survive from the Anglo-Norman period. Notable among them are the sacristy door at Kilcooley Abbey in Co. Tipperary, Dean Odo's door at Clonmacnoise and the west door of Clontruskert Priory in Co. Galway.

Form and Function

The west doorway at Clontruskert is decorated with simple ribs and topped with figures and plant forms in relief. It was the main – formal – door to the church.

Technique

The arches of the doorway are accurately carved in clean, crisp lines. The figures and foliage are carved in relief inside a rectangular frame.

Decoration

The figures above the door represent (from left): St Michael the archangel, weighing souls; St John the Baptist, holding a lamb; St Catherine, with a wheel peeping out from behind her dress; and an unidentified bishop with an impressive crosier. Plant forms outline the arch and make a kind of tree between the figures. A little angel holds a shield in each of the bottom corners of the frame. These figures are in a style that you might find anywhere in Europe: there is no trace of the Irish Insular style.

On each side of the doorway, there are additional carvings. On the left, a rosette, a lion fighting a griffin, and a pelican in her piety. On the right,

Figure 27.15 The west doorway of the Augustinian Priory at Clontruskert, Co. Galway, *c.* 1471.

starting at the top, are a grotesque face, a piece of strap-work, a star, a mermaid with a mirror, two creatures with entwined necks, and what may be a pair of dragons. The number of strange and peculiar images is notable: if fact, these were quite common symbols in medieval times.

> **RESEARCH** Using the internet or the library, try to find out what some of the fantastical carvings on the Clontruskert doorway symbolise. Are any still relevant today? Can you think of any modern equivalents for these symbols?

Secular Architecture

As the Normans took territory from the native Irish, they built strongholds at strategic places to help them hold it. At first, these were just earthen mounds with wooden defensive walls, known as 'motte and bailey' castles. However, as the Normans' grip on the land strengthened, they began to build fortified stone keeps. Castles surrounded by a curtain wall with defensive towers were built at Carrickfergus, Dublin, Limerick, Trim and many other places.

In the 15th century, smaller tower houses were built to defend the borders of the Pale. The Gaelic chiefs copied this style of construction, building more that 2,000 of them. Larger castles were built by the MacNamaras at Bunratty, Co. Clare, in 1425, and taken over by the O'Briens in 1475. Another large castle was built at Cahir, Co. Tipperary.

Figure 27.17 Dunguaire Castle at Kinvarra, Co. Galway, is a good example of the type of larger tower house built by Irish chieftains. It was built by the O'Hynes in 1520.

Sculpture

We have already seen that decorative carving on architecture was practiced to a high standard. Figure carving was becoming more prominent in its own right.

The Cantwell Knight, Kilfane Church, Co. Kilkenny
Form and Function

The Cantwell Knight is a tomb figure carved from a single piece of limestone. It was originally from the top of the stone chest-tomb of a Norman knight, Thomas de Cantwell, who died in 1319.

Figure 27.16 Carrickfergus Castle, Co. Antrim, is defended by a curtain wall with towers.

Figure 27.18 The Cantwell Knight, Kilfane Church, Co. Kilkenny. *c.* 1320. This sculpture is from before the Black Death, when the Normans dominated large areas of the country. The figures from the cloister arcade in Jerpoint Abbey are of a later date.

Technique

The over-size sculpture was carved in the round using iron chisels. The work is of good quality, although some of the rendering of fabrics is a little stiff. It compares very closely with contemporary English examples.

Decoration

The knight is dressed for battle, wearing an iron helmet and chainmail. His cloth surcoat is held closed by his sword belt (the end of the sword can be seen behind his leg). His shield carries the Cantwell family crest. Spurs on his feet show that he fought on horseback. The right leg crossed over the left may indicate that he went on the Crusades.

Chest-tomb at Kilconnell Franciscan Friary, Co. Galway

The figures laid out on tombs, which were a feature in the Pale, are much less common in the Gaelic parts of the country. There, chest-tombs with

Figure 27.19
The little figures carved between the pillars of the cloister arcade at Jerpoint Abbey, Co. Kilkenny, illustrate the style of dress worn by the English settlers in the 14th and 15th centuries.

elaborate tracery over them were the preferred style. These can be found in many churches and abbeys of the 14th and 15th centuries.

Form and Function

The chest-tomb at Kilconnell Franciscan Friary has flamboyant tracery over it, and an area enclosed in a stone frame.

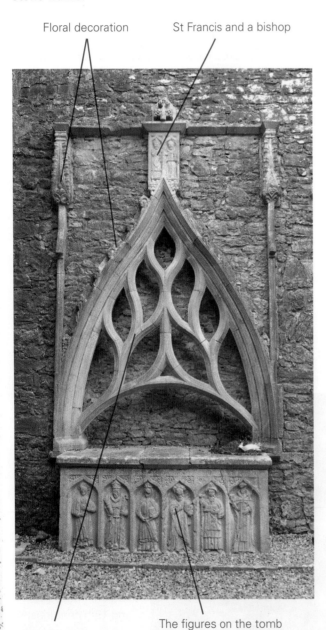

Floral decoration

St Francis and a bishop

Flamboyant tracery

The figures on the tomb chests are sometimes called 'weepers'

Figure 27.20 The chest-tomb and tracery at Kilconnell Friary, Co. Galway, late 15th century.

Technique

The high-quality stone is carved with framework and tracery. Small figures adorn the front of the chest in medium relief. This is a well-executed carving by competent masons.

Decoration

The little figures set in arches on the front of the tomb are St John the Evangelist, St Louis of Toulouse, the Virgin, St John the Baptist, St James of Compostela and St Denis of Paris. These figures compare in style with the figures over the door at Clontruskert priory. The flamboyant tracery is well made and has floral decoration along its outline. Above the arch there are two more figures: St Francis, the founder of the Franciscan order of monks, and an unidentified bishop, both smiling.

Wood Carving

Statues carved in wood were probably common in late medieval times, but little has survived to today. A quite rigid-looking Madonna and child in painted wood from Kilcorban is now in the Diocesan Museum in Loughrea, Co. Galway. It is about 90 cm tall and dates from the 13th century.

The Misericords in St Mary's Cathedral, Limerick

Form and Function

A late 15th-century set of folding seats made for use in the choir can be found in St Mary's Cathedral in Limerick (Fig. 27.21). The seats are made of solid oak, and are carved on the undersides with images of the exotic animals mentioned in the bestiaries. The carved decoration was a reminder of the moral lessons they represented. A small lip on the top of the lifted seat allowed a person standing for a long ceremony to lean back and take a little rest while still appearing to be standing.

Technique

The wood carving is carried out to a high technical and artistic standard, comparing favourably with contemporary English work.

Figure 27.21 The Misericords from St Mary's Cathedral, Limerick. The carvings in dark oak date from the late 15th century.

Decoration

The strange creatures in the carvings are balanced on each side with leaf patterns, creating a harmonious design in the space. Movement and texture are well handled in the designs.

> **RESPOND**
>
> Respond to the figure sculpture of the Gothic period, comparing figures like the Cantwell Knight with the figures from the Kilconnell chest-tomb. Make sketches and take notes to use with your written work or as a starting point for some artwork.

Manuscripts

During the Gaelic Revival, Irish scholars compiled information from older sources, creating genealogies, law tracts and medical and astronomical treatises. Much of the work was written in Irish, in a style of script that had its sources in the 9th century. At the same time, books in Ireland were also being written in the European style. One of the last books to be commissioned in the Gaelic tradition – the Book of the Burkes – was mostly European in style, but with some Irish elements.

The Book of the Burkes
Form and Function

The Book of the Burkes, dating from between 1571 and 1580, was written in Irish and Latin on 75 vellum folios, 22 of which are still blank. It is a genealogy, and attempts to prove the Burke family's connection to kings of England and continental Europe. Some praise poems and law tracts are also included.

Technique

The book was written in the traditional way in pen and ink in the Irish minuscule style. The full pages of decoration are illuminated in bright colours.

Decoration

The fully decorated pages include four scenes from the Passion of Christ, nine Burke portraits and the family coat of arms.

Figure 27.22 A portrait of a knight of the Burke family from the Book of the Burkes, Trinity College Library, Dublin.

Metalwork

Much of the metalwork that survives from the late medieval period was made by Irish craftsmen for Irish patrons, but the style and design of the work was based on European models. Older objects like book shrines were sometimes reworked, replacing work in the Insular style.

The Domhnach Airgid Book Shrine
Form and Function

The Domhnach Airgid ('Silver Church') Book Shrine is a wooden box decorated with metal plates of different dates. The box was made to hold a gospel book associated with St Patrick and a relic of the true cross.

Technique

The shrine was remodelled by the craftsman John O'Bardan for John O'Carbri, the abbot of Clones, in about 1350. This information comes from the inscription, which runs around the border of the box. The Christ figure and the panels on the front are made of cast silver, which has been gilded. A square crystal above Christ's head once held a relic of the true cross.

Decoration

The panel on the top left of the face of the shrine shows the Archangel Michael and the Virgin and Child. On the top right are three apostles, probably James, Peter and Paul, while on the bottom right are three Irish saints, St Columcille, St Brigit and St Patrick. The scene on the bottom left shows St Patrick presenting the book, which was enclosed in the shrine, to St MacCartan.

The figure of the crucified Christ is very worn, probably from pilgrims touching the shrine as a mark of respect. A little dove beside his head represents the Holy Spirit. All the figures are in the Gothic style and can be compared with figures from the Kilconnell chest-tomb and the doorway at Clontruskert.

The O'Dea Crosier

Bishop Cornelius O'Dea of Limerick commissioned Tomas O'Carryd to make him a crosier and mitre in 1418. These objects are still in the ownership of the bishop of Limerick, and are on display in the Hunt Museum. The O'Dea Crosier (Fig. 27.24) is the only one of its kind in Ireland.

Form and Function

This richly decorated crook is a symbol of the bishop's authority, which would be displayed on special occasions. The crosier is made of silver, and stands at 197 cm tall.

Figure 27.23
The silver-gilt panels on the front of the Domhnach Airgid book shrine were made in the Gothic style by an Irish craftsman in *c.* 1350.

Figure 27.24
The O'Dea
Crosier.

Technique

The crosier has been cast in silver with areas of gold, outlined in a cast floral pattern. Enamel is used for the background colour behind the figures, and as a floral pattern along the side of the crook.

Decoration

Inside the loop of the crosier is a tiny nativity scene. Below this, little canopies shelter images of six female saints incised into metal plates on a background of enamel. Larger, more richly-decorated canopies below these house three-dimensional figurines of the Trinity, St Peter and St Paul, St Patrick, the Virgin Mary and an unknown bishop. An enamel knob below the crook has an inscription on it. The style of the crosier is Gothic, comparable with English examples from the same period.

The Lislaughtin Processional Cross

Form and Function

This decorated metal cross with a figure of the crucified Christ was made for the Franciscan friary at Lislaughtin, Co. Kerry (Fig. 27.25). The inscription on the cross says that Cornelius O'Connor and his wife, Avlina, had it made for the friary in 1479. It was found in 1871 by a farmer ploughing near the monastery.

Technique

The cross is made of sheet silver, which has been pierced to create areas of openwork. The Christ figure and the knob below the cross have been cast in silver, but all parts of the cross are gilded. The lozenge-shaped projections on the knob once held enamel.

Figure 27.25
The Lislaughtin Processional Cross, National Museum of Ireland, Dublin.

Decoration

The roundels at the ends of the arms of the cross contain images of the evangelists: the winged lion of St Mark, the ox of St Luke and the eagle of St John. The central roundel over Christ's head is empty, but it would probably have held the winged man symbol for St Matthew. The Christ figure, head inclined, is in the Gothic style.

Other Late Medieval Work

The deBurgo-O'Malley Chalice, the O'Dea Mitre and priest's vestments from Waterford are among the other treasures that have survived from this time. All were designed and made in the Gothic style.

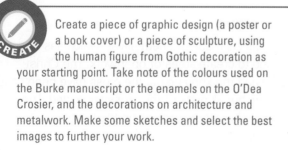

Create a piece of graphic design (a poster or a book cover) or a piece of sculpture, using the human figure from Gothic decoration as your starting point. Take note of the colours used on the Burke manuscript or the enamels on the O'Dea Crosier, and the decorations on architecture and metalwork. Make some sketches and select the best images to further your work.

Analysis

The Gothic style became dominant in Ireland in the 13th century. Try to work out the causes for this change. Look at examples of architecture and craftwork, see who the work was being made for and who was making it. Look at the style of the human figure on architecture, in sculpture, in manuscript design and in metalwork: what do they have in common? There were changes in the use of line and form, in texture and colour. Look for examples like the Book of the Burkes or the misericords in Limerick Cathedral to explore these differences, which can also be found in sculpture and metalwork.

The Gothic style likely came to Ireland through the influence of the European monastic orders and the Church reforms that had begun to take root in the early 12th century. The Norman-English influence was strong, particularly in the east of the country, where they imposed their culture on the region with no concessions to native traditions. The Gaelic Revival of the 1400s had lost the link to the Irish Insular style, so the buildings and craftwork were carried out for the most part in the Gothic style.

After the Late Medieval Period

The Anglo-Norman period in Ireland was scarred with invasion and struggles between Gaels and the European knights who had taken over large parts of the country. When King Henry VIII of Britain and Ireland broke with the pope in 1533 and took the Church into his own control, he set in motion a process that would lead to the dissolution of the monasteries in both kingdoms.

The efforts by the English crown to subdue rebellion in Ireland went on for centuries. People from England and Scotland were given land in Ireland and the natives were invited to go to Connacht. With all this conflict in the country, it is unsurprising that little in terms of art and architecture has survived.

Chapter Review

1. Describe the 'full Gothic treatment' in a building you have studied: the three-stage elevation, the vaulting and the decoration. Use sketches to help make your points.

2. Write an account of a building in the Gaelic Revival style. Describe its structure and decoration in words and sketches.

3. Using words and sketches, describe a piece of Gothic sculpture that appeals to you, noting style, subject and technique.

4. What differences do you notice between sculptures made in the Norman areas of Ireland and the sculptures of the Gaelic Revival? Compare two examples using words and sketches.

5. Describe an example of a piece of metalwork in the Gothic style, noting its structure and decoration in words and sketches.

6. Compare the metalwork of the Gothic era with Romanesque examples. What were the main changes in style and technique? Describe an object in each style, using sketches to illustrate your points.

7. 'The art of the Anglo-Norman period was about memorialising and glorifying people who considered themselves important.' Discuss this statement, using examples to support your viewpoint.

Further Research

www.history.com/topics/middle-ages/black-death – Learn more about the causes and results of the Black Death

www.virtualvisittours.com/christ-church-cathedral – Explore Christ Church Cathedral, Dublin, remotely on a phone or computer

www.stpatrickscathedral.ie – Click on 'Learn' then 'Life and History' for a short video introduction to St Patrick's Cathedral, Dublin

monastic.ie – Photographs and some information on Kilconnell Friary and Clontruskert Priory, Co. Galway

www.holycrossabbey.ie – The official website of Holycross Abbey, Co. Tipperary

www.thejournal.ie – Search for 'best medieval statue Ireland Kilkenny' for an article on some of the medieval sculptures in the Kilkenny area

www.misericords.co.uk/limerick.html – Close-up photographs of the misericords in St Mary's Cathedral, Limerick

limerickdioceseheritage.org – Search for 'O'Dea Crozier' to learn more about the bishop's crook

irisharchaeology.ie – Search for 'Domhnach Airgid' to see a 2015 article about the book shrine

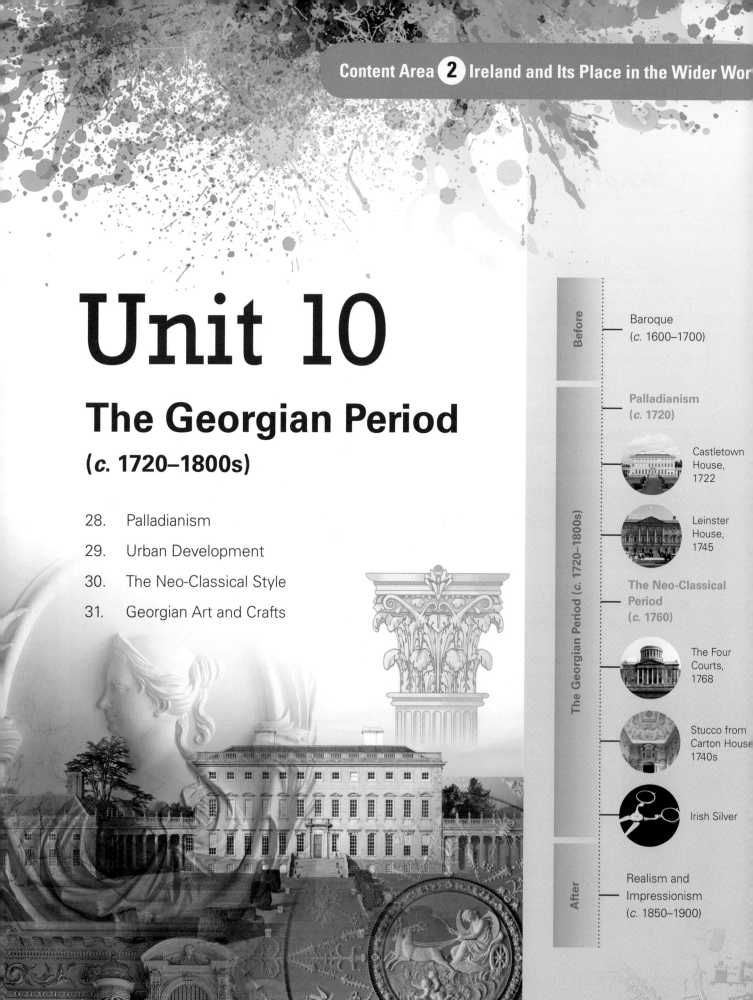

Unit 10

The Georgian Period

(*c.* 1720–1800s)

Before

Baroque
(*c.* 1600–1700)

Palladianism
(*c.* 1720)

Castletown
House,
1722

Leinster
House,
1745

The Neo-Classical
Period
(*c.* 1760)

The Four
Courts,
1768

Stucco from
Carton House
1740s

Irish Silver

The Georgian Period (*c.* 1720–1800s)

After

Realism and
Impressionism
(*c.* 1850–1900)

Chapter 28

Palladianism

By the end of this chapter I will ...

* understand the social and political background to the arts and culture of the Georgian era
* understand suitable terminology to explain the structure and decoration of architecture at the time
* be familiar with the construction and decoration of large country houses
* be familiar with some public buildings built in the expanding city of Dublin
* be able to describe two buildings by Sir Edward Lovett Pearce and Richard Cassels
* understand the contrast between the exteriors and interiors of Palladian buildings.

Before the Georgian Period

In the early 1700s, Ireland was beginning to recover from a long period of war and social unrest. The Cromwellian campaigns and the war between William III (William of Orange) and James II ended when the Catholic Irish and Anglo-Normans were finally defeated at the Siege of Limerick in 1691. Land was confiscated from Catholics and given to English, Scottish and Welsh settlers. Landless Irish people were banished to Connacht.

Poyning's Law, dating from 1494, forbade parliament meeting in Ireland without the permission of the English king. The Penal Laws, drawn up in the 16th and 17th centuries, limited the rights of Roman Catholics and Presbyterians in England and Ireland. They could not hold public office, vote, be a member of one of the professions, own land or be educated. Priests could be put to death. These laws were enforced to varying degrees. Catholics still owned up to 20 per cent of the land and Catholic priests operated under license.

Against this background there was not much development in the arts in Ireland. One of the few innovative buildings was constructed to accommodate wounded and disabled soldiers. The Royal Hospital (now the Irish Museum of Modern Art) in Kilmainham, Dublin, built between 1679 and 1687, was designed by Sir William Robinson with some classical features (Fig. 28.1).

Context

The term 'Georgian' refers to a variety of styles in architecture and the decorative arts. It was a development of styles flexible enough to allow for changes in taste and fashion, including Baroque (see Chapter 7, p. 106), Rococo, Greek, Neo-Classical, Egyptian and Oriental design, each of which held sway for a time.

Figure 28.1
The Royal Hospital at Kilmainham, Dublin, was based on the design of the Hôtel National des Invalides in Paris, which also housed invalid soldiers. It is one of the earliest Irish buildings to have classical features.

The name Georgian comes from the successive King Georges of England, from George I, who became king in 1714, to George IV, who died in 1830. The style is characterised by good craftsmanship in a classical system of design and proportion (Fig. 28.2).

Classical proportions: The principles of design and proportion used in Greek and Roman architecture. They were revived in Renaissance times and again in the Georgian period.

Figure 28.2 The classical orders

Labels: Pediment, Cornice, Frieze, Architrave, Doric capital, Fluted column, Base, Doric, Ionic capital, Corinthian capital, Composite capital, Tuscan capital

Political and Social Background

Following the final defeat of the Irish chieftains in 1691, there was a period of peace and prosperity in Ireland where the Anglo-Irish landlords became wealthy. There was a strong export trade in wool, linen and agricultural produce, particularly salt beef, pork and butter. Trading and export centres in the towns and ports of Ireland often have well-built streets of Georgian buildings and market houses. While the wealth and patronage was largely in the hands of the Protestant minority, the artisans and tradesmen were often native Irish Catholics. Dublin became one of the largest and most prosperous cities in Europe.

Organisations were set up for the improvement of agriculture, industry and the arts. The Dublin Society, founded in 1731 (it later became the Royal Dublin Society, which still operates in Ballsbridge in Dublin), sponsored research and awarded prizes to encourage industry and crafts. The Wide Streets Commission, set up in 1757, regulated planning

Figure 28.3
The Irish House of Commons,
1780, by Francis Wheatley.
This is the only record of what
the interior of the Irish House
of Commons looked like.
The painting shows Grattan's
famous speech on the repeal
of Poynings' Law. The public
gallery is full of spectators.

and street design in Dublin city, which was going
through a phase of expansion.

A Dublin parliament, run by the Protestant Anglo-
Irish gentry, gained independence from the English
parliament at Westminster for a short period,
following a motion proposed by Henry Grattan in
1782. However, Grattan's parliament was short-lived
because, following the Irish rebellion of 1798, the
Act of Union was passed in 1800, which created
the United Kingdom of Britain and Ireland, with one
parliament in Westminster.

The Grand Tour

This was the age of the 'Grand Tour', when people
of wealth and education visited the sights of Europe,
with particular attention given to Classical and
Renaissance arts and architecture. The sights of Rome
and Florence and the works of art being revealed
at Pompeii influenced returning tourists to attempt
classical design in their own public and private
buildings.

Search for 'Grand Tour of Europe' on
www.thoughtco.com and read the article
'Grand Tour of Europe in the 17th and 18th
Centuries' for a short account of the origins of the
Grand Tour. This may help your understanding of the
classical influences coming to Ireland at the time.

Andrea Palladio

Andrea Palladio (1508–80) had an enormous influence
on architecture through his books *I Quattro Libri
dell'Architettura*, which were published in 1570
and translated into *The Four Books of Architecture*
in England in 1715–20. These books contained
drawings of plans and elevations of Palladio's
buildings and advice on proportions, building
materials, the 'correct' classical orders, porticos,
columns and other useful details. Palladio offered
a system of proportions 'as immutable as the
harmonies of music', which harmonised all parts
of his designs. His theories were based on the
books by the Roman architect Vitruvius and his own
measurements of classical buildings in Rome.

Palladio designed houses for wealthy Venetians in
the surrounding countryside. The houses combined
elegant living space for the owner with outbuildings
for animals and farm work, a self-sufficient unit. This
arrangement proved popular with Irish and English
country gentlemen, who built a great number of
houses, both large and small, in the style.

Innovation and Invention

The style and design that we see in this chapter
was really the great innovation of the Georgian

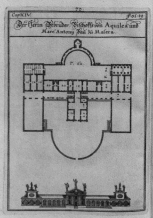

Figure 28.4 The Villa Barbaro, Maser, Italy, 1558, by Andrea Palladio. The photograph of the house shows some changes from Palladio's design in his *Four Books of Architecture*, which was an important source of ideas for Georgian architects.

period. There were no new materials or techniques developed in the fine arts, but the quality of craftsmanship improved in all fields.

Technology was also improving, for instance accurate clocks allowed sailors to work out longitude which had been a problem until then. This allowed for the making of accurate charts and voyages of exploration around the world.

New iron-casting techniques made building bridges and other structures possible. Iron railings, balconies and street furniture are a feature of Georgian terraces.

The construction of the first canals began in Ireland in 1756, improving trade and transport.

Literacy rates were improving, and daily and weekly newspapers improved communications.

These improvements in transport and communications helped the spread of new ideas in the arts and crafts and the movement of tradespeople and heavy materials.

Media and Areas of Practice

The Palladian Style in Ireland

Palladian buildings in Ireland were often truer to Palladian ideals than English examples; this may be because some of the architects came directly from Europe and were not influenced by the English version of the style. Irish interiors were often more elaborate with Baroque and Rococo style plasterwork in high relief.

Note: **The Layout of a Palladian-style House**

The central block was often square in plan, with a temple front of columns and a triangular pediment forming a portico over the formal entrance, generally of two floors over a basement.

The basement was often of rusticated stone, containing the kitchen, services and minor rooms.

The ground floor, referred to as the *piano nobile* ('noble floor'), would have been reached by a flight of steps leading to the entrance. Inside were the main reception rooms and master bedroom. This floor would have the tallest windows and most spacious rooms.

The top floor had lower ceilings and contained bedrooms and rooms of lesser importance. The windows were often square on this level.

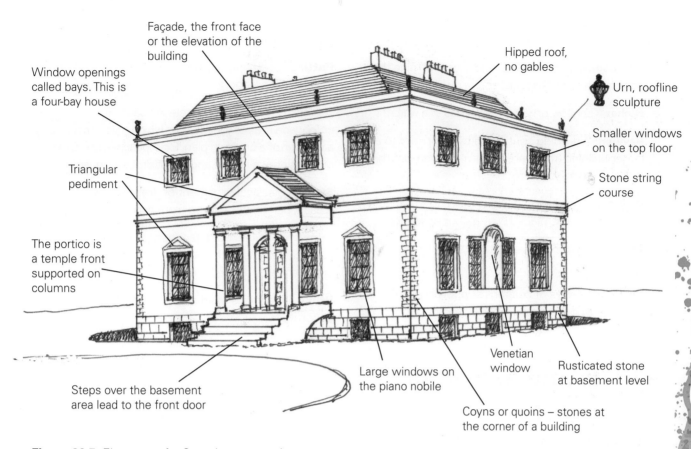

Figure 28.5 Elements of a Georgian country house.

Labels on figure:
- Façade, the front face or the elevation of the building
- Window openings called bays. This is a four-bay house
- Triangular pediment
- The portico is a temple front supported on columns
- Steps over the basement area lead to the front door
- Large windows on the piano nobile
- Coyns or quoins – stones at the corner of a building
- Venetian window
- Rusticated stone at basement level
- Stone string course
- Smaller windows on the top floor
- Urn, roofline sculpture
- Hipped roof, no gables

Terminology

There is a lot of terminology associated with classical architecture. We will introduce some here that may help your understanding of the buildings in this chapter.

Arcade: A row of arches, supported on columns or pilasters.

Architrave: A formal beam or lintel which is the lowest part of an entablature.

Balustrade: A row of upright 'balusters' supporting a hand-rail in a stairs or supporting a cornice to form a parapet.

Bay: Often used to describe a window opening in a building. A house with four windows across its front elevation might be described as four bays wide.

Cherub: A chubby, winged, male infant or winged infant's head.

Colonnade: A row of columns.

Cornice: The top, finishing element on a classical structure.

Cupola: A small dome.

Elevation: Another word for a façade, or a drawing of any vertical aspect of a building.

Engaged: Applied or attached. Most often an engaged column, which is physically attached or embedded in the surface of a wall.

Entablature: The horizontal elements resting on top of a row of pillars, comprising the architrave, frieze and cornice.

Façade: The external face of a building, particularly the front.

Fanlight: A glazed window over a door, semi-circular in shape, with radiating glazing bars, suggesting an open fan.

Frontispiece: An elaborate entrance forming the central element in a façade.

Niche: A shallow ornamental recess in a wall.

Pavilion: A building connected by a corridor to a larger building (there are other meanings, but this is the relevant one here).

Pediment: A projecting gable, with a low triangular or curved shape, placed over a door or window.

Pilasters: A decorative rectangular pillar attached to a wall.

Portico: A series of columns supporting a roof, creating a porch on the façade of a building.

Putti: Chubby male babies, without wings, used in classical decoration.

Quadrant: Quarter of a circle. A quadrant colonnade is a row of columns which follow a curve, a quarter of a circle, in plan. Examples can be seen on Castletown House and Russborough House.

Swag: A classical ornament of drapes, flowers, or foliage, hanging in a curve from two points.

Temple front: Part of a façade resembling a classical temple, with columns carrying an entablature and a pediment.

Urn: A lidded vase used as an architectural decoration.

Artists and Artworks

Sir Edward Lovett Pearce (1699–1733)

Born in Co. Meath, Pearce went to England to study architecture after the death of his father in 1715. He studied with his father's cousin, the famous English Baroque architect Sir John Vanbrugh who was working on the design of Blenheim Palace at the time. After a spell in the army, Pearce travelled to France and Italy for three years to study architecture. He had a copy of Palladio's *Quattro Libri*, which he annotated with his own sketches and observations on the buildings he saw. He met Alessandro Galilei, the designer of Castletown House, in Florence.

Pearce was one of the most influential architects of his day and is credited with bringing the Palladian style to Ireland. Castletown House, Drumcondra House (All Hallows College), Bellamont Forest and Cashel Palace were among the large country houses that he worked on. The Parliament House (Bank of Ireland) in College Green, Dublin, was his greatest and most influential public building.

Castletown House, Co. Kildare

Castletown House is the earliest and largest of about two dozen large country houses that were built in Ireland between 1716 and 1745. It was built for William Conolly, who had risen from humble beginnings to become one of the richest and most powerful men in Ireland. He made a vast fortune from land deals and rose to political prominence as the Speaker of the Irish House of Commons.

The Italian architect Alessandro Galilei was commissioned to design the house. He came to Ireland in 1719. He spent less than a year on the job, producing drawings of the front elevation and probably the plan, and then he departed, leaving others to carry out the work, which was begun in 1722. Sir Edward Lovett Pearce took over the project in 1724 on his return from his Grand Tour in Europe. He designed the quadrant Ionic colonnades that join Galilei's central block, built in pale limestone, to the two end pavilions, which are in a warm brown limestone (Fig. 28.6).

Castletown is the first large country house in Ireland to be designed by a professional architect using classical proportions.

Exterior

The central block is in the style of an Italian town palazzo, 13 bays wide. The building is three storeys over a basement. A set of broad steps reaches the main entrance across the open area in front of the basement. The tallest windows are on the ground floor. The first-floor windows each have a pediment, alternately curved and triangular. The windows on the top floor are square. A balustrade at roof level helps to conceal the hipped roof. A matching balustrade runs along the top of the colonnades and continues along the roof level of the wings, creating unity and symmetry in the whole composition.

Interior

There is a double-height entrance hall, which was designed by Pearce (Fig. 28.7). He used Ionic columns around the walls and to support a balcony that connects to the central corridor on the first floor. The columns in the hall match the colonnades outside. This balconied hall, with its black and white stone floor tiles, was frequently copied in other Irish houses and is the only part of Castletown that survives unchanged from Speaker Conolly's time.

Many of the features of Castletown's interior date from the late 1750s when Tom Conolly, grandnephew of the Speaker, inherited the estate. He married Lady Louisa Lennox in 1758; she was the daughter of the Duke of Richmond and a granddaughter of Charles II of England. Louisa was only 15 at the time of her marriage, but she took over the management and decoration of the house with some enthusiasm. She ordered the beautiful

Stone floor tiles   Ionic columns

Figure 28.7 Castletown House entrance hall, designed by Sir Edward Lovett Pearce. In this double-height hallway, you can see windows from ground and first floor levels.

cantilevered stairway (the end of each stair tread was built into the wall without external supports) built in Portland stone, and the plasterwork on the walls of the stairwell, which was carried out by Filippo and Paulo Lafranchini, the Swiss-Italian stuccadores (see p. 449). The plasterwork consists of floral swags, cherubs and family portraits in a high-relief Rococo style. In the 1760s, Louisa, with her sister and friends, decorated the walls of one of the ground floor rooms with mezzotints and engravings, creating the only 'print room' still surviving in Ireland.

Figure 28.6 Castletown House, Co. Kildare (front elevation), designed by Alessandro Galilei and Sir Edward Lovett Pearce.

Quadrant colonade

Pediments, alternately curved and triangular

Balustrades

Roofline sculptures in the form of urns

Figure 28.8 The Long Gallery at Castletown House. The large room had a carefully balanced decoration scheme.

In the 1770s, the Long Gallery was completely redecorated. The room, which is more than 24 m × 7 m, is at the rear of the first floor (Fig. 28.8). The walls are decorated with paintings in the Pompeian style by Thomas Ryder. The room has eight windows overlooking the gardens; Conolly's Folly (1740) can be seen in the distance. The wall opposite the windows has two doors with a niche between them, which contains a statue of Diana the Huntress. Above the doors is a large semi-circular (lunette) oil painting, a version of Guido Reni's *Aurora*. Other oil paintings are incorporated into the decoration scheme, including portraits of Tom and Lady Louisa Conolly over the fireplaces at each end

of the room. All the elements of the room design – including paintings, niches, sculptures, mirrors and even the coloured glass chandeliers specially ordered from Venice – were carefully balanced in a symmetrical arrangement of all the parts. The Conollys used this enormous room as their family living room where they could have family meals, play games or music and entertain close friends. Several activities could go on at the same time without interfering with each other.

Bellamont Forest, Co. Cavan

Begun in 1730, Bellamont Forest (Fig. 28.9) is a smaller villa that Pearce designed for his uncle, Thomas Coote, who was Lord Justice of Ireland. Compared to Castletown it is a very plain structure, almost square in plan.

Exterior

The building is constructed of locally fired red brick, with details picked out in cut limestone. The entrance front has a portico, which consists of a pediment supported on Doric columns approached by broad steps. The windows on the ground floor are also pedimented. Pearce used stone to outline the *piano nobile*. A stringcourse that runs around the building at portico level and corner stones (quoins) create a kind of frame to emphasise the most important rooms of the house. The basement is of rusticated stone, with deep joints and a roughened

Figure 28.9 Bellamont Forest, Co. Cavan. The entrance front is a pediment supported on Doric columns.

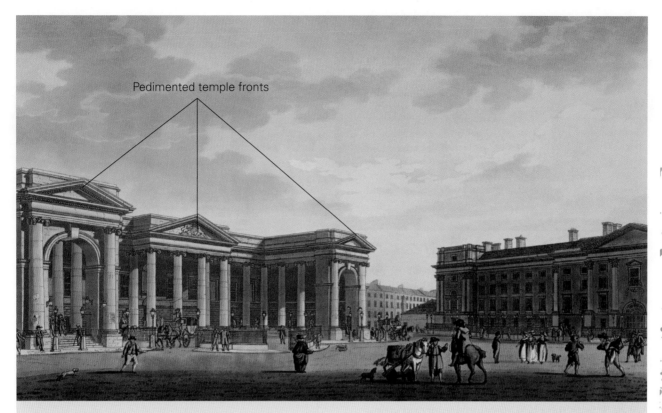

Pedimented temple fronts

Figure 28.10 The Irish Parliament (now the Bank of Ireland), College Green, Dublin, designed by Sir Edward Lovett Pearce. The three fronts and the forecourt can be seen clearly in this print.

surface. The upper floor has square windows. The Venetian windows on the side elevations were often copied by later architects.

Interior

The colonnaded lobby on the top (bedroom) floor, which is lit from above by a lantern window, was also frequently copied. There is some good high-relief plasterwork in the interior.

The Parliament House (Bank of Ireland)

Parliament House (Fig. 28.10) is considered to be the most important early Palladian public building in Britain or Ireland. It was the first structure designed to hold two houses of parliament: it contained chambers for the Commons and the Lords of the Irish parliament.

Interior

The House of Commons (see Fig. 28.3) was at the centre of Pearce's design. A large octagonal space

covered by a dome, it was damaged by fire in 1792 and removed when the building was converted to a bank in the early 19th century. This chamber was surrounded on three sides by a corridor of top-lit domed squares, which became a feature of Pearce's work.

The House of Lords, which is set off to the east side of the Commons, retains many of its original features (Fig. 28.11). In plan it is quite like a church with an apse (a semi-circular area projecting from the wall of a building) at the eastern end. It still retains its original plasterwork and a carved oak fireplace. The decoration includes large tapestries of the Battle of the Boyne and the Siege of Derry by Jan van Beaver and a Waterford crystal chandelier made of over 1,000 pieces of glass.

Exterior

Pearce's design for the entrance incorporates three temple fronts. The ends facing the street combine round-headed arches with pediments overhead. The central portico supports a pediment on four Ionic columns, with roofline figure sculptures by

Figure 28.11 (left) The interior of the House of Lords. This chamber has many of its original features.

Figure 28.12 (right) Parliament House, Westmoreland Street entrance, designed by James Gandon in 1782 as a separate entrance to the House of Lords.

Edward Smyth (who we will learn about later in the unit) representing Commerce, Fidelity and Hibernia. An Ionic colonnade connects these three temple fronts; in plan it is like a letter *E*. The central portico is set back from the ends, creating a forecourt where parliamentarians could make a formal entrance in their horse-drawn carriages. The Parliament House would have been the most impressive building in Dublin of its day. It influenced the design of other public architecture in Britain and Ireland.

Later Additions

The building in its present form includes a Corinthian temple front entrance on the east (Westmoreland Street) side, designed by James Gandon in 1782 as a separate entrance for the House of Lords (Fig. 28.12). Gandon also designed the curved wall with niches, which connects his entrance to Pearce's colonnade. Later, a portico and screen wall were built on the west side and pilasters were added to Gandon's wall to harmonise the whole composition.

A Short but Influential Life

Pearce spent only seven years working in Ireland, but in that time he changed the direction of Irish architecture. He died in 1733 at the age of 34, with some of his work unfinished. Richard Cassels, who had been his assistant on a number of projects, took over the practice and became the leading architect in the country working in the Palladian style.

Design a piece of craftwork using classical design elements. Make sketches of some of the internal and external decorations on Palladian buildings as your source material.

Find out more about the decorative elements found on Palladian buildings. The best way to see these elements is by visiting a Palladian building, but you can also research decorative features online.

Richard Cassels, Cassel or Castle (1690–1751)

Born in Hesse-Kassel in Germany of a Huguenot family with a background in architecture, Cassels trained originally as a military engineer but became interested in Palladian architecture when he was working in England in 1725. Sir Gustavus Hume brought him to Enniskillen in Co. Fermanagh in 1728 to design a house for him; he was also working with Pearce on the Parliament House that same year.

Cassels was an innovator in his plans for country houses. He designed an oval drawing room at the rear of Ballyhaise in Co. Cavan (now the Agricultural College) and he put semi-circular bay windows on the side elevations of Belvedere House in Co. Westmeath. These features became popular in Ireland and England, but not until years later.

Russborough House near Blessington, Co. Wicklow

Russborough House (Fig. 28.13) is a high point in Irish Palladian country house design. It was begun in 1741 for Joseph Leeson, the first Earl of Milltown, and built in local granite.

Exterior

The façade is over 200 m long and includes a central block, six bays wide, connected by quadrant arcades to two pavilions, each seven bays wide. Walls continue beyond the pavilions to outbuildings at each end. There is a Baroque arch, topped with a cupola, at the centre of each wall to add interest and relief to the composition.

It is a perfect example of Palladio's idea of combining the master's house within the structures of a working farm. The buildings on the west side contained the stables. The kitchens and other out offices were on the east side. Many of the original features have survived intact. Stone, statuary, inlaid floors, mantles and plasterwork are all original and in good condition.

The central block of Russborough is two storeys over a basement. The entrance is reached by a stairway, which is the full width of the frontispiece, which consists of four engaged Corinthian columns with floral swags between the capitals. These support a triangular pediment, which is applied to the wall. There is a semicircular fanlight over the door. String courses at pediment and roof level create a horizontal emphasis. Cassels used urns as roofline sculptures on the main house as well as on the arcades and the wings.

Interior

The simplicity, even severity, of the exterior of Russborough is in contrast with the lavish Baroque and Rococo interior. There are seven interconnected reception rooms on the *piano nobile*, all 6 m tall. Apart from the dining room, each room has coved ceilings (curved where the ceiling meets the wall). Dado rails in carved mahogany 1.2 m high help to reduce the apparent height of the rooms. Carved mahogany is also used on the doors, stairs and banisters. The floor of the saloon is also mahogany with satinwood inlay (Fig. 28.14).

The Lafranchini brothers, whose work we noted at Castletown, decorated several of the ceilings. In the saloon, *The Loves of the Gods* are represented by cherubs and figure groups framed by plant forms and swags. The plasterwork at Russborough is considered to be the finest in the country.

Other Country Houses

Cassels designed many of the great Georgian country houses in Ireland including Powerscourt House, Co. Wicklow, Carton House, Co. Kildare and Westport House, Co. Mayo. He also designed some large town houses in Dublin, the first to be built in cut stone in an otherwise brick streetscape. These included Newman House in St Stephen's Green, Tyrone House in Marlborough Street (now part of the Department of Education and Skills), Powerscourt Townhouse (now a shopping centre) and the largest of them, Leinster House, in Kildare Street (which is now the Dáil, the seat of the Irish government).

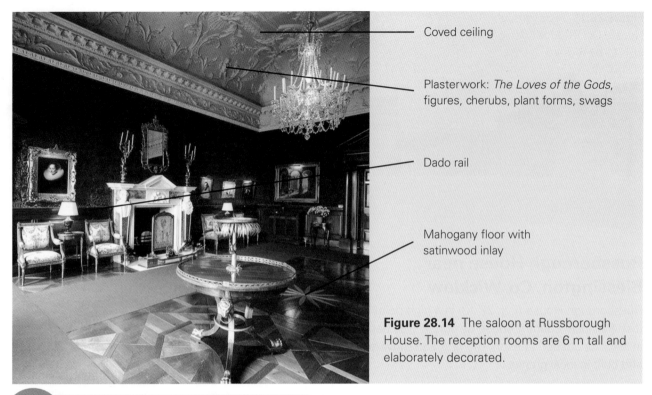

Coved ceiling

Plasterwork: *The Loves of the Gods*, figures, cherubs, plant forms, swags

Dado rail

Mahogany floor with satinwood inlay

Figure 28.14 The saloon at Russborough House. The reception rooms are 6 m tall and elaborately decorated.

Discuss with your classmates both the merits and the problems with the way of life represented through the design and decoration of these large country houses.

Leinster House

Originally built in 1745 as a town house for the 22-year-old James Fitzgerald, the 20th Earl of Kildare and the 1st Duke of Leinster, Leinster House is basically a Palladian country mansion relocated into the city (Fig. 28.15). The entrance front on Kildare Street is built in fine Ardbraccan limestone and the simpler Leinster Lawn front is built in granite. It is set back from the building line behind its own forecourt.

Exterior

The central block is three storeys tall and 11 bays wide. The entrance is emphasised by a three-bay

Curved pediment

Three-bay breakfront

Corinthian columns

Triangular pediment

Balustrade

Rusticated ground level on breakfront

String course

Fig. 28.15 Leinster House (Kildare Street front), designed for the Duke of Leinster by Richard Cassels.

breakfront, which runs the full height of the building. The ground floor of this section is rusticated, and a plain moulding surrounds the doorway. At first-floor level a balustrade connects four Corinthian columns, which support a triangular pediment at roof level. The windows of the first floor have curved and triangular pediments like those on the *piano nobile* at Castletown.

Interior

There is a double-height hall with a balcony, like the one at Castletown. A surprising amount of the original decoration survives, considering its changes of use over the years, including some good plasterwork by the Lafranchini brothers.

Davis Ducart (Daviso de Arcort)

A Sardinian architect and engineer, he worked mainly in the south of Ireland in the 1760s. The Custom House, now the Hunt Museum, in Limerick is thought to be one of his earliest designs (Fig. 28.16). His style was a Franco-Italian version of Palladianism, which sometimes looked more modern than contemporary work.

The entrance front of the Custom House faces the river. It has a rusticated ground floor with three arches at the centre supporting the frontispiece, which has fluted pilasters supporting a simple entablature. He uses a straight arcade as the connection to the end pavilions rather than the curved versions used by other architects in Ireland.

Ducart designed several buildings in Cork: the Mayoralty House, Lota and Kilshannig, which has beautiful plasterwork by the Lafranchini in their later, lighter style.

Ducart's masterpiece is considered to be Castletown Cox in Co. Kilkenny. Castletown Cox is seven bays wide and three storeys over a basement, built in fine cut limestone. Straight arcades again connect the house to domed pavilions, which form the corners of two L-shaped courtyards at the rear of the house. There is a very fine interior, with plasterwork by Patrick Osborne of Waterford.

Art Elements and Design Principles

These were the first buildings formally designed by architects in Ireland. Great care was taken with the symmetrical arrangement of all the parts of the buildings, outside and in. Decoration followed classical models. Pillar capitals were in the classical styles seen in Figure 28.2. Columns were used in balanced groups to develop depth and interest in the surface of the buildings. These architects were very conscious of shape, form and texture, balancing areas of plain wall with framed hollow

Figure 28.16
The Custom House, Limerick (riverfront), now the Hunt Museum, designed by Davis Ducart.

spaces like windows and niches and contrasting smooth wall surfaces with rusticated stone. Inside plasterwork was used to decorate and add texture to wall surfaces with symmetrical arrangements of natural forms.

In summary, Palladian architectural design includes: classical proportion, symmetry, temple fronts, Venetian windows, and the use of classical orders on columns.

Chapter Review

1. What was Palladio's influence on Irish architecture? Use words and sketches to describe two buildings that show Palladio's influence.

2. Describe in words and sketches a public building designed by Sir Edward Lovett Pearce. You should note features of the exterior and interior decoration of the building.

3. Richard Cassels designed a number of country and city houses. Write an account of a country house designed by him and use sketches to describe some decorative features from the exterior and the interior.

4. What were the influences that gentlemen brought back from the Grand Tour? Did it change their taste in art and architecture? Explain.

5. Compare a country mansion to a public building, noting differences in scale and decoration. Use words and sketches to make your comparisons.

6. Look at the building in the photograph opposite (Fig. 28.17) and describe its style and decoration. Use sketches to help you describe the elements of the design.

Analysis

To describe a Palladian building properly, you will need a lot of terminology. Pick one or two buildings and practise sketching them and filling in the names of the parts on your drawings.

During this period of prosperity in Ireland, architecture and design caught up with what was happening in Britain and Europe. People of means brought ideas back from their Grand Tours and tried to recreate the standards in classical art and architecture they had seen in Europe.

Figure 28.17 The Rotunda Hospital south façade by Richard Cassels.

Further Research

www.vam.ac.uk/articles/palladianism-an-introduction – A guide to the characteristics of Palladian design

www.russborough.ie – The official site of Russborough House. Look through the gallery to see more of the interior of this house

www.youtube.com – Search for 'Castletown House' (5:57) to learn more about the building and to see more of the details of the interior

www.youtube.com – Look up 'Russborough House – Palladian Splendour in Ireland' (5:41) to see more of the exterior and some of the rooms inside Russborough House

Chapter 29

Urban Development

By the end of this chapter I will ...

* understand how Dublin city expanded in the 18th century
* know about the Wide Streets Commission
* be able to describe the structure and decoration of a Georgian terrace house
* know some examples of Georgian street houses.

Context

At the beginning of the 18th century, Dublin was still a small walled medieval city with narrow streets and alleys. Houses were built of stone and wood. By the end of the century it was the second city of the British Empire, with elegant streets and squares and impressive public buildings. The city developed outwards from the area around Dublin Castle.

The Duke of Ormond set land aside for the Phoenix Park, which was to be a deer park surrounding a royal residence. He approved the development of houses on both sides of the Liffey set back from the river behind broad paved quays.

North of the Liffey

Much of the early development began north of the Liffey. Sir Humphrey Jervis developed lands around Capel and Jervis Streets. The Earl of Drogheda owned lands that were developed into Henry, Mary and Earl Streets. Luke Gardiner bought out many of the interests and became the main developer north of the Liffey from 1714 onwards.

South of the Liffey

On the south side, Sir Francis Aungier and the Earl of Meath were the early developers. Joshua Dawson, who was the Viscount Molesworth, planned Dawson, Molesworth, Nassau and Kildare Streets from 1710 onwards. The Fitzwilliam family (Lords Mountjoy) were the main developers on the south side after 1780.

Other Towns

Other towns in Ireland have Georgian elements. For example, the red-brick terraces of Newtown Pery in Limerick, the Mall in Cork, much of Birr in Co. Offaly and parts of many towns contain Georgian streets or civic buildings.

The Wide Streets Commission

The Wide Streets Commission was established to control planning and to create order and uniformity in the development of Dublin city. They had powers of compulsory purchase of land and to enforce regulations. The commission was made up of members of parliament and the mayor, so they had considerable political clout. They cut through old parts of the city to create Parliament Street, which connected Dublin Castle to Capel Street

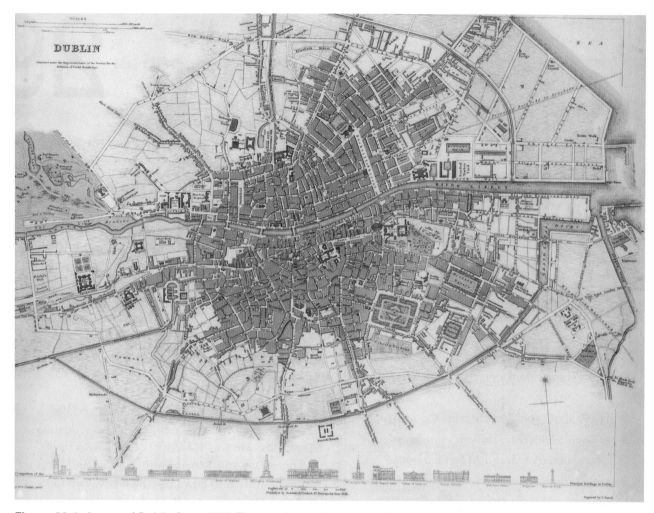

Figure 29.1 A map of Dublin from 1836. The canals created a boundary for the growing city.

Bridge and the north side of the city, where the earliest Georgian streets were built. Later they built another bridge (Carlisle Bridge, now O'Connell Bridge) further down the river, connecting Sackville (now O'Connell) Street with new developments at Westmoreland and D'Olier Streets. These streets were designed in the 1790s with integrated shop fronts, a feature that did not appear in London until later.

The Development of Streets and Squares

The earlier squares like St Stephen's Green and Parnell Square were developed piecemeal, a few buildings at a time, but later squares like Mountjoy on the north side and Merrion and Fitzwilliam Squares on the south side were laid out in advance.

Most streets and squares had a continuous building line, but there are streets that have houses that vary in height, width, size of windows and doors and the colour of the bricks. Some houses have basements and first floors in cut stone and a few of the larger houses were completely stone built. The North and South Circular Roads outlined the urban area, which was later redefined by the Royal and Grand Canals (Fig. 29.1).

Innovation and Invention

Urban planning was the great innovation of the Georgian period in Ireland. Streets and squares were laid out on a grid pattern, wherever possible, creating a spacious environment and easier movement of people and traffic.

Figure 29.3 Merrion Square was designed as a unit. This aerial view shows the park, which was private to residents of the square.

storage areas for the houses. Circular coal holes on the pavements opened into chutes where coal, which was used to heat the houses, could be poured into the stores below. The streets were cobbled and the footpaths in the better parts of Dublin had granite kerbs. An open area between the street and the houses allowed light into the basement windows. This area was protected by a cast-iron railing set in a low stone plinth at street level. Railings continued up the sides of the steps to the front door. The steps formed a bridge over the area. Cast iron was also used for balconies and for foot-scrapers and other street furniture.

This was a time before motorised transport or electricity and everything was moved by horse and cart. Candles or oil lamps provided the only source of light. There was no public street lighting.

Media and Areas of Practice

Architecture

Houses vary in size from a single bay wide, which was rare, to five or even seven bays for some of the largest houses. The basements were at natural ground level. The streets were built on brick arches. The spaces beneath the arches were used as

Terraces and Squares

Exterior

The doorways provide one of the main decorative features of the Georgian street house. They come with a variety of fanlights and porticoes made up of classical elements (Fig. 29.4). Some houses have a small window each side of the door to help light the hallway inside. The sash windows vary in size according to the importance of the rooms within. The tallest windows were on the first-floor reception rooms and the smallest on the top-floor bedrooms.

The houses were often built of red Bridgwater Brick, which came as ballast in ships trading with Bristol.

Figure 29.4 Some examples of the range of styles used on Georgian doors.

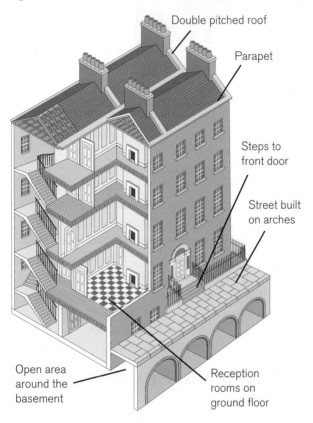

Double pitched roof

Parapet

Steps to front door

Street built on arches

Open area around the basement

Reception rooms on ground floor

Figure 29.5 Cutaway view of a Georgian terrace house.

The plainness of the façade is emphasised by the parapet, which partly conceals the roof. The parapet was required by fire prevention regulations, to avoid rising sparks catching in the eaves and setting fire to the roof. Roofs were double pitched; rainwater was carried through to the rear of the house and collected in down pipes. Houses had a garden at the rear with a carriage house at the far end; this could be accessed from a mews lane, which ran along behind the houses.

www.auctioneera.ie/georgian-house-architecture offers information on how to recognise a Georgian house. Some images are not typical, but the information is good. Use this site to help you recognise Georgian houses in your area or online.

Interior

Most Georgian terrace houses were family residences, lived in by successful merchants and members of the professions. Some gentry used them as town houses. They were most often four storeys over a basement with two reception rooms on the ground and first floors, one at the front and one at the rear, with a stairway and passage running down one side (Fig. 29.5). The formal stairs normally stopped on the second floor where the bedrooms of the master and the lady of the house were located. Smaller stairs gave access to the top floor, which was usually divided into four smaller bedrooms for children or servants.

Arrangement of the Rooms

The basement contained the kitchen and rooms for servants to work and live in. Ceilings were relatively low and there was little or no decoration. Ground-floor and first-floor rooms were taller and had decorative plasterwork. The quality and quantity of the stucco depended on the wealth of the owner and the skills and talents of the builder or architect. The drawing room was normally more elaborately decorated; some of the finer houses have fully patterned ceilings surrounded with a frieze up to 30 cm deep. Dining rooms were less elaborately decorated.

Figure 29.6 A three-bay red-brick Georgian terrace house with a cast-iron balcony (left). The roof cannot be seen from street level. A Georgian-style bedroom (right).

Rooms in the reception areas of the more ordinary houses would have had a plaster ceiling rose as a centrepiece and elaborate cornices. The ceilings of the basement and the top floors would have been quite plain. Stucco or wood carving was used for 'overdoors', which decorated the doorways of the main rooms. Swags, urns, heads or simple fluting were in the range of designs used in these areas. Fine joinery was a feature of Georgian houses: panelled doors and shutters, decorative door frames and balustrades, well-made sash windows with thin glazing bars, fine-patterned framing on fan lights all carried out to the highest standards.

 www.numbertwentynine.ie has an introduction to the Georgian Museum which will help you understand life in a Georgian house. Video and virtual reality are used to explain the house. Take notes or, better still, visit the house.

Artists and Artworks

Henrietta Street, which is just off Bolton Street on the north side of the city, was the earliest example of the Georgian terrace (Fig. 29.7). Large four-storey houses, which were four or five bays wide, had big

Figure 29.7
Henrietta Street, Dublin.

areas of plain brick between their well-proportioned windows. Door cases and pediments were in stone (London houses had wooden door cases) and the spacious interiors were based on country house designs. Sir Edward Lovett Pearce designed No. 9 and No. 10. A Palladian compartmented ceiling in a colonnaded entrance hall can be seen at No. 9, a scaled-down version of Castletown. No. 2 to No. 5 Henrietta Street were built by the banker Nathaniel Clements, one for his own use and the others for speculation.

Robert West's house, No. 20 Dominick Street (see p. 449), has the strongest contrast between plain exterior and decorated interior with the flamboyant plasterwork he created in the stairway and reception rooms.

The plain façade of No. 7 Ely Place conceals the exotic plasterwork by Michael Stapleton that represents the labour of Hercules (see p. 450).

These are just some of the more outstanding early red-brick houses that line Dublin city's streets and squares.

Later in the century, houses became more standardised. They were mainly three windows wide, with a wide arch enclosing the door case.

 Try making a painting based on your impression of life in Georgian Dublin.

 Research Georgian dress, design and lifestyle through images of paintings and prints of the time. The National Gallery has a good collection of 18th-century paintings you could see on a visit.

Art Elements and Design Principles

Harmony in proportions was an important element of urban design. The height of the buildings was related to the width of the street, so a spacious scale was created. Windows and doors were designed using mathematical formulas to create harmonious shapes.

Room sizes were normally two cubes in area, which was believed to be an ideal space.

Outside, terraces were quite plain red brick structures, relying on painted doors and window frames for a change of colour and form on the flat surface. The doorways provided the main decorative focus with their porticoes, fanlights and pillars.

Inside, pattern and symmetry were harmonised into schemes of decorative plasterwork on walls and ceilings.

Analysis

Town planning, quality craftsmanship and good materials were all part of urban architecture in Ireland. Who were the buildings made for, and who developed them?

Although many of the architects and designers came from outside Ireland, there was a short period when Dublin in particular had finer public buildings and more elegant streets than London. Only a privileged few led the life of culture and refinement that is represented by the architecture, decoration and furnishings that we associate with the Georgian period, but this social inequality was true of any country at that time.

Chapter Review

1. What kind of people were the developers of Georgian Dublin?

2. Do you think that town planning worked well in Irish Georgian towns and cities? Give some examples of well-planned streets and squares using words and sketches.

3. Describe the structure and decoration of a Georgian street house. Make sketches of exterior and interior features and describe their style and function.

4. What classical elements do you see in a typical Georgian street doorway? Make a sketch and note the parts with classical roots in a written answer.

5. Can you imagine life in a Georgian terrace house? Do you know how it was heated and lit? Where would you have washed and gone to the toilet? Where was the food cooked and how did it get to the table? Can you imagine other aspects of life at the time?

6. Describe the typically Georgian features you see on the door in the photograph opposite (Fig. 29.8). Use sketches to illustrate the details.

Further Research

www.theculturetrip.com/europe/ireland/articles/a-tour-of-the-buildings-of-georgian-dublin/ – Some text and images of Georgian Dublin

www.youtube.com – Watch the video 'Georgian Dublin' (5:14) by Trinity College Dublin. It may help you understand this period in greater detail

www.google.ie/images – Search for '20 Dominick Street Dublin' to see photographs of this street in Dublin today

Figure 29.8 A Georgian doorway in Fitzwilliam Square.

Chapter 30

The Neo-Classical Style

By the end of this chapter I will ...

* note the changes in style from Palladian to Neo-Classical design

* be able to describe a building designed by William Chambers, Thomas Ivory and James Gandon

* know terminology that will help me describe the architecture I study.

Context

In the late 18th century, there was a change of style in architecture. Original Roman and Greek designs were preferred to the Renaissance interpretation of them through architects like Palladio.

A Patron of the Arts

James Caulfield, Lord Charlemont, spent a number of years on the Grand Tour in Europe. His cultural interests led him to spend a lot of his time in Rome, where he was friendly with artists and architects. On his return to Dublin in 1755 he wanted to bring Italian style to his Irish properties, so he employed William Chambers, a friend that he made in Rome, to make the designs for him.

Innovation and Invention

The Neo-Classical period is referred to as the Age of Enlightenment. There was an interest in scientific theory, reason and individuality. Voyages of discovery, like Captain Cook's exploration of the South Pacific, and Isaac Newton's theories on gravity and planetary movements were opening discussion on all aspects of the arts and sciences.

Visit *www.study.com* and search for 'Enlightenment's Influence on 18th- & 19th-Century Art & Architecture'. Do you think new scientific thinking affected the arts?

Media and Areas of Practice

The precise designs and decorative elements of Neo-Classical architecture created a demand for skilled tradesmen and stone carvers. Some designers came from abroad, like the Lafranchini brothers who worked in stucco and Simon Vierpyl, a sculptor, who supervised the building of the Casino at Marino, but the demand was met mainly by Irish workmen trained through apprenticeships or through the Dublin Society Schools.

Many designers copied freely from books of engravings, which showed Roman ruins or reconstructions of them. Giambattista Piranesi (1720–78) produced several very influential books of engravings, which exaggerated the size of Roman buildings. Another book of engravings, *The Antiquities of Athens*, which was published in 1762, led to a Greek Revival. The discoveries at Pompeii and Herculaneum helped create the Etruscan style which influenced the Adam and Empire styles.

 Research the Adam and Empire styles. Compare these versions of Neo-Classical style.

Artists and Artworks

Sir William Chambers (1723–96)

Chambers was the leading English architect of his day. He designed a town house and a garden temple for the country estate of Lord Charlemont, who renamed the estate at Donnycarney 'Marino' in memory of an Italian town he had visited on the Grand Tour. Marino House was demolished long ago, but the garden temple, the Casino at Marino, and his town house, Charlemont House in Parnell Square, now the Hugh Lane Gallery, still stand.

Charlemont House

Charlemont House, which was built in 1763, formed

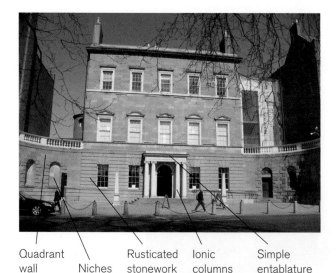

Quadrant wall | Niches | Rusticated stonework | Ionic columns | Simple entablature

Figure 30.1 Charlemont House, Dublin (now Hugh Lane Gallery) was designed for Lord Charlemont by Sir William Chambers.

the centrepiece for the north side of Parnell Square (originally Rutland Square). The house is connected to the red brick terraces on each side by quadrant walls, which are decorated with niches (Fig. 30.1). The ground floor is of rusticated stone, while the two upper floors are finished in smooth cut stone. The entrance has a simple entablature supported on Ionic columns. It is a relatively simple exterior when compared with the early Palladian town houses of Dublin such as Leinster House.

The Casino at Marino

Casino means 'little house'. The Casino at Marino was built during the 1760s and is basically a garden ornament on the grand scale (Fig. 30.2). Chambers designed it as an architectural gem first; function was not of primary importance. The building is deceptively large; a second attic storey is almost hidden above the cornice. In plan it is a Greek cross inside a Doric colonnade.

Exterior

The Casino stands on a podium that is stepped on the north and south sides and has a balustrade on the east and west sides. The columns support an entablature decorated with ox skulls and concentric circles. The walls are rusticated to create a contrast with the smooth columns. A pediment creates a centrepiece on the north and south sides, and the attic storey decorated with swags and figure sculptures forms part of the centrepiece on the east and west sides.

Chambers never came to Ireland, so Simon Vierpyl, an English sculptor, who had also befriended Lord Charlemont in Rome, supervised the work. Vierpyl was in charge of the stone carving and the exquisite detailing of the building, as well as having overall responsibility for the construction. All the functional parts are incorporated into the design – the urns on the roof are chimney pots and four of the pillars are hollow to bring rainwater from the roof into cisterns in the basement where it could be used for household needs.

Interior

The glass in the windows is curved, which causes

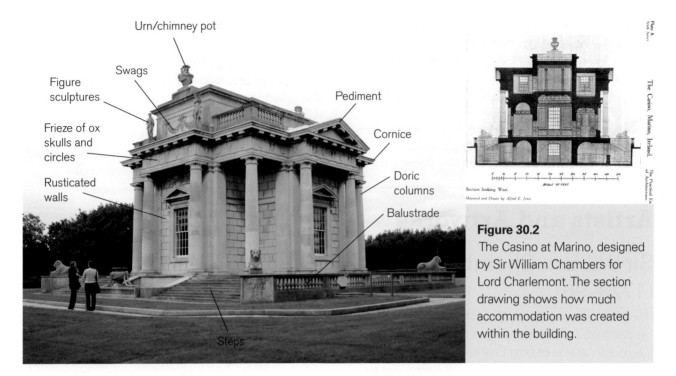

Urn/chimney pot

Swags

Figure sculptures

Pediment

Frieze of ox skulls and circles

Cornice

Rusticated walls

Doric columns

Balustrade

Steps

Figure 30.2
The Casino at Marino, designed by Sir William Chambers for Lord Charlemont. The section drawing shows how much accommodation was created within the building.

a reflection that prevents someone on the outside seeing in. This provides some privacy and disguises the fact that partitions and stairs, which form part of the ingenious interior, cross some of the window spaces. The basement has a kitchen and workrooms for the servants. The ground floor has a formal entrance hall and three reception rooms, with geometric patterned floors in exotic woods and fine plasterwork by Cipriani, another of Lord

Charlemont's friends from Rome. The highlight of the interior is the stateroom on the first floor, which is richly coloured in contrast with the pure white interiors on the ground floor (Fig. 30.3).

Sir William Chambers designed other buildings in Ireland – the Chapel and Theatre at Trinity College and Lucan House in Co. Dublin – but none compare with the refinement and perfection of the Casino.

Figure 30.3
The Casino at Marino, interior.

Built with the best materials and to the highest standards, it cost £20,000 at the time, which was a considerable fortune. The Casino was an influential building and aspects of its design appeared in several important buildings in following years.

Thomas Ivory (1732–1786)

Born in Cork, Ivory worked as a carpenter before turning to architecture. He had picked up some Neo-Classical ideas from the drawings exhibited at the time of the Royal Exchange competition and put these new ideas to good use for another competition to design a school for the King's Hospital students.

The Blue Coat School

Now home to the Law Society of Ireland in Blackhall Place, Dublin, the Blue Coat School was so called because of the colour of the uniform of the King's Hospital students (Fig. 30.4).

Exterior

The layout follows the plan of Palladian country mansions, with the main central block connected to two wings by curved walls with niches. The entire ground floor, including the quadrant walls, is rusticated except for the frontispieces on the wings.

The central block is still generally Palladian, but the wings are treated differently, relying more on their structural form than on detail for their effect. Round-headed niches create hollow spaces at first-floor level, as do the large relieving arches over the central windows. Recesses with swags and oval niches also form part of the design. Balustrades at the windows and niches on the first floor support a string course that runs the full length of the building, tying all the elements together.

Master of the School of Architectural Drawing

Ivory had a major influence on Irish architecture through his role as the first Master of the School of Architectural Drawing at the Dublin Society. One of his pupils, James Hoban, designed the White House in Washington, DC.

James Gandon (1743–1823)

An Englishman and a student of Sir William Chambers, Gandon became the leading architect of the Neo-Classical period in Ireland. He was brought over to design a new Custom House in 1781, almost a mile downriver from the old building. This was part of the eastward development of the city away from the medieval centre around Dublin Castle.

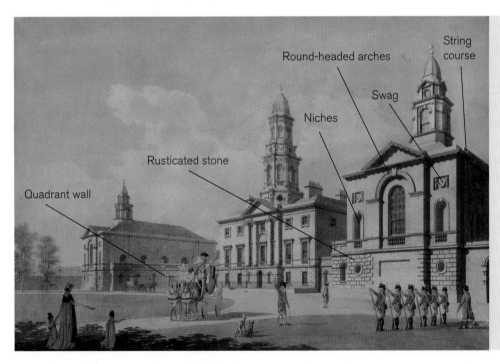

Round-headed arches

String course

Swag

Niches

Rusticated stone

Quadrant wall

Figure 30.4
The Blue Coat School, a print by Thomas Malton, National Gallery of Ireland, Dublin. The towers shown in the print were never built.

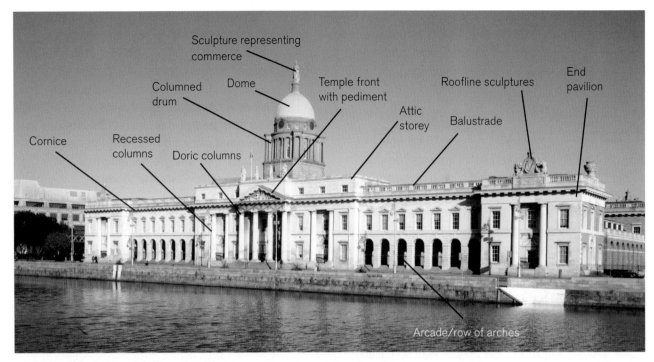

Labels on image:
Sculpture representing commerce
Columned drum
Dome
Temple front with pediment
Roofline sculptures
End pavilion
Attic storey
Balustrade
Cornice
Recessed columns
Doric columns
Arcade/row of arches

Figure 30.5 The Customs House, Dublin (riverfront), designed by James Gandon in 1781.

The Custom House

The Custom House was built on previously undeveloped, marshy ground, which made for complicated and expensive construction. In plan the building is a square with long façades on the north and south sides connected to corner pavilions (Fig. 30.5).

Exterior

The riverfront, which faces south, is two storeys tall. The entrance is a temple front with a pediment supported on freestanding Doric columns reaching over two storeys. An attic storey helps to emphasise the slightly projecting central block. Arcades at ground level make a bridge between the central block and the end pavilions. Columns set in recesses create a feature on the end pavilions and on each side of the entrance. A cornice runs the full length of the building. Above this, balustrades connect the roofline of the pavilions to the attic storey.

Enormous sculptures of coats of arms and urns on the rooflines of the pavilions continue the vertical emphasis created by the columns below, making a contrast with the horizontal nature of the building. The riverfront can be seen reflected in the surface of the Liffey, which also helps to increase the apparent height of the building. A tall columned drum supports the dome, which has a figure representing Commerce on the top. Edward Smyth was responsible for the sculpture on the Custom House.

The Four Courts

Built in 1786, the Four Courts (Fig. 30.6) is considered by some to be one of the finest Neo-Classical buildings in Britain or Ireland.

Exterior

The building has a central block, which is square in plan, supporting a large pillared drum with a saucer-shaped shallow dome. The façade has a large pedimented portico with Corinthian pillars rising over two storeys. Niches on the first floor are deeply recessed. A balustrade decorates the roof line and figure sculptures of Moses, Mercury and Justice surmount the portico; seated figures of Wisdom and Authority mark the corners of the façade. Screen walls with triumphal arches at the centres connect the main building to the wings. Large carved crests are mounted on these arches, again sculpted by Smyth.

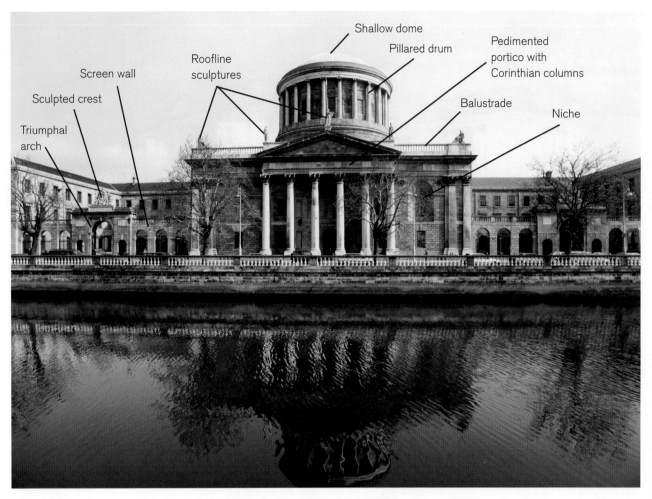

Triumphal arch

Sculpted crest

Screen wall

Roofline sculptures

Shallow dome

Pillared drum

Pedimented portico with Corinthian columns

Balustrade

Niche

Figure 30.6 The Four Courts, Dublin (riverfront), designed by James Gandon in 1786.

Interior

The ground floor has a large circular reception area with four courts leading diagonally off it. Originally the courts were only separated from the hall by pillars. Curtains were hung shortly after construction and then timber and glass screens were built. The partitions were built in masonry when the building was reconstructed following its burning in 1922, when all the interior decoration was lost.

Visit *www.buildingsofireland.ie* and search for images of the interior and exterior of the Four Courts building. Make notes and sketches to help your understanding of the building.

Other projects

Gandon was commissioned to design many of the major buildings in Dublin and a number of the

projects ran simultaneously, including the extension to the House of Lords, the Four Courts, Carlisle (O'Connell) Bridge and the King's Inns.

Gandon also designed some buildings outside Dublin: Waterford Courthouse, which is now demolished, Coolbanagher Church in Co. Laois and Emo Court nearby, a fine country mansion that was only just begun at the time of Gandon's death. Emo was one of a few houses that Gandon designed, mainly for his patrons. Abbeville, which was built for Sir John Beresford, and Emsworth are both in Co. Dublin.

James Wyatt (1746–1813)

By the end of the century, houses were generally smaller than the palaces we saw earlier. They were also less lavishly decorated. Interiors were often in the Adam style. James Wyatt was the leading figure in country-house design in the later part of

Figure 30.7 (above)
Castle Coole House,
Co. Fermanagh.

Figure 30.8 (left)
Gothick façade of Slane Castle.

the century. He supplied designs for the renovation and alteration of many houses, and schemes for the decoration of others. He designed Castle Coole in Co. Fermanagh for the Earl of Belmore in 1793 (Fig. 30.7). The house is nine bays wide and is simply finished, with no window mouldings and little decoration. Four Ionic columns reach over two storeys to support the plain pediment over the entrance. Straight Doric colonnades make the connection to the end pavilions. Wyatt was also responsible for the design and furnishing of the elegant interior.

The Gothick style

Wyatt designed a renovation of Slane Castle in Co. Meath in 1785, which demonstrates a new romantic fashion in Gothic decoration (Fig. 30.8). Towers and battlements were added to a classical building in a style known as 'Gothick', with a 'k' to differentiate

it from the more serious Neo-Gothic of the next century.

Art Elements and Design Principles

There was a movement away from Baroque and Rococo in favour of classical design. New ideas came directly from buildings seen on the Grand Tour and from books of engravings showing classical buildings.

Form and outline were considered to be the primary elements in good Neo-Classical design. This can be seen in the clean lines and simple decoration of the front of Charlemont House, which was designed as a centrepiece for the north side of Parnell Square, bringing symmetry to that block of buildings.

The highly decorated Casino at Marino uses all the elements of form, texture, shape and pattern to separate areas of the design and to emphasise the symmetry and harmony of the all the elements of the building.

The mass of the Custom House and the Four Courts is broken up by the clever use of forms projecting and receding from the surface, creating patterns of light and shadow that reduce the bulk of these large buildings.

Interiors were not as heavily patterned in the Neo-Classical style; finer more symmetrical plasterwork relied on the colour of painted ceilings and walls for its effect.

Analysis

> The Neo-Classical style borrowed elements from ancient Greece and Rome. Can you identify these elements in some of the buildings in this chapter?

The change in taste from Rococo to a more classical style created some of the most iconic public buildings in Dublin.

The influence of architects and designers from Britain and Europe in the early part of the century and the training available in the Dublin Society School led to a generation of Irish designers who could hold their own in any company at home or abroad.

Chapter Review

1. What are the main differences between Palladian and Neo-Classical design?

2. Describe the structure and decoration of the Casino at Marino. Use words and sketches to describe some of its unique features as well as the art and design elements.

3. Write an account of a building by James Gandon. Use sketches and words to describe the structure and decoration of the building.

4. Compare a public and a private building from the Neo-Classical period, describing the differences in scale and decoration in words and sketches.

5. What do you think of the standard of workmanship in Neo-Classical buildings? Use words and sketches to show details of structure and decoration that demonstrate your points.

6. Using words and sketches, describe the Neo-Classical features of the building in Fig. 30.9 below.

Figure 30.9 The façade of Dublin City Hall, designed by Thomas Cooley.

Further Research

www.casinomarino.ie – The official site of the Casino at Marino

www.hughlane.ie – Click on 'About Us' and then select 'Charlemont House' for further information about the building

www.archiseek.com – Contains accounts of buildings designed by Thomas Ivory, James Gandon, William Chambers and James Wyatt

www.youtube.com – Look up 'Casino Marino – Culture Night 2012 – Dublin' (10:31) for a guided tour of the building

Chapter 31

Georgian Art and Crafts

By the end of this chapter I will ...

* know about the quality of craftsmanship in Georgian Ireland
* have some terminology to describe the craftwork I see
* be able to describe the work of two stuccodores
* know the work of Edward Smyth, sculptor.

Context

At the beginning of the 18th century, Irish craftwork followed the English style, but usually a few years behind the fashion. A number of things changed around 1750, when some trade restrictions between Ireland and England were lifted and the first students who had been trained in the Dublin Society School were now beginning to offer their work for sale in Ireland. A good deal of the work by Irish craftsmen was of high quality. There was an Irish style, stronger in form and decoration and slightly heavier than English or European work.

A new middle class had developed in Ireland; large farmers and professional people wanted to furnish their town and country houses in style.

Irish stuccodores produced the decorative plasterwork for the larger houses and public buildings in the country. There were silversmiths, glassmakers and joiners in most of the larger urban centres in Ireland providing quality products for their local markets.

The Dublin Society School

The Dublin Society School was founded in the 1740s, under its first master Robert West (d. 1790). He taught figure drawing, which he had learned in Paris. James Mannin (d. 1779), a French artist living in Dublin, taught Ornamental Landscape Drawing and Thomas Ivory (1732–86) took over the teaching of Architectural Drawing in about 1759. Most Irish artists from this time on got some education in the school. The standard in the school seems to have been very high; many of its pupils had successful careers in Britain and Europe, as well as at home.

Innovation and Invention

The idea of training artists, designers and craft-workers in schools rather than through the apprentice system was quite new and helped to create greater numbers of skilled people to work in all the crafts.

The Neo-Classical style was more controlled and refined and used simpler decoration than we have seen in the Palladian style.

Mass production of decorations began in plasterwork, ironwork and woodwork. Individual pieces were still made for individual clients, but ready-made designs were more common.

Media and Areas of Practice

Silverwork

Silverwork in the late Rococo style was produced in workshops in Dublin and Cork and Limerick. *Repoussé* and chasing, which created areas in relief and open work, were features of this style. Country scenes, flowers, birds and masks were among the designs that appeared on silver work. Dish rings, three-legged sugar bowls and helmet-shaped cream jugs were particular to the Irish market and are much sought after by collectors today.

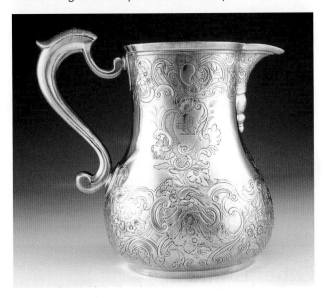

Figure 31.1 Irish silver jug with engraved decoration.

Stucco Decoration

Eighteenth-century decorative plasterwork is more correctly referred to as stucco. Stuccowork was developed in ancient times and made into an art form during the Renaissance, Baroque and Rococo periods.

Stucco: A quick setting, flexible material made of very fine sand, crushed white Carrara marble, gypsum, alabaster dust and other, sometimes secret, ingredients, which were mixed with water to create the stucco. It could be cast in moulds or applied freehand. When it was dry, the surface could be polished to a smooth finish.

Decorative stucco was introduced during the 18th-century building boom in Ireland, first in the compartmented style, which was a continuation of 17th-century design, where the ceiling was divided into decorated geometric shapes. In the 1740s, the Lafranchini brothers introduced a Baroque style with human figures in high relief surrounded by Acanthus leaves, swags of flowers and putti. Their later work was more Rococo, lighter and with more movement, and the human figure was less evident (Fig. 31.2).

Sources for Stucco Designs

The classical scenes and decorations were probably borrowed from French and Italian engravings. It was the practice in the 18th century to use engravings as a reference for all kinds of decoration. Books of patterns and designs were produced so that architects and craftsmen could copy from them.

Mass-produced Plasterwork

Towards the end of the 18th century, commercially mass-produced moulds brought an end to

Figure 31.2 Lafranchini Brothers' stucco work.

Figure 31.3 A piece of Irish Georgian furniture.

hand-crafted work. Decorative mouldings could be obtained quickly and cheaply, which suited the needs of Irish developers in a market where prices were falling following the Act of Union in 1800.

Furniture

Trade with the West Indies brought new and exotic timbers to Britain and Ireland. Mahogany, which is a dark, fine-grained wood, was ideal for turning and carving; it produced strong elegant furniture (Fig. 31.3). Irish carvers developed a style of high-relief decoration in the form of foliage, animals and masks. They often finished the ends of table and chair legs with large paws. Chairs, cabinets and particularly side tables carved by Irish joiners are highly regarded by collectors worldwide.

Household Woodwork

The standard of woodwork on doors and windows was high; door frames and overdoors were carved and sash windows had light, finely made glazing bars.

Glass

Irish glassmakers got a boost in 1780 when trade restrictions were dropped and a tax was put on English glass. A period of great productivity

followed; glass factories in Dublin, Belfast, Cork and Waterford all produced thick, deeply cut glass work. A typically Irish product was a large serving dish with a turnover rim with deeply cut designs (Fig. 31.4).

Figure 31.4 A piece of Irish Georgian cut glass.

 Go to *www.penrosecrystal.com* and click on 'History of Penrose' to learn about the history of the original Waterford glass company. Do you think Georgian glass is superior to modern designs? Discuss with your classmates.

Other Crafts

Ceramics, bookbinding and fabric printing were also flourishing industries in Ireland, which produced work of the highest quality, equal to any in Europe.

Artists and Artworks
The Painters

A number of the graduates of the Dublin Society School had successful careers. Hugh Douglas Hamilton (*c.* 1739–1808) was a successful society portrait painter in London and Rome, where he was a friend of the Italian sculptor Canova. He also painted subject pictures like *Cupid and Psyche in the Nuptial Bower*, which is in the National Gallery of Ireland with some of his other work (Fig. 31.5).

Other artists had careers in landscape and subject paintings.

Figure 31.5 *Cupid and Psyche in the Nuptial Bower*, 1792–3, by Hugh Douglas Hamilton, oil on canvas, 198 × 151 cm, National Gallery of Ireland.

High relief figures of gods and goddesses

Swags

Patterns from natural forms

Figure 31.6 The stuccoed ceiling of the Gold Salon at Carton House by the Lanfranchini brothers.

The Stuccadores

The Lafranchini Brothers

Born in Ticino in the Italian-speaking part of Switzerland, Paulo (1695–1770) and Filippo (1702–1779) were the most influential stuccodores (plaster modellers) to operate in Ireland. They worked in an Italian Baroque figurative and ornamental style on about 15 Irish houses. They are often associated with the buildings of Richard Cassels.

At Carton House (Fig. 31.6) and Newman House they produced figures of classical gods and goddesses surrounded by swirling Acanthus cartouches and swags. Classical figures are used again at Riverstown House in Co. Cork, where personifications of the virtues decorate the walls. A copy (in plaster), of Nicolas Poussin's painting of an allegory on truth appears on the dining room ceiling and is the highlight of the stuccowork in the house. Copies of the plasterwork at Riverstown were made for Áras an Uachtaráin in 1948 (Fig. 31.7).

There are figure scenes at Kilshannig House, also in Co. Cork, made in 1766, but these are unusual as the Lafranchini brothers had generally changed to a lighter, more Rococo style from the 1740s on. At Russborough House the lighter style is more evident. Acanthus leaf and floral swags with occasional putti make up the rhythmic patterns that decorate the ceilings of the saloons (see Fig. 28.14, p. 428). The walls in the stair hall at Castletown are also decorated in this lighter, lively, asymmetrical Rococo style (Fig. 31.8). While Paulo went to work in England in the 1750s for a number of years, Filippo remained in Ireland into the 1770s.

Robert West (d. 1790)

West came from a family of stuccodores whose work was recorded from the early 17th century. He was also a master builder. West's best work is high-relief birds and human heads emerging from curved plant forms in the Rococo style. These almost freestanding birds appear at his own house, No. 20 Dominick Street, and at No. 28 St Stephen's Green. The birds are surrounded by leaves, flowers, fruits and musical instruments. West or his studio also decorated some country houses, such as Dowth Hall, Co. Meath, and Dunsandle, Co. Galway.

Figure 31.7 (left) Some of the plasterwork copied from Riverstown House at Áras an Uachtaráin.

Figure 31.8 (right) Plaster portrait from Castletown House. The bust in classical drapery is surrounded in an oval frame decorated in leaf patterns.

Michael Stapleton (1747–1801)

Stapleton was a master builder and stuccodore in the Neo-Classical style. He was a pupil of West's and was able to do creative freehand plasterwork as well as copies of English designers like Robert Adams. A large collection of Stapleton's drawings and engravings survive in the National Library of Ireland. These show that he designed original compositions as well as copying from published sources. Stapleton's Neo-Classical designs look like lace or embroidery. Delicate white plant forms arranged in geometric patterns against a coloured background form the basis for most compositions. Figure scenes and classical devices like urns or musical instruments are used as centres of interest in the designs (Fig. 31.10).

Stapleton's work appears in the exam hall in Trinity College, Powerscourt House on South William

Figure 31.9 (left) An example of Robert West's plasterwork from his house at 20 Dominick Street, Dublin. West's high-relief plasterwork can be almost freestanding.

Figure 31.10 (right) A detail of the stairwell ceiling in Belvedere House, Dublin. In Michael Stapleton's Neo-Classical plasterwork, figure scenes and musical instruments are combined with plant forms in geometric patterns.

Figure 31.11 Stairway at Belvedere House, Dublin, by Michael Stapleton.

Figure 31.12 Keystone from the Custom House representing the River Blackwater, carved by Edward Smyth.

Street, Dublin, Lucan House, which is now the Italian Embassy, and Mount Kennedy House. His masterpiece is considered to be Belvedere House in Great Denmark Street in Dublin, which he completed for the 2nd Earl of Belvedere in 1786. (The Jesuit Order bought the building as a school in 1841 and it has been run since as Belvedere College; James Joyce was its most famous past pupil.) Stapleton was the architect and stuccodore of this project; he produced some of his most creative work for the stairs and the main reception rooms (Fig. 31.11).

Stone Carving

Several students of the Dublin Society School had careers in sculpture. For example, Christopher Hewetson (*c.* 1739–94) ran a successful studio in Rome and produced some work in Ireland also. The memorial to Provost Baldwin in Trinity College is his work.

Edward Smyth (1749–1812)

An Irish sculptor, and graduate of the Dublin Society School, Smyth was responsible for much of the carving on the Custom House and other buildings designed by Gandon. The riverine heads that decorate the keystones of the arches on the riverfront show Smyth's bold style to advantage. Carved in high relief and classically proportioned, they are based on Greek and Roman models. Fourteen heads represent the rivers of Ireland: the Foyle, the Erne, the Liffey, the Boyne, the Nore, the Blackwater (Fig. 31.12), the Atlantic, the Ban, the Shannon, the Lee, the Lagan, the Suir, the Barrow and the Slaney. The hair or headdress of each head carries symbols in the form of plants and animals to represent each river. The keystone over the main door represents the Liffey, the only female figure in the group.

Smyth also carved the figures and decoration on the Four Courts.

Art Elements and Design Principles

Georgian craftwork was of the highest quality. Skilled stone carvers like Edward Smyth used shape and form to create the bulk of their sculpture and then used texture and pattern to separate different areas within it.

Irish silver and glass were strongly modelled; forms had clear outlines and the surfaces were boldly marked with decoration. Glass had deeply cut patterns and silverwork was often pierced with open spaces. Designs were symmetrical and balanced.

Furniture was deeply carved in high relief and decorated with animal, plant and other natural forms. Backgrounds were sometimes textured to create a contrast with the carved decoration.

Figure 31.13 The arms of Ireland from the Custom House in Dublin by Edward Smyth. The design is symmetrical and the surfaces are separated into textured and smooth areas. Hollow spaces create dark areas to contrast with the light falling on the surfaces.

Analysis

Form, texture, colour and symmetry were all important elements in Georgian design. Look for these features in some examples of the arts and crafts of the time.

During the 18th century, Irish architecture and design joined the mainstream of European development. It came out of the backwater that it had been in for centuries and enjoyed a period where it was at the forefront of fashionable taste.

The Dublin Society Schools played an important role in creating high standards for their students of painting, sculpture, architecture and crafts. Many graduates of the schools went on to successful careers, not just in Ireland, where the pool of patrons was small, but in England and further afield.

After the Georgian Period

At the close of the century, Ireland was again in political turmoil. The sense of national pride that had grown with the achievements in architecture and the arts, and the prosperity that had developed, led some to believe that Ireland would be better off separate from Britain. The French and American revolutions created an atmosphere of rebellion, which led to a rising in 1798. The rebellion was quickly put down and the Act of Union was signed in 1800, which made Ireland part of the United Kingdom of Great Britain and Ireland. With Dublin's parliament closed, politics and influence moved to London, again leaving Ireland at a financial disadvantage and in a political and cultural backwater.

With the wealthier patrons gone, many of the older Georgian terraces became tenements, rented out to poor people and not properly maintained.

Building continued in the classical style. The General Post Office on O'Connell Street in Dublin is an example of the many public buildings from the 19th century with classical features.

The Dublin Society Schools continued to produce good painters and sculptors; many made their living in England due to a lack of patrons at home.

Chapter Review

1. Describe two pieces of craftwork from different crafts and note in words and sketches the style and techniques involved in their making.

2. Describe some work by the Lafranchini brothers. Make sketches of two examples of their work and explain the process by which they were made.

3. What affect did the Dublin Society School have on the arts in Ireland? Name two graduates and give an example of their work.

4. Describe the characteristics of the stucco work of Robert West or Michael Stapleton. Sketch an example of their work and explain the style they worked in.

5. Where might you find the work of the sculptor Edward Smyth? Give examples in words and sketches of some of his work.

Further Research

www.askaboutireland.ie – On this website click into the 'Learning Zone' and then the 'Secondary Students' section. From here you can search for 'Dublin Silver' and read an article on Dublin Georgian silver

www.visual-arts-cork.com – Click on 'Irish Arts' under the 'Page Contents' section on this website. Click the link to 'history of Irish art' then click on the 5th link of the '10 Key Stages' – 'Painting: The Rebirth of Irish Art (1650–1830)'. From here you can learn more about the Royal Dublin Society and read accounts of a number of 18th-century artists

www.youtube.com – Go to YouTube and search for 'House of Waterford Crystal: An Introduction' (3:55) to watch a video showing the cut-glass-making process

www.irishtimes.com – Click on the search bar and type the keywords 'Dominick Street', then set the search date to 22/08/2017. Click on the article titled 'One of Dublin's "grandest buildings" opens to public for first time' to see a short video showing some of West's plasterwork

Unit 11

Irish Art and Modernism

(*c.* 1880–1960s)

32.   Continental Influence

33.   The Celtic Revival

34.   The Early Moderns

Continental Influence

By the end of this chapter I will ...

* know about the continental influence on Irish painting

* be able to describe work by Nathaniel Hone, Walter Osborne, Roderic O'Conor, William Orpen and William John Leech

* to be able to observe the differences and similarities between *plein air* painting and Impressionism.

Before Modernism

In 1800, the Act of Union united Britain and Ireland as one nation with a parliament in London. Social and economic conditions changed for the worse, as power and decision-making was now a long way from Ireland and it was not a priority in the English parliament.

Ireland had a large population of small farmers and labourers living in subsistence conditions. A potato blight in 1845 took away the main food source, and many poorer people died or emigrated in the following years. Most of the famine victims were Irish speakers, and as a result the Irish language went into decline with their passing. By the late 1800s, there was some indication of economic

recovery, but commissions for artists were hard to come by, so many had to go abroad to make a living.

RESEARCH Visit *www.britannica.com/topic/land-league* for a short account of the Land League and Home Rule movements. Use this information to compare social conditions in Ireland with Europe at the time and the effect it had on the arts.

Art continued in the Classical style: accurate drawing and careful finish were still the norm well into the 19th century. Towards the end of the 1800s, however, influences from mainland Europe led Irish artists to question their subjects, style and techniques.

In Europe, this was the time of the *Belle Époque*, when the prosperity that followed from the Industrial Revolution led to a building boom in many European cities. In Ireland, The Land Reform and Home Rule movements created an interest in a new Irish identity separate from the British Empire. A new middle class had the money and leisure time to pursue an interest in the arts. New styles of art and architecture flourished in this atmosphere of exploration and invention.

Context

From about 1850, Irish artists began to find their way into European art academies, particularly those in Antwerp and Paris. A new approach to painting was developing in the French academies and in the artists' colonies that sprang up in the small towns around the forest of Fontainebleau, south of Paris.

The Royal Hibernian Academy (RHA), founded in 1823, was the main supporter of the arts in Ireland. The RHA ran an art school and awarded prizes and scholarships at their annual exhibitions to encourage young artists.

Media and Areas of Practice

Oil painting was still the preferred medium for most artists, but due to changes in subjects and style, brushwork became looser and paint was applied thickly to allow artists to work more quickly and expressively. This enabled artists to capture changing light and colour as they worked increasingly out of doors.

As the 19th century came to a close, Irish artists were becoming influenced by the Impressionist and Post-Impressionist styles becoming popular in Europe. The Impressionists used a colour palette based on theories of light. They excluded earth colours and black, using colours close to the visible spectrum colours – red, orange, yellow, green, blue, indigo and violet.

 Compare the colour scheme in a painting by Nathaniel Hone with one by Roderic O'Conor and note the difference Impressionist colours make.

Innovation and Invention

Modern synthetic paints produced a better colour range than artists previously had access to. Newly invented tin tubes allowed artists to carry paint outdoors more easily, while prepared canvases could be bought, which saved artists the time it took to make their own.

Flat paintbrushes were more frequently used in preference to traditional round brushes, as they allowed for broader strokes and the 'square brush' technique that became popular with the Impressionists and later artists.

Art Elements and Design Principles

Subjects changed from formal Classical or Romantic themes to scenes from the everyday lives of ordinary people, as well as simple landscapes.

This latter subject was first addressed by the Barbizon School, a group of artists who lived and worked near Fontainebleau. The artists worked on studies and sketches outside – *en plein air* – painting what they observed, but produced finished paintings, based on their outdoor work, in the studio (see Unit 4).

The Impressionists were a ground-breaking group, offering paintings made quickly from direct observation as finished works. Subjects and composition changed, influenced by the invention of photography. Paintings often captured a fleeting moment, like a camera does, and were less formally composed than the subject paintings of the previous generation.

Artists and Artworks
Nathaniel Hone (1831–1917)

Nathaniel Hone came from a wealthy family and did not need to work to make a living. This allowed him to follow his interests freely. After a few years working as an engineer, he went to Paris in 1853 to study art in the workshops of Adolphe Yvon and, more importantly, Thomas Couture, who was a figure painter influenced by the new trends in Realism. He had a conventional training, copying pieces in the Louvre and drawing directly from the human figure. Couture emphasised drawing and painting skills, so an artist could put down first impressions quickly with confidence.

In 1857, Hone moved to Barbizon, where he worked among the *plein air* painters Corot, Millet, Harpignies and Manet (see Unit 4). Here, he painted *The Banks of the Seine* (Fig. 32.1), which features a human subject; this is notable as Hone's later work rarely includes people.

Following his marriage in 1872, Hone spent most of his time in Ireland, although he still frequently

Figure 32.1
The Banks of the Seine,
1882, by Nathaniel Hone,
oil on canvas,
62 x 100 cm, National
Gallery of Ireland, Dublin.

travelled abroad. He exhibited at the RHA and became a member of the academy in 1880. *The Banks of the Seine* was exhibited there in 1882.

In his later life, Hone lived on the family estate in Malahide, where he found the subject matter for most of his work: landscapes, seascapes, boats and farming activities. He also taught at the RHA where he was an influence on a generation of Irish painters.

Pastures at Malahide

Composition and Colour

A simple series of horizontal lines separate the land and sky. Low diagonals lead the eye from the nearest cow to the left of the horizon, then back up through the cloud shadow to the right of the format, emphasising the sense of space in the painting.

Hone uses subtle, natural colours, often featuring the light and shade typical of the Irish climate. The dark green of the pasture contrasts with the bright light on the clouds. The eye is drawn to the yellow ochre in the far background through the pale highlights of the cows.

Style and Technique

Hone's mature work was in the *plein air* style that he had learned in France: simple landscapes, freely

Figure 32.2
Pastures at Malahide,
1907, by Nathaniel Hone,
oil on canvas,
82 × 124 cm,
National Gallery of
Ireland, Dublin.

painted, with attention paid to changing light and weather.

Hone made a lot of watercolour sketches direct from nature, but his exhibition pieces were completed in the studio in oil paint on canvas. His brushwork was quick and vigorous, using the thickness of the paint for textures and description of form and volume.

Influences

Hone's early training with Couture gave him the skills and confidence to work quickly. He used these skills to capture the effects of light and nature he learned with the Barbizon artists he met in France.

Walter Osborne (1859–1903)

Educated at the RHA School, Walter Osborne won many prizes as an art student, including the Taylor Scholarship in 1881 and 1882, which allowed him to study in Antwerp and spend a year painting in Brittany. *Apple Gathering, Quimperlé* (Fig. 32.3), a scene in the *plein air* style, is from this time. As his work developed, Osborne's style became looser and moved towards Impressionism.

Osborne was a popular and successful portrait painter and it was an important part of his living. He taught at the RHA School, where William Leech

Figure 32.3 *Apple Gathering, Quimperlé*, 1883, by Walter Osbourne, oil on canvas, 58 × 46 cm, National Gallery of Ireland, Dublin.

was one of his pupils. His final unfinished work, *Tea in the Garden*, which is on display at the Hugh

Figure 32.4
In a Dublin Park, Light and Shade, 1890s, by Walter Osborne, oil on canvas, 71 × 91 cm, National Gallery of Ireland, Dublin. This is a moody painting both in colour and subject matter.

Lane Gallery, shows that his style was becoming more Impressionistic before his sudden death from pneumonia at the age of 44.

In a Dublin Park, Light and Shade

This group of figures is an allegory for life, from babyhood to old age. It is unsentimental; the mother figure looks tired and unwell and no one looks well-off or jolly. It is an observation of the lives of ordinary people in Dublin of the 1890s.

Composition and Colour

The line of faces is about a third of the way down from the top of the format, and the figures of the man and woman are each about a third in from the sides, but it is the use of light that mainly draws our focus to the faces of the characters.

The colours are natural; Osborne uses warm earth colours and bright greens in the sunlit areas, which contrasts with the browns, dark greens and black in the shadows. These are the colours of the *plein air* style rather than the brighter colours of the Impressionists. The skin tones are in earth colours, sienna and ochre, mixed with white. Touches of red are used in lips and cheeks. Subtle tones are used in the shadow areas on faces and hands.

Style and Technique

There is a mixture of styles in this painting. It can be classified as a genre piece because of its subject, as a *plein air* piece through the observation of landscape and also approaches the Impressionist style in the free brushwork and the observation of light.

From his early work in Brittany, Osborne showed an interest in the effects of light. In this richly textured oil painting on canvas, he contrasts deep shadow with white highlights, literally spotlighting points of interest. Large brushmarks quickly applied are characteristic of Osborne's later work, yet none of the accuracy is lost.

Influences

His early education at the Royal Dublin Society and in Antwerp gave him the skills to take on the *plein*

air style he discovered in France. His friendship with English artists and visits to France broadened his experience and gave him a taste for a more modern style.

Create some life drawings of people in different lighting situations. Try using a colour medium like oil pastels to express light and shade without using black.

Roderic O'Conor (1860–1940)

Born in Roscommon to a land-owning family, Roderic O'Conor had independent means and did not need to make his living by his art, which left him free to experiment with the most advanced styles and ideas of his time. He became integrated with French art and did not often exhibit with other Irish artists.

O'Conor's early art education was in the Dublin Metropolitan School of Art. He furthered his education in Antwerp and then worked under Charles Carlous-Duran in Paris in the 1880s. He was aware of the Impressionists and admired Sisley in particular. He would have seen the work of Gauguin and van Gogh in the *Salon des Indépendants* in

Figure 32.5 *Field of Corn, Pont-Aven*, 1892, by Roderic O'Conor, oil on canvas, 38 × 38 cm, Ulster Museum, Belfast.

Figure 32.6 *Bretonne*, 1890s, by Roderic O'Conor, oil on canvas, 54 × 45 cm, National Gallery of Ireland, Dublin.

1889. O'Conor exhibited for many years at the *Salon des Indépendants*, as well as the *Salon d'Automne*.

By 1892, O'Conor was working in Brittany in an advanced Post-Impressionist style. *Field of Corn, Pont-Aven* (Fig. 32.5) owes a lot to the style of van Gogh – bold stripes of colour contour the landscape, emphasising its form, while the powerful colours radiate heat. He continued working in this 'stripe' technique for the next ten years while he lived in Brittany, painting landscapes, seascapes and local women in traditional costumes.

Bretonne

Composition and Colour

The traditionally placed figure creates a triangular composition. The complimentary reds and greens used to create tones make for a 'hot' colour scheme often found in his work.

Style and Technique

This oil painting on canvas is strongly marked with broad brushstrokes thickly painted. O'Conor's boldly painted brushwork shows the influence of van Gogh, and anticipates the Fauves and Expressionists. The painting was made during the time O'Conor was working in his striped technique. Complimentary colours are laid down side by side and the eye is allowed to mix them visually into areas of light and shadow. His style was unique among the group of painters he worked with at Pont-Aven.

Impressionists and Intimists

When O'Conor moved to Paris in the 1880s, he came in contact with the Impressionists and Post-Impressionists and immediately adopted aspects of their style and techniques. He was particularly impressed by van Gogh, leading O'Conor to create his 'stripe' technique, which he developed over his ten years in Brittany.

Paul Gauguin was the leading artist in the group of painters who lived around Pont-Aven. When he returned from his first Tahiti trip in 1894, he became friendly with O'Conor and they were close for a few years, although O'Conor maintained an independent style. He did not exhibit for ten years from 1893 to 1903.

When he moved back to Paris in 1904, O'Conor's painting changed course and developed into a more Intimist style. He painted interiors, still life and nudes in a style more like that of Bonnard and Vuillard. His style gradually became more traditional, although strong colour was still a feature. *Iris* (Fig. 32.7), painted in 1913, is one of a series of flower studies he made.

> **Intimism:** A genre of intimate domestic scenes painted in an Impressionist technique, particularly associated with the French artists Bonnard and Vuillard.

O'Conor died in 1940 in Nueil-sur-Layon, in the south of France. His studio remained closed for fifteen years until his wife died. A large body of his work was discovered in the studio when it was reopened, along with a collection of paintings by Impressionists and Post-Impressionists that he had purchased over the years.

Figure 32.7 *Iris*, 1913, by Roderic O'Conor, oil on canvas, 61 × 50 cm, Tate Gallery, London.

Figure 32.8 *The Mirror*, 1900, by William Orpen, oil on canvas, 50 × 40 cm, Tate Gallery, London.

Sir William Orpen (1878–1931)

The son of a Dublin solicitor, William Orpen was a child prodigy. He began studying at the Metropolitan School of Art in Dublin at just 12 years of age.

Orpen went on to study at the Slade School in London, where he was greatly influenced by his teacher, Henry Tonks. Orpen was knowledgeable about art history and often included references to the work of the masters in his own paintings. Unlike many of his contemporaries, he did not study abroad, although he did make trips to Europe. where he visited galleries and was familiar with the work of the Impressionists.

From 1899, he exhibited with the New English Art Club in London and with the RHA in Dublin. His early paintings were mostly interiors in dark tones in the Dutch style. Convex mirrors, like the one in the *Arnolfini Portrait* by Van Eyck (see Fig. 5.3, p. 82), were sometimes used as a centrepiece in these paintings. *The Mirror* (Fig. 32.8) is one of these genre pieces.

From 1902 to 1914, Orpen taught part-time at the Metropolitan School of Art in Dublin, and proved very influential to a generation of students. He spent his summers at Howth, where he painted scenes of the gravel beach and the cliffs.

During World War I, Orpen acted as an official war artist and was troubled for the rest of his life by the things he saw. Many of his paintings show No Man's Land under winter snow or blooming with spring flowers, although some depict the wounded and dying, and the terrible conditions the soldiers fought in. There is a large collection of his war paintings at the Imperial War Museum in London.

He was made a Knight of the British Empire in 1918, and made a very good living as a portrait painter in London after the war, which he continued right to the end of his life.

Figure 32.9
Midday on the Beach,
1910, by William Orpen,
oil on canvas,
89 × 117 cm.

Midday on the Beach
Composition and Colour

The figures are placed in the bottom left corner of the format, a diagonal drawn from the top left corner to the bottom right would enclose them. This is balanced by the clothes and picnic hamper in the top right. The diagonal from bottom left to top right catches the mothers hand and legs and the child's face. This is quite a modern arrangement, a little bit unbalanced to create tension for a more dramatic effect.

Orpen uses mainly spectrum colours in the Impressionist way, in the shaded areas as well as in the brighter spots. His normal palette of colours was more traditional, featuring ochres, earth colours and black as well as spectrum colours.

Style and Technique

This painting is Impressionistic both in composition and colour; outlines are reduced and the effects of

light are closely observed. The oil paint is applied in dabs, freely painted, direct from the brush, without blending. Outlines are reduced to a minimum, allowing changes of colour to create the forms. The brushmarks are particularly clear in the highlights on the mother's dress.

William John Leech (1881–1968)

Leech studied at the Metropolitan School and the RHA in Dublin under Walter Osbourne before going to Paris where he was influenced by the Post-Impressionists. He moved to Brittany in 1903 and lived at Concarneau for a few years. He continued to visit France throughout his life. Leech exhibited in Dublin and Paris all through his career.

Convent Garden, Brittany

Composition and Colour

The off-centre placing of the main figure, who looks as if she is about to leave the scene, is modern for the time. The row of figures at the top of the composition seem suspended in space. The foreground flowers create a diagonal, taking up almost half the picture space, although their lightness only adds to the sense of space.

William Orpen acted as a war artist during World War I. Find an example of one of his war artworks, and compare it to *Midday on the Beach* in terms of colour, composition, style and technique. Which painting do you prefer? Why?

Figure 32.10 *Convent Garden*, Brittany, 1913, by William John Leech, oil on canvas, 132 × 106 cm, National Gallery of Ireland, Dublin. This painting shows the strong influence the Impressionists had on Leech. It was first exhibited in the Paris Salon of 1913.

Leech was a colourist, and he used spectrum colours in the Impressionist way. Note the delicate shades in the areas of white clothes and flowers. Little spots of orange and red enliven the green areas. It is a masterful rendering of light and shade.

Style and Technique

This painting has a mix of styles – the loosely painted foreground is made of large, dashed-off brushstrokes, while the face of the young woman is carefully painted from accurate drawings. This is a large studio painting, different from his smaller, looser paintings, which were made *en plein air*. The thickly-painted grass and flowers contrast with the delicate brushwork on the figures.

Influences

Aspects of van Gogh's brushwork can be seen in the foreground. The asymmetrical composition, with the central figure about to leave the picture, is a feature in many Impressionist paintings. The more

Figure 32.11 *Un Matin*, 1918–20, by William John Leech, oil on canvas, 112 × 127 cm, Hugh Lane Gallery, Dublin. This boldly painted picture shows the influence of Impressionism and Post Impressionism.

carefully drawn and detailed figures, however, are in the English tradition.

Un Matin

Un Matin is almost abstract in its sense of pattern and shape. It is painted in a limited palette of blues and greens. The influence of the Post-Impressionists can be seen in the brushwork, which is again in the style of van Gogh (see p. 187). The flat, decorative pattern is reminiscent of Gauguin (see p. 190).

Leech did not have much effect on the development of Irish art, as he lived outside Ireland most of his life.

Research the work of some Impressionists you will find in Unit 4. Compare them with the artists in this chapter. Do you think the Irish artists compare well with their French contemporaries?

Analysis

Choose some paintings by your favourite artists from this period. Observe the changes in colour and technique in their work over time.

As Irish artists began to study more on the continent, the new European styles began to make their way back into Ireland. Hone, Osborne and Orpen, who taught in Dublin art schools, were very influential on the following generation of art students. Irish artists were often at the forefront of the new styles and techniques developing in France.

Irish artists were thus less influenced by what was happening in art circles in London, and now looked to the continent for their further education and inspiration.

Chapter Review

1. Name two Irish artists who learned the *plein air* style of painting in France. Using words and sketches describe a painting in the style by each artist.

2. Look at the painting *In a Dublin Park, Light and Shade* (Fig. 32.4) by Walter Osborne. Describe its composition and use of light in words and sketches. Do you think there is an emotional message in the painting?

3. Roderic O'Conor was one of the most advanced painters of his day. Using words and sketches, describe one of his paintings which shows his style and technique to advantage.

4. Using words and sketches, analyse the composition of William Orpen's *Midday on the Beach* (Fig. 32.9). Where did the influences for this painting come from?

5. Look up another painting by William Leech and describe in words and sketches the composition, the use of colour, and the style you think the work is in.

6. Describe the work of your favourite artist from this period, using words and sketches to illustrate the aspects of their work that appeals to you.

Further Research

www.visual-arts-cork.com – Navigate the A-Z index to find out more about any of the artists featured in this chapter

www.youtube.com – Search for 'Walter Fredrick Osborne' (2.20) by KistoDreams for an overview of the artist's works

ww.youtube.com – Search for 'William Orpen' (3.29) for an overview of the artist's works

www.youtube.com – Search for 'William John Leech - Is this Ireland's Favourite Painting?' (4.13) to learn more about *Convent Garden, Brittany*

www.visual-arts-cork.com/artist-paints/colour-theory-painting.htm – Learn more about colour theory and how to apply it to your own artwork

Chapter 33

The Celtic Revival

By the end of this chapter I will ...

* have learned about the Celtic Revival
* be able to describe the work of Jack B. Yeats, Paul Henry, Seán Keating and Harry Clarke
* have learned about the Irish artists working in stained glass.

Context

By the early 20th century, historical research and archaeology were turning up evidence of an artistic and literary past that was uniquely 'Irish'. This corresponded to the search for a national identity in literary circles; plays, poetry and novels sought the 'real people' of Ireland. The subject soon found its way into art, and before long themes from mythology, alongside the people and landscape of Ireland, were taken up by the new generation of artists. The art of the past, particularly Insular Art (see Unit 8) became a popular reference for artists and craft workers.

Media and Areas of Practice

Painting

Dublin art schools continued to teach formal drawing and painting techniques in the Classical tradition, but new techniques were beginning to come in from the continent. This influenced some artists more than others.

Sculpture

Stone carving and bronze casting continued in a conservative style, although subjects followed the Celtic Revival theme. Oliver Sheppard's The *Death of Cúchulainn* (Fig. 33.1), a scene from an Irish legend in the GPO in Dublin, is one of the best-known examples of this.

Figure 33.1
The Death of Cúchulainn, by Oliver Sheppard, General Post Office, Dublin.

Stained Glass

An Túr Gloine (The Tower of Glass) was a co-operative stained-glass studio set up in Dublin in 1910. It was managed by portrait painter Sarah Purser, although she herself did not design many windows. Michael Healy (1873–1941), Catherine O'Brien (1881–1963) and Wilhelmina Geddes (1888–1955) were among the most important members of the group.

Alfred E. Child also set up a stained-glass department in the Metropolitan School of Art in Dublin. He had trained in the studios of William Morris, the leading designer in the Arts and Crafts movement in England. Stained-glass design was taught to a very high technical standard at the school.

Harry Clarke, who was a student of A.E. Child, ran an independent glass studio and was technically – and artistically – the most adventurous of the stained-glass artists.

Crafts

There was a great revival in handicrafts using designs based on the Celtic past. The Yeats sisters Elizabeth and Lily joined Evelyn Gleeson to create the Dun Emer Guild, making all kinds of crafts for public and private use. They too were influenced by William Morris and the Arts and Crafts movement.

The Yeats sisters also ran Dun Emer Press, hand-printing and -binding literary works by Irish writers. Their brothers, W.B. Yeats and Jack B. Yeats, were the editor and illustrator respectively. Evelyn Gleeson ran the craft studio, training and overseeing the young women of the guild. They mastered weaving and embroidery, creating carpets, wall hangings, lacework, clothing and other craftwork. Their work can be seen in the Honan Chapel, Loughrea Cathedral and the National Museum of Ireland.

Create a design for poster, album cover or book cover inspired by the work of the Dun Emer Guild.

Art Elements and Design Principles
Architecture

The growing nationalist feeling at the turn of the 20th century lead to a desire to build in a distinctively Irish style. The most suitable model was considered to be the Irish Romanesque style of the 12th century. Numerous churches and some secular buildings were built in a version of this style. The most complete example is the Honan Chapel at University College Cork, designed in 1916 by James F. McMullen (Fig. 33.2). All the exterior and interior elements are in the Hiberno-Romanesque Revival style, including windows by *An Túr Gloine* and Harry Clarke. The Hiberno-Romanesque Revival style was frequently used by architects in the Celtic revival period.

Figure 33.2 The Honan Chapel, University College Cork.

Innovation and Invention

The new interest in the Celtic past as a source of design and subject matter was the main innovation of the period.

Renewed interest in handicrafts and stained glass were the main areas of invention.

Artists and Artworks

Jack B. Yeats (1871–1957)

Son of the portrait painter John Butler Yeats and brother of the poet W.B. Yeats and Lily and Elizabeth Yeats of the Dun Emer Guild, Jack B. Yeats was born in London but spent much of his childhood in Co. Sligo with his grandparents.

He went to art school in London and spent his early career as an illustrator of magazines, papers and books. These illustrations were tightly composed, drawn in strong lines, with an impish sense of humour.

From the 1890s to the early 1900s, Yeats painted watercolours of everyday characters and events in England. *The Man from Aranmore* (Fig. 33.3), painted on a trip to the Aran Islands, dates from this period.

In the early 1900s, Yeats moved back to Ireland and began painting in oils, although his subjects – everyday scenes of people and place – remained the same.

By the 1920s, Yeats had developed a more fluent painting style. His 1923 painting *The Liffey Swim* (Fig. 33.4) won a silver medal in the Arts and Culture section of the Paris Olympics of 1924. The painting shows the strong brushmarks and brighter colours of this stage of his development.

Note: The Olympics were not always solely about athletic achievement. Events at the 1924 Olympics in Paris included competitions in architecture, literature, music, painting and drawing. This was also the first Olympics in which Ireland was recognised as an independent nation.

In the 1930s, Yeats began to paint more from memory than direct observation. He was developing a signature style with bold brushmarks, thick paint

Figure 33.3 (left) *The Man from Aranmore, c.* 1905, by Jack B. Yeats, black chalk and watercolour on board, 38 × 27 cm, National Gallery of Ireland, Dublin.

Figure 33.4 (above right) *The Liffey Swim*, 1923, by Jack B. Yeats, oil on canvas, 61 × 91 cm, National Gallery of Ireland, Dublin.

Figure 33.5
Grief, 1951,
by Jack B. Yeats,
oil on canvas,
102 × 153 cm,
National Gallery of
Ireland, Dublin.

and strong colours that combined to create a sense of movement and change.

Yeats was a very private person. He did not allow anyone to watch him paint, he took no pupils and gave no lectures, preferring his art to speak for him.

Grief

Grief may be based on one of Yeats's sketches, *Let there be no more war*. There are buildings in the background, suggesting a street. The central figure is a man on a white horse surrounded by armed soldiers. In the right foreground is a figure of a woman holding a blond child, to the left an old man reaches out his arms in despair. The painting seems to be an anti-war statement.

Composition and Colour

Our eye is drawn to the figure on horseback through the dark triangular group of figures in the left foreground. The mother and child on the right complete a pyramid, with the rider at its top.

Violent reds and yellows dominate the top left half of the picture, while the lower right is mainly blues. Colours are used in the Expressionist way to show emotion: blues for sorrow, and reds and yellows for more violent emotions.

Style and Technique

This is one of Yeats's later works in the Expressionist style, where colour and brushwork are used to express ideas and emotions. The thin underpainting shows through in many areas, but is generally overlaid with strong marks loaded with oil paint. Yeats used palette knives and scrapers as well as brushes to apply paint. It is easy to see the large gestures the artist made with the paint.

Paul Henry (1876–1958)

Belfast-born artist Paul Henry moved to Paris to further his artistic education in 1898, first to the Académie Julian and then to the studio of American artist James McNeill Whistler. He later moved to England, where he worked as an art teacher and illustrator. In 1910, he went on a holiday to Achill Island with his wife Grace, who was also an artist, and fell so in love with it that they lived there for the next nine years.

Critics say that Henry did his best work at this time. He made small paintings of local people going about their daily tasks, farming and fishing. *The Potato Diggers* (Fig. 33.6), which Henry painted in 1912, shows an influence of Millet as well as the more modern van Gogh and Daumier. Henry was clearly

Figure 33.6 *The Potato Diggers*, 1912, by Paul Henry, oil on canvas, 51 × 46 cm, National Gallery of Ireland, Dublin. Henry's early work in Achill often featured the local people going about their daily tasks.

developing an individual style of impasto painting, giving careful thought to composition and colour. As time went on, he moved into painting pure landscape, with figures appearing less often.

> **Impasto:** Thickly applied paint which retains the marks of the brush or other instrument of application.

Dawn, Killary Harbour

Composition and Colour

The high point of view creates an unusual composition; a small foreground area of heathery hillside and rocks creates a contrast to the increasingly pale distance stretching out below. The delicate shades of blue used in the receding hills create an atmosphere of misty light. The increasingly cool and pale colours create distance.

Figure 33.7 *Dawn, Killary Harbour*, 1921, by Paul Henry, oil on canvas, 69 × 83 cm, Ulster Museum, Belfast. This atmospheric landscape shows the influence of Whistler in the delicate colouring and smooth finish.

Style and Technique

This painting shows the flat surface and delicate tones that Henry was exposed to in Paris, under the influence of Whistler and the Art Nouveau style. He made a number of these paintings of moody light, which contrast with his more boldly painted work. The oil paint is applied thinly and is more brushed out than in much of his work.

Society of Dublin Painters

Henry moved to Dublin in 1920 and was involved with the more modern painters in the Society of Dublin Painters, who exhibited together because of their dissatisfaction with the RHA.

Two of his paintings of cottages were used as railway posters, which made his work very popular with the public. Some critics felt that Henry became a victim of his own success, forced to repeat the scene with cottages, mountains and a huge sky to meet public demand.

For a number of years, Henry's work was so familiar through reproductions that it became devalued. Now it is understood as a well-painted and important record of a disappearing way of life, and is taken seriously.

Figure 33.8
A Connemara Village, 1930–3,
by Paul Henry, 76 × 91 cm,
National Gallery of Ireland, Dublin.
Henry's landscapes with huge
skies and cottages were very
popular with the public. They
showed a way of life that was
beginning to disappear
in rural Ireland.

A Connemara Village

A Connemara Village, painted between 1930–3, is a skilful work. The forms of the turf stacks, cottages, and the clouds are almost sculpted from differently-angled brushstrokes.

Grace Henry (1868–1953)

Born in Scotland, Grace studied in Brussels and then Paris, where she met her husband, Paul. She was sadly overshadowed by her husband's reputation in her own lifetime, but she is well regarded by critics today for her bold painting style and modern approach. *Top of the Hill* (Fig. 33.9) in the Limerick City Gallery of Art is one of the paintings made during their stay on Achill Island. After her marriage to Paul ended in the 1930s, she painted in various places around Europe, coming back to Ireland at the beginning of World War II. She continued to paint and exhibit to the end of her life.

Seán Keating (1889–1977)

Born in Limerick, Keating got a scholarship to the Dublin Metropolitan School of Art in 1911. Like many of his contemporaries, he was strongly influenced by his teacher, William Orpen. He won the Taylor Scholarship in 1914 and went to visit the Aran Islands, where he was very impressed with the lives and culture of the people. The islanders became symbolic of the 'real' Ireland for him, and he continued to use figures in traditional Aran dress in paintings throughout his life.

Figure 33.9 *Top of the Hill*, c. 1920, by Grace Henry, oil on linen, 60 × 50 cm, Limerick City Gallery of Art. This painting shows a casual meeting of a group of women in traditional dress. Figures and features are outlined in a modern style.

Keating was a nationalist and wanted to record the development of the new Republic. He painted a series of allegories, which were not always successful, to highlight the changes in society and

Figure 33.10
Men of the West, 1915, by Seán Keating, oil on canvas, 97 × 125 cm, Hugh Lane Gallery, Dublin.
The group includes a self-portrait of Keating on the left.

the development of the state. *Night's Candles are Burnt Out* (1928–9) and *An Allegory* (1952) are examples of this style.

Keating tried to record the progress of the Irish state from the poverty and backwardness of the newly independent state to the proud new republic he hoped it would become. He exhibited regularly in Ireland, England and the USA. He believed the artist to be a craftsman and a worker, and he took on all kinds of projects, from posters to portraits to floats for pageants. More than anything, Keating was an academic painter who was proud to trace his art links back to Ingres through a succession of student-teacher relationships.

Men of the West

A group of three figures dressed in the traditional clothes of Aran Islanders are armed with rifles, and positioned in front of a tricolour. They represent the people of the west, ready to take up arms for Ireland. Keating used himself as the model for the man on the left, staring boldly at the viewer. His brother and a friend modelled for the other figures.

Composition and Colour

This formally arranged figure group stands out sharply from the simple background. It is constructed around a series of triangles based on the diagonals of the canvas. The colours are quite

traditional: earth colours form the basis of the under drawing and flesh tones. Reds are used for emphasis here and there. Blues and greys are used to contrast with the warmer colours.

Style and Technique

Keating's style owes a lot to his teacher Orpen; he was little influenced by the European art movements and was quite hostile to Modernism. This studio painting uses traditional painting techniques built on drawing. Brushwork is used to describe surfaces and forms and is not emphasised for its own sake.

Upstream of Powerhouse with Drilling Gang and Wagon Train

Some critics consider the 26 paintings and numerous drawings that Keating was commissioned to make for the construction of the Shannon Hydro Electric Scheme from 1926 to 1929 to be his best work. Painted on-site, they are bold and direct, contrasting the huge, overpowering machinery used in the construction of the dam and canal with the small human figures. *Upstream of Powerhouse with Drilling Gang and Wagon Train* (Fig. 33.11) is one of this series. Painted in a limited colour scheme of earth tones and greys, quick brushmarks describe the form of the landscape. In contrast, the huge machine in the top left is executed in sharp outline.

Figure 33.11 *Upstream of Powerhouse with Drilling Gang and Wagon Train*, 1926–27, by Seán Keating, ESB collection. This painting in earth colours and black shows the huge scale of the machinery being used on the project.

Harry Clarke (1889–1931)

Clarke's father Joshua had a church-decorating and stained-glass business in North Frederick Street in Dublin. Clarke's secondary education was with the Jesuits in Belvedere College, which was close to his home. He left school at the age of 14 following his mother's death. He began an apprenticeship in his father's workshop and went to night classes at the Dublin Metropolitan School of Art under A.E. Child. He won a full scholarship in Stained Glass in the School of Art in 1910 and won a gold medal for stained glass at the Board of Education National Competition in London three years in a row from 1911.

Book Illustration

Clarke began to get commissions for book illustrations early in his career. The first to be published was Hans Christian Andersen's *Fairy Tales* for Harrap Publishers of London, which was well received when it came out in 1916. The book had 40 full-page illustrations, 16 of them in colour. He illustrated several books for Harraps, including 96 drawings for a 1925 edition of Goethe's *Faust*. The 'Walpurgis Night' page shows Clarke at his macabre best: a sniggering devil pushes a victim into the festering zoomorphic mass at the bottom right (Fig. 33.12). An arc of hair connects to a witch at the

Figure 33.12 'Walpurgis Night', 1925, by Harry Clarke from *Faust* by Goethe.

top of the composition, grasping pieces of people who have led less than virtuous lives. The drama of the dense black background contrasts with the fine line and texture marks that Clarke uses to describe fur, fabrics and fantasy. The drawing and decoration is beautiful, which makes the weird subject even stranger.

Clarke's style can be described as Symbolist, but it includes elements of Celtic Revivalism and Romanticism.

His figures are stylised and have a characteristic look – large eyes, long, separated fingers and toes, and elongated proportions.

Use white chalk or paint on black paper to create your own Harry Clarke-style mythical character.

Stained Glass

His success in competitions led to the commission for nine windows for The Honan Chapel of Saint Finbarr at University College Cork, which he worked on between 1915 and 1918. *An Túr Gloine* got the commission for the other eight windows.

A bequest from the Honan family allowed the church to be built to the highest standards in the Celtic Revival style.

The St Gobnait Window

St Gobnait, the patron saint of beekeepers, had a church in medieval times on Inisheer in the Aran Islands in Co. Galway. Clarke spent many summer holidays and sketching trips on the island, where he learned about the saint. Scenes at the top and bottom of the window show Gobnait and her companions driving off thieves who came to rob her

Figure 33.13
The St Gobnait Window, 1916, by Harry Clarke, a single stained-glass lancet window, one of nine in Honan Chapel, Cork.

church. The main panel shows St Gobnait in profile, a church in her left hand and a staff in her right. Thieves cower behind her robes and bees surround her.

Composition and Colour

Our attention is drawn to the pale profile of Gobnait, with her flowing red hair outlined by a dark halo with a green cross, echoing the semi-circular curve of the arch of the window. In the arch, another curve of bright stars and crosses surrounds the nuns in the top left. Yet another curve connects the faces of the nuns and the thieves in the bottom section. The large patterned area of Gobnait's robe is almost abstract; we need the face and hands to identify her figure.

Clarke was famous for his careful choice of colour. He went to London several times a year to get the coloured glass he needed for each project, and even had special coloured glass made for him. In this window, the royal blue of Gobnait's robe dominates, contrasted with the white veil she wears. Gem-like beads of red and blue form a screen behind the figures. Clarke used green to separate areas of red, while bright areas like hands and faces are set against areas of darker glass.

Style and Technique

Clarke was a very talented craftsman, and he used acids to thin coloured glass and create a range of subtle tones. His painting of details and shading was very skilful. He used leading as strong line to emphasise areas of the composition: note the honeycomb patterns in Gobnait's robes.

Influences

Clarke saw an exhibition of International art in Dublin in 1905 and was impressed by the work of Aubrey Beardsley and the Pre-Raphaelites. He kept in touch with movements in art and craft through magazines and trips to London and Paris.

Secular Glass

Clarke designed some secular windows as well as church windows. *The Eve of St Agnes* window, now on display in the Hugh Lane Gallery in Dublin, won a gold medal when it was exhibited at the Aonach Tailteann art exhibition in 1924. *The Geneva Window*, 1930, commissioned by the government for the

International Labour Court in Geneva as a gift from the Irish state, was ultimately rejected, as some of the subjects and images were considered to be too controversial by the conservative Irish politicians who had commissioned the window. It is now in the Wolfsonian Art Museum in Miami Florida, USA.

Later Life

Clarke suffered from ill health all his life and for his last few years was seriously ill with tuberculosis, in spite of this he worked extremely hard. He produced 130 windows, several illustrated books, graphic designs, fabric designs, schemes of decoration for the family church-decorating business and was involved in organising and judging exhibitions.

Analysis

> Subject rather than technique was often the focus of these artists. Examiine these two areas of focus in some of the works in this chapter.

The Celtic Revival, which began late in the 19th century and continued into the early 20th century, was closely related to the nationalist movement that ultimately culminated in an independent Irish Republic in 1949. During these years, Ireland became somewhat isolated from the new art movements in Europe.

The life and work of the ordinary people of Ireland was a recurring theme with painters of this group. The search for the 'real Ireland' that came with the struggle for independence sent artists to islands and the west of Ireland, where they sought a 'traditional' way of life. The continental influence was less obvious in this group and a kind of conservatism evolved in the newly independent state.

Chapter Review

1. Describe two pieces of work in words and sketches that show the characteristics of the Celtic Revival.

2. Do you think the interest in Ireland's Celtic past and the struggle for independence were related? Use words and sketches to show the perceived link between these two interests.

3. Jack B. Yeats's reputation has grown over the years and he is now considered to be the most important Irish painter of his generation. Do you find his work easy to understand? Write an account of one of his works, using sketches to illustrate features of his style and technique.

4. Do you think that the artists that went to paint the people and places of the west of Ireland found the 'real people' of Ireland? Explain your opinions, using words and sketches to illustrate examples of their work.

5. Some people think Harry Clarke's windows and illustrations have a dream-like quality. Would you agree? Explain your point of view using words and sketches to describe two examples of his work.

6. Who is your favourite artist from this period? Using words and sketches, describe two of their works, explaining what it is you like about them.

Further Research

celticrevival.wordpress.com – A wide-ranging blog about the Celtic Revival movement

www.nationalgallery.ie – Search for 'Jack B. Yeats 1871–1957' to learn more about this member of the artistic Yeats family

www.visual-arts-cork.com/irish-artists/ paul-henry.htm – Learn more about Paul Henry, arguably the first Irish post-Impressionist artist

www.youtube.com – Watch 'Harry Clarke - Is this Ireland's Favourite Painting?' (4.14) by RTÉ to learn about his masterpiece, *The Eve of St. Agnes*

Chapter 34

The Early Moderns

By the end of this chapter I will ...

* understand how Modern Art was introduced into Ireland
* be able to write an account of the work of, Mary Swanzy, Mainie Jellett, Evie Hone and Norah McGuinness
* have learned about the Cubist influence in Ireland
* be able to describe stained-glass work by Evie Hone
* understand Eileen Gray's role as a Modernist designer.

Context

Due to the social and economic upheaval that followed World War I, the Irish War of Independence and the Irish Civil War, Ireland had become isolated. This was mostly due to travel restrictions and a determination that the new state would be self-reliant.

The movements in Modern Art that followed each other in quick succession in Europe in the early years of the 20th century went largely unnoticed in Ireland.

In 1918, two young artists – Evie Hone and Mainie Jellett – met at art school in London. They decided to go to Paris together to learn what they could about the new styles of art that were developing

there. They studied first with André Lhote and then with Albert Gleizes, and worked together to develop distinct theories on Cubism.

Hone and Jellett exhibited their Cubist work in Dublin in 1923–4, but the work was little understood by the more traditional audience. However, the artists soon went on to raise awareness of modern artistic theories among the younger Irish artists.

Media and Areas of Practice

Oil paint was still the medium of choice for most artists, although Evie Hone did use gouache for smaller pieces.

> **Gouache:** an opaque watercolour that produces areas of flat, matte colours. It was frequently used by designers and illustrators.

Art Elements and Design Principles

Cubism took many forms throughout Europe. Hone and Jellett, alongside Mary Swanzy and Norah McGuinness, brought to Ireland a form of Cubism that they evolved with their French tutors. This style was based on observations and adaptations of the natural world, rather than pure Abstraction (see Unit 5).

Innovation and Invention

This group of women, known as the Early Moderns, were the innovators of their generation. They brought new ideas and working methods to a reluctant academic art education system in Ireland.

Women had only been allowed to attend art schools since the 1880s. Art was not considered to be a suitable career for ladies, although they might do arts and crafts to keep themselves entertained. The Early Moderns were ground-breaking in their achievements, showing that women too were serious and committed artists.

Artists and Artworks

Mary Swanzy (1882–1978)

Dublin-born Mary Swanzy was probably Ireland's first modern painter. She went to classes in May Manning's studios at an early age, where she was taught by the portrait painter John Butler Yeats, father of William, Jack, Elizabeth and Lily. She went on to the Dublin Metropolitan School of Art and spent time copying old masters in the National Gallery of Ireland. She exhibited portraits in the RHA from 1905 to 1910.

Swanzy moved to Paris, where she worked in a number of studios. During this time, she visited Gertrude Stein, an American writer and art collector who hosted a *Salon* for the leading artists and writers of the time. Swanzy would have seen work by Gauguin, Picasso and Matisse there, and it is clear that the young artist was influenced by them from her later works.

Swanzy was a well-travelled woman. A trip to Hawaii and Samoa in the 1920s resulted in paintings of the people and landscape in bold colours and simplified forms. *Samoan Scene* in the Ulster Museum is one of this series (Fig. 34.1).

Swanzy's style continued to evolve over her lifetime. She was influenced by a variety of styles, including Fauvism, Cubism, Futurism, Symbolism and Surrealism (see Unit 5). She continued to paint throughout her life, changing styles as she progressed. Some of her later works are allegories, commenting on morality and human weakness.

Figure 34.1 *Samoan Scene*, 1920s, by Mary Swanzy, oil on canvas, 153 × 96 cm, Ulster Museum, Belfast.

Propellers
Composition and Colour

Dark propeller shapes on red poles come in from the bottom right-hand corner of the format, getting smaller and paler as they progress through the centre. Darker colours frame the composition. Pale pink rectangles create a feeling of open space in the left centre. Curves create a sense of movement throughout the composition. Warm tones, reds, pinks, oranges and yellows create a contrast with the dark propeller shapes and framing elements, suggesting open space in the centre of the composition.

Figure 34.2 *Propellers*, 1942, by Mary Swanzy, oil on canvas, 54 × 46 cm, National Gallery of Ireland, Dublin. This demonstrates Swanzy's version of the Futurist style, which aimed to represent technology and movement.

Style and Technique

Swanzy blended colours with brushstrokes working away from dark or light edges. Although geometric shapes and straight lines make up much of the composition, this is not a hard-edge painting.

Influences

Swanzy experimented with many styles, beginning as an accomplished academic portrait painter and becoming progressively more modern. This painting follows the Futurist style, an Italian movement that emphasised speed and technology.

Mainie Jellett (1897–1944)

Born in Dublin, Mainie Jellett began her education in art at the Metropolitan School of Art before moving to London. She met Evie Hone at Westminster School of Art and together they went to Paris in 1920 to study Cubism. They worked in Paris for

10 years, on and off, in collaboration with Albert Gleizes, who credited them with being important contributors to his theories on Cubism.

Jellett exhibited an abstract Cubist 'decoration' in the 1923 exhibition of the Society of Dublin Painters. Unfortunately, her work was ridiculed and criticised by both critics and the public.

By the 1930s, Jellett had developed a more personal, less theoretical, Cubist style, and she exhibited with the *Art Non-Figuratif* group in Paris from 1932. She remained in touch with the cutting edge of European art throughout her career.

Despite the geometric style of her paintings, Jellett did not reject nature or representation in her work. She took the forms she wanted and built her compositions around them.

Jellett contributed much through her teaching at the Metropolitan School of Art, her writing and publicity for Modern Art. She was a founding member of the Irish Exhibition of Living Art in 1943, which exhibited the work of artists who had been rejected for their Modernism by the RHA.

Abstract Composition

Figure 34.3 *Abstract Composition, c.* 1935, by Mainie Jellett, oil on canvas, 104 × 82 cm, Crawford Gallery, Cork. An abstract composition based on the holy family.

Jellett was a religious person and often based her paintings on the work of old masters, particularly Fra Angelico.

Composition and Colour

The shapes seem to radiate out from a central point, dividing into three figures based on curves. The whole composition combines straight lines and curves.

Harmonies rather than contrasts form the basis for her colour palette. Blues, purples and violets move to reds, oranges and yellows. The tones provide a sense of depth, highlights provide a foreground, while darks offer depth.

 Can you find the three figures in Mainie Jellett's *Abstract Composition*?

Figure 34.4 *Deposition*, 1939, by Mainie Jellett, oil on canvas, 121 × 69 cm, Hugh Lane Gallery, Dublin.

Style and Technique

A personal style based on abstract Cubism. Jellett took elements from her naturalistic sketches and repeated them to create harmonies which became the abstract work of art.

This is an oil painting on canvas, finished to a smooth surface without textures. The colour areas meet abruptly, without blending, in a style that later became known as hard-edge painting.

Deposition, painted by Jellett in 1939, is strongly coloured and more clearly figurative than her earlier work, though still composed on Cubist principles. (Fig. 34.4).

 Make a drawing from a primary source, human figure or natural form. Repeat some elements of the forms or outlines as arcs or straight lines. Echo some of the shapes you have taken from your drawings, developing outwards from the centre of your format.

Evie Hone (1894–1955)

Born in Dublin, descended from the painters Nathaniel Hone the Elder and the Younger, Evie Hone went to London to study art under Walter Sickert. It was here that she met her lifelong friend and fellow artist, Mainie Jellett. Together, they went to Paris where they studied Cubism, first with André Lhote and then Albert Gleizes.

Cubist Composition

Composition and Colour

A group of concentric circles broken into small areas of colour creates a focal point in the top centre of the painting. A large area of green and mid-blue creates a kind of figure, made of curves, which connects to the circles. This 'foreground' element is set against a background of deep blues, purples and greys, framed by straight-edged right angles and lines of various lengths and colours.

The green area dominates the darker colours surrounding it. A sense of detail and focus is created in the small, brightly coloured areas within the circles. Some of the bright colours are echoed in the linear areas that surround the dark background. The layered and overlapped colours create a sense of depth and movement in the work.

Figure 34.5 *Cubist Composition, c.* 1931, by Evie Hone, gouache, 91 × 60 cm.

Style and Technique

This painting is in the abstract Cubist style Hone developed when working with Jellet and Gleizes in Paris.

This painting is oils on canvas; subtle changes happen where colours are brushed together within the geometric areas of the composition, although the borders of the coloured areas are clearly defined.

Stained Glass

Evie Hone was a very religious person. She entered an Anglican convent in 1925 but returned to painting quickly. In 1937, she converted to Catholicism and changed her focus to stained glass, a medium in which she could express her faith. Hone trained in the studios of *An Túr Gloine*, particularly with A.E. Childs and Wilhelmina Geddes.

She set up her own studio in Rathfarnham in Dublin later on, and designed *The Four Green Fields*, with symbols of the four provinces, for the Irish pavilion at the 1939 New York World's Fair. It is now in the Government Buildings in Dublin.

Her largest and most ambitious work was the east window at College Chapel, Eton School in Windsor, England (Fig. 34.6). She was commissioned to replace the glass that had been destroyed in a bombing raid during World War II. The huge composition includes images of the Crucifixion and the Last Supper. The rich reds and blues that are characteristic of her work give way to greens and browns, which frame the composition.

Hone was influenced by the medieval stained glass she had seen in Europe on a trip with members of *An Túr Gloine*. She also saw a connection between modern abstract art and Celtic art in the use of non-representational pattern and colour.

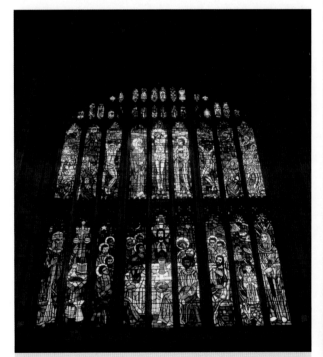

Figure 34.6 The east window at College Chapel. Eton School, Windsor, by Evie Hone. Reds and blues dominate the colour scheme of the large window in the style of medieval glass she had seen on visits to Europe.

Hone joined forces with her best friend Mainie Jellett to attempt to bring Modernism to Ireland. She was also a founding member of the Irish Exhibition of Living Art in 1943.

Although she was a revolutionary artist, always in touch with the latest movements in art, she is best remembered for her stained-glass work.

> Evie Hone's artwork was often inspired by religion, a subject she was passionate about. Design a stained-glass window based on a theme or subject you are passionate about.

Norah McGuinness (1901–1980)

Norah McGuinness was born in Derry and studied art at the Dublin Metropolitan College. In 1929, on the advice of Mainie Jellett, she went to Paris to study with André Lhote. McGuinness spent time working in London and New York during the 1930s, but returned to Dublin in 1939.

She was a working artist all her life, designing costumes and sets for the Abbey and Peacock theatres. She also illustrated books and was the window dresser at luxury department store Brown Thomas for 30 years.

McGuinness was a founding member of the Irish Exhibition of Living Art, for which she served as chairman for almost 20 years.

A Quiet Place, one of McGuinness's landscapes, is based on direct observation, but the artist uses geometry and multiple viewpoints to create a Cubist style (Fig. 34.7).

McGuinness's reputation grew over the years, and she represented Ireland alongside Nano Reid in the 1950 Venice Biennale. She was awarded an honorary membership of the RHA in 1957 and an honorary doctorate at Trinity College in 1973.

Garden Green

Composition and Colour

A selection of household objects arranged on a table in front of a window. Some objects are seen from

Figure 34.7 *A Quiet Place*, 1959, by Norah McGuinness, 50 × 60 cm, Crawford Art Gallery, Cork. Direct observation and multiple viewpoints are combined in this landscape.

Figure 34.8 *Garden Green*, 1962, by Norah McGuinness, 102 × 71 cm, Hugh Lane Gallery, Dublin.

above; others are viewed from a variety of angles. The white objects – bottle and cloth, cup and saucer – lead the eye through the window to the little girl in the garden. The harmonies of greens connect all the areas of the composition. It takes a moment to separate table from grass, plants and windows.

Style and Technique

Norah McGuinness had a personal style based on Cubism. *Garden Green* is still representational, but we are offered alternative viewpoints and harmonies in colour and shape that take the work beyond Realism. Colour blending and brushwork are an element in this oil painting on canvas. It is a more painterly approach than most Cubist pieces.

Eileen Gray (1878–1976)

Eileen Gray was born in Enniscorthy and grew up between Wexford and London. She attended the Slade Art School in London, and at the same time took lessons in lacquer work with a furniture restorer, Dean Charles.

In 1902, Gray went to Paris with friends, studying at the Académie Colarossi and at the Académie Julian. In 1907, she studied lacquer work with Seizo Sugawara, who was restoring Japanese lacquered furniture in Paris. In 1910, they opened a workshop together, producing screens and other pieces for wealthy clients.

Furniture and Interior Design

In 1917, Gray was hired to design the interior of a Paris apartment for wealthy fashion and millinery shop owner, Juliette Levy. *Harper's Bazaar* magazine wrote a rave review of it, describing the 'thoroughly modern' interior as the epitome of Art Deco.

The furniture included the Bibendum Chair, which was a take on the Michelin Man, featuring tyre-like shapes on a tubular chrome steel frame (Fig. 34.9). The Pirogue Day Bed, which was gondola-shaped, with a patinated bronze lacquer finish, was also included in the interior.

Gray's style became simpler in the late 1920s, moving away from the exotic woods, ivory and furs

Figure 34.9 The Bibendum Chair by Eileen Gray.

that she used in earlier work. She was fascinated by lightweight, functional, multipurpose furniture, and is now believed to be the first designer to use chrome tubular steel in furniture design (Fig. 34.10).

Figure 34.10 The adjustable table E-1027 by Eileen Gray.

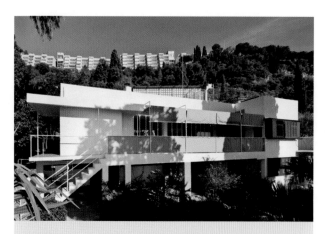

Figure 34.11 E-1027 by Eileen Gray. The concrete construction raised on pillars has simple Modernist lines very advanced for the 1920s.

Figure 34.12 Gray furnished the interior of E-1027 with her own furniture. She wanted to create a harmonious atmosphere for living in.

Architecture

Gray began a romance with the Romanian architect Jean Badovici in 1921 and spent the next six years teaching herself architecture from technical and theoretical books. She also had drafting lessons and visited building sites.

E-1027

In 1926, Gray began a design for a holiday home near Monaco, staying on-site for three years while the house was built. The house was in Badovici's name because Gray was not a French citizen. He also took part of the credit for it when it was finished, and published an edition of his magazine on the house design.

Note: Why E-1027? It's a code for the names of the owners: E for Eileen, 10 for J, the tenth letter of the alphabet, 2 for B and 7 for G. So, Eileen, Jan Badovici, Gray.

E-1027, as the house is known, is a masterpiece of Modernist design. The design is based on cubes, raised over the sloping stony ground on pillars. It seems to be based on Gray's then-friend Le Corbusier's 'Five Points of the New Architecture'. The two fell out later because Le Corbusier tried to take some credit for the design of E-1027.

The building is open plan, standing on pillars, has horizontal windows, an open façade and a flat roof accessible by stairs (Fig. 34.11).

Gray furnished the interior with her own pieces (Fig. 34.12). She stated that 'the interior plan should not be an incidental result of the façade; it should lead to a complete, harmonious and a logical life.' The building has now been restored and is open to the public.

In 1931, Gray separated from Badovici and began a new house called Tempe à Pailla, above the nearby town of Menton. It is a small two-bedroom house with a large terrace, designed to make the best of the panoramic views and to create air flow to keep the house cool in summer. The furniture was designed to be multipurpose, filling changing needs.

Gray was pretty much written out of design history until the late 1960s and early 1970s, when she was rediscovered, written about in design magazines and given a retrospective exhibition of her work in London and Dublin. She is now recognised as a ground-breaking Modernist designer, and many of her furniture designs are still being produced under license.

Analysis

Most of the innovators at this time were women. Why do you think this was? Choose some examples of their work and examine subject and technique.

The Irish Cubists were not appreciated in the first half of the 20th century. It took time for the public and the more conservative teachers in the art colleges to accept that traditional Realism was no longer the main focus in the world of art. The perseverance and example of the Early Moderns led to an opening up of minds and attitudes to Modern Art.

Because Eileen Gray lived and worked in Paris most of her life, she was unknown in Ireland until the 1970s. Her contribution to the world of design is now well recognised.

Organising exhibitions like the Irish Exhibition of Living Art and writing publications on Modern Art got the public more engaged in modern movements. It was largely through the efforts of Hone, Jellett, Swanzy, McGuinness and Gray that Modern Art got a foothold in Ireland.

After Modernism

In the years following World War II, Ireland became a bit isolated and conservative due to the government policy of self-sufficiency and the trading difficulties caused by the war. In the 1960s, there was a change of policy and Ireland became a trading nation and experienced a period of prosperity. This new prosperity created a demand for the arts and a new generation of artists got public and private commissions.

Art education was also changing and, by the mid-1970s, art schools had finally modernised their curriculums. More secondary schools offered art as a Leaving Certificate subject, since it was accepted by the universities as an entry subject.

Some artists were able to make a living in Ireland, but many still went abroad, where Modern Art was better understood and appreciated.

Chapter Review

1. How did the Cubist influence come to Ireland? Was it well received? Write about two artists who worked in the Cubist style, using sketches to illustrate your answer.

2. Mary Swanzy changed her style throughout her life. Do you think this is a good thing, or should artists stick to one style? Use words and sketches to make your points.

3. Trace the educational development of Mainie Jellett and Evie Hone and show what it brought to their art.

4. Evie Hone tried to express her religious faith in her stained-glass windows. Do you think this is evident in the work? Use words and sketches to describe one of her windows.

5. Norah Mc Guinness created an individual style of Cubism. What do you think of it? Sketch and write about examples of her work to make your points.

6. Do you think Eileen Gray's designs hold up in the 20th century?

Further Research

www.visual-arts-cork.com – Search for 'Mary Swanzy' to learn more about one of the earliest abstract painters in Irish art

www.visual-arts-cork.com – Search for 'Norah McGuinness' for more on the Irish landscape artist, graphic designer and illustrator

www.manresa.ie – Click on 'Evie Hone' in the 'About Manresa' menu to see some close-ups of Hone's stained glass

www.youtube.com – Watch 'Irish Women Artists 1870–1970' (5:00) for an overview of the Early Moderns

www.eileengray.co.uk – Designer Eileen Gray's official website

www.youtube.com – Search for 'A brief introduction to Eileen Gray' (23:13) for a video presentation on Eileen Gray's work

Unit 12
Post-1960s Art in Ireland

Post-1960s Art in Ireland

Second-Generation Moderns
(1960 to present)

Isolated Bei
1952,
le Brocquy

The Childrer of Lir, 1966,
Kelly

Hard-Edge Painting
(1958 to present)

Une Nature Morte à la M Irlandaise, 19
Farrell

Photo-Realism
(late 1960s to present)

Portrait of No Brown, 1985
Ballagh

Installations
(mid-1970s to present)

Ghost Ship,
1998, Cross

Minimalism
(late 1950s to present)

Meditation Painting, 200
Scott

Proclamation
2007, Gillespi

Performance and Mixed Media
(late 1960s to present)

Cassandra's Necklace, 20
Maher

Tremble Trem
2017, Jones

Chapter 35

The Second Generation of Modern Artists

By the end of this chapter I will ...

* understand the changes in society and art education that promoted Modernism
* be familiar with the changes in media and techniques that were introduced at this time
* have seen examples of a variety of styles of painting and sculpture
* be able to give an account of the life and work of at least four painters
* become familiar with the work of at least two sculptors.

Before 1960

Following World War II, Ireland went through a period of austerity and rationing. The country had become very conservative in the years following independence from Britain, and the arts were at a low ebb. It was hard to have a career as an artist unless you had another means of support. As a result of all these factors, many Irish artists went abroad, where they felt Modern Art was better understood and appreciated

Context

The 1960s were the time of the Cold War between the Soviet Union and the USA, when there was a real fear of a nuclear war. In Ireland, this was a time of economic expansion, when the self-sufficiency and isolation of the 1950s was overtaken by free trade and foreign investment. National output and employment were at record highs.

In 1961, the newly founded television station, Raidió Teilifís Éireann (RTÉ), began creating a forum for new ideas and debate. Worldwide, new styles of music, literature and art, were replacing the conservatism and censorship of the previous generation.

Free secondary education was made available from 1967, creating new possibilities for people who did not have these opportunities before.

The Civil Rights movement, which began in Derry in the late 1960s, was followed by the Troubles in Northern Ireland, overshadowing all political and social development.

An oil crisis in the 1970s triggered a global economic downturn, with unemployment and reduced opportunities in Ireland. The country, alongside Britain and Denmark, joined the European Economic Community in 1973, bringing a much-needed boost to the Irish economy.

A series of referendums on the social issues of abortion and divorce in the 1980s created new political and social priorities. Following further expansion of the EEC in the 1980s, the Maastricht Treaty created the foundations for European Union in 1995 and the single currency, the Euro, in 1999.

Media and Areas of Practice

New materials and techniques were introduced in the 1960s. Acrylic paint was good for the hard-edge painting that was popular internationally, while being more budget-friendly than oils. Screen printing and other print media were more frequently used in mainstream art.

New experimentation with media included dripping, throwing, diluting, spraying, layering, scraping and a host of other processes, which challenged the conventions at the time.

Figure 35.1 Liberty Hall, Dublin, designed by Desmond Rea O'Kelly. It was completed in 1965, then the tallest building in Ireland.

Industrial and environmental elements were introduced into sculpture, which underwent radical change in this era. Photography, film, video and other kinds of lens art entered the realm of fine art.

A belief that the art idea was more important than the art object led to all kinds of experiments with performance art and other events that did not end with a product, but were *themselves* the art.

Architecture, too, underwent radical change. The first Modern buildings appeared in Ireland in the 1960s (Fig. 35.1).

Art Elements and Design Principles

The notion that artworks needed subjects or titles seemed unimportant in this age of experimentation; numbers were often used to identify a series of pieces rather than names. Abstraction of all kinds – hard edge or gestural or produced by any method – was the most common form of expression.

Innovation and Invention

Art colleges finally conceded that Modern Art was a valid form of artistic expression, and changed their courses in the 1970s to accommodate new thinking. Materials, techniques and ideas were going through a period of rapid change, as outlined above.

Artists and Artworks
Painters
Louis le Brocquy (1916–2012)

One of the leading figures in 20th-century Irish art, le Brocquy actually studied chemistry in Trinity College and spent a number of years working in the family oil refinery business before studying the old masters of art in the galleries of Europe.

Le Brocquy returned to Dublin in 1940, at the beginning of World War II, working as a self-taught painter. He was a founder member of the Irish Living Art Exhibition in 1943 and had his first solo exhibition in London in 1947. In 1948, he married another Irish artist, Anne Madden, and they moved to live in the south of France.

His busy painting career can be divided into a number of periods, during which he worked on similar subjects or series. The first was a series of 'Tinker' paintings in the late 1940s. In the early 1950s, he moved on to his 'Grey Period', which evolved into a 'White Period' in the late 1950s. This then made way for a series of 'Heads', which continued on and off until 2006.

RESEARCH Go to YouTube and search for 'Louis le Brocquy Ancestral Head 1965' (2.11). Watch the video and pay careful attention to the brushwork that le Brocquy used. Make a series of studies using the same brush technique.

There was a 'Procession' series in the 1980s and 1990s; 'Human Images' from the 1990s into the new millennium; and finally a 'Homage' series, where le Brocquy worked from images of his favourite artists.

Isolated Being

In this painting from the White Period, a human figure is emerging from or disappearing into the background. It may have been influenced by x-rays of the artist's wife's back and ideas of isolation.

Composition and Colour

The central figure takes up about one-third of the width; the head is located one-third down from the top and a strongly coloured and textured area features about one-third up from the bottom. It is a very balanced conventional composition.

Some bold red marks in the middle of the figure contrast with the muted tones of the rest of the painting. A blue-grey background is overpainted with white, merging with the blue in some areas.

Style and Technique

This oil painting on canvas is from le Brocquy's White Period. The smooth surface of the delicately

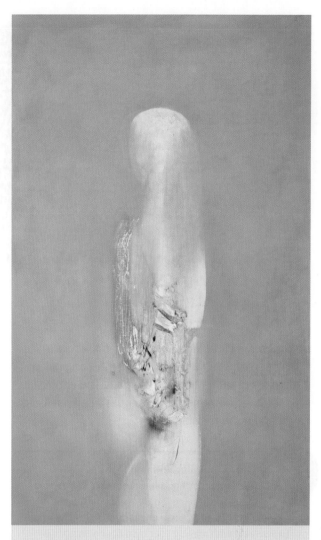

Figure 35.2 *Isolated Being*, 1962, by Louis le Brocquy, oil on canvas, 152 × 91 cm, Hugh Lane Gallery, Dublin.

coloured background appears to be attacked with bold marks and scratches in the centre of the canvas. A heavy application of paint in the centre of the figure is faded out to the sides, creating the impression of the figure emerging or being absorbed into the background.

Other Works

Over the course of his seventy-year career, le Brocquy illustrated books, designed theatre sets and costumes, and re-introduced tapestry as an art form. *Hosting of the Táin* (1969) in the Irish Museum of Modern Art is one of his beautifully coloured Tapestries.

Figure 35.3
Army Massing,
1969, by Louis le
Brocquy, from Thomas
Kinsella's translation
of *The Táin*. Gestural
brushmarks, made
with printer's ink,
were used to make
the figures.

Le Brocquy's illustrations for Thomas Kinsella's translation of *The Táin* (Fig. 35.3) in the original in 1969 have great strength and vigour. The controlled brushstrokes demonstrate the artist's sensitivity to any medium he is using.

> Go to YouTube and search for 'The Táin Collection by Louis le Brocquy' (3.03). While you're watching the video, pay particular attention to the artist's use of descriptive brushmarks. Experiment with making your own scene using this technique.

His 'Heads' series of paintings was his longest lasting and, some would say, most important body of work. He painted images of writers and artists trying to reveal the spirit and imagination of his chosen characters. W.B. Yeats (Fig. 35.4) and James Joyce were both featured many times, while Samuel Beckett, Francis Bacon and Seamus Heaney were among the artist's acquaintances who found themselves subjects of his artwork.

Image of W.B. Yeats

Composition and Colour

The face dominates the 70 × 70 cm space: le Brocquy may have been influenced by Celtic spirituality, in which the head houses the spirit.

Figure 35.4 *Image of W.B. Yeats*, 1976, by Louis le Brocquy, oil on canavs, 70 × 70 cm, Irish Museum of Modern Art, Dublin.

Primary colours are used to create the structure and modelling of the face. The unexpected colour and application of paint distort the image.

Style and Technique

Le Brocquy's painting style is unique, and does not fit into to any school or group. The face emerging from the almost white canvas is painted wet into wet – that is, paint is applied and smudged or moved with the brush on the wet surface. More paint is added or moved while the surface is still wet.

Le Brocquy is regarded as one of Ireland's greatest artists. His work has been shown all over the world and is featured in some of the great international collections.

Abstract Painters

Patrick Scott (1921–2014)

Scott came from a farming background in Co. Cork, but grew up in Dublin and went on to study architecture. He exhibited his paintings as early as the 1940s, but continued in architecture until 1960, when he represented Ireland at the Venice Biennale and also won a Guggenheim award.

In the 1960s, Scott painted a series of 'Large Solar Device' compositions, which protested against the continued testing of nuclear weapons. One of these, measuring 234 × 153 cm, is on display in Dublin's Hugh Lane Gallery.

 Go to Vimeo and search for 'Artists Stories / Patrick Scott' (14:05). Watch the interview with the artist and make notes on his artistic process.

Scott felt that simplicity was an essential part of his work. He often used circles or parts of circles as the focus in his compositions. He was interested in Zen and meditation and this came across in his paintings, which are often very calming to look at.

Throughout his life, Scott was a designer as well as an artist, and produced tapestries and prints in addition to paintings. He was one of the first Irish artists to produce completely abstract work.

Meditation Painting 28
Composition and Colour

A circle of gold leaf dominates the upper portion of the work. The top edge of the circle is close to the

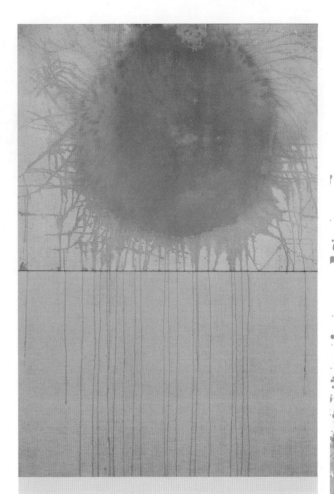

Figure 35.5 *Large Solar Device*, 1964, by Patrick Scott, 234 × 153 cm, Hugh Lane Gallery, Dublin. Liquid tempera paint was applied to untreated canvas and allowed to run.

top of the canvas and the lower edge is close to the black rectangle at the bottom of the canvas. There is some space to left and right of the circle. The lower part of the canvas is divided into an area of black and an area of untreated canvas.

All the divisions are unequal; the black band is larger than the space below, and the upper portion, with the circle in it, is bigger than the lower area. Do you think that these proportions create a tension or a harmony?

Style and Technique

This is a pure geometric abstraction. The materials are reduced to the basics: unprimed canvas, black acrylic paint and gold leaf.

Figure 35.6 *Meditation Painting 28*, 2007, by Patrick Scott, gold leaf and acrylic on unprimed canvas, 120 × 81 cm, Irish Museum of Modern Art, Dublin.

Figure 35.7 *Hawk and Quarry in Winter, in Memory of Peter Lanyon*, 1964, by Tony O'Malley, oil on board, 53 × 72 cm, Crawford Art Gallery, Cork.

Tony O'Malley (1913–2003)

Born in Callan, Co. Kilkenny, O'Malley drew and painted from an early age. He began a career as a bank official, but in 1940 he became ill with tuberculosis and painted a lot during his convalescence. He went back to banking, but resigned and took up painting full time in 1958.

O'Malley found it difficult to get his work noticed in Ireland, so he went to live in St Ives in Cornwall, England in 1960. There was a thriving artistic community in St Ives and O'Malley kept a studio there for 30 years.

In 1973, he married the artist Jane Harris, who had connections with Lanzarote and the Bahamas. The light and colour in Lanzarote and particularly the Bahamas changed O'Malley's colour palette in his paintings. He used brighter and more saturated colours in his later work.

Hawk and Quarry in Winter, in Memory of Peter Lanyon (Fig. 35.7) is an abstraction based on landscape; the cool colours suggest winter. He said of his work: 'Abstraction does enable you to get under the surface, to get beyond appearance, and express the mind.'

O'Malley had a very successful career; his work is in collections all over the world. He was made a Saoi of Aosdána in 1990 and given an honorary doctorate by Trinity College in 1994.

Mid-Summer Window with Moths
Composition and Colour

This is a colourful abstraction based on nature and landscape. Natural greens and browns are decorated with small areas of yellow and red. A yellow dotted stripe almost halves the square panel. One could try to explain this painting in terms of creatures and nature, but that would be imposing a type of realism that is not the point of the work.

Style and Technique

O'Malley sometimes applies textures and scratches to the surface of his work. In this painting, brushmarks and surface scratches create a sense of movement and depth.

Figure 35.8 *Mid-Summer Window with Moths*, 1992, by Tony O'Malley, oil on board, 126 × 126 cm, Hugh Lane Gallery, Dublin.

O'Malley uses texture to great effect. Using oil pastels, create a landscape or still life, then use the end of a paintbrush or another pointed object to scratch into the pastel, picking out details or adding texture to your work.

Camille Souter (b. 1929)

Born in England but raised in Ireland, this artist was named Betty Pamela Holmes before her first husband, Gordon Souter, gave her the nickname Camille.

Souter trained as a nurse in London, where she spent much of her spare time visiting galleries. She began painting in the 1950s while recovering from an illness, spending some time working in Italy and Ireland. Her early work is Abstract Expressionist (see Unit 6), but a figurative element crept in, so some objects can be recognised amid the textured surfaces of the paintings. In *Washing by the Canal* (Fig. 35.9), we can see the washing of the title hanging between trees at the top of the picture. The rest of the painting is more obviously abstract; surfaces are marked and textured and colours, although natural, do not clearly belong to real objects.

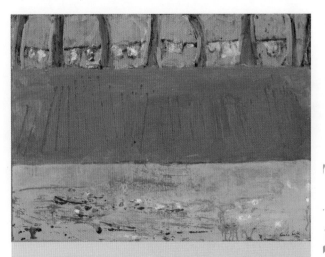

Figure 35.9 *Washing by the Canal*, 1964, by Camille Souter, oil on board, 58 × 79 cm, Limerick City Gallery of Art.

Souter is a prolific painter, generally working in a fairly small size. She has created series of paintings based on themes as different as flying, the circus, the Gulf War, meat and still life. Her loose painting technique, rich colours and observations of nature make her work accessible and attractive. She has received recognition and awards throughout her career, and has exhibited in the Irish Exhibition of Living Art, Independent Artists and the RHA annual exhibition.

Old Wheel Gate Entrance to Estate
Composition and Colour

This is an abstract painting based on observations of real objects. The dark hub of the wheel is the focus of the piece.

The upper half of the format is loosely painted in a buff colour, which does not draw attention to itself. The lower half is more richly coloured and textured. Natural, muted greens and greys create the background for the blue-black drawing of the wheel shape. The colours are rich, though not bright, suggesting weather and light conditions. What season and time do the colours suggest to you?

Style and Technique

This small oil painting is on paper. The loose brushwork and texture marks are typical of Souter's work.

Figure 35.10 *Old Wheel Gate Entrance to Estate*, 1967, by Camille Souter, oil on paper, 50 × 33 cm, Irish Museum of Modern Art, Dublin.

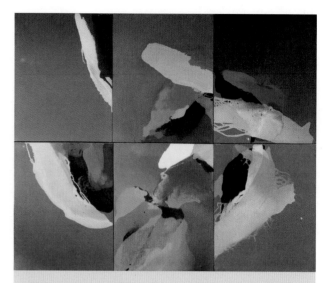

Figure 35.11 *Big Red Mountain Series, sixpartite,* 1967, by Anne Madden, oil on canvas, 185 × 220 cm, Collection of Trinity College, Dublin. The paintings were made by pouring pigment and sometimes adding sand for texture.

Anne Madden (b. 1932)

Daughter of an Irish father and an Anglo-Chilean mother, Anne Madden spent her earliest years in Chile. The family moved to England in 1936, and, as a young woman, Madden went to college in the Chelsea School of Arts and Crafts in 1950. However, she found the courses very traditional, and was excited by an exhibition of American Abstract Expressionist paintings she saw in London in 1956. A series of spinal operations following a riding accident interrupted her career, but after her marriage to Louis le Brocquy in 1958 and a move to the south of France, she was able to paint full time.

Early works in muted colours and based on the stony Burren landscape were followed by more colourful compositions like *Big Red Mountain Series*

(1967), which hangs in Trinity College, Dublin (Fig. 35.11). Madden also represented Ireland in the Paris Biennale in 1965.

A lot of Madden's works were painted in series. Megaliths and other monuments in the landscape provided the inspiration for paintings where the format was divided into a series of unevenly spaced verticals on a densely painted surface. A series of 'Openings' followed, where architectural frames lead to dark, uncertain spaces created in thinly layered paint. This was followed by a series based on Pompeii – people and buildings frozen in time and the ever-present possibility of death.

Madden has continued painting in series throughout her career. Gardens, boats, an Icarus series, time and space and the Northern Lights have all been sources of inspiration for her. She is a prolific painter, and exhibits solo or as part of a group every year. She has exhibited in many European cities most often in Paris, in Dublin almost every year, all over Ireland, and in several American cities.

Opening with Figures
Composition and Colour

This 225 × 220 cm canvas is almost square, broken into a grid of six rectangles, each suggesting a door

Figure 35.12 *Opening with Figures*, 1985, by Anne Madden, oil on canvas, 225 × 220 cm, University College Dublin.

or window frame leading to an internal opening or space. There is an image of a curled-up human figure in the top central section of the grid: a reminder of the bodies found during the excavations of Pompeii.

The frames on the six rectangles are in warm tones – violets, reds, oranges and yellows – which contrast with the cool blues and darks inside. The colours blend into each other, progressing from one colour to the next and from light into dark.

Style and Technique

This is oil paint on canvas, thinly painted in layers over a framework of hard-edge rectangles. The blended colours and sketchy brushwork soften the sharp edges of the framework. Madden usually paints with her canvases on the floor, applying paint quickly and working on more than one canvas at a time.

Pop Art into Photo-realism: Michael Farrell (1940–2000)

Born in Kells, Co. Meath, Michael Farrell had his secondary education in England. He did not enjoy his education, partly due to his dyslexia. He went on to study Commercial Art in St Martins, London, and enjoyed the artistic community in Soho.

Farrell's early work was in a style he called Celtic Abstraction, using images from Celtic art combined with the current international preference for minimalist hard-edge abstraction. During the 1960s he was very successful commercially and represented Ireland in the Paris Biennale in 1967.

Farrell became politically conscious as a result of the Civil Rights movement in Derry in 1968. In 1969, he won a prize at the Irish Exhibition of Living Art in Cork and, in his acceptance speech, declared that he would not exhibit his work in Northern Ireland 'until the state has achieved the basic fundamentals of a decent society'. He adapted his 'Citron Pressé' series of paintings to try to express some of these political ideas (Fig. 35.13).

In 1971, he moved to Paris, enjoying the bohemian life there, but remaining focused on the political situation in Ireland. He created a series of paintings, prints and drawings on the theme of 'Miss O'Murphy', based on the painting *A Female Nude Reclining on a Chaise-Longue* (1752) by the French artist François Boucher (1703–70), which shows Miss Marie-Louise O'Murphy, a mistress of King Louis XV. In Farrell's work she is a metaphor for

Figure 35.13 *Une Nature Morte à la Mode Irlandaise*, 1974, by Michael Farrell, acrylic on paper on board and acrylic on wood, 73 × 73 cm, Irish Museum of Modern Art, Dublin.

Ireland, *Madonna Irlanda*, scandalously exposing herself, and yet exploited and abused.

Farrell lived most of his life in France, working in Paris and Provence. He painted very critical self-portraits and another series challenging his struggles with alcohol. Paintings with a political message were part of his ongoing subjects. In later years, he painted more freely, often inspired by his surroundings in Provence.

Madonna Irlanda or the Very First Real Irish Political Picture

Composition and Colour

Farrell creates a false frame which he incorporates into the painting to challenge the convention of framed pictures. The female figure is placed on the crossing point of the diagonals of the painted area. A version of Leonardo da Vinci's *Vitruvian Man* is in the upper left, covering his private parts. A self-portrait of Farrell is in the upper right corner, observing the scene. The composition is busy with images and symbols which direct our focus to the nude figure in the centre.

Blues and greys are contrasted with areas of warmer greys and browns. Small areas of red create highlights.

Style and Technique

Farrell mixes the hard-edge abstract qualities of his earlier work with more gestural marks to create movement and texture in areas of the surface. There is a Pop Art element to the piece. He chose the figurative images to allow him express political ideas he could not show through abstraction.

A selection of Farrell's work can be found at *www.mutualart.com*. Think about how the artist presents political issues. How could you interpret the political issues in the world today through your artwork? Sketch out some ideas addressing the issue that concerns you most.

Figure 35.14
Madonna Irlanda or the Very First Real Irish Political Picture, 1977, by Michael Farrell, acrylic on canvas, 174 × 186 cm, Hugh Lane Gallery, Dublin. The female figure represents Ireland in this satirical commentary on Irish politics and society.

Robert Ballagh (b. 1943)

Painter and designer Robert Ballagh was born in Dublin. He qualified as an architect and worked as a show-band musician before taking up a full-time career in art and design in 1967. He worked with Michael Farrell for a while, and had some early success; he represented Ireland at the Paris Biennale in 1969.

His early style was influenced by Pop Art. He made a number of paintings based on old masters simplified to outlined shapes and flat colour. *The Third of May – After Goya* (1970) is in the Hugh Lane Gallery, Dublin.

Following the Rosc Exhibition of International Modern Art in Dublin in 1972, Ballagh made a series of paintings of people looking at paintings from the exhibition. *Two Men and a Lichtenstein* is part of the series (Fig. 35.15). It was painted in acrylics on 16 small canvases joined together.

Later in the 1970s, a more hyper-realistic style emerged as Ballagh painted scenes from his own life and surroundings. He was commissioned to paint several portraits over the years and began a series of paintings of people he admired from the worlds of culture and politics.

Ballagh's work hangs in many important collections around the world. His design work includes 70 Irish postage stamps and the last set of Irish pound banknotes before the Euro. He also designed stage sets, including one for *Riverdance*.

Portrait of Noël Brown

Composition and Colour

This is an unusual arrangement of six canvases in a cruciform shape. Dr Browne takes up the full height of the four centre panels, while the panels on each side show views of his Connemara home. Sea stones and books are placed on the floor at the foot of the canvas. A reason for the cruciform shape might be that Dr Browne was forced out of office through the influence of the Catholic Church, who were against the reforms he was trying to bring in to the Department of Health in 1948.

Figure 35.15 *Two Men and a Lichtenstein*, 1973, by Robert Ballagh, acrylic on canvas, 244 × 244 cm, Irish Museum of Modern Art, Dublin.

Figure 35.16 *Portrait of Noël Browne*, 1985, Robert Ballagh, mixed media, 183 × 137 cm, National Gallery of Ireland, Dublin.

Style and Technique

The painting is in the 'hyper-realistic' or 'photo-realistic' style. The painting is in oils on canvas with the addition of stones and books. The painted surface is smooth.

> **Photo-realism:** Also known as 'hyper-realism' or 'super-realism', this term describes a style of extremely realistic art based on photographic images, begun in the USA in the 1970s.

A Figurative Artist: Brian Bourke (b. 1936)

Born in Dublin, Bourke studied for a short time at the National College of Art and Design in Dublin and St Martins and Goldsmiths colleges in London, but he is largely self-taught. He travelled in Europe for a couple of years but kept in touch with the young modern artists in Dublin and was part of the Independent Arts and Projects Arts groups, which young artists organised to support each other and promote their work.

He has had a continuing interest, throughout his life, in portraits and landscapes. He represented Ireland at the Paris Biennale in 1965 and at other exhibitions in London, Europe and the USA.

Drawing is the basis for a lot of Bourke's work. He produces etchings and lithographs as an extension of this process. Descriptive line and hatching are part of all his work. His painting *Knock a Lough* (Fig. 35.17), is typical of the landscapes he was making in the 1970s and 80s. The painted surface is busy with abstract marks as well as description. The colours are bold and sometimes unexpected. A sense of movement swims over the whole image.

Bourke, like many artists, often works in series. Don Quixote has been a recurring theme and he created the Sweeney series in the 1980s, based on an old Irish legend. Twelve paintings from this series were exhibited at the Rosc '88 exhibition, which displayed the work of 50 international artists in the Guinness Hop Store and The Royal Hospital at Kilmainham,

Figure 35.17 *Knock a Lough*, 1979, by Brian Bourke, mixed media, 48 × 40 cm.

now the Irish Museum of Modern Art. Bourke is a prolific artist who works in a range of media including sculpture in wood and metal. Heads cast in bronze relate to the portraits and figure drawing that are so much part of his work.

Self-Portrait with Blue, Red and Green
Composition and Colour

This is a self-portrait, one of many in Bourke's lifelong exploration of his own image, which are often humorous and self-critical.

The face is centrally placed, in the foreground, looking directly at the viewer. The background is loosely marked and has a colour wash in the upper portion of the format. The colour wash in burnt sienna creates a skin tone and a background. Black, red and brown lines create the description of the face. Areas of white highlight emphasise structure and depth. The blue, yellow and red areas of flat colour, on the little hat, make a stark contrast with the strongly marked surface of the face.

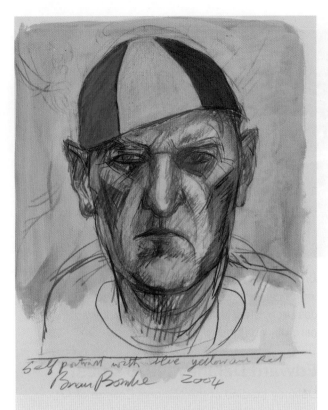

Figure 35.18 *Self-Portrait with Blue, Red and Green*, 2004, by Brian Bourke, mixed media on paper, 65 × 56 cm, Irish Museum of Modern Art, Dublin.

Style and Technique

This is an observational drawing made with expressive marks and gestures. Likeness is not the primary concern; it is as much about the marks and surface.

Sculpture

Figurative Sculpture
Oisín Kelly (1915–81)

Oisín Kelly worked as a teacher for 20 years, and made sculptures in his free time. Eventually, he attended night classes in the National College of Art and spent nine months studying in Chelsea Polytechnic under Henry Moore (see p. 261) in 1947–8.

Much of Kelly's early work was in woodcarving. In particular, he received a lot of commissions from churches, who noted the genuine religious feeling in his figures.

In 1964, Kelly became artist-in-residence at the Kilkenny Design Workshop and produced designs for textiles, ceramics and metalwork.

The Children of Lir

The Children of Lir is a memorial to the freedom fighters of 1916 that takes the form of four children and four swans. It may be an allegory for the fall of the old regime and the new state rising from it.

Composition

The four children spiral down in increasing degrees of collapse into the pool that the sculpture stands in. The swans rise from within the figure group, moving upward in a tighter spiral. One needs to walk around the sculpture to appreciate the complicated interplay of shapes and forms and the sense of movement that is achieved.

Style and Technique

This is a large sculpture cast in copper and bronze. The original work would have been modelled in clay and scaled up to the final size.

Figure 35.19 *The Children of Lir*, 1966, by Oisín Kelly, copper and bronze, the Garden of Remembrance, Dublin.

Figure 35.21 Thomas Davis Memorial, 1966, by Edward Delaney, College Green, Dublin.

Most of Kelly's work is figurative, but not realistic. Forms are simplified and movement is often suggested.

Other Works

The Children of Lir was the first of a number of public sculptures that Kelly was commissioned to do. *The Working Men* statue that stands outside the City Hall in Cork, the *James Larkin* statue on O'Connell Street in Dublin, the *Roger Casement* statue at Ballyheigue in Co. Kerry and the *Chariot of Life* statue outside the Irish Life Centre in Dublin are just a few of Kelly's large sculptures.

Kelly also made smaller pieces for private sale and exhibition. He made dancers, animals and more abstract work. His *Marchers* is one of his smaller works, full of energy, as many of his smaller pieces are. (Fig. 35.20).

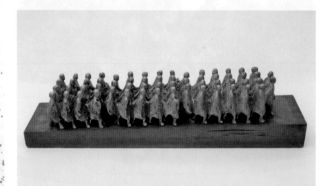

Figure 35.20 *The Marchers*, 1969, by Oisín Kelly, 18 x 78 x 7 cm, Irish Museum of Modern Art, Dublin.

Bronze was not the only medium Kelly worked in; he carved stone and wood and also worked in cast iron, steel and cement. His work was always carefully adapted to the medium.

Edward Delaney (1930–2009)

Delaney studied at the National College of Art, and was awarded scholarships and funding to study in Germany and Italy. He then spent some time working in sculpture foundries in Germany and France, where he learned the skill of lost wax bronze casting. He represented Ireland at the Paris Biennale in 1959 and 1961 and at the New York World's Fair in 1965. His return to Ireland in the 1960s coincided with the expanding art market that followed economic growth and cultural change.

Delaney established a studio in Dún Laoghaire and a foundry capable of casting monumental sculpture, the first in Ireland. He received a number of public commissions in the 1960s and 1970s, including the Thomas Davis Memorial located on College Green, Dublin (Fig. 35.21).

In the 1980s, Delaney moved to Connemara, Co. Galway, at which point his work began to get more experimental. He also founded an open-air sculpture park in Carraroe, where he exhibited his steel trees and other works.

Thomas Davis Memorial

Delaney's monument to the activist features a larger-than-life sculpture of Thomas Davis behind a *Fountain of the Four Angels*, blowing their trumpets to awaken the four provinces of Ireland.

Composition

The figure of Davis is elevated on a tall plinth so he can be seen over the heads of the angels. The fountain is placed a distance away from the statue to create a sense of space in the composition.

Style and Technique

The angels are in the Expressionist style typical of Delaney's work at this time. They are heavily textured, with slim limbs and small heads. The Davis figure is more monumental: more a statement than a portrait. The figures are cast in bronze, using the lost wax technique that Delaney had learned in Germany.

John Behan (b. 1938)

Son of a grocer in inner-city Dublin, young John Behan made frequent visits to his grandfather's farm in Leitrim, where he developed a love of animals that continued all his life.

When he left school, Behan trained as a metalworker, which gave him a deep, functional understanding of sculpting materials and techniques.

Behan attended the National College of Art in Dublin and, while he found the life classes very useful, the culture was very conservative. In 1960, he attended Ealing Art College in London, supporting himself by working in metal workshops.

Behan returned to Dublin in 1961 and was a founding member of New Artists. At this time, he was mainly painting and designing theatre sets, but

Figure 35.22
The Beast, 1972, by John Behan, bronze, 38 x 60 x 21 cm, Crawford Art Gallery, Cork.

by 1966 he was back working with metal in sculptor Edward Delaney's workshop.

In 1970, Behan started the Dublin Art Foundry, where attendees developed their casting skills in the lost wax technique. *The Beast* in the Crawford Art Gallery, Cork, is typical of the small animals and figures he was producing at the time (Fig. 35.22).

As technology improved, so did the quality of Behan's work, and the ability to work on a larger scale. He has exhibited and travelled widely around the world and his work is in many important collections.

Famine
Composition

This large bronze memorial to the victims of the Great Famine is located on the shores of Clew Bay in the shadow of Croagh Patrick, Ireland's holy mountain. The sculpture is set in the centre of a large circular paved area and takes the form of a

Figure 35.23 *Famine*, 1997, by John Behan, bronze, Murrisk, Co. Mayo.

three-mast sailing ship. For some viewers, the three masts represent the crucifixion. Emerging from the hull of the boat, skeletal figures seem to fly among the masts, representing the departing souls of the victims.

Style and Technique

Like most of Behan's work, *Famine* is figurative but not realistic. The ship is the largest bronze ever cast in Ireland, while the figures attached to the mast are made of assembled bronze bars welded together.

This ship is matched by a companion piece outside the UN building in New York, *Arrival: New Dawn*, which shows the survivors of the coffin ships arriving in America. Unsurprisingly, Behan considers the Famine to be the most important event in Irish history.

Abstract Sculpture
John Burke (1946–2006)

John Burke studied at the Crawford School of Art in Cork, where he was awarded a fellowship to study sculpture at the Royal College of Art in London. In London, he worked in the studio of the abstract sculptor Bryan Kneale three days a week while attending life-drawing classes at the RCA two days a week.

Burke spent a year traveling to North Africa, the Greek Islands, Italy and the Netherlands before returning to Ireland.

In the 1970s, he set up a studio near Blarney, Co. Cork and taught two days a week in the Crawford School. He had an influence on the sculpture students there, including Eilis O'Connell, Vivienne Roche, Maud Cotter, James Scanlon, John Gibbons and Jim Buckley.

His work was exhibited in Ireland and internationally, including exhibitions in New York, Munich and Brussels. He also produced smaller gallery pieces for private sale.

Red Cardinal
Composition

In this abstract sculpture, interlocking curves of sheet steel are set at right angles to each other. As the viewer moves around the sculpture, the spaces and relationships of the parts change, creating a sense of movement.

Figure 35.24 *Red Cardinal*, 1978, by John Burke, steel, Baggot Street, Dublin.

Style and Technique

Red Cardinal is a Minimalist Abstract work in the Modernist tradition. Sheet steel is cut to shape, bent to the correct curve, then welded and riveted together to create the intersecting shapes. Bright red paint adds drama and creates a smooth finish. It is obvious from this work that knowledge and appreciation of materials was important to Burke.

Influences

Burke was influenced by the work of Anthony Caro and Phillip King, whose work he had seen as a student in London. They were both working with painted steel at the time.

Other Works

Burke was commissioned for large public sculptures, like the one at the Wilton Roundabout in Cork. He also produced smaller pieces like *Gallery* with *Sliding Doors* (Fig. 35.25) in the Crawford Gallery. He was a founding member of Aosdána, an organisation set up to support people in the visual arts, music and literature.

Figure 35.25 *Gallery with Sliding Doors*, 1997, steel, 26 x 88 x 22 cm, by John Burke, Crawford Art Gallery, Cork.

Analysis

Changing styles and techniques were an important feature in the art of the late 20th century. Keep this in mind as you analyse the motives and meanings behind the works in this chapter.

The second half of the 20th century was a time of great change in the visual arts in Ireland. By the 1970s, art colleges had modernised their courses so students had an education similar to that in other European countries. Galleries and museums were supporting artists and public commissions were given to Modern and Abstract artists for the first time. In 1969, Minister of Finance Charles Haughey introduced a tax-exemption scheme for artists working full time, which is unique to Ireland. It means that the money earned by composers of music, writers and visual artists from creative and original works is exempt from tax.

Chapter Review

1. Describe some of the changes in art media that were introduced in the 1960s and 1970s. Use words and sketches to make your points.

2. Using words and sketches, give an example of a work of pure abstraction in painting or sculpture, naming the work and the artist. What materials and techniques were used in its making?

3. Select a portrait or self-portrait by one of the artists in this chapter. Describe the technique and materials used by the artist, using words and sketches.

4. New mediums and techniques were being introduced in sculpture. Using words and sketches, give some examples of the work of artists you know.

5. Elements of the landscape were still evident in some paintings from this time. Using examples from paintings you are familiar with, describe some of these works in words and sketches.

6. Some artists included the human figure in their work. Describe the work of a figurative painter and a figurative sculptor that you know, using words and sketches.

7. Describe the work of an artist who created an emotional response in you when you studied their work. Use words and sketches to show what aspects of the work affected you.

Further Research

www.publicart.ie – Browse Ireland's public art

www.rte.ie/archives – Search for 'Profile Artist Tony O'Malley' for an insight into the artist's personal life and artistic inspiration

www.youtube.com – Search for 'Anne Madden Painter & Muse - RTE Arts Lives' (56.43) to watch a fascinating documentary on Anne Madden's work and life

www.robertballagh.com – Robert Ballagh's official website

Chapter 36

Contemporary Artists

By the end of this chapter I will ...

* know how political and social changes have made a difference in the world of art

* have seen new media, and different ways of using traditional media, that came with new thinking and technology

* have learned about the different ideas of what it is that makes a work of art

* be able to describe the work of at least four contemporary artists.

Context

Over the course of the last 50 years, there have been extraordinary and radical changes in the world order. New scientific discoveries and technologies of all kinds have made changes that would have been unimaginable just one generation ago.

* The fall of the Berlin Wall in 1989 and the democratic revolutions that followed in Eastern Europe has altered the political landscape.
* The launching of the Hubble Space Telescope in 1990 changed our view of the universe and our place in it.
* The Human Genome Project, an international scientific research project, completed sequencing of human DNA in 2003, increasing understanding of human development and the nature of our existence.
* The development of the internet changed communication and distribution of knowledge and ideas forever.

All of these innovations and changes in politics and thinking, worldwide, have created a whole new set of possibilities for artists.

Media and Areas of Practice

Up to the turn of the 20th century, painting, drawing and sculpture covered most of what was popularly considered to be 'art'. During the 20th century, this definition expanded to include found objects, photography, performance, film and video and some other media. In a gallery today, an artist might exhibit video, dioramic vitrines (things displayed in glass or plastic boxes), found objects, digital prints and live performances as well as the more traditional artistic forms.

Art Elements and Design Principles

In the past, an art historian could follow movements and styles as they evolved, as we have done in this book. Impressionism followed Realism, and Cubism evolved into Surrealism and Abstraction. This sequencing of styles no longer operates in today's art world. Individuals find their own means of expression and often use a range of media that might have been specialised in a previous generation.

World centres of art are also a thing of the past, in the way that Paris was at the centre of new developments during the 1880s and New York in the 1950s was where the new ideas were being tried out. Now due to instant communication worldwide, there is no particular central geographic focus for artists.

Innovation and Invention

Art in the 21st century incorporates a greater variety of media and ideas than at any time previously. The whole notion of what art is and who should make it has been challenged at every level.

Artists and Artworks

There are many contemporary artists living and working in Ireland today. Here we have made a small selection of well-established artists who demonstrate some of the range of work being practised today. You will find many more on the Arts Council website and the Irish Museum of Modern Art website.

Dorothy Cross (b. 1956)

Cork-born Dorothy Cross works in sculpture, photography, video and installation. She began her art education at the Crawford Municipal School of Art, then went to Leicester Polytechnic (now De Montfort University) in the UK and the San Francisco Art Institute in the USA.

Cross has been a regular exhibitor since the 1980s, and her 1991 installation *Powerhouse* was exhibited in Dublin, London and Philadelphia.

Cross's installation pieces usually combine found objects from different environments into 'poetic amalgamations' of unlikely combinations of materials and ideas. She creates unexpected connections between different materials and combines ideas that are not obviously related into works of art that are thought-provoking and sometimes surprising.

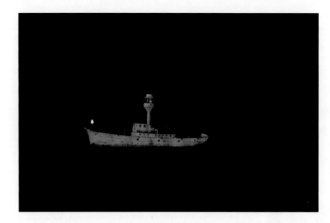

Figure 36.1 *Ghost Ship*, 1998, by Dorothy Cross.

Ghost Ship (Fig. 36.1) is one of Cross's best known pieces, as it got a lot of attention when it was first revealed. An old light ship, the *Albatross*, was coated in phosphorescent paint and anchored in Scotsman's Bay off Dún Laoghaire. It lit up so that it glowed a fluorescent greenish-white at night. The light glowed and faded over a three-hour period. The idea was to commemorate the 11 lightships that had marked dangerous rocks off the Irish coast, and the courageous crews that manned them. They had all been decommissioned and replaced by automatic buoys by then.

Basking Shark Currach
Composition

For this piece, Cross combined shark skin with the frame of a currach, creating an unexpected mixture of objects and viewpoint. The currach becomes the skeleton of the shark, and the shark skin covers the structure of the boat (Fig. 36.2).

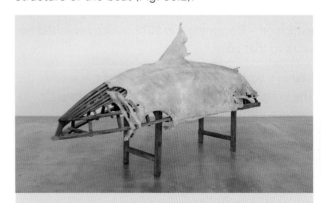

Figure 36.2 *Basking Shark Currach*, 2013, by Dorothy Cross, shark skin and wood.

Style and Technique

Basking Shark Currach is an assembly, a form of sculpture traceable back to Picasso (see p. 205). A currach frame with a shark skin stretched over it. This type of assembly, where objects are combined in an unexpected way, has been part of Crosse's practice from early in her career. The combination of shark skin and currach frame offers thoughts on the sea, human interaction with the sea, and the animals that live in it.

> **RESPOND**
> Cross combines two or more unrelated items together to create a unique and thought-provoking artwork. Make two lists – one of natural forms and one of man-made forms – and combine them at random to find your own unique 'poetic amalgamation'.

Alice Maher (b. 1956)

Alice Maher was born in Cork and studied in art schools across the British Isles and the USA. In 1986, she was awarded a Fulbright scholarship to the San Francisco Art Institute, and in 1994 she represented Ireland at the São Paulo Biennial.

Maher combines painting, sculpture, photography, animation, digital media and installation in her pieces, often combining media in an unexpected way.

Part of Maher's practice is conventional drawings, sometimes of long strands of hair loosely interwoven, for example *Andromeda* (1999) or the drawings of a girl doing a series of tasks in *The Thicket* (1991).

The Irish Museum of Modern Art, Dublin, hosted an exhibition – Becoming – in 2013, which reviewed her work to that point.

Maher's work is in collections around the world. The wide range of her practice gives her freedom to express ideas in any number of ways.

Berry Dress
Composition and Colour

This little dress is displayed on a glass shelf above eye level so that the viewer can see inside the structure (Fig. 36.3). The pins that hold the berries

Figure 36.3 *Berry Dress*, 1994, by Alice Maher, rosehips, cotton, paint, sewing pins, Irish Museum of Modern Art, Dublin.

in place stick through to the inside. This creates a contradiction between the purpose of the dress – to keep a child warm – and the injuries that might be inflicted by the pins.

The relationship between the vermillion red of the painted dress and the original red of the rosehips is constantly changing over time as the berries dry out and decompose.

Style and Technique

There is no particular 'style' to attribute to work of this nature. It is conceptual, where the thoughts provoked in the viewer are more important than the physical presence of the work.

The dress form is made of painted cotton. The rosehips are affixed with sewing pins. The whole construction is very delicate and will probably disintegrate over time, which is another calculated part of the work.

Interpretation

This work has been interpreted as an illustration of the innocence and cruelty of childhood. Fairy tales such as Snow White, Little Red Riding Hood and Sleeping Beauty have explored similar themes.

Cassandra's Necklace

Cassandra's Necklace was a collaborative video installation based on a script for a play by Anne Enright. The music was composed by Trevor Knight, it was filmed by Vivienne Dick and the editing was completed by Connie Farrell.

The Cassandra of the title was the daughter of King Priam and Queen Hecuba of ancient Troy. The god Apollo admired Cassandra, and gave her the ability to predict the future. Cassandra annoyed Apollo, so he cursed her so that her prophecies would not be believed.

The lambs' tongues worn round the neck of the actress in the video are a metaphor for the stilled tongue of the prophetess. She cannot tell people her prophecies, because they won't believe her.

Figure 36.4 Still from *Cassandra's Necklace*, 2012, by Alice Maher.

 Visit *www.alicemaher.com* to see Maher's range of work. Can you find any common themes linking the pieces? Make notes and sketches to help with your studio and written work.

Eilis O'Connell (b. 1953)

Born in Derry, Eilis O'Connell grew up in the Donegal countryside with the freedom to explore her surroundings. This turned out to form the basis for her creativity.

The O'Connell family moved to Cork when Eilis was 10, and her first art education was in the Crawford School of Art. She went to Massachusetts College of Art in 1974, returning to Cork, where she received a distinction in sculpture in 1977.

In the following years, O'Connell won awards and travelling scholarships that allowed her to further her studies in Europe and America.

O'Connell is best known for her large public sculptures in Ireland, England and mainland Europe.

Secret Station

The title comes from the Seamus Heaney poem 'The Diviner'. The conical shapes are 11 metres tall and produce plumes of steam, which serve as a reminder of the coal exporting trade from Cardiff during the steam age (Fig. 36.5).

Composition

The structure's main components are two towering bronze cones with curved, galvanised steel beams fixed horizontally on top. Steam generators inside the cones create plumes of steam, and fibre optics light up the sculpture at night. It is set in open ground near the harbour and can be seen from roads nearby.

Style and Technique

This is a large abstract sculpture that includes mechanical devices (steam generators and fibre optics). The construction of large sculptures like this has to be carefully engineered and planned to meet planning and safety regulations. The artist's

contribution is in the design of the object, rather than the construction itself.

Other Works

Many of O'Connell's sculptures are on display in public spaces around Ireland. *Chroma* (2014) can be seen at the new Science building at University College in Dublin, *Atoms and Apples* (2013) is at Trinity College, Dublin and *Reedpod* (2005) is found on Lapps Quay in Cork.

O'Connell's smaller-scale works often relate to natural forms and everyday objects like tools and clothes, which people are in frequent contact with.

Each Day, on the grounds of the Crawford Art Gallery, Cork, is a simple bronze form that could represent a cloak or the bow of a boat (Fig. 36.6). The multiple meanings and possibilities leave something for the viewer to work out for themselves. O'Connell stated that some of her work can be seen as 'an extension of the body, an extra shell or layer to protect the human spirit'.

O'Connell was a founding member of The Sculpture Factory in Cork, and is a member of Aosdána and the RHA.

Figure 36.6 *Each Day*, 2003, by Eilis O'Connell, bronze, 240 x 120 x 120 cm, Crawford Art Gallery, Cork.

Rowan Gillespie (b. 1953)

Gillespie was born in Dublin. He spent his early years in Cyprus and studied in York School of Art, Kingston College of Art and the Statens Kunstole in Oslo, Norway. He returned to Dublin in 1977 and set up a studio and foundry in Blackrock, Co. Dublin.

Gillespie is unusual in that he carries out the whole design, modelling and casting process completely by himself. He uses the lost wax process to produce his bronze sculptures.

Many of Gillespie's sculptures are site specific: they are made to be placed in a particular location and are designed for that environment.

His greatest artistic influences are Henry Moore and Edvard Munch.

Famine

Famine is a memorial to the victims of the Irish famine who had to emigrate from the Dublin quays (Fig. 36.7).

Composition

The group of figures extends along the quay, each isolated in their own misery. A man carries a limp child; others carry small parcels of their possessions. A skinny dog follows.

Style and Technique

The figures are recognisably human, but their features and anatomy have been elongated for dramatic effect. The finish is rough: the bronze was not cleaned or polished after it came out of the mould. This crude treatment adds to the ragged look of the people on their way to the ship that will hopefully take them to a new life.

There is a companion piece to this sculpture in Toronto, Canada. It represents the surviving refugees arriving off the coffin ships, hoping for a new start in life.

> **RESPOND**
>
> Compare the Famine memorial by Rowan Gillespie with the sculptures on the same theme by Edward Delaney and John Behan. Look at their use of materials, the composition of the piece and its location. Think about the emotional impact of the work.

Other Works

Gillespie produces smaller work for private sale and for some unusual locations. In *Aspiration*, a figure climbs the wall of the Treasury Building, while *Birdy* sits on the windowsill of 3 Crescent Hall in Mount Street, Dublin.

Figure 36.7
Famine, 1997, by Rowan Gillespie, bronze, Customs House Quay, Dublin.

Figure 36.8 *Proclamation*, 2007, by Rowan Gillespie, bronze, Kilmainham Gaol, Dublin.

Proclamation is one of Gillespie's most striking works. Located opposite Kilmainham Gaol in Dublin, it commemorates the signatories of the Declaration of Independence and the executions following the 1916 Easter Rising (Fig. 36.8).

The figures are more abstracted than those in Gillespie's other works because they represent the idea of an imagined ideal world rather than the specific people who were shot.

The bronzes are arranged in a circle. They are simplified down to leaf or flame shapes with a blindfolded head on top – no limbs or human features. The Declaration of Independence, inscribed on a bronze plaque, is placed in the centre of the circle. At the foot of each figure is a name and the death sentence passed by the British Military Tribunal. Each figure is pierced with

a different pattern of holes representing the bullet holes of the firing squad.

Michael Quane (b. 1962)

Cork native Michael Quane studied Science at UCC before attending to the Crawford College of Art. He continues to live and work in Co. Cork today.

Quane is mainly a stone carver, working in Kilkenny limestone and marble. He produces a range of both small- and large-scale pieces.

Horses and Riders

Quane says that *Horses and Riders* represents 'a sense of the connectedness of individuals through their culture, history, evolution, dependency and need, amid their own personal isolation and indivisibility'.

Composition

The figures in *Horses and Riders* are arranged so that they come gradually into focus as you approach the roundabout (Fig. 36.9). When you arrive your eye is led on to the next horse and rider as you move around the roundabout. Quane says he designed it this way to follow the flow of traffic as it moves around the traffic island. The viewer needs to make a full circuit of the roundabout to see the complete composition.

Figure 36.9 *Horses and Riders*, 1995, by Michael Quane, Kilkenny limestone, 220 x 220 x 180 cm, Mallow, Cork.

Style and Technique

The style is a modified realism, wherein human and animal forms are distorted to fit into the shape of the design.

This sculpture began as a 23-ton block of stone and was carved down to 11 tons finished weight. Like much of Quane's other works, there are areas of roughly finished surface where tool marks are used to denote form and texture. This contrasts with areas of smoothly finished stone.

Other Works

Quane's sculptures appear in private and public collections across Ireland, the UK, mainland Europe and the USA. An unusual figure outside Mayorstone Garda Station in Limerick, *Persona* (Fig. 36.10), is based on the idea that everyone is an actor on the stage of life and we all wear masks to carry out our roles as criminals, police, judges, or just ordinary citizens.

Equality is a theme that runs through Quane's work. His figures are often naked, to remove any hints of class or social position.

 Create a three-dimensional work of your own that explores the human form. You could work from life or from a concept.

Sean Scully (b. 1945)

As a young man, Irish-born Sean Scully worked a series of jobs in London to support himself while doing evening classes at the Central School of Art. During his lunch breaks, he went to the Tate Gallery, where *Van Gogh's Chair* had a particular impact on him.

In 1965, Scully decided to study art full time, first at Croydon College of Art and then at Newcastle University, where he remained as a teaching assistant. At this time, his painting style was influenced by Op Art and based on a complicated grid system of lines and bands, where colour contrasts created a sense of depth.

Scully soon won a fellowship allowing him to study at Harvard University in America in 1972–73. Here,

Figure 36.10 *Persona*, 2000, by Michael Quane, Kilkenny limestone, 210 x 91 x 65 cm, Mayorstone, Limerick.

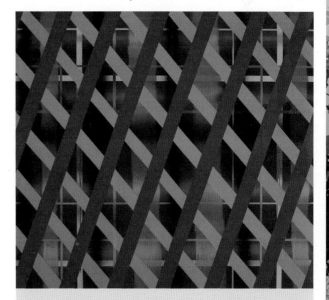

Figure 36.11 *Newcastle Bridge*, 1972, by Sean Scully, acrylic on canvas, 244 × 274 cm.

he took on a hard-edge style with spray-painted bands and stripes – vertical, horizontal and diagonal – which excluded all expressive marks (Fig. 36.11). On his return to London, he sold out a solo exhibition of these paintings.

Scully moved to New York in 1975 and continued to paint and teach there for most of his career, exhibiting regularly in Europe as well as America. He was nominated for the Turner Prize in 1989 and 1993.

Dorothy

Dorothy is an Abstract painting in memory of the artist's friend, Dorothy Walker, who had been a member of the board of the Irish Museum of Modern Art, where the painting is now exhibited.

Composition and Colour

The painting is composed of an arrangement of rectangles. At first glance, they seem regimented and regular in size, but they are individual and irregular, creating rhythms within the composition. In *Dorothy*, Scully uses cool pastel shades of blues and greys, contrasted here and there with areas of ochre and navy to create the sadness he feels at the death of his friend. In this, *Dorothy* is a marked contrast with the majority of Scully's pieces, which

Figure 36.12 *Dorothy*, 2003, by Sean Scully, oil on linen, 275 × 335 cm, Irish Museum of Modern Art, Dublin.

are warm in tone, often featuring deep reds with earth colours and black accents.

Style and Technique

This is an oil painting on linen. The rows of stripes and rectangles are drawn and painted freehand in layers with large brushes. The overpainting of one colour on another – with areas of the canvas left exposed – creates a depth and luminosity in the pastel colours.

Other Works

Scully made a gift of eight paintings to the Hugh Lane Gallery in Dublin in 2006 and an additional painting in 2018. A one-man exhibition, Sean Scully: Sea Star, in which the painter responded to works by Turner, went on show in the Tate Gallery in London in 2019.

Scully continues to work in a variety of media, painting, sculpture, printmaking and installations. His work is more widely appreciated now than at any other time in his life.

Brian O'Doherty, a.k.a. Patrick Ireland (b. 1928)

A key figure in conceptual art in Ireland and America, Brian O'Doherty grew up in Roscommon and studied medicine at UCD, followed by extensive post-graduate research in the UK and USA. O'Doherty changed career in the 1960s, becoming an art critic, a writer, a television presenter and an artist.

In 1972, O'Doherty took on the pseudonym Patrick Ireland in a performance at the Irish Exhibition of Living Art, watched by 30 invited 'witnesses'. He was assisted by the artists Robert Ballagh and Brian King, who splashed him with green and orange paint as a protest at the Bloody Sunday killings in Derry. The artist said he would sign his artwork with his new name 'until such time as the British military presence is removed from Northern Ireland' (Fig. 36.13) Following the Northern Ireland peace process, in 2008, he held a symbolic burial of his alter ego Patrick Ireland in the grounds of the Irish Museum of Modern Art (Fig. 36.14).

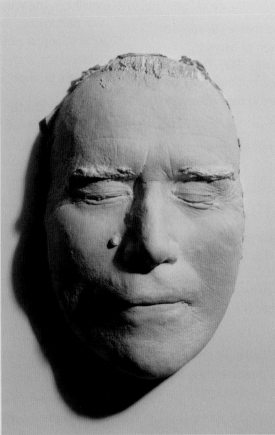

Figure 36.13 (left)
Documentation of Performance Entitled Name Change, 1972, by Brian O'Doherty/ Patrick Ireland, Irish Museum of Modern Art, Dublin.

Figure 36.14 (right)
The Burial of Patrick Ireland, Death Mask, 2008, by Brian O'Doherty, plaster and paint, Irish Museum of Modern Art, Dublin.

O'Doherty has had a lifelong interest in Ogham script, a 20-character Celtic system of writing based on Roman letters. For him, Ogham represented concerns about Irish identity and language.

O'Doherty's works and writings are held in high regard in America and form part of many important permanent collections worldwide.

One Here Now
Composition and Colour

One Here Now is a series of nine murals based on Ogham script that cover the walls of the Sirius Arts Centre in Cobh (Fig. 36.15). They address Irish identity and are intended to be a memorial to those who were forced to leave Ireland from ports like Cobh.

Figure 36.15 (right)
One Here Now, 1996 (restored 2018), by Brian O'Doherty, a.k.a. Patrick Ireland, Sirius Arts Centre, Cobh, Cork.

Style and Technique

These are hard-edge paintings that were applied directly to the walls. A selection of essays accompanied the original work in 1996. The work was designed to be temporary, but the Arts Centre preserved it under layers of lining paper, allowing it to be seen again in 2019.

This is a site-specific piece, created specifically for the rooms in the Arts Centre.

Jesse Jones (b. 1978)

Dublin-born Jesse Jones graduated with an MA in Visual Arts Practice from Dún Laoghaire Institute of Design and Technology in 2005. Her work has taken many forms, from gallery-based films and installations to large-scale public events.

NO MORE FUN AND GAMES, a 2016 event in The Hugh Lane Gallery, combined a selection of paintings by women artists from the gallery's collection with a huge screen, printed with an image of a woman's arm (Fig. 36.16).

The idea was to challenge the way in which art history and galleries had marginalised women artists. Jones invited a number of women to collaborate in the selection of the paintings, which were exhibited together for the first time. The walls of the gallery where the paintings were hung were papered with a shiny silver paper, referencing the 'silver screen' of cinema. The curtain was moved by attendants each day, hiding and revealing different aspects of the exhibition. The whole exhibition consisted of tours with performers, lectures, discussions, events and publications. A cinematic score was composed in collaboration with Gerald Busby, which was played on speakers throughout the gallery.

Jones was chosen to represent Ireland at the Venice Biennale in 2017. She filled the large space of the Irish Pavillon at the Arsenale in Venice with an installation called *Tremble Tremble* (Fig. 36.17).

Tremble Tremble

Tremble Tremble addresses issues of human rights, information and gender equality through a film theatrical production of a creation myth. The title comes from 'this trembling sense of being on the precipice of massive political change' that Jones feels.

Composition

The space was enclosed with black voile curtains printed with the image of a woman's bare arm. The curtains were closed round the audience, enfolding them as they watched the film projected on screens. Large sculptures based on the fossilised bones of Lucy, the earliest known human skeleton, which was found in Ethiopia in the 1970s, help to focus attention on the screens.

Style and Technique

This type of production is not in a specific style. The artist uses a range of media to express the ideas she has in mind. Film, print, performance, sculpture

Figure 36.16 *NO MORE FUN AND GAMES*, 2016, by Jesse Jones, Hugh Lane Gallery, Dublin.

Figure 36.17 *Tremble Tremble*, 2017, by Jesse Jones, The Arsenale, Venice (temporary installation).

and other media are combined with input from other artists to create the experience.

Other Works

Jones likes to work in collaboration with other artists. For example, Tessa Giblin helped curate the Venice installation, and actress Olwen Fouéré helped to devise the script and texts, as well as performing in the film.

Political and social issues, particularly hidden problems, form the inspiration for much of Jones's work.

Analysis

The concept or idea behind the work is often the most important element for contemporary artists. Pay particular attention to this when you are examining the art of this period.

In the 21st century, artists are not limited by the traditional designations of painter, sculptor, designer, film-maker, photographer or craftworker. While all these disciplines exist and people work within them, artists also combine aspects of all the disciplines and none in their work. The boundaries of what makes a work of art are not confined to made objects. The art 'idea' is at the centre of many artists' practice.

Chapter Review

1. Note some of the social, political and scientific changes that have affected contemporary artists.

2. Describe some of the new media that contemporary artists use. Use words and sketches to give examples by artists you have studied.

3. Describe, in words and sketches, an installation by an artist you have studied. Note the location, subject, and the materials and equipment used in the work.

4. Performance art can be a one-time event or it can be filmed, photographed or written about. Write an account of a performance you have learned about, using words and sketches, to describe the event and any materials or equipment involved.

5. Write a description and make sketches of a public sculpture by an artist you have studied. Note how it suits its location, the subject and materials used and how successful you think it is as a public monument.

6. Traditional materials are often used in contemporary art. Describe the work, in words and sketches, of an artist you have studied who works with traditional materials used in a contemporary way.

Further Research

www.kerlingallery.com/artists/dorothy-cross – View Dorothy Cross's works at the Kerlin Gallery online

www.eilisoconnell.com – On O'Connell's official website, her sculptures are classified as 'inside' or 'outside'. Aside from their location, what are the differences between these two sets of sculptures?

www.youtube.com – Search for 'Sean Scully: Why this, not that?' (52.12) to watch an engaging documentary about the artist and his perspective on art

rowangillespie.net – Rowan Gillespie's website features a selection of his expansive works

www.michaelquane.com – Browse Quane's stone sculptures by selecting 'Work' from the menu bar

www.vimeo.com – Search for 'Jesse Jones, interview Tremble Tremble' (14.02) to watch an interview with the artist at the Venice Bienniale

Units 13–16

Today's World

Unit 13

Artists: Theory and Thinking

By the end of this unit I will ...

* have studied the practice of a number of artists
* understand what Conceptual Art is
* be able to describe the practice of a designer
* know about the work of a filmmaker
* have opinions about what makes some photographs art
* have explored who art is made for: patrons, locations and self-expression.

Figure 37.1 Aboriginal rock painting of a turtle at Ubirr, in the UNESCO World Heritage Site of Kakadu National Park, Northern Territory, Australia.

Introduction

Professional art practice takes many forms today. Creators of fine art can be involved in an amazing range of ideas and media. Artists continue to work in traditional media like painting and sculpture, but even here the range of materials used has expanded in the 20th and 21st centuries.

In early times, artists worked with the materials that they found in the environment, such as wood, stone and earth colours. In some remote parts of the world, people still work in this way.

As society became more sophisticated, so did art media, processes and practices. In ancient Greek and Roman culture, artists were considered to be essential members of society with a critical function – making beautiful objects and memorials for important citizens.

Through the Middle Ages and into relatively modern times, artists and craftworkers went through an apprenticeship system where the student spent many years learning the techniques of the trade and working with a master before they qualified to work for themselves.

In the 18th century, Academies, which were something like modern art colleges, began to take over from the apprenticeship system. Artists learned their craft and had to reach certain standards before qualifying to practise on their own. The Academies had annual exhibitions where a

Figure 37.2 An illustration from the Boccacio manuscript showing the artist Thamar painting a Madonna while her apprentice mixes colours.

Figure 37.3 *Still Life with a Violin and a Pitcher*, 1909–10, by Georges Braque, oil on canvas, 117 × 74 cm. The Cubist break with conventional perspective started artists questioning all aspects of traditional art.

committee selected the work that they considered to be of a high enough standard to go on public display. It was difficult for an artist to get public or private commissions if their work was not exhibited in an Academy.

By the late 1800s, artists were breaking out of the Academic system and working together in groups, sharing ideas and inspiration. The Realists and Impressionists (see Unit 4) were among the first to organise independent exhibitions.

In the 20th century, art practice changed a lot as there was a move away from traditional methods,

Figure 37.4
A Private View at the Academy 1881, 1883, by William Powell Frith, oil on canvas, 103 × 196 cm. This image shows the dense hanging of paintings and the large numbers of wealthy clients attending an Academy exhibition.

subjects, materials and techniques. Artists challenged all the conventions of art that had been accepted for 500 years (see Units 5 and 11 on Modernism). The artist's role in society changed from being a service provider – producing paintings, sculptures and designs for people and society to enjoy – to challenging aspects of society and conventions.

The Contemporary Artist

In contemporary art, artists and designers are not limited by choice of media or the disciplines of a craft or skill. If you look at the piece on Conceptual Art on page 519, you will see that all the self-imposed limits of technique and design have been abandoned.

That does not mean that all artists have abandoned skills-based work. Many artists still enjoy the disciplines of drawing or the technical challenge of

difficult techniques; they are just no longer seen as an essential part of a work of art.

The whole range of media has increased in the last century; photography, film sound and video, as well as performance and installation, are now all considered to be mainstream media for the artist to use.

Identity and Self-Expression

An artist's identity almost always comes through in their work, if they are truly involved in the process. We can understand a lot about an artist like Vincent

> RESPOND
>
> How do you think Van Gogh is feeling about himself in the self-portrait illustrated here? Write a short piece giving your opinion on how the artist's identity can be seen in the way they express themselves in paint.

Figure 37.6 *Self-Portrait as a Painter*, 1888, by Vincent van Gogh, oil on canvas, 65 × 50 cm, Van Gogh Museum, Amsterdam. The colour scheme and brushwork in this painting express mood almost as much as the facial expression.

Figure 37.5 *Coma Berenices*, 1999, by Alice Maher, etching, 92 × 73 cm.

van Gogh (see Unit 4, p. 187) just by observing the colours and brushwork he uses. His subjects are often simple landscapes, but it is the way that he paints these subjects that expresses his personality. His self-portraits give a further insight into his emotional state (Fig. 37.6).

An artist's political and religious beliefs, as well as their views on society and their personal history, are often expressed through their work. In modern art this can be the primary reason for an artist to make a work of art, to show their audience what they are thinking and feeling about issues that are important to them. Earlier in art history the artist was not allowed such freedom of expression; however personality and character often show through in their work. See if you can find an early artist whose personality shows through in their art.

Modern Artists Using Conventional Techniques

Some Irish artists still work in a broadly traditional way; the painters Robert Ballagh (p. 495), Anne Madden (p. 492) and Sean Scully (p. 509) all in Unit 12, and many others you can find on the Arts Council and Irish Museum of Modern Art websites. Lucien Freud (p. 269) and Jenny Saville are English painters who use traditional techniques to make modern paintings.

Sculptors working in a traditional art practice include Rowan Gillespie (p. 507) and Michael Quane (p. 508) in Unit 12. Kara Walker produces cast sculptures that challenge traditional art values.

Art Outside the Gallery

Many artists feel that exhibiting their work only in galleries limits what they can do and who will see their work. Environmental artists (see Unit 16), performance artists and street artists sometimes put their art in public places to get a wider audience. This is also done to argue against the idea that art is important only because it has monetary value and can be owned by private individuals in the hope that its value will increase and result in a profit.

The anonymous street artist Banksy (see Unit 16, p. 567) creates work that is often controversial, asking questions about social values and the meaning of art.

> **Aesthetic:** Concerned with beauty or the appreciation of beauty.

Figure 37.7 Banksy's *Washing Away of Cave Paintings* discovered on Leake Street in London in May 2008 and painted over by August 2008.

Art Prices

Traditionally art has been bought and sold by dealers and collectors with some artists' work getting enormous prices and others not so much. To some people this is what art collecting and appreciation is about: the price of the work is its value. To others the value of art is not about price but its aesthetic qualities or the response it creates in the viewer.

Figure 37.8 *Balloon Dog (Orange)*, 1994–2000, by Jeff Koons, stainless steel with transparent colour coating, 307 × 363 × 114 cm.

Research: On YouTube, watch the video 'Jeff Koons on *Balloon Dog (Orange)*' (4:19). This video offers some insights into his art practice. Make notes and sketches to use in your written work.
Respond: Respond to the $58,405,000 price of Jeff Koons's sculpture, *Balloon Dog (Orange)* by having a classroom debate on the value of art, money or artistic values.

Conceptual Art

Conceptual Art had its beginnings in Dadaism (see Unit 5, p. 208), where the art idea was seen as more important than the art object. In the 1960s a movement towards the art concept began in several parts of the world at the same time. An Australian artist Sol LeWitt wrote an article in 1967 for the important art magazine, *Artforum*, stating that the ideas and planning in preparation for making a work of art were the real art, not the object that resulted from the plan. The article was entitled 'Paragraphs on Conceptual Art', which gave the movement its name.

Joseph Kosuth's *One in Three Chairs* (Fig. 37.9) showed a chair in three different ways. An ordinary chair, a photograph of a chair and a dictionary definition of a chair. He felt the meaning 'chair' could be shown equally well by an object, a photograph and words.

Figure 37.9 *One in Three Chairs*, 1965, by Joseph Kosuth.

On YouTube, watch the video 'The Case for Conceptual Art' (11:25). You could have a discussion with your classmates about Conceptual Art, considering whether you think it was a valid form of art or not.

Once the notion that an idea could be art took hold, it challenged the traditional foundations of art, where artistic skills and precious objects were at the centre of the art market. Conceptual Art allows anything to be considered art and many artists today feel free to switch from one medium to another, choosing the form and materials, for each occasion, which will express their ideas best.

Many modern artists work in this way, Dorothy Cross (p. 503) and Alice Maher (p. 504) in Unit 12, and Ai Weiwei in Unit 6, are just a few examples.

Respond to the work of one of the artists you have studied using the information above.
Create a work that develops from their way of practising art.
Research the work of the artist, making notes and sketches to help you develop your own work.

We could continue looking at different ways that artists make art, but you can find examples in the contemporary art sections of this book in Units 6 and 12.

Architecture

The discipline of architecture is the art, science and business of building. An architect has knowledge of the aesthetic and technical aspects of building in the public and private sectors.

Architects design a whole range of things, including homes, office blocks, schools, churches, theatres and museums, sports stadiums, bridges and urban spaces. They need to be aware of social trends, understand the law and engineering principles, and have a good business sense.

The Royal Institute of Architects in Ireland (**www.riai.ie**) and the Irish Architecture Foundation (**www.architecturefoundation.ie**) have information on careers in architecture and award-winning buildings. You can use these sites to do research for written work on architecture in the Chapter Review.

It used to be said that architects design machines for living in, but, more recently, form is often considered to be a primary design consideration. The needs of the people using the building should be at the centre of the architect's considerations.

- Form is the visible shape and make of something. In architecture, shapes can be based on simple geometry. The circle is the basis for spheres and cylinders. The triangle creates cones and pyramids. Squares form cubes. Architecture is created from these basic forms.

- Function is a basic part of architectural design. The building must work for the client, keeping people warm and dry, and creating the spaces for work, rest or play that are needed. The phrase 'form follows function' was the guiding principle for architects and designers in the 20th century. This puts the purpose of the building first before any decoration or aesthetic ideas. Postmodernist architects have moved away from a pure interpretation of this idea; you will see more stylish and dramatic buildings in the 21st century.

An example of an Irish architectural practice with an international reputation is O'Donnell & Tuomey (visit **www.odonnell-tuomey.ie**). They have won national and international prizes for their work, which you can find on their website.

You can find a list of prominent Irish architects at **www.culturetrip.com** by searching 'top 10 Irish architect studios to watch'. You can then make your own choices about your preferred style of building. Take notes and make sketches to use with your studio work and written work.

Figure 37.10 The Convention Centre, Dublin Docklands. Designed by the Irish-American architect Kevin Roche, the Convention Centre combines the simple forms of the cylinder and the cube as the basic elements of the design.

Figure 37.11 (left)
The Pompidou Centre in Paris shows its functional parts on the outside, leaving the internal spaces free for people to move in.

Figure 37.12 (right)
The Shard in London has sections at the top that are aesthetic and do not have a human function.

Design some preliminary sketches for a school gym big enough for a basketball court, changing rooms and toilets, storage for equipment, office space and a viewing area. Consider that it might be a multifunctional space; gyms can also be used as school assembly areas, theatres and exam halls.

Research the size and shape of the space you will need, the kind of construction methods that might be used and the surfaces and finishes you would like.

Create some sketches showing internal and external views and note ideas for materials on the drawings.

Respond to your work by comparison with the ideas that your classmates have come up with. Exhibit your drawings.

Designers

The term 'design' covers a wide area of activities: architecture, product design, graphics for print and the web, fashion, interior design, crafts and more.

The Design Brief

This is a document developed between the client and the designer and may include the following points:

1. **Objectives and goals:** What is the purpose of the project and what do we expect to achieve from it?

2. **Budget and schedule:** How much will be spent and will the project be delivered in sections or complete? Will there be deadlines for parts or all of the project?

3. **Target audience:** Who is the work designed to engage with? Who is the client trying to reach?

4. **Scope of the project:** Are client and designer clear about the size of the project, the stages of production and how much design content will be produced?

5. **Available/required materials:** Does the company already have a logo and identity or will the designer provide these? What products and services are being designed?

6. **Overall look:** Understanding the design preferences of the client, in dialogue with the designer, will help to make the overall style clear. They may prefer minimalist modern design or more traditional styles.

7. **Any definite 'don'ts':** What the client does not want is just as important as what they do want.

Design for Craft

Artists who design and make craftwork are following in an age-old tradition where the whole process is completed by the same person, from the initial idea through the creative process (see Introduction to Visual Studies, p. xxi) to the finished piece of craftwork.

Gold Zipper Link Ring
by Emer Roberts

Made of solid gold, this is a cast sculptural piece inspired by architecture and the Art Nouveau style (Fig. 37.13). There is a tension between the thin band and the strongly patterned surface of the ring. The contrast between raised and hollow elements allows the light to catch the top surfaces, leaving the lower areas in shadow. The band is an incomplete circle, which leaves an open area at the top of the ring where the band connects to it; a surprising break in the symmetry of the design. The smooth surface and warm colour of the gold harmonise the interlinked forms of the design. Emer Roberts won Irish Jewellery Designer of the Year in 2019.

Figure 37.13
Gold Zipper Link Ring, by Emer Roberts Design, Dublin.

Design an item for presentation to finishers in a charity fun run.

- **Research** the creative process (p. xxi) to help develop your ideas. Choose a craft you think would be most suitable and give reasons for your choice.

- **Create** a range of sketches and explorations leading to a design for a suitable object.

- **Respond** to the limitations and possibilities of the craft you have chosen and the nature of the object to be made.

Product Designers

These are the people who design everyday objects from cars and furniture to hand tools for home and work.

Examining a Designed Object

From the beginning of the Industrial Revolution to the invention of many modern products, designers have been involved in improving the look and function of man-made objects.

To design a useful and stylish object, the following four points must be kept in mind:

1. **A product should suit the needs of the people it was made for.**

   The science of ergonomics has developed out of this need for products to be safe and user-friendly. To design an ordinary item, like a chair, you will need a good deal of information: is it a dining room chair, an office chair or an armchair? All have different requirements and will probably be made of different materials.

2. **A product should function properly and efficiently.**

   A product needs to be mechanically sound and safe. We might take an example of an electric lawn mower; it should obviously cut grass, but it must be safe to use. On/off switches should be at the user's hand and safety cut-off should operate when hands are taken off the machine.

   If it operates on a cable, it should have a device to prevent it cutting its own cable. A rechargeable electric mower can operate without cable and would be safer (Fig. 37.15).

Search online for 'product design chair images' to get an idea of the range of possible designs which may help you with ideas for your studio product-design project.

- **Respond** to the chair designs you found online.

- **Research** the most suitable materials you might use for each of the different types of chair above and consider the variety of people that might use them.

- **Create** some alternative designs, noting your ideas for structure and decoration on the drawings.

Figure 37.14 Chair sketches by designer Spencer Nugent.

Figure 37.15 A cordless lawnmower.

3. A product should be made of suitable materials.

Modern materials have made the work of the product designer easier. We now have heat-resistant plastics that can be used for electric kettles, for instance. Carbon fibre is lighter and stronger than steel and can be made in almost any shape.

> **RESEARCH** Go to **www.sciencedirect.com** and search 'ergonomic design'. There is a good explanation of ergonomics on this site which you will need to understand if you are making product designs or writing about them.

Figure 37.16 Shockproof carbon fibre cases for iPhones.

RESEARCH CREATE RESPOND

Using the creative process (p. xxi) make some designs for a vacuum cleaner to be used in the home.

- **Research** the position of switches and safety features in your drawings and point out the choice of materials and colours you would use and why you would choose them.

- **Create** some alternative designs and select the best one for development.

- **Respond** by displaying your design and comparing it with your classmates' work.

RESEARCH CREATE RESPOND

Design some pieces of coloured tableware that might be used for picnics or barbecues.

- **Research** the shapes and materials you might use and explain your choices. Consider recyclable or sustainable materials.

- **Create** some designs for cups, plates, bowls, knives, forks, spoons and any other equipment you would like.

- **Respond** to designs by professionals and compare your work to theirs.

4. A product should look good in shape, colour and texture (it should be aesthetically pleasing).

This is where styling and colour choice is taken into account. What looks good to the public can change over time and in different parts of the world. Culture and fashion partly dictate, but well-designed objects should be ageless.

Figure 37.17 An angle-poise lamp by Herbert Terry & Sons. It was first manufactured in 1935 and is still in production.

Search online for 'timeless product designs images' and find some examples of designs which have stood the test of time. Take notes and sketches of the designs you like to use as inspiration for your studio work, or as reference for written work.

- **Create** a design for a freestanding bedside-table lamp for reading at night.
- **Research** the choice of materials and type of lighting to be used.
- **Respond** to your ideas with sketches and notes of a selection of design options and select a final design.

Graphic Designers

Graphic design is the art of visual communication through typography, images, colour and space. The designer can work in a broad area, from advertising and company identity/branding, to design for print (books and magazines, etc.), posters, billboards (large advertising hoardings), website graphics and art posters and prints.

Go to **www.creativeblog.com** and find the article called 'names designers should know'. Select a designer whose work appeals to you as an inspiration for your studio work and as an example for your written work.

Posters

Lithography, a new method of printing large pages in colour, sparked a very creative period in poster design in the 1880s and 1890s. Jules Chéret

Figure 37.18 *Palais de Glace* (The Ice Palace), a poster from the 1890s by Jules Chéret.

(1836–1932) developed a three-colour system which produced full-colour prints cheaply and quickly, revolutionising poster making. Chéret would have completed all stages of the design and printing process by hand.

Palais de Glace (*The Ice Palace*)

This is a poster typical of the 1890s in Paris (Fig. 37.18). The happy young woman at the centre of attention displays the new freedoms being experienced by women at the time.

Composition

The brightly coloured skater creates a diagonal across the page. The figures in grey tones in the background balance the movement. The lettering at the top and bottom frame the composition.

Typography

All the artwork for lithographic prints was made by hand, including the letters. You can see that they are individually shaped to fit the spaces they occupy. The large letters could be read from a distance.

Colour

The reds and oranges in the skaters' clothes express fun and excitement. These colours contrast with the blues and greys of the lettering and the background.

Design Practice

Having a clear idea of the design brief is vital, so the designer and client have the same goals in mind. Once the subject has been agreed, the designer will choose the images, colours and typography (the shape, size and style of the letters), and put them together in a design.

Modern designers will work out rough ideas in a sketch book, progressing the design to a stage where they begin to try out some of the designs on computer.

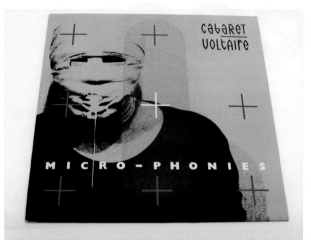

Figure 37.19 Cabaret Voltaire's *Micro-Phonies* record cover designed by Neville Brody, 1984.

Neville Brody (b. 1957)

An English graphic designer, typographer and art director, Brody is famous for his magazine covers for *The Face* and *Arena* in the 1980s. He also designed ground-breaking album covers for Cabaret Voltaire (Fig. 37.19), The Bongos and Depeche Mode.

He designed his own typography and was a founder member of Fontworks and the website FontShop, which sells original typefaces. His work has been published in bestselling books by Thames and Hudson, and his art has been exhibited in the Victoria and Albert Museum. He was the Dean of the School of Communications at the Royal College of Art until 2018.

His design company, Research Studios, was founded in 1994 and has branches in a number of cities in Europe. They design packaging, websites, on-screen graphics and corporate identity. They did work for Paramount Studios and other international corporations and redesigned the look of *The Times* newspaper in 2006 and the BBC in 2011.

Search online for 'graphic design sketchbook images'. You will see some designers' rough work. You can find some international poster design projects at *www.line25.com*. This site may help you understand how designers work and how you could work in a similar way. Make sketches and take notes to help you remember the process.

- **Create** a poster design to promote a concert by a band or singer you like. Make some sketches of alternative images, colours and lettering, and decide on the best combination to progress towards a finished poster.
- **Research** images and lettering that will help express the type of music and the style of the singer/band.
- **Respond** with an effective design and message to the style of music and the performer.

Design a logo for a sports club, real or imagined.
- **Research** the areas where the logo might be used, e.g. letterheads, signage, on clothes or equipment.
- **Create** a series of annotated sketches to explore some possibilities and develop towards a finished logo.
- **Respond** to the choices you have made in the process and see if you might change any aspects of your design. Discuss the results with your classmates.

Company Identity

There are many famous international companies that have a clear identity. The Coca-Cola lettering is recognised worldwide. The Nike swoosh and the McDonald's golden arches are recognised without words. Most car manufacturers have a badge that people recognise.

Logo: A sign, symbol, trademark or badge that identifies the commercial enterprise, organisation or individual that it represents. A logo that is made of letters, like the IBM logo, is called a logotype. A logo that is purely graphic, like the Nike swoosh, is called an ideogram.

Logos

Logos can be used in a variety of sizes and locations. For example, the Aer Lingus logo (Fig 37.20) appears on letter heads, tickets, staff uniforms, signage, on vehicles, in their advertising and on their aeroplanes.

Figure 37.20 The Aer Lingus logo and typography have to fit a range of products from small to large.

Advertising Design and Packaging

The graphic designer has to link a range of media together in an advertising campaign. The images used in print media (newspapers, magazines, etc.) will be repeated on television, roadside hoardings, packaging and on the internet, so that the viewer gets the same message, slogans and images repeated wherever the product is mentioned. Humour can be an effective way of advertising; can you think of any humorous advertisements that you think were effective?

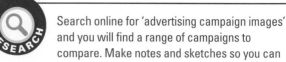

Search online for 'advertising campaign images' and you will find a range of campaigns to compare. Make notes and sketches so you can use these images as reference for your studio work or for your written work.

Figure 37.21 An image of a humorous advertisement.

Function

The purpose of most advertising design is to promote or sell the product or idea behind the design. The designer uses the art elements and design principles in a creative way to draw attention to the product or message they are promoting for their client.

Design an advertising campaign for a new perfume produced from natural ingredients.

- **Research** suitable names, colour schemes and graphics.
- **Create** a series of sketches of the container and the typography.
- **Respond** to the natural ingredients, the type of user the product is designed for and the advertising outlets you would use.

Website Design

The principles of design and layout for a website are similar to design for print media except that websites will have active areas and links to other pages or media.

The designer needs to be familiar with a wide range of disciplines. User-experience (UX) design tries to make a user-friendly website which meets the client's needs.

User-interface design (UI) lays out the pages and buttons that the user will see on-screen, this is known as 'the front end'.

The designer usually begins with sketches of the layout and typography and then moves on to a wireframe which shows the layout and contents of each screen page, where the logo goes, how navigation is handled, etc.

Layout is almost always based on a column grid (usually 12 columns), which helps the designer plan where content will be on the different-sized screens of different devices.

The designer makes a design for each page, a home page, a contact page and a shopping page for

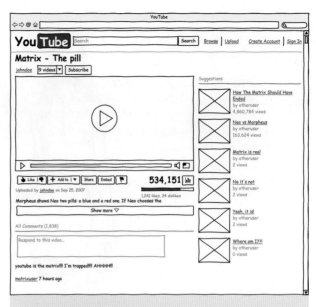

Figure 37.22 Web design wireframe layout of a YouTube page.

example, which shows the rest of the team how the complete site will look. The developers then code the site with the active areas to complete the project.

Go to **www.graphicdesignjunction.com** and search for 'best award-winning websites'. This site will give you an insight into website design. Select an example you like and make notes as reference for your written work.

Design a web page for a real or imagined adventure sports club.

- **Research** the sport and find or draw suitable images.
- **Create** a page layout for a home page.
- **Respond** to the nature of the sport and the kind of person you think would be involved in it.

Fashion Design

Fashion design is an artform that tries to combine the natural beauty of fabrics with design to create clothing and accessories.

Fashion is influenced by culture and social attitudes, which can create very different looks in various

Figure 37.23 A rough sketch of a dress evolving into a final coloured version.

times and places. A fashion designer tries to design clothes that function comfortably, as well as being attractive to their clients.

A designer can begin with an idea or theme, such as an aspect of nature or part of design history. They usually have a client or market in mind when they are working on their ideas. They will think about who will wear the garment and when it will it be worn, every day or for a special occasion.

Sketches, fabrics or models might be the starting point for an idea.

Search online for fashion-design images and you will find the kind of drawings that fashion designers make. Write notes and make sketches to use as reference for your studio work or written work.

RESEARCH **CREATE** **RESPOND**

Design an outfit for a friend for a Debs Ball.

- **Research** the types of fabric that would be suitable, how they move and hang.
- **Create** a selection of drawings to show to your client.
- **Respond** to the shape of your client, their colouring and sense of style.

Figure 37.24 Hats by Irish milliner Philip Treacy.

Accessories like shoes, hats, bags, scarves, ties, belts, gloves, jewellery, watches, sashes, shawls, socks and stockings are often designed by separate designers.

There are many other fields of design that might be of interest, but we do not have room to explore them all here. Please feel free to follow up any area that you are interested in.

Photography and Film
Photography

Fine art photography is different from just capturing an image in an artistic way. The artist uses photography as a medium to express an idea, an emotion or an artistic intention.

Search online for 'fine art photography artists'. You should be offered a long list of international artists. Select one or two that appeal to you; make notes and print out some images that you can use in research for your studio work or written work. Some of the more contemporary artists have video links.

Photographs can be analysed in the same way as paintings or other forms of art; the art elements and design principles apply in the same way.

Search online for '10 up and coming photographers from Ireland'. Respond to the work of a photographer by analysing two of their photographs using the headings: composition; colour or tone; texture; balance; light and space.

Take some photographs using a mobile phone of people, places or objects that you think show joy, sorrow or another emotion that appeals to you.

- **Research** the possibilities of editing colour or superimposing images through the editing programme in your phone.
- **Create** an image you can print, project or view on-screen.
- **Respond** to the possibilities of your editing programme to express your idea.

Film

Some commentators may think that film is the most powerful art medium. The combination of sound with moving images makes it a very complete artistic experience. Film is also readily available; you can see it on your TV, on DVD, downloaded from the internet onto any device, or you can get the fuller experience in your local cinema, quite cheaply when compared to other entertainments.

The first moving films were made by the Lumière brothers in the 1890s, lasting only a minute or so. By the 1920s, they were about 15 minutes long and were becoming a popular entertainment, shown in theatres between acts. *The Cabinet of Doctor Caligari*, a German horror film written by Hans

Figure 37.25 A photograph by Ruth Maria Murphy.

Figure 37.26 A still from the German horror film, *The Cabinet of Doctor Caligari*, 1920, director Robert Wiene.

Figure 37.27
A still from *The Wizard of Oz*, 1939, an early colour film directed by Victor Fleming.

Janowitz and directed by Robert Wiene, included painted sets, special effects and editing in one of the first consciously artistic productions (Fig. 37.26). You can see it on YouTube.

As technology improved, editing, special effects, zoom lenses, sound, colour and camerawork added to the language of film. *The Wizard of Oz*, made in 1939, was an early colour film (Fig. 37.27).

Colour became more common in the 1960s, when film had to compete with the growing popularity of television. Some movies are still shot on film, but digital video is more frequently used because it is easier to edit and create special effects with.

Analysing a Film

When looking at film you should try to be aware of how the elements of sound, colour, lighting, camerawork, special effects, direction and editing affect our enjoyment and understanding of the film.

Sound

Sound helps with atmosphere in a film. A scene in a darkened room with traffic noise and sirens can place us in a city. Bird song, running water or the sound of a breeze in the trees can locate us in the country. An actor's accent or tone of voice can suggest location or mood.

Music creates atmosphere; the screeching violins in a horror film or a gentle ballad give us an idea of what to expect on-screen. Music written for film can be as well-known as the film.

Sound effects are added at the editing stage, where all the necessary sound – slamming doors, footsteps, sounds from nature, explosions, music, etc. – are all synchronised with the action on-screen.

Colour

Colour can be important for mood and atmosphere. Red may suggest heat or violence; blue might suggest cold or sadness. Scenes can be colour enhanced to create a particular effect.

Lighting

Some documentaries and small-budget films can be filmed in natural light, but most film scenes are artificially lit so that light direction and intensity

Figure 37.28 A lighting crew at work.

Figure 37.29 A steady-cam operator in action.

can be relied on and the technical aspects of focus and aperture (the amount of light getting into the camera) don't have to be continually changed.

Camera Work

Camera work is important in helping the viewer to engage with the scene. You might see the world through the character's eyes, or the camera might move from one face to another so you could see the reaction to what is being said or happening on-screen.

A **pan** shot is where the camera moves horizontally from a fixed position. It can be used to follow movement or to show a wider context in a scene. The **tilt** is used to follow vertical movement from a fixed position. A **tracking** or **dolly** shot is used to follow action. The camera is mounted on a little truck (dolly) usually on rails so that it can be kept steady while it moves along with the action.

A **zoom** lens allows the camera user to change from a wide-angle view to a close-up or vice versa, without moving the camera or changing the lens. It can be very useful for explaining context or showing a detail in a scene.

A **steady-cam** is a counterbalanced unit that allows smooth movement with a hand-held camera. It is a heavy piece of equipment used to follow complicated movement and camera angles.

A **drone operator** controls the movement of the remotely operated flying camera that is used to get overhead shots and follow cross-country action.

The **camera angle** can have a dramatic effect on a scene. A **low-angle** shot can make the characters in a scene look dominant or threatening. A **high-angle** shot can put the viewer in a controlling position, where they may feel sympathy for the characters in the scene. **Flat or eye-level** shots are often used to record conversations or confrontations where the viewer is eye-to-eye with the actors.

A bird's eye view is filmed from directly overhead. In **an oblique angle shot**, the camera is tilted so the horizon is at an angle.

Figure 37.30 A still showing a low-angle shot from a film.

Special Effects

CGI (computer-generated imagery) is now more frequently used than sets or models. 3D computer graphics can be used to create structures and environments that would be impossible in the real world. Blue or green screens can be used when human action needs to be superimposed on an imaginary background or in a physically impossible

Figure 37.31
A scene from
Paddington, 2014, using
special effects.

location, like Spider-Man flying from building to building. Explosions, car crashes, falling buildings and huge crowds can all be created by 3D computer animation.

The Crew

The director is responsible for guiding the creative vision and the style of a film. They often have combined role with a title like producer/director or writer/director. In a smaller production the director can control the whole process, from writing the script, arranging finance and casting the actors to filming, editing and looking for outlets to show the film. The director is the link between the production, creative and technical teams in a bigger production and provides the ideas that turn the script into the images and sounds that the audience see on-screen. Organising and advising the actors during rehearsals and filming is an important part of the director's role.

Figure 37.32 Director Steven Soderbergh working on set.

Figure 37.33 A makeup artist working on an actor between scenes on a film set.

The art director supervises makeup, costumes, sets and props to support the storyline and atmosphere of the film.

The editor works closely with the director to assemble shots into scenes. They check technical standards, continuity of lighting and colour and the actor's performance. An editor needs to be creative, noting moments of spontaneity from the actors that might improve the story. The editing team mixes the sound, music and images, adding any special effects that might be needed.

There are so many practitioners and functions within the film industry that we could not hope to cover them here. To get some idea of the range of jobs and careers involved, you could look online.

The scale of the production usually determines the number of staff and the levels of specialty involved. One individual can make a complete film on their

Go to **www.careersinfilm.com**. You could make notes on the various jobs that people do in the film industry and draw a web or flowchart to show how the specialists work together.

own. They can be the writer, producer, director, actor, cinematographer, editor – the whole show. At the other extreme, hundreds of people can be involved in a production, from studio bosses through the layers of production and technical experts to actors and extras.

Some of the people involved in filmmaking are well-known to the public. Actors and directors are often household names, whereas some others involved may never come to the public's attention, though they would be well-known in the industry.

Film Production

Film production usually begins with writing a story line and script. A novel or a piece of history might be the starting point. There are so many genres to choose from that almost any topic can be considered.

> **Genre:** A word used in all the arts to describe the subject, category or style of a work. Action, drama, comedy, fantasy and horror would be examples of film genres.

> Search for 'famous Irish film directors' on the internet. Make notes and sketches of the work of one director for reference in your studio or written work.

Analysis

The practice and function of art and design have completely changed in what is now the information age. Many large 21st-century industries are based on information and ideas rather than physical products. In the same way, art has responded to change as it always does: by exploring the boundaries of what is possible with new technologies and ideas.

Make a short film about environmental challenges in your school or neighbourhood.

- **Research** your topic and write a story line.
- **Create** a short film using phones as cameras; get friends involved and shoot the action from a number of viewpoints.
- **Respond** to your film through the editing process.

Chapter Review

1. Describe the work of a contemporary artist who uses drawing skills and technical media to create their work. Use words and sketches in your answer.

2. Write and sketch a description of a building that you like, noting how it fits into its location. Give some background information on the architect.

3. Find an artist you would describe as an innovator and write an account of their work, illustrated with sketches.

4. Conceptual Art opens up an almost limitless range of possibilities in art. Discuss the work of an artist that you think explores these possibilities, using words and sketches.

5. Design takes many forms. Discuss the work of a designer you admire, pointing out the features of their work. Use sketches to illustrate your points.

6. Do you think craftwork is still relevant in the 21st century? Use words and sketches to identify examples to support your points.

7. Film can be art or just entertainment. How would you describe the difference? Give examples in words and sketches to illustrate your points.

8. Before the modern era, most art was made with an audience in mind. Describe a work of modern art that you think was made for a particular audience, using words and sketches to make your points.

Further Research

www.khanacademy.org – Search for 'contemporary art intro' for a simple introduction to contemporary art

www.virtosuart.com – Search for '30 most influential contemporary artists' to read about acclaimed artists from around the world

www.visual-arts-cork.com – This website offers a comprehensive look at Irish contemporary artists

www.designwanted.com – Accounts of some of the most influential designers, which may inspire you with ideas for your own studio work

www.designireland.ie – Profiles on a range of Irish craft designers

www.dccoi.ie – The Design Council of Ireland website may help you decide on your choice of craft and give background for written work

www.irish-art.com – Search for 'Irish artists' for a comprehensive list of Irish artists

www.imma.ie – The Irish Museum of Modern Art website

Artists: Processes and Media

By the end of this unit I will ...

* to be able to understand what 'process' and 'media' are
* know how to interview an artist in person or online
* respond to a gallery or museum visit
* know something about the role of a curator.

Art elements and design principles (see p. xiv) are used by all art and design practitioners. Architects may begin with line drawings, developing these into 3D models on-screen, or actual models, to show the client how light and space work on the design. In fact, most artists and designers begin with pen or pencil line drawings, as this is the quickest method to put down ideas.

Artists and designers will develop their work using the art elements and design principles that best express their ideas.

Art Can Take Many Forms

New processes and media are evolving all the time as materials and equipment are being developed. Artists work in new ways, combining media like video, sculpture, performance, or anything that their imagination can conjure up. You will find artists in

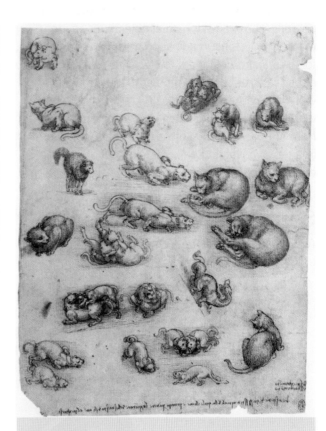

Figure 38.1 Drawings of cats from Leonardo da Vinci's sketchbooks in the Royal Collection in London show how artists can explore a subject with drawings.

Unit 16 who work directly with nature, allowing the things they make to return to nature over time. Other artists take their work directly to the public, in the form of street art and public performance. Artists like Jesse Jones (see Unit 12, p. 512) combine video, sculpture, performance and other disciplines together to express their message.

Research

Some artists like to work spontaneously, responding directly to a physical stimulus like a landscape, a person, man-made or natural objects, or an idea that forms in their imagination. It is more common for artists and designers to do some research either as a response to problems they encounter while they are working or as a starting point in their working process. Research can take many forms, from simply making sketches, exploring ideas and images to collecting objects, taking photographs or examining other artists' work.

Sources for Artists' Ideas

Almost anything can be a starting point for a work of art. Many artists work from the environment, using the many forms of nature from the universe to microscopic images as a source of ideas. Social commentary (see Unit 15) and the human condition also frequently stimulate the artist's imagination. Some artists do not need a specific subject, responding to marks they make themselves or objects they find to begin a process of exploration, adding to and subtracting from the work in progress until a conclusion is found.

When you are searching for topics for your own work, it is best to look for primary sources, working directly from the environment. You might research man-made or natural materials from your surroundings as your starting point.

Process

The art process is the making of art, collecting, sorting, organising, making connections between objects, and ideas, and noticing patterns and contrasts. The act of making art is also part of the process: drawing, photographing, joining, constructing, applying, assembling – any process can be involved.

The artist researches the subjects and ideas for their work. Different artists work in different

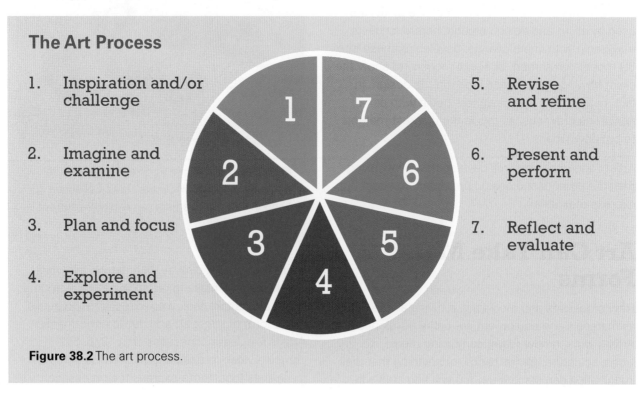

The Art Process

1. Inspiration and/or challenge
2. Imagine and examine
3. Plan and focus
4. Explore and experiment
5. Revise and refine
6. Present and perform
7. Reflect and evaluate

Figure 38.2 The art process.

ways, but most will have developed a method of organising their work process. Here is an example of how the creative process can be organised. You do not have to follow the sequence shown; you could start at any point and go in any direction you liked.

1. **Inspiration and/or challenge:** This is where the impulse to make or design something comes from. You might have seen something or had an idea that inspires you to make a piece of art or craftwork. You might have been set a challenge by your teacher or a client.

2. **Imagine and examine:** In this part of the process, you might be developing ideas through sketching, researching, discussing, taking photographs, collecting objects – anything to feed your ideas and examine possibilities.

3. **Plan and focus:** When you have gathered information, it is time to make a plan. What will I make and how will I go about it? What skills and materials will I need? You could annotate plans and sketches with ideas for materials and working methods.

4. **Explore and experiment:** At this stage you might try out ideas with different materials, techniques and colours to see what things work well together and what does not. You may

have to rethink your earlier ideas in light of your experiments.

5. **Revise and refine:** Examine your various experiments and select the best ones for further development. Make the best version of your plan using the most suitable materials and techniques.

6. **Present and perform:** Present your work to your teacher, client or classmates. You could make a verbal presentation explaining the thinking and process that brought you to the final piece of work. The work could be exhibited in your school or in a more public space.

7. **Reflect and evaluate:** Comments from your teacher, classmates or clients might help you to think about your work and how to develop techniques and ideas for future projects. It is difficult to be objective about our own work, but try to give some thought to progressing your skills and ideas.

Go to YouTube and watch the video 'Exploring Sketchbooks – Animating the Archives' (9:40). The explanations of how some artists use sketchbooks may help you to understand how to use your own sketchbook.

Two drawings by Picasso show how his style changed throughout his working life.

Figure 38.3 (left) The atmospheric *Mother and Child*, 1904, shows how he explored the detail of the hand.

Figure 38.4 (right) His style in 1933 was very different; a simple linear treatment describes form, texture and pattern in the *Two Dressed Models*, 1933.

Media

The materials or forms used by an artist are called their 'media'. Contemporary artists feel free to use almost anything as their medium. The days of paint on canvas or murals, and sculptures in stone, wood or bronze being the only accepted types of fine art media are long gone. The artist is now free to explore the real or virtual environments and use their imagination to find their mode of expression.

> You will find a long list of media that may help you think of alternative approaches to your studio work at **www.creativity-innovation.eu/list-art-media**. Make notes to remind yourself of different media you might use.

Encountering Artists

To understand how artists work and what motivates them, it is best to have a first-hand conversation where you can ask the questions that interest you.

> *Note:* Sometimes it is possible to have an artist, designer or architect working in your school under one of the Artists in School programmes. These are run by a number of organisations:
>
> The Arts Council – **www.artscouncil.ie**
>
> Irish Architecture Foundation – **www.architecturefoundation.ie**
>
> NAPD Creative Engagement programme – **www.creativeengagement.ie**
>
> Creative Ireland programme – **www.creativeireland.gov.ie**.

It might be possible to arrange a visit by an artist to your school, or better still, some artists and designers are open to having students visit them in their studios.

Should you be lucky enough to have a meeting with an artist, you might consider the type of questions you would ask them. For example:

- How/Why did you become an artist?
- How do you find your subjects?
- How do you begin a piece, and what is your process?
- Where do you show your work?

This is just a small sample of the type of questions you could ask. You will need to adapt to the artist/designer/architect and their work, and the answers they give to your questions.

Meet the Artist

Laura Callaghan

Figure 38.5 Laura Callaghan.

Laura is an Irish illustrator based in Belfast. She has many well-known brand names among her commercial clients and her work has been featured in *The Guardian*, *NYLON*, *Seventeen* and *The Sunday Times*, among others.

Her colourful female characters are much more than 'pretty girls'. They are part of a thought-provoking social commentary.

She makes drawings of women in power, women in repose and women in everyday settings, which offer a refreshing slice of reality. Instead of using them as objects, as was traditional in the advertising industry,

Figure 38.6 *Cleithrophobia*, 2019, by Laura Callaghan, gouache on watercolour paper.

Laura's work reinforces the humanity of the characters.

No topics are off the list for these modern-day women dealing with all the ups and downs of being a female. They address issues of autonomy, self-love and delusion. The characters make examples of themselves in the privacy of their homes.

Interview

Q. Hi Laura! How did you become an illustrator?

Laura: I studied Visual Communications at NCAD in Dublin as there was no Illustration course at that time. I was always incorporating illustration into my projects, but after an internship at a design studio in my final year, I realised graphic design wasn't really for me.

Q. How did your career progress from there?

Laura: I moved to London in 2010 to do a one-year Masters in Illustration in Kingston University, and then I worked in South London before moving to Belfast in 2019.

Q. What process do you use when creating these illustrations?

Laura: I sketch out a few initial ideas super quickly in a sketchbook. I start out with scribbles that probably wouldn't make sense to anyone looking at them, but it helps me get a feel for the composition.

I then narrow it down to a few compositions and I work these up as small pencil sketches. I check with the client before making a few tweaks to the design.

Then I sketch the characters more fully, adding clothing details and refining facial features. Once I am happy with the sketch, I enlarge it and print it out. This is so I that I can use a lightbox to draw the outlines in pen for the final illustration onto paper – this means there are no messy pencil lines to rub out and, if I mess up the inking, I still have an intact pencil sketch to work from if I need to restart.

Once the characters are inked in with a drawing pen, I scan the image and colour it digitally in Photoshop.

> **Photoshop:** Adobe Photoshop is a software programme widely used in digital art.

Q. What characters do you like to draw best?

Laura: I like to draw women with strength, but that's not to say they're perfect and together characters. Their lives and environments are messy – sometimes they're working dead-end jobs, stuck in a rut or a terrible relationship. But I don't think having that vulnerability makes them any less strong.

Q. Is there a reason why you only draw women?

Laura: My work is very narrative in nature and a lot of the issues and experiences I'm exploring are personal, so I tend to tell those stories from a female perspective. I didn't start out intending to only draw female characters, but it's definitely where my interest lies.

$\mathcal{N}ote$: Laura Callaghan can be found on Instagram (@lauracallaghanillustration), Twitter (@lauramcallaghan) and on her website ***www.lauracallaghanillustration.com.***

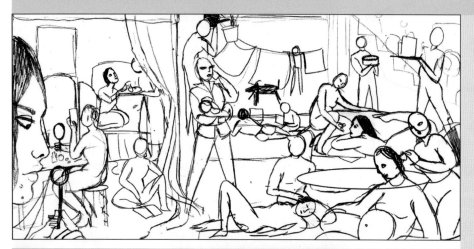

Figure 38.7
Fact, 2019, by Laura Callaghan. (top) Sketch version of the piece; (middle) the drawing; (bottom) the finished mural.

Online Interviews

There are many YouTube interviews with well-known artists that give insight into their practice and use of media.

- Dorothy Cross (p. 503) works with whatever materials or processes seem appropriate to the work in progress. Go to YouTube and watch the video 'Art Encounters: Dorothy Cross at TEDxDUBLIN' (18:27).

- Sean Scully (p. 509) uses more traditional media in a modern way. Go to YouTube and watch the video 'Sean Scully: Painting' (34:17). This video includes some short scenes of Scully involved in the painting process.

- Judy Chicago talks about her art practice in the YouTube video 'Meet the Artists | Judy Chicago | The Birth Project' (5:50) and Damien Hirst takes us through his modern exhibitions in the YouTube video 'Artist Damien Hirst at Tate Modern | Tate' (12:51).

Make notes and sketches to use as research for your written work and studio practice.

Find an online interview you like and write a description of the working methods and materials used by the artist, using examples of their work to illustrate your points.

Art Galleries and Museums

You can see the work of historical artists or contemporary artists in galleries and museums. Gallery spaces have evolved from large rooms full of paintings and sculptures in Victorian times, to the 'white cubes' of the 20th century, where all architectural features are screened off so nothing distracts from the work on display.

Commercial Galleries

These are businesses that represent artists in the way that music companies represent musicians. The gallery gets exclusive rights to the artist's work

Figure 38.9 Charles Gilmore Fine Art, a gallery in Belfast.

Figure 38.8 A modern white gallery space with a few artworks on display.

in a region. Major international artists might be represented by galleries in America, Europe and Asia. Galleries can have six to eight exhibitions a year featuring the different artists that they represent.

The gallery takes up to 50 per cent of the net value of the work to cover expenses like rent, staff, entertaining clients, keeping records and all the expenses and arrangements that go with displaying and promoting the work. The artist is then free to get on with their work. Gallery owners are nearly always art lovers and collectors who invest a lot of time and money in the project.

www.irish-art.com and **www.visualartists.ie** have directories of public and commercial galleries that you might visit. You could record your visit for use with your written work.

Cooperative Galleries, Pop-up and Temporary Galleries

Groups of artists can get together to organise their own exhibitions and studio spaces. Sometimes these can be sponsored by government organisations or other patrons. For many artists who are starting out and have not yet made a reputation, this can be a way of getting some exposure for their work.

Go to **www.irish-art.com/irishartgroups.php**. This website has a list of studios, cooperatives and art groups. You might look for local galleries to visit where you could meet the artists and ask questions to help with your written work and studio practice.

Open Call Exhibitions

These can be organised by any gallery or group. Any artist can make a submission and the work is selected by a committee or a curator. Some of the big Biennial exhibitions are organised in this way and many local and group exhibitions also use this process.

Public Galleries and Museums

The public gallery has a different function from private enterprises. Some museums, like the National Gallery of Ireland, house historical collections; others, like the Irish Museum of Modern Art, display modern and contemporary art. These are publicly funded institutions responsible to a board and public authorities. Galleries of this kind would have a mission statement to guide the nature of their collection. It might be to create a local or national collection or an international collection. They might concentrate on a particular time in history or a specific type of art, like the Chester Beatty Library, which specialises in Oriental art. Most public galleries have a permanent collection and display parts of it at a time. They also run temporary exhibitions focused on a theme or an individual artist.

Figure 38.10 The interior of the National Gallery of Ireland, Dublin.

These galleries are collecting work that is significant for the time in which it was made for future generations. For an artist to have their work exhibited in a public gallery could be life-changing; it marks their work as being judged to be important in the development of art in their time.

 www.ireland.com/magazine/culture/galleries-and-museums includes museums and galleries all over the country. Many of these institutions will offer guided tours and may be able to cover special topics for you. You should arrange a visit to a gallery near you, recording what you see and learn for your written work.

- **Respond** to a gallery visit where you have focused on a particular artist or work of art and made notes and sketches.
- **Create** a work, using your sketches and notes, dealing with issues that strike you as a result of your visit.
- **Research** the work, the artists and the gallery to help you decide on the theme of your work.

Visiting Galleries and Museums

A visit to a gallery or museum is an opportunity to engage with art directly. The work can be seen up close and features that might be missed in photographs or on-screen can be noticed.

The Building

The size, shape and style of the building that houses an exhibition can be important. One criticism of the Guggenheim Museum in Bilbao, Spain, is that the gallery spaces inside are too big and important work can look insignificant (Fig 38.11).

At the same time, the building itself, designed by the Canadian-American architect Frank Gerhy, has had such impact internationally that a significant tourist industry has emerged in Bilbao.

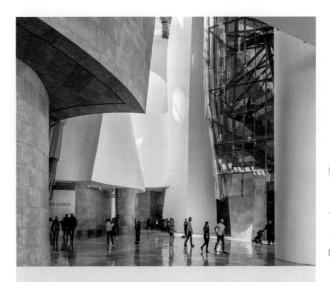

Figure 38.11 The interior of the Guggenheim Museum, Bilbao.

Smaller galleries may be restricted to a certain size or type of work by the nature of their space.

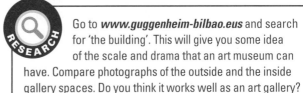 Go to *www.guggenheim-bilbao.eus* and search for 'the building'. This will give you some idea of the scale and drama that an art museum can have. Compare photographs of the outside and the inside gallery spaces. Do you think it works well as an art gallery?

What to Look for During a Visit

Before you visit an exhibition, see what you can find out about it online. This will help to prepare you with

Figure 38.12 The Clare Street entrance to the National Gallery of Ireland, Dublin, designed by Benson and Forsyth.

a background about the gallery or museum and the ideas behind the exhibition you intend to see.

Look at the building and note its architectural style. See if there is easy access for people with disabilities and what facilities they provide, e.g. toilets, café, shop, reception, signage and other information like catalogues and digital media stations.

> Create some annotated sketches of the layout of the exhibition space and particular works that interest you. Make notes to remind yourself of features of the work and the gallery. These notes should help you with written work later and remind you of elements you might include in a school exhibition.

Type of Work Exhibited

You should note the type of work that is on exhibition in the gallery, e.g. 2D or 3D; modern media, like video or installations. Exhibits from a different time or culture may need some research to appreciate them more fully. Some modern and contemporary art can be challenging and may need an explanation or research to help understand it.

Does the exhibition have a title or a theme? This information will usually be covered in the artist's statements or in an exhibition catalogue.

Is the work on display by an individual or a group? If it is a group, what is the connection between them?

Layout

Pay attention to the way the work is displayed. In a large gallery, like the National Gallery of Ireland, the work may be divided into large headings like 'European Art' or 'Irish Art' and then further broken down into sub-groups like 'European Art 1300–1650' and so on. In smaller galleries, work could be divided by style, technique or any number of alternative categories. See if you can work out reasons for the groupings you see on a gallery visit.

Note the arrangement of the work within the gallery space. How is art displayed on the walls: is it in groups or widely spaced? Where are 3D pieces placed? Is there room to walk around them and see them from all angles? Some 3D work may be placed on a plinth or inside a vitrine (a glass box). Rooms may be darkened for video or screen displays.

Lighting

Make note of how the paintings are lit. When good natural light is available, purpose-built galleries will often have glazed areas in the roof to let in natural light. Artificial lighting is often concealed so it does not distract the viewer. In the older parts of the

Figure 38.13 Crawford Art Gallery in Cork. If you drew a line along the wall at eye level through the centres of the larger paintings, the paintings would be distributed in a balanced way above and below this line. A space has been allowed for the sculpture on a column, about a third of the way from the end of the wall. North-facing glass panels concealed in the roof allow gentle, natural light into the space.

Figure 38.14 The Grand Gallery in the National Gallery of Ireland, Dublin. This was the main gallery, filled with paintings and sculptures when the building was initially opened in 1854.

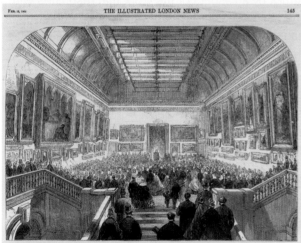

THE ILLUSTRATED LONDON NEWS

Figure 38.15 *The Lord Lieutenant of Ireland, George William Frederick Howard, 7th Earl of Carlisle, (1802–1864), opening the National Gallery of Ireland.* A wood engraving from the National Gallery of Ireland.

National Gallery, glass roofs with obscure glass fill the rooms with soft natural light (Fig. 38.14).

Modern artificial light can be very unobtrusive; small lighting units can be kept out of sight, throwing gentle light on the exhibits. You should try to find out how it is arranged in an exhibition that you visit so you can appreciate what good lighting can bring to a display.

Sources of Information

Large museums and galleries will have a catalogue of their permanent collection and maps of the layout of the galleries. Temporary exhibitions may have a smaller catalogue and the work can be identified by a number or an information label beside the work.

Some galleries have interpretive media and technology that you can interact with, which may provide audio or video information on the exhibition (Fig. 38.16). Phone apps are available in some galleries to guide you round the exhibits and provide background information.

Figure 38.16 A virtual reality experience at an art gallery.

The Curator

The curator brings art to the public. They can propose an idea for an exhibition, research the availability of the artworks, oversee arrangements for loans and transport, organise the catalogue, decide on wall colours and texts and decide on the layout and hanging of the work.

Large galleries will have a curatorial team, with specialists in historical periods such as the Renaissance or cultural areas like the Middle East.

Figure 38.17 A curator and her assistant at work, organising an exhibition.

Independent curators can be artists, critics, academics, writers and dealers, who have a reputation for creating exciting exhibitions. Many of the big biennial and triennial (every two or three years) exhibitions are curated by independents.

Search for 'best art biennials' on the web and you will be offered a long, clickable list of worldwide exhibitions to explore. Some have virtual tours that you could use to give you an idea of what to expect when visiting an exhibition.

EVA International is an Irish biennial exhibition based at Limerick City Gallery of Art. The website **www.eva.ie** will connect you with their archive of past exhibitions and future plans. You might visit this site before a gallery visit to help you prepare notes and questions to answer on your visit.

This may work best with a group. **Research** the material for a student exhibition in your school. Decide on a theme, like drawings from life or ceramics, for instance. Decide on the group to be involved, one class or all the art students. Will the exhibition be open to the public or just for the school? **Create** an exhibition space within the school; put up stands, clear furniture and set up lighting. Make a catalogue and decide on signage. **Respond** to the work in progress and adjust your layout for best viewing and access.

Using Art as Inspiration

Sometimes when we come across the work of an artist in a book, online or in a gallery, we can be struck by an aspect of the work that resonates with thoughts, ideas or images we have had ourselves. It can be good to use these parallel themes and ideas in our own work, not merely copying aspects of the work but sharing an understanding of what the artist was doing and using it to progress our own ideas and techniques. Many artists make references to the work of other artists and designers in their art, not copying but building on their ideas and techniques.

During the Renaissance, Raphael developed ideas that he got from the work of Leonardo and Michelangelo, creating his own style and technique from these foundations. The Impressionists (see Unit 4, p. 160) were influenced by Oriental art and photography, while Picasso (see Unit 5, p. 205) was influenced by African masks and early Spanish art. In more recent times, the Irish artist Robert Ballagh (see Unit 12, p. 495) made paintings of people looking at the paintings of other artists at an exhibition, directly quoting the paintings but putting them in a different context. In the same way you could use works that you like to help develop your own artistic process.

Respond to a work of art that you like by adapting the themes or techniques that impress you into a work of your own. Use the art process on page 536 to help you with the project.

Analysis

Visiting a gallery or museum is the best way to become familiar with the art process. You can see the media and techniques up close and have a more complete experience of the work. Photographs in books or images on-screen do not reveal the true colours, texture, size or presence of an original work.

Exhibitions often provide the context of the era or style to a work you are interested in. Context often shows up features you would not have observed with just one example.

The processes and media that artists use to produce a work of art continue to develop and change. The work that is now in the main stream would not have been considered to be art a couple of generations ago.

Chapter Review

1. What do the words 'process' and 'media' mean?

2. What does a curator do?

3. Following a visit to a gallery or museum, discuss your opinions with a small group within your art class and elect a spokesperson to explain your views to the class.

4. Prepare a list of questions that you might ask an artist visiting your school. Research their work and make your questions relevant to it.

5. Write an account of a visit to a gallery or exhibition. Note the building outside and in, describe the gallery space, and select two pieces (naming the artist and the title of the work) you think represent the character of the exhibition.

6. What do you think could be done to make galleries and museums more interesting for young people? Write suggestions and make sketches of your ideas.

Further Research

www.visual-arts-cork.com – Search for 'Irish art galleries' for a comprehensive list of galleries around Ireland

www.youtube.com – Search for 'Visual Artist Joe Caslin discussing his artistic process' (9:38)

www.youtube.com – Search for 'National Gallery of Ireland Virtual Tour' (4:50) to learn more about each room in the National Gallery of Ireland

www.kitchentableclassroom.com – Search for 'virtual tours' to learn more about a number of international galleries

www.the-talks.com/interviews/art – Contains interviews with international artists

Unit 15

Art as Social Commentary or Commentator

By the end of this
unit I will ...

* be able to describe a work of art that makes comments on the society of its time
* know how to discuss the role of fine-art prints in creating awareness of social issues in society
* understand how to identify some of the innovations that Dadaism brought to Modern Art
* be able to recognise the role of the designer in creating new social standards
* be able to interpret the impact film can have on people's understanding of social issues.

Context

It could be said that all art is a commentary on the society it is made in. In this unit, however, we will be looking at the work of some artists who consciously decided to make comments and judgements about society and the issues it faces.

Many artists today feel that their work should hold up a mirror to society, reflecting issues and events that they see as important. What the issues are and how to approach them is something each artist has to work out for themselves.

Figure 39.1 *Napoleon at the Saint-Bernard Pass*, 1801–2, by Jacques-Louis David, oil on canvas, 261 × 221 cm, one of five versions of the painting. David represents Napoleon as a heroic, windswept figure controlling his spirited horse, a man in command. The perspective places the viewer at the hero's feet, looking up in admiration. A number of versions of this painting were made to promote this image of Napoleon.

Social Commentators Throughout History

Artists and designers can create an awareness of social issues among a wide audience.

In the past, powerful people used artists to enhance their status and promote their achievements (Fig. 39.1). The Pharaohs of ancient Egypt built enormous tombs and temples to demonstrate their god-like status, while the ancient Romans created triumphal arches to celebrate famous victories and emperors. Most art and architecture in the post-Renaissance period was commissioned by powerful patrons of Church and State, so the artists and designers had little say in what subjects were depicted.

Following the Protestant Reformation, artists in Protestant countries were allowed to choose their own subjects and we begin to see more social commentary. Pieter Bruegel the Elder pointed out human foolishness, and often illustrated proverbs like 'the blind leading the blind' (Fig. 39.2).

Dutch genre paintings, too, sometimes offer lessons in human behaviour through scenes in family homes and inns (see p. 79).

In the early 1700s, Jean-Antoine Watteau made paintings illustrating the lives of the rich and privileged.

Prints

Printmaking began in Europe in the 15th century as a way of illustrating books. Soon, printed leaflets and pamphlets were produced to inform – and influence – the public. Illustrations could be understood even by people who could not read; illiteracy was the norm in that era. These printed illustrations became popular when they were sold in the street and at fairs and markets. They often had religious or moral themes, and were one of the few ways in which ordinary people were exposed to art.

Albrecht Dürer created a series of woodcuts and engravings illustrating the horrors of war and sin (see Fig. 39.3).

Search online or in a library for more of Bruegel's proverb paintings to see how the artist represented human foolishness.

Who – or what – points out foolish behaviour and actions in the modern world?

The Chester Beatty Library in Dublin has a collection of Dürer prints that illustrates a range of drawing techniques. If you are able, visit the library and make some quick line sketches of your favourite print.

Figure 39.2
The Blind Leading the Blind, 1568, by Pieter Bruegel the Elder, tempera on canvas, 86 × 154 cm, Museo Natzionale di Capodimonte, Naples. Bruegel illustrated many proverbs both as lessons and as entertainment.

UNITS 13–16 TODAY'S WORLD

Figure 39.3 *The Four Horsemen of the Apocalypse*, 1498, by Albrecht Dürer, woodcut, 39 × 29 cm, Chester Beatty Library, Dublin.

Engraving: A print-making technique produced by incising (cutting in) a design into a metal plate, usually copper, using a burin (a sharp steel tool that can cut fine lines into the metal). Tones are produced by cross-hatching and textures are achieved by making lines and marks with the burin.

William Hogarth produced several series of prints which he hoped would influence people's attitudes to some of the dangers in the society of his time. The pair of engravings *Gin Lane* and *Beer Street* illustrate the dangers of alcoholism. They were accompanied by poems that pointed out the consequences of indulging in too much alcohol.

Francisco de Goya recorded the French invasion of Spain (1807–1814) in the 'Disasters of War', a

RESPOND ➤ Compare the responses of artists to alcoholism in London of the 1700s with modern artists' responses to substance abuse. Which do you find more compelling?

Figure 39.4 *Gin Lane*, 1751, by William Hogarth, etching and engraving on paper, 36 × 31 cm, Tate Britain, London.

Figure 39.5 *And it Cannot be Helped*, from The Disasters of War, 1810–20, by Francisco de Goya, drypoint etching, 14 × 17 cm, Metropolitan Museum of Art, New York.

series of 82 etchings and aquatints. These were not published until after his death; some people think Goya may have feared a violent reaction from the public, as he had received following the publication of his previous series, 'Los Caprichos', which mocked traditional practices and superstitions. People were outraged by the prints, and thought the artist was making fun of ordinary people.

RESPOND

- Type 'Goya prints' into a web search and you will find many of his social commentary works. Do you find them shocking, funny or insulting?
- Who do you think are the social commentators of the 21st century?

Etching: a printing method. A metal plate is covered with a waxy medium before it is drawn into with a needle or sharp point. The plate is placed in an acid bath where the acid bights into the areas where the protective surface has been scratched away. The plate is then inked up and printed.

Aquatint: a type of etching where powdered resin is melted onto a metal plate creating areas of tone. Etching and aquatint are usually used together, combining line and tone.

Prints commenting on social issues continued to be popular through the 19th century. The most notable artist-commentator of this time was the printmaker, painter and sculptor Honoré Daumier. In his most infamous piece, *Gargantua*, Daumier portrayed the French King Louis Phillipe as a greedy giant, consuming all the resources of France. Daumier spent six months in prison for creating this image, and the magazine that published it, *Le Caricature*, was closed down.

Figure 39.7 *Street (Strasse)*, from the portfolio *Nine Woodcuts*, 1919, by Otto Dix, 24 × 18 cm. This simple woodcut is an observation of city life.

Figure 39.6

Gargantua, 1831, by Honoré Daumier, lithograph, Bibliothéque nationale de France, Paris.

Figure 39.8
The Volunteers, 1921–2, by Käthe Kollwitz, 49 × 35 cm, Tate Britain, London. This woodcut shows a group of young men arm in arm rushing forward in their enthusiasm to do their patriotic duty.

In the early 20th century, artists like Emil Nolde and Otto Dix illustrated the unhappy state of German society after World War I. The Expressionists (see Unit 5, p. 215) continued to make prints commenting on social issues.

Käthe Kollwitz: The Volunteers

Käthe Kollwitz, who we looked at in Chapter 15, was a German artist who chose printmaking as her primary form of expression. Her prints show the hard lives led by ordinary people in Germany following World War I.

In the 1920s, Kollwitz produced a series of prints called 'War'. One of these prints is *The Volunteers*, an Expressionist woodcut with simplified forms and large areas of black space. The large areas of dark in the print suggest a foreboding of the evil that war brings.

The group of young men in the print are arm-in-arm, rapidly moving forward and upward in their enthusiasm to join the war. All appear to be singing – except the figure in the middle, whose eyes and mouth are closed. Kollwitz had names for the young men in the image, who she said were friends of her son, and were all killed in the war.

Kollwitz's social commentary is made by creating prints based on personal experiences rather than battle scenes or dramatic events.

 Create a print which represents your thinking on current social problems.

Impressionism

The Impressionists (see Unit 4, p. 160) were social commentators insofar as they portrayed the everyday lives of middle-class people in and around Paris. Renoir, in particular, catches a party atmosphere in his *Dance at the Moulin de la Galette* and *Luncheon of the Boating Party* (see p. 172), which show young Parisians enjoying themselves in the open air. Such relaxed freedom had not been possible in earlier generations, when working on the land and at manual trades left little time for recreation.

Dadaism

In the 20th century, social commentary became a much more common element in artistic practice.

Figure 39.9 *L'Absinthe* (The Absinthe Drinker), 1875–6, by Edgar Degas, oil on canvas, 92 × 68 cm, Musée d'Orsay, Paris, a commentary on the use of alcohol in society.

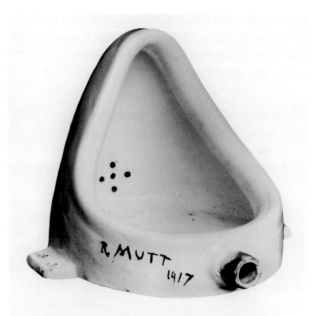

Figure 39.10 *Fountain*, 1966 (replica of original, 1917), by Marcel Duchamp, Philadelphia Museum of Art. Presenting found objects as art was meant to challenge the art establishment, who admired art for its monetary value rather than its beauty or truth.

Dadaism, which was prominent from 1916 until 1922, proved to be one of the most influential art movements in the 20th century. It was anti-establishment, protesting at the pretentious and ignorant attitudes of most artists, dealers and critics in the face of war and social problems. Dadaists poked fun at the idea of art as a precious or valuable thing. They exhibited found objects – a bottle rack, a urinal, an iron with tacks stuck to its smoothing surface – declaring that they were 'art'. They ridiculed the absurdity of existence ('What does it mean to exist?'), a sentiment echoed in the plays of Samuel Beckett.

The most famous Dadaist work is Marcel Duchamp's *Fountain*, a factory-made urinal displayed on a pedestal and signed 'R. Mutt, 1917'.

After an exhibition in New York at which *Fountain* had been hidden from public view, Louise Norton wrote in the magazine, *The Blind Man*, 'Whether Mr

Mutt with his own hands made the fountain or not has no importance. He chose it. He took an ordinary article of life, placed it so that its useful significance disappeared under the new title and point of view – created a new thought for that object.'

 RESPOND Do you agree with the Dadaist idea that any item an artist chooses and displays in a new context is a work of art? Why or why not? Draw a mind map of your ideas and discuss them with a partner.

Conceptual Art (see Unit 13, p. 519) is a descendant of the Dada movement.

Picasso's *Guernica*, (see Unit 5, p. 207) is one of the most famous paintings commenting on war and conflict. It has become an icon of anti-war movements, with its images of destruction and chaos.

Design

Designers have been at the forefront of creating public opinion since the origin of the poster. The poster has been used as a propaganda tool by almost every state. During World War I, each one of the warring nations used posters to promote their nation and vilify their opponents.

Propaganda: Information, especially of a biased or misleading nature, used to promote or publicise a particular political cause or point of view.

Figure 39.11 *Lord Kitchener Wants You* poster, 1914. Armies on both sides used posters for propaganda during World War I.

A web search for 'World War I posters' will bring up many examples of wartime propaganda posters. These large pieces of public art, easily reproducible and instantly recognisable, were one of the most effective ways of getting an idea across before the invention of television and before colour images were possible in newspapers.

Figure 39.12 *War is not healthy for children or other living things* poster, 1966. The handmade look of this poster is typical of the anti-commercial hippy culture that was part of the anti-war movement worldwide.

Protesting against war was a criminal offence in most countries as recently as the late 20th century. Public protests against the Vietnam War in the 1960s may have helped to bring this ban to an end in the West. Artists and designers were very involved in the protest movement, producing posters, t-shirts and artworks to highlight the injustice of war. Look for anti-Vietnam war posters in a web search to see the range of mostly hand-designed posters that challenged the government position on the war.

Handmade art and craft was part of the protest against the big commercial and industrial interests that were profiting from the war. People continue to protest using a wider range of media.

Have a classroom debate on the most effective ways of protesting against war. Consider a design campaign that you could organise against a current war.

Social Issues

Effective design can be an important contribution to the effective promotion of the goals of any organisation. There are over 9,000 registered charities in Ireland, so creating an identity and appealing to the public can be quite a challenge. Charities can indicate the social issues that people feel are not being adequately addressed by the state.

Homelessness has been an issue in many parts of the world as a growing gap in incomes makes it difficult for people who are not in well-paid jobs to afford any kind of accommodation. In Ireland there are eight charities that deal with housing and homelessness – The Simon Community, Focus Ireland, the Peter McVerry Trust, Cope, Threshold, Crosscare, St Vincent de Paul and the Irish Council for Social Housing – each with their own identity and services.

Look at the logos for a variety of charities. Pick one that you think could be improved and sketch some ideas for a new design. Select your favourite and add it to a finished product, such as a t-shirt, packaging, marketing material like posters or even stationery.

Designers need to be conscious of social issues and make designs that are sensitive to all members of society, no matter what their race, sexual orientation or gender. In the past, sexism in particular was often an issue in advertising.

Environmental design issues are dealt with in Unit 16: Art and the Environment.

Modern Artists

Many contemporary artists are affected by environmental issues. You will find a number in the Art and the Environment section (see Unit 16), where will also find reference to street artists, who are often politically motivated.

Politics, in its broadest sense, is a great motivator for artists, who often find themselves in

disagreement with the social and governmental norms of the day. Artists Like Michael Farrell and Brian O'Doherty (aka Patrick Ireland; see Unit 12, p. 510) responded to the fighting and bloodshed in Northern Ireland during the 1970s by creating works of art that highlighted the issues and by speaking out in public about them.

In 2010, Chinese artist and activist Ai Weiwei created a work called *Sunflower Seeds*. He recruited 1,600 workers from the town of Jingdezhen in eastern China, famed for its porcelain, to make 100 million ceramic sunflower seeds, the same size and shape as real seeds. The ceramic seeds were put in a gallery space where the viewers could get up close to them. Many of the people who made the ceramics were unemployed in a town which had made ceramics for the Chinese Emperors for a thousand years. Ai Weiwei says the work relates to China's past and the inequalities that industrialisation can create.

Visit *www.widewalls.ch/art-and-politics* for some background on art and politics and an interview with Ai Weiwei.

Do you think art can influence politics? Discuss the topic with your classmates using examples from this video and other examples you have found.

Figure 39.13 *Sunflower Seeds, 100 million ceramic husks for social change*, 2010, by Ai Weiwei. The ceramic sunflower seeds look real, and they represent the work of many skilled hands in a mass-produced world.

Figure 39.14 *Everyone I Have Ever Slept With*, 1993–5, Tracey Emin.

Figure 39.15 Marching banner for the Artists' Campaign to Repeal the Eighth Amendment, 2018, Limerick.

Gender equality has been an issue for many artists like Judy Chicago and Tracy Emin (see Unit 6). Groups like Pussy Riot and Guerrilla Girls create and document feminist performance art, and have large followings on social media.

Judy Chicago challenged the male-dominated art world and drew attention to 'women's work' in crafts, such as needlework and ceramics, which were traditionally dismissed as being less important than fine art (see Unit 6, p. 255, Figure 17.16). Tracey Emin also used women's handicraft techniques to make her point in *Everyone I Have Ever Slept With*, aka *The Tent*. Emin used appliqué to inscribe the names of lovers, friends and family within a small tent.

Irish artists also used sewing and embroidery during a street procession in Limerick as part of the Campaign to Repeal the Eighth Amendment in May 2018. Sarah Cullen, Rachel Fallon, Alison Laredo, Alice Maher, Breda Mayock and Áine Phillips refused to play into 'the dirty politics of shock value', but instead used 'the beauty of the art' to make their point. The artists, along with students of Limerick College of Art and Design, created a marching banner, hand-made aprons and large ghost-like figures of Cassandra, the prophetess of ancient Greek myth who spoke the truth but no one believed.

Figure 39.16 *Aprons of Power*, 2018, by Rachel Fallon for the Artists' Campaign to Repeal the Eighth Amendment Procession. The Aprons of Power are held in the Collection of the Arts Council of Ireland.

Figure 39.17 *The Cassandras*, 2018, Áine Phillips and students of Limerick School of Art and Design for the Artists' Campaign to Repeal the Eighth Amendment Procession, Limerick.

Stephen Doyle

Stephen Doyle is a visual artist whose work focuses on the LGBTQ+ community and its interaction with the rest of society.

Figure 39.18 Artist Stephen Doyle.

A graduate of Crawford College of Art and Design, Doyle's work references queer identity and queer culture through painting and installation. He received the Student of the Year Award upon graduating in 2017, which included a solo exhibition – Alt Masc, which was held in the Lavitt Gallery – and a residency at Backwater Studios in Cork.

Seán Kissane, the Curator of Exhibitions at the Irish Museum of Modern Art, was guest speaker at the opening, of the exhibition. He said:

'Doyle's work takes the contemporary concerns of his generation, and, using the traditional medium of portraiture, has brought it right up to date and made it relevant to all of us.'

Since graduating, Stephen has won various international awards and has been shortlisted for many more.

Dylan Is Ainm Dom...

In 2018, Stephen Doyle was shortlisted for the prestigious Zurich Portrait Prize for *Dylan Is Ainm Dom...*, on show at the National Gallery of

Figure 39.19 *Caihong at an Intersection in the Changning District*, 2019, by Stephen Doyle.

Figure 39.20 *Dylan Is Ainm Dom...*, 2018, by Stephen Doyle, oil and neon light on board, 120 x 120 cm, National Gallery of Ireland, Dublin.

Ireland. This was the first artwork in the national collection to openly address transgender identity.

The inspiration for *Dylan Is Ainm Dom…* came when Stephen attended the Rainbow Ball fundraiser for BeLonG To, at which he heard Kirsty Donoghue speak about her son Dylan and transgender identity. Further to this, it was to highlight a part of the LGBTQ+ community that has remained invisible within our museums.

Interview with Stephen Doyle

Q. Hi Stephen! Did you always want to be an artist?

Stephen: I was always interested in making things, but art college allowed me the freedom to be myself.

Q. Why did art college suit you so well?

Stephen: Continuous assessment and independent learning suited me perfectly. I felt secure to be myself there, which allowed the work to flow.

Q. Why do you paint portraits?

Stephen: I tell a person's story. I discuss sexual orientation and sexual identity and the body is a perfect vessel to explore those subject matters.

Q. What issues do you identify as an artist?

Stephen: Queer culture is what I know. To date, I've discussed hypermasculinity, drag and ball culture, gender fluidity and non-binary identity, autonomy in contemporary China and more.

Q. What inspired you to paint Dylan's portrait?

Stephen: Kirsty's speech really got to me. I found Dylan a very inspiring young man – the kid I wanted to be at that age. I began to wonder how many of us are that sure of ourselves and that confident at 17.

Q. What do you hope it achieves?

Stephen: I hopes his portrait makes Dylan feel valued, because that was my only real intent for the piece.

Q. How did you choose the title?

Stephen: The title is very important; it has to sum up the entire work. *Dylan Is Ainm Dom…* is a self-declaration – 'This is who I am', plain and simple. To have it in Gaeilge echoes the connection to his Irish roots.

Q. What does the background represent?

Stephen: The woods are symbolic of his Irish heritage and the neon element mimics the curves of the natural environment and gives the piece a juxtaposing energy. Like the traditional and the new, wider society and queer culture.

Jesse Jones

Irish artist Jesse Jones (see Unit 12, p. 512) explores many social issues in her work, including the place of women in the arts and art history. The role of women in society, their exploitation in domestic service, inequality, the pay gap between men and women – all these issues were included in *No More Fun and Games*, an installation in the Hugh Lane Gallery in Dublin in 2016.

Tremble Tremble, which was the Irish entry at the 2017 Venice Biennale, had many references and messages. The title was borrowed from an Italian feminist social movement in the 1970s, which sought payment for domestic labour and abortion rights. One of the slogans (translated from Italian) was 'Tremble tremble, the witches have returned'. Jones used this as a focus for her work, which addressed the referendum on the eighth amendment to the Irish constitution regarding the right to have an abortion.

A range of other feminist issues are also referred to in this complicated and multi-layered presentation. *Tremble Tremble* incorporated film, sound, sculpture and performance and was exhibited in the Project Arts Centre in Temple Bar in 2018 before travelling to other parts of the world.

Figure 39.21
Tremble Tremble, 2018, by Jesse Jones, Project Arts Centre, Dublin.

Film

Most films comment on some aspect of society, and everyone has their own preferences when it comes to genre and acting style.

In this section, we will look at the career of just one Irish director and screenwriter who has dealt with social issues throughout his career.

Lenny Abrahamson was born to a Jewish family in Dublin and studied Physics and Philosophy in Trinity College in Dublin. He left his PhD in Philosophy at Stanford University, California, to return to Ireland and begin his filmmaking career.

Abrahamson's first film was *Adam and Paul*, co-written with Mark O'Halloran in 2004. It is a dark comedy that follows a day in the lives of two heroin addicts in Dublin. It is set in a bleak inner-city location. The colours are grey and dull to add to the message of the film, which is a commentary on the lives of addicts and the hopeless situation they are in. Abrahamson uses comic moments contrasted with harsh realities to bring the viewer into a world that few, hopefully, will ever have to deal with. His second film, *Garage*, in 2007, also written with Mark O'Halloran, looks at the life of a simple country man who has difficulties with his relationships. Both films were well received and won the Irish Film and Television Award for best film.

Figure 39.22 A still from *What Richard Did*, 2012, dir. Lenny Abrahamson.

In 2012, Abrahamson won his third IFTA for *What Richard Did*, a film that deals with issues of privilege and responsibility among young people.

Frank, released in 2014, is about an eccentric musician and stars Michael Fassbender, Domhnall Gleeson and Maggie Gyllenhaal. In *Frank*, Abrahamson again uses dark humour to deal with issues of mental health and friendship.

In 2015, Abrahamson's film adaptation of Emma Donoghue's novel *Room* was nominated for four Academy Awards, winning one for Best Actress (Brie Larson). The harrowing plot of a woman and her five-year-old child held captive is chilling, but the film manages to make it a tale of growing up and coming to terms with the world in spite of the circumstances the characters find themselves in. In 2020, Abrahamson directed *Normal People*, a coming-of-age television series about the relationship between a young Irish man and woman, based on Sally Rooney's novel.

In all of his films, it seems that Abrahamson manages to deal with serious social issues without putting the audience through an unpleasant experience.

Analysis

Social commentary has long been an element of the inspiration of the artist. After the Reformation, the paintings and prints made by the artists of the time told tales of the dangers of sin, bad social behaviour and alcohol. The artists pointed out the terrible things that could happen if you strayed from living a good and virtuous life.

In the 1800s, artists like Goya and Daumier put their living and even their lives in danger by protesting injustice and abuse in the society they lived in.

In the 20th century, political and social protest became more common with the spread of democracy and what people understood as a right to protest.

In today's world, artists like Ai Weiwei stake their freedom against a right to protest at what they see as social injustice. Outside of democratic societies, artists who voice protests or different opinions can be silenced and removed from society. Artists continue to bring their concerns to public attention by whatever means they can.

Chapter Review

1. What were the subjects chosen by social commentators following the Reformation? Give two examples of works by artists you have studied using words and sketches.

2. Prints were an important way of communicating ideas in the 17th, 18th, 19th and 20th centuries. Do you think they could be relevant today? Give examples using words and sketches to make your points.

3. Do you think Impressionism was real social commentary or were the artists just looking for pleasant subjects to paint? Your comments should include sketches of relevant paintings.

4. Dadaism and its descendant Conceptual Art did a lot to change the way artists comment on society. Give some examples, in words and sketches, of works that demonstrate that view.

5. Do you think there are social issues important enough for artists to risk their freedom for? What do you think these issues could be? You could have a class debate to see how others feel about freedom of expression and its consequences.

6. Write an account of a film that brought important social issues to your attention. Describe how camera work, colour, sound, special effects and direction affected your appreciation of the film.

Further Research

www.format.com/magazine – Search for 'A Short History of Protest Art' to learn more about artists' responses to social issues

www.widewalls.ch/art-and-politics – An article assessing the relationship between art and politics

www.thedrum.com/topics/sexism – A variety of articles on sexism in advertising

www.guerrillagirls.com – The official website of the feminist art group

www.youtube.com – Search for 'Exclusive Interview: Lenny Abrahamson Talks Room' (10.25) for an insight into the director's artistic process

Art and the Environment

In this unit, we will look at the importance of the environment to artists throughout history and around the world. Artists have always responded to their environment as a source of materials and inspiration.

Context

When people first began to make art, they used the materials available in their environment – charcoal from their fires, and earth colours from different coloured clays and soils. With these basic materials they decorated the walls of caves and probably their own bodies. These materials and tools are still in use around the world – as are stone, bone and wood – for making three-dimensional art.

As culture progressed, people began to create their own environments in the shape of buildings, towns and cities. Through medieval times and later, architects,

> **By the end of this unit I will ...**
>
> * know how artists can use the environment as an art medium
> * be able to write an account of work by a street artist
> * have examined and analysed a piece of public art
> * understand how designers consider environmental issues when designing a product
> * have thought about online environments and their uses.

Figure 40.1
Polychrome (multi-coloured) paintings of Eland antelope made by San hunter-gatherers between 1,500 and 2,000 years ago at uKhahlamba-Drakensberg National Park, South Africa. Drawings made with charcoal and earth colours are evidence of a human understanding of the materials and subjects that the environment provided.

...k at the art of the Stone Age in Ireland in ...it 7. This art was a response to the artists' ...urroundings, as well as observations of the ...s of stars and planets. Make notes and sketches ...ge of tools and structures that Stone Age people creat... directly from their environment.

artists, designers and craftworkers continued to collect their materials and inspiration, in a direct way, from the environment. Wood and stone are used for buildings, furniture and sculpture; clay for ceramics; and metals for tools, weapons, sculpture and a variety of other uses. Glass was also a natural product.

The Industrial Revolution brought great change to people's interaction with the environment.

Figure 40.2 *Sun Breaking through the Fog, Houses of Parliament*, 1904, by Claude Monet, oil on canvas, 81 × 92 cm, Musée d'Orsay, Paris. The fog obscuring the buildings is a result of the smoke from domestic coal fires and factories. This painting is one of a series that Monet painted while he lived in London. His work was an observation of the environment rather than a commentary on it.

www.biographyonline.net/facts-about-the-industrial-revolution will give you some background on the social and economic changes that came with a growing exploitation of the environment. You could use this information in your written work on the environment.

Artists responded to polluted and unsafe industries by forming groups like the Arts and Crafts Movement. Such groups promoted hand-made crafts and natural materials which they believed gave dignity and value to the workers' efforts.

As we get closer to our own time, you will be familiar with the environmental issues that face this generation, primarily the abuse of the environment through our use of fossil fuels, plastics, chemicals and other damaging materials. Artists continue to try to point out these problems and suggest solutions. They work with man-made materials, chemically produced pigments and modern technology (video and computers) to effectively catch the public's attention and raise awareness.

Art from Recycled Materials

The exhibition design and model-making company Cod Steaks, with lead artist Sue Lipscombe, designed and built models of a humpback and blue whale for the city of Bristol, the European Green Capital 2015. The whale heads and tails were made from wickerwork (willow rods), a natural material. The splashing sea around them was made of single-use plastic water bottles to symbolise the damage plastics are doing to the ocean.

Figure 40.3 *The Bristol Whales*, 2015, by Sue Lipscombe and Cod Steaks, willow and recycled plastic, a temporary installation made for Bristol's year as European Green Capital.

The enormous sculptures were placed in Millennium Square in Bristol for just six weeks to emphasise the short time we have to take action and preserve life in the oceans. The contrast between the natural materials the whales were made from and the man-made material of the sea, was just one focus of the project.

The Czech artist Veronika Richterová makes her art from recycled plastic bottles. Many artists use recycled materials of all kinds to produce their pieces.

Lin Evola creates sculptures of angels from recycled weapons. She lived in Los Angeles, USA in the 1990s and was horrified at the level of gun crime in the city. She visited local communities and persuaded people to give up their weapons, melt them down and turn them into cast angels. The first ones she made were small, poured from bronze and were less than a metre tall, but as support for the project grew, she was able to make larger pieces created primarily from decommissioned nuclear stainless steel.

The *Renaissance Peace Angel* (Fig. 40.4), at almost four metres tall, was created in 1995, with a plaque added in 1997, and was moved to the Ground Zero site in New York just weeks after the 9/11 destruction of the Twin Towers. There, it was appreciated as a peace symbol and the base was signed by many of the firefighters, police officers and rescue workers who had been there on the day of the plane strikes. The sculpture is now permanently sited in the September 11 Memorial & Museum in New York.

Evola now works with communities around the world decommissioning weapons and recreating them as angels. She has worked in Mexico, Korea and Jerusalem.

Figure 40.4
Renaissance Peace Angel, 1995–97, by Lin Evola, recycled metal, September 11 Memorial & Museum, New York.

Land Art

Artists often work directly in and with the environment, so design principles like space and scale are often important in their art. *Spiral Jetty* by Robert Smithson (see Unit 6, p. 257) takes art out of the gallery and connects it directly to the environment.

Figure 40.5
A Circle in Ireland, 1975, by Richard Long is an example of Land Art that uses materials from the landscape to create the art form.

...rd Long records his movement ...ironment by 'drawing' on the ...the materials (usually stones) he finds ...s sculptures are then photographed for

A Circle in Ireland was photographed in the Burren in Co. Clare, and the Cliffs of Moher can be seen in the distance (Fig 40.5). Long described the Burren as 'my kind of landscape, a sort of stony, wet desert, also with a lot of nice people and a lot of humour and beautiful music'. In the photograph the circle breaks the natural straight lines of the cracks in the stone surface, and the patterns of nature are contrasted with the human, abstract idea of a circle. Long describes his work as 'art made by walking in landscapes, photographs of sculptures made along the way. Art about mobility lightness and freedom. Simple creative acts of walking and making, about place, locality, time, distance and measurement. Works using raw materials and my human scale in the reality of landscapes.'

Long also makes exhibition pieces, often of stones, laid out in simple geometric patterns.

Architecture

Architecture is a human response to controlling our environment; we make houses to protect us from the climate. Larger buildings can function as meeting places, like churches or temples, or as places of refuge, like walled cities.

The Great Wall of China was built to protect the Chinese Empire from outside forces. Buildings can represent a certain style or status, like the Palace at Versailles in France or the Guggenheim Museum in Bilbao. Buildings have traditionally had a local style which responds to available technology and materials. Georgian Dublin (see Unit 10) was built of red bricks, which were available cheaply, and to a size that was technically possible at the time. Most cultures and societies produce an architecture that suits their climate and environment.

Note: Go to **www.worldatlas.com** and search for the article '15 traditional house types from around the world'. This will provide you with further information on the topic of architectural styles of building.

Great advances have been made in building technology in the last generation. Buildings with zero energy running costs are being built, contributing to the national grid from their

Figure 40.6 Carcassonne, a city in southern France. People used to build walled cities to protect their environment from outside interference.

renewable energy resources. As well as that, environmentally friendly buildings are increasing in numbers worldwide.

 **www.processindustryforum.com/energy/20-most-eco-friendly-buildings-on-earth** has a list of eco-friendly buildings. Take notes and make sketches for reference in your studio work or written work.

Increasing the scale of urbanisation is one of the major environmental concerns facing people today. There are sometimes conflicting views about the consequences of urbanisation.

Figure 40.7 The Bank of America building, New York, designed by Cook and Fox. This building was built with recyclable materials. It provides its own solar-powered heating and uses captured rainwater and recycled waste water.

 Go to **www.hdr.undp.org** and search for 'rapid urbanisation opportunities and challenges to improve the wellbeing of societies'. On a different tab, go to **www.nationalgeographic. com/environment/article/urban-threats**. Read these two contrasting views on urbanisation. You could have a classroom discussion on urbanisation and its environmental implications and create posters to support your viewpoint. Review the poster designs with your classmates and assess the strength of their messages.

Landscape Design

Landscape architecture is the designing of outdoor spaces, like parks and gardens, to harmonise with the built environment or road systems.

Figure 40.8 Central Park, New York. Frederick Law Olmsted designed the complete scheme for Central Park – the land forms, water features, planting layout, paving and other structures. He was the first to use the title 'Landscape Architect'.

Modern designers need to have a knowledge of environmental science and ecology as well as design and plants.

You will find information on the profession of landscape architect and designers at **www. arch2o.com/landscape-architecture-profession**. You could use this information in written work on the topic.

Environmental Design

Environmental design includes many of the disciplines we have looked at above. It is a process that addresses environmental concerns, blending nature and technology when making plans, programmes, policies, buildings or products.

Many environmental designers work on large projects like motorways and large industrial or urban constructions, trying to reduce the environmental impact of human interference as much as possible. Ecology has to be the primary concern in this type of development, allowing the natural elements like water, trees and air quality to be of primary importance. Efforts have to be made to reduce the impact of noise, light and air pollution during construction and later when the project comes into use.

An example of a building that won prizes for its environmental sustainability is the School of Art, Design and Media in Singapore, designed by CPG Consultants. The five-storey building is on the Nanyang Technological University Campus in a little valley that was supposed to be kept as a green-lung space (Fig. 40.9). It is a concrete structure with high-efficiency glass curtain walls mainly facing north to reduce heat gain. The grass roof is a public space that can be accessed by steps along its edge. The roof also collects rainwater that is used for irrigation of the green space. The building has low operation and maintenance costs due to super-efficient air conditioning and lighting systems. The glass walls reflect the trees and green spaces surrounding the building, and create a feeling of transparency inside and outside the building.

Conservation of built heritage is also part of environmental design. Designers try to incorporate existing buildings of architectural or social merit into renewal projects. Sometimes buildings can be repurposed and brought up to modern standards of insulation and heating, but this is not always possible or desirable. The environmental designer will make every effort to use suitable materials and techniques to match with the original construction of the building, researching its history and deciding on the best features to retain and restore. In Ireland, the Office of Public Works manages historical buildings in public ownership and is responsible for their restoration and upkeep.

Street Art

Street art began as illegal political graffiti, spray painted on empty buildings, public places and hoardings around construction sites. From there it has developed into an artform, frequently associated with political or social commentary. It has become a worldwide phenomenon and some artists have combined it with a more conventional art career.

 **www.streetartcities.com** has a world map with street art locations you can click on. You can find artists whose work appeals to you that can be used as references in your studio or written work.

Figure 40.9
The School of Art, Design and Media, Singapore, designed by CPG Consultants. The green-roofed building was designed to have minimum impact on the environment, replacing the grass taken up by its footprint with a grass roof.

Figure 40.10
Graffiti on the Berlin Wall. The wall was built in 1961 to separate East and West Berlin during the Cold War. After the wall height was raised in the 1980s, artists from all over the world began to paint on the western side. The eastern side was blank because no one was allowed near it.

The anonymous British artist Banksy has become known worldwide, his gallery works selling for large sums. He continues to be a subversive and controversial figure, and his art is often mentioned and commented on in mainstream media, fulfilling one of the main purposes of his work.

RESEARCH There are a number of Irish street artists working here and internationally. You can search for '10 Irish street artists' on *www.culturetrip.com*. Choose an artist whose work you like and research their work to use in your studio work or written work.

Figure 40.11 *What Are You Looking at?* 2015, by Banksy, London

Maser is a Dublin-born street artist who has worked internationally and is now based in the USA. He studied Visual Communications in Dublin and began making murals based on typography in the 1990s. This work evolved into abstract geometric compositions created with a limited colour palette of bright colours, which he always uses to maintain continuity in his work. *The City is My Garden* was a project he worked on in collaboration with the National Botanic Gardens and Arnotts in 2017 (Fig 40.12). The idea was to increase awareness of green areas in the city and to involve the public in creating green spaces.

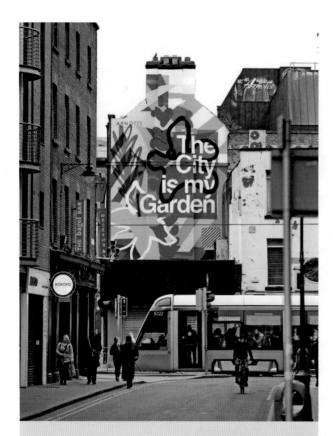

Figure 40.12 *The City is My Garden*, 2017, by Maser, Liffey Street, Dublin.

Maser painted the outside of the Tara Building, a co-working creative space in Dublin, making a bold colour statement in an otherwise dull streetscape. Maser often works in collaboration with other artists and likes to involve local people when he is painting a mural in a community. Works on canvas and fine-art prints are also part of his practice.

Street art is often used to raise awareness of public issues. It can brighten up a derelict area, create a festive atmosphere and become a tourist attraction. Waterford holds a street-art festival every two years called Waterford Walls.

  In small groups, research the work of a street artist you like. Agree on a theme, create some rough sketches to work out your ideas and decide tasks for each member of the group. Create a mural on a wall or a large panel. Review your work by comparing with the murals of other groups in the class. You could then exhibit your work.

Public Art

Public art has been a feature of our environment from ancient times in which the Greeks and Romans erected memorials to great citizens or events. In modern times, public art has become much more accessible – we are even expected to interact with it. You can walk among the figures of Rowan Gillespie's *Famine* along the Custom House Quay in Dublin (see p. 507).

 Search online for 'public art in Ireland images' and you will find further information on examples of public art from around the country.

Figure 40.13 *The Spire (The Monument of Light)*, 2002, designed by Ian Ritchie, Dublin. At 120 m tall, the Spire is one of the tallest pieces of public art in the world.

Figure 40.14
Woven branch circular arch, 1986, by Andy Goldsworthy, Dumfriesshire. Goldsworthy uses natural materials that decay over time as is the way of nature.

You should try to engage directly with a piece of public art. If you go to ***www.publicart.ie***, there is a directory of the projects that have been funded by the state. You should be able to search your own county for projects you can access easily. Try to analyse the work using art elements and design principles, make sketches, take photographs and make notes. You should find sizes and materials on the website. Walk around the work so you can see it from different angles and note changes that develop from different viewpoints.

Create a design for a public sculpture to go in your school grounds. Decide on size and materials that will withstand weather and human contact. Think about a subject/theme suitable for your environment. You could discuss options with your classmates. Review your design and the impact it could have on the school environment.

Environmental art is designed to enhance the environment or to become an integrated part of it. It may also make a statement on environmental issues.

Environmental Art

www.tate.org.uk/art/art-terms/e/environmental-art has a definition of the term 'environmental art', and a list of works and artists from their collection that could be a useful reference for your written work.

The Scottish artist Andy Goldsworthy uses natural objects like leaves, stones, branches and ice to make site-specific installations, and observe their natural changes over time (Fig. 40.14). He uses beautiful colour photography to record the process of change that nature brings to his work.

Snaking lines, spirals, circles and holes are the elements he works with most frequently. The making process is important to him; handling the pieces and making connections with natural materials are an essential part of the work.

Figure 40.15 *Sycamore leaves edging the roots of a sycamore tree*, 2013, by Andy Goldsworthy, Hampshire.

Goldsworthy feels that his outdoor sculptures are not a commodity to be exhibited and sold; they return to nature over time. He believes that 'people also leave a presence in a place even when they are no longer there'. This is reflected in some of his more monumental work in stone.

Find out more about Goldsworthy and his art by visiting **www.theartstory.org/artist/goldsworthy-andy**.

Eileen Hutton is American artist living and working in Ireland. Her work is ecologically based. In 2012, she developed a Masters in Art and Ecology at the Burren College of Art. This is accredited by National University of Ireland, Galway and provides an immersive education in the development of professional practice as an ecologically oriented artist.

Eileen's practice centres on the notion of ecology, in the broadest sense as a study of relationships and the interconnectedness of the natural world. Her work explores the invisible relationships that exist within a given place: between human beings, animal species and plant life. She is interested in the critical role that honeybees and birds play within ecosystems and has built various artificial habitats in order to support them and the surrounding biodiversity. In collaboration with these priority species, she creates sculptures within their nesting boxes and beehives, and sees this practice as crossing the boundaries between ecological and artistic intervention.

You can find some environmental artists at **www.mymodernmet.com/environmental-art**. Look at the range of work they do and discuss the possibility of creating your own environmental piece with your classmates. Experiment with materials, find a location and create an environmental piece using materials from your environment. Respond by recording the natural effects of weather and time on your work.

Environmental Design

Environmental design includes many of the disciplines we have looked at above. It is a process that addresses environmental concerns when making plans, programmes, policies, buildings or products.

Consumer/Product Design

There is an increasing awareness of the importance of our choice of materials when designing products and packaging.

When designing for the environment, designers should consider:

- evaluating the human health and environmental impacts of the processes and products

Figure 40.16 Local community members engaging with vibrating solar-powered bee sculptures at the Ennis Street Arts Festival.

Figure 40.17 *Inside Out Hive*, by Eileen Hutton. Located amongst other traditional national hives, the sculpture in situ reflects the optimal role of sustainability: that it functions best when integrated into existing systems and not isolated from them.

Figure 40.18 An eco-friendly phone case by Pela Case. Recycled or environmentally friendly materials can be used in creative ways to make useful designs.

Figure 40.19 Philips steam iron. Designers revaluated the traditional materials and shape to make a safer, more efficient iron.

Some companies have sustainable design policies which create good practice and awareness of environmental issues. Phillips, a company that produces electrical goods, have had a 'sustainability in manufacturing' policy for the last 20 years.

CREATE   RESEARCH   RESPOND

- **Create** an eco-friendly design for a household product that you think needs environmental improvement. Discuss some options with your classmates.
- **Research** the possibilities of changing materials and processes.
- **Respond** to the design needs of the client/consumer and share your results with your classmates.

- ensuring that people or environment are not harmed by any aspect of the product
- identifying the information that is needed to make good environmental decisions. You need the best scientific and engineering information to help make the right design choices
- assessing the alternatives in case there is a more environmentally friendly solution
- reducing or eliminating toxic emissions in the process or product, and using cleaner technologies or chemicals
- designing products that can be reused and recycled
- monitoring the impact and cost of each part of the process
- continually evaluating the process and product, and making improvements that decrease environmental impact.

These are just the environmental considerations; the usual design criteria is outlined in Unit 13: Practice and Function still have to be considered.

Good design should reduce industrial waste, use the most environmentally friendly materials, and manage waste and resources.

Online Environments

Online environments allow us to communicate, learn and interact with individuals and communities on an international scale. We have used web and video links in this book that allow us to learn from sources around the world.

Public services are mainly online now; for example, you can renew your passport, pay taxes, apply for grants and permissions, receive benefits, and many other services if you have some kind of computer device with internet access.

Online learning is becoming a normal way of delivering education from primary schools to higher level university courses. While sometimes it is just an addition to work in the classroom, it can also involve online courses that can be delivered and examined remotely without the teacher and the student ever meeting in person.

Figure 40.20
Many services and resources are available to everyone with access to the internet.

RESEARCH *www.tate.org.uk/visit/tate-modern* will take you to the Tate Modern website, which offers a lot of information about its collection. Note how the information is arranged. Is this a user-friendly website? Discuss with your classmates.

Galleries and museums can be visited remotely and many institutions allow online access to their material too.

Shopping online can be done from home and is a great service for people who are housebound. Most supermarkets deliver goods purchased online; anything from clothes and sports equipment to washing machines and DIY tools can be remotely ordered and delivered to your door within a matter of days. However, there are also negative effects to this modern shopping behaviour. Small, independent shops without an online presence may find it difficult to compete with larger establishments who have accessible websites. As a result, towns and cities have an increasing number of empty or out-of-business shops.

Entertainment can take many forms online: you can watch TV or listen to the radio, listen to any music you like, have video chats using Zoom and Skype, play multi-player games and watch social entertainment channels like YouTube. Traditional TV channels are being overtaken by online services, and the video rental business has been wiped out by Netflix and other streaming platforms.

Online entertainment allows the viewer to choose their own time and place to access the entertainment they would like. Artists use websites to promote their work and to gain a wider audience for their art.

Information-gathering is the most common use of the internet. People can find out about events and entertainment, check facts, follow up on their interests and hobbies, and get in touch with organisations.

For people with phones, there are applications (apps) that can be used for entertainment or information on sports and hobbies. Voice-activated systems allow quick access to any material online. The web can be a great resource for art and design research too. Many artists find inspiration and information on the web.

Note: Social networking has become one of the most popular uses for of the internet. It is an aspect of human contact that did not exist before the internet and some people have mixed feelings about it.

Many artists have Facebook, Instagram, Twitter and other accounts where they can share ideas and have conversations with other artists around the world. How do you feel about social-networking sites? You could discuss it with your class group.

RESPOND Respond to the positive and negative effects of online communication with a classroom discussion on the benefits and dangers of online exposure for artists.

Analysis

Environmental art is a relatively modern addition to the range of topics and media that artists use to express their ideas. Artists like Christo and Jeanne-Claude (see p. 272) draw attention to features of the urban or rural landscape, their work developing into a commentary on environmental issues. Artists emphasise a greater sensitivity to the natural environment through their work, and challenge the general public to be conscious of the dangers of environmental change. Architects and designers have raised awareness of the issues facing the human environment and have responded with ideas on how to improve our use of resources.

Chapter Review

1. Do you think that making art is a natural human response to our environment? Write and sketch some illustrations to support your points.

2. Can you find some of the art elements and design principles in a work of environmental art? Make sketches and notes to explain your findings.

3. Architecture is a human effort to control our environment. Describe, in words and sketches, a building you think creates a good human environment.

4. Do you see street art as vandalism or a legitimate art form? Use examples of the work of two street artists to make your points.

5. Write and sketch an account of a piece of public art that appeals to you.

6. What do you think are the most important environmental issues that face designers? Illustrate, in words and sketches, two examples of environmentally well-designed products.

Further Research

www.africanrockart.org/rock-art-gallery/south-africa – A gallery of African rock art

www.widewalls.ch/environmental-artists – A group of artists involved in environmental art

www.youtube.com – Search for 'Cave Art 101 | National Geographic' (3:18) to learn what prehistoric art can tell us about our world

www.youtube.com – Search for 'The Case for Land Art | The Art Assignment | PBS Digital Studios' (9:29) to gain a better understanding of Land Art

www.greentech-news.org/most-amazing-eco-friendly-buildings – Contains an informative video on the most amazing eco-friendly buildings in our contemporary world

www.youtube.com – Search for 'This street art is absolutely breath-taking' (15:02) to watch a video about how street art can inspire, surprise and transform a boring urban environment

www.youtube.com – Search for 'Public Art Documentary in Dublin Ireland' (4:08) to learn more about public art in Ireland

www.youtube.com – Search for 'Creative public sculptures in the world' (5:34) to watch a video with a selection of public art from around the world

www.youtube.com – Search for 'Being in the Land - A Sculptural Investigation of Ecology – Eileen Hutton' (2:16) to see how one artist is blurring the lines between ecology and art

www.youtube.com – Search for 'How product design can change the world | Christiaan Maats | TEDxUniversityofGroningen' (13:06) to learn more about how products can embody a change in our world

Glossary

A

Abbot: The head of a monastery. His role was to lead and inspire all the monks, and they had to obey him. The word 'abbot' comes from the Greek abbas, which means 'father'.

Absolute monarchy: A monarchy that is not limited or restrained by laws or a constitution.

Abstract art: Art that does not attempt to represent an accurate depiction of a visual reality, but instead uses shapes, colours, forms and gestural marks to achieve its effect.

Abstract Expressionism: A post-World War II art movement in American painting, which developed in New York in the 1940s.

Academy: Artist-run organisation whose aim was to improve the professional standing of artists as well as to provide teaching.

Aesthetic: Concerned with beauty or the appreciation of beauty.

Aisle: The side of a nave separated by a colonnade.

Allegory: Art that uses figures or objects to represent abstract qualities or ideas, often used to symbolise a deeper moral or spiritual meaning, such as life, death, love, virtue or justice. Renaissance allegories frequently refer to Greek and Roman legends or literature.

Altarpiece: A work of art that decorates the space above and behind the altar in a Christian church.

Amber: Fossilised resin that is honey-yellow in colour.

Anatomy: The science of the bodily structure of animals and plants. During the Renaissance, some artists dissected bodies to better understand their structure.

Annals: A year-by-year record of events. Medieval monasteries often kept records of important events.

Antiquity: The classical age of Greece and Rome.

Applied art: The application of design and aesthetics to objects of function and everyday use.

Arcade: A series of arches supported by piers or columns.

Arcadian: Arcadia refers to a vision of an unspoiled wilderness that is in harmony with nature. The term comes from the Greek province of Arcadia, which dates to antiquity.

Architecture: The art or practice of designing and constructing buildings.

Architrave: A formal beam or lintel that forms the lowest part of an entablature.

Artefact: Something created by humans, usually for a practical purpose; an object of cultural or historical interest.

Articulation: A method of styling the joints in the formal elements of architectural design.

Ashlar: Hewn or cut-square stone or stone facing.

Assemblage: Art made by assembling disparate elements often found by the artist and sometimes bought specially.

Astronomy: The study of the stars and planets.

Atelier: A French word that translates literally as 'studio' or 'workshop'.

Atmospheric perspective: A method of creating the illusion of depth or recession in a painting or drawing by modulating colour to simulate changes affected by the atmosphere on the colours of things seen at a distance. Also called aerial perspective.

Austere: Severe or strict in manner or attitude.

Automatism: The performance of actions without conscious thought or intention.

Avant-garde: In art history, used for a group of people whose ideas are considered to be ahead of their time.

B

Balustrade: A row of upright balusters supporting a handrail in a staircase or supporting a cornice to form a parapet.

Baptistery: A detached part of a church where baptisms are performed. Baptisteries are usually round or octagonal in shape.

Baroque: Relating to or denoting a style of European architecture, music and art of the 17th and 18th centuries that followed Mannerism and is characterised by ornate detail.

Barrel vault: A simple, continuous vault, typically semi-circular in cross-section.

Basilica: A building similar to a Roman basilica (public meeting hall), used as a Christian church. An important church, sometimes with special privileges from the pope.

Basin stone: A large stone carved into the shape of an open basin.

Bay: A division of a building, defined by features like windows, arches or columns.

Belle Époque: French for 'Beautiful Epoch'. A period of French and Western history conventionally dated from the end of the Franco-Prussian War in 1871 to the outbreak of World War I in 1914.

Bestiary: An illustrated book of animals, real and imagined, which was popular in medieval times. A moral lesson went with each animal.

Bifolium: A leaf of vellum or parchment folded to make two pages.

Blind arcade: A series of arches against a flat surface with no openings, usually a decoration on a wall.

Bohemian: A term used to describe a way of life for artists and intellectuals. It is suggested they are unconventional in habits and dress, and sometimes in morals.

Breakfront: A slightly projecting central section of a building.

Bronze: An alloy (mix) of copper and tin.

Bulla: Latin word for 'bubble'. A round or teardrop-shaped object.

Byzantine: Relating to or having the characteristics of a style of art and architecture developed in the Byzantine Empire, especially in the 5th and 6th centuries.

C

Camera obscura: A darkened box with a convex lens or aperture used to project the image of an external object onto an internal screen. A forerunner of the modern camera.

Capital: A separate, wider piece at the head of a column, pilaster or pillar that provides a base for the structures above.

Carolingian Empire: A large area of north-western Europe with a capital at Aachen in modern Germany, ruled by the Frankish dynasty, which included the Emperor Charlemagne, from *c.* AD 800–888.

Carpet pages: Pages with an all-over pattern; looks like a Persian carpet.

Cartoon: A full-scale preparatory drawing for a painting, tapestry or fresco.

Cast: A form created by pouring liquid material, such as plaster or molten metal, into a mould.

Cathedral: From the Latin word *cathedra*, meaning 'seat'. A cathedral houses the seat of the bishop and is the central church for a wider area or diocese.

Chalice: A large cup or goblet, typically used for drinking wine.

Chamber: A room or enclosed space.

Champlevé: Enamelwork in which hollow areas made in metal sheet are filled with coloured enamels.

Cherub: A type of angel that is usually shown in art as a beautiful young child with small wings and a round face and body.

Chevron: An ornamental device made of a series of V shapes.

Chiaroscuro: Meaning 'light-dark' in Italian, the term refers to fine gradations from light to dark in painting.

Chi-Rho: A Christian symbol made up of the first two letters, Chi and Rho, of the Greek word *Christos* (Christ).

Chivalry: A code of conduct associated with the medieval Christian institution of knighthood. This moral system established the notion of honour and courtly manners.

Cinquecento: An Italian word that means 'five hundred' but is used to refer to the 16th century in Italian art.

Cist: An underground box-like burial chamber made of stone slabs.

Cladding: A thin layer of one material used externally on a building.

Classical: Something related to the civilisation of ancient Greeks and Romans, especially in literature, art and architecture.

Classical orders: The Doric, Ionic and Corinthian decoration of ancient Greek and Roman architecture.

Clerestory: A row of windows in the upper part of a church wall above the roof level of the aisles.

Cliché: A phrase, opinion or art that is overused and shows a lack of original thought.

Cloisonné: Metal wires or strips soldered to a base, creating areas that are filled with coloured enamel.

Cloister: A covered walk or arcade surrounding a square enclosure, usually attached to a church or monastery.

Codex: A book made of separate leaves, as opposed to a scroll.

Co-extensive space: The space of the object itself as well as the space all around it. It extends outward as an object, but at the same time it draws the viewer inward and unifies the experience.

Collage: A piece of art made by sticking various different materials, such as photographs and pieces of paper or fabric, onto a backing.

Colonnade: A row of columns supporting an entablature or a series of arches.

Column: A freestanding pillar, typically cylindrical, supporting an arch, entablature or other structure, or standing alone as a monument. Often built in accordance with one of the orders of architecture.

Complementary colours: Any two hues positioned exactly opposite each other on the basic colour wheel. Complementary colours contrast with each other more than any other colour, and, when placed side by side, make each other look brighter.

Composition: The arrangement of elements within a work of art.

Concentric: Multiple shapes sharing the same centre, usually referring to circles within circles.

Concept: The idea behind a work of art.

Conceptual Art: In which the idea (or concept) behind the work is more important than the finished art object. This emerged as an art movement in the 1960s and the term usually refers to art made between the mid-1960s and the mid-1970s.

Conservation (of art) and restoration: The preservation and repair of architecture, paintings, drawings, prints, sculptures and objects of the decorative arts.

Continuous narrative: A type of visual story that illustrates multiple scenes of a narrative within a single frame. Multiple actions and scenes are portrayed in a single visual field without any dividers.

Contrapposto: Meaning 'placed opposite'. In art it refers to a human figure standing with most of its weight on one foot so that its shoulders and arms twist off-axis from the hips and legs.

Contre-jour: Painting or photographing a subject against the light.

Corbelling: The process of making a dome or arch using overlapping layers of stones.

Corinthian: Relating to one of the five classical orders of architecture. Characterised by a bell-shaped capital with carved ornaments based on acanthus leaves.

Cornice: The uppermost ornamental moulding that crowns an architectural composition.

Council of Trent: An ecumenical council of the Roman Catholic Church that was held in three parts, from 1545 to 1563.

Counter-Reformation: Also called Catholic Reformation or Catholic Revival. The Roman Catholic Church's efforts in the 16th and early 17th centuries directed against the Protestant Reformation and towards internal renewal.

Crossing: The area of a church where the nave is intersected by the transept.

Cruciform: In the shape of a cross.

Crypt: An underground chamber, usually vaulted, beneath the floor of a church.

Cubism: a highly influential style invented around 1907 by artists Pablo Picasso and Georges Braque. It emphasises the flat, two-dimensional surface of the picture plane.

Cupola: A small dome. An evenly curved vault on a circular or polygonal base.

Curator: Someone employed by a museum or gallery to manage a collection of artworks or artefacts.

Cusp: The pointed end where two curves meet. It can be a projecting point in Gothic decoration.

D

Dada: An art movement formed during World War I in Zurich in reaction to the horrors and folly of the conflict.

Dado rail: A moulding that separates the lower part of an interior wall.

Damask: A rich, heavy silk or linen fabric with a pattern woven into it.

Decorative: Serving to make something look more attractive or ornamental.

Degenerate art: A term used by the Nazi Party in Germany to describe art that did not support the ideals of Nazism.

Depict: To represent by a drawing, painting or other art form.

Deuterocanonical: 'Second canon' in Greek. It usually means the parts of the Bible that are only used by some Christian Churches.

Diagonal: A straight line joining the opposite corners of a square or rectangle. A slanting straight line.

Didactic: Intended to teach, particularly in having moral instruction.

Diminuendo: Letters decreasing in size at the beginning of a passage in an Irish manuscript.

Diptych: Meaning 'folded twice' in Greek; this is an altarpiece made of two panels hinged together.

Distortion: Something being warped out of shape, but still recognisable.

Divine: Of God; god-like.

Divisionism: The characteristic style in Neo-Impressionist painting, defined by separation of colours into individual dots or patches that interact optically.

Dolmen: A megalithic tomb where large flat stones are laid on top of upright stones.

Doric: Relating to or denoting a classical order of architecture characterised by a sturdy fluted column and a thick square abacus resting on a rounded moulding.

Drapery: Depiction of the folds of fabric in drawing, painting and sculpture.

Dressed stone: Smoothly finished blocks of stone.

Dry-stone construction: Stones laid without mortar to construct a wall.

E

Elevation: Another word for a façade, or a drawing of any vertical aspect of a building.

Elongated: Something made longer, especially in relation to its width.

Empirical perspective: What an artist directly observes, without observing the careful rules of linear perspective.

Enamel: An opaque or translucent glossy substance that is a type of glass. It is applied in powdered form to metal and is melted and bonded by heat. It is used for ornament.

Engaged: In architecture, applied or attached, most often an engaged column, which is physically attached or embedded in the surface of a wall.

Engraving: To cut or carve into a hard surface.

Entablature: The upper part of a classical building supported by columns or a colonnade, comprising the architrave, frieze and cornice.

Ergonomics: The study of people in their working environment. The interaction of people with structures and equipment.

Encaustic art: Also known as hot-wax painting. This involves using heated beeswax, to which coloured pigments are added, applied to a surface – usually prepared wood, although canvas and other materials are also used.

Evangelist: A writer of one of the four Gospels of the Christian Bible: Matthew, Mark, Luke and John.

Expressionism: An art movement in which the image of reality is distorted in order to make it expressive of the artist's inner feelings or ideas.

F

Façade: The front or main face of a building.

Fanlight: A window over a door, often semi-circular, where the glazing bars look like the ribs of a fan.

Fascia: A long, thin board that covers the area where a wall joins a roof. The sign above the window of a shop where the shop's name is written.

Fauvism: A style of painting with vivid expressionistic and non-naturalistic use of colour that flourished in Paris from 1905. Although short-lived, Fauvism had an important influence on subsequent artists, especially the German Expressionists.

Fibula: A type of dress fastener. Gold objects made of a bow and end cups or discs from the Bronze Age in Ireland were also called fibulae.

Figurative: Referring to any form of modern art that retains strong references to the real world and particularly to the human figure.

Filigree: Ornamental work in fine gold or silver wire.

Finial: A boss or knob used as the top, finishing piece on an architectural decoration. It can be used to finish a spire, canopy or gable.

Foil: A leaf shape. A trefoil is three foils. A quatrefoil is four foils.

Folio: A single sheet, front and back, of paper or vellum.

Foreshortening: The technique of depicting an object lying at an angle to the picture plane by using perspective devices.

Form: The visible shape or configuration of something.

Fresco: Wall painting on wet plaster.

Frieze: In classical architecture, the middle division of an entablature featuring a strip of decoration or figures. A decoration in painting or sculpture in a long, horizontal format.

Frontispiece: The decorated entrance area on the façade of a building.

Function: The practical use or purpose of a designed object.

G

Genre: A style or category of art or film. In painting, it refers to small-scale paintings showing narrative scenes from everyday life.

Georgian: A style of architecture from the time of the English kings George I, 1714, to George IV, who died in 1830.

Gesamtkunstwerk: A work of art that makes use of all or many art forms or strives to do so. The term is a German word which has come to be accepted in English as a term in aesthetics.

Gesso: The dense and brilliantly white base used in tempera paintings.

Gestural: Loose sketching or quick brushstrokes to capture a subject's basic form and to express movement.

Gild: To cover with a thin layer of gold.

Glaze: In oil painting, a thin coat of transparent colour laid over another.

Gold leaf: Gold beaten into thin sheets and used to cover surfaces.

Gold tooling: Embossing a decorative design through a sheet of gold leaf. The surface beneath may be 'tooled' over to form a pattern.

Gorget: A U-shaped gold collar from the Irish Bronze Age with a disc attached to each end.

Gothic: A style of architecture prevalent in western Europe in the 12th to 16th centuries (and revived in the mid-18th to early 20th centuries), characterised by pointed arches, rib vaults and flying buttresses, together with large windows and elaborate tracery.

Gouache: A type of water-soluble paint that, unlike watercolour, is opaque, so the white of the paper surface does not show through.

Granulation: An effect that can be achieved with wash work when using colours with heavy pigment particles.

Graphic arts: The visual arts based on the use of line and tone rather than three-dimensional work or the use of colour.

Greek cross: A cross where all four arms are of equal length.

Gregorian chant: Hymns sung in unison to accompany mass or other religious services. It is named after Pope St Gregory I (AD 590–604).

Guilds: Associations of artists, craftsmen or tradesmen. These organisations regulated the financial, social and political interests of their members.

Gum arabic: A binder for pigments in watercolour paints. It is made from the gum of the acacia tree, which is traditionally associated with (now Saudi) Arabia.

H

Happening: A partially improvised or spontaneous piece of artistic performance, typically involving audience participation.

High relief: So deeply carved or modelled that the main elements are almost free from their background.

Historiated initial: An enlarged letter at the beginning of a paragraph or other section of text that contains a picture.

History painting: A painting with a serious narrative portrayed in a dramatic way, often with a moral message. The word 'history' relates to the Italian *istoria*, meaning narrative or story, and does not necessarily relate to actual events from history.

Hue: A colour or a shade of a colour.

Humanism: An intellectual movement in Italy that started in the 14th century. It suggested the ideal of an education based on Greek and Roman thought, emphasising the value, potential and goodness in humans, which turned away from medieval God-centred scholarship.

I

Iconography: The use or study of images or symbols in the visual arts.

Identity Art: Focusing on the moment and the body of the artist. It can also involve the body of the audience. Performance art is often considered the most important form of art that explores the identity question.

Idolatry: The worship of an idol or cult image, being a physical image, such as a statue or a person, in place of God.

Île-de-France: The compact region immediately surrounding Paris. It includes the city and its suburbs as well as several large, surrounding towns.

Illumination: Decorations and illustrations found in medieval manuscripts.

Illusionist: A term used to describe a painting that creates the illusion of a real object or scene, or a sculpture where the artist has depicted a figure in such a realistic way that they seem alive.

Impasto: In oil painting, colour thickly applied (like paste) to a canvas or a panel.

Incision: Cutting into a surface with a point or blade.

Infrastructure: The basic equipment and structures (such as roads and bridges) that are needed for a country, region or organisation to function properly.

Initial: The first capital letter of a passage in a manuscript.

Installation (art): Used to describe mixed-media constructions or assemblages that are usually designed for a specific place and for a temporary period of time.

Insular style: A version of the La Tène style that developed in manuscript illumination and the decorative arts in Britain and Ireland in the 8th century.

Interlace: Decorative patterns made by weaving strands together, like plaiting or basketwork.

International Gothic: An artistic style during the late 14th and early 15th centuries, characterised by elegant stylisation of illuminated manuscripts, mosaics, stained glass, etc., and by increased interest in secular themes.

Ionic: Relating to one of the five classical orders in ancient Greece, characterised by a fluted column with a moulded base and a capital composed of four volutes.

J

Jamb: The side of a window, door or other wall opening. In medieval or classical architecture, they sometimes contain columns or statuary.

Japonism: From the French *Japonisme* (first used in 1872), it refers to the influence of Japanese art, fashion and aesthetics on Western culture.

Jellinge: A style of Viking art from the 9th and 10th centuries featuring intertwined animals with curled lips and long pigtails.

Juxtaposition: Two things being seen or placed close together with contrasting effect.

K

Kaleidoscopic: A changing pattern or scene. Relating to a tube that has mirrors and loose pieces of coloured glass or plastic inside at one end so that you see many different patterns when you turn the tube while looking through the other end.

Kerbstone: In the Stone Age, the large stones that surrounded the base of passage mounds.

L

La Tène: A style of art developed by the Celts in Central Europe. It combines natural forms, leaf and vine shapes with spirals, scrolls and trumpet shapes into a flowing Abstract art.

Latin cross: A cross where the vertical shaft is longer than the crosspiece.

Lapis lazuli: A semi-precious stone that is greatly valued for its deep blue colour. It is traditionally the source of the pigment ultramarine in art.

Linear: A style that relies on line for its main effect rather than colour or tone.

Linear perspective: A system of creating an illusion of depth on a flat surface. All parallel lines in a painting or drawing using this system converge in a single vanishing point on the composition's horizon line.

Lintel: A horizontal piece of stone or timber inserted at the top of a door, window or other opening to take the weight of the wall above.

Lithograph: A method of printing. An image is drawn onto the surface of a smooth, level piece of limestone using an oil-based crayon.

Lock rings: Ornaments made of gold wire and sheet metal formed into cone shapes. They may have been hair decorations.

Loggia: A gallery open at one or more sides.

Low relief: Sculpture that projects less than half its true depth from the surface.

Lozenge: Shaped like the diamond shape in playing cards.

Luminous: Giving off light; bright or shining.

Lunula: A sheet-gold neck ornament from the Bronze Age, shaped like a crescent moon.

M

Majuscule: Large capital or uncial letters that are usually the same height. The Irish version has some small ascenders and descenders.

Mandorla: Almond-shaped stylised glory of light enclosing sacred figures like Christ.

Mannequin: A dummy used to display clothes in a shop window.

Mannerism: Also known as Late Renaissance. A European art style that emerged in the later years of the Italian High Renaissance, around 1520, spreading by about 1530 and lasting until about the end of the 16th century in Italy.

Manuscript: A document written by hand.

Medium: This can refer both to the type of art (e.g. painting, sculpture, printmaking), as well as the materials an artwork is made from.

Megalithic: A period in the Stone Age when people built monuments with large stones.

Memento mori: An object kept as a reminder of the inevitability of death, such as a skull.

***Millefiori* glass:** Meaning 'thousand flowers', this refers to little sections cut from multicoloured glass rods of enamel used to decorate areas in metalwork or to create jewellery.

Minimalism: An extreme form of Abstract art developed in the USA in the 1960s. Typified by artworks composed of simple geometric shapes based on the square and the rectangle.

Minuscule: Smaller lower-case letters with ascenders and descenders, like modern handwriting, developed in the 7th century.

Modelling: The convincing representation of three-dimensional forms in two dimensions. The use of a malleable material like clay or wax to make a three-dimensional form.

Modernism: A global movement in society and culture in the early 20th century that sought a new alignment with the experience and values of modern industrial life.

Monochrome: A painting or drawing executed in shades of a single colour.

Monumental: Something great in size, ambition or importance, or serving as a monument.

Motif: A distinctive feature in a design. The subject of a painting.

Mould: A hollow container that gives shape to molten liquid (wax, plaster or metal) when it hardens.

Mythological: Relating to a collection of myths or mythology.

N

Narrative art: Art that tells a story.

Naturalism: A true-to-life style that involves the representation or depiction of nature (including people) with the least possible distortion or interpretation.

Nave: The main area of the church between the aisles.

Neo-Classical: A style of decoration based on ancient Greek and Roman examples popular in the 1770s.

Neolithic: The new Stone Age, when polished stone axes and other tools came into use *c.* 3700 BC in Ireland.

New Testament: A collection of the books of the Bible produced by the early Christian Church that included the Gospels.

Niche: A recess in a wall often used to hold a statue.

Nimbus: The disc or halo behind the head of a saint.

Non-representational art: Also called non-objective art, this style consisted of works that had no reference to anything outside themselves. In practice, it was mainly geometrically abstract.

Nymph: A creature from Greek mythology. A nymph is described as a nature spirit in the form of a young woman, usually found in the woods.

O

Ogham: An alphabet of 20 characters consisting of parallel lines across a vertical line or edge. It was used in Ireland from the 3rd or 4th century AD.

Oil paint: A medium where pigments are mixed with drying oils, such as linseed. Oil paint became popular during the 15th century in Northern Europe.

Old Testament: The Hebrew Bible as interpreted by Christianity.

Optical mixing: Pure primary colours in small touches placed close together so that they seem to merge, creating secondary colours in the eye of the beholder. This technique was used by Impressionists and Neo-Impressionists.

P

Painterly: Form is not represented by outline, but by the application of paint in patches of colour, resulting in the appearance of visible brushstrokes within the finished painting.

Pale, the: An area of strong English influence between Drogheda and Dublin.

Palladian: In the style of the Renaissance architect Andrea Palladio.

Parchment: Animal skin, especially from a goat or sheep, prepared for writing.

Paten: A plate, usually made of silver or gold, used to hold the bread during the Eucharist in Christian ceremonies.

Patronage: Financial or moral support given to an artist or craftsman by someone with wealth or power.

Pavilion: In architecture, a building connected by a corridor to a larger building.

Pedestal: A base supporting a statue or other object.

Pediment: A gable-like decoration over a portico, door or window.

Pelta: An ornamental motif made of arcs, often elaborated on in Celtic art.

Penannular brooch: A brooch where the ring has an opening – it is not a complete circle.

Pentecost: An event after the death of Jesus when the Holy Spirit in the form of tongues of fire descended on his disciples.

Perspective: A method of representing a three-dimensional object on a flat or nearly flat surface. Perspective gives a painting a sense of depth.

Piano nobile: The main floor containing the reception rooms in an Italian palazzo or a large townhouse.

Pier: A large, solid and freestanding support, usually square or round in section.

Pietà: Meaning 'pity' in Italian, it refers to the representation of the Virgin Mary holding the dead Christ on her lap.

Pigment: The dry, usually powdered form of colour.

Pilaster: A rectangular column, especially one projecting from a wall.

Pilgrimage: To go on a journey to a famous place. In medieval times, it was a place associated with a Christian saint.

Pillar: A freestanding upright in architecture, of any regular shape.

Piloti: A column of iron, steel, or reinforced concrete supporting a building above an open ground level.

Pinnacle: A small turret-like roof decoration. It is often richly ornamented.

Plane: A flat surface. Any distinct flat surface within a painting or sculpture can be referred to as a plane.

Plein air: Meaning 'out of doors', this refers to the practice of painting pictures outside.

Plinth: A square base for columns, statues or vases.

Poesia: Sixteenth-century Italian paintings that have a poetic quality.

Pointillism: The theory or practice in art of applying small strokes or dots of colour to a surface so that, from a distance, they blend together.

Polyptych: Many panels together.

Porcelain: A hard, fine-grained white ceramic ware.

Portal: A doorway. A portal was often set back several steps in Romanesque and Gothic architecture. This gave doors a considerable emphasis on the façade.

Portico: A structure consisting of a roof supported by columns at regular intervals, typically attached as a porch to a building.

Portray: To make a likeness of by drawing, painting or representing in a work of art.

Postmodernism: A late 20th-century style and concept in the arts, architecture and criticism, which represents a departure from Modernism. It is characterised by the self-conscious use of earlier styles and conventions, mixing different artistic styles and media, and a general distrust of theories.

Post-painterly Abstraction: A term covering a range of new developments in Abstract painting in the late 1950s and early 1960s, characterised by a more rigorous approach to Abstraction.

Predella: A painting or carving beneath the main scenes or panels of an altarpiece.

Prefiguration: An early indication of something that will happen in the future.

Proportion: The relationship of a part to a whole object. In painting, sculpture and architecture, it can describe the ratio or ideal proportions of the various parts of the human body.

Proto Renaissance: Refers to the pre-Renaissance period (c. 1300–1400) in Italy and the activities of progressive painters such as Giotto.

Pseudo-penannular brooch: A brooch that looks like a penannular brooch, but the ring is closed, usually with decoration.

Psychedelic art: An art movement that emerged in the 1960s based on psychedelic experiences induced by hallucinogenic drugs.

Putti: Chubby male babies, without wings, used in classical decoration.

Q

Quadrant: One-quarter of a circle. A quadrant colonnade is a row of columns that follows a curve, a quarter of a circle in plan.

Quatrefoil: A form of tracery composed of four foils.

Quattrocento: The 15th century in Italian art. It was preceded by the *Trecento* in the 14th century.

Quill pen: A pen for writing with ink made from the flight feathers of a goose or other large bird.

R

Readymades: A term used by the French Dadaist Marcel Duchamp to describe works of art he made from manufactured objects.

Realism: The accurate, detailed, unembellished depiction of nature or contemporary life.

Reformation: A 16th-century movement for the reform of abuses in the Roman Church ending in the establishment of the Reformed and Protestant Churches.

Relic: A part of a deceased holy person's body or belongings kept as an object of reverence.

Relief: A composition or design in which parts stand out from a flat surface. See also **high relief** and **low relief**.

Reliquary: A container, often richly decorated, for sacred relics, usually parts of a saint's body or possessions.

Repoussé: Metal hammered into a relief design from the back.

Representational art: Art that attempts to show objects as they really appear, or at least in some easily recognisable form.

Retrospective (exhibition): Retrospective means 'looking back', so a retrospective art exhibition looks back at the work that a living artist has produced over their entire career.

Rococo: A light, sensuous, intensely decorative French style developed in the early 18th century after the death of Louis XIV and in reaction to the Baroque grandeur of Versailles.

Romanesque: A term used to describe pre-Gothic art and architecture from roughly the 9th to the 12th century. It is characterised by round arches and heavy construction.

Romanticism: The early 19th-century movement in art and literature distinguished by a new interest in human psychology, expression of personal feeling and interest in the natural world.

Rose window: A large circular stained glass window divided into leaf-like shapes by spokes of tracery.

Rubrics: Instructions or explanations written in red in a manuscript.

Rustication: Masonry treated to resemble huge blocks with a rough surface and emphasised joints.

S

Salon: The official French art exhibition held from 1667 in the Salon d'Apollon in the Louvre. The exhibition was later moved to the larger location of the Palais de l'Industrie but kept the title of the 'Salon'.

Scholasticism: A way of thinking and teaching knowledge in the Middle Ages. It was influenced by the Italian Dominican friar, St Thomas Aquinas (1225–1274). This influential theologian combined the thinking of Aristotle, the ancient Greek philosopher, with Christian religious doctrine.

Scumble: In painting, the various overlaying of thin coats of opaque or dry paint – the opposite of glazing. It produces a slightly broken effect.

Secession: The action of formally withdrawing from membership of a federation or body, especially a political state. In Germany, it refers to a number of Modernist artist groups that separated from the support of official academic art.

Semiotics: The study of signs and symbols in works of art.

Sfumato: Derived from the Italian word for 'smoked', this is a well-controlled and subtle method for the graduation of tone and outlines. It creates a soft, hazy effect.

Shrine: A place considered holy by association with a sacred person or relic.

Sinopia: The preparatory drawing used to map out the composition of a fresco in red-brown chalk.

Site-specific: Refers to a work of art designed specifically for a particular location and that has a relationship with the location.

Spanish Inquisition: A judicial institution established to combat beliefs or opinions contrary to Catholic teaching. In practice, it served to consolidate power in the monarchy of the newly unified Spanish kingdom, but it achieved that end through infamously brutal methods.

Spire: A tall, conical-shaped roof on a church tower or turret.

Stereotype: A widely-held but fixed and oversimplified idea of a particular type of person or thing.

Stucco: A quick-setting semi-liquid material that sets hard. It can be modelled or moulded. It is not simply plaster – it is a more complex mix of materials.

Stylised: Treated in a mannered or non-realistic way, using artistic forms and conventions to create effects. Not natural or spontaneous.

Surrealism: A 20th-century avant-garde movement in art and literature that sought to release the creative potential of the unconscious mind, for example by the irrational juxtaposition of images.

Swag: A classical ornament of drapes, flowers or foliage, hanging in a curve from two points.

Symbolism: The use of symbols to express or represent ideas or qualities in art.

Symmetry: An exact match of parts of a design on either side of an axis. Harmony, proportion or uniformity between parts of a design or building and the whole.

T

Tache: The clamped metal ferrule or collar that made flat brushes available to the French Impressionists. The mark made by a flat paintbrush was called the *tache* brushstroke. *Tache* means 'spot', 'smudge' or 'patch' in French.

Tapestry: Wall hanging of silk or wool with a non-repeating pattern or narrative design woven in by hand.

Tectonics: In architecture, this is the science or art of construction, both in use and artistic design. It refers not just to the activity of construction, but the raising of this to an art form.

Tempera: The form of painting used before oil painting. Traditionally, colour pigments were mixed with egg yolk or glue.

Temple front: A façade that looks like a Greek temple, with pillars and a pediment or portico.

Tenebrism: A style of painting, especially associated with the Italian painter Caravaggio and his followers, in which most of the figures are engulfed in shadow, but some are dramatically illuminated by a beam of light, usually from an identifiable source.

Tondo: A circular painting or relief sculpture. It derives from classical medallions.

Tone: The lightness or darkness of something – this could be a shade or how dark or light a colour appears.

Torc: A neck, wrist or waist ornament consisting of a band of twisted metal.

Torso: Trunk of the human body, sometimes a sculptured figure that lacks head or limbs.

Triptych: Picture made up of three panels. The outer ones are usually hinged so that they can be moved.

Triskele: A Celtic symbol consisting of three curves radiating from the same point and turning in the same direction.

Trompe l'œil: Means 'trick of the eye' and refers to the technique of using realistic imagery to create an optical illusion of depth.

Tympana, plural of tympanum: The word comes from Latin and Greek meaning 'drum'. This is a semi-circular or triangular decorative wall surface over an entrance, door or window, which is bounded by a lintel and an arch.

Typography: The art or procedure of arranging type or text.

V

Vanishing point: The point at which receding parallel lines viewed in perspective appear to converge.

Vanitas: A painting that is a reminder of death and the futility of earthly achievements.

Vault: A roof based on the structural principles of the arch.

Vellum: The skin of a calf prepared for writing.

Visual culture: Visual culture is a way of studying a work that uses art history, humanities, sciences and social sciences. It is intertwined with everything that one sees in day-to-day life, including advertising, landscape, buildings, photographs, movies, paintings and apparel. Anything within our culture that communicates through visual means.

Vitrine: A large glass cabinet used for displaying art objects.

Volute: A scroll-shaped architectural ornament often found on pediments or capitals.

Voussoirs: The wedge-shaped stones forming an arch.

W

Woodcut: A method of relief printing from a block of wood cut along the grain.

Z

Zoomorph: Animal shapes changed into designs.

Image Credits

For permission to reproduce photographs, the authors and publisher gratefully acknowledge the following:

© Aer Lingus: 526L; © akg-images: 226T, 226B, 462; © akg-images/© Estate of Michael Farrell, IVARO Dublin, 2021: 494; © akg-images/Erich Lessing: 179R; © Alamy: iiiTR, iiiBR, xiiTL, xiiCL, xiiiT, xvR, xviiiL, xixT, xixB, 1R, 2, 3B, 5L, 9, 10, 12TL, 12TR, 16T, 16C, 16B, 19BL, 23, 26R, 28T, 28C, 28B, 35T, 37T, 37B, 39R, 40T, 40B, 42L, 43, 44, 45, 46L, 46R, 47, 49e, 49f, 49C, 50T, 54TL, 57R, 59TL, 67, 69TL, 69TC, 69TR, 69B, 70L, 73B, 79, 80, 81, 82, 84L, 84R, 86, 87L, 88BL, 88BR, 90L, 90R, 91T, 91B, 92T, 94L, 95L, 95R, 96B, 97, 98R, 99T, 100L, 101, 103L, 104, 106a, 106c, 106d, 106e, 106f, 106BL, 106BR, 107T, 107B, 109, 110L, 110R, 111, 113T, 113B, 115, 119T, 121T, 121B, 122T, 122B, 123, 124, 125, 126, 127L, 127R, 128, 129L, 129R, 130T, 131, 132, 134T, 135L, 135R, 138T, 139, 140, 143L, 143R, 143b, 143c, 143d, 143e, 143f, 145L, 145B, 144, 147, 148, 150, 151T, 151C, 152, 153T, 154T, 154B, 156, 157T, 157B, 158, 161, 162T, 162B, 163, 164T, 164B, 165, 167, 168T, 168CL, 169TL, 169TR, 170T, 171, 172T, 172B, 173T, 160, 173B, 175, 176T, 176B, 177L, 178, 179L, 180, 183, 184, 185, 186L, 186R, 187T, 187BL, 188, 189T, 189B, 190, 191, 193, 195a, 195b, 196T, 199L, 200R, 201, 202L, 203T, 214, 215, 220L, 220R, 221L, 221R, 222, 224C, 225R, 229, 240BR, 240b, 241, 265R, 293CR, 314BL, 325BL, 353R, 358, 362R, 388, 400T, 400B, 401, 402, 403BL, 404B, 408B, 409T, 416BR, 416e, 419, 424B, 425, 426L, 426R, 427, 430, 430B, 435TL, 435TR, 437, 438T, 444T, 445, 446T, 447T, 448R, 449L, 454a, 450BR, 466B, 486, 515, 516TL, 517R, 518, 520, 521L, 521R, 514C, 524L, 524R, 525, 526R, 528C, 529R, 530, 531TR, 531B, 532T, 532B, 532C, 535C, 540TR, 540BR, 541C, 542, 543T, 543B, 545B, 546, 550TL, 551B, 553L, 554L, 561B, 562L, 567T; © Alamy/© 2021 Helen Frankenthaler Foundation, Inc., IVARO Dublin, 2021: 238; © Alamy/© Ai Weiwei: 283; © Alamy/© Anish Kapoor, DACS London/IVARO Dublin, 2021: 277; © Alamy/© Anselm Kiefer: 275T; © Alamy/© Aram Designs, world licence holder for Eileen Gray Designs: 482L; © Alamy/© Claes Oldenburg and Coosje Van Bruggen: 252, 259; © Alamy/© Eilis O'Connell, DACS London/IVARO Dublin, 2021: vBR, 484C, 502T, 506T; © Alamy/© Estate of Andrew Wyeth, ARS NY/ IVARO Dublin, 2021: 243B; © Alamy/© Estate of Christo V. Javacheff: 240h, 273T; © Alamy/© Estate of Constantin Brâncuși, ADAGP Paris/ IVARO Dublin, 2021: 202R; © Alamy/© Estate of Edward Hopper, ARS NY/IVARO Dublin, 2021: 240c, 243T; © Alamy/© Elaine de Kooning Trust, ARS NY/IVARO Dublin, 2021: 230T, 236; © Alamy/© Estate of Evie Hone, IVARO Dublin, 2021: 454B, 479B; © Alamy/© Estate of Francis Bacon. All Rights Reserved, DACS London/ IVARO Dublin, 2021: 260, 268L; © Alamy/© Estate of Georges Braque, ADAGP Paris/IVARO Dublin, 2021: 208; © Alamy/© Georgia O'Keeffe Museum, ARS NY/IVARO Dublin, 2021: 243C; © Alamy/© Pollock-Krasner Foundation, ARS NY/IVARO Dublin, 2021: 195f, 240d; © Alamy/© Successió Miró, ADAGP Paris/IVARO Dublin, 2021: 211; © Alamy/© The Easton Foundation, ARS NY/IVARO Dublin, 2021: 240g, 254; © Alamy/© Association Marcel Duchamp, ADAGP Paris/IVARO Dublin, 2021: 553R; © Alamy/© 2021 Kate Rothko Prizel & Christopher Rothko, ARS NY/IVARO Dublin, 2021: 239; © Alamy/© Estate of Max Beckmann, Bild-Kunst Bonn/IVARO Dublin, 2021: 227R; © Alamy/© Estate of Jean Tinguely/The Niki Charitable Art Foundation, ADAGP Paris/IVARO Dublin, 2021: 278; © Alamy/© Estate of Oisín Kelly, IVARO Dublin, 2021: 484b, 497R; © Alamy/© Estate of René Magritte, ADAGP Paris/IVARO Dublin, 2021: 212; © Alamy/© R. Hamilton. All Rights Reserved, DACS London/IVARO Dublin, 2021: 245; © Alamy/© Salvador Dalí, Fundació Gala-Salvador Dalí, VEGAP Madrid/ IVARO Dublin, 2021: 195e, 210; © Alamy/© Jasper Johns, ARS NY/IVARO Dublin, 2021: 240C, 246; © Alamy/© John Behan, IVARO Dublin, 2021: 499B; © Alamy/© Succession Picasso/DACS, London 2021: 205; © Alamy/© Succession Picasso/ DACS, London 2021: 195c, 195T, 206TL; © Alamy/© Tracey Emin, All rights reserved, DACS London/IVARO Dublin, 2021: 276; © Alamy/2021 The Andy Warhol Foundation for the Visual Arts, Inc., ARS NY/IVARO Dublin, 2021: 248; © Alamy/Barbara Hepworth © Bowness/Tate: 262TL; © Alamy/Element Pictures – Irish Film Board: 559C; © Alamy/Maurice Harron: xviiB; © Alamy/Sue Lipscome, Cod Steaks: 562R; Illustration recreated from original by Alexander Ganse, 2000: 120; © Amtuir/ RATP/Wikimedia Commons: 197C; © Andy Goldsworthy: 569T, 569B; © Annora Callaghan: 570L, 570; © Anonymous/AP/ Shutterstock: 230B; © Anthony Murphy/mythicalireland.com: 292L; © Antiques World: 448L; © Image courtesy of Áras an Uachtaráin: 450TL; © Images supplied by Aram Designs, world licence holder for Eileen Gray Designs: vTL, 454L, 454f, 481; © Armagh Public Library/St Patrick's Church of Ireland Cathedral: 315TC; © Arnotts/Maser: 568L; © BnF, Dist. RMN-Grand

Alfred and Ingrid Lenz Harrison and the Regis Foundation/Bridgeman Images/© Estate of Otto Dix, Bild-Kunst Bonn/IVARO Dublin, 2021: 227L; © Museumslandschaft Hessen Kassel, Neue Galerie/Arno Hensmanns/© Estate of Joseph Beuys: 273B; © National Gallery of Art, Washington, D.C./© Succession H. Matisse: 203B; © National Gallery of Denmark (SMK)/© Succession H. Matisse: 204; © National Gallery of Ireland: 72, 146, 174, 441, 457T, 457B, 458T, 458B, 454b, 460, 467R, 545C; © National Gallery of Ireland/© Estate of Jack B. Yeats, DACS London/IVARO Dublin, 2021: 467L, 468; © National Gallery of Ireland/© Estate of Mary Swanzy: 477T; © National Gallery of Ireland/© Estate of Paul Henry, IVARO Dublin, 2021: 469L; © National Gallery of Ireland/© Estate of Paul Henry, IVARO Dublin, 2021: 470T; © National Gallery of Ireland/© Estate of William John Leech, 2021: 454R, 463L; © National Gallery of Ireland/© Robert Ballagh, IVARO Dublin, 2021: 484d, 495R; © National Museum of Ireland: ivBL, 286BR, 286CR, 286b, 286c, 286e, 293TL, 298, 299C, 300TL, 300C, 303T, 303B, 304CL, 304CR, 305C, 305BL, 305BR, 306, 308, 309T, 310C, 311T, 311C, 315TL, 315B, 315CR, 316, 317, 319C, 319BL, 319e, 329B, 331T, 334, 335, 342BR, 342BL, 344T, 344C, 345C, 345BL, 346R, 369, 370L, 370R, 371T, 371C, 374BL, 375T, 379, 392, 393CL, 393BL, 393BR, 394, 395L, 395R, 412, 414; © National Museums Northern Ireland/© Estate of Mary Swanzy: 476; © National Museums Northern Ireland/© Estate of Paul Henry, IVARO Dublin, 2021: 469R; © National Museums Northern Ireland, Collection Ulster Museum: 289, 459; © Neil Jackman, Abarta Heritage: 406B, 407; © Nicolò Orsi Battaglini/ Bridgeman Images: 61R, 65R; © Nina Leen/The LIFE Picture Collection via Getty Images: 232; © Pela Case, visit pela.earth: 571L; © Peter Macdiarmid/Getty Images/© Ai Weiwei: 555; © Philadelphia Museum of Art/Gift (by exchange) of Mrs. Herbert Cameron Morris, 1998/Bridgeman Images/© Association Marcel Duchamp, ADAGP Paris/IVARO Dublin, 2021: ivTL, 195BR, 209L; © Philadelphia Museum of Art/The George W. Elkins Collection/Bridgeman Images: 187BR; © Phillips: 571R; © Photographic Archive, National Monuments Service, Government of Ireland: ivB, 286C, 286a, 286d, 292R, 293TR, 296L, 296R, 313, 314TR, 319BR, 319c, 319f, 324, 325CL, 327T, 338L, 338R, 350, 354, 357C, 357B, 359L, 359R, 360L, 360R, 361, 362L, 380, 381, 382, 383T, 383B, 404T, 405L, 416C, 423T, 423B, 424T, 442, 443, 451R; © Photographic Archives Museo Nacional Centro de Arte Reina Sofia/Succession Picasso/DACS, London 2021: xiv; © Print Collector/Getty Images: 364TL, 364TR, 364C, 365, 367, 368L, 516B; © Rachel Fallon/photo © Darren Ryan: 548T, 556CR; © Raffaello Bencini/Bridgeman Images: 49B, 56, 59R, 60T, 60BL, 60BR, 61L, 64R, 70R, 74; © Richard Long, DACS London/IVARO Dublin, 2021: 561T, 563B; © RMN-Grand Palais (musée de l'Orangerie)/Michel Urtado/Benoit Touchard/© Succession H. Matisse: 213; © Robert O'Byrne, theirishaesthete.com: 411T, 447B; © Robert Rauschenberg Foundation: 247; © Rolls Press/Popperfoto via Getty Images: 261T; © Ros Kavanagh, courtesy of Sirius Arts Centre/© Brian O'Doherty: 511B; © Rowan Gillespie, photo: Liam Blake: 484g, 507, 508L; © Royal Irish Academy: 319b, 320T, 327BL, 327BR, 328; © Ruth Maria Murphy: 529L; © Saatchi Gallery/© Tracey Emin, All rights reserved, DACS London/IVARO Dublin, 2021: 556TL; © Scala, Florence 2020/© Succession Picasso/DACS, London 2021: 206B; © Sean Scully, 2021: 484BL, 509R, 510; © Shutterstock: 13C, 29L, 41T, 117B, 195d, 216C, 217B, 403T, 403CR, 405R, 409B, 433C, 523C, 567B; © Shutterstock/© 2021 Holt/Smithson Foundation and Dia Art Foundation, Licensed by Artists Rights Society (ARS) NY: 257B; © Sotheby's/© Estate of Louis le Brocquy, IVARO Dublin, 2021: 488T; © Spencer Nugent: 514TL, 523TL; © Staatliche Kunstsammlungen Dresden/Bridgeman Images/© Estate of Otto Dix, Bild-Kunst Bonn/IVARO Dublin, 2021: 216B; © Stair na hÉireann | History of Ireland. All rights reserved. Originally published at stairnaheireann.net/2020/03/30/the-legend-of-cu-chulainn-4/: 465B; © Stan Honda/AFP via Getty Images/© Judy Chicago, ARS NY/IVARO Dublin, 2021: 255T; © Stephen Doyle: 557TL, 557BL, 557BR; © Succession Picasso/DACS, London 2021: 537R; © Tate: 269, 455T, 461L, 461R; © Tate/© Claes Oldenburg: 240TR, 251; © Tate/© David Hockney: 271, 272; © Tate/© Estate of Francis Bacon. All Rights Reserved, DACS London/IVARO Dublin, 2021: 267; © Tate/© 2021 Kate Rothko Prizel & Christopher Rothko, ARS NY/IVARO Dublin, 2021: 237; © Tate/© Estate of Roy Lichtenstein, ADAGP Paris/ IVARO Dublin, 2021: 250; © Tate/2021 The Andy Warhol Foundation for the Visual Arts, Inc., ARS NY/IVARO Dublin, 2021: 240e, 241T, 249; © Tate/The estate of R. B. Kitaj: 263; © The Board of Trinity College Dublin: 390, 398T, 411B; © The estate of Jean-Michel Basquiat: 265L; © The Fine Art Society, London, UK/Bridgeman Images/© Estate of Marianne Brandt, Bild-Kunst Bonn/IVARO Dublin, 2021: 217C; © The Henry Moore Foundation, All Rights Reserved, www.henry-moore.org, 2021: 262TR; © The Hunt Museum and the Diocese of Limerick: 413; © The Metropolitan Museum of Art/Art Resource/Scala, Florence 2020/© Anselm Kiefer: 274; © The Museum of Modern Art, New York/Scala, Florence 2020: 552; © The Museum of Modern Art, New York/Scala, Florence 2020/© Pollock-Krasner Foundation, ARS NY/IVARO Dublin, 2021: 234B; © The Museum of Modern Art, New York/Scala, Florence 2020/© Estate of Max Beckmann, Bild-Kunst Bonn/IVARO Dublin, 2021: 218L; © The Museum of Modern Art, New York/Scala, Florence 2020/© Estate of Otto Dix, Bild-Kunst Bonn/IVARO Dublin, 2021: 551C; © The Museum of Modern Art, New York/Scala, Florence 2020/© Joseph Kosuth, ARS NY/IVARO Dublin, 2021: 255B, 519R; © The Office of Public Works: vCR, 416CL, 450TR; © The Phillips Collection, Washington, D.C.: 199R; © The Solomon R. Guggenheim Foundation/Art Resource, NY/Scala, Florence 2020/© Frank Stella, ARS New York/IVARO Dublin, 2021: 240BL, 240f, 253; © Trinity College Library Dublin/Bridgeman Images: 319d, 319g, 333, 340L, 340R, 341L, 341R, 349T, 366, 368R; © Una Healy Graphic Design, unahealydesign.com: xviiiR; © Universal History Archive/Universal Images Group via Getty Images: 138B, 554R; © University College Dublin, published by UCD Digital Library: digital.ucd.ie/view/ ivrla:31490: vTR, 450BL; © VCG Wilson/Corbis via Getty Images: 49c, 143a, 149; © Werner Forman/Universal Images Group

NEW APPRECIATING ART